FIGHTING: INTELLECTUALISING COMBAT SPORTS

KEITH GILBERT

FIGHTING: INTELLECTUALISING COMBAT SPORTS

KEITH GILBERT

First published in 2014 in Champaign, Illinois, USA
by Common Ground Publishing LLC
as part of The Sport and Society book series

Copyright © Keith Gilbert 2014

All rights reserved. Apart from fair dealing for the purposes of study, research, criticism or review as permitted under the applicable copyright legislation, no part of this book may be reproduced by any process without written permission from the publisher.

Library of Congress Cataloging-in-Publication Data

Fighting : intellectualising combat sports / Keith Gilbert, editor.
    pages cm. -- (Sport and society)
  Includes bibliographical references and index.
  ISBN 978-1-61229-431-5 (pbk : alk. paper) -- ISBN 978-1-61229-432-2 (pdf : alk. paper)
  1. Hand-to-hand fighting--Training. 2. Mixed martial arts--Training. I. Gilbert, Keith, 1950-

GV1111.F54 2014
796.81--dc23

2014005667

Table of Contents

Acknowledgements x

Chapter 1: Striving for Lucidity against the Tide of Opinion 1
Keith Gilbert

Part I: Education

Chapter 2: Professionalization and Experiential Learning in Higher Education: The University of Derby's (Buxton Campus) Development of a B.A. (Hons.) Degree in Martial Arts 12
Charles Spring

Chapter 3: Modifying Pupils' Attitudes and Behaviors in the Classroom through Access to Regular Martial Arts Training 21
James R. Lee-Barron

Chapter 4: Learning 'in' and 'through' Amateur Boxing 29
John Fulton

Chapter 5: Martial Arts and Youth: For Better or Worse? 38
Marc Theeboom & Jikkemien Vertonghen

Chapter 6: How Do Fighters Learn How to Fight: An Insiders' Critique of Traditional Martial Arts Pedagogy 49
Richard Bailey

Chapter 7: Teaching Close Quarter Combat to Military Personnel: A Pocket Guide for New and Inexperienced Instructors 58
Jamie Lee-Barron

Part II: Body

Chapter 8: Body-experience Lineages in Martial Art Cultures 67
David Brown

Chapter 9: Constituting the Fighter's Body: On *Being-with* in Brazilian Jiu-Jitsu 78
Bryan Hogeveen & Jennifer Hardes

Chapter 10: The Female Fighter Phenomenon in Denmark and Greece: Exploring Gender Dynamics in Judo 87
Anna Kavoura, Marja Kokkonen, & Tatiana V. Ryba

Chapter 11: Weight Management and Weight Cutting for Competitive Grapplers 97
Brian Jones

Chapter 12: The Idea of (UN) Winning in Martial Arts as Opposed to Combat Sports 105
Baris Sentuna

Part III: Rhythm and Balance

Chapter 13: Shaping the Rhythms of Mixed Martial Arts Practice.117
Stanley Blue

Chapter 14: Competitive Balance in Olympic Boxing: 1904–2012 ..125
David Chaplin & Sergio Mendoza

Chapter 15: Can Martial Arts Training Protect from Fall Down Accidents? 136
Hannu Leinonen

Chapter 16: Rhythm Skills Development in Chinese Martial Arts ..144
Colin McGuire

Part IV: Boxing

Chapter 17: Professional Boxing: Law and Self-regulation 155
Ian Warren

Chapter 18: Democratizing the Noble Art 165
Kath Woodward

Chapter 19: 'Pugilistic Pastoring': Volunteering in Amateur Boxing as Missionary Work 173
David Chaplin & John Harris

Chapter 20: Boxing and Religion: Faith and Heritage in the Sweet Science 181
Kevin Grace

Chapter 21: The Martial Science of Boxing and Its Contribution to Military Close Combat 189
James R. Lee-Barron

Chapter 22: The Sweet Science: Boxing as Sport and Spectacle 198
Guy Spriggs

Part V: Capoeira

Chapter 23: A Multi-dimensional Model of the Martial Arts: How Biological, Psychological, Social, and Spiritual Factors Interact in Brazilian Jiu-Jitsu & Capoeira 207
John T. Sorrell & Itaborá Ferreira

Chapter 24: Female Regional Capoeira Masters in Rio de Janeiro: The Fight as a Male Dominated Area 230
Eliane Glória Reis da Silva Souza, Fabiano Pries Devide, Sebastião Josué Votre, & Mauricio Murad

Chapter 25: Capoeira: An Example of Sustainable Sport 240
Andrea Cristiane Alves da Cunha & Renata Osborne

Chapter 26: Capoeira as an Art of Living: The Aesthetics of a Cunning Existence 247
Greg Downey

Part VI: Social Issues

Chapter 27: The Highway to Hooliganism? An Evaluation of the Impact of Combat Sport Participation on Individual Criminality .. 267
Craig Jenkins & Tom Ellis

Chapter 28: Synchronizing Modernity: Panama Al Brown and the Fight Game in France, 1926–1938 290
Bennetta Jules-Rosette

Chapter 29: Mixed Martial Arts [MMA]: Social Interactions and Inclusion in the Brazilian Favelas 312
Orestes Manoel da Silva & Carla Rocha Araujo

Chapter 30: Developing Emotional Intelligence through the Martial Arts 328
Chris Moser and Cheri Hampton-Farmer

Part VII: Research on the Individual Martial Arts

Chapter 31: Approximately 'As Real as It Gets': Naturalistic Mythologies, Biological Determinism, and MMA's Symbolic Environment of Originary Violence 338
Matthew P. Ferrari

Chapter 32: Approaches to the Historical Acculturation of Judo ... 355
Haimo Groenen

Chapter 33: Understanding Martial Arts in the Light of Japanese Mesology and Systemic: The Case of Shintaido's W*akametaiso* *Kata* 365
Pierre Quettier

Chapter 34: Mixed Martial Art Viewership Motivation: An Analysis of Motives in Mixed Martial Arts Viewership 376
Yongjae Kim

Chapter 35: The Importance of Education and Morality in the Martial Arts 390
Keith Gilbert

Notes on Contributors 396

Index 400

Acknowledgements

The development of this book provides a much needed addition to the practical and research literature surrounding the relationship between martial arts, intellectual discovery, and research. As such this book is the first of its kind and I hope that it is used as an initial baseline text to further stimulate research and practice into this association.

There is no doubt that without the support of the authors in this text it would not have come to fruition. In this respect I would like to take this opportunity to thank each individual author. I understand that many interrupted their own work schedules in order to be able to provide the chapters for *Fighting: Intellectualising Combat Sports* and I am indebted to them for their professionalism and determination to provide some of their original work for this text.

I fully understand the current problematics placed on academics, practitioners, and writers who labour in universities and the profession across the world. Indeed, I realise that for some, the development of a chapter for this book was a herculean effort as many pressures had been placed on them in their own separate work environments. Again I thank the authors for their efforts and hopefully I have set the seed for them to join me and be involved in writing for a further text in five years' time to review the research on martial arts. Also my thanks go to the authors who I called upon later in the piece who happily assisted me with chapters that have strengthened and allowed me to broaden the scope of the text by giving it a truly international flavour.

There have been others who have kindly spent time and effort supporting the development of this book. One such person is Ian Nelk, the enthusiastic books editor from Common Ground Publishing who has been supportive and with me every step of the long and often arduous process towards maturity of this text. As such I would like to personally thank him for his insightful ideas and suggestions which ensure the quality of the text.

My thanks go to the University of East London and the individuals, too many to mention within UEL, who have provided library, statistical, and financial research support for the fine-tuning of the book. Without this constant backup and support from my own organisation, research work of this kind would not be possible. I thank the academic staff, in particular Nick Bourne and James Beale, and also my postgraduate students and the many practitioners who have influenced my thinking and caused me to redirect initial thoughts and ideas.

My thanks go to SportAccord, and in particular Vlad Marinescu, the director general, for his support and approval for the use of the photograph for the front cover, which is truly spectacular. My gratitude also goes to photographer Augusto Bizzi who took the wonderful photograph at the SportAccord World Combat Games in St. Petersburg, Russia in 2013.

Finally, it would be remiss of me not to thank my partner Dr. Yuen Ching Ho, who provided me with moral, psychological, academic, and editorial advice throughout the development of this book.

Keith Gilbert

Chapter 1

Striving for Lucidity against the Tide of Opinion

Keith Gilbert

'You must not fight too much with one enemy, or you will teach him all your arts of war.'

Napoleon Bonaparte

'He who is not courageous enough to take risks will accomplish nothing in life.'

Muhammad Ali

'A bit of violence never hurt anybody.'[1]

Graffiti in a London Underground Station

Introduction

'I don't philosophically believe in fighting of any kind. In fact if there was a war I would probably become a 'conscientious objector'. These were the words of a work colleague who is also a sociologist and he refused to become involved in this book because of his arguably somewhat misguided thinking regarding the notion of the benefits of fighting versus the problematics of fighting. There is no denying that many academics and indeed many people feel this way. In-fact it is something of a misnomer for me to write a book about fighting and as such I feel

---

[1] In Tutt, N. (1976). Violence, U.K. Department of Health and Social Security publication. London.

strangely hypocritical after lecturing to my students over the past years when living in Australia about the negative aspects of violence in sport. I argued vociferously that contact sports of all kinds are deleterious to humans and that contact sports were the cause of many injuries in children and youth which significantly increased the public health bill in Australia and across the world. I never let on to the students that I loved boxing and used the negative case to provoke thinking and argument and discussion amongst my students. Even in tutorials I argued strongly against violent sports like rugby union and rugby league and opted to promote non-contact sports like swimming and tennis for children and youth. Of course like my colleague I was metaphysically wrong because the many and various types of martial arts are utilised around the world to develop sound morals, values and belief systems in many children and youth and the fitness benefits far outweigh the minimal demands made on society's health systems, structures and funding.

In fact my love of boxing manifested itself in the early year of the Muhammad Ali era and I followed his career through the major fights which were broadcast in television in the U.K. and the U.S.A. with great gusto. Although I never attended a fight until I was on sabbatical leave in Boston where I witnessed the sweat and efforts behind preparation of the fighters and the training required to sustain multiple punches and the draining of human energy in ten short rounds. During this period I was also lucky to meet Muhammad Ali personally and understand that this man was not just a boxer but an American and global icon. It was about this time in Boston that I began to think about the nature of martial arts and their relationship to scholarly, cerebral and intellectual thought. Hence the great need for a book such as this in both the academic and practical martial arts communities. It is clear when elaborating on this point that there is little work in the area of fighting or combat sports in the higher education sector and if you go to any good bookstore you will find work on the martial arts and combat sports but these books are grounded for the most part in the practical domain. As such there is an obligation by academics to support the international federations and reinforce their thirst for knew knowledge development and of course to support postgraduate and undergraduate students and courses in the higher education realm. Teachers and parents need this book to enable them to understand the nature of fighting and its benefits for their children. Most importantly this book provides a voice for younger academics that are beginning their careers and also to support the burgeoning area of sports for development where boxing in particular has much to offer. Indeed, what follows is a collection of the thoughts of others which I synthesis and pull together, in a coherent fashion, in the final chapter of this book - 'Fighting: Intellectualising Combat Sports'.

Definitions and Agencies

There is no solitary definition or theory of fighting that stands out traditionally or culturally in the context of world sports. The general definition however, may be classed as a construction of specific terminology and text but more importantly different martial arts and combat sports construct the definition according to their particular philosophies and in different ways. Indeed, it could be argued that because of the ethical and moral nature of the meaning of fighting in different societies and the historical nature of the martial arts in different societies that the definition and also the nature of the culture of fighting is inherently political in nature. As such the various definitions are highly contested and have their own political intent as most martial arts feel that their form of fighting is superior to others. The only overriding and conjoint fact which is prevalent across disciplines of martial arts is the physical nature of the various forms and practical component of the art itself. Therefore the term physical seems as though it should be a relevant term grounded in all the definitions of the martial arts. This is important as each carry buried explanations which in turn underpin the nature of the sports themselves and add to the individual nature of the differing forms of martial arts. Thus implicit in the martial arts are the sociological notions of historical struggle, power relationships and preparation for self defence and as each individual behaviour varies across the disciplines then the nature of the individual martial arts lays open to outside criticism and debate. In practice fighting definitions are mediated by different agencies and individual exponents grasp of the nuances of their martial art. Indeed, if there is no longer a definition of a particular martial art then the sport ceases to have the individual concepts which separate it from other martial arts. Therefore if the definition changes then the sport could be in danger of dying out or being subsumed along with its aging proponents. Thus the terms 'concepts' and 'definitions' are often used interchangeably causing some confusion and dismay amongst various components and traditions.

When it comes to the discussion of the definition of martial arts then there is no possibility of me appeasing everyone with my thoughts and perspectives and one single definition? The main reason for this is that there are so many competing factors in the defining of the term martial arts and so many differing martial arts and so many differing aspects such as contact, no contact, partial contact, with weapons, without weapons, those that strike, those that educate, those that improve mental skills, those that exercise the body, those that promote health, those that include dance movements, others which include choreography, those that are mixed, those that are designed specifically for war, those for peaceful purposes, those for self protection or self defence, those with spiritual or religious dimensions, those that include meditation, those to show self control, those which are traditional, those which are modern, those that promote respect, those that promote discipline, those that develop youth, those that provide confidence, those that have an aesthetic quality, those which employ brute force, those which are more technical, those which employ leverage, those which exude certain values and ethics, those which require strength, agility and skill development, those with Asian traditions, those which are regional, those which are hybrid. However, if the truth be known and as hinted previously, we have a situation where every martial art has its own definition grounded in historio-graphical contexts.

So is it possible to define the martial arts? Authors such as Buekler, Castle and Peters (2009)[2] early in their landmark paper argue that the definition of the martial arts is purely semantic and simply put includes the following Oxford English Dictionary definitions for the two separate words:

---

[2] See the excellent paper by Buekler, S., Castle, P., & D.M.Peters (2009). Defining the Martial Arts: A proposed Inclusive CI system. *Journal of Sports Science & Medicine*, p.p. 1-9 ISSN 1303-2968.

Martial: belonging to war

Art: skill acquired by experience, study or observation

They further argue that these basic statements define martial arts as 'the skill of warfare'[3]. At the end of their paper they state that there appears to be some difficulty in defining 'the martial arts' and argue that '....it is time that such an accepted term as 'martial art' was redefined so that an enhanced, generic definition may be offered which encompasses differences of the various combat systems'. The definition of martial arts then seems to be difficult to deliver and I feel lacks the main aspect of the arts which often gets left behind and is seen as periphery but in my mind is very important. The hidden perspective is endemic to human movement and in particular dance which could be argued as being inherent to the skill development which is found in all sports. In other words all sports movements could be classified as forms of dance. This point is controversial of course and I am prepared for this to be a contentious issue which can be reasoned and discussed further. However, if I argue that there is a direct link between the worth of movement and our existing comprehension of our differing life worlds then we can easily understand the nature and importance of shape, form, harmony, rhythm, flow and movement in space from a chorographical perspective in the martial arts. If we add kinesiological concepts of verticality and centre of gravity to the equation then we can argue, as Rudolph Labans[4] theories espouse, that all types of movement have forms of dance components and support the notion that the body becomes an instrument of expression. Indeed, Laban viewed life as a dynamic movement experience and he looked upon movement as a two way language process through which the body could communicate by giving and receiving messages. He believed that movement stems from the inter-dependence of body, mind and spirit and he understood that our inner life relates to the outer world. Laban could have been speaking about the martial arts and in doing so he created a theoretical language in order to help the observer understand and record movement objectively. Why then can we not define the martial arts in terms of movement and in particular dance movements as the skills learned in dance need to be practiced and are repetitive and the skills learned in martial arts also need to be practiced and are repetitive. The movements produce strong intrinsic feelings whether kinaesthetic or spiritual and they are aesthetically pleasing and the issues of time, space and flow are very important to the development of skilled exponents of the martial arts as they are to dancers.

The ***first general*** definition for martial arts with an emphasis on ***movement*** could include all of the above movement words and appear something like the following:

---

[3] This paper can be found online at the following URL address: https://eprints.worc.ac.uk/621/

[4] The following book is very informative and the key to much of the development of the working definition on martial arts above: Bradley, K., (2009). Rudolph Laban, Routledge books, Abington, U.K.

Martial Arts:

> Martial arts consist of a conglomeration of complex body movement patterns grounded in the notions of space, time, flow, form, rhythm, harmony, speed, equilibrium, and power which can all be separately choreographed forming each individual martial art and possessing the essentially symbiotic elements of dance.

In other words each martial art has its own series of movements related to dance and in practice can be choreographed to produce as argued a language for their particular method. Indeed, all the elements of dance could also be the elements of martial arts and in this manner the two areas of expertise are symbiotic in nature. Many of you will disagree with this perspective and the above 'first general' definition and the following might support our opposing perspectives. There are of course other perspectives which need to be discussed and these include the uncertainty re the definition of the term 'art'. Here again there are endless possibilities in relation to the definition which are philosophically external to the realms of the development of this book but none the less important. Indeed, if there were to be a definitive definition of the martial arts developed then a clear understanding of the definition of art would need to be put forward as an initial concept. Although it is safe to say that any definition of art[5] must include the importance of history, cultural features and trans-historical characteristics that revolve around a clearly stable aesthetic core. It could be argued that the martial arts possess all of these characteristics. For example some definitions and comments regarding martial arts which emphasis the arts are as follows:

> '…the art of war: the strategies, tactics and techniques of combat'

Oxford English Dictionary[6]

And the notion of art itself:

> '…the various branches of creative activity, such as painting, music, literature, and dance'.[7]

The above definition relates specifically to the performing arts and that seems highly relevant to the martial arts as they all include movement as their major component.

The ***second general*** definition for martial arts which emphasises the ***arts*** could include all of the above and other *'art'* words and might appear something like the following:

---

[5] See Stanford Encyclopaedia of Philosophy: [Available at:] http://plato.stanford.edu/entries/art-definition/ [accessed November 1st 2013]
[6] http://www.oxforddictionaries.com/definition/english/art [accessed November 1st 2013]
[7] http://en.wikipedia.org/wiki/Definition_of_art [accessed November 1st 2013]

Martial Arts:

> Martial arts are a set of intellectually challenging historically grounded movements which relate to performance art and refer specifically to creativity, design, aesthetics, expression, appreciation and like painting, architecture, writing, poetry, creative style and music every martial arts organisation belongs to a distinctive art-form.

Again this is controversial and open to debate and thus far I have concentrated on the terms 'movement' and 'art' and not the term 'martial' and this distinction needs explanation. In point of fact to lean directly towards the arts and to discount the martial would be frankly idiotic as that is the one area which is dominant when expressing the relationship between the terms martial and arts.

Defining Martial

There is fundamental perspective underpinning the term 'martial'. This revolves around the following statement from work colleague who is a black belt in karate: '…..*the bottom-line with true martial arts is to kill and the main idea is not to choreograph anything when fighting'*. In other words the entire dance moves, practice choreography and art statements add up to nothing when engaging another fighter. In other words the nature of fighting as a 'martial art' is not always to provide an aesthetic experience for the fighter or spectator but to achieve domination over your adversary which is clearly primitive, elemental and designed to protect yourself and destroy the opposition. Hence the term 'Martial'. As Bolelli (2008:3) comments:

> 'The martial arts bring us back to something more primal. In the fighting arts, it is our own physical well-being that is on the line'.

In line with this statement Frantzis (1998:1) notes that '…the word 'martial' comes from Mars the ancient Roman god of war'[8] and thus any discussion of the martial arts must always include the terms warfare or combat. Some have argued that their is a certain 'beauty' to the movements displayed in the martial arts but frankly as Frantzis (1998:10) further argues '…who cares whether the movements are beautiful or ugly? Beautiful movements may or may not be martially functional' as the purpose of the Martial arts is to win at all costs. Thus in the heat of the moment functionality, technique and skilled movement might be replaced by the ugliest strike and aesthetics becomes subsumed in favour of surprise and winning. Martial also provides other perspectives which differ from the arts such as the notion of 'fear'. The fear of violence and also the overcoming of that fear are endemic to the very nature of most forms of martial arts and every fight not only becomes a battle against your opponent but also a battle against your own

---

[8] Please see the following URL for further basic information regarding the term 'Martial': http://en.wikipedia.org/wiki/Martial_arts

weaknesses. As Bolelli (2008)[9] mentions: 'The very physical nature of our existence makes it impossible to completely escape this primordial fear'. Indeed, '…it takes a certain kind of courage ….. and willingness not to be afraid of either being hit or thrown or hitting and throwing a fellow human being (Frantzis, 1998:34)[10]'. Fear and courage go hand in hand in the martial arts - yet they are diametrically opposed in other aspects of life. Another marked difference between the terms 'movement', 'art' and 'martial' is the concept of 'pain'. Indeed for some athletes pain is addictive and something which they need to experience to know that they have been in a fight and it has been scientifically proven that athletes can become desensitised to pain overtime. In other words pain thresholds increase and it becomes more difficult for an opponent to hurt you and the human body needs more stimuli, in the form of increased force, in order for the body to feel increased pain. There is also a positive factor if you are psychologically trained and in tune with your body. The body's ability to cope with pain can therefore be a deciding factor in the development and consequent success of martial arts athletes. Green (2011: 74) argues that the martial arts '…hurts so it is real' and the notion of pain is of great importance in defining the 'Martial' component of 'martial arts'. Green (2011)[11] further argues 'pain attracts participants' in that:

1. It provides confidence that the experience is real.
2. It is in itself an avenue to encounter the body as a united 'self' with clear limits and boundaries.
3. It establishes intimacy between participants, which is necessary for the formulation of community within site.

I argue here that pain is in fact related to the mind/body dichotomy and can be addictive and pleasurable. In other words as mentioned previously fighters get accustomed to pain. Indeed, an interesting study would be to discover what happens to fighters after they retire – do they still need the stimulation which pain provides and if so how do they get this 'shot of pain'? After all as Frantzis (1998:10) argues 'It is the intellect which masters the actions of the body' and in the same way it is the brain which masters the levels of pain which the body can endure. And as Bolelli (2008) mentions '…every fight is a battle against your own weaknesses' whether physical or mental. Indeed, how do the fighters cope mentally after their careers are over? An additional perspective to be taken into account which does not exist in the area of the arts is that in some martial arts activities there are open displays of blood through blows or cuts caused by head clashes and other drills designed to injure the body. Martial arts can therefore be brutal and highly dangerous.

---

[9] Noted in Bolelli, D. (2008). On the Warriors Path: Philosophy, Fighting & the Martial Arts, Blue Snake Books, California U.S.A.

[10] Further interesting points regarding primordial fear are found in the paper: Frantzis, B.K. (1998). The Power of Internal Martial Arts, Combat Secrets of Ba Gua, Tai Chi and Hsing-I. Energy Publications, California. U.S.A.

[11] Green, K. (2011) It Hurts so it's Real: Sensing the Seduction of Mixed Martial Arts. *Social and Cultural Geography*. Vol. 12 Issue 4 p.1

The definition of 'Martial' as distinct from the previous definition of Buekler, Castle and Peters (2009) who argue basically that it is 'belonging to war' is far more complex and involves issues concerning armed combat and unarmed combat which are the two main martial arts variation's. A distinction perhaps from other variations such as the use of art and traditional Japanese dance oriented martial arts – blending armed and unarmed and aggressive unarmed attack. Buekler, Castle and Peters (2009) in their excellent paper doubt that it is possible to define martial arts and they argue that there are two types of which have been transformed into sporting and spiritual manifestations. These are: 'martial' and 'civilian' and they note that 'The martial arts are thus one aspect of the debate and it is time that such an accepted term as 'martial art' was redefined so that an enhanced, generic definition may be offered which encompasses differences of the various combat systems'. Clements[12] (2009) views the defining of the martial arts from an historical perspective and mentions that '…there is a debate within martial arts circles today over the differences between combat-sports and fighting-arts' and this highlights the fact that it is difficult to define the term 'martial arts' because of the competing interests of differing groups and their contradictory philosophies. All forms of martial arts however, contain the variables of striking (whether contact or non-contact) and the use of leverage to throw or off balance an opponent. Clements (2009) takes this one step further by stating that:

> 'The function of fighting techniques is to effectively cause injury or incapacitation to another person so as to end a fight. The purpose of martial art however, can be to improve the individual's capacity when necessary to efficiently and humanely defend themselves by fighting techniques and, where possible, potentially make use of such violent force superfluous. It's the *martial* that provides the *how*, but it's the *art* that decides the *why*.

Clements (2009) however, falls short of providing a definition of the 'martial arts' but provides some interesting perspectives in his short paper.

As such any definition of the 'martial' in 'martial arts' should be socially, culturally and historically defined and mediated and interrelated to the notions of pain, injury and the 'waging of war'[13]. For example historically forms of martial arts were utilised to ensure that individuals survived the 'kill or be killed'[14] mentality and incorporated notions of human dignity and mental strength. Indeed, a definition of martial arts should provide a more precise statement of the 'martial' that distinguishes it from the 'art' without being too narrow which diminishes the impact of the terms and without being too broad as this runs the danger of losing sight of the distinctive core notions of martial arts. Given that at the beginning of this chapter I argued that a definition is used to differentiate

---

[12] See http://www.thearm.org/essays/Defining-A-Martial-Art.html (accessed 20/11/2013)
[13] http://www.thefightgame.tv/MAhistory.htm (Accessed 20/11/2013)
[14] Please see 'The Fight Game TV' http://www.thefightgame.tv/MAhistory.htm for a poignant definition of the martial arts. This website provides a good view of the history of martial arts and freely admits that defining the martial arts 'is a tricky subject'. (Accessed 21/11/2013)

between the conditions defined – in this case – martial and arts, it makes sense to pitch the definition between the two ends of the narrow/broader end of the spectrum. I wish to reiterate that there is no single 'correct' definition but any definition must include historical, social and cultural perspectives which attempt to be inclusive of both the term art and martial. My aim is therefore to provide a *working definition* which can be utilised and discussed in further research papers and projects and although I am arguing for a focused material definition of the martial arts I am not naive enough to think that my definition will cover all aspects of the martial arts. Moreover, my definition needs to be understood in the wider scientific context concerning all of the aspects of fighting and indeed combats sports so as not to ghettoize martial arts in a residual category of inflexibility and attempts to make it available to the wider community. In other words definitions cannot be divorced from the political use to which they are used and I have no control of the how the definition may be utilised in the future – whether it is for political or social reasons.

With the previous thoughts in mind what is my definition of martial arts? I only trust it opens up new debate and enhances the martial arts:

The ***third*** general definition for ***martial arts*** could include all of the above '*martial*' words and might appear something like the following:

> Martial arts are grounded in history, highlighted by harmony between the mind and body and in all forms consist of a prearranged group of physical activities involving domination, supremacy and controlled aggression which is manifested in differing arrangements of complex, coordinated, powerful contact and non-contact skilled movements (often including weapons) which in extreme forms can lead to pain and bloodletting but certainly in defeat or victory over an opponent.

This definition is again controversial and far too long. I make no apology for it being controversial but agree that it does need to be reshaped and argue that if you take your own martial art whether it is boxing, judo or another the definition should fit nicely with your own form of martial art.

The following definition is therefore an attempt at defining 'martial arts' in this book and is divided into 6 separate sections which when combined make up the whole. **Martial Arts**:

1. Are grounded in history and possess as their core element - harmony between the mind and the body.
2. In all forms consist of an established group of physical activities and values which differentiate the particular martial art.
3. Involves domination of an opponent and controlled aggression displayed by often complex, coordinated, powerful contact and non-contact skilled physical movements.
4. Participation can lead to pain and bloodletting but certainly in personal defeat or victory over an opponent.
5. Involves elements of courage, fear, chivalry and is increasingly recognised as a means to enrich people's lives through personal and community development.

6. Practice increases physical, mental, emotional, spiritual health and consequent overall fitness gains in its participants[15].

This chapter has thus attempted to deconstruct the term 'martial arts' and view it from the perspectives of movement, dance, art and martial. In completing this mission there has been an attempt to define martial arts which in itself is a very difficult task and I expect the above definitions aka 'first', 'second', and 'third' general definitions to challenge students and academics and practitioners well into the future. The final definition I expect to be the beginning of discussion. After-all it is controversial and each of the 6 sections, I am sure, can be reworked to provide a solid basis for the future of martial arts research.

The remainder of this book contains chapters which have been written by 34 practitioners and academics from across the world and as such the work is global in its reach and content. The book is the first of its kind which incorporates theories and practices from a range of academics and practitioners within differing disciplines of the martial arts. I am grateful for the support which I have been offered from my peers and colleagues who have never failed to respond to my many requests for further information, slight changes in chapter outline and in some cases total rewrites and reference corrections. This book is divided into 7 different parts which highlight the strengths of the authors and also develops area which might be opened up for further research into the future. These parts are:

Part I Education
Part II Body
Part III Rhythm and Balance
Part IV Boxing
Part V Capoeira
Part VI Social Issues
Part VII Individual Martial Arts

These are the separate parts which make up the backbone of the book and throughout these parts are dealt with in a highly sensitive manner by the authors and the writing which follows is a credit to their professionalism and determination to have their voices heard. The final chapter provides a meta-synthesis of the previous chapters and attempts to provide further research ideas and questions and solutions for future research in the martial arts domain.

---

[15] See Martial Arts http://en.wikipedia.org.wiki.Martial_arts [Accessed September 12th 2013]

Part I: Education

Chapter 2

Professionalization and Experiential Learning in Higher Education: The University of Derby's (Buxton Campus) Development of a B.A. (Hons.) Degree in Martial Arts

Charles Spring

Introduction

Although other sports are a popular choice for undergraduate study, the study of Martial arts in traditional U.K. higher education institutions is rare. This is surprising because it is currently ranked the 5th most popular club sport in the UK and 13th for participated sports activities (Sports England, 2006). This positions the martial arts above weight training, cricket, rugby union and athletics.

While the study of Martial Arts in higher education is an unusual concept in the U.K. within Japan and China there is a history of acceptance of martial arts based degrees in their Universities. Institutions offering martial arts degrees in Japan and China have helped professionalise martial arts coaching in these countries. Unfortunately, the lack of similar programmes in the U.K. has arguably left the martial arts industry in Britain in chaos and professional disarray. It should be identified here that in terms of the term professionalise; this is not the idea of being a professional sports person, but someone who adheres to particular standards in their teaching and instruction.

In an attempt to address the problem of professionalization the UK's first martial arts degree programme was developed by the sports department at the University of Derby in Buxton. Research funding for the project gave the University an Opportunity to investigate the martial arts degrees at the National Institute for Fitness and Sports in Kanoya (NIFS) in Japan and the Tianjin Sports University in China. The findings from the study helped shape the curriculum and teaching methods used in Buxton. It is also perhaps worth noting here that the teaching methods and philosophies that emerged from the programme have also been delivered at institutions in Finland and Germany. With its foundations supported by experiential learning rather than sports science, this programme is perhaps unique in the world of U.K. higher education. The author believes the knowledge and insights gained from this approach is far-reaching and worthy of special attention.

Experiential Learning

Experiential learning is defined by Beard and Wilson as '…the sense- making process of active engagement between the inner world of the person and the outer world of the environment.' (Beard and Wilson 2007: p.2). Martial arts provide numerous experiential learning opportunities for students, and uses the "sense making" process of active engagement to learn the arts and develop experiential knowledge. For example, rather than use some of the dictionary version to answer the question of "what is martial arts"? I rely instead on the experiential knowledge of our students to provide a definition. This process usually creates a range of ideas. These are:

> 'Ways of training the physical and mental aspects of humans.
> They include hands, feet and other bodily weapons
> They also include weapons systems
> They can include sports orientated fighting systems
> They can include softer systems such as Tai Chi'

>   (Spring, 2005)

And also I believe that:

> 'The martial arts are about skills that are developed for fighting, that include the recognised oriental and western hand to hand styles but also encompass weapons systems from around the world. These are not necessarily military based arts and include 'hard' and 'soft' styles'.

>   (Spring, 2005)

When the degree in martial arts theory and practice was proposed at the University of Derby questions were asked by quite a few martial artists about the intentions of it, for instance, I was often asked was it expected to replace the black belt? This was a foolish notion, and of course it was not the case. Instead it was to give an opportunity for developing knowledge and practical abilities, such as teaching and coaching more effectively and to develop a more professional approach to delivering martial arts. The development of the programme involved representatives from the martial arts, including the heads of two organisations as well as input from several other external bodies. One aspect these advisors were keen to have included was the practice of martial arts and experiential opportunities to develop teaching and coaching skills. This made a 30% contribution to the programme and was a major influence that attracted the majority of the students to our course.

However, before we developed the curriculum of our degree there was a need to research institutions that had similar programmes. Our starting point was to analyse how martial arts is taught in the countries of Japan, China and Thailand. This led to a tour of these countries and extensive talks with the educators that manage their martial arts degrees. Our general findings from our research were the curriculums of these programmes have a strong focus on their culture a finding also identified by Hamguchi (2006). In contrast, the teaching of sport in the UK and Europe tend to be influenced by sports science and has a focus on its historical rather than cultural origins.

Historical Perspectives

In the Eastern world Martial arts in China flourished because of the Shaolin Temples which has a rich history of training and supplying warriors. In Japan there were Bushido warriors, in China the 'warrior tradition' was adopted by the Shaolin monks. In the western world the 'warrior tradition' was adopted by the Baronial Knights. The knights served their masters and had a code of chivalry similar to the warrior monks. In all these cases the development of fighting ability was primarily due to the need to defend one's self and prepare for war. Over time, however, it can be argued, that martial arts became the development of the self rather than the need to prepare for war.

Observations by the author at a recent U.K. Karate competition suggest chivalrous behaviour is still flourishing. Competitors have to bow onto the mat and to each other, they adhere to rules and regulations and anyone straying from these gestures of respect is penalised. Respect is also shown by handshakes at the end of the competitions. On one particular occasion at a competition a young boy forgetting to shake hands whilst leaving the competition mat realised his mistake and created a scene of apology, ensuring everyone in the arena could see he regretted his mistake.

In Bushido the ethics and belief system encompassed a range of military values such as, loyalty, courage, compassion, duty and obligation. Duty and obligation is seen by many in the martial arts as the most important *Giri and Gimu.* This is what some of the older writers see as the most vital attributes of a good samurai (Turnbell, 2010). Giving these to your Lord and master was an economic as well as obligational contract, for this obligation and loyalty the Lord looked after the samurai's basic needs (Turnbell, 2010). Similarly the 'English Knights' were expected to adopt the 'code of chivalry' and value 'loyalty' (Turnbell, 2010). In the U.K. we still have a connection to our chivalrous past, it is rumoured that we drive on the left-hand side of the road so our Knights passing on horseback would have a better chance of using their weapons (James, 2002). Military values from the past are evident in other contemporary traditions. For example, in Japan they bow, showing deference and respect, in the UK we shake hands to show our respect it also shows we are not going to attack one another. In another example, the Royal family and the titles of Lords still pass on through the hereditary system. Many families have coats of arms, and ancient laws regarding training with bows and arrows still exist. Even the idea of democracy resonates from Knights wanting to see justice for the majority.

Historically, the 'Warrior class' in both western and eastern societies were seen as law keepers. In the U.K. the term Sheriff was given to the main responsibility, this tradition still exists in America today. The 'Maisters of Arms' were the main people responsible for localised training in the UK (James, 2002). Every town in the UK would at one time have a school of training similar to the Japanese Ryu and the Chinese Wushu schools (Castle, 2003). Indeed, military style training is evidenced very early on in both eastern and western history.

Education through Martial Arts

The idea of analysing and developing Martial Arts practice into programmes of study is not a new one. Martial Arts was introduced into the school curriculums of Japan nearly 100 years by professor Kano in Japan (Webber and Collins, 2005. Hamaguchi, 2006). The Martial arts such of Judo and Karate, have essentially been used to accentuate a student's physical, mental and emotional development. In China the martial art of Wushu was moved into the school system after the Cultural Revolution; although there were schools prior to these Martial arts was never part of the mainstream educational system (Spring, 2010). In contrast, Thailand has a long established programme of physical educational studies aligned with Thai Boxing and this has evolved into a standardised approach across their higher educational sector.

In the U.K. physical education (P.E.) programmes have been part of the school curriculum system since the mid 1800's and was adopted by every school the early 1900's (Beasheal and Taylor, 1996). Until the 1960's boxing was a part of most PE programme. Interestingly boxing is making a return, and there are now several schools making a concerted effort to prove its educational values (BBC news report 2007, Harris S. on Daily Mail 2009). Although a high number of Martial arts coaches regularly attend and work with schools the teaching of martial arts in the UK has not been professionalised. In Japan and China the professors that lead their schools have Budo and Wushu on their curriculum, they also have professionally qualified instructors that are usually educated to postgraduate level (Spring, 2010). These establishments turn out highly qualified students that inform practice in the schools system (Kusaka 2006). The destination of the vast majority of these students is the educational system (Spring 2010 & Kusaka, 2006).

In the U.K. university level sports programmes tend to focus on sports coaching and it can be argued this is the same in P.E. programmes, the focus on active learning is on coaching of different sports. Sports coaching degrees, however, have received mixed reviews. Knowles et al (2005) for example, highlights that the vast majority of sports coaches believe their trade is not learned through the undertaking of academic programmes but through actual coaching practice. In the case of martial arts this is done within the training halls and dojos around the country; where grading and other short courses may be undertaken by practitioners. Hammond and Perrys (2005) analysis of the effectiveness of academic programme delivery of sports coaching in the UK, concludes a balance has to be struck between the practical and the academic. They argue coaches would benefit from programmes of study that enable them to develop an intimate knowledge of their profession. The same could be said for martial arts instructors. Martial arts instructors are not just coaches they have a teaching role too. Indeed, Kernspecht (1984 and 2011) believes that teaching is the main role of martial arts as predominantly martial arts are taught for other things not just sports. As mentioned above in Japan, Thailand and China this is the main destination of those studying in higher education in those countries. Therefore it could be argued that in the school system in the UK there is professional development for those entering schools but for all the teachers/coaches externally it is not yet the same. From this point the developing notion of professionalising sports coaching and hence martial arts teachers/coaches will be discussed.

Professionalization

In the United Kingdom the concept of professionalization of sports coaching has already received large support. A vision statement put out by U.K. Sport in 2001 expresses this succinctly:

> 'By 2012, the practice of coaching in the U.K. will be elevated to a profession acknowledged to central to the development of sport and the fulfilment of individual potential'.
>
> (UK Vision for Sport (2001) in Taylor and Garret, 2010)

The particular report that the above statement was within assessed the issues around professionalization of a very wide ranging industry. They identified a number of key barriers, these being, internal resistance, changing governmental policy, profession fragmentation and changes in leisure markets. All of the above are concerns within the martial arts industry, as identified above there issues with the wide range of martial arts, thus it could be argued fragmentation. Fragmentation and resistance are areas that Karate in the United Kingdom, as one discipline within martial arts, has had real problems with. A recent endeavour to create one overarching national governing body has met with much resistance. Several organisations recently got together for talks and this collapsed when one group left the talks (AMAUK 2012). Both Sport England and the Sport and Recreation Alliance want Karate to have one governing body to enable better focus, increased competence in coaching and a generally more professional attitude amongst Karate coaches; this feeds into a wider governmental strategy to professionalise sports coaching (AMAUK 2012, Taylor and Garret, 2008). This point as well as the point made above on changing governmental policy highlights something to develop further, that of what is meant by the term professionalization.

The first hint towards a widening professionalization agenda in education was Estelle Morris's drive for professionalising of the role of head teachers (Woods, Armstrong and Pearson, 2011). This happened alongside the same governments push towards a more coherent policy for developing sports (Taylor and Garret, 2008). professionalization is seen as important for particular sectors to give credibility to work being undertaken by the individuals in the respective sectors. Some argue it a very positive action for a number of reasons, self-confidence, job satisfaction and effectiveness (Woods, Armstrong and Pearson, 2011). Others argue against believing it is just a remodelling of teachers role and increasing workloads by stealth (Stevenson, Carter and Passey, 2011). Whatever the case? The concept has evolved and gained momentum. Other areas have followed the professionalization agenda, one of these being sports coaching, possibly because of its proximity to P.E. and their working closely with schools and the educational system (Taylor and Garret, 2010). Taylor and Garret (2010) also note that the sports coaching industry equally supports and resists the professionalization agenda that is increasingly being implemented. They recognise the fractured nature of the coaching field, which is also an on-going issue in the martial arts as previously discussed. Despite this as indicated by Sports England there has been a need to try and raise the professional identity of coaches so that they get the credibility and rewards they deserve (Sport England, 2004). Unlike the educational sector which many argue was already professional and undertook a serious approach to their daily work already (Stevenson, Carter and Passey, 2011) sports coaches are often seen as voluntary, may often be unpaid and have a mixed bag of credentials that allow them to coach (Sport England 2004, Taylor and Garret, 2010). However many of the main stream sports including Judo have recognised Sports Coach United Kingdom (SCUK) coaching awards. Others such as boxing have set qualifications that have to be undertaken prior to being able to coach. In the wider Martial arts field, however, this is even more disparate, to ascertain the credentials of a Martial arts coach is often complex and difficult. Magazines in the field of Martial Arts Illustrated and Combat frequently discuss this area and instructors featured in these magazines go to great pains to evidence their backgrounds. This would not be required if there was a standardised approach to qualifying instructors. This need for standardisation is the approach taken in Japan, China and now Thailand, in all these countries the levels are set and all instructors go through the same qualifications to be able to teach within the governmental sectors, in Thailand they are trying to implement that an individual cannot teach/coach unless they do the University qualification. If Martial arts are going to develop in the context of the drive for professionalism within the field of sports coaching then it can be argued that there is a need for a qualification that is standardised, that there is growing recognition for this is noted in kickboxing where recently the main governing bodies featured an editorial in the September 2011 Martial Arts Illustrated promoting a BTEC course in coaching for their members that all instructors would now have to do. I have been approached by a number of organisations interested in higher education for the same purposes, to develop a standardised approach to ensure professional consistency in martial arts coaches and indeed worked with the Thai University sector to set the parameters for their award. To further develop the concept of higher educational professional programmes for martial arts requires the support of the martial arts organisations and the wider martial arts fraternity. In Japan, China and Thailand this is the case, the governing bodies of the martial arts support the idea of higher educational study. In earlier research undertaken the author of this chapter found the educationalists at the institutions attended where all very active in the martial arts organisations as well as the universities (Spring, 2010).

Therein lies the rationale behind developing a degree in martial arts. The BA (Hons) Martial Arts Theory and Practice was delivered at the University of Derby Buxton for seven years. The programme leader for that period was the author of this chapter. Through study of the grades, retention rates and other available data from the student body several observations can be recorded. One observation on the collective that came to study was the wide range of abilities both martial and in the sense of coaching/teaching, the students, who came onto the programme possessed. The programme had been designed to enable the students to develop coaching skills through experiential learning applying theory in practice sessions. Some were incredibly able; both martially and in the dojo at coaching or teaching (generic use here for training hall from my karate bias). Others were not as capable in both and because of the nature of the programme being experientially bias did not stay on the programme. This then leads to the question, why is this? They all had several years of experience, some more than others. They were mostly black belts or very close to being. Well, not a large sample one might say, and one would agree, however it could also be argued that it was an extremely random sample of those particularly dedicated individuals, in the martial arts who chose to come to university. They were from a range of different disciplines not selected by the author or researcher. This is a question that the notion of professionalization could answer, those who get their black belts do so on merit of what a particular instructor determines is the standard to be achieved, some refer back to others within their respective organisations, some do not. What an independent programme could do is change that subjectivity and give a standardised qualification that indicated an authority to teach.

Other findings during the period of time the degree has been delivered was the percentage of students gaining a 1st or 2:1 has been high, over 70% in all years that students graduated, one year 100% of those graduating. Students found the experiential nature of the degree beneficial, they also recognised that in the industry their degree would matter; but not be more valuable than the black belts the majority owned. So part of any programme of study, needed to be, practical experiential aspects of martial arts that were developed alongside theory. So the name Martial Arts Theory and Practice was a key component of what students wanted. Several have gone on to become teachers or work in education.

To develop the programme further in the U.K. it was necessary to collaborate with a host organisation as this initial degree was fast becoming a full honours degree; this was an observation by many of the students who studied on the programme that a wholly dedicated martial arts programme would be better. Such a body for collaboration was the European Wing Tsun Organisation (EWTO). The EWTO and the University of Derby [Buxton] developed a full honours programme as opposed to the old joint honours to make it wholly applicable to Martial arts in 2012. This has had the same focus of applied aspects alongside theoretical underpinning. At the time of writing it is running very successfully and will have graduates by 2015. There have also been approaches made by several other organisations who are interested in following this model.

Conclusive Statements

In conclusion, as discussed above, arguably Martial arts could benefit from a higher educational programme of study that is accepted and accessible by all who wish to teach. This would be impartial and generic and enable all practitioners to benefit from this study. It would help professionalise the area of Martial arts and create individuals that could lead the martial arts much as teachers do the educational system. Any programme though would benefit from the approach of experiential learning. This approach enables individuals to learn by doing and applying what it is they are interested in to the arena they are about to enter. They develop a professional approach that is recognised in a much wider context and equally applicable to kendo as it is kung fu or karate. It would also enable Martial artists to be comparable to each other by other organisations such as schools and leisure centres and would be of huge benefit to children, communities and university graduates.

References

Beasheal, P. & J. Taylor (1996). *Advanced Studies in Physical Education and Sport*, Thomas Nelson & Sons Ltd. UK.

Beard, C. & J.P. Wilson (2007). *Experential Learning; A best practice guide for Educators and Trainers,* Kogan Page. London. UK

Castle, E., (2003). *Schools and Masters of Fencing; From the middle ages to the eighteenth century,* Dover. UK.

Dohrenwend, R. E., (2005). The Walking Stick. *Journal of Asian Martial Arts*, Vol 14 No 4. Via Media. USA.

Goodman, F. (2010). *The Ultimate Book of Martial Arts,* Hermes House. London.

Gratton, C. and I. Jones (2004). *Research Methods for Sport Studies,* Routledge. London.

Hamaguchi, Y. (2007) *Innovation in Martial Arts,* in Maguire J. and M. Nakayama Eds., (2007) *Japan, Sport and Society: Tradition and change in a globalising world,* Routledge. London

Hammond. J. & J. Perry (2005). A multi-dimensional assessment of soccer coaching effectiveness, *Ergonomics, Vol. 48.* Taylor Francis

Harris. S. (2009). *Boxing back on the timetable in state schools* (Available at http://www.dailymail.co.uk/news/article-1205080/Boxing-timetable-state-schools.html) (Accessed 08/11/2012)

Hurley, J. (2002). *Tom Spring: Bare-Knuckle Champion of All England,* Tempus. Stroud. UK.

James, L. (2002). *Warrior Race: A History of the British at War,* Abacus. London.

Kerspecht, K. (1984). *On Combat,* EWTO-Verlag. Heidleberg. Germany

Kerspecht, K. (2011). *Kampflogik 3!,* EWTO-Verlag. Heidleberg. Germany

Kernspecht, K. and Konig, O. (2012) Personel communication

Knowles, Z., Borrie, A. & H. Telfer (2005). Towards the Reflective Sports Coach: issues of context, education and application. *Ergonomics, Vol.48. nos 11-15 15 Sept-15 Nov,* Taylor Francis

Kolb D.A, Boyatzis R.E, & C. Mainemelis (1999). *Experiential Learning Theory: Previous Research and New Directions* in R. J. Sternberg and L. F. Zhang (Eds.), (2000). *Perspectives on cognitive, learning, and thinking styles.* NJ: Lawrence Erlbaum.

Kusaka, Y. (2006). *The emergence and development of Japanese school sport* in Maguire J & M. Nakayama Eds., (2007) *Japan, Sport and Society: Tradition and change in a globalising world* Routledge London

Lewis, P. (1990). *The Way to the Martial Arts,* Marshall Cavendish. London
Marshall, G. (Ed). (1998). *Dictionary of Sociology,* Oxford. UK
Martial Arts Illustrated (September 2011). Martial Arts Limited. Huddersfield
McCarthy, P. (1995). *The Bible of Karate Bubishi,* Tuttle Boston USA
Reid H. & M. Croucher (1983). *The Way of the Warrior: The paradox of the Martial Arts,* Century Publishing. London
Sport England. (2004) Sport England Communications
Sport England. (2006). *Active People Survey Factsheet* Sport England Communications
Spring, C. (2005). *Martial Arts; Inclusion in Higher Education in the UK.* Conference Paper June 2005, HAMK Hamenlinna. Finland
Spring, C. (2010). *Application of Martial Arts in Higher Education: Case study of Undergraduate Degrees at the University of Derby UK.* Combat Sports Conference September 17-19th 2010 Rzezsnow Poland.
Stevenson, H., Carter, P. & R. Parry (2011). *'New professionalism,' workforce remodeling and the restructuring of teachers' work'* International Electronic Journal for Leadership in Education
Taylor P. & Garret. (2010). The *Professionalization of Sports in the UK.* Routledge
Turnbull, S. (1995). *The Book of the Medieval Knight,* Arms and Armour Press. London
Woods, C. Armstrong, P. and D. Pearson (2011). (Available at http://www.icsei.net/icsei2011/Full%20Papers/0028.pdf) (Accessed 08/11/2012)
http://www.amauk.co.uk/attachments/267_Formation%20of%20the%20English%20Karate%20Council.%20Statement.pdf (Accessed 04/06/2013)
http://news.bbc.co.uk/1/hi/education/6312589.stm (Accessed 20/02/2013)

Chapter 3

Modifying Pupils' Attitudes and Behaviors in the Classroom through Access to Regular Martial Arts Training

James R. Lee-Barron

Introduction

Teaching, as a lot of people reading this will already know, is not the easiest thing in the world. However, whatever difficulties we might occasionally experience as martial arts instructors is as nothing when compared to what some school teachers have to put up with. Being a teacher in a modern school can be an extremely stressful profession, one that can eventually take its toll upon a person's mental and physical wellbeing. The attitudes and behaviors encountered by modern day teachers are often insulting and threatening, with some even resulting in personal violence against teachers. The teachers having to cope with these issues "on the front line" as it were, are under huge and consistent pressure, and this can lead to a massive breakdowns in both confidence and competence, even causing bouts of depression. All of this negativity is largely due to a minority of students behaving in a completely unacceptable manner towards their teachers, peer-groups and even the wider local community, due to them having what is termed "Emotional and Behavioural Difficulties" or EBD.

    This chapter will share some important observations I have made regarding the positive effect martial arts training can exert upon troublesome" or "difficult" children and young people. It will recount how I noticed that regular training can dramatically increase not only the health and fitness of pupils, but also boost their levels of confidence and self-esteem, inner discipline, and important social abilities such as interpersonal skills and teamwork, etc. All of which serves in reducing some of the more classical traits of EBD. Naturally, because of these improvements, they also aided in the students overall academic performance by instilling a strong sense of self-worth, discipline and respect in the individual, helping to reduce instances of disruptive behavior such as bullying and so aiding teachers in maintaining control in the classroom during their mainstream schooling.

I have been involved with the martial arts for over forty years, and education and training for the past thirty. During that considerable period of time, I have taught all types of things to all types of people and I still enjoy the tremendous buzz I get whenever I see my students learning and achieving. I first taught in a Special Educational Needs setting way back in the early 1980's when I had the privilege of working with Students with Learning Disabilities (Autism/Down's Syndrome) and found the task to be both challenging and rewarding. I later underwent special training to become better at what I was doing (yes, for any responsible teacher CPD has always been there: We didn't have to wait to be told to update our training and qualifications. Back then, we just did it!) with the City Literary Institute in London, and pursued this specialism for several years, both in the UK and elsewhere.

Then, in 1999, I began teaching some special classes for children and young people with Emotional and Behavioural Difficulties. These pupils attended a local special school, and their PE Teacher had contacted me to see if such a venture might be possible. Naturally, I jumped at the chance and commenced giving lessons to them very shortly thereafter.

An Eye-opening Experience

The classes were to take place at a martial arts club in a town neighbouring their school, this meant that the pupils would have to be "bussed" in for their training and, on more than one occasion, the class had to be postponed due to some sort of disturbance that took place on the minibus during the short trip between their school and the training venue which was literally only a scant few miles away! In other words: So frequent and serious was the disruptive behaviour of this group that, sometimes, they never even managed to make it to the class!

I also had an interesting time when they did actually turn up to the venue: I was initially subjected to an almost constant stream of verbal abuse, had my instructions completely ignored and, during one seemingly quite subdued training session, wherein I was lulled into a very false sense of security, one bright young fellow thought he would take it upon himself to try and set light to the building by making use of the toilet rolls in the Gents conveniences! So, you can take it from me that these classes can be extremely eventful, to say the least. Yet, it must be remembered that this disruptive (and, at times, even destructive) behavior is not deliberately directed at any particular person or object. Rather, it is a symptom of a deeply troubled human being, an expression of the anguish and turmoil they feel deep inside of themselves for a whole variety of different and extremely complex reasons. Therefore, it should be perceived as being a very loud cry for help and attention. If an instructor wishing to work with this type of group is unable to accept this, and begins taking the abuse that will is hurled at them in a personal way, then they will actually end up playing the students game rather than encouraging them to play theirs. Consequently, no one will end up getting anywhere. Be that as it may, "forewarned is forearmed" as they say and, as I had been informed that this group was known to consist entirely of pupils with EBD, this is precisely how I expected them to behave, and had prepared myself accordingly.

I found that the old, reliable tools worked best: I completely ignored the negative behavior (in this sort of situation, you simply must be prepared to endure a certain amount of abuse and negativity, and allow it to wash off you like water from a ducks back. It would be very foolish, especially at the early stages, to challenge and confront every little thing, as you would end up filling up the whole lesson in this way and nothing concrete or positive would be achieved) while ensuring that I noticed and praised the positive. Now, at this early stage, there was precious little "positive", I can tell you. Therefore, I had to lower my sites somewhat and become a lot more realistic as to what could actually be taught, learnt and achieved in these preliminary sessions.

I made sure I noticed and praised the very smallest of things: A posture that was sloppy but at least attempted, a kick that was done badly, but tried, a break-fall that made far more noise than sense, but was executed on cue, etc. I praised these small things not just because I wanted to encourage them, but because I had come to realise that, to them, they were not "small things" at all. Quite the opposite in fact: They were making a very real effort to listen, observe, imitate, and practice: To learn, in other words. And this was a very big thing for them to do. I also had to be very careful as to how and when I praised them. Members of this group possess their own strict sub-culture, wherein the respect of their peers is absolutely everything. Consequently, getting any sort of praise from any sort of teacher is not looked upon as being the coolest thing in the world and, if given in too obvious a way, it can seriously damage their "Street-cred" and even compromise their position in the pecking order. From a teacher's point of view, praise given at the wrong time and/or in the wrong way can actually end up encouraging rivalry, jealousy and bullying, and we need to always be mindful of this when dealing with such groups. A simple nod or a wink in the right place will normally suffice. It is best to try and completely avoid acknowledging anyone as a "teacher's pet" so don't over do it.

The same can be said about the person you use to help you in class: DON'T! Instead, try and use everyone in the group at different times and for different things (the bow, the warm up, helping you to demonstrate a technique, etc.) This helps maintain motivation and enthusiasm while also avoiding causing too much friction amongst the group. You should also be prepared for a student you choose to help to occasionally decline your kind offer, in no uncertain terms! If and when this should happen, then maintain your composure and choose someone else (while keeping your fingers firmly crossed) It was by recognising and appreciating these often extremely tiny positives that could so easily have gone completely unnoticed, that I gradually began to establish a more positive rapport with these students. Building upon this smallest of foundations, I gradually began to notice a slight, almost imperceptible, change in the way this group behaved.

They began lining up by themselves, even though they would still fidget, talk and mess around. They would listen to what I was saying, even if they sometimes looked completely bored with the whole thing, and started to genuinely make an effort to learn, remember and practice the techniques, even if they did still swear at each other (and me) on the odd occasion. To help this continue in this trend, I ensured that I never spent too long upon one thing. We would practice solo kicking and/or striking techniques for about five minutes, then change to practicing a throwing technique for the next few minutes, then break-aways, etc. By the fourth week of lessons, things had improved so much that I even introduced an element of weaponry (in the form of foam-rubber safety nunchaku) and this went down very well indeed.

From that point on, the group became very self-regulating: They all made an effort to behave, listen and learn and, if anyone started to get a little too disruptive the rest of the group would ask them (perhaps not always in the politest of ways) to shut up and behave. Even more surprisingly, the person would normally just come out with something like "oh yeah, okay!" whereas, a few weeks earlier, there would have probably been a physical encounter. By the end of the term, this group was finally ready for their grading exam. Despite everyone's reservations, they had managed to modify and regulate their attitudes and behaviour to such an extent that they had learnt just as much as any of the other mainstream groups I was teaching of a similar age and ability.

Yes, they were still hyper-active and, again yes, there was still the occasional lapse in concentration. The difference was that the students themselves had, by now, made the conscious decision to not mess about so much and to try to pay attention when they were shown something. Yes, I had used every trick I knew (and even learned a few more) to help them reach these conclusions and make this decision but, in the end, it was their hard work that had finally paid off. As we all know: When a person achieves well in one area, it often has a knock-on effect upon other areas of their life. And this, according to the feedback I received from this groups school teachers, proved no exception. I was told that they had become a lot less disruptive in class, and, while they were still far from what you might call "perfect", it was noticed that they seemed to be "trying harder", and were achieving more because of this.

Unfortunately, due to both budget-constraints and the school having to relocate to another building, and also to certain changes in my own situation, these classes were discontinued after only a couple of terms. This was disappointing not only for the students themselves, but also for the fact that any form of serious, localised research could not be conducted. The reasons for a young person developing and demonstrating the symptoms of EBD are both numerous and complex, and so lay well outside the parameters of this paper. We do, however know that EBD often manifests itself in Antisocial Behaviour and aggression, and it is important that any instructor considering such work understand a little about these.

Recent research into aggression has managed to identify a variety of traits and indicators. Among these are the following:

- Impulsiveness
- Short attention span
- Hyperactivity
- Anxiousness
- Depression
- Low levels of confidence and self esteem
- Troubled relationships with family members
- Paranoia

Some of the above traits might well be inherited (nature) while others will be the products of the persons social environment (nurture). Other important influences could be the type, frequency and intensity of some form of personal abuse, and the misuse of certain substances, etc. For example, it has been proved that violence and cruelty can leave a very real "scar" upon the brain chemistry itself, with the person typically having quite low levels of serotonin (a neurotransmitter that inhibits aggression). Therefore, a young person who has (again, for example) suffered abuse is often very quick to anger.

To help them, teachers need a patient, respectful appreciation regarding this complex predicament, and to develop the skills necessary to have a positive impact while at the same time establishing firm boundaries around aggressive behaviour without the pitfalls of punishment, shame and humiliation. After all, most of these children will have been through an extremely hard time, so there is no need for us to add to their distress any further. We are there to help, not to hinder.

As far as the martial arts instruction goes: A training environment should be established wherein opportunities for learning and achievement are provided within a climate of encouragement and recognition of progress. These young pupils require intense educational interventions, but any form of improvement should not be expected to manifest themselves overnight: It has taken a sustained period of time to cause the young person's behavior to deteriorate to such an extreme extent, and it will most probably take an equal amount of time to begin to modify it in a more positive way. Martial arts can play a vital role in this intervention as it allows these students to begin expressing themselves in a more positive way through providing an outlet for their more negative behaviors, channeling their energies and emotions into something that is enjoyable, meaningful and worthwhile.

In my own opinion, the study and practice of the martial arts tends to differ quite dramatically from other sorts of physical activities in that their influence upon children and young people with EBD, simply because they are structured in a very different way, with both short and very long-term targets of achievement already identified and put
in place.

- respect
- discipline
- confidence
- self esteem
- interpersonal skills
- teamwork
- lengthened attention span
- acceptance of authority
- control of stress levels
- anticipation of next grade
- eventually achieving the black belt (or equivalent).

In short, it would seem that they are an absolutely excellent tool for encouraging both cognitive and behavioral modification. Martial arts tend to appeal to children and young people. They allow us to reach out and connect with them, engaging them where other subjects, sports and pastimes might have failed, exerting profound, meaningful and long lasting lessons that allow for a positive change for the better.

Conclusion

In addition to the above, I have also taught a variety of special educational needs in mainstream college subjects, and have taught a martial arts class in a hostel for young ex-offenders recovering from substance abuse these experiences, if included them here, would mean this becoming a thesis rather than a short, concise piece of work. Therefore, I have chosen to limit myself to the most relevant situation and experience befitting this brief piece of work.

Hence, it is based entirely upon my own personal experiences and observations and, as such, must be viewed and evaluated as being purely anecdotal. While there has been some far more serious research projects conducted concerning this area, this has been somewhat sporadic in nature. However, what empirical evidence does exist would seem to serve in backing up my own opinion: Strongly indicating that martial arts are, indeed, a very powerful and important tool in aiding these youngsters to improve themselves and achieve far more than they would otherwise. One thing we do certainly know is this: Positive interventions at the earliest possible opportunity is the key to realizing good outcomes for children and young people with any kind of emotional and behavioral difficulties. The government (in the UK at least) is, at last, beginning to lend more support to the structures that bring together various agencies such as education, social services and the NHS, etc. in a model of positive intervention, the common goal of which is to help and support young people. I believe that martial arts training also have a lot to offer and, in my opinion, should be included as an integral part of this initiative.

After all is said and done, it is wrong to expect our students to learn from the way we teach. Instead, we must teach in the way that they learn.

Martial arts have a huge amount to offer both special and mainstream education, and it is one of the ambitions of the IMAS to see martial arts included in the national curriculum both here in the UK and elsewhere. From an education standpoint, martial arts tend to tick several important boxes all at once, and can be easily and directly linked to certain core subjects which are already a part of the national curriculum such as PE and Science. While, from a pupils point of view, martial arts are exciting and fun to learn, as well as imbuing their practitioners with a certain amount of "street-cred". In addition, such training includes aspects of self-defense, which can assist with personal safety and crime reduction, etc. As well as helping to keep our children and young people healthy and fit, a very important consideration for a world facing the prospect of coping with an increasingly aging population who we will need to keep as active as possible in the future. Since the experiences I have related above, I have been asked to deliver special classes to young people undertaking the Duke of Edinburgh's Award, and have worked with a national advisory service on teaching, delivering personal safety courses to teaching staff and managers, thus demonstrating further the numerous useful applications that both regular martial arts training and its extended aspects, such as self-defense and personal safety, can have. In short, they are, in my own humble opinion, a veritable goldmine as to what they have to offer not only as a stand-alone subject in their own right, but in their ability to enrich and enhance others as well. And this is especially the case when it comes to engaging children and young people with emotional and behavioral difficulties.

References

Daniels K., & E.W. Thornton (1990). An Analysis of the Relationship Between Hostility and Training in the Martial Arts, *Journal of Sports Sciences*, 8: 95-101.

Daniels K., & E.W Thornton (1992). Length of Training, Hostility and the Martial Arts: A Comparison with Other Sporting Groups, *British Journal of Sports Medicine*, 26: 118-120.

Fuller J.R. (1988), Martial arts and psychological health, *British Journal of Medical Psychology*, 61, 317-328.

Gleser J., & P. Brown (1988). Judo Principles and Practices: Applications to Conflict-Solving Strategies in Psychotherapy, *American Journal of Psychotherapy*, 42: 437-447.

Jasnoski M.L., Corday D.S., Houston B.K., & W.H. Osness (1987). Modification of Type A Behavior Through Aerobic Exercise, *Motivation and Emotion*, 11: 1-17.

Jin P. (1989), Changes in Heart Rate, Noradrenaline, Cortisol and Mood During Tai Chi, *Journal of Psychosomatic Research*, 33: 197-206.

Jin P. (1992), Efficacy of Tai Chi, Brisk Walking, Meditation, and Reading on Reducing Mental and Emotional Stress, *Journal of Psychosomatic Research*, 36: 361-370.

Konzak B., & F. Boudreau (1984). Martial arts training and mental health: An exercise in self-help, *Canada's Mental Health*, 32, 2-8.

Leith L.M., & A. H. Taylor (1990). Psychological Aspects of Exercise: A Decade Literature Review, *Journal of Sport Behavior*, 13: 219-239.

Parsons M. (1984). Psychoanalysis as vocation and martial art, *International Review of Psychoanalysis*, 11(4):453462.

Richman, C.L., & H. Rehberg (1986). The development of self-esteem through the martial arts, *International Journal of Sports Psychology*, 17(3), 234-239.

Trulson M.E. (1986). Martial arts training: A novel 'cure' for juvenile delinquency, *Human Relations*, 39, 1131-1140.

Reiter H. (1975). A Note on the Relationship Between Anxiety and Karate Participation, *Mankind Quarterly*, 16: 127-128.

Richman C.L., & H. Rehberg (1986). The Development of Self-Esteem Through the Martial Arts, *International Journal of Sport Psychology*, 17: 234-239.

Weiser M., Kutz I., Kutz S.J., & D. Weiser (1995). Psychotherapeutic Aspects of the Martial Arts, *American Journal of Psychotherapy*, 49: 118-127. [1]

---

[1] In addition to the above, I would highly recommend Edward De Bono's work to any type of teacher, particularly "Six Thinking Hats", which is always readily available in several formats.

Chapter 4

Learning 'in' and 'through' Amateur Boxing

John Fulton

Introduction

This chapter is based on an ethnographic study which explored amateur and professional boxing in the North East of England with a particular focus on 'amateur boxing'. The main aim of the study was to examine ways in which involvement in boxing could interact with other areas of the boxers' lives. A useful approach to the study of learning and its impact on people and their life is the concept of capital. Bourdieu's notion of capital served as a theoretical underpinning for the study, and to put the aims in another way the focus was on how the learning which took place in the boxing clubs could interact with the development of capital. Capital can be defined as: the resources or attributes possessed by an individual which can increase his or her life chances.

Central to Bourdieu's notion of capital is cultural capital which represents the ruling classes and their particular dispositions, habits, tastes, values etc. These are the standards against which people are judged and the more power people have in society the closer their dispositions are to those of the ruling classes. The more academic qualifications a person has the more economic capital they can have (although not always). Cultural capital can determine opportunities in life. The boxers in this study, coming from mainly working class areas, did not have a high degree of cultural capital but the participation in boxing did add to their life chances and develop capital. This chapter will explore the ways in which participation in boxing can increase capital of those who participate.

The Boxing Scene

Amateur boxing is of course an Olympic sport and as such is both structured and organised. The Amateur Boxing Association (ABA) England is the organising body. England is divided into regions and the North East of England is one of these regions stretching from the Scottish borders to the Yorkshire borders. The most northerly area is Amble in Northumberland and the furthest south is Redcar. All clubs are approved and registered with the Amateur Boxing Association. This means, in practice they are approved as being appropriate in terms of qualified coaches and appropriate premises.

Boxing clubs were found largely in urban areas or in former mining villages, areas in which manual labour in heavy industry was valued. This is an important factor as certain dispositions and backgrounds are associated with this. The clubs formed a clear hierarchy and at the top were the well-established clubs who had produced a number of champions. The clubs had national and international links and attracted sponsorship. Clubs lower down the pecking order were often one man shows and were regarded with suspicion by the ABA officials. There were all sorts of nuances with the rules and these clubs were never quite sure of which had to be followed and which ones could be ignored.

The boxing clubs were seen as an asset to the locality and yet, there was also ambivalence as was characterised by the two contradictory discourses which can be summarized as:

- Boxing is inherently good and is a constructive thing for young males; it prevents them getting into trouble and is a constructive outlet for aggression
- Boxing is inherently harmful and there is something distasteful about two people hitting each other and it also carries the potential for serious injury

The people running the clubs clearly adhered to the first of the discourses. Many of the coaches and those involved see boxing, considerably wider than the activity but rather as a preparation for life; as one club programme sated in its introduction:

> 'We try to keep the kids off the streets and instil in them self-discipline and character building. Boxing is a combative sport and as such requires a high degree of courage, self-dedication, physical fitness etc. It also provides an excellent outlet for their natural aggressive instincts, this is excellent training for "the Battle of Life" which the boys will soon be facing, modern life is very hard and the ability of a boy to accept good and averse conditions and decisions in a sporting manner is excellent preparation'.

> Programme for Tournament,
> Sunderland, October 2004

The common perception was that many were heading for a life of crime and boxing prevented this from happening. This statement from a gifted amateur boxer typifies this…

> 'Hung around on street corners and just drifted, into.... a gang of street kids hanging around. I drifted into the local boxing club and ...looking back it's the best thing I ever did'.

It was difficult to confirm this, as many of the boxers came from stable working class homes with a high degree of organisation (....this was similar to Wacquant's (1992) findings in Chicago). However one thing which was universally acknowledged was the inclusivity of boxing:

> 'Boxing is a sport you can do where you don't have to have much money you only have to pay £1.30 as a sub, and some places if you can't afford that they will let you in. You don't need to buy football boots or a strip you just need to go there and train... You know, it's not as easy to go to a football club because you've got to be half way decent to get in the team. It's a bit confident blowing not to get in the team. Whereas boxing you go there whether you are good or not good. You can go there and do the training you don't have to compete...'

It was a continual conscious choice for the young people who had to make a clear decision as to choose constructive activities or drift into hanging around street corners with alcohol issues and potential confrontations with neighbouring groups or with the police. There are a number of activities available and it was a matter of personal choice which one they engaged with, of course people could and did choose more than one. Boxing appealed to them because it was a traditional masculine sport which involved the display of considerable prowess and in which they could prove themselves as men.

This was not to suppose that all the boxers were 100% dedicated or committed and stayed the course, many fell by the wayside. The pattern of involvement was that as described by Sugden (1987). A hiatus of young people joined the clubs at the ages of 11 -12 and many dropped out between 12 and 16, as one respondent put it when they discovered drink and girls. A smaller number stayed the course, some going on to win national championships and a smaller number going onto the Commonwealth and Olympic games. A smaller number would go onto become professional boxers. This chapter will focus on those boxers who participated during their teenage years rather than the ones who went on to be amateur champions or entered the professional ranks. However, many people I meet, such as colleagues, and to whom I mentioned I was carrying out a boxing study recognised both discourses but despite this supported boxing, and saw it as a good and purposeful activity. This following statement, from a youth worker, typifies much of what I heard...

> 'I'm stuck in the middle of this in terms of the benefits of boxing versus the aim of a boxing match which is to punch someone in the jaw so it rattles their brains renders them unconscious for at least 10 seconds. It's a very crude description of it and when you're dealing with young people who've got anger management problems and issues around that there's just a doubt in me mind but then for years I've worked in youth clubs and stuff like that beforehand where there was big boxing sections

and you see some really tough kids who've had a hard time, come in and they get the discipline of a good set out training session where they're getting good physical fitness, again camaraderie with other boxers. They've got goals, they've got aspirations and stuff like that and it's done in a very disciplined fashion...'

It is clear that there is the assumption both from politicians, the general public and the boxers themselves that this participation can prevent the boys from getting into trouble. Involvement in sport makes for a structured, time occupying activity and also has character building properties (Bourdieu, 1978). My study shows that whilst this could be the case, some respondents, whilst acknowledging boxing as a good character building thing to do, saw amateur boxing as an end in itself. Whether it actually prevented the young men from getting into trouble is difficult to ascertain. Arguably, the boys and young men, involved in boxing, would have found some other constructive way of spending their time; also some did fall by the wayside and drop out of boxing. However, one boxer who dropped out was found guilty of "mugging" someone, and this was remarkable enough to made the headlines of the local paper, expressing horror at this. The perceptions are, nevertheless, boxing is a way of preventing trouble and, to some, it gives it a raison d'être.

The gender issue is interesting in the context of this study. Female boxing has, in the past 10 years or so become increasingly common, and certainly after the 2012 Olympic Games. Yet at the time of the study female boxers were so rare as to be non-existent. As regards the ethnic mix: the North East does not have a particularly strong mix but in certain areas there was a sizable Asian community (mainly Pakistani and Bangladesh), which did have a boxing presence. The local mosque approved of boxing and indeed organized trips to a gym 30 miles away run by a Muslim trainer. They informed me that the Koran mentioned wresting as an appropriate sport, and they were comfortable with boxing as a sport akin to wrestling.

Body Capital

The working class and middle class can view their bodies differently (Bourdieu, 1997); Schilling (1992) refers to this as physical capital. The middle class look on the development of their body as a project or an end in itself whereas for the working class the body is important and can be a means to an end; for example increased physical prowess can lead to more job opportunities (Bourdieu, 1978).

In the context of his Chicago boxing study, Wacquant (1995) referred to the attributes developed through boxing as "body capital". Body capital refers to the way in which the boxer builds up his body which can be used as a fighting machine. This takes endless discipline both in terms of keeping the body at the correct weight, maintaining a high level of physical fitness and level of physical fitness and in various other ways such as looking after the hands, as despite the protection of hands by warps and gloves, injuries to the hands were not uncommon. An additional feature is maintaining weight and, in practice, this meant exerting self-discipline to eating and drinking, in not eating unhealthy foods and abstaining from alcohol. The British boxer Ricky Hatton (2008) wrote of when he was preparing for a match he would stop eating fast foods and enter into a vigorous training regime and exclude himself to gain this body capital. Participation in boxing necessitated the development of a high degree of fitness, and this fitness is central to body capital. In the tournaments and in sparring it became immediately apparent in a boxer neglected his fitness levels, although in amateur boxing the rounds were only two minutes in length it was surprizing how tiring these two minutes could be and how much energy they could expend.

Boxing also required a degree of resilience and a training of the body both to react quickly and to take physical pain. I only engaged in light sparring which was more of a simulation that the real thing and a light punch was not at all pleasant, whereas a full scale punch would come as quite a shock, as one respondent put it:

> "It's a shock all right. I have experienced it on smaller levels myself".

Reflexes were highly toned, as Joyce Carol Oates (1987) wrote; when punched the natural reaction is to turn away, yet the boxer reflexes make him hit back; or when knocked down the easiest thing is to continue lying on the ground, rather than get back up and start fighting again. Other than in boxing or in some form of combat sports, it can be argued that the skills of body capital are of no real use. Wacquant (2004) makes the point that:

> "….the specific capital he possesses is entirely embodied, and once it has been used, devoid of value in any other domain". (Wacquant, 2004:59).

However, it is worth differentiating between physical and body capital and whilst the boxers did develop a high level of body capital they also developed physical capital. One can take body capital to refer to the development of the body through and for boxing and physical capital as the development of the body per se. The boxers developed both body capital, and in the sense they developed a high level of physical fitness, physical capital. This physical capital could impact of other areas of their life. The physical capital gave the young men a certain confidence which was conveyed through their appearance, and the ways in which they held themselves and related to their peers, with a certain confidence. An important aspect of Bourdieu's theories is the concept of habitus or disposition, Bourdieu (1997) does not differentiate between internal and external dispositions, for example, one's gender is conveyed through the body, for example men and women have different ways of sitting and holding themselves.

Bridges (2009), writing in the context of body building, discusses gender capital; by this he means the closer the individual is to society's idealised concept of male and female. Within this context the idealised male is that of hegemonic masculinity (Connell, 2005). This captures the notion of physical capital; the boxers in the study were developing their male bodies and in doing so were becoming more masculine or more like the idea of the hegemonic male.

The study took place in boxing clubs in the North East of England and the economic changes are well documented, in that the traditional heavy industry of coal mining and ship building have all but disappeared. Rather than a stable employment pattern it has now become much more precarious and much of the employment is in the service industry such as call centres; and with the decline of heavy industry young men can no longer express their masculinity through this type of work. Nayek and *Kehily*. (2008) express this as: masculinities which are economically and culturally displaced and the young men need to find other ways of expressing their masculinity. It is logical to relate this to Nayak and *Kehily*.'s findings and argue that participation in boxing is a way of developing and maintaining a masculine identity, in a situation of economic change where traditional masculine roles are absent. Through participation in boxing the young man gained a disposition, physique and status as a boxer, which often included a damaged or broken nose, which gave him a degree of kudos both with his peers and with different generations.

Learning

Physical capital was something which had to be actively worked at and involved a high degree of learning. People learn in all sorts of ways, not only in formal educational settings. A useful way of conceptualising this is in formal, non-formal and informal learning; this also allows for interaction between the three. If we take formal education to be school based, the participants in the gym engaged in non-formal and in-formal learning. Non-formal learning is organised and structured but does not lead to a formal qualification; whereas informal learning refers to things picked up and takes place due to interaction with others. It can be constructive and purposeful and can also lead to the development of bad habits. (Colley et al, 2002:10)

A central issue is that learning is implicit in the development of capital, although Bourdieu's theory is not explicitly a learning theory (although is highly influential in the sociology of education). Arguably the development of capital involves learning through socialisation. For example, a large part of the process of joining the club was socialisation into the world of boxing which involves the acceptable norms of behaviour within the particular setting. Importantly, a degree of discipline was required like turning up on time, attending regularly, and showing a degree of commitment to the boxing club. The situation of the amateur boxing clubs was a form of non-formal learning; as learning the skills of amateur boxing was taught in structured manner, although mostly learning came through the body. Informal learning was also an important aspect; the adoption of the attributes of hegemonic masculinity had to be learned. There were many unwritten rules of behaviour and if this behaviour was deviated from the boxer would be ridiculed and called names like a "big girl", often in a teasing way but the underlying message was clear (Fulton, 2011). This helped with developing a masculine identity in an area and at a time when masculinity was being eroded in all sorts of other ways.

There was a predominance of young school age boys and certainly the largest numbers involved were under 18. The relationship of learning and the development of capital were of interest, as was how the informal and non-formal learning could interact with formal learning in the educational setting. The discipline instilled through boxing was perceived to be a very important aspect of boxing or could be the background to the development of capital.

Direct engagement with schooling was fairly rare although one boxer made an interesting comment which typified the ways in which the non-formal and informal learning could be used in other areas. He, although was involved in amateur boxing looked to professional boxers for role models; both those boxing now and previous boxers. His hero was the African American boxer Muhammad Ali, and this he held in common with many others; he spoke at length of how in an interest in Mohammad Ali lead him to read about Ali and he became involved in reading further about race relations in the US. Much of the learning which happened in boxing in all sorts of ways, could (and perhaps should) be transferred to their school and students encouraged explicitly to relate their learning of some mainstream subjects to boxing. This is one example; but there are numerous others. However, there was clear links between engagement in boxing and the development of social capital. Social capital is the network of relations an individual has in society, which can be both in terms of emotional support and practical benefits for the individual. It is an increasingly popular term and is used widely and is increasingly being represented in policy documents. This was an important aspect of the boxing scene. There were numerous examples of social capital and its development. The degree of camaraderie which was built up and the sense of community is difficult to encapsulate in words but there were numerous examples of the ways in which people would help each other out. For example, through my involvement I built up a network of tradesmen.

The boxing clubs tended to be in self-contained areas, but many of the clubs put on regular shows or tournaments and through these shows the boxers could gain a higher profile in the area, and if they performed well a degree of respect. Through the network of relations the young boxers had a variety of people to turn to gain help. A good example of this is one of the respondents, a business man who ran an amateur boxing club, helped a boxer out who was in trouble with his employers:

> 'Like take to-day I'm going to-day, I am going to defend a lad against a local authority; sadly, I have to be careful when I say local authority because it is likely to be individuals acting within a local authority. But here you have a lad who has boxed since he was 10 years old, who has boxed at every level other than Olympic and he has had the opportunity to do that. He is an absolutely top flight professional who appears on television, who has appeared on TV in every contest he has had, has the potential to raise the morale of the whole of the area and promote the area. He was injured in his last contest, a genuine injury, a broken hand and after two weeks of sickness they stopped his pay. His contract of employment he's entitled to 6 months on full pay and he's not a shirker. And the sad thing is they cannot see the potential'.

Conclusions

Alheit (2002:3) describes capital particularly succinctly:

> "......in a well-known television interview Bourdieu used the metaphor of a casino. We gamble not only with the black chips that represent our

economic capital, we also use the blue chips symbolising our cultural capital, our exams and titles, what we know about people, about our minds and bodies, about our society. The red chips represent perhaps the social capital we own, our connections the social access that everyone has. Taken together all these different chips represent our capital".

If one's capital is akin to chips in a poker game, social capital are the yellow chips, body or physical capital are the red ones and cultural capital are blue. Then engagement in boxing does give the boxer some red and yellow chips, and his social capital leads to increased greatly body capital. These two forms of capital interact as body capital, and the confidence and recognition adds to his social capital. The relationship with boxing and cultural capital is a little more nebulous, but skills of self-discipline do assist with the development of cultural capital. More direct links could be made with the informal and non-formal learning in boxing gym to schooling with could benefit learning and engagement.

References

Alheit P. (2002). The double face of life long learning; Two analytic perspectives in a "silent revolution". *Studies in the Education of Adults* 34(1):3-22, 2002.

Bourdieu P. (1978). *Outline of a Theory of Practice*. Cambridge: Cambridge University Press.

Bourdieu P. (1997). *Pascalian Meditations*. Cambridge: Polity Press.

Bourdieu P. (1978). Sport and Social Class. *Social Science Information* 17(6):819-840.

Bridges, T. S. (2009). Gender capital and male bodybuilders. *Body & Society* 15.1 83-107.

Colley, H, Hodkinson P & Malcolm J. (2002). *Non-formal learning: Mapping the conceptual terrain*. A Consultation Report. Leeds: University of Leeds Lifelong Learning Institute. 2002.

Connell, R (2005) *Masculinities*. Cambridge: Polity Press (2nd Edition).

Fulton, J. (2011). "What's your worth?" The Development of Capital in British Boxing *European Journal for Sport and Society 8(3), 193-218.*

Hatton, Ricky (2008) *Ricky Hatton: The Hitman*. London: Random House.

Nayak, A. & *Kehily*. M.J. (2008) *Gender, Youth and Culture: Young Masculinities and Femininities*. Basingstoke: Palgrave Macmillan.

Oates Carol Joyce. (1987) *On Boxing*. New Jersey: The Ecco Press.

Schilling C. (1991) Educating the Body: Physical capital and the production of the social. *Sociology* 25(4):653-672, 1991.

Sugden John (1987). The exploitation of disadvantage: The occupational subculture of the boxer. in: *Sport, Leisure and Social Relations*. Horne J and Jacy D & Tomlinson A. London:Routledge & Kogan Paul.

Wacquant L. (1992). The social logic of boxing in Black Chicago: Towards a sociology of pugalism. *Sociology of Sport* 9:221-254, 1992.

Wacquant L. (1995) Pugs at work: Bodily capital and bodily labour among professional boxers. *Body & Society* 1 (1):65-93 .

Wacquant L. (2004) *Body and Soul: Notebooks of an Apprentice Boxer.* .New York:Oxford University Press.

Chapter 5

Martial Arts and Youth: For Better or Worse?

Marc Theeboom & Jikkemien Vertonghen

Introduction

Sports participation studies consistently indicate that martial arts (e.g., judo, karate, taekwondo, kickboxing) are among the most practised sports in many countries (e.g., Australia: Australian Bureau of Statistics, 2009; Canada: Ifedi, 2008; Europe: van Bottenburg, Rijnen, & Sterkenburg, 2005). In many cases, martial arts are listed in the ten most practiced sports among youth in particular (Ministère de la jeunesse des sports et de la vie associative, 2005; Nederlandse Hartstichting & NOC*NSF, 2007; Tammelin et al., 2003; Warren, 2008; Wolt et al., 2007). It is interesting to note however, that despite this high popularity among youngsters, there is controversy regarding the desirability of youth martial arts practice. While advocates indicate that martial arts have a positive impact on the behaviour of youngsters (e.g., Jaspers, 2007), opponents claim that this involvement can lead to increased aggression (e.g., Marks, 2008). Today, many examples of controversial statements regarding the value (or danger) of martial arts practice for youth can be found on the internet. According to some, the perceptions of outcomes of martial arts practice are largely generated by the media and entertainment industry (e.g., martial arts movies) (Cynarski & Walczak, 2009; Fuller, 1988; Grady, 1998; Smith, 1999; Stickney, 2005). It is indicated that this kind of popular media often creates a distorted image of martial arts practice, because some aspects (e.g., the ethical values of martial arts) are underexposed, while other more spectacular elements are highlighted.

The paradox in which two opposite outcomes are linked to youth involvement in martial arts, has resulted in an ambiguous public discourse on their value and legitimacy as a youth activity. By and large, there is a general notion that a dichotomisation exists between, on the one hand, specific martial arts styles that are associated with positive outcomes and, on the other hand, styles that result in negative effects. There is a common view that Asian (traditional) martial arts (e.g., karate, taekwondo, aikido) with a distinct emphasis on philosophical and spiritual aspects next to physical elements, are more associated with positive and educational outcomes. At the same time however, there is a negative perception of 'harder' martial arts styles (referred by some as 'combat sports') (e.g., boxing, Thai and kickboxing, mixed martial arts or 'MMA') which is often more linked to aggressive, violent and health-compromising behaviour. The latter is well depicted in 'Strictly Baby Fight Club', a Channel 4 Cutting Edge TV documentary from 2008, which highlighted the growth of cage fighting among children in the UK[1]. The documentary showed children engaging in hard martial arts contests in their own country and also travelling with their parents to Thailand to be allowed to fight with less restricted competition rules and protective gear.

Consequently over the years, a number of concerns have been formulated based on medical, philosophical and ethical grounds with a plea for a ban or restriction of youth involvement in harder martial arts (e.g., Bledsoe, 2009; Buse, 2006; Carr, 1998; Kochhar et al., 2005; Sheard, 1997; Pearn; 1998). However, this public debate is often based on strong personal beliefs and, with the exception of physical health-related issues, with little or no reference to scientific research. Although it can be expected that common views on the personal and social impact of martial arts involvement on youth can benefit from looking at research findings, it is important to understand the extent to which conclusive scientific evidence can be provided at all.

Where is the Evidence?

To date, a range of topics in a variety of disciplines have been studied in relation to martial arts involvement (e.g., physiology, biomechanics, injury epidemiology, psychology, history, sociology, pedagogy). Since long, a major topic has been the prevalence of injuries as it is often assumed that martial arts participants are more susceptible to injury (e.g., Lystad, Pollard & Graham, 2009; Ngai, Levy & Hsu, 2008; Pieter, 2005; Rechel et al., 2008). However, based on research findings, it remains unclear whether or not there is a higher occurrence of injuries in martial arts compared to other sports or even between different styles. For example, while some studies reported higher injury rates in martial arts (e.g., Falvey et al., 2009; Junge et al., 2009), other research did not (e.g., Belechri et al, 2001; Darrow et al., 2009). Injury rates between different martial arts have also been compared (e.g., Cynarski & Kudlacz, 2008; Zetaruk et al., 2005). Findings however have not always pointed in the same direction. While some studies reported a higher injury incidence among harder styles compared to other martial arts (e.g., Gartland et al., 2005), other research resulted in no differences (e.g., Gartland et al., 2001).

Another major topic in martial arts research has been on investigating socio-psychological outcomes among young martial arts participants (see Vertonghen & Theeboom, 2010). Undoubtedly, this interest is generated by the general notion that involvement in martial arts can have an effect on youth's attitude and behavior (e.g., in terms of psychological well-being; level of aggression; social

---

[1] http://www.channel4.com/programmes/strictly-baby-fight-club

skill development). Here too, the actual impact of martial arts involvement on young participants remains obscure (Theeboom, 2012). While most studies have pointed in the direction of the appearance of positive effects of martial arts involvement (e.g., higher levels of self-regulation; increased psychological well-being; decreased violence levels among young participants), negative outcomes have been reported as well (e.g., increased antisocial behavior and aggression). For example, while some longitudinal studies did not report an increase in aggressiveness among the participating youngsters in selected Asian martial arts (e.g., Reynes & Lorant, 2001), other research findings did (Delva-Tauiliili, 1995; Reynes & Lorant, 2002).

It is also interesting to note that one Norwegian study in particular conducted by Endresen and Olweus (2005) received considerable media attention and was referred to in a number of public internet fora (e.g., Bullshido.net, 2007; van Dongen, 2005; Weel, 2005; Veganfitness.net, 2008). The study examined possible effects of participation in so-called 'power sports' (i.e., boxing, weightlifting, wrestling and Asian martial arts) on antisocial involvement among preadolescent and adolescent boys. Endresen and Olweus' results suggested that participation in power sports leads to an increase of violent as well as non-violent antisocial behaviour outside sport, compared to a non-participation control group. The fact that this particular study received more attention than most other studies, seems to underline the negative image that exists among many with regard to youth involvement in some martial arts (e.g., boxing).

As indicated earlier however, the extent to which existing research provides a better understanding of the impact of martial arts involvement on youth is limited. One of the reasons for this is the fact that most studies investigating the outcomes of youth martial arts practice make use of a broad classification of martial arts (e.g., 'traditional' versus 'modern'; 'soft' versus 'hard'; 'defensive' versus 'offensive'; 'competitive' versus 'recreational')(e.g., Cynarski & Kudlacz, 2008; Zetaruk et al., 2005). Although it makes sense to take the wide variety of martial arts that exists into account, dividing them only into broad categories or disciplines to determine their impact will not be sufficient. This is illustrated by the fact that several studies - as earlier described - have produced opposite findings (sometimes even within the same styles). We have therefore indicated elsewhere that a better understanding of the social-psychological impact of martial arts involvement on youth can only be obtained if several specific influential factors are taken into account (Vertonghen & Theeboom, 2010). These factors relate, among other things, to the participants' characteristics, the type of guidance or coaching, the social context of participants, as well as to the structural and inherent qualities of the particular martial art style. In other words, there is a distinct dependency on the specific context in which martial arts are practised. This view is in line with Pawson's (2001) configurational approach to causality of social interventions in which outcomes can only be understood as a result of the interaction of a particular combination of circumstances. Consequently, insight into the actual conditions and processes of martial arts practices are equally important to determine outcomes.

In fact, one wonders whether the latter is even possible to determine at all. For there are a number of reasons why this is not an easy task. For example, the very fact that different contextual factors can be expected to have an impact (or not) on youngsters' attitudes and behaviour, makes it very difficult to empirically determine the actual effects of martial arts involvement. It is clear that a number of these factors are not directly related to the martial arts practice as such (e.g., the role of the social context of youngsters involved, such as peers and family relations). It therefore becomes difficult to determine the relative contribution of the specific martial art youngsters are practising.

Another issue which makes it difficult to measure the actual impact of martial arts involvement relates to the 'problem' of determining causality. It is not because two variables occur at the same time (e.g., prolonged martial arts involvement and high self-esteem) that one is the cause and the other the effect. It may very well be the other way around. For example, youngsters with high self-esteem might be more attracted to martial arts or are more motivated to continue their involvement than others. As most of the existing research on that matter uses a cross-sectional design (comparing beginners with more experienced martial artists), it is difficult to rule out these type of errors. Moreover, as mentioned earlier, even longitudinal studies have been shown to be inconclusive (e.g., Reynes & Lorant, 2001; Reynes & Lorant, 2002). With this in mind, the fact that harder martial arts in general are regarded as causes for, among other things, increased levels of aggression of youngsters, becomes much harder to prove. The same, however, can be said for the opposite claims about the positive socio-psychological and pedagogical functions of (traditional) martial arts.

Martial Arts and Sport Development

Over the years, a wide range of positive effects as a result of martial arts involvement has been described in the literature. Among other things, these benefits relate to increased levels of self-control (Madden, 1995), self-confidence (Konzak & Klavora, 1980), aggression regulation (Wisse, 2007), self-perception (Finkenberg, 1990), pro-social behaviour (Lakes & Hoyt, 2004), stress reduction (Wall, 2005) and school violence prevention (Smith et al., 1999; Zivin et al., 2001). This is in line with a growing belief among many regarding the social role of sport in general. This increased trust in the 'good of sport' is illustrated by the fact that today in many countries sport is viewed by policy makers and sports providers as an effective means to help realise social objectives that go far beyond sports related goals. For example, 2004 was announced as the 'European Year for Education through Sport' (Janssens et al., 2004) and even the United Nations regards sport as a powerful tool to help attain the Millennium Development Goals (United Nations, s.d.). Consequently, an increasing number of 'sport for development' projects have been set up over the past years in many countries all over the world[2]. Similar to what we mentioned earlier regarding the lack of conclusive evidence for the impact of martial arts involvement on youth, the cumulative evidence base for the developmental potential of sport in general remains weak. Long and Sanderson (2001) pointed out that, to date, there is limited empirical evidence indicating a direct causal relationship between doing sport and social integration or any other beneficial social outcome for that matter. Coalter (2007) argued that the underlying causes for this 'knowledge gap' need to

---

[2] See e.g., http://www.sportanddev.org

be found in the often taken for granted beliefs or storylines on the social beneficial outcomes that are attributed to sports participation. In light of this, Green (2008, p. 132) argued that *"....the belief that sport builds character is so ingrained that neither providers nor participants feel it necessary to do anything more than to provide opportunities"*.

However, despite the lack of empirical evidence, as mentioned before, a growing number of 'sport for change' initiatives have been set up in many parts of the world. And while not exclusively, it is fair to say that a majority of these sport-based developmental programmes are aiming for specific target groups.

Socially Vulnerable Youth and Martial Arts

One of the groups that is often targeted are youngsters coming from socially deprived neighbourhoods and/or ethnic minorities. Many of these youngsters are characterised by a situation of so-called 'social vulnerability'. A situation which is defined as the risk to repeatedly experience negative aspects such as control and sanctions when coming in contact with social institutions (school, labour market, justice system; Vettenburg, 1998). According to Walgrave (1992), the term refers to the vulnerable position of specific individuals or groups in society living in economically deprived urban neighborhood's that cannot benefit from organized educational and welfare opportunities.

Today, there is an increasing number of sport-based developmental initiatives that are set up to reach out and to work with socially vulnerable youth (Holt, 2008). Literature describes a number of strategies that are being used in these developmental programs (e.g., 'positive youth development' - Holt, 2008; 'life skills approach' – Gould et al., 2006; 'responsibility model' – Hellison, 1995). And while a wide variety of sports is organised within this type of programmes, it is interesting to note that a considerable amount of these programmes include one of more martial arts. A recent inventory of martial arts based developmental programmes aimed at socially vulnerable youth shows that harder martial arts (i.e., boxing, Thai and kickboxing) in particular are more organised than traditional martial arts (i.e., judo, karate, taekwondo; Theeboom & Verheyden, 2011). Some authors have tried to explain this interest in harder martial arts by referring to the existence of a (symbolic) association with fighting or class struggle (e.g., Lagendijk, 1991, Wacquant, 1992) or its masculine identity (Woodward, 2007). The working or lower class image of harder martial arts is believed to bridge the gap that often exists between educators and youth (Theeboom et al., 2008). This fact, however, brings about the odd situation that the most socially contested types of martial arts (i.e., the harder ones) are the most preferred in sport-based developmental initiatives for socially vulnerable youth. So in other words, these martial arts that are often believed to instigate aggressive and delinquent behaviour of youngsters, are in fact the ones that are used most in behaviour changing strategies aimed at youth who are believed to show more frequent antisocial behaviour.

Some Further Thoughts!

The above-described position of hard martial arts in sport-based developmental initiatives brings about a number of issues that require further thoughts. As a way to conclude this chapter, we will elaborate on two of these issues. One is situated on the policy level, the second is a research related one.

On a policy level, the paradox can best be illustrated by a specific case. For this we have chosen to look at the governmental sports policy context of Flanders, the northern Dutch-speaking part of Belgium. Since more than a decade, one of the pillars of the Flemish sports subsidisation policy relies on the existence of a selected list of 54 sports that are eligible for official recognition and financial support by the Flemish government. The list was highly debated and it took a long time to come up with the final selection. It includes 10 different martial arts (aikido, amateur boxing, fencing, jiu-jitsu, judo, karate, kendo, taekwondo, wrestling and wushu). Apart from amateur boxing (because of its Olympic status), no other hard martial arts are included. This is mainly because of distinct medical and moral concerns that were raised. Flemish sports policy is now facing two problems: one is related to the increased popularity of Thai and kickboxing over the last decade. As a consequence, there is a high demand for official recognition of these particular sports and for support of teachers formation, as well as for a legislative framework in relation to medical and ethical issues. But as long as these sports are not on the list, the government is restricted in taking decisive actions. And while expanding the list would seem like a logic step, few government officials are in favour because it would open up the debate again, as well as incite demands from other sports that are not on the list either. A second problem the Flemish government is facing relates to the fact that on the one hand no recognition and support is allowed for participants of Thai and kickboxing (because they are not on the official sports list). However on the other hand, the same government supports a number of sport-based developmental initiatives that make use of these sports. To date, it is still unclear how this can fit into one coherent official government policy regarding harder martial arts.

A second issue relates to the actual status of martial arts research. More in particular, the extent to which the evidence base regarding the impact of martial arts involvement on youth can be expanded. As earlier described, at present there is limited insight into the actual outcomes of martial arts participation. Today however, there is a growing notion that research faces several methodological problems. Again, this is line with more general literature on sport for development. Coalter (2011) for example argued that sport-based social practices are mostly guided by '...*inflated promises* and *lack of intellectual clarity*'. He referred to Pawson's (2004) comment that much social policy intervention can be characterised as '...*ill-defined interventions with hard to follow outcomes*'. The fact that most research reports only mention the type of martial art under study (or in some cases the teaching approach), does not allow anyone to draw firm conclusions regarding the actual impact of martial arts involvement. We therefore concur with Patricksson (1995) that there is a need to stop generalising about such a heterogeneous, summative, concept as sport (or martial arts for that matter) and examine issues relating to particular types of sports and how they are exactly delivered and experienced. It will be the only way to begin to understand what conditions are necessary for martial arts involvement to have beneficial outcomes for young people.

References

Australian Bureau of Statistics (2009). Children's participation in cultural and leisure activities (Cat. No. 4901.0). www.abs.gov.au/AUSSTATS/abs@.nsf/DetailsPage/4901.0Apr%202009?

Belechri, M., Petridou, E., KediKoglou, S., & D. Trichopoulos (2001). Sports injuries among children in six European Union countries. *European Journal of Epidemiology*, 17, 1005-1012.

Bledsoe, G.H. (2009). Mixed martial arts, in R. Kordi, N. Maffulli, R.R. Wroble & W. A. Wallace (Eds.), *Combat Sports Medicine*, (pp.323-330). Springer, London.

Bottenburg, van M., Rijnen, B. and J. van Sterkenburg (2005). *Sports participation in the European Union. Trends and differences*, W.J.H. Mulier Institute - Arko Sports Media, 's Hertogenbosch – Nieuwegein.

Bullshido.net (2007). www.bullshido.net/forums/showthread.php?t=59083&page=3

Buse, G.J. (2006). No holds barred sport fighting: a 10 year review of mixed martial arts competition. *British Journal of Sport Medicine*, 40, 169-172.

Carr, D. (1998). What moral significance has physical education? A question in need of disambiguation, in M.J. McNamee (Ed.). *Ethics and Sport*, (pp.119-133). E&FN Spon, London.

Coalter, F. (2011). Sport development's contribution to social policy objectives. The difficult relationship between politics and evidence, in B. Houlihan & M. Green (Eds.), *Routledge Handbook of Sport Development*, (pp. 561-579). Taylor & Francis Ltd., London-New York.

Coalter, F. (2007). *A Wider social role for sport: Who's keeping the score?*, Routledge, London.

Cynarski, W.J. & Kudlacz, M. (2008). Injuries in martial arts and combat sports - a comparative study, *Archives of Budo*, 4, 91-97

Cynarski, W., & Walczak, J. (2009). Karate casus in Poland – towards sociology of martial arts. *Journal of Combat Sports and Martial Arts*, 1, 59-63.

Darrow, C.J., Collins, C.L., Yard, E.E. & R.D.Comstock (2009). Epidemiology of Severe Injuries Among United States High School Athletes 2005-2007, *American Journal of Sports Medicine*, 37(9), 1798-1805.

Delva-Tauiliili, J. (1995). Does brief Aikido training reduce aggression of youth?, *Perceptual and Motor Skills*, 80(1), 297-298.

Endresen, I.M. & D. Olweus (2005). Participation in power sports and antisocial involvement in preadolescent and adolescent boys, *Journal of Child Psychology and Psychiatry*, 46(5), 468-478.

Falvey, E.C., Eustace, J., Whelan, B., Molloy, M.S., Cusack, S.P., Shanahan, F. & M.G. Molloy (2009). Sport and recreation-related injuries and fracture occurrence among emergency department attendees: implications for exercise prescription and injury prevention, *Emergency Medicine Journal*, 26(8), 590-595.

Finkenberg, M.E. (1990). Effect of participation in taekwondo on college women's self-concept, *Perceptual and Motor Skills*, 71, 891-894.
Gartland, S., Malik, M.H.A. & M.E. Lovel (2001). Injury and injury rates in Muay Thai kick boxing, *British Journal of Sports Medicine*, 35, 308-313.
Gartland, S., Malik, M.H.A. & M.E. Lovel (2005). A Prospective Study of Injuries Sustained During Competitive Muay Thai Kickboxing, *Clinical Journal of Sport Medicine*, 15(1), 34-36.
Grady, J. (1998). Celluloid katas: Martial arts in the movies - A practitioner's prejudices, *Journal of Asian Martial Arts*, 7(2), 86-101.
Gould, D., Collins, K., Lauer, L. & Chung, Y. (2006). Coaching life skills: A working model? In D. Lavallee (Ed.), *Sport and Exercise Psychology Review*, 2(1), 4-12.
Green, C. (2008). Sport as an agent for social and personal change, in V. Girginov (Ed.), *Management of sports development*, Butterworth-Heinemann, Oxford.
Hellison, D. (1995). *Teaching responsibility through physical activity*. Human Kinetics, Champaign, IL.
Holt, N.L. (2008)(Ed.). *Positive youth development through sport*, Routledge, London.
Ifedi, F. (2008). Sport Participation in Canada, 2005 (Catalogue no. 81-595-MIE2008060). Ottawa: Culture, Tourism and the Centre for Education Statistics.
Janssens, J. et al. (2004). *Education through sport. An overview of good practices in Europe*, Arko Sports Media, Nieuwegein.
Jaspers, R. (2007). Vechtsport goed voor zelfbeheersing [Martial arts good for self-control]. De Gelderlander. www.gelderlander.nl/voorpagina/nijmegen/2329348/Vechtsport-goed-voor-zelfbeheersing.ece
Junge, A., Engebretsen, L., Mountjoy, M.L., Alonso, J.M., Renström, P., Aubry, M.J & J. Dvorak (2009). Sports Injuries During the Summer Olympic Games 2008, *American Journal of Sports Medicine*, 37(11), 2165-2172.
Kochhar, T., Back, D.L., Mann, B. & Skinner, J. (2005). Risk of cervical injuries in mixed martial arts, *British Journal of Sports Medicine*, 39, 444-447.
Konzak, B. & P. Klavora (1980). Some social psychological dimensions of karate participation: An examination of personality characteristics within the training context of a traditional martial art. In P. Klavora, & K. Wipper (Eds.), *Psychological and sociological factors in sport*, (pp. 64-86), University of Toronto, Toronto.
Lagendijk, E. (1991). De zwarte band van etnische minderheden. Over kleur, macht en kracht van lichaamscultuur [The black belt of ethnic minorities. On colour, power and strength of body culture], *Vrijetijd en Samenleving*, 9(2), 45-62.
Lakes, K.D. & W.T. Hoyt (2004). Promoting self-regulation through school-based martial arts training, *Journal of Applied Developmental Psychology*, 25(3), 283-302.

Long, J. & I. Sanderson (2001). The social benefits of sport: Where's the proof?, in C. Gratton & I. Henry (Eds.), *Sport in the City*, (pp. 187-203), Routledge, London.

Lystad, R.P., Pollard, H. & P.L. Graham (2009). Epidemiology of injuries in competition taekwondo: A meta-analysis of observational studies, *Journal of Science and Medicine in Sport*, 12(6), 614-621.

Madden (1995). Perceived vulnerability and control of martial arts and physical fitness students, *Perceptual and motor skills*, 80, 899-910.

Marks (2008). Aggression in the Martial Arts. www.markstraining.com/2008/11/aggression-in-martial-arts.html

Ministère de la jeunesse des sports et de la vie associative (2005). *Les jeunes dans la pratique sportive licenciée en 2003* [Youth in licenced sport activities in 2003], STAT-Info Bulletin de statistiques et d'études, Paris.

Nederlandse Hartstichting & NOC*NSF (2007). *Sportparticipatie en evaluatieonderzoek* [Sport participation and evaluation research], Sportscan, Zwolle.

Ngai, K.M., Levy, F. & E.B. Hsu (2008). Injury trends in sanctioned mixed martial arts competition: a 5-year review from 2002 to 2007, *British Journal of Sports Medicine*, 42(8), 686-689.

Pawson, R. (2001). *Evidence Based Policy, vol. 1, In Search of a Method*, ESRC UK Centre for Evidence Based Policy and Practice, Working Paper, 3, Queen Mary University of London, London.

Pawson, R. (2004). *Evaluating ill-defined interventions with hard–to-follow outcomes*. Presentation to ESRC seminar. Leeds Metropolitan University, Leeds.

Patriksson, G. (1995). *Scientific Review part 2. The significance of sport for society – health, socialization, economy: a scientific review*, Council of Europe Press, Strasbourg.

Pearn, J. (1998). Boxing, youth and children, *Journal of Paediatrics and Child Health*, 34, 311-313.

Pieter W. (2005). Martial arts injuries, *Medicine and Sport Sciences*, 48, 59–73.

Rechel, J.A., Yard, E.E. & R.D. Comstock (2008). An epidemiologic comparison of high school sports injuries sustained in practice and competition, *Journal of Athletic Training*, 43(2), 197-204.

Reynes, E. & J. Lorant (2001). Do competitive martial arts attract aggressive children?, *Perceptual and Motor Skills*, 93(2), 382-386.

Reynes, E. & J. Lorant (2002). Effect of traditional judo training on aggressiveness among young boys, *Perceptual and Motor Skills*, 94(1), 21-25.

Sheard, K.G. (1997). Aspects of boxing in the Western 'Civilizing Process', *International Review for the Sociology of Sport*, 32(1), 31-57.

Smith, R. (1999). *Martial musings: A portrayal of martial arts in the 20th century*. Via Media Publishing, Erie, PA.

Smith, J., Twemlow, S. & D. Hoover (1999). Bullies, victim, and bystanders: A method of in-school intervention and possible parental contributions, *Child Psychiatry and Human Development*, 30(1), 29-37.

Stickney, J.J., (2005). *Discourses of Empowerment: Female martial artists on the martial arts.* Paper presented at the annual meeting of the American Sociological Association, Philadelphia, PA.

Tammelin, T., Näyhä, S., Hills, A. & M. Järvelin (2003). Adolescent Participation in Sports and Adult Physical Activity, *American Journal of Preventive Medicine*, 24(1), 22-28.

Theeboom, M. (2012). A closer look at effects of martial arts involvement among youth, *International Journal of Sport Management and Marketing*, 11(3/4), 193-205.

Theeboom, M. & E. Verheyden (2011). *Vechtsport met een plus. Kansen voor kwetsbare jongeren* [Martial arts with a plus. Chances for vulnerable youth], Academic & Scientific Publishers, Brussels.

van Dongen, M. (2005). Wie leert vechten, zal ook gaan vechten [Who learns to fight, will fight], *De Volkskrant*, September, 29.

Veganfitness.net (2008) www.veganfitness.net/viewtopic.php?p=258885

Vertonghen, J. & M. Theeboom (2010). The social-psychological outcomes of martial arts practise among youth: a review, *Journal of Sports Science and Medicine*, 9, 528 – 537.

Vettenburg, N. (1998). Juvenile Delinquency and Culture Characteristics of the Family, *International Journal of Adolescent Medicine and Health*, 3, 193-209.

Wacquant, L. (1992). The social logic of boxing in Black Chicago: Toward a sociology of pugilism, *Sociology of Sport Journal*, 9, 221-254.

Walgrave, L. (1992). Maatschappelijke kwetsbaarheid van jongeren als een opdracht [Social vulnerability of youngsters as a task]. In P. De Knop & L. Walgrave (Eds.), *Sport als integratie. Kansen voor maatschappelijk kwetsbare jongeren.* Koning Boudewijnstichting, Brussel.

Wall, R.B. (2005), Tai Chi and mindfulness-based stress reduction in a Boston public middle school, *Journal of Pediatric Heath Care*, 19(4), 230-237.

Warren, C. (2008), Kids' sports, *Canadian Social Trends*, 11, 54-61.

Weel, I. (2005). Jongens worden agressief van vecht- en krachtsport [Boys become aggressive from martial and power sports], *Trouw*, September, 28.

Wisse, E. (2007). *Onderzoek naar de rol van betekenisgeving in thai/kickboksen en de invloed hiervan op de integratie van allochtone jongeren* [Investigation into the role of giving meaning in thai-/kickboxing and the influence on the integration of immigrated youth], Mulier Instituut, 's-Hertogenbosch.

Wolt, K., Bosveld, W. & J. Slot (2007). *Sportmonitor 2006: Inzicht in het sportgedrag van Amsterdammers* [Sport monitor 2006: Insight in sport behavior of the citizens of Amsterdam]. Amsterdam: Dienst Maatschappelijke Ontwikkeling.

Woodward, K. (2007). *Boxing, masculinity and identity. The 'I' of the tiger*, Routledge, London.

Zetaruk, M.N., Violan, M.A., Zurakowski, D. & Micheli, L.J. (2005). Injuries in martial arts: a comparison of five styles, *British Journal of Sports Medicine*, 39, 29-33.

Zivin, G., Hassan, N., DePaula, G., Monti, D., Harlan, C., Hossain, K. & K. Patterson, (2001). An effective approach to violence prevention: traditional martial arts in middle school, *Adolescence*, 36, 443-459.

United Nations. (s.d.). Sport for Development and Peace. The UN system in action.
www.un.org/wcm/content/site/sport/home/sport/history

Chapter 6

How Do Fighters Learn How to Fight: An Insiders' Critique of Traditional Martial Arts Pedagogy

Richard Bailey

Tradition

During World War II in Britain when armaments were becoming scarce and the use of manpower was critical, time-and-motion studies were made of gun crews in the army to see if the speed of operating could be increased. One of these studies looked specifically at artillery crews. In many ways, the operation was impressive, with each of the soldiers smoothly following the well-choreographed process. But one thing puzzled the observers: at a certain point, just before the firing of the gun, two of the men stood at attention away from the gun. Once the gun was fired, they stepped back in to help.

Nobody seemed to know why the soldiers simply stood while the others carried on. They just knew that it had to be done that way because it had always been done that way. Then one day, the researchers met an old artillery Colonel. He immediately knew the reason for the immobile soldiers. He said that 50 years earlier, horses had been used to haul the big guns, before motor vehicles took over. The time-and-motion people looked confused: "So how does that explain the two soldiers standing to attention, Sir?" "Simple: they're holding the horses!"

It seems to me that the martial arts have more than their share of horses! Even in this era of martial sports, Mixed Martial Arts, and street self-defense, the center of gravity of combat activities lies firmly in the styles that sell themselves (whether explicitly or implicitly, honestly or dishonestly) as traditional. Indeed, the appeal of these systems comes largely from the sense that they have survived for a very long time. This sense is bolstered by the paraphernalia of training clothes based on the daywear of Japanese or Chinese peasants, the insistence that lessons take place in a foreign language, and the maintenance of a code of conduct often alien to most host countries.

The fact that hardly any of the styles taught in the West are as old as they imply is an awkward truth. For example, three of the most popular styles, Shotokan Karate, Aikido, Tae Kwon Do were all invented during the Twentieth Century (Funakoshi, 1973; Park, Park, & Gerrard, 2009; Ueshiba, 1988). Much the same can be said of versions of Chinese 'kung fu'. Whilst their students might like to think they are successors to a line that can be traced back to the mystical Shaolin Temple, they are much more likely to be a member of a school dating back just a few decades, the result of one of the endless splits and feuds that have characterized the history of Asian martial arts (Green & Swinth, 2003). The medium is the message, and tradition continues to be a dominant feature of most martial arts. This is not necessarily a problem. Quite the contrary: traditions are indispensable components of learning and knowing, and we would barely be able to function at all without accepting some sorts of authority, custom and tradition. Tradition can show us what has worked well in the past, and what has kept our predecessors alive. However, in the words of the great Lemony Snicket (2004), "Just because something is traditional is no reason to do it, of course". Difficulties begin to rise when tradition becomes a thing in itself; when it is recognized as tradition. Then tradition ceases to be an adaptable and 'living' repository of learning and becomes a source of deadening force of authority.

What Has Happened in the Martial Arts Pedagogical Realm?

Traditional Martial Arts Pedagogy

There is an inherent danger facing anyone criticizing practices that they describe as 'traditional', or 'standard', or conventional, and that is that they merely construct a 'straw man' to knock down. A straw man argument occurs when the critic re-interprets a position in such a way that it is so weak or absurd than no sensible person would hold it. And dishonest strategy is particularly easy to play in the martial arts, which are characterized by a huge degree of variation, contradictions, and tensions. The martial arts are not a coherent clan, unified by a shared passion; they are a loose group of warring tribes!

Nevertheless, I maintain that not only is there such a thing as the traditional martial arts pedagogy, but that its influence is so great it is practiced even in styles that explicitly distance themselves from the past, such as Bruce Lee's Jeet Kune Do, kickboxing and modern self-defence systems [1]. This traditional pedagogy happens when most or all of the following criteria are met:

- a considerable amount of the session time is spent with players practicing basic techniques without an opponent;

---

[1] To be clear on this point, I am not suggesting that all instructors in these systems adhere to traditional approaches, but that many of them cannot separate themselves from them. For example, one JKD school I once attended taught the usual mixture of Kali, boxing and Wing Chun, using teaching methods that were indistinguishable from Classical Karate!

- when an opponent is involved, s/he is relatively immobile and compliant;
- predetermined, choreographed drills and patterns, such as kata, hyeong, or forms form a central feature of training.

That these elements can be sensibly described as the traditional approach to teaching martial arts is supported by numerous textbooks and academic studies (e.g., Cox, 1993; Layton & Bell, 1997; Lorge, 2011; Nakayama, 1977; Ohlenkamp, 2006; Theeboom & Knop, 1998). It is also supported by practitioners themselves. In preparation for this chapter, I engaged in a series of conversations with martial artists of different styles from around the world via social media (specifically Twitter and LinkedIn). If anything, their views of the importance of basic techniques and kata where more fundamentalist than those of the textbooks. "Basics are everything", I was told, and "…they lay the foundation for all that follows". "Kata is the time-honored method for practicing these techniques", and "It must work because it has been around for centuries". In the words of one popular karate text, kata and their associated basic techniques represent the "key" to the martial arts, and traditional practice gives the student that key (van Weenen, 2002).

At this point, one thing needs to be made clear. As my title suggests, my primary concern is the effectiveness of martial arts pedagogy as a preparation for fighting. I do not for a moment believe that this is the only, or even main reason why people would wish to undertake such activities. There is little doubt that regular martial arts training can make positive contributions to participants' health and well-being (Abbott & Lavretsky, 2013; Woodward, 2009). It also seems capable of contributing to a much wider personal, creative, and spiritual development (Nicol, 1975; Yuasa, 1993; Zarrilli, 1998). However, my concern here is with what might arguably be considered the defining characteristic of the martial arts - combat. In this respect, I claim, traditional pedagogy is ineffective.

Learning

Pedagogy - the arts, crafts and science of education - is a hotly contested topic among theorists (Hansen & Laverty, 2010). But some themes are not controversial. For example, it is beyond doubt that pedagogic practice is built upon theories of learning; that some of these theories are mistaken; and that's decades of research have taught us a great deal about effective and ineffective pedagogy.

We also know that the long-standing view of the brain as a kind of blank slate (or empty container) onto which is written experiences is plain wrong (Pinker, 2003). Babies enter the world hard wired with countless sources of knowledge and insight gleaned through thousands of years of evolution. From that moment, the young child voraciously consumes information, seeking to understand, adapt to, and control issues or her environment. By the time a student enters a martial arts club, therefore, he/she has an extensive biography of experience and knowledge which cannot help but influence any learning that takes place. This is why the much-prized "beginner's mind" of Zen Buddhism is an idealized aspiration rather than an everyday reality (Suzuki, 1970).

Consequently, no two people will leave a pedagogic encounter with the same learning, and the learning that does occur is not necessarily that which was intended by the teacher. Learning is essentially an active process, in which the learner struggles to construct meanings that are relevant to them from the situation. As the great psychologist Jeremy Bruner put it, "Stimuli ... do not act upon an indifferent organism" (Bruner & Postman, 1949, p. 206).

This point has an implication that is of enormous importance: teaching and learning have no necessary connection. Most of my social media informants simply assumed that what was taught was what was learned. But just because an activity aims to teach a certain skill or knowledge does not mean that it will. No matter how skilled or impassioned the teaching, unless the learner understands it and engages with it, there is no reason to suppose that he or she has learned and that he or she will be able to apply it. The philosopher Karl Popper (1974) offered a useful way of understanding how this might work in practice. Learning, he suggested, has the character of problem solving, and is most likely to occur when teaching and experience provides solutions to problems that are real and meaningful to the learner. So, if a martial artist is struggling to defend him/herself from a certain type of attack, and the instructor provides a workable solution, learning is very likely to take place, it will be remembered, and applied in future. However, if the same instructor merely demonstrates a series of apparently arbitrary techniques that are then imitated by the students, those techniques are much less likely to be retained and applied (Bailey, 2000)[2].

Consequently, people learn best when learning situations are real and meaningful. How does the teacher or instructor make sure that these conditions apply? This is where another group of findings from research become relevant. Situated learning emphasizes that learning is most effective when it is specific to the situation in which it is learned. In other words, learning is most likely to occur when the context of teaching closely reflects the context of learning (Ramsden, 1984). Swimming on dry land, for example, is a poor preparation for swimming in water because it lacks many of its defining characteristics. Likewise, many people claim that schools fail to prepare their students because life in a classroom shares few of the features of the world into which the young people will enter.

Situated learning is actually made up of a number of claims, and each of them highlights the difficulties for traditional martial arts pedagogy (see Table 1).

Principles of Situated Learning	Traditional Martial Arts Pedagogy
Effective learning tends to be situated in the situation in which it occurs	Sessions tend to take place in settings very different from the situation in which they would be applied

---

[2] Since my focus in this chapter is on martial arts pedagogy, I have not gone into the sometimes bizarre techniques that actually make up many kata and forms! Indeed, I will save these arguments for another day.

Principles of Situated Learning	Traditional Martial Arts Pedagogy
Skills and knowledge do not transfer easily between tasks	Skills and knowledge developed in kata in training in other basic skills learning are assumed to transfer to fighting
Effective training is concrete, realistic and meaningful	Training is usually abstract, unrealistic and not reflective of fighting situations
Teaching is most effective when it is done in dynamic, ever-changing environments	Training is usually done in stable, not changing environments.

Sources: Anderson, Reder, & Simon, 1996; Greeno, 1998; Lave & Wenger, 1991

From the perspective of situated learning, then, traditional martial arts pedagogy fares rather badly because it fails to resemble the situations in which its skills will be applied. Simply put, we learn what we do. If any martial artist wishes to prepare for the complexity and chaos of a street fight, he or she will be badly served if the training is simple and ordered.

Techniques or Skills?

It was a traditional martial artist who first and most effectively translated the practical implications of this type of research for the martial arts, and for sport in general. Geoff Gleeson was the UK's National Coach for Judo, and as a young man had lived and studied with the family of the founder Jigaro Kano. Gleason made a number of innovations and provocative ideas, but the one that is of most relevance to this discussion is his distinction between techniques and skills (Gleeson, 1983; 1989). Gleeson's initial target was what judo players call Uchikomi, or repetitive technical training. It is worth remembering that, unlike most martial arts, practice of techniques necessarily involves interaction with another player. So, from the perspective of learning theory, judo (and other grappling sports) already have a significant advantage over other (punching and kicking) systems. Nevertheless, Gleeson was critical of the use of Uchikomi for three main reasons:

1. Fixed routines: Uchikomi is often practiced as habitual patterns of movement. However, Gleeson argued that judo is the practice and application of a skill, and habit and skill are not synonymous. Gleeson further maintained that there was no necessary connection between the static repetition of a throw as Uchikomi and the dynamic performance of a throw when the players are in motion.
2. How the completion of a skill movement affects the improvement of the skill: the throw is rarely completed in Uchikomi practice. In fact, practice is often carried out with no movement of the players, non-completion of the throw and no realistic resistance from the partner. Therefore, the player never really knows if he or she is performing the

techniques correctly and effectively since there is no genuine feedback. Gleeson's conclusion was that not only will Uchikomi not help to improve throwing skill, but will actually impede any skill improvement.
3. Rhythmic pattern differences in static and dynamic movement: Non-movement of the partner and a stereotypical movement in and out of the position by the throw leads to a regular beat rhythm. This never happens in competition fighting. The movement patterns associated with fighting in training and competition are complex and contain endless variations of movement by both of the players. Therefore, the transfer rents of skills between the practice and performance is non-existent.

Indeed, Glesson concedes that the practice of Uchikomi may help to increase stamina and strength, but its value as a method of improving throwing skills in fighting situations is extremely limited (Gleeson, 1967).

Traditional martial arts pedagogy focuses on the development of technique (as do almost all martial arts textbooks), and simply assumes that this will transfer into skilled performance against an opponent. Gleeson's central insight is that technique cannot be treated in isolation, for there are many other things which affect and modify all techniques when they are converted into a competitive skill. Ultimately, skill is much more about context than it is about technique, and it is context that needs to be taught, experienced and understood. Uchikomi - which is actually a rather more dynamic and interactive form of basic technique training that is common in the majority of martial arts - is limited precisely because it confuses skilled performance with the repetition of mere technique. Skill "can be defined only in terms of success, of achievement, of a goal" (Guthrie, 1952, p. 136). So, skills are actions with some outcome in mind (Schmidt and Wrisberg, 2000), rather than mere physical actions.

The philosopher Hubert Dreyfus - as far as I am aware, not a martial artist - offered another argument, which seems to support Gleeson's position. Dreyfus took issue with the widespread view that road to expertise begins with the development of isolated elements (what Gleeson would call techniques) he argued that they were:

> "....meaningless, atomistic elements.....Nothing is intelligible to us unless it first shows up as already integrated into our world, fitting into our coping practices".

> (Wrathall, 2000, p. 95).

Dreyfus argued that if we were to go straight to the actual phenomena we are studying, and undertook a very detailed observation of the activities that they make up, it would be evident that we are not processing bits of information as we deal (or cope) with them. In addition, Dreyfus introduces what he calls the 'argument from skills' (Wrathall, 2000) to show how the traditional view of learning by building up discrete bits of technique is problematic. His argument can be paraphrased and reframed like this: if we are to understand how people learn to perform martial arts, and we follow the assumptions of traditional pedagogy, we will need not only rules for performing the techniques, but also a specification of the rules that allow us to know when specific techniques apply in different contexts. The different techniques that make up the different skills necessary for successful fighting mean that we are talking about a huge number of rules. But still further rules would seem to be needed to direct these rules, and so on for an infinite regress.

It is difficult to see how to escape this client, without abandoning the traditional assumption that skilled performance is the result of acquired, developed and applied techniques. However, the argument does not apply if performance in fighting is understood in terms of the learning of real and meaningful skills in real and meaningful contexts. In a nutshell: there is only one way to learn how to fight in the martial arts: fighting. Of course, this need not always be fighting in the sense of "the real thing". It is possible (and sensible) to construct a program of teaching and learning that simulates fighting contexts, and encompasses many of the defining characteristics of fighting situations, which would include unpredictability, emotion, and contact.

Conclusion

This chapter has suggested that fighters learn to fight by fighting. So, martial arts pedagogy, at least as it relates to preparation for fighting, is much simpler than is usually presented both in textbooks and by instructors. Basic training, in the way practiced around the world, and kata, have many virtues, but they are extremely limited as preparations for fighting. They survive not because they work, but because of the power and mythology of tradition in the martial arts. They also gain sustenance by the fact that they all rarely tested in the crucible of real fighting. Systems that are regularly tested, even in the relatively safe arena of full contact sport, are much less likely to rely on traditional martial arts pedagogy. They have learned that tradition is only of value to the extent that it keeps you fighting.

References

Abbott, R., & Lavretsky, H. (2013). Tai chi and qigong for the treatment and prevention of mental disorders. *The Psychiatric clinics of North America*, 36(1), 109-119.

Anderson, J. R., Reder, L. M., & H.A. Simon (1996). Situated learning and education. *Educational Researcher*, 25(4), 5-11.

Bailey, R.P. (2000). Education and the Open Society: Karl Popper and Schooling. Aldershot: Ashgate.

Bransford, J. D., Brown, A. L., & R.R. Cocking (1999). How People Learn. Washington, DC: National Academy Press

Bruner, J. S., & L. Postman (1949). On the perception of incongruity: A paradigm. *Journal of Personality*, 18(2), 206-223.

Cox, J. C. (1993). Traditional Asian martial arts training: A review. *Quest*, 45(3), 366-388.

Funakoshi, G. (1981). Karate-Dō: My Way of Life. Tokyo: Kodansha International.

Gleeson, G. R. (1967). Judo for the West. Kaye & Ward.

Gleeson, G. R. (1983). Judo inside out: a cultural reconciliation. London: Lepus Books.
Gleeson, G. R. (1989). Judo Games. London: London: A & C Black.
Green, T. A., & J.R. Swinth (2003). (Eds). Martial arts in the modern world. Westport, CO: Greenwood Publishing Group.
Greeno, J. G. (1998). The situativity of knowing, learning, and research. *American Psychologist*, 53(1), 5.
Hansen, D. T., & Laverty, M. J. (2010). Teaching and Pedagogy. In R.P. Bailey, P. Barrow, & Carr, 2010). The Sage Handbook of Philosophy of Education. London: Sage Publishing, p. 223.
Lave, J., & Wenger, E. (1991). Situated Learning: Legitimate peripheral participation. Cambridge: Cambridge University Press.
Layton, C., & V.C. Bell (1997). Slow movement as a function of advancement in the shotokan karate kata set. *Perceptual and Motor Skills*,84(3), pp. 1009-1010.
Lorge, P. A. (2011). Chinese martial arts: from antiquity to the twenty-first century. Cambridge: Cambridge University Press.
Nakayama, M. (1977). Best karate: comprehensive. Tokyo: Kodansha international.
Nicol, C. W. (1975). Moving Zen: karate as a way to gentleness. London: Bodley Head.
Ohlenkamp, N. (2006) Black Belt Judo. London: New Holland Publishers.
Park, Y. H., Park, Y. H., & J. Gerrard (2009). Tae Kwon Do: The ultimate reference guide to the world's most popular martial art. New York: Facts on File Publishing.
Pinker, S. (2003). The blank slate: the modern denial of human nature. New York: Penguin.
Popper, K. R. (1974). The Philosophy of Karl Popper (Vol. 1). La Salle, IL: Open Court Publishing Company.
Ramsden, P. (1984). The context of learning. In F. Marton, D. Hounsell & N. Entwistle (eds), The Experience of Learning. Edinburgh: Scottish Academic Press.
Snicket, L. (2004). A Series of Unfortunate Events: The Blank Book. New York: HarperCollins.
Suzuki, S. (1970). Zen Mind, Beginner's Mind. Boston, MA: Shambhala Publications.
Theeboom, M., & Knop, P. D. (1998). Asian martial arts and approaches of instruction in physical education. *European Journal of Physical Education*, 4(2), 146-161.
Ueshiba, K. (1988). The spirit of Aikido. Tokyo: Kodansha International.
van Weenen, J. (2002) The Beginners Guide to Shotokan Karate. Bedford: Paul Hooley and Associates.
Yuasa, Y. (1993). The body, self-cultivation, and ki-energy. New York: SUNY Press.
Woodward, T. W. (2009). A review of the effects of martial arts practice on health. *Wisconsin Medical Journal*, 108(1), 40.

Zarrilli, P. B. (1998). *When the body becomes all eyes: Paradigms, discourses and practices of power in Kalarippayattu, a South Indian martial art.* New Delhi: Oxford University Press.

Chapter 7

Teaching Close Quarter Combat to Military Personnel: A Pocket Guide for New and Inexperienced Instructors

Jamie Lee-Barron

Introduction

We are now in the 21st century, a time of stealth technology, smart munitions, satellite surveillance and surgical strikes executed by unmanned aerial vehicles. With all of these scientific advances, it would be very easy to assume that modern warfare has little or even no need for the traditional "boots-on-the-ground" approach to combat. However, as we have all witnessed in the last few years, this is certainly not always the case. The contemporary conflicts that now rage all around us are often very complicated and dirty affairs that demand all of the advanced technology mentioned above be deployed and used to the maximum effect but, the simple truth is, these technologies cannot ever hope to bring about a favorable outcome all by themselves. In fact, all of these wonderful "super-weapons" are usually employed in tangent with, or in direct support of, the ground troops, be they either special forces or a larger contingent of more conventional formations. This is because even in this day and age there is absolutely no substitute for the "boots-on-the-ground" approach. There never has been and (probably) never will be a substitute for this form of fighting.

Even at the very height of the cold war, when everyone thought that the third world war was imminent and would be thermo-nuclear in nature, large numbers of ground troops were still maintained by both sides. These consisted not only of commando-type forces to carry out raids on targets of strategic importance, but mostly huge numbers of regular troops for (what was loosely termed) the "mopping-up" operations. In other words, both sides recognised and accepted the fact that before, during and after the nuclear engagement, the good old boots-on-the-ground would still be sorely needed. As I stated above, there really is no substitute for them.

Now that we have established this premise, we can move on to the 'meat and potatoes' of this guide:

> The primary role of the combat soldier, at least when deployed in a war-zone is, today, precisely the same as it always has been historically: To close with and destroy the enemy. To do this, the soldier needs to be properly prepared (selected and trained), well-equipped (weapons and resources) and highly motivated (positive mental attitude). Fighting in battle is one of the most harrowing events any human being can experience. Basically, a human being is an animal and, like any other animal, self preservation is our primary motivation. Hence, whenever we are faced with any type of situation which might compromise our personal safety, our immediate response is to extricate ourselves as quickly as possible. One method for helping to overcome this most primeval of instincts is to re-program the brain somewhat through careful selection and training, so channeling the stress hormones it is secreting into the "fight" rather than the "flight" response and, therefore, effectively triggering an aggressive type of mind-set rather than a fearful one (but never to the detriment of other important attributes, such as common sense and sound judgement, of course).

Training in close combat helps enormously with this process, as it toughens up the soldier both physical and mentally, therefore preparing them more effectively for the rigors of battle, instilling them with the aggressive determination they need in order to survive and also serves to equip them with the knowledge and skills required in order for them to successfully fulfill their primary objective as stated above: To close with and destroy the enemy. However, in recent years the important military skill of hand to hand combat has become somewhat neglected due to far too much faith being placed in fancy pieces of kit and ever more lethal technologies, and far too little effort being directed toward the correct selection and training of personnel. As commented by one wise old warrior:

> "Wars may now be fought with technology, but they are still won by people"

Close combat training is, in my own opinion, and the opinion of certain other "old sweats" the world over, an absolutely essential part of the training and selection of a combat soldier. Yet, because of the apathetic view taken by the powers that be, it is almost a dying specialism. Hence, there is a very serious lack of instructors in these skills, and this shortage needs to be addressed, sooner rather than later. As it is, we are forced to make the best of a bad situation (not an uncommon thing for any soldier) and to make the best use of what we have by way of "alternative provision" if you will (same sentiment as above). And this is precisely why this pocket-guide has been penned.

The Problem

It is becoming increasingly common in different units of various armies around the globe for them to become committed to an operational role in a combat environment and, lacking any kind of formal Hand to Hand (H2H) combat syllabus, they desperately turn either to the local martial arts instructor or, more usually, to someone actually already in the unit who happens to possess some experience in the martial arts, for some urgently needed help and guidance. The third choice would, of course, be someone who purports to teach "military close-combat" but who might never themselves have actually served in the armed forces in any way, shape or form. Sometimes, these people can still be reasonably well trained individuals but they have had to rely solely upon their instructors (and sometimes the instructor of their instructors) experiences rather than their own. Therefore, good as it may be, it is still very much "second" or even "third" hand information and, as such, has been accepted with a certain amount of trust and faith on their part. (There is always be a lot to be said for the actual "been there and done that" type of experience when it comes to anything to do with the military, but especially close combat.)

These people often get thrown in the deep end. Yes, they might well have a certain amount of expertise in the martial art/self defence/close combat system they have learned, practiced and taught, but now they have been asked to help prepare people for battle, and that is a very different type of learning outcome than they are used to.

Keeping it Real

Fighting in combat, against an enemy who is well trained and whose sole purpose is to try and kill you is very different from defending yourself against some drunken fool in a bar, or even trying to restrain/arrest a violent mugger, simply because, although each of these situations do still present a certain amount of danger, the prime motivation of the person involved has NOT been to engage and attempt to destroy you: The encounter is just an unfortunate occurrence. Nor is it likely that they will have trained specifically for the purpose of killing you. Sorry if this upsets some people, but that's the simple truth of the matter: Very different indeed!

Rising to the Challenge

Being requested to help teach the armed forces should always be viewed as being a great honor, but it is also a great responsibility that can prove a little daunting for a new or inexperienced instructor. This situation is far from ideal but is, none the less, increasingly common in the modern world, where some armies have almost completely disregarded close combat as being a serious military skill. Now, though, the troops of several countries are engaged in wars wherein close combat is increasingly becoming the norm. Therefore, for those brave few who do step up to the mark and are prepared to roll up their sleeves when called, the guidance below might prove to be of some use, if it is followed and implemented correctly.

Adapting

Just as military close combat differs widely from mainstream martial arts, so too, must the teaching and learning methods employed in their instruction. Martial arts are a hobby and pass-time. They are intricate, complicated and beautiful, demanding a lifetime of dedicated study and practice. Indeed, it can require literally years of painstaking practice in order for the student to grasp even the basic fundamentals of a system, which also usually comes wrapped –up in its very own peculiar set of philosophies and traditions. Military close combat, on the other hand, needs to be learned quickly and effectively over a very short space of time. Because of this, the technical content must be kept select, simple and effective. As in any learning, the subject should be of some use to the student or they simply will not retain it. What motivates the martial artist is the idea of training hard towards eventually understanding the various techniques of the system they are learning, gradually progressing through the different grades until they reach the coveted black belt level and beyond. They are both patient and determined, at once understanding and accepting that this goal will take them many years to realize.

In direct contrast to this, a soldier's motivation is simple: To close with and destroy the enemy, and to (preferably) survive while doing so. A new recruit in the military is required to take in lot of information very quickly indeed and, while the time spent on combat skills might vary somewhat depending upon the type of unit they have joined, even if it is a combat infantry regiment, they will only be allocated a certain amount of time to learn what they need to survive on the battlefield.

Even elite assault troops such as commandos and paratroopers will only be given a few hours of training in which to master some basic moves of close quarter fighting that might help them to stay alive when the chips are down. Is this possible? Yes, but only if certain rules and guidelines are strictly adhered to. When an instructor is teaching the Close Combat, it is vitally important that they remember the following seven rules:

1. Prepare and Plan

Know what you are going to teach them. Tell them what they are going to learn, help them to learn it well then tell them what they have learned. In the military, this process is colloquially known as the "7 P's" These are as follows:

>PRIOR
>PLANNING AND
>PREPARATION
>PREVENTS
>P**S
>POOR
>PERFORMANCE

This is an extremely useful and effective formula to follow. Think about what your students need to learn, how long you have to teach it to them, what resources will be required to do this effectively, what budget has been allocated and how you intend assessing their learning.

2. Don't Make it Too Complicated

Remember you are teaching soldiers to kill other soldiers. You are not preparing martial artists for a display, getting a team ready for a competition, or even teaching police officers how to restrain a suspect, all of the above are very specialist-skills, and so must be allocated adequate amounts of time. Your students, on the other hand, have to learn how to neutralise the enemy as quickly and efficiently as possible in as short a time as possible. Therefore, you should utilise what is termed the KISS principal:

> Keep it simple stupid.

Don't waste their valuable time and yours going too much into the "whys" and "wherefores" of the techniques. Just make sure they can do what they need to do well enough to get the job done. Answer any questions if you are asked but remember, they are not there for a lecture, they are there to learn how to fight and win. You will find that soldiers make good students, as they are well aware that their very life may depend upon learning what you are teaching them. However, they will question anything they think might be superfluous to requirements, so don't go over the top as regards either technical or theoretical content.

Don't teach them what you think might work. Teach stuff that will work.

3. It's Better To Practice a Few Techniques a Hundred Times Than To Practice a Hundred Techniques a Few Times!

Give them only what they need. Don't make the mistake of over-loading them with a lot of useless information they cannot use or are even interested in. These techniques must be able to be used by a soldier when they are hungry, tired, cold/hot/wet and (above all) scared out of their wits! They need to be practiced and practiced until they become an ingrained part of their gross- motor skills. An instinctive reaction that is second nature, completely void of any and all intellectual reasoning and complicated thought processes. Remember: it's not about what YOU can do well. Rather, it's about what you can teach them to do well! And it must always be "Fit for Purpose".

4. Repetition, Repetition, Repetition. And You Can Say That Again!

Really drum the moves into them. Recap often, ensuring you assess their learning, skill and ability each and every step of the way. Use the SAS principle:

> Speed – In combat, you only get one chance. Make sure you grab it and use it FAST!

Aggression – Do unto them before they can do unto you. And make sure it stays DONE!

Suprise – Never "telegraph" whatever you are going to do, instead: Just DO IT!

5. Methods of Instruction

Methods of Instruction (MOI), is a simple but effective system of teaching and learning. It has its origins in the armed forces, wherein NCO's (Non-Commissioned Officers) have to turn raw-recruits into trained, capable and confident service people in a very short period of time. MOI utilises something called EDIP. EDIP stands for:

Explanation: (TELLING them what to do) Try not to use too much "jargon". Keep it short, sweet and to the point.

Demonstration: (SHOWING them what to do) Demonstrate from different angles, pausing to emphasise what is important.

Imitation: (letting them DO it for themselves) Observe, correct and advise them.

Practice: (Getting it RIGHT) Evaluate and assess their learning and performance.

As stated before, MOI this is a very simple, effective method indeed that, if employed properly, can definitely help in making your job a little easier.

6. Listen!

Listen to what the soldiers say, especially the older veterans, either by "ear-wigging" in the mess after training, or simply paying careful attention to them whenever they try to tell you something. You will find them to be an invaluable source of useful information that will aid you in further refining your technique, so ensuring that what you are teaching remains fresh, relevant and of real worth.

7. Continue with Your Own Training!

Always take the time and trouble to learn more yourself. This might be swapping stories with other instructors in the Mess, attending relevant courses and seminars, reading good material to do with the subject and swapping information, ideas and opinions on certain forums.

If you don't do this, then you will stagnate, and your teaching will become a boring chore for you rather than an interesting experience for the students. Consequently, you will be letting everyone including yourself down by not fulfilling your duties to the best of your ability.

Stay fresh, enthusiastic and, above all be PROFESSIONAL.

Application and Use of Close Quarter Combat Training

Training in close combat/hand to hand has applications in literally all operational theaters, and lends itself particularly to those environments wherein the enemy combatants are more able to get within a much closer proximity before they can be detected and engaged, such as fighting a built-up areas (street-fighting/house-clearing) or jungle warfare (where it comes as a surprise to many to find out that the dense, damp vegetation can sometimes cause rounds to bounce of it harmlessly!) etc.

Conclusion

This pocket guide is not meant to cast any aspersions upon anybody's particular style, training, technique or ability, and I know most people that read it will have the good sense and maturity to recognize and accept this.

Teaching soldiers hand to hand fighting is an enormous responsibility. These are students who really need what you are teaching them and who will, more than likely, have to use it in very real life or death situations. They will actually be going into hostile environments wherein what they have learned from you could be the determining factor in them returning home in one piece.

That's why it needs to be done properly. And that is the reason why this little guide has been written, to help new or inexperienced instructors do a better job than perhaps they would otherwise. I sincerely hope it will prove of some use to these good people, and wish them every success in their very worthwhile endeavors. Please remember:

MILITARY CLOSE COMBAT IS NOT:

SELF DEFENCE - It is about "offending" the enemy rather than "defending" oneself.

MARTIAL ARTS - There is very little "art" in close combat. A lot of the "martial" though.

CONTROL AND RESTRAINT – an enemy who has been efficiently disposed of does not usually require "controlling" or "restraining" in any way as they should already be dead. Note: The nature of modern military operations is such that troops are often deployed in roles other than that of general or open warfare. These non-combat roles would include internal/external security operations and UN peacekeeping deployments, etc. In such cases, instruction will usually be both necessary and supplied in various methods of control and restraint. Due to these changing roles, many modern soldiers will probably be required to undergo such training, especially if they are to be involved in riot-control and/or "policing" types of operation, usually in support of the civil authorities, etc.

In addition, these techniques are of definite use in certain "snatch" operations, and for those service people tasked with military security and investigation, such as the provost units, etc.

Author Anon.

Author Anon is a former member of the military where he was trained in both conventional and unconventional warfare. He has a wealth of experience in the operational sense and as an instructor in close quarter fighting, having worked with the security forces of several NATO Aligned countries as an advisor and consultant.

Suggested Further Reading

Note: There is a huge amount of literature available on this subject matter, most of which may be filed under the heading "the blind leading the blind", as it is not worth the paper it has been written on. The selected works below are, again in my own humble (but somewhat educated) opinion, the "real deal". They were written by people with the necessary training, background and mindset, and have been helping soldiers to survive for years.

Get Tough, by Capt. W. E. Fairbairn (1942) Paladin Press; New edition edition 1996 ISBN-13: 978-0873640022
Do or Die, by Colonel A.J.D. Biddle
The Leatherneck Association Inc, 1937, 1944
Cold Steel, by John Styers (1952) Paladin Press; Reprint edition Jun 1 1979 ISBN-13: 978-0873640251
Deal the First Deadly Blow. The encyclopedia of unarmed and hand to hand combat.
Headquarters, Department of the Army, 1971
Kill Or Get Killed, by Col. Rex Applegate Paladin Press 1976 ISBN-13: 978-1581605587
Close Combat (United States Marine Corps) USMC, MCRP 3-02B. 1999
U.S. Army FM 3-25.150, Combatives Headquarters, Department of the Army, 2002

Part II: Body

Chapter 8

Body-experience Lineages in Martial Art Cultures

David Brown

> 'Does your instructor have a direct lineage to a first generation instructor of JKD? In other words, did he [sic] ever study for a good length of time with one or more original students of Bruce Lee or one of the direct second generation students? This is important because this is one way to be sure that the instructor you are studying with has some basis for his knowledge other than books and movies'.

http://www.bruceleefoundation.com

Introduction

The opening epigraph is illustrative of a consistent feature within many martial art cultures: A preoccupation that there is a lineage of teachers based on some form of direct intergenerational connection between present and previous masters/teachers. This chapter explores martial arts lineages and highlights that underpinning this practice is the cultural imperative of transmitting embodied experience. Drawing on Shilling's (1993) consideration that, '...it is only in the context of the body's inevitable death that we can understand its full social importance,' (Shilling, 1993, p. 175) it is argued that the transient relationship between bodies and martial arts drives the logic of practice of lineages of embodied experience or, as they shall be more succinctly referred to: body-experience lineages. In what follows, the chapter first illustrates the practical logic underpinning body experience lineages. Next, it considers, the issue of body-experience lineages, incorporated capital and legitimate succession of Master practitioner/teachers. Following this, the focus shifts to consider some practical modalities of body-experience lineage involving silent codes, family heredity, technical authority and bureaucracy. The final two topics concern the idea of body-experience lineage as pedagogy and the language and symbolism of body experience lineage. The chapter concludes by connecting the notion of cultural transmission via body-experience lineages in martial cultures with the emerging public issue of intangible cultural heritage.

Body Experience Lineages as Practical Logic in Martial Art Cultures

Shilling (1993) concludes that one of the few certainties about our bodies is that they will eventually grow old and die, and along with the passing of our bodies will be the passing of embodied knowledge, so painstakingly developed over a lifetime. This 'problem', Shilling explains, raises particular issues for the transmission of valued body knowledge. Elaborating the point, Shilling (1993, p.142) draws upon Bourdieu's concept of incorporated (physical) capital commenting:

> 'Physical capital cannot be directly transmitted or inherited...because of the un-finished-ness of the body, its development is a complex and lengthy process which can last for years...physical capital...declines and dies with its bearer (Bourdieu, 1986: 245). Consequently, the possession of physical capital can be seen as a more transient resource than the possession of economic capital'.

Such underlying existential corporealities are faced by all individuals, social groups, cultures and societies in everyday life and, according to Giddens (1984), form part of a complex of reasons why people tend to orientate towards ontological security in their social behaviour. However, the loss of incorporated capital becomes even more acutely realised when something embedded in the body needs to be passed on to the next generation in order for a collective socio-cultural practice to survive. One such instance is the passing away (or cessation of teaching due to infirmity) of a celebrated master martial artist. Therefore, this biological moment is also a profoundly social moment. The a priori realisation of the consequences and inevitability of this moment is deeply embedded in the practical logics of many martial art cultures. Moreover, these practical logics lead to specific practices such as constructing "family trees," "lineage maps", or "genealogies" of martial art cultures to illustrate the body-experience connection between the Master practitioner teachers from successive generations[1].

---

[1] A few critical caveats are worth making of the representational claims being made by lineage maps. These maps don't show variations of pedagogy or style; the often significant influence a senior student / teacher may have on a class or entire martial art; Experienced teachers may have had several teachers; meaning that they do not have a 'pure' martial habitus from one particular lineage; teachers may pass down different versions of the art as they age and evolve their art; Lineage maps usually do not show the time spent training with a Master; Lineages are often the subject of strong debate within martial arts

While these lineages are in "lived experience" much more diverse than maps such as these indicate, they serve to imply the transmission of incorporated capital. This is because, without body lineages, specific bodily knowledge, such as use of energy, sensitivity, touch, "feel", specific solutions to the problem of body combat, idiosyncratic body ritual, martial choreographies, and the mythologised notions of "secret" techniques such as dim mak[2], contained within the myriad martial arts cultures would "die" with the bodies of the last practitioner of that lineage.

These brief conceptualisations and illustrations begin to highlight how the transmission of valued embodied experience as incorporated capital provides a necessary foundation for the practical logic of many martial art cultures, if they are to survive the enduring problem of bodily transience. Attention is now turned to consider some of the more specific social functions and processes that such a logic gives rise to Body-experience lineages, incorporated capital and legitimate succession Body-experience lineage's principle purpose is to provide a modality to legitimately articulate the succession of the Masters of a given martial art, which, following Bourdieu (1990) can be understood as a form of incorporated capital which in turn is readily converted into social, economic and ultimately symbolic capital. Embodied martial knowledge is taken to be incorporated by those martial artists who have trained with the most culturally esteemed master practitioners of the previous generation (developing incorporated capital) and then been ratified by these Master's as "worthy" (the incorporated is converted into symbolic capital). The ratification gives this incorporated capital symbolic value by being culturally authentic in the specific delimited field of martial arts. The possessor in turn can "profit from" this in numerous ways, and of course keep the art form / lineage going by being in a position to attract students. However, this process does not happen without struggle. Transplanting the term martial art for sport in Bourdieu's (1993, p. 121) in the following analysis of the field of sport as a field of struggle of body legitimacies illustrates the point:

> 'The field of [martial arts] practices is the site of struggles in which what is at stake, inter alia is the monopolistic capacity to impose the legitimate definition of [martial art] practice and of the legitimate function of [martial arts]...And this field is itself part of the larger field of struggles over the definition of the legitimate body and the legitimate use of the body'.

Therefore, we can begin to see that struggles within the martial art fields are in fact struggles over what constitutes the legitimate martial body and the legitimate uses of the martial body (via legitimate techniques of the body, acceptable attack and defence codes of conduct, how and when combat techniques should used, what the goal of violent confrontation should be, the appropriate style of movement, acceptable pedagogies for practice etc.). The outcome of these struggles can be seen in the current practical configuration of the martial arts field

---

communities, there are many versions. The specific examples here have been provided as they are in the public domain already and their use of Wikipedia indicates an appeal is being made that these lineages are authentic and therefore "legitimate."

[2] Dim Mak or "touch of death" refers to techniques that attack pressure points in the body.

and has considerable significance for the identities of martial arts and martial artists themselves[3]. The Master (and his/her senior teachers) are the principle conduits who embody a lineage and must strategically manage this struggle for legitimacy. Subsequently, the close attention paid by many martial artists to their embodied heritage, is neither a mystical (although it may have quasi mystical representations) nor cynical action (although clearly some use this modality in instrumental ways for commercial or egotistical enhancement etc.) but, rather, following Bourdieu (1990), can be seen as following a very practical logic, in relation to struggles for the arts precedence in a field of martial arts in which a given martial art(ist) is currently positioned.

Furthermore, this struggle for legitimacy is made all the more pertinent, yet elusive and problematic given the intensification of inter-culturality that has evolved from the diffusion of what were once localised martial arts into global networks of martial practices. Transmission and succession has to take place across very diverse cultures and socialised bodies and minds of its global community of practitioners. The dynamics at play in this situation lead to a rapidly increased sense of concern for "authenticity" for some. These concerns are particularly well captured by the writings of the Tai Chi teacher John Leporati:

> 'What constitutes an "authentic" transmission in terms of martial arts and which individuals received that transmission from their teachers is one of the most controversial topics in martial arts today. Countless articles in martial publications have discussed it. Internet chat rooms, list servers and newsgroups devoted to the subject seem obsessed with it and I've seldom read a martial arts magazine that didn't have at least one letter to the editor in which a practitioner claimed that "my sifu can beat your sifu" because my teacher got the "real" or "secret" transmission... As we enter an age where many of the learned masters of the older generation are dying off, how does one decide who to study with? Whose "transmission" can be said to be "authentic"?'
>
> Leporati, John:
> http://www.patiencetaichi.com/

This authenticity/legitimacy concern and the practical logic of body-experience lineages seems to hold for more modern martial arts as well (who do not have a single direct lineage to connect to) stimulating new body lineages and invented traditions[4]. Lastly, body-experience lineages are not particular to Asian martial arts but also present with arts of an intercultural origin as in the case of Ed Parker's Kempo Karate[5]. In each of these scenarios the stimulus of globalisation,

---

[3] This is well illustrate by the Vale Tudo era where the combat effectiveness of a number of martial art's were called into question, thereby restricting the legitimacies claims that could be reasonably be made.

[4] For an example see Kook Sul Kwan at:
http://www.ockoreanmartialarts.com/about/lineage/ (last accessed 1.07.2013)

[5] Again A senior student of Parker was Larry Tatum and his "Black Belt Family Tree" can be seen here: http://www.ltatum.com/familytree.html (last accessed 1.07.2013)

change and interculturality is also countered simultaneously with glocalisation, and (re)invention of tradition (Hobsbawm & Ranger, 1983).

Practical Modalities of Body-experience Lineage: Silent Codes, Family Heredity, Technical Authority and Bureaucracy

Chu, Ritchie and Wu's (1998, p.83) historical research suggests that 'in order to prevent abuse' many Kung Fu styles, such as in their case, Wing Chun were initially practiced under a silent code which meant the art 'was passed down to only a few chosen disciples and was never documented.' This silent code was one of the strongest means through which martial arts were guarded, conserved and evolved in the bodies and minds of a chosen few. However, as Reid and Croucher (1983, p.19) point out this modality is also the most fragile form of lineage and transmission:

> 'A master who has made a decision to reveal his [sic] art will often withhold a central core of advanced teaching that he will pass on only to an approved successor. Should a suitable candidate never appear, the technique dies unless one of the followers is able to rediscover or reinvent it'.

Skoss' (1994) historical investigation of transmission practices in traditional Japanese martial arts suggests the widespread use of explicit and formalised processes of body-experience lineage by way of either heredity (isshi sodden) or technical authority (yuiju ichinin). The first, isshi sodden means the complete transmission of a ryu's (art's) techniques and principles to one's blood heir and as such is clearly built upon legacy of the social and symbolic capital accorded heredity in feudal Japan. The second yuiju ichinin, refers the practices of passing all the ryu's secrets to a single designated inheritor who was not a member of one's family. This practice was only invoked in circumstances where a family heir to the art was either not forthcoming or deemed insufficiently expert. History illustrates that both these modalities of transmission have been used together with examples of both (at different times) evidenced in the histories of Judo and Aikido. Japanese martial arts are not the only context where heredity is in evidence. Elsewhere, the Brazilian martial art of Gracie Jui jitsu is an emphatic illustration of how heredity continues to play a central part in a modern martial arts lineage. This illustration is all the more poignant given the significance of this particular martial in the world of combat sport today.

In the late modern era, the practical logic of transmission through body experience lineage in many martial arts has also become a bureaucratic institutionalised process that is managed by international committee structures. Larger institutionalised "state sanctioned" arts such as Judo (Villamon, Brown, Espartero & Gutierrez, 2004) Shotokan Karate, Taekwondo and increasingly Wushu (DeKnop & Theeboom, 1997) have instigated modernised and bureaucratised processes in which the institution is fronted by socially sanctioned (often elected) presidential figureheads, and the technical authority is deferred to a "technical committee of experts" who research and modify technique in response to a range of exigencies, including commercial, sporting and media pressures. Arguably, key elements of the body-experience lineage are removed from influence here, although the emergence of teacher/coach/practitioner "camps" in the Mixed Martial Arts, such as Cesar Gracie Jiu-Jitsu , Blackhouse and Jackson's is indicative that body-experience lineage is an practical logic. With such a variety of processes in evidence today, caution needs exercising when generalising about transmission in martial arts cultures. However, it is probably fair to say that struggles remain observable between potential successors (family members or individual / group technical "authorities") and these constitute a micro politics of body-experience lineage that help illuminate the practical issues of transmitting a lived art. The reactions and subsequent trajectories of the sometimes disgruntled "failed successors" who see no option but to split from the art and start up their own art based on their interpretation exposes one powerful source of proliferation and change of body-experience lineage within martial arts culture.

Body-experience Lineage as Pedagogy: Direct Experience and Collective Embodied Identity

There are four conceptually interrelated points that help illuminate body-experience lineage as pedagogy. First, the construction of a collective identity through body-experience lineages, can be shown more clearly by Frank's (1995) notion of ideal types (body-selves) of body usage[6]. As Frank (1995 p.43) articulates 'The mirroring body defines itself in acts of consumption. [Emphasis original]...This body-self is called mirroring because consumption attempts to recreate the body in the images of other bodies.' In this sense, the practical focus on body-experience lineages encourages martial arts practitioners to consume the idealised "example," of the living embodiment of their chosen art form, that example being the Master and/or senior level teachers. Large amounts of technical and personal scrutiny, respect, and even forms of devotion (religious connotation intended [7]) are often paid to these "master bodies," thereby setting up a relationship of mirroring through mimetic consumption of martial technique, interactional gesture, emotional comportment, speech patterns, martial style, dress style, ritual style, and in a less embodied sense interpretations of philosophy, martial history, religious association and even broader cultural tastes. Transmission through mirroring shows how Masters and senior teachers carry responsibility for preserving what Bourdieu (1998, p. 76-77) refers to as the *illusio* of an art, making sure students get 'caught up in and by the game,' and come to believe 'the game is "worth the candle."'

Second, at the level of daily training practice, body-experience lineages assumes a focus on direct practical experience and transference of "feel" through the communion of bodies training, "grading" and competing together, a process that directly connects master practitioners to senior teachers to students. This a process which connects the bodies practitioners of an art across time and space with the senior teacher training occasionally with the Master and then returning

---

[6] Frank (1995) outlines four ideal types of body uses: "Disciplining" "dominating" "mirroring" and "communicative".

[7] For discussions of religious and spiritual implications of martial practices see Brown et al 2008; 2011, Jennings, Brown & Sparkes 2010, Brown 2013.

with new ideas to pass this on to his/her students. This is precisely the process implied by lineage maps. Such a view is given further support from Mellor and Shilling's (1997) notion of sensual solidarity (a sensation of unity through shared experiences) which helps articulate practices through which martial artists begin to feel "united" by their shared sensual social conditioning. In particular, the experiences of particular types of pain, discomfort or humility induced by training, learning and competition.

Third, Durkheim's ([1917]2001) notion of collective effervescence remains according to Shilling and Mellor (1998, p. 196) valuable, because

> 'It captures the idea of social 'force' at its birth; when embodied humans feel themselves and are transformed through an emotional structuring of their sensory and sensual being...This force is experienced mentally and physically, and binds people to the ideals valued by their social group'.

The ritualized practices of class training, grading's and competitions are productive of various types of (intended) collective emotional states valued within this particular art ranging from the relaxed awareness of a Tai Chi class, the disciplined focus of the Karate grading or the explosive adrenaline of a Judo tournament. Fourth, these ideas of mirroring, sensual solidarity and collective effervescence combine to illustrate what Merleau-Ponty (1964) refers to as intersubjectivity. Intersubjectivity suggests that the restricted notion of discrete martial artists (as monadic beings) "influenced" by practical social encounters should give way to the idea of martial artists as "relational beings" (Mauthener & Doucet, 2003) in which, 'the subject is his [sic] body, his world, and his situation, by a sort of exchange' (Merleau-Ponty, 1964, p.72). Jennings' (2010) ethnography of a Wing Chun association showed that intersubjectivity found expression in positive dispositions towards shared cultivation in which practitioners came to recognise their own improvement was bound with their helping others improve (due to the need to have more and better partners to train with). These relational, intersubjective senses become incorporated as dispositions in the collective and individual habitus of practitioners providing a distinctive and valued identity for practitioners, which is also necessary if the art itself is to survive.

The Language and Symbolism of Body-experience Lineages

While irreducible to linguistic and semiotic forms, these elements nevertheless strongly augment the corporeal practices of body-experience lineages. The first of these worthy of mention relates to the discourses of martial arts training pedagogy, which are traditionally minimal. For example, applying Bernstein's concepts ([1975] 2003) of restricted / elaborated discursive codes in instructional contexts (such as during training and grading sessions at the dojo or kwoon) helps to better articulate the pedagogy of transmission. For example, in traditional martial arts the linguistic codes are often highly restricted at the beginning of training (where explanations are often minimalistic or left out altogether) to deliberately focus on the practical mimesis/mirroring of a technique or movement concept, free from the intellectual distraction of 'understanding'. Only later are these codes elaborated (once the student has acquired technique or choreography) to show the application, "reasoning", limitations, alternatives for the movement etc. Of course, this also serves a second functions which is to preserve the "secrets" of the art for those who have shown loyalty and commitment.

Second, martial arts are replete with a plethora of symbols, creeds, maxims (many of these are "vestigial" remnants of the oral cultures they emanated from) and classic scholarly texts all of which serve as important sources to augment body-experience transmission. Notable examples of these are provided by the Wing Chun code of conduct (written by grandmaster Yip Man); Master Gichin Funakoshi's 20 principles of Karate; The code of Hwarang (adopted and elaborated but many Taekwondo associations); Wu Yuxiang's (1812-8) Mental Understanding for the Practice of the Thirteen Actions, concerning martial principles of Tai Chi. Lastly, notable symbolism includes the widespread use and adaption of The Taiji (Yin Yang) symbol and a virtual bestiary of fighting animals (Tiger, Dragon, Crane, Snake, Monkey etc). While detailed examinations of each of these is not possible here, it is possible to suggest that their use is an attempt to signify in words or symbols, idealised bodily dispositions that should guide the types interoception, exteroception and proprioception experienced and valued by advanced practitioners of these arts.

Finally, the explosion of interest in narrative research (see for example Herman, Jahn & Ryan, 2007) has led to quite profound transformations in academic interpretations of the "story" and "history". These developments implicate how we might view the multitude of body experience lineage stories. For example, Somers (1994) proposes a range of "levels of narrative" ranging from the personal, to the public, to metanarratives. These levels help to show how certain stories circulating in martial arts cultures act as metanarratives of legitimacy and transmission. A prominent illustration is provided by the metanarrative of the "origin" of South East Asian martial arts, involving the activities of the legendary fighting monk Boddidharma. Another metanarrative focuses upon the "ancient" origin stories that circulate in relation to prototypes of Tai Chi Chuan and the Taoist masters of Wudang Mountain in China. Attached to these metanarratives, are invariably more (g)localised public narratives that provide explanations of how a particular martial art(ist) is connected with this ancient history, through the body-experience lineages of their teachers. Finally, the increasing interest in (auto)biographical testimony (personal narratives) also serves as part of the process of linguistic narrative transmission of an art. These range from "testimonial" stories in discrete sections of texts on martial arts techniques, to full (auto)biographies (see Jacob, 2005).

These brief illustrations, contain a range of narratives types and levels which what Murray (1999) refers to as narrative resources implicitly used by martial artists to provide coherence to their collective identities. These narrative resources are often deemed sufficiently important to be required to reproduce in gradings and to promote on publicity material.

Closing Comments

This chapter has highlighted the phenomenon of body-experience lineages. As with any kind of embodied, practical knowledge, it is elusive due to the difficulties in accessing precisely the transmission of bodily experiences in martial arts cultures, as they take place. In spite of, and to an extent because of these difficulties, cultural sustainability and the processes that underpin it is an increasingly important and recognised issue. Martial arts are beginning to be identified under UNESCO's (2003) convention on 'intangible cultural heritage' which includes:

> 'Traditions or living expressions inherited from our ancestors and passed on to our descendants, such as oral traditions, performing arts, social practices, rituals, festive events, knowledge and practices concerning nature and the universe or the knowledge and skills to produce traditional crafts....While fragile, intangible cultural heritage is an important factor in maintaining cultural diversity in the face of growing globalization'.

(www.unesco.org/culture/ich/)

To this end, many traditional martial arts (such as the Korean art of Taekkyeon that was registered in 2011) are being beginning to be recognised as much more than just culturally esoteric forms of fighting. Instead they should be seen as a culturally rich and valuable genre of performing arts, social practices, rituals and traditional knowledges that form part of a simultaneously diverse and common human cultural heritage. Therefore, better understanding the function and process of body-experience lineages in increasingly globalised and glocalised martial art cultures is an imperative not just for academic enquiry but also for the practical purposes of sustaining these practices as valued intangible cultural heritage.

Notes:

An Earlier version of this chapter entitled "La lignee corporelle: conceptualisation de la transmission des arts martiaux traditionnels en Occident" was published in STAPS (2011) 93, pp. 61 - 71.

References

Bernstein, B. ([1975] 2003). *Class, codes and control, vol. 111: Towards a theory of educational transmission.* London, Routledge, Taylor & Francis.
Bourdieu, P. (1990). *The logic of practice.* Cambridge, Polity Press.
Bourdieu, P. (1993). *Sociology in question.* London, Sage Publications.
Bourdieu, P. (1998). *Practical reason: On the theory of action.* California, Stanford.
Brown, H. & K.Brown (2013). "Seeking spirituality through physicality in schools: learning from 'Eastern movement forms'". *International Journal of Children's Spirituality*, 18(1): 30-45.
Brown D.H.K, Molle, A, & G. Jennings (2009). *Belief in the martial arts: Exploring relationships between Asian martial arts and religion.* Stadion, 35, pp.47-66.

Brown, D.H.K., Jennings, G., & A. Leledaki (2008). "The changing charismatic status of the performing male body in Asian martial arts films". *Sport in Society*, 11(2), 174 - 194.

Brown, D.H.K., & A. Leledaki (2010). "Eastern movement forms as body-self transforming cultural practices in the West: Towards A sociological perspective". *Cultural Sociology*, 4(1), 123-154.

Chu, R., Ritchie, R., & Y. Wu (1998). *Complete Wing Chun: The definitive guide to Wing Chun's history and traditions*. North Clarendon, Turtle.

Durkheim, E. (2001). *Elementary forms of religious life* (C. Cosman, Trans.). Oxford, Paperbacks, Oxford U.K.

Giddens, A (1984). *The constitution of society: Outline of the theory of structuration*. Cambridge: Polity Press.

Frank, A. W. (1995). *The wounded storyteller: Body, illness and ethics*. London, University of Chicago Press.

Herman, D., Jahn, M., & Ryan, M.-L. (2007). *Routledge encyclopedia of narrative theory*. Oxford, Routledge.

Hobsbawm, E., & Ranger, T. (1983). *The invention of tradition*. Cambridge, Cambridge University Press.

Jacob, R. (2005). *Martial arts biographies: An annotated bibliography*. Lincoln, NE, iUniverse, Inc..

Jennings G. (2010). *Fighters, Thinkers, and shared cultivation: Experiencing transformation through the long-term practice of traditionalist Chinese martial arts*. Unpublished PhD, University of Exeter, Exeter.

Jennings, G., Brown, D., & Sparkes, A. C. (2010). "It can be a religion if you want": Wing Chun Kung Fu as a secular religion. *Ethnography*, 11(4), 533-557.

Leporati, J. (2009). "The true transmission: Exploring the controversy". http://www.patiencetaichi.com/public/120print.cfm. Accessed: 25/06/2009.

Mauthner, N. S., & A. Doucet (2003). "Reflexive accounts and accounts of reflexivity in qualitative data analysis". *Sociology*, 37(3), 413-431.

Mellor, P., & C. Shilling (1997). *Re-forming the body: Religion, community and modernity*. London, Sage.

Merleau-Ponty (1964). *Sense and nonsense*. trans. Dreyfus, Dreyfus, and Allen, Evanston Ill, Northwestern U. Press.

Murray, M. (1999). "The storied nature of health and illness", in, M. Murray & K. Chamberlain (Eds.), *Qualitative Health Psychology*, London, Sage, pp. 47-63.

Reid, H. & Croucher. M. (1983). *The way of the warrior: The paradox of the martial arts*. London, Century Publishing.

Shilling, C. (1993). *The body and social theory*. London, Sage Publications.

Skoss, M. (1997). "Transmission and succession in the classical arts". from http://koryu.com/library/mskoss4.html. Accessed 28.06.2013.

Shepherdson, C. (2008). *Lacan and the limits of language*. New York, Fordham University Press.

Somers, M. (1994). "The narrative construction of identity: A relational and network approach". *Theory and Society*, 23, 605-649.

Sparkes, A.C. (2009) "Ethnography and the senses: Challenges and possibilities". *Qualitative Research in Sport and Exercise*, 1(1), pp. 21-35.

Theeboom, M., & P. De Knop (1997). "An analysis of the development of Wushu". *International Review for the Sociology of Sport*, 32(3), 267-282.

UNESCO (2003) *Intangible Cultural Heritage*. Available at: http://www.unesco.org/culture/ich/ . Last accessed 28.06.2013.

Villamón, M., Brown, D.H.K., Espartero, J., & C. Gutiérrez (2004). "Modernization and the disembedding of Judo from 1946 to the 2000 Sydney Olympics". *International Review for the Sociology of Sport*, 39(2), 139-156.

Chapter 9

Constituting the Fighter's Body: On *Being-with* in Brazilian Jiu-Jitsu

Bryan Hogeveen & Jennifer Hardes

Introduction

Brazilian Jiu-Jitsu (hereafter BJJ) is a primarily ground based martial art where participants attempt to choke, strangle and manipulate large joints. It emerged in *fin de siècle* Brazil when the Gracie family adapted lessons they received from Mitsuyo Maeda who was, because of his fighting prowess, widely known as Conde Koma or the Count of Combat (Peligro, 2003). According to the official history of BJJ written by Kid Peligro (2003), Maeda was one of Jigoro Kano's, the founder of Judo, best students. The Gracie's took what they learned from Maeda and adapted the techniques to their body types and the needs of street protection in Brazil. Their modifications were motivated by their understanding that fights typically end up on the ground where the struggle is ultimately decided (Peligro, 2003, 1).

Not until recently did the art breach its national borders. In fact, it was not until 1995 that the first non-Brazilian was awarded a black belt. Since this time, and buoyed by the success of Royce Gracie in the first iteration of the Ultimate Fighting Championship (UFC), the numbers of schools and academies that teach BJJ has multiplied exponentially. Academic study has not kept pace. While martial arts like Karate, Judo and Taekwondo have seen much ink spilled about their strictures, BJJ has received relatively scant attention. Nevertheless, we are convinced that this art offers a rich site from which to theorize how fighters' (and perhaps other athletes) bodies are constituted. There are many other lessons that might accrue from studying this art in detail (i.e. ethical relations). In this essay, however, we call on our martial arts experiences and interviews conducted with BJJ athletes to discern how the fighter's body is forged in relations *with* accomplished and skillful others. To this end we draw on Jean-Luc Nancy's theorizing on touching and being-with.

Our analysis joins a burgeoning literature concerning the sporting, martial, or combative fight space where corporeal engagement occurs (Downey 2005; Hogeveen, 2013; Spencer, 2009; 2012; Wacquant, 2004, 2011). Such accounts of the body have generated rich insight into the phenomenological experience of the fighter and a deeper awareness of how the fighter's body is crafted through its interactions 'in the world' (Hogeveen , 2013). We turn to Jean-Luc Nancy in this chapter for several reasons. Nancy allows us to engage in a carnal sociology that not only generates insight into these rich bodily experiences, but actively foregrounds how the body and its experiences are relationally constituted (Crossley, 1995). We suggest that Nancy's (2000, 2002, 2008) lexicon of the body, the centrality of 'being-with', touching, and his concept of the 'singular-plural', gives us new theoretical elements to more fully engage with and comprehend the fighter's embodied experiences (Spencer 2012). To the uninitiated combative space might appear devoid of philosophical traces. But this oversimplified interpretation belies a rich site for thinking more deeply about the body.

Being-with, Moving-with

We begin with a simple premise – 'there is no pure presence of the fighter'. They do not materialize out of the void. Instead fighters are forged in connection with and to skilled others who impart martial lessons passed down to them. To one extent or another, relations between bodies and ghosts always already condition martial arts. In addition to training BJJ, I regularly teach classes. From where do the 100s of techniques and movements I inculcate and instill come? Did I invent them? Did they materialize in a dream? I learned them from my instructor who acquired them from hers and so on back to Maeda, to Kano and beyond.

Willing training partners and generous teachers are fundamental to disseminating martial arts traditions. This is especially true in BJJ. Referred to often as the game of human chess, BJJ combines qualities of posture, timing, leverage and feel. With these qualities at its center, rather than strength, aggression and force, BJJ is appealing to the young and the elderly, to the affluent and the marginalized, and to bodies ranging in abilities.

Contemporary times have seen a virtual explosion of BJJ instructional material. Students motivated to supplement their tutelage were, until very recently, hard pressed to secure competent resources aside from traveling to the many academies that dot Rio's streets. The dearth of resources stemmed from how closely many academies and schools closely guarded their secrets and how few qualified instructors were located outside of Brazil. With the refinement of electronic recording devices and the ability to almost instantaneously disseminate images from place to place on a massive scale, BJJ instructional materials have propagated at an unprecedented rate. Throwing caution to the wind and eager to circulate the latest techniques in hopes of cashing in on their celebrity, world champions and highly acclaimed practitioners are now providing martial artists from around the world a window into their academies. Multiple time world champion, Andre Galvao, for example, charges $150 a year for access to 'allgalvao.com'. Through this venue, BJJ practitioners can '…..hear directly from Andre... his thoughts on matches, his mindset, his preparation and his training.

See and learn the techniques taught daily in his San Diego academy ... [and] get an insider look at his lifestyle and what it takes to be a champion and world-renowned instructor'.

BJJ is an open martial art. Unlike other traditions that might close themselves off to innovation, BJJ is rapidly evolving. Partially fueled by the internet and other electronic media, new techniques, submission set-ups and movements emerge every year. However, grooving these into a body that understands requires a willing and learned other. An athlete can watch Galvao perform an arm-lock and scroll through it in their minds hundreds of times, but their body will not truly grasp the position unless studied relationally - preferably alongside a more experienced body. The poverty of learning from two dimensional images becomes evident when new students who have been nourished on a steady diet of YouTube clips and UFC events enter the academy. All quickly realize that a significant distance separates watching techniques and performing them with precision on a resisting opponent. Before attending my first BJJ class I too had watched several UFC events that convinced me I could easily replicate the top athlete's performances. When it came time to spar that first night I attempted an arm-lock, a tactic I had seen fighters perform so effortlessly on TV, and fell flat on my back at a considerable distance from my opponent and successful application of the technique. All students' arms were safe that night, with the only real damage being to my ego.

Viewing techniques on video or reading about them in books goes only a short distance toward forging a body that understands or one that can adeptly apply the concepts. Learning is relational and perceptual. Significant educative dimensions are lost in exchanging a touching and sensing body for a two dimensional object where there is no spatial and temporal convergence of bodies. The distant other is absent and unavailable at the point of execution. Archiving knowledge in print, video or on the internet assures the perpetual circulation of knowledge. This is certainly laudable. Nevertheless, observation and study of these media do not at once fabricate an understanding and cooperative body. In the absence of intermingling proximal and touching bodies that anchor the movement in contemporary space and time a fissure remains.

For several years we experimented with a relatively popular BJJ technique without much success. We had witnessed several high level practitioners employ this strategy with exceptional proficiency and artistry at tournaments and on instructional YouTube clips. Yet, it remained elusive to our bodies. Something was absent. From the relevant materials at my disposal we attempted to observe the entirety of the position - the grips, the angles, the spacing, & etc.. But to no avail. Each time we ventured to perform the technique, the anticipated result would sometimes materialize, but would more often collapse under the weight of my partners' defense. We were fully aware of the expected result, yet a deficiency remained. Last August we were invited to a seminar conducted by the originator of the technique. Although he did not teach this particular position, we approached him during a lunch break to inquire about my lack. He spent half an hour instructing us on how to obtain the proper angle, pressure and leverage. While we have yet to master the position (if there is even such a thing), we have made considerable progress to this end. More than would have ever been the case had the space between our bodies remained separated by a page or screen.

Residue that evades the camera's eye was at the center of our foundering. Digitization connected us with an expert across the globe. However, physical distance that precluded touch rendered such important elements to the success of this particular movement - e.g. angle, pressure and leverage - equally remote. Being with, *touching* this expert and feeling his body's comportment as he performed the technique added core dimensions absent from the two dimensional rendering. Our later competence was derived from immediate relational touching bodies.

After demonstrating a particular choke one of my students complained that "she didn't understand" how to make this technique effective. I directed her to perform the move on me and was immediately aware of her problem. Visually she could point to no difference between the technique I demonstrated and what she had performed. Her declaration is not unusual among my students. It is not that I am a particularly poor instructor. The matter lies in the substance of BJJ and at which I hinted in the above example. Much of what contributes to the efficiency of BJJ techniques is imperceptible. Considered among the greatest BJJ practitioners of all time, Rickson Gracie emphasized this point, he notes: "good Jiu Jitsu is invisible" (Alonso 2005). Gracie is here drawing our attention to the unseen and inconspicuous that can only be grasped through the touch of someone much more experienced. Only when I applied the technique to my student with instructions to attend to the pressure and angles of my arms was she better equipped to apply the choke on her training partner.

We are very much aware that some individuals have employed various two dimensional media to acquaint themselves with novel positions and strategies. In fact, before the dissemination of BJJ outside of Brazil and a few notable schools in the United States, videotapes were the only access many interested students could convene. Throughout my years in the art I have listened to many practitioners brag about the old days where they would huddle around the television to watch the *Gracies in Action* videotapes featuring individuals from the Gracie clan - who, according to the official history, founded BJJ - besting representatives from Kung Fu, Judo, Kickboxing and Karate. These veterans grumble about how fortunate contemporary students are to have access to a mountain of material. "Tapes" were all they had - and each other. In 1993 UFC 1 introduced BJJ to the world and whetted the appetite of martial artists from across North America. When Royce Gracie, son of Helio Gracie (one of the founders of BJJ), prevailed over representatives from various martial arts that night, it sparked off a quiet revolution. Interest was fervent and sweeping. The problem for the would be students was that there were very few qualified black-belt instructors living outside of Brazil and that video cassettes were not only in short supply, but also very expensive. However, this shortfall added to both the mystique and the craving for BJJ instructional content.

Terry has practiced and trained in various martial arts for most of his 50 years and earned black-belts in several of them. Akin to many other martial artists with whom I have spoken, after UFC 1 he soon scaled back his practice of these fighting styles to spend more time learning the twists and holds of BJJ. However, lack of resources (both financial and human) seriously obstructed his intention. Terry explains:

'....the first instructional videos started coming out, and they were just ridiculously expensive, this was back in the days where a hundred bucks gave me chest pains. I got hooked up with a bunch of guys from different martial arts, and we also agreed that it was important to learn to roll on the ground. At that time, like it was unheard of that anyone had a blue belt, like, "oh, so-and-so has gone and done two classes at the Gracie's academy, I've got to go and pick his brain'.

Motivated to learn but unable to locate experienced others who could assist him in his endeavor, Terry searched in earnest until he finally secured a group who would meet on Saturdays for "BJJ" training. However, as Terry explains, because only a few people had any skill or practical knowledge the experience was chaotic: "I had a friend who had a club with mats. There was nobody there on Saturday. On Friday night we'd start calling around. Saturday morning we'd show up and beat the shit out of each other."

Training under these conditions soon grew tiresome. Even though they had watched some MMA bouts and the *'Gracies in Action'*, none of Terry's friends were adept at applying holds or securing submissions. That was until Bob starting buying all the instructional VHS tapes that were slowly making their way out of Brazil and onto the international market. Together Terry and Bob would attempt these positions, locks and holds. Synergistically they would slowly unscramble what they were gleaning from the videotapes. After watching an arm-lock or choke they would attempt the positions on each other. Over several years their cooperative interaction helped them to become slightly more proficient during their anarchic sparring sessions. Their bodies understood the macro and easily observable details of each position, but the finer details that get lost in translation when the position is transferred to VHS tape escaped them. It was not until many years after their humble beginnings when a Brazilian BJJ black belt settled in their home town that Terry's skills "exploded." He reports that even though he almost wore out his video collection inspecting them for the finer details, it was not until this black belt arrived in town that he was given the missing "pieces of the puzzle".

Much is forfeited in swapping an experienced other who we can touch and who can touch us for those who are distant in space and time. Two-dimensional images furnish a general orientation, but edification comes most acutely when anchored in an accomplished other whose spacing is much more intimate. It is not the case that we cannot learn at a distance. As a novice, Terry benefitted considerably from VHS tapes and his synergistic experiments with Bob. Without him and in the absence of a willing training partner on which to experiment, Terry's revelations would have remained trapped in a cognitive cul-de-sac. Nevertheless, the arrival of his black belt instructor sling-shotted his erudition. We are always *with* many others, but it is those willing to share knowledge greater than our own and who are in immediate proximity that are pivotal to intricate, precise and exhaustive skill acquisition.

Fighters' bodies are forged through touch in intimate space and in relation with other bodies (Hogeveen, 2013). There is no meaning in BJJ that is not shared between and among other bodies. More to the point, there is no BJJ without a plurality of individuals - near and distant - interlaced together in a common end.

This brings our discussion full circle back to Jean-Luc Nancy. In his seminal book, '*Being Singular Plural*' Nancy (2000) confronts the question of relational Being and sets his lofty sights at "the order of philosophical exposition" (30). To him, "there is no meaning if meaning is not shared. ... Being cannot *be* anything but being-with-one-another circulating in the '*with*' and as the '*with*' of this singularly plural coexistence" (2-3). This insight strikes at the heart of '*being*' and what has heretofore been obfuscated in philosophical debate and discourse. For his part, Nancy aims to re-order philosophy, "....for which it has been a matter of course that the 'with' - and the '*other*' that goes along with it - always comes second" (30). Heidegger preserved and ensconced what Nancy believes is an antiquated discourse when "....he does not introduce the co-originality of *Mitsein*" (30-31). By contrast, Nancy claims that the multiplicity and heterogeneity of beings is the justification for '*being*'. He maintains that "...a single being is a contradiction in terms. Such a being, which would be its own foundation, origin and intimacy, would be incapable of *Being*" (Nancy 2000, 12).

Nancy further claims that we cannot describe an experience of the body without considering how the body is constitutively relational. He recently argued "above all, body means in presence of other bodies" (Nancy 2010, 86). Nancy (2000) calls this the "singular-plural" of '*being*', which implies that there is no essence of '*being*' that is not a co-essence or '*being-with*' (Nancy, 2000, 30). At the heart of his argument is the contention that, "...if being is being-with, then it is ... *the 'with' that constitutes Being*; the with is not simply an addition ... to some prior being; instead, the 'with' is at the heart of Being" (Nancy, 2000, 30).

By accenting the relationality of '*being*' we are highlighting how fighters' bodies are forged in interaction with others. Their bodies are more than an 'extension of the self'. Training *with* others provides the milieu and backdrop in which skill is acquired. However, if improving and learning technique is the end to which we practice, it is paramount to interface with those more skilled than ourselves. Terry's foundering is a case in point. Exceptional instructors open out to their students. I have been fortunate to learn from a world-class athlete who has pushed me beyond myself with grace and openness. Although they have certainly twisted, choked and contorted my body in a manner that it was unaccustomed, it was not out of malice or with sadistic purpose. Rather, my fighter's body was engendered with the help of my instructor who extended and altered the limits of my perception through the violent interlacing of our bodies.

BJJ study hinges upon touch. Let us be clear, touching is not confined to one sense, but spreads out through the body and is coupled with others. If we were to privilege the optical over all other sense it would only serve to invalidate all that is excluded by that particular sense (Derrida 2005). Recently, I was struck by a visually impaired competitor being led to the mats. The unavailability of optical stimuli did not obstruct his ability or hamper his chances for a medal. In fact, he placed third. Throughout his matches, the competitor's coach bellowed instruction and relayed positional details. This competitor, like all others that participated, counted on and put their faith in 'an other'; in someone who could usefully guide them through BJJ's strictures and subtleties, both in the immediate context of the competition and every day in the academy. It this kind of intimate relationality that undergirds effective and positive martial arts tutelage.

Intertwining sensory stimuli emanating from his opponent and his coach equipped him to deftly navigate the grappling milieu. Sight is but one sense. Touching opens out to and envelopes the world - even if we are not always consciously aware of the minutiae of its input. Our touch glides along through "slits, holes and zones" (Nancy 2008, 45). It is necessarily diverse, distinct and interwoven. Touching, for Nancy, is a "mobile, unstable caress, seeing the image in slow motion, fast-forwarded, or frozen, seeing as well with *touches* from other senses smells, tastes, timbres, or even with sounds, from the senses of words" (Nancy 2008, 45-47). Circulating senses and touch orient us toward our world and provide clues to unscramble its meaning. Although the optical is one form of touch that tunes us into our world, it is only one in what Nancy (2013) usefully calls an "anarchic exuberance" of the senses.

Touching is conditioned by movement and spacing. Nancy (2008, 135) writes, "what touches, what we are touched by, is on the order of *emotion*, ... which implies "set in movement, in motion." While emotion might begin to capture what Nancy is after, he prefers the term "commotion" because "this word has the advantage of introducing "with" (*cum*). Commotion is being set in motion with" (Nancy 2008, 135). During sparring sessions movement is not mine alone. It is not an extension of 'myself'. Rather, it is the other's gesture that signals my body to respond. I am touched by an "anarchic exuberance" of sight, sound, tactile, smell and even taste that stimulates my reaction. Rillion Gracie (2009, 32) explains the importance of touch and sensing when he argues that over time and through experience, "…you start to develop sensibility where you can guess your adversary's thoughts. A second before the the guy makes a move your hook is in there blocking him. That's what Jiu-Jitsu's about."

"Rolling" is intimate. Bodies intertwine and contort as each attempt to gain an edge over the other. As my partner advances I use their cues to thwart, reverse and make headway toward securing a submission hold and ending the match. To this end, I listen intently to the sound of their breathing. Laboured breath betrays my opponent – she is tiring. I hear the sound of her feet shifting as she feints one direction and moves in another in anticipation of finding a hole in my defenses. Her hips shift and their grips move from my collar to my pants signaling their attempt to create a dominate position. My trained body responds and moves with the movement of the other. It *senses* their intention. This (co)-motion does not belong to me, nor to the other. Together we dance, struggle, fight and improve our technique and ourselves.

Conclusion

Coming to terms with Nancy's understanding of being-with and touching go some distance in helping us discern how the fighter's body is constituted. In this chapter we have endeavored to use this rich insight Nancy provides to explicate a phenomenological account of the fighters' bodily experience. In doing so we have demonstrated, by way of various examples, how a fighter's body is always already constituted through its relationality to and with others. As we have noted, if we did not move and learn together, we would be two individuals doing separate things, and therefore not responding to one another. The movement in the fight is not merely of the *'I'*: the movement is not merely *'one's own'*.

The fighter's body and corporeal experience is forged through responses to something or someone other in proximity and anchored in technique developed through time, space, and a ghostly history. Through this exploration of BJJ we have foregrounded the importance of capturing the fundamental relational experience that constitutes the body and its comportments, describing how fighter's bodies are forged *with* others. In doing so, we have opened up a relationally-paved avenue for understanding and describing both martial arts experiences, as well as sporting experiences more broadly.

References

Allen-Collinson, J., & J. Hockey (2011). 'Feeling the way: Notes Toward a Haptic Phenomenology of Scuba Diving and Distance Running'. *International Review for the Sociology of Sport*, 46(3), 330-345.

Alonso, M. (2005). 'Quebra Silêncio'. *Tatame*. June.

Bourdieu, P. (1990). *The Logic of Practice*. Stanford: Stanford University Press.

Breivik, G. (2013). 'Zombie-like or Super-conscious: A Phenomenological and Conceptual Account of Consciousness in Elite Sport.' *Journal of the Philosophy of Sport,* 40(1): 85-106.

Crossley, N. (1995). 'Merleau-Ponty, the Elusive Body and Carnal Sociology.' *Body and Society* 1(1): 43-63.

Derrida, J. (2005). *On Touching: Jean-Luc Nancy*. Stanford: Stanford University Press.

Downey, G. (2005). *Learning Capoeira: Lessons in Cunning from An Afro-Brazilian Art*. New York: Oxford.

Gracie, R. (2009). 'The Guard.' *Gracie Magazine* 143: 29-32.

Heidegger, M. (2008) [1962]. Being and Time. John Macquarrie and Edward Robinson (Trans). New York: Harper Collins.

Hockey, J., & J. Allen-Collinson, (2009). The Essence of Sporting Embodiment: Phenomenological Analyses of the Sporting Body. *The International Journal of Interdisciplinary Social Sciences*, 4(4): 71-82.

Hogeveen, B. (2013). 'It is about your body recognizing the move and automatically doing it': Merleau-Ponty, Habit and Brazilian Jiu-Jitsu. In Raúl Sánchez García and Dale C. Spencer (Eds.), Fighting Scholars: Habitus and Ethnographies of Martial Arts and Combat Sports. Anthem Press.

Nancy, J-L. (2000). Being Singular Plural. Stanford: Stanford University Press.

Nancy, J-L. (2002). L'Intrus, *The New Centennial Review*, 2(3), 1-14.

Nancy, J-L. (2008). Corpus. Translated by Richard Rand. New York: Fordham University Press.

Nancy, J-L. (2010). Dialogue on the Philosophy to Come. *Minnesota Review*, 75(3): 71-88.

Nancy, J-L. (2010). 'On Touching, Sense, and Mitsein'. Lecture delivered at the European Graduate School. Accessed May 15th at: http://www.egs.edu/faculty/jean-luc-nancy/videos/on-touching-sense-and-mitsein/

Nancy, J-L. (2013). Extraordinary Sense. *Senses and Society*, 8(1): 10-13.

Parry, J. (1998). 'Violence and Aggression in Contemporary Sport'. In. M.J. McNamee and S.J. Parry (Eds.), Ethics and Sport, pp. 205-224, New York: Routledge.

Peligro, K. 2003. *The Gracie Way: An Illustrated History of the World's Greatest Martial Arts Family*. Montpelier: Invisible Cities Press.

Spencer, D. (2009). 'Habitus, Body Techniques, and Body Callousing: An Ethnography of Mixed Martial Arts', *Body & Society*, 15(4), 119-143.

Spencer, D. (2012). Ultimate Fighting and Embodiment: Violence, Gender, and Mixed Martial Arts. New York & London: Routledge.

Wacquant, L. (1995a). 'The Pugilist Point of View: How Boxers Think and Feel About Their Trade', *Theory & Society,* 24(4): 489-535.

Wacquant, L. (1995b). 'Pugs at work: Body Capital and Bodily Labour Among Professional Boxers', *Body & Society*, 1(1): 65-93.

Wacquant, L. (2004) Body and Soul: Notebooks of an Apprentice Boxer. Oxford & New York: Oxford University Press.

Wacquant, L. (2011). 'Habitus as Topic and Tool: Reflections on Becoming a Prize Fighter'. *Qualitative Research in Psychology*, 8: 81-92.

Chapter 10

The Female Fighter Phenomenon in Denmark and Greece: Exploring Gender Dynamics in Judo

Anna Kavoura, Marja Kokkonen, & Tatiana V. Ryba

Introduction

Bodies flying through the air and pinned to the ground is what a newcomer sees when entering a judo *dojo* (training school). Wearing their blue or white, heavy cotton *judogi* (training uniform), male and female *judokas* (judo athletes) are practicing together throws, immobilizations, chokes, and joint locks. As Olympic sport for men since 1964, judo has a high emphasis on competition. In addition to mastering a number of techniques, students have to practice their active attack and defense skills in every training session. Beyond technical and mental skills, physical skills are also important in determining who will dominate the fight. On the mats, bodies are tested and physical skills (such as strength, speed, explosive power, and endurance) are contested and celebrated. All these features are traditionally associated with the male physique. How do female athletes fit in this male arena? What are the gender power dynamics that they have to cope with?

In theory, judo was founded by Jigoro Kano to be an inclusive sport that could be practiced by every citizen, regardless of age, size or gender (Miarka, Marques, & Franchini, 2011). However, Miarka and colleagues argue that the social and cultural male-oriented judo context discriminated against women since the very beginning. The authors give evidence that from 1882 until the late 1960's, women were restricted to softer forms of training *(kata)* and they were not allowed to practice fighting *(rantori)*. Moreover, because of their 'fragile' biological nature, women were not allowed to compete and it was only in 1992 that women's judo joined the Olympic program (Miarka et al., 2011).

Ideas of biological determinism are so deeply embedded in our (sporting) culture (Vertinsky, 1994a) that it is always by reference to biology that male superiority is naturalized. As Vertinsky argues, the asymmetrical gender power is built upon 'natural' differences between two sexes, engaging scientists and medical doctors, from antiquity until now, in the construction of 'an ideology of female bodily incapacity' (Vertinsky, 1994b, p.149). This seems to be the case in judo as well, where sport physiology and psychology scholars insist on examining the differences between female and male judokas, based mainly on quantitative methods. Female judokas have been found to be shorter, lighter and have smaller body surface area (Karagounis, Maridaki, Papaharalampous, Prionas, & Baltopoulos, 2009), suffer from abnormal eating habits and problematic (body) self-esteem (Rouveix, Bouget, Pannafieux, Champely, & Filaire, 2007), score lower in many self-concept variables, such as physical condition, body attractiveness, sport competence, physical self-worth, and global self-esteem (Le Bars, Gernigon, & Ninot, 2009) and might respond hormonally stronger to pre-competition stress (Umeda et al., 1999). Thus, in light of the current quantitative research evidence, the picture looks quite depressing for the female judoka who is presented as biologically inferior to her male counterpart. Whether female inferiority is a biological fact or a socially constructed belief, it makes one wonder how it affects women's positioning and experiences in judo.

Previous sociological research has contributed to our theoretical knowledge of gender dynamics in martial arts and combat sports (Guerandel & Mennesson, 2007; Halbert, 1997; Hargreaves, 1997; Macro, Viveiros, & Cipriano, 2009; Mennesson, 2000; Sisjord, 1997; Sisjord & Kristiansen, 2008, 2009; Young, 1997). Feminist scholars have pointed out that the values and expectations of being a woman are in contrast with those of being a fighter (Halbert, 1997; Hargreaves, 1997; Mennesson 2000) and female martial artists experience discrimination and have to use several strategies to manage their identity (Halbert, 1997). An inquiry that shed some light to the construction of gender in interactions between judokas was published by Guerandel and Mennesson (2007), who argue, based on observation of trainings that the judo framework conflicts with that of gender expression, whereas the female competitors must position themselves as women but also be recognized as judokas.

The tensions between femininity and the sporting body have been pointed out in the past by critical scholars of sport psychology (e.g. Choi, 2000; Krane, Choi, Baird, Aimar, & Kauer, 2004; Markula, 1995). While the experiences and identity negotiations of the female athlete are not new research topics, the subject of women's judo remains conspicuously absent from sport and gender studies (Miarka et al., 2011). Aiming to fill this void, in this essay we provide some insights on the ways that gender dynamics affect the experiences of women judokas. To add on previous feminist cultural studies on the interaction of gender and culture (e.g. Markula, 1995; McGannon, Courtin, Schinke, & Schweinbenz, 2012), we follow an ethnographic approach to examine how gender is enacted particularly in the sociocultural contexts of Denmark and Greece.

Comparative Ethnographic Study of Female Judo Athletes' Experiences

Sport ethnography has been advanced as a research approach in the study of contemporary sport cultures (Sands, 2002). Particularly, in cultural sport psychology and in feminist scholarship, ethnographic methods have been favored for holding the potential to examine how power and privilege operate in different sport fields (Ryba & Wright, 2010). Giving a voice to the female athlete who remains in the margins of the male-dominated judo culture is central to our study. Thus, ethnography was selected as an approach for gaining insights into the experiences, behaviours and values of women judokas.

Similarly to other ethnographic studies of sport cultures (see for example Thorpe, 2010), this inquiry draws upon multiple sources, including personal observations and experiences, interviews and informal personal communication, articles in sport magazines and websites, as well as discussion in related forums. Instead of focusing upon a particular site, a multisited approach was adopted with the aim to examine the influence of the cultural context on the female athlete's experiences and psyche. As we have previously argued (Kavoura, Ryba, & Kokkonen, 2012), female judokas cannot be understood as a homogeneous group. Having been socialized in various cultures as well as being subjects of multiple discourses such as class, ethnicity, gender, sexuality, religion, and age, female judokas make different sense of their sporting experiences. Thus, in our ongoing research, data are constructed during ethnographic visits in various judo clubs in two different countries. The ethnographic visits lasted from couple of weeks to six months, depending on the circumstances and the travelling resources of the ethnographer. Data collection started in November 2010 and is still in process.

Ethnographic fieldwork has been conducted by the first author, who is also a judo athlete and a Greek woman. This was important in gaining access in the sport culture, as well as trust from the cultural members. As an ethnographic insider, the field researcher packed her judogi, travelled to the various judo clubs, trained with the club members and hanged out with them in seminars, competitions and other activities. During the course of the research, she sweated with them, bled with them, and shared the same frustrations (such as performance anxieties, injuries, and diet). Observations were made on and off the mats, switching roles from one of the athlete to the researcher, based on the demands of the particular moment.

The choice for these specific ethnographic sites was made because of the diversity that these social contexts offer. Investigating the experiences of women fighters in the egalitarian social context of Denmark on the one hand, and in the Greek patriarchal society on the other hand, enables us to explore the impact of the social setting on the psychological processes of the female athlete. Moreover, comparative data allow us to examine whether and in what ways the male underpinnings of judo culture are manifested in various sociocultural contexts. To illustrate our arguments we refer to the interviews conducted with two Danish and two Greek female athletes, whose names we have changed to protect their identity. The particular interviews were selected as case studies because the athletes belong to the same age and the same training level. They are all between 17 and 19 years old, champions of their weight category in their respective countries, with a training age between 6 and 11 years. The interviews lasted from 20 to 45 minutes and were audio recorded and transcribed. We work with feminist poststructuralist and Foucauldian theories to glean analytical insights into how our participants' experiences are framed by gender.

Female Athlete Identity Negotiations and the Male Underpinnings of Judo

In the remainder of the chapter we offer some insights from our ethnographic research. Two issues came out from our analysis: (a) the different ways that young female judokas negotiate their identity in Greece and in Denmark and (b) the male dominance of judo that is manifested in both cultures. Below we discuss these issues.

Greece: 'Try to act like a girl'

> **Eleftheria:** "I don't lift that many weights to become too muscular, but neither I am not lifting at all. I am lifting moderately in order to have a nice body and look and act like a girl".

In cross-cultural research (Hofstede, Hofstede, & Minkov, 2010), Greece is represented as a collectivist and masculine culture, in the sense that society is 'we' defined and success oriented and driven. Moreover, it is stereotypically perceived that in Greek culture hierarchy is respected and inequalities amongst people are acceptable (Hofstede et al., 2010). Kavoura, Ryba, and Chroni (2011) have previously argued that there are specific expectations of how women can behave, think, or look like in Greece, and the values of being a woman are in contrast with those of being a competitive judoka.

The female versus athlete paradox has been pointed out by feminist scholars in the past (e.g. Krane et al. 2004). Findings from our ethnographic study in Greece give support to previous findings of feminist research, indicating that women are influenced by dominant discourses of gender and femininity. This can be especially problematic in the case of young female athletes who struggle to find a balance between being a successful competitor, but in the same time a feminine and beautiful young woman. The following quote from Alexandra indicates that while she wants to keep up with all the requirements of being an elite athlete, such as incorporating strength training sessions to her training schedule, she is also concerned with keeping up with the requirements of being a woman.

> **Alexandra:** "Sometimes I was thinking that I also started looking like...how to say it...to gain muscle from the weight training. But then I thought about it again and I said that I like this [judo]. And since I like it and I do it well, I don't care what other people say, or how do I look. And, if you do not do excessive training, [judo] has nothing to do with if you are feminine or not".

> **Anna**: "So, if you do excessive training you think that you are not feminine anymore?"

> **Alexandra:** "No, just, usually, from the athletes [older successful female judokas] I see that when you do too much weight training your body starts becoming more like...more like male".

It is very interesting the way that Alexandra is trying to rebel against dominant discourses of femininity (against 'what other people say'), but then she is associating herself the athletic body with the male body. Choi (2000) argues that the 'sporty' type has always been associated with masculinity and while the female athlete is now more acceptable than ever before, what remains questionable is the relationship between femininity and physicality.

> **Eleftheria:** "When I first started [judo], they [my friends] were teasing me, saying that judo is not for girls, judo is only for boys".

> **Alexandra:** "My friends never had anything to do with this kind of sports [martial arts] and they always consider me like…let's say a tomboy…because I was stronger and more physically active than the rest".

Behaving in a way that is not considered to be feminine appropriate, may lead to the girl's femininity being questioned and sporty girls may be viewed as 'tomboys' or lesbians (Choi, 2000). Moreover, Choi argues that traditional notions of gender are still influencing how the female athlete is viewed, as well as how she might view herself. 'If the girl or woman wants to play the masculine game of sport she must do so in conformity with the patriarchal rules that ensure she is first and foremost recognized as a heterosexual feminine being' (Choi, 2000, p. 8)

> **Eleftheria:** "My first boyfriend was from judo and he could understand me more. He was telling me that judo is good and I should continue training, but I should also try to act like a girl. And since I was able to balance both [being an athlete and being a girl] he had no problem".

Denmark: Being the 'cool girl'

> **Mia:** "I'm good at what I'm doing and I just like what I do and stuff…instead of all the girls. Most of the girls just sit at home and do their homework and going to party and get really really drunk. I am a little different".

Denmark is represented as an individualistic and feminine society, in the sense that individuals are expected to take care of themselves, and good relationships, co-operation, and modesty are appreciated and emphasized (Hofstede et al., 2010). Danes are stereotypically considered to be very egalitarian mindset, believing in independency and equal rights (Hofstede et al., 2010). In addition, keeping the life/work balance is considered to be an important quality.

Danish girls are brought up to become strong, autonomous and independent women, that can manage equally well domestic and career responsibilities. Newell (1996) has described that phenomenon as the 'superwoman syndrome'. In contrast to the rigid gender role schemas that exist in Greece, gender roles in Denmark often overlap, leaving more space to women for gender performativity and identity negotiation. Mia and Sofie, the young female elite judokas that participated in our study, reject the traditional model of passive womanhood. They differentiate themselves from the 'ordinary' and 'girlish' girls and they construct the identity of the 'cool' girl.

> **Sophie:** "The girls from my class are really 'girlish'. We [girls from judo] do things in a different way".

> **Mia:** "Almost the whole high school knows me. Everybody talks about "judo Mia"..."she is so cool"...and stuff like that. People are very nice to me. Some [people] at school will come over to me to tell me that I am the coolest girl in school".

However, even though young judokas reject the passive womanhood model, it seems that they are aware that they are challenging the norms, and that 'male' and 'female' activities still exist.

> **Sophie:** "I just really thought it was cool doing a sport that wasn't quite normal for girls".

It's a 'Male Sport'

> **Mia:** "Sometimes the boys in the national team are like...they think they are better than the girls. It's like... "Oh girl judo is just bad"... and stuff like that they say. They say it's as a joke, but at the same time I still think they mean it. But I just told them to shut up. I don't care what they say. It's not like they are doing better results than girls, so..."

Even though, female judokas cannot be understood as a homogeneous group (they have different stories to tell and their experiences in judo might differ a lot), one thing remains the same in all judo clubs all over the world: judo is a male dominated sport and female athletes remain an outnumbered group. Men's judo is the 'real judo' or the norm, while women are trying to keep up.

> **Alexandra:** "It is definitely a male dominated field, because few women will manage to cope with the training...with the coaches...with the fact that you are alone among so many men. In the beginning it is difficult, because when you are younger you feel bad being the only girl among all these boys. Your friends are teasing you...they say stuff. But, as the time goes, and the relationships get better...you create bonds....then it's good. So now, that I am doing [judo] many years, I have no problems. I feel the same comfortable with both girls and guys".

As previously stated, this male domination of judo has been justified and naturalized by biological-based reasoning. In order to cope with the gender power dynamics and the established male superiority, female athletes need to 'get used to it'. As illustrated in the previous quote, another coping strategy is the creation of good relationships and bonds in the training.

> **Sophie:** "What keeps us going through all these things is that we are in this together".

In answering the previously raised question of how do women get access to this male dominated sport culture, findings from our study indicate that there needs to be a male to open the way for the female judoka. Three out of four informants had brothers and/or fathers that were also doing judo or other martial arts.

> **Mia:** "I have two older brothers. The oldest one started judo because of my dad [ ] and he liked it. And then my other brother and I started together".

> **Alexandra:** "I started [judo] because my family urged me, when I was around six years old. And just so, my brother went first and then me after him".

In addition, all the informants perceived that they received more support from their fathers than from their mothers, who perceived judo as a dangerous sport for their daughters. Support from significant males seems to be very important for the integration of the young female athletes to the male domain of judo.

> **Mia:** "My mother is really afraid of it [judo]. She is proud of us, she doesn't want us to stop, but she is like…why couldn't you just start dancing. She is afraid of all the injuries and stuff like that".

> **Eleftheria:** "All my boyfriends do some kind of martial art (the ones I had) so they don't say anything about my appearance".

Conclusion

Our comparative ethnographic research suggests that dominant cultural beliefs within a society permeate the experiences of young female judokas. Greek athletes struggle to find a balance between being a competitive judoka, but also a beautiful woman. They can do the masculine sport of judo as long as they 'try to look and act like a girl'. In addition, because Greek culture is rather patriarchal, girls and women experience more pressure to 'act like a girl' from their families, which in turn not only perpetuate cultural beliefs but also under collective pressure to raise their daughters properly. On the other hand, the egalitarian Danish culture offers more space for gender performativity and young judokas seem to be comfortable with challenging the norms. They differentiate themselves from the 'girly' girls and they construct the identity of the 'cool girl'.

Indeed, sport in general and martial arts in particular allow girls and women to broaden the spectrum of 'acceptable' gender performativity and identity; therefore, judo participation is potentially beneficial for women. Yet, as our empirical data suggests, the culture of martial arts is framed by gender, privileging 'male' characteristics and predispositions. The male domination of judo is naturalized by reference to biology and consist an international phenomenon. Thus, we would not be true to our research and serve well for future generation of female athletes if we ignore the gender inequality as lived and narrated by female judokas.

There is evidence that the complexity of living the female versus athlete paradox might lead to negative behaviours, such as poor body image, disordered eating, and low self-esteem (Krane et al., 2004). Through their identity negotiations, young female judokas redefine the acceptable female behavior. By constructing the identity of a girl like all others, or an exceptional being, a 'cool girl', they are trying to find their place in the male domain of judo. Judo, or sport in general, is one of many traditionally male fields that when women are trying to enter are viewed as an anomaly:

> "The *savante* – the woman of science – like the female athlete is simply an anomaly, an exceptional being, holding a position more or less intermediate between the two sexes. In one case the brain, as in the other the muscular system has undergone an abnormal development".
> (Fine, 2010, p xx).

In conclusion, while we are moving towards gender equality, we are far from achieving it in every day practices and collective phenomenological understanding of gender. Even in egalitarian countries (such as Denmark), where gender equality policies have been adopted, we are far away from real progress toward equal opportunities. As Newell (1996) argues, while women have expanded their roles outside of the house and family sphere, there is little evidence that men are expanding their roles too. Domestic work and child care remain on the shoulders of women, who now have to invent all sorts of coping strategies in order to combine them with sport and work careers. The sport field, as well as the labour market, remain structured around the male norm. The topic of equal opportunities in sport remains a provocative and sensitive subject even in countries that score high in gender equality, and there is a general attitude that the problem of gender inequality is 'old-fashion' and it will just 'solve itself' (Habermann, Ottesen, & Skirstad, 2005). We believe that in order for a progressive social change to happen in judo, we need to overcome patterns of male dominance which are, ironically, often reproduced by women themselves. So far, positivistic research on biological differences has tried to 'educate' women how to use their 'fragile' body in female appropriate activities. Future research needs to assist female athletes to find the space they deserve and to teach them that they are only limited by their own prescriptive meanings of vulnerability and frailty.

References

Butler, J. (1990). *Gender trouble.* London: Routledge.
Choi, P. Y. L. (2000). *Femininity and the physically active woman.* London: Routledge.
Fine, C. (2010). *Delusions of gender: How are minds, society, and neurosexism create difference.* New York: W.W. Norton & Company, Inc.
Foucault, M. (1995). *Discipline and punish: The birth of prison* (Trans. A. Sheridan). (2nd ed.). New York: Vintage.

Guerandel, C., & C. Mennesson (2007). Gender construction in judo interaction. *International Review for the Sociology of Sport, 42*(2), 167-186.

Habermann, U., Ottesen, L., & B.Skirstad (2005). It will solve itself (?). In Hofmann, A. R., & Trangbaek, E. (Eds.), *International perspectives on sporting women in past and present* (pp. 189 – 211). Copenhagen: University of Copenhagen.

Halbert, C. (1997). Tough enough and woman enough: Stereotypes, discrimination, and impression management among women professional boxers. / suffisamment fortes et suffisamment feminines: Stereotypes, discrimination et perception concernant l'encadrement chez des boxeuses professionnelles. *Journal of Sport & Social Issues, 21*(1), 7-36.

Hargreaves, J. (1997). Women's boxing and related activities: Introducing images and meanings. *Body and Society, 3*, 33.

Hofstede, G., Hofstede, G. J., & M. Minkov (2010). *Cultures and organizations: Software of the mind.* (3rd ed.). New York: McGraw-Hill.

Karagounis, P., Maridaki, M., Papaharalampous, X., Prionas, G., & P. Baltopoulos, (2009). Exercise-induced arterial adaptations in elite judo athletes. *Journal of Sports Science and Medicine, 8*, 428-434.

Kavoura, A., Ryba, T. V., & S. Chroni (2011). *Negotiating a female judoka identity in Greece*. Paper presented at the 13th European Congress of Sport Psychology, Madeira, Portugal.

Kavoura, A., Ryba, T. V., & M. Kokkonen (2012). Psychological research on martial artists: A critical view from a cultural praxis framework. *Scandinavian Sport Studies Forum, 3*(1), 1-23.

Krane, V., Choi, P. Y. L., Baird, S. M., Aimar, C. M., & K. Kauer (2004). Living the paradox: Female athletes negotiate femininity and muscularity. *Sex Roles, 50*, 315-329.

Le Bars, H., Gernigon, C., & G. Ninot (2009). Personal and contextual determinants of elite young athletes' persistence or dropping out over time. *Scandinavian Journal of Medicine & Science in Sport, 19*, 274-285.

Macro, E., Viveiros, J., & N. Cipriano (2009). Wrestling with identity. An exploration of female wrestlers' perceptions. *Women in Sport & Physical Activity Journal, 18*(1), 42-53.

Markula, P. (1995). Firm but shapely, fit but sexy, strong but thin: The postmodern aerobicizing female bodies. *Sociology of Sport Journal, 12*, 424-453.

McGannon, K. R., Courtin, K., Schinke, R. J., & A.N. Schweinbenz (2012). (De)Constructing Paula Radcliffe: Exploring media representations of elite running, pregnancy and motherhood through cultural sport psychology. *Psychology of Sport and Exercise, 13*, 820-829.

Mennesson, C. (2000). 'Hard' women and 'soft' women: The social construction of identities among female boxers. / femmes 'dures' en femmes 'douces': La construction sociale des identites chez des femmes boxeuses. / 'harte' frauen und 'weiche' frauen: Die soziale konstruktion von identitaet bei boxerinnen. / mujeres 'duras' y mujeres 'blandas': La construccion social de las identidades entre las mujeres boxeadoras. *International Review for the Sociology of Sport, 35*(1), 21-33.

Miarka, B., Marques, J. B., & E. Franchini (2011). Reinterpreting the history of women's judo in Japan. *The International Journal of the History of Sport, 28*(7), 1016-1029.

Newell, S. (1996). The superwoman syndrome: A comparison of the "heroine" in Denmark and the UK. *Women in Management Review, 11*(5), 36-41.

Rouveix, M., Bouget, M., Pannafieux, C., Champely, S., & E. Filaire (2007). Eating attitudes, body esteem, perfectionism and anxiety of judo athletes and nonathletes. *International Journal of Sport Medicine, 28*, 340-345.

Ryba, T. V., & H.K. Wright (2010). Sport psychology and the cultural turn: Notes toward cultural praxis. In T. V. Ryba, R. J. Schinke & G. Tenenbaum (Eds.), *The cultural turn in sport psychology* (pp. 3-28) Morgantown, WV: Fitness Information Technology.

Sands, R. S. (2002). *Sport ethnography.* Champaign, IL: Human Kinetics.

Sisjord, M. K., (1997). Wrestling with gender: a study of young female and male wrestlers' experiences of physicality. / Lutte et identite sexuelle – Etude des experiences de la "physicalite" chez des lutteurs et lutteuses. *International Review for the Sociology of Sport, 32*(4), 433-438.

Sisjord, M. K., & E. Kristiansen (2008). Serious athletes or media clowns? Female and male wrestlers' perceptions of media constructions. *Sociology of Sport Journal, 25*(3), 350 – 368.

Sisjord, M. K., & E. Kristiansen (2009). Elite women wrestlers' muscles. *International Review for the Sociology of Sport, 44*(2), 231 – 246.

Thorpe, H. (2010). The psychology of extreme sports. In T. V. Ryba, R. J. Schinke & G. Tenenbaum (Eds.), *The cultural turn in sport psychology* (pp. 363-386). Morgantown, WV: Fitness Information Technology.

Umeda, T., Nakaji, S., Sugawara, K., Yamamoto, Y., Saito, K., Honjo, S., Sakurai, Y., & M. Totsuka (1999). Gender differences in physical and psychological stress responses among college judoists undergoing weight reduction. *Environmental Health and Preventive Medicine, 4*(3), 146-150.

Vertinsky, P. A. (1994a) *The Eternally Wounded Woman: Women, Doctors, and Exercise in the Late Nineteenth Century.* Urbana: University of Illinois Press, 1994.

Vertinsky, P. (1994b). The social construction of the gendered body: exercise and the exercise of power. *The International Journal of the History of Sport, 11*(2), 147-171.

Young, K. (1997). Women, sport and physicality: Preliminary findings from a Canadian study. *International Review for the Sociology of Sport, 32*(3), 297 – 305.

Chapter 11

Weight Management and Weight Cutting for Competitive Grapplers

Brian Jones

Introduction

Grappling, and other combat sports such as mixed martial arts and boxing, are almost always divided into weight classes so that athletes can compete against others their own size. This is done to prevent heavier athletes from gaining an unfair advantage and to reduce the risk of injury. In some tournaments there may be an open, no weight class, division but these are the exception rather than the rule. The range of weight within each class varies depending on the grappling style and is typically 5 – 10 kg [1] (Artoli et al 2010; Kiningham & Gorenflo 2011).

The use of weight classes makes weight control an important aspect of competitive grappling. Staying within one's optimal weight category requires attention to diet and an appropriate training regimen. Unfortunately far too many athletes, whether due to personal decision or pressure from coaches, use severe and potentially dangerous methods of weight reduction to get into lighter classes in hopes of gaining a competitive advantage. Studies report that as many as 67% of wrestlers may engage in rapid weight reduction to make weight for competition (Artoli et al 2010; Kiningham & Gorenflo 2013). In addition a number of medical conditions related to dehydration, heat, and overexertion may be associated with attempts to cut weight. Deaths have even been reported in wrestlers from extreme voluntary dehydration.

---

[1] American College of Sports Medicine Position Stand on Weight Loss in Wrestlers. *Med. Sci. Sports Exerc.* 28(2):ix-xii. 1996.

Body Composition

Lean athletes tend to perform best in weight class sports. Maintaining low levels of body fat allows grapplers to have high relative strength and power. Low body fat is also associated with greater aerobic and anaerobic endurance. Research on elite competitors has found that male wrestlers tend to maintain an in-season body fat of 4 - 9% body fat and range between 8-16% off-season. Elite level judoka are typically between 6.7 – 15.8% with a mean of 9.3%. Recommendations based on numerous studies suggest that the optimal range of body fat for male grapplers is 5 – 16% (Callister, Staron, Fleck, Tesch, & Dudley 1991; Yoon, 2002). Although scientific data is lacking on the levels of body fat in elite female grapplers, research from the sport of Olympic weightlifting, suggest that relative strength and power in women is maximized at around 10 – 18% body fat (16). These recommendations do not apply to heavyweights who generally have significantly higher levels of body fat. It is well known that excess body fat tends to diminish athletic performance and endanger health so even heavyweight grapplers should keep fat mass to reasonable levels (Petosa, & Zupan, 1995).

Although leanness is associated with better performance, it should not drop below 5% for men or 10% for women (Wilmore, & Costill 1994). Levels lower than this will not help performance and may pose serious health risks for athletes. This is especially true for female grapplers because excessively low body fat is associated with disrupted menstrual function (amenorrhea) and low bone density (osteoporosis) (Wilmore, & Costill 1994).

The American College of Sports Medicine's position statement on weight loss in wrestling stresses the need for athletes to maintain competitive body weight through sound nutritional practices[2]. This includes a diet high in complex carbohydrates, low in fat, and with adequate amounts of protein. The minimum calorie requirements for high school and college age grapplers are 1700 – 2500 kcal/day and hard training may increase this by up to 1000 kcal/day[3]. To insure proper nutrition athletes should not consume fewer calories than the daily minimum. Gradual fat loss will occur by consuming the daily caloric minimum and keeping up with workouts. Extremely low calorie and crash dieting for rapid weight loss should be avoided.

The NCAA has instituted a weight certification program so that wrestlers cannot compete below a minimum healthy weight. This weight is defined as "no less that 5% body fat in a hydrated stated with hydration being measured by a specific gravity urinalysis" (Shirreffs, 2003). Grapplers in styles other than wrestling where weight certification is not required are encouraged to use this definition as a guideline for determining a healthy minimum competition weight. In cases where urinalysis is not possible, hydration status can be determined by examining the color of the urine as described in the following section.

---

[2] American College of Sports Medicine Position Stand on Weight Loss in Wrestlers. *Med. Sci. Sports Exerc.* 28(2):ix-xii. 1996
[3] ACSM Position Stand on Weight Loss in Wrestlers. *Med. Sci. Sports Exerc.* 1996

Dehydration

One of the most common methods used by grapplers to cut weight before competition weighing-in is dehydration (Kiningham & Gorenflo 2013). Dehydration to a state known as hypohydration is usually accomplished by fluid restriction, exercise, plastic sauna suits, sitting in the sauna, or a combination of these techniques. In some cases drugs such as diuretics, laxatives, or stimulants are used. Athletes attempt to shed as much water as possible prior to weighing-in so they can get into the lightest weight category possible. They attempt to rehydrate as much as possible in the period between the weigh-ins and competition. The idea is that competing at a lower weight will provide an advantage of size, strength, and power over opponents who compete at their normal weight. Dehydration for weight-cutting purposes has become so widespread in grappling and other fighting sports that some coaches and athletes see it as necessary for success. This is the case, as one published report details, even for wrestlers as young as five years old (Sansone, & Sawyer, 2005).

Hypohydration has numerous detrimental effects on physiological and psychological function. Research shows that fluid loss $\geq 2\%$ of body weight causes significant reductions in maximal strength, aerobic capacity, and anaerobic endurance (Jones 2008). It can also decrease alertness and ability to concentrate, cause headaches, and increase negative mood states such as anger and tension (Hall & Lane 2001). Dehydration interferes with the body's ability to cool itself during exercise and can lead to an increased likelihood of potentially deadly health problems such as heatstroke or rhabdomylosis. Alterations in electrolyte balance, particularly from the use of diuretics, may lead to muscle cramping (Coris et al 2004; Kiningham & Gorenflo 2001).

Maintaining adequate hydration is vital for both health and performance. Sweating, the body's primary means of temperature regulation during exercise, can result in the loss of 0.5 to 2.0 liters of fluid per hour (Anastasiou, 2009). Environmental factors such as high heat and humidity, and the wearing of heavy equipment or clothing (such as a gi) can dramatically increase sweat rate. Athletes who do not take measures to drink plenty of water before, during, and after practice and competition can quickly become dehydrated. The American College of Sports Medicine's position statement on nutrition for athletes recommends that 14-22 oz. of fluid be drunk before training and 6-12 oz. every 15-20 min during the workout. For rehydration after training athletes should drink 16-24 oz. of fluid for every pound of body weight lost[4].

Research has shown that urine color has a relatively linear relationship to urine concentration (19). In a state of adequate hydration, a large volume of urine will be produced and will be clear or a light straw color. Dehydrated individuals will produce less urine less frequently and it will tend to be darker and more concentrated. It should be noted that some vitamin supplements may cause urine to be a bright yellow color independent of hydration state. Body weight can also be used as a quick measure of hydration. Grapplers should weight themselves

---

[4] See - American College of Sports Medicine Position Stand, American Dietetic Association, and Dietitians of Canada Joint Position Stand on Nutrition and Athletic Performance. 2000. Retrieved on July 11, 2007 from www.ms-se.com.

when properly hydrated so that they have a reference weight. Values substantially below this weight occurring within the span of hours or days represent fluid loss. Body weight should also be taken immediately before and after practices to determine how much fluid should be replaced (1,19).

Dropping a few pounds of water weight prior to weighing in can be accomplished safely and effectively by adhering to a few guidelines. First, losing water weight should only be done if there are several hours or more between weigh-ins and competition. It is possible to rehydrate effectively in 2-hours if weight loss is minimal however, it can take much longer to recover from severe dehydration (Artoli, 2010). Water weight loss should be kept under 2% of bodyweight to prevent decrements in performance. Although one research study on experienced judoka found that these athletes were able to adequately rehydrate from a 5% body mass weight loss within 4-5 hours and suffer no significant drop in performance (Artoli, 2010). Finally, the method used to drop water weight is important. Research suggests that exercise for rapid weight loss impaired performance less than a sauna or diuretics (Judelson, 2007). Light exercise then may represent a superior strategy for those cutting weight.

Heat Illness

Exertional Heatstroke

Exertional heatstroke can occur in any circumstance involving prolonged exercise. These illnesses occur most frequently in hot-humid environments but may also be present in cool conditions. Incidence of heatstroke among grapplers is not known but it may be most likely to occur during episodes of weight cutting. Factors that may increase the risk of heat illness include:

1. dehydration
2. sitting or exercising in saunas
3. prolonged exercise
4. exercising in plastic 'sauna' suits or other heavy clothing
5. medications
6. workout stimulants such as ephedrine, synephrine, or ma huang
7. sleep deprivation
8. low fitness levels
9. diarrhea
10. viral illness

In exertional heatstroke core temperature rises to above 40 deg C and is accompanied by nervous system disturbances and organ system failure. The high internal temperatures present in heatstroke can cause damage and dysfunction to the nervous system, heart, and other body tissues. Without proper medical intervention heatstroke can lead to death. The extent and reversibility of the damage caused by heatstroke depends on the how quickly care is received. Any case of heatstroke should be considered a life-threatening medical emergency.

Symptoms differ from the classic, non-exertional type of heatstroke in that patients will normally exhibit sweaty and skin rather than flushed and dry. Signs are often non-specific and can include disorientation, confusion, dizziness, unusual behavior, irritability, headache, loss of balance or muscle function, collapse, vomiting, seizures, or coma. Particularly in hot-humid conditions, any major change in personality, behavior, or performance is cause to evaluate an athlete for heatstroke (Coris, 2004). Treatment involves rapid whole body cooling by immersion in ice water. In cases of heatstroke, cooling should be initiated on site by placing cold towels on the head, trunk, and extremities and rotating them as they warm. Ice packs can be used on the neck, armpits, and groin. Even if the patient appears to recover, cooling treatment should be continued until medical help is obtained.

It is recommended that athletes who suffer a bout of heatstroke wait for at least a week after release from medical care before returning to training. Workouts should resume in a cool environment and the duration, intensity, and temperature gradually increased over a 2-week period to build heat tolerance. Grapplers who demonstrate adequate heat tolerance can resume full training and competition after 2-4 weeks (Chinevere, 2008).

Exertional Heat Exhaustion

Heat exhaustion is the most common heat illness in athletic populations and normally occurs during prolonged exercise in hot-humid environments. The incidence of heat exhaustion among grapplers is not known but may be comparable to rates among other athletes. One study reported incidences of 85 per 10,000 and higher among youth soccer players playing in an outdoor summer tournament (Coris, 2004). The likelihood of heat exhaustion increases with increased ambient temperature, exercise intensity and duration, and dehydration. The risk of heat exhaustion may therefore, be higher during attempts to rapidly cut water weight.

Heat exhaustion results from severe central fatigue causing a widespread dilation of blood vessels in the skin and extremities. Normally these vessels are constricted during exercise so that blood can be shunted to working muscles and blood pressure can be maintained. Vasodilation leads to cardiac insufficiency, reduced work capacity, and in many cases, collapse. The symptoms of heat exhaustion include elevated heart rate and breathing; a sweaty, pale appearance; headache; weakness; dizziness; chills; nausea; vomiting; diarrhea; irritability; muscle cramping; and decreased muscular coordination. Core temperature may or may not be elevated[5].

Heat exhaustion often resembles heatstroke and the most reliable field test is rectal temperature. Temperatures of >40 deg C are indicative of heatstroke and those of <40 deg C of heat exhaustion. In the case of uncertainty, it is recommended that the rapid cooling procedures described under heatstroke be applied. Grapplers with heat exhaustion should be moved to cool, air-conditioned or shaded area, have excess clothing removed, and be placed lying down with the feet elevated. Monitor heart rate, blood pressure, breathing rate, temperature, and central nervous system status closely. Oral fluids should be given for rehydration

---

[5] See - American College of Sports Medicine Position Stand on Weight Loss in Wrestlers. *Med. Sci. Sports Exerc*. 28(2):ix-xii. 1996

if the athlete is conscious, able to swallow, and is not vomiting. Those unable to rehydrate orally should seek medical attention.

Athletes should not return immediately to training or competition following a bout of heat exhaustion. Training can resume in 24-48 hours assuming proper rehydration. A physician follow-up is recommended for any grappler who suffers heat exhaustion.

Exercise-Associated Muscle Cramps (Heat Cramps)

Grapplers training for prolonged periods in hot-humid environments may experience painful muscle cramps in the arms, legs, or abdomen. The incidence of cramps in grappling is not known but one study investigated the incidence of cramps requiring medical attention in marathoners over a 12-year period and found 1.2 cases per 1000 runners. Factors that are associated with the development of heat cramps include prolonged exercise, loss of body water, and loss of sodium from sweating. The likelihood of cramping may increase when multiple daily practices are held or at tournaments when grapplers are cutting weight and could have several matches (Anastasiou, 2009).

Muscle cramps involve tight contractions that can be extremely painful and debilitating. The cramp may seem to move around in the muscle as one group of fibers contracts then another. Individual muscles usually spasm for 1-3 minutes but the entire bout of cramping may go on for up to 8 hours.

Muscle cramps can be treated by rest and by stretching the affected muscle groups in the fully-lengthened position. Fluids and sodium should be provided in the form of sports drinks with added table salt (1/8-1/4 tsp. per 300-500ml of fluid) or salty broth. Salt tablets or salty snacks may also be provided to increase sodium levels. Severe cramps may be treated medically with and intravenous saline solution or muscle relaxants. It is possible for some athletes to return to practice or competition in the same day following rest and fluid replacement while others may need a day or more to recover[6].

Prevention of Heat Illness

The likelihood of heat-related illness can be decreased by remaining well-hydrated and keeping sodium levels adequate. Always replace fluid and salt after practices and competitions and track hydration status using urine color and body weight as described above.

Heat acclimatization may provide the best protection against heat related illness. By gradually increasing the duration and intensity of exercise in hot environments over a period of 10-14 days, athletes become better able to tolerate heat exposure (Chinevere, 2008). A number of positive physiological changes occur such as earlier onset of sweating and higher sweat rate that allow the body to more effectively cool itself. In the absence of heat exposure, tolerance quickly

---

[6] American College of Sports Medicine Position Stand on Exercise and Fluid Replacement. 2007. Retrieved on July 5, 2007 from www.ms-se.com.

declines. Coaches and grapplers should keep this in mind, particularly when training outdoors or during a change of seasons.

Some grapplers train and compete with and without the gi while others specialize in one or the other. Wearing a heavy grappling gi may cause a substantial increase in an athlete's thermal load and increase the likelihood of heat illness. For this reason a gradual, 10-14 day acclimatization period may be prudent for those grapplers using a gi for the first time.

References

American College of Sports Medicine Position Stand on Exercise and Fluid Replacement. 2007. Retrieved on July 5, 2007 [retrieved from www.ms-se.com].

American College of Sports Medicine Position Stand on Exertional Heat Illness during Training and Competition. 2007. Retrieved on June 24, 2007 [retrieved from www.ms-se.com].

American College of Sports Medicine Position Stand, American Dietetic Association, and Dietitians of Canada Joint Position Stand on Nutrition and Athletic Performance. 2000. Retrieved on July 11, 2007 [retrieved from www.ms-se.com].

American College of Sports Medicine Position Stand on Weight Loss in Wrestlers. *Journal of Medical. Science. Sports & Exercise.* 28(2):ix-xii. 1996.

Anastasiou, C.A. et al. (2009). Sodium Replacement and Plasma Sodium Drop During Exercise in the Heat When Fluid Intake Matches Fluid Loss. *Journal of Athletic Training.* 44(2):117-123.

Artoli, G.G. et al. (2010). Rapid weight loss followed by recovery time does not affect judo-related performance. *Journal of Sports Science.* 28(1):21-32.

Callister, R. Staron, R.S. Fleck, S. J. Tesch, P. & C. A. Dudley. (1991). Physiological characteristics of elite judo athletes. *International. Journal of Sports Medicine.* 12(2):196-203. 1991.

Chinevere, T.D. et al. (2008). Effect of Heat Acclimation on Sweat Minerals. *Medicine, Science & Sports Exerc*ise 40(5):886-891.

Cisar, C. J., Johnson,G.O., Fry, A.C., Housh, T.A., Hughes, R.A., Ryan, A.J. & W. G. Thorland (1987). Preseason Body Composition, Build, and Strength as Predictors of High School Wrestling Success. *Journal Applied Sport Science Research* 1(4):66-70.

Coris, E.E., Ramirez, A.M. & D.J. Van Durme. (2004). Heat Illness in Athletes: The Dangerous Combination of Heat, Humidity, and Exercise. *Sports Medicine.* 34(1):9-16

Hall, C. J. and A. M. Lane. (2001). Effects of rapid weight loss on mood and performance among amateur boxers. *British Journal of Sports Medicine.* 35:390-395.

Jones, L.C., et al. (2008). Active Dehdyration Impairs Upper and Lower Body Anaerobic Muscular Power. *Journal of Strength and Conditioning Research.* 22(2):455-463.

Judelson, D.A., et al. (2007). Hydration and Muscular Performance: Does Fluid Balance Affect Strength, Power, and High-Intensity Endurance? *Sports Medicine.* 37(10):907-921.

Kiningham, R. B. & D. W. Gorenflo. (2001). Weight loss methods of high school wrestlers. *Medicine, Science & Sports Exercise.* 33(5):810-813. 2001.

Moeckel-Cole, S.A. & P.M. Clarkson. (1995). Rhabdomylosis in a Collegiate Football Player. *Journal of Strength & Conditioning Research.* 23(4):1055-1059.

Petosa, P. S., & M. F. Zupan. (1995). Aerobic Training, Lean Body Mass, and Athletic Performance. *NSCA J.* 17(3):11-17.

Rosner, M.H. (2009). Exercise-associated Hyponatremia. *Seminal Nephrology.* 29:271-281,

Sansone, R. A. & R. Sawyer. (2005). Weight loss pressure on a 5-year old wrestler. *British Journal of Sports Medicine.* 39(1):e2. 2005.

Shirreffs, S. M. (2003). Markers of hydration status. *E. J. Clinical Nutrition.* 57(Supp 2):S6-S9.

Wilmore, J. H. & D. L. Costill. (1994). *Physiology of Sport and Exercise.* Champaign, IL: Human Kinetics.

Yoon, J. (2002). Physiological Profiles of Elite Senior Wrestlers. *Sports Medicine.* 32(4):225-233

Chapter 12

The Idea of (UN) Winning in Martial Arts as Opposed to Combat Sports

Baris Sentuna

Introduction

There has been an ambiguity whether to name eastern sports or arts as martial arts or combat sports. By people unaware of the insight of those arts do name it as sports and on the contrary unaware of the sports name it as arts. One of the discussions in this chapter is based on this problematic. To what extend bodily physical acts are named as sport and to what extend they are named as arts. The second part of this chapter is based on the winning situation. Winning or losing is an important aspect of sports. In today's modernized societies there is also a new concept I name as "as if winning" as being a spectator or watching on screen, which created a new emerging martial arts which turns out to be combat sports.

Arts or Sports

"What is the relation between art and sports?" This is a philosophical question that is very much discussed in the Philosophy of Sports. There are also different naming as well, based on the physical activity. For preliminary memorandum it is also hard for the practitioners to name what are they practicing. Is it arts or is it sports? Aikido is sports without competition. From the view point of practitioners beginners saying that it is not sports but an art of war. Only at the advanced level, does it become a martial art. Nonetheless, it is quite hard to drive a clear line between arts and sports even for the practitioners. (Sentuna B. McNamee M. Korkusuz, F. & E. Kiraz 2010).

Artistic / Aesthetic

The main discussion on sports and art comes from two distinguished philosophers: Best, in his book "Philosophy and Human Movement" (1979), and Wertz, in his book "Talking a Good Game" (1991). Best is very straightforward "I contend that no sport is an art form." (Best, 1980, p.69). A distinction is important for this discussion between purposive sports where "there are a variety of ways to achieve the purpose"; on the other hand, an "Aesthetic sport is one which the purpose can be specified only in terms of the aesthetic manner of achieving it." (Best, 1980, p.71) Best gives a very good example of a sunset:

> "It is not necessary, since clearly all or most physical education activities are not primarily, if at all, of aesthetic interest; it is not sufficient, since most phenomena which are of aesthetic interest (such as a sunset) are obviously not part of physical education".

(Best, 1980, p.72)

The second distinction in Best is this: "....there is a tendency to differentiate purposive and aesthetic activities in terms of competition." It is a misconception, for Best, to equate aesthetic activity with competition. He gives the example of Korean violinist Kyung Wha Chun's statement, which is also important for Aikido, made after winning one of the best prizes. "It was one of the worst experiences of my life, because competitions bring out the worst in people." For Best, this is what Wertz misses. According to Best, this problem can easily be overcome by making the distinction between purposive and aesthetic sports "recognizing there can be competition in both activities" (although it can bring the worst).

Best then discusses spectators and contemplation, and argues that there still can be room for aesthetic considerations without spectators for a sportsperson. For him, it is "important to try to locate the source of this misconception that the aesthetic is exclusively a spectator enjoyment." Then, he gives the example of an ace tennis service :

> "I can, if sufficiently competent, have the aesthetic experience of producing a perfect ace service, but not if there were no game of service, not if I have not learned how to play, and not if I do not perform the requisite action in the appropriate context. The action is observable, but I do not have to observe it,. Indeed I may be practicing alone, so no one observes it. but that does not preclude the possibility of my having the experience."

(Best, 1980, p.75)

Best continues with what he thinks he agrees with Wertz about: sport as art in objet trouvé, meaning found art. Then Best discusses his most fundamental disagreement with Wertz: the difference between "aesthetic" and "artistic". He thinks that they are used synonymously by Wertz. Best argues that the term "Aesthetic applies for sunsets, birdsong…, whereas the artistic tends to be limited, at least, in its central uses, to artifacts or performances intentionally created by human beings." (Best, 1980, p.75) On "artistic" and "aesthetic", Best points out a main difference: "It is certainly a central factor in the ways in which the arts have influenced society . By contrast, such possibility is not intrinsic to any sport, even of the aesthetic kind, since the performer cannot, within its conventions, express a view of life issues." (Best, 1980, p.78)

I think it is sufficient to understand the thinking of Best in its general terms at the least. I would like to quote one more paragraph where he summarizes himself:

> "In contrast to Professor Wertz, I would insist that the aesthetic sports do not, as he puts it, 'have more claim of art' than purposive sports but rather their claim is more plausible-which, of course, is by no means the same thing. That plausibility depends upon a misconceived and misleading elision of the aesthetic and the artistic." (Best, 1980, p.79)

Wertz in his book "Talking a Good Game" gives his ideas on Wertz claims, "Our notion of art is far richer than just the notions of representation and expression" (Wertz, 1991, p.178) According to Wertz, the philosophy of art begins with these concepts and the relationship of sports to them must be mapped out. Wertz also straight-forwardly explains his idea, "At the outset I want it to be clear that I do believe that sport (or at least some of it) is or can be art" (Wertz, 1991, p.178) On Best, Wertz argues, "Best's view of art is what Jacques Barzun has described as art from 'the classical -sector, gilt-edged, consecrated art.' Best reiterates an 'old dogma of art'" (Wertz, 1991, p.179) Wertz gives the Living Theatre example where audience can also become players. According to Wertz, Best's argument from the objet trouvé could have been true 20 years ago. Wertz gives examples from Ludic Art, where Ludic interfaces are playful interfaces. Furthermore, Wertz gives the example of a baseball player.

> "It is quite possible that in pursuing artistic goals (like a baseball game) an athlete might well incur failure in his/her sport's end. (defined by the non-artistic goals-points, runs, goals, .etc.) This suggests that art may be tangentially present in these sports but not necessarily that sport is art"

(Wertz, 1991, p.183)

From this argument, Wertz moves on to discuss symbolical things that make something art even if it is actually a sport. When a tennis match is played in Wimbledon, it is symbolical and it is art. He also asks, "Could village cricket be art?" For Wertz, "Usually village cricket is not art. But under appropriate circumstances it could be" (Wertz, 1991, p.183)

Wertz gets into the Best's line of argument on the distinction between "aesthetic" and "artistic". The aesthetic value of a game is perceived in the visual value alone whereas its artistic value is based on history, context, etc. Unlike Best, Wertz thinks that the spectacular aspect of sports cannot be ignored. He asks, "Why then do we build stadiums, arenas?" and continues, "It may not be the principal goal of sports but it is one of the principal goals of sport (i.e. Aristotelian goals)." (Wertz, 1991, p.186) For Wertz, "categories like art and sport change by the very fact that people who employ these categories apply them to different objects" (Wertz, 1991, p.187)

About martial arts, from Best's argument about life and art, Wertz makes a cunning claim as well. "Best claims that life issues that make up an imaginative work of art have no analogue in sport. In other words sports have no content or subject matter. But why not?" (Wertz, 1991, p.189) Wertz here gives a very clever example of body-builders, who shape their bodies like a sculpture from ancient Greece. Wertz continues with the example of a gymnast: a former student of his performed gymnastics with the music "The Lord's Prayer" and made his movements accordingly.

Another point they disagree on is that while Best claims that sports do not represent anything, Wertz argues that they do. He gives examples that also come to my mind. Jessie Owens's four gold medals in the Nazi Olympics (1936) gave strength to Americans. Wertz then asks, "Can athletes be expressionists in their play?" (Wertz, 1991, p.194) Wertz gives the example of Boris Becker, the 1985 Wimbledon champion, whose play revealed sadness and remorsefulness, according to journalists, after learning about his grandfather's death at the break of a game.

Other Ideas

There are other articles written on the point of art and sports as well, which I will mention very briefly. Cordner (1988) discusses both Best and Wertz, and gives his view on the point. Platchias (2003) in his article entitled "Sports is Art" argues against Best through Kantian aesthetics. In another article, Young (1999) discusses it from a Heideggerian point of view. In order to defend my thesis, I want to discuss in more detail an article of the distinguished philosopher Allan Bäck (2009), entitled "The way to Virtue in Sport".

Serious Business

Bäck starts with the claim that the idea that sports develop moral virtues is supported by many philosophers; nevertheless, he thinks that sports might promote more vices than virtues. He claims, "Moreover there are other activities that actually do provide the benefits claimed erroneously for sports: the traditional martial arts." (Bäck, 2009, p.217) Bäck continues by giving brief definitions of both: "A sport is a form of play involving a contest or competition, typically measuring physical things" and "A (traditional) martial art (Japanese: Budo; Korean: Moodo) is a 'way of do' or method of enlightenment on the human condition through the ritualized practice of techniques designed to neutralize violence." (Bäck, 2009, p.217)

For Bäck "martial arts are not sports". He states, "war is serious not playful business...Yet! Unlike Western combat traditions, Eastern ones alloyed the combat with a quest of non-violence and spiritual enlightenment" (Bäck, 2009, p.217); and continues with his arguments against certain martial arts, "In contrast, a martial art sport like Olympic Taekwondo stresses the game of competition. Its goal is to win the athletic contest. The training here places little emphasis on combat applications, ritual or formal patterns." The point that Bäck makes here I totally agree with. When competition is involved in martial arts or any arts, as Best suggested with an example, things become worse:

> "The martial art training (bugei) evolved from merely being jutsu (skills) to being also "do" (Chinese: Tao): ways to enlightenment. As the military application of martial arts waned in modern times, the focus shifted from jutsu to do, from skill to art. Many martial practices changed their names accordingly: jujitsu became judo; kenjutsu became kendo."

[Aikijitsu became Aikido, but why did he not mention it?]

Bäck summarizes different views of sports and makes his point as follows: "defining sport as a mutual quest for excellence fits all modern sports." (Bäck, 2009, p.221) However, as we will discuss in the writings of Parry below, this is not always the case. Bäck then discusses his argument in the context of dangerous (I prefer risky") sports and states in response to both Russell (Russell, 2005) and Fischer (2002), which is important for us:

> "...still they both have a better than average chance of acquiring certain values or virtues through the practice of dangerous sport. So we have the dilemma either we pursue this dangerous path or we lessen our chances for excellence..Yet I will argue that this is a false dilemma: there are other options, other ways to acquire those same virtues. The option I will explore is training in martial arts".

(Bäck, 2009, p.224)

On this point I totally agree with Bäck. Bäck states, "For despite the common claim, the evidence given in studies in the social sciences is that sport does not produce a good moral character. On the contrary, it tends to produce a bad one" (Bäck, 2009, p.226)

Then, Bäck shifts back to martial arts again and discusses the empirical data on martial arts as well as the moral character of martial arts. He claims, "Outside of Korea and other Asian countries the decline in the moral character of martial arts competitors has already been noted by many involved." (Bäck ,2009, p.228) This important and interesting fact presumably proves why the founder of Aikido insisted that Aikido stays away from any form of competition so as many other martial arts. Bäck cites the trainer of the U.S. Olympic Taekwondo team: "I don't train martial artists, I train athletes" and states they are not interested in self-defence but winning."

Bäck thinks that "A lot of things are lost. Traditional martial artists are good people well grounded. They have good morals, good ethics, good family values, and are aware of culture and society." (Bäck, 2009, p.228) I cannot agree with Bäck, I think that Bäck misses the fact that Aikido still remains as a traditional martial art without competition and still preserves the values Bäck considers as "lost". Bäck then proceeds to an argument on martial arts that is germane to our purposes. He writes:

> "Above I have claimed that a martial art as traditionally practiced is not a sport. To be sure, there is martial art, sport. A martial art can be practiced as a sport. It is a physical activity and we can arrange contests and make rules to judge who is more proficient at this or that aspect of the sport: breaking; speed of strikes; expertise in the formal patterns (kata; poomse [in Aikido there is only simple Katas in weapon training]) On the Olympic level we have judo and taekwondo. Yet many martial arts traditions [like Aikido] reject the sport competition. And even sparring (jiyu-kumite) just for practice. Here I am focusing on martial arts, not on martial art sport".

(Bäck, 2009, p.229)

For that reason we will have another part discussing the winning an loosing interns of today's media and spectatorship. Bäck also divides martial arts into three stages. At the first stage, there is violence and injury, however, "the third and final stage resembles Gandhi's ahimsa: the total elimination of or absence of violence and struggle." (Bäck, 2009, p.232)

Finally, Bäck makes the point on which we built our thesis: that at the beginner and intermediate levels Aikido or any martial art in general is a sport, whereas it is an art at the advanced level. For our thesis we take Bäck's following argument:

> ".. a sport remains cut off from the serious business of real life as it is a type of play. It focuses on artificial contest. [This sentence we ignore since it is Aikido with no contests] In contrast martial art is not a type of play. Rather it supports the serious part of life—and its transcendent contests. It has no winners or losers, [as we will discuss in the next label] just as life ultimately does neither. The martial arts have a meditative and spiritual tradition of a sort that Western sports lack".

(Bäck, 2009, p.232)

I again partly agree with Bäck. While what Bäck says is true, I believe that at the advanced level of Aikido or other martial artist even though all attacks are real, generally no one gets hurt. From my point of view, it is in the form of play that I take Loland and McNamee's definition of sports for granted: "if voluntarily engaged in sport games-keep the ethos of the game if the ethos is just ..." (Loland and McNamee, 2000, p.69) In Aikido, beginners and intermediate students are learning the practice. It takes a lot of time in martial arts even to learn the basic movements. For that reason, the attacks in the beginner and intermediate levels are semi-real, meaning that they are not that serious as long as the practitioner learns the basic movements. Therefore, at the beginner level Aikido and other martial arts are sports game, voluntarily engaged in, whose ethos comes from the code of Samurai.

We can prove this point with the meaning of the black belt as well. In Aikido and (also other martial arts) there are only two belts (white and black) in order to prevent "belt wars". The black belt in Aikido means "Sho-Dan". Sho in Japanese means beginner. It shows that you have just begun training Aikido. The black belt practically means that you have learned all the forms. Now you are going to practice them with "reality". This reality we have mentioned above.

From those aspects, Aikido and other martial arts at the beginner and intermediate levels is a sports game; only at the advanced level is it an art. I would like to end this discussion by again quoting from Bäck: "One might continue to wonder whether the Way of the martial arts is the best way, especially due to some side effects of the intermediate level on many practitioners." (Bäck, 2009, p.234) This also proves our point about the "intermediate" because it is a transition level to reality. When they are not properly trained by the instructor, many practitioners give up at this level. We would like to end like Bäck by a quote from Spinoza: "The path to virtue is as difficult as it is rare." (Bäck, 2009, p.234).

Wining and AS IF Winning

Here we need to discuss another aspect of combat sports. This is the winning or in my terms the fake winning or un-winning. It is necessary for us to understand what makes martial arts apart from its origins and transforms them into combat sports. For that reason we need to understand the case of UFC. Different forms of "winning" except from the sports game context are analyzed in this part. For the sake of argument we named the "winning in the sports pitch" as a result of bodily act and game, as "real winning". There are two main arguments related to this, in this part. First argument is on "un-winning" and the other one is the argument of "as if winning". In this analysis different concepts used, such as "constructed winning", "fake winning", "shallow winning" interchangeably with those different forms of winning since they do share much more than they differentiate. In "as if winning" the concentration is on the spectatorship, "fake" and "shallow" feelings, the act "as if you won", seem to be created willingly, in modern society. One more important differentiation for "as if winning" and winning, the feeling is "real" in case of idea of winning. It has its own reality, which is a different set of reality, is a hypothetical reality when compared to winning in sports games. The feeling, of that sort we name in this text, is: "as if winning", "constructed winning", "fake winning". The second argument un-winning, concentrates on the un-winning discourse. We named it as un-winning because the concept of "losing" is the opposite of winning in the sports pitch, where as "losing" in the un-winning discourse as fact of so-called "modernity", losing is rarely used and un-winning is not the exact opposite of "winning". We do deeply analyze this point. Before getting into these arguments, we do analyze an intimate act happening as result of "real winning" that could be useful for a differentiation point and analyses. This intimate act is "hugging" especially in martial arts or combat sports.

Hugging

For differentiation between two kinds of winning we named as "real" and "constructed", we should take a closer look at the act of hugging. Hugging is the act of intimacy happening in the case of "real pitch". The intimate "hugging" takes place and is recognized more sharply, especially when the winner suppresses the loser. There is the unpredictable act of hugging; even there is the glory and ritual of "winning" taking place by the winner on the pitch. There are two types of hugging, happening on the pitch. One is formal, before the match and the other one is "intimate" after the match. To make differentiation between those two types of hugging we need to take a closer look to the nature of the game and fair play. This act of intimacy, is much more than "fair play", it can include fair play, where fair play turns out to be something in the game and acting as if the explanation of actions inside the game which are quite unacceptable, in normal life situations and making them legitimate by arguments where it also turns out to be a code of conduct and "learned behavior". While playing with your opponent and winning to prove that I am acting "fair" inside the game and giving a preliminary idea of the so called "justice" in the context of the game play. Hugging is outside of this context. Action out of fair play are most of the time concern for a penalty. If we think it negatively, if a player, does not give a hug, it is even understandable and no one is ever blamed for that. The differentiating point is, there is a ceremony before and after the match. Before the match there is that formal, "created" ceremony. Whereas, after the match players are mostly free to do whatever they want. It is because you do not want to give an intimate hug to someone, you are going to punch, kick, and tackle, within minutes. The difference is based on the idea of winning and losing. Even those mostly uneducated football players, do share the loosing of the opponent team where they are not obliged to do so as in form of fair play.

In "real" sports games; there is that interesting sense of "sharing". You share the "loosing of the opponent" caused by your game play, although you are the "winner". Even in highly professional level, it turns out to be code of conduct, -I am sure you remember cases- where these millions of dollar earning, snobbish young players, as the winners come and hold the hand of the "losers" and giving them "hug" at least changing uniforms. If we raise the wilderness of the game there is raise in the intimacy level as well. It is very hard to understand, the boxers, going on each other in deathly punches, after the match these, two deadly, scary man giving hug to each other. In same pattern, the game that could be interpreted, as most violent sports of modern times, cage fights (UFC – Ultimate Fighting Championship), those people in this violent and crazy thing, bleeding from eyebrows, nose, and having deadly punches, kicks and locks; after the match, come and give the most intimate hugs to each other. This intimate act is not fair play since it is happening outside the match and pitch, it is something else. It is based on sharing. A hug is a form of physical intimacy. And more closely as we stated before this comes from the martial arts training of those people. Levinas suggests that "responsibility for the other is rooted within our subjective constitution" (Levinas, 1961) The intimate act of hugging takes place in this responsibility. On the other hand in the "fake" and "constituted" winning and in the discourse of "un-winning" there is no room for sharing. It is such an un-winning human condition from the start. "Feels like winning" is an important concept for workers of the society and team members of modern firms. It has to be kept alive in that sense, the idea that you are winning. The real difference between those two kinds of "winning", winning in the modern society firm as a modern worker and winning on the sports games is, where in one situation you can dig your opponent's grave, on the other, you go and give a hug. One can argue that the latter one is the hypothetical since there is not money. This argument is not true in the professional sports. There is a lot of money. What makes the real difference is, one is constructed and one is pure. One important question about this is, if there are no spectators or media coverage, will UFC still be in progress. Another one is, is there a misusage of martial arts.In order to create that sense of "winning" and use the performance created as a "result of the game play" for winning and to make it continuous, sips of winning by games of various kinds are created. The physically inactive games, like gambling, TV spectator ship & video games for that sake, are more plausible from various perspectives since they require low costs to create when compared to active games. There is also a discussion of those kind of games be included in concept of "sports". Those kinds of games do have the "hypothetical" sense when compared to "real pitch" games and the physical conduct with the opponent is not possible, ontologically different than the pitch games. There is the sense of the hypothetical, in comparison to "real" in those sort of ontology.

It is very hard to give a will to a worker, who saw himself in a kind of competition all the day in the workplace, a kind of sporting event in its real sense. To make people in an active life style, could be hard, wanting the workforce, to compete after the work is quite hard in that sense. On the other hand , there is a need for a winning workforce as well. For the creation of this sort of ideas, watching of sports is a solution. It works as both in positive and negative aspects for the closed system, positively, spreading the "fake idea of winning" to the spectators and also negatively and not praising any kind of physical activity and making them inactive. Based on this, there is creation of the new kind of sports area, it is passive spectatorship, as being in front of TV-Screen. It is to create martial artists or combat sporters without ever engaging them into the game.

Spectatorship & Hypothetical Winning

Current structure on winning as constructed, is a kind of theory based on, the "fake" and shallow concept of winning which is "feels like as if winning" 'to feel like as if won'. As we stated above, the idea of winning is an important tool to create a demanded "ready to compete" workforce for the system. One reason of supporting a big club; is the idea of "as if/fake winning". Who wants to be on the loser side? From that simple distinction we can explain, an act of "unpredictable" happening in supporters as well. Strange kind of spectatorship occurred in modern society. People most of the time, have two clubs in Turkey or around the world. They support their "local team" as well as a bigger club with a bigger chance "not to lose". A fan of a "Bandırmaspor" FC of Bandırma a small city club of 100.000 habitants, opens up his local team's flag in Champion's league final match between Barcelona and Manchester United at the same time wearing Barcelona shirt. This is quite a new kind of spectatorship, lately created by the spectators based on the condition of winning we are trying to explain above.We also can explain one big problem, of football and violence which is hooliganism. The idea tied to "family" is the idea in football of 12th player is created on this basis. You are like a player on the pitch where in reality you are not. The problem of this kind of idealization is , those kind of spectators act, with those kind of ideas; as warriors of the same family. This results in hooliganism. This is -in a sense- the "virus" of the system. While creating "warrior spirit" without a war, there can turn out to be "actual warriors" since they hold the spirit.

Philosophy of Winning "As If"

In addition to "spirit", action and manipulation in its very essence, how can it be possible "watching sports" in front of a TV screen, with an inactive life style, go beyond the real experience, of playing on the pitch which is desired "act" ? The spectator in front of TV screen can be manipulated, advertised, and even be made to "pay for" that in active event. That is a "real" victory in the sense that, both earning money and manipulating the passive spectator. "Inactively" being on the pitch and acting "as if" you are. The main question here is that: How can this hypothetical spectatorship be valuable for some people than the real pitch? This is deeply rooted philosophical question and position. The idea of experiencing an "As if" situation. The spectator in front of TV is watching sports in the form of As If. As If he is the one who plays. This 'As If' position can be exemplified by another bodily act. People also "pay" for watching. That 'As If' is like pornography. Where the bodily act sex is to pornography, TV spectatorship is like to sports. There is the act of as if you were doing the act, which also has its own kind of reality in itself. Is UFC an ultimate form of "as if".

Conclusion

In first part of this chapter we have tried to figure out the difference between arts and sports regarding martial arts using the argument between Wertz, Best and Back. The difference between sports and arts is problematic where as in martial arts or combat sports there is that being togetherness. In second part of this chapter we have tried to analyze the different aspects of winning, together with different concepts like hugging and spectatorship. The analysis of un-winning and winning as if together with the concepts has revealed that, winning is a very rich concept deeply rooted in our everyday life. For that reason we have tried to differentiate between the "real winning" we call in sports pitch and the other kinds of winning and un-winning. There are of course other types and forms of winning, in everyday life, which also need to be clarified and put into bracketing in the sense of philosophical concern. The case of screening martial arts has this kind of problematic.

References

Bäck, A. (2009) The Way to Virtue in Sport. Journal of Philosophy of Sport, 36:217-237

Bäck, A. & Kim, D. (1979) Towards A Western Philosophy of the Eastern Martial Arts.

Best, D. (1980) Art and Sport. Journal of Aesthetic Education, 14: pp.69-80

Cameron, J. (1999). Kants Categorical Imperatives as Foundation for Development Studies and Action. *European Journal of Development Research*, Vol. 11:2 p.p. 43-52

Cooky, C., Wachs, F. L. Messner, M. & S.L. Dworkin (2010). It's Not About the Game: Don Imus, Race, Class, Gender and Sexuality in Contemporary Media, *Sociology of Sport Journal* 27: p.p.139-152.

d'Anjou, P. (2010). Beyond Duty and Virtue in Design Ethics, *Massachusetts Institute of Technology Design*. Issue 26, Volume 1,Winter.

Derrida, J. (1997). *Politics of Friendship,* Translation byGeorge Collins. Verso Press. London, U.K.

Derrida, J. (1994). *Specters of Marx, the state of the debt, the Work of Mourning, & the New International*, Translated by Peggy Kamuf, Routledge, London, U.K. p.150

Leibenstein, H. (1980). *Beyond Economic Man: New Foundations of Microeconomics*, Harvard University Press. U.S.A.

Kant, I. (1993). *Grounding for the Metaphysics of Morals* (3rd Ed). Translation. James W. Ellington Hackett Press. p. 30

Levinas, I. (1961). *Totality and Infinity: An Essay on Exteriority*. Transltion. Alphonso Lingis. Pittsburgh: Duquesne University Press, p. 21

Sentuna B, McNamee M, Korkusuz F, & E. Kiraz (2010). Qualitative Enquiry of Aikido Practitioners from different levels to the Philosophical Discussion between Arts and Sports – The Case of Aikido in-between, *International Journal of Eastern Sports & Physical Education*, Vol 8:2, pp. 35-43.

Wertz, S.K. (1991). *Talking a good game: Inquiries into the principals of sport*. Southern Methodist University Press. U.S.A.

Part III: Rhythm and Balance

Chapter 13

Shaping the Rhythms of Mixed Martial Arts Practice

Stanley Blue

Introduction

In one out of only a handful of academic titles to be published on the sport of mixed martial arts, Dale Spencer (2012) describes rhythms of practice in the following:

> MMA competitions feature competitors in a ring or caged-in area inflicting pain on their opponents, *inter alia*, by punching, kicking, elbowing and kneeing their opponents into submission'.

(Spencer 2012, p.3)

Thus, the image pervades of 'ultimate fighting' or 'cage fighting', both in the media and in academic studies, as one of participants committed to the giving and receiving of pain and 'violence'. Rather than perpetuate an already sensationalised image of the blood and 'violence' of MMA competition through a study of this sport as spectacle, I turn in this text to an analysis of the demanding, changing and highly co-ordinated and synchronised rhythms of practice of MMA training, of the intense preparations that are arduously endured in order to peak on fight day through what Loïc Wacquant, in his famous study of Woodlawn's Boxing Gym describes as:

> '... the minute and mundane rites of daily life in the gym that produce and reproduce the feeling, this very peculiar corporeal, material symbolic economy that is the pugilistic world'.

(Wacquant 2004, 6)

I argue here that these rhythms of practice, that is, the re-production of the changing 'world' of mixed martial arts training can be particularly well conceptualised through Henri Lefebvre's theoretical schema of 'Rhythmanalysis' ([1992] 2004). Building on Lefebvre's understanding of rhythms, I draw on empirical examples from an immersive and 'rhythmanalytical' study of MMA, in order to outline three conceptual tools: 'arrhythmia', 'training' and 'syncopation', that can provide not only a model for conceptualising the shaping of rhythms of mixed martial arts practice; but also more generally point towards a theory of social action that has an understanding of ongoing social change at its heart. Therefore, in closing this chapter, I suggest that the conceptualisation that I outline here has significant implications for both public and policy guidelines and may be particularly well suited to offering an accessible and alternative approach to dominant models in health, nutrition and exercise studies that predominantly rest on a theoretical framework of 'cognitive psychology' and behaviour change rhetoric.

What is MMA?

So, what is MMA if it is not a blood thirsty and barbaric practice that is intent on commodifying 'violence' and pain? For Rosi Sexton, who made her debut in the 'Ultimate Fighting Championship' (UFC) recently (June 2013), the rhetoric of 'violence' and pain is a far cry from her experience of the sport. In a recent interview with the BBC, she says:

> 'For me it is not about beating up another human being, it's about challenging myself, the technical challenge... In a sense, it's no different to trying to score a goal in football or a point in tennis. What some people from the outside might perceive as brutal, doesn't feel the same way when you're in there...'
>
> (Rosi Sexton in Osborne 2013)

Rosi Sexton draws our attention to a different kind of discourse about MMA. Indeed, it is a discourse that is much more prevalent within the 'world' of MMA and from my own studies and experience; it is one that much more accurately reflects these rhythms of practice. It highlights a (perhaps more traditional) understanding of martial arts as training the body and as disciplining the 'self' (and we might well consider this in the Foucauldian sense (see Foucault 1975) to develop technique, to improve fitness and athleticism and to adjust and adapt routines to rise to the challenges of training and competing in this sport. Indeed, mixed martial artists are challenged to master not one; but a variety of martial arts disciplines and need to be able to move seamlessly between techniques from a variety of arts. Building on the fundamental systems of Thai Boxing, for stand up fighting, Wrestling, for transitioning between fighting on the feet to fighting on the ground and Brazilian Jiu-Jitsu, for ground fighting, MMA practitioners have to develop their own styles that fit their own body shapes, strengths and weaknesses, with their game plans and abilities by drawing on all manner of martial styles from Karate to Kung Fu, Sumo to Judo and Taekwondo to Capoeira.

In stark contrast to the Olympic Judoka, who is required only to master one particular discipline; mixed martial artists have to train, adapt to and improve their 'knowledges' and abilities in all areas of unarmed combat and have to have the physical strength and conditioning to constantly transition between Boxing and Wrestling, between fighting on the feet and fighting on the ground.

In order to compete for up to five, five minute rounds of unarmed combat, mixed martial artists maintain strict and ever changing training schedules, strength and conditioning programmes and nutrition and supplementing regimes, often training three times per day, every day of the week. This study asks the questions, how is it that these rhythms of practice change, how is it that these rhythms become strict and hard wired for practitioners and what can this tell us about shaping rhythms of practice?

A Rhythm Analytical Methodology

It is important to note here that the empirical foundation of these ideas is in no way separate from its theoretical orientation. Significantly, to study the *rhythms of practice* of mixed martial arts requires a particular methodological approach that is consistent with understanding practice as both temporally and spatially situated and as becoming, that is constantly changing and made different through repetition, through rhythms of practice. Elsewhere (Blue Forthcoming 2013), I have argued that it is problematic to define 'a practice' of MMA, that due to its continuous development and evolution it becomes increasingly difficult to draw a boundary around and label 'a practice' of MMA. Instead, I have suggested, following Allen Pred's (1990) argument that it may be more useful to consider the situated-ness and becoming-ness of social practice. However, understanding practice in this way, as in the 'moment' of doing, as happening, free from re-presentation through the subjects and objects of social action, defies study as an *object* practice of MMA by a *subjective* researcher. If we consider practice in this way, as the 'moment' of doing, then there is no *object* to which to become close to in an attempt to remove the distance between the *subject* researcher and the *object* of study.

Instead, following Lefebvre's ([1992] 2004) suggestion, I employ a rhythmanalytical methodology, recognising my position as historically and geographically situated as both researcher and participant in order to study the rhythms of mixed martial arts. This has involved training for over three years in this sport. From humble beginnings taking only one or two classes per week, to training up to three times per day through gruelling and complicated workouts, strictly dieting and maintaining complex supplementing regimens (sometimes monitored at minute intervals) to manage my weight and to prepare for peak fitness for competition and finally competing at the highest amateur level in the U.K. This processes required dedicating significant amounts of time to and organising other practices around gym workouts and training sessions, becoming obsessive with food and travelling to various destinations, including Thailand and Japan to take seminars and classes with specialists in particular styles. In a similar vein to Loïc Wacquant's (2004) famous study of the 'world' of Boxing, I provide a part ethnographic, part auto-ethnographic, immersive study of the changing rhythms of MMA practice. However, where this study differs from Wacquant's is that he took his academic studies to be separate from his boxing practice. Rather this study provides a re-presentation of my own rhythms of practice of both MMA and academic study, in order to show how these rhythms shape each other.

Rhythms of Practice of MMA

It is in this way that I take up an analysis of the rhythms of MMA from a reading of Henri Lefebvre's 'Elements of Rhythmanalysis' ([1992] 2004) in order to move beyond re-presentation and mediatisation and to recognise practice as both presencing and becoming. Importantly the concept of rhythm is not intended to capture change over linear time; but instead to capture the form of the production of difference through repetition, that is rhythm (see Deleuze [1969] 1994). Therefore, for Lefebvre, rhythm consists of repetition, of the re-production of 'moments' of situated and becoming practice. However, this is never repetition of the same. When a 'moment' of practice is repeated, it is necessarily different due to the fact that it follows. Thus, rhythms are made up of constantly changing repetitions. Further, we can never conduct an analysis of a rhythm devoid of contextual and supporting rhythms. Instead Lefebvre contends that every rhythm is already 'polyrhythmic', both made up of and always in concert, co-ordinated and synchronised with other rhythms. Thus we might consider the 'polyrhythmia' of the 'world' of MMA as made up of rhythms of training, sparring, strength and conditioning, drilling techniques, stretching, having physiotherapy, eating, recovering, running, swimming, competing, managing weight and so on. Not to mention that these rhythms are also in concert with, that is to say co-ordinated and synchronised with, rhythms of family life, working, studying and all the rest.

When these rhythms are in a state of health, in 'normal' (and in this sense normed!) 'everydayness', Lefebvre refers to this as 'eurhythmia', that is, when rhythms are in co-ordination and concordance, in their 'normal', 'everyday' and routine state. Thus, we might recognise the mixed martial artist's rhythms of training, sparring, weight lifting, eating and resting all being in a healthy and 'normal' routine state as 'eurhythmia'. However, 'polyrhythmia' can also become discordant. This is what Lefebvre refers to as 'arrhythmia'. It is the de-synchronisation of 'eurhythmia' caused by and causing a state of suffering and absence. This is where rhythms break apart, alter and bypass synchronisation. Importantly though, every 'arrhythmia' is already always replace by another 'eurhythmia'. Doing, or social action, never ends. Rather this is a conceptual analysis for understanding the continuous and ongoing shifts in rhythms of practice.

For example, a common 'arrhythmia' that occurs within the rhythms of practice of MMA is injury. Due to the physical rigours of the sport and the high intensities of training, injuries can and do occur fairly often. Injuries such as ligament tears, lower back problems, pulled muscles and twisted ankles are all common injuries and can lead to a de-synchronisation of a practitioner's rhythms and thus a desistence from practice. Being injured and missing out on training often disturbs rhythms of eating, of strength and conditioning and so on. This de-synchronisation can make it difficult, especially for beginners, to re-establish 'eurhythmic' rhythms of MMA practice and there becomes almost a 'eurhythmia' of not practicing MMA, which itself becomes very difficult to break. However, for many MMA practitioners, especially those who are more experienced, injury is a well understood part of the sport so that these 'arrhythmias' become accounted for and adjusted to, so that they fall in to the 'eurhythmia' of MMA practice.

How then is it possible to shape and steer rhythms of practice that are constantly changing? I argue that the study of MMA can provide us with three conceptual tools, 'arrhythmia', 'training' and 'syncopation' that illustrate an approach to strengthening eurhythmia and shaping the rhythms of practice in 'everyday' life.

Arrhythmia

First, MMA offers an intriguing approach to dealing with 'arrhythmias' such as injuries. Precisely because they are a common part of the sport, MMA fosters an understanding of injury as at the same time, a break in 'eurhythmia'; but also as common, repeated and 'everyday'. Thus, injury may well lead to desistance from rhythms of practice of MMA for the novice practitioner; but Shane, a professional mixed martial artist who has been fighting for over five years, recognises that accommodating injuries is simply a part of the rhythms of MMA practice. He spoke to me in an interview conducted after an afternoon training session:

> 'Injuries are just a part of the job. You have to learn how to manage them and learn how to work around them. If I have hurt my leg, I come in and work my boxing, or if my arms are hurt, I come and train my kicks. If I've knocked my head I don't spar but I work on my technique and my cardio. A lot of injury management and prevention is about listening to your body to know what to work and when'.

> (Shane)

Thus we can see in the rhythms of MMA practice an almost preventative approach to dealing with 'arrhythmia'. Rather than reacting to a problem or break in rhythms of practice, as a change that exists between two fixed states, it might also be possible to recognise that what people do is continually changing, for example injuries happen, and that this continual changing can be strengthened and supported by accommodating breaks, by accommodating and adjusting to 'arrhythmia'. This ability to accommodate arrhythmia, I argue, is built up through 'training'.

Training

For Lefebvre, every time there is 'arrhythmia', there is also an opportunity to imprint rhythms, that is, to shape rhythms of practice through 'training'. In a chapter entitled 'Dressage', Lefebvre describes, in similar terms to Foucault (1975), how human beings come to 'discipline' themselves, to train themselves to act in particular ways through repetition:

'Humans break themselves in like animals. They learn to hold themselves. Dressage can go a long way as far as breathing, movements, sex. It bases itself on repetition. One breaks-in another human being by making them repeat a certain act, a certain gesture or movement'. ([1992] 2004, 39)

Nowhere is this breaking in through repetition more clearly evident than in the continuous 'drilling' and 'training' in MMA practice. Techniques are 'drilled' over and over again until they become ingrained, embodied and 'natural'. Even the so-called free sparring that tends to be done at the end of the session comes to take on a habitual and repetitive cast, always sparring three, four minute rounds, first of kick boxing, then of wrestling, then of ground fighting, constantly rotating through the same partners. This 'drilling' or 'training' does not simply apply to rhythms of bodily movements in the gym; but comes to fix and schedule weekly timetables and routines as well. Monday night becomes ju-jitsu night, Friday morning is for strength and conditioning and Friday night becomes the night that is looked forward to the most because it is 'cheat meal' night.

Thus, in this model it is 'training' through repetition that shapes rhythms of practice. Rather than approaches that consider changing people's attitudes to get them to 'choose' to change their behaviours (approaches that informs much policy guidance on issues of public health for example), this model argues that shaping rhythms of practice, requires 'training' through repetition of doing and at the same time an understanding of accommodating 'arrhythmias' in order to strengthen 'eurhythmic' rhythms of practice. Finally, I go on to show how these two conceptual tools might be employed to 'syncopate' the rhythms of 'everyday' life.

Syncopation

In musical terms, 'syncopation' refers to a disturbance of the regular flow of rhythm as emphasis is placed on the off-beat of the rhythm to create an unexpected rhythmic pattern. I argue that this idea is an intriguing notion for considering the shaping of rhythms of practice. It requires first and above all an opportunity, a break in rhythms or practice and second an understanding of the rhythms of practice to be altered as 'trained', that is, repeated to the extent that they are experienced by the practitioner as routine and 'everyday' practice. It is then potentially possible to recognise the extra-everyday, the non-routine and that which has not been 'trained' or disciplined in the same way and to emphasise, to highlight or accent this 'moment' of practice, this 'arrhythmia', in order to overcome the 'everyday' and the 'disciplined'. Through repetition of this 'moment' of arrhythmiatic, of non-routine practice through 'training' would then allow this rhythm to 'fall in', for itself to become recognised as the 'everyday' and as routine. For example, when I first started training at the MMA club, there was no time at the end of the session that was left over for stretching. When this arrhythmiatic rhythm of practice was brought to the coaches' attention, it became a rhythm that was emphasised, that we repeated every night at the end of each class until it because a fundamental and eurhythmic part of our 'everyday' rhythms of practice.

Nevertheless, it is important to recognise that any attempted 'syncopation' is still rooted in the understanding of rhythms as constituted by *difference* through repetition (Deleuze [1969] 1994) and that of course the production of differences as 'polyrhythmic' and existing across multiple scales is not predictable nor is it open to design. Merely it is possible to recognise 'eurhythmia' and attempt 'training' that might imprint different rhythms. Lefebvre warns us:

> 'But it should not be necessary to see in these innovations only progress, creations. This positive aspect is not without the so-called negative side: impoverishment, and weakening, through the loss of spontaneity etc.' (p.64)

Thus, as conceptual tools, 'syncopation', 'training' and 'arrhythmia' are ways of getting a handle on continual change, on becoming. They do not however, offer an analysis of how to change one state of affairs into another. On the contrary, they suggest how continual change, that is, rhythms of practice might be steered or shaped.

Conclusion

In summary, I have argued, through a rhythmanalytical study of mixed martial arts, that shaping the rhythms of practice of MMA can be understood through the concepts of 'arrhythmia', 'training' and 'syncopation'. However, these ideas, whilst prompted through my engagement in this sport could well be employed to challenge dominant models and paradigms that exist in a variety of fields from sustainability to health, from deviance to education. In particular current health policy and guidance, particularly in the U.K. is built on an understanding of the rational, economic and independent 'agent' that chooses between healthy and unhealthy behaviours based on certain held attitudes and beliefs. Further research could help to complicate that picture by examining the 'polyrhythmia' of 'everyday' healthy and unhealthy routines, in order to demonstrate their tight knit, synchronised and co-ordinated dependence on all manner of other rhythms in 'everyday' life and thus demonstrate how healthy or unhealthy rhythms of practice might well be shaped through understanding 'arrhythmia', 'training' and 'syncopation'.

References

Blue, S. Forthcoming (2014). "Ongoing Change in the Rhythms of Mixed Martial Arts Practice." *The International Journal of Sport and Society*.

Deleuze, G. [1969] 1994. *Difference and Repetition*. Translated by P. Patton, *Athlone Contemporary European Thinkers Series*: Continuum International Publishing Group.

Foucault, M. (1975). *Discipline and Punish*: Random House of Canada.

Lefebvre, H. (1992) 2004. "Elements of Rhythmanalysis: An Introduction to the Understanding of Rhythms." In *Rhythmanalysis: Space, Time and Everyday Life*, edited by S. Elden. London, New York: Continuum.

Original edition, Éléments de Rhythmanalyse: Introduction à la Connaissance des Rythmes, Paris: Éditions Syllepse.

Osborne, C. (2013). "UFC: Rosi Sexton To Be First British Female Ultimate Fighter." *BBC Sport*, 12.06.13.

Pred, A. R. (1990). *Making Histories and Constructing Human Geographies: The Local Transformation of Practice, Power Relations, and Consciousness*: Westview Press.

Spencer, D. (2012). *Ultimate Fighting and Embodiment: Violence, Gender and Mixed Martial Arts*: Routledge, Taylor and Francis.

Wacquant, L. J. D. (2004). *Body and Soul: Notebooks of an Apprentice Boxer*: Oxford University Press.

Chapter 14

Competitive Balance in Olympic Boxing: 1904–2012

David Chaplin & Sergio Mendoza

Introduction

Studies of competitive balance hold a prominent position in literature on sport. As one example, a scan of the "most cited" and "most read" articles in *Journal of Sports Economics* (conducted June 2, 2012), reveals that three of the ten most frequently-cited articles deal explicitly with competitive balance. By rank, these are: #1 (Kesenne 2000), # 3 (Humphreys 2002) and #4 (Schmidt and Berri 2001). Two of the ten most read articles deal explicitly with competitive balance: #5 (Zimbalist 2002) and #10 (Dietl et al. 2011). Furthermore, beginning with the paper generally regarded to be the first in the field of sports economics (Rottenberg 1956), a steady stream of articles dealing with competitive balance in sports have followed (Neale 1964; El-Hodiri and Quirk 1971; Noll 1974; Scully 1989; Fort and Quirk 1995; Kesenne 2000; Schmidt and Berri 2001; Humphreys 2002, etc.). Lastly, in reaching a far broader audience than professional economists, both Fort (2011) and Leeds and von Allmen (2011), dedicate an entire chapter to competitive balance in their popular sports economics textbooks. With such a strong emphasis on both measuring the degree of competitive balance existing in sport and extolling the virtues of greater competitive balance in the literature (that of, *ceteris paribus,* greater outcome uncertainty and thus higher attendance at sporting events), it is surprising that competitive balance in boxing (professional or amateur) has to this point been practically ignored by sports economists. In fact, since the first article emerged in the sub-field of "boxing economics" (Balbien et al. 1981), only five other book chapters or articles in this field (all focused on professional boxing) are indexed in the EconLit database (Tenorio 2000; 2006; Amegashie and Kutsoati 2005; Rosca 2012; Chaplin 2012) as of this writing. Only the articles by Balbien et al. (1981)

and Chaplin (2012) perform multivariate regression analysis on real-world data; the others are theoretical or descriptive in nature. This relatively paltry output indicates there is still much work to be done to bring analyses of boxing in the sports economics literature in line with the majority of other sports. While Sanderson and Siegfried (2003) and Tenorio (2006) make brief and qualitative mention of competitive balance in professional boxing and Balmer, Nevill and Williams (2003) deal tangentially with the issue in a quantitative analysis of home-field advantage in the Summer Olympic Games, this study marks the first comprehensive quantitative analysis of competitive balance in amateur boxing and is believed to be only the third article in the sports economics domain related to amateur boxing (following the work of Chaplin, 2011 and Chaplin, Halbert and Knapp, 2011).

In the second segment of the paper, a more in-depth review of the competitive balance literature is provided, with the study divided between team and individual sports. Differing methods employed and findings on the degree of competitive balance in each category will be presented. Section Three provides the methods employed to evaluate the degree of competitive balance in Olympic Boxing and draws comparisons (where available) with other sports. Section Four provides a discussion of the statistical findings and their future research and policy implications.

Literature Review on Competitive Balance

Beyond the recent popularity of issues of competitive balance in the sports economics literature, as documented in the previous section, it is interesting to note that the first article attributed to dealing explicitly with the economics of sports (Rottenberg 1956) stresses the importance of competitive balance in Major League Baseball (both for individual teams as well as the league as a whole) as follows:

> "But in baseball no team can be successful unless its competitors also survive and prosper sufficiently so that differences in the quality of play among teams are not "too great."…In one sense, the teams compete; in another, they combine in a single firm in which the success of each branch requires that it be not "too much" more efficient than the other. If it is, output falls". (pp. 254-255).

Rottenberg, therefore, "threw down the gauntlet" for future researchers in the field of sports economics to keep issues of competitive balance at the forefront of their analyses. The foci of the vast majority of the research on competitive balance in sports has been on professional team sports; however, a limited number of studies have tackled the topic of individual sports. As Fort and Maxcy (2003) indicate, "Different measurements are of different use, and all lines of research into competitive balance have, to date, proven quite instructive" (154). In this context, a review of the different measurements used and conclusions drawn in analyses of competitive balance will be provided with the review of the literature subcategorized into "Previous Studies of Competitive Balance in Team Sports" and "Previous Studies of Competitive Balance in Individual Sports".

Previous Studies on Competitive Balance in Team Sports

Leeds and von Allmen (2011) provide several broad measures of competitive balance leagues: within-season variation (measured by a ratio of actual-to-idealized standard deviation of winning percentages), between-season variation (which can be measured as "frequency of championships," using the Herfindahl-Hirschman Index or the "distribution of wins" using the Lorenz Curve). Schmidt and Berri (2001) and Fort and Quirk (2011) add to Leeds and von Allmen's work on the topic by adding Gini coefficient analysis, while Humphreys (2002) provided an alternative to the standard measures of competitive balance in sports used at that time, which he titled the "Competitive Balance Ratio" (CBR). Results point to greater overall competitive balance in Major League Baseball, National Hockey League and National Football Association relative to the National Basketball Association and English Premier League Football over the period 1998-2008 (Leeds and von Allmen 2011, 156). Employing a ratio of actual standard deviation of winning percentages to the idealized standard deviation and comparing sports across different time frames, however, Berri et al. (2005, 1032) find that competitive balance was better in English Premier League Football (from 1976-2003) than any of the four major American team sports: Major League Baseball (1901-2003), National Football League (1922-2003), National Hockey League (1917-2003) and National Basketball Association/American Basketball Association (NBA: 1946-2003; ABA: 1967-76). The authors' findings are consistent with Leeds' and von Allmen's work in that they find greater competitive balance in Major League Baseball, National Hockey League and National Football Association than in the NBA or ABA. In their paper on the relationship between competitive balance and attendance in Major League Baseball, Schmidt and Berri (2001), found that competitive balance was the best it had ever been in the 1990s (in an analysis dating from 1901-1999). Forrest et al. (2005) take the analysis of competitive balance in a somewhat different direction than the majority of studies, as they factor-in home field advantage. The authors find that significant home field advantage exists in the English Football League (EFL), such that uncertainty of outcome is maximized when a weak home team plays a strong away team. In their simulation, they find equalization of quality differences across teams would actually reduce outcome uncertainty and therefore reduce EFL attendance by over 25% (445).

Previous Studies on Competitive Balance in Individual Sports

In his analysis of men's and women's Grand-Slam Tennis Tournaments, del Corral (2009, p.567) explains the difficulties in using conventional competitive balance measures applied to sports leagues (for example, the Gini coefficient or dispersion of winning percentages) in an individual sport with single-elimination tournaments. To deal with this problem, the author develops an alternative competitive balance measure based on the relative frequency with which the 16 seeded players reached the 4th round in Grand-Slam Tennis Tournaments. In an analysis spanning 1994-2008, the author found that the 2001 ruling to increase in the number of seeded players from 16 to 32 decreased competitive balance significantly for men, but not for women. In their study on outcome uncertainty in NASCAR, Berkowitz et al. (2011) find evidence of declining competitive balance over the period 2007-2009. Due to many of the same limitations cited by del Corral (2009) regarding traditional competitive balance measures for individual sports, the authors use both a version of the "standard" Herfindahl-Hirschman Index (HHI) employed in this paper and an "adjusted-churn" measure designed to reflect the starting and finishing positions of the drivers and encompasses the entire field of drivers.

Methods and Statistical Results

Data from the 24 Summer Olympic Games in which boxing was contested (1904-2012, with 1912 excluded as the sport was illegal in Sweden at the time) are analyzed. The metric of "standardized medal points" (in which a gold is worth 3 points, silver worth 2 points and bronze worth 1 point) employed by Ball (1972) and Balmer et al. (2003) is utilized here. Three different measures of competitive balance are employed. First, a "standard" Herfindahl-Hirschman Index (HHI) is computed by decade for Olympic Boxing (with the 1910's excluded – the 1912 Games for reasons mentioned above and the 1916 Games were not held at all due to WWI). Using this measure, well-known in the industrial economics literature as a measure of overall concentration in an industry, the sum of squared market shares provide a rough gauge for how competitive an industry is. With a maximum value of 10,000 (monopoly), the following ranges for the HHI are associated with the different degrees of industry competitiveness: below 1,000 = competitive marketplace; 1,000-1,800 moderately-concentrated marketplace; above 1,800 = high concentration in the marketplace (Rhoads 1993, 188-189; NationalGrid 2009, 4). One notes from the Appendix, Table Two, that in terms of the concentration of boxing medal points awarded across all nations, the 1950s, 1970s-2000s and the 2012 Olympics all demonstrate a competitive marketplace; the 1920s-1940s and 1960s demonstrate moderate concentration and the 1900s have high concentration. Interestingly, the results found herein for Olympic Boxing are consistent with competitive balance in the entire Summer Olympic Games (1896-1996), as Baimbridge (1998, 162) indicates that competitive imbalance is a problem in the Summer Olympics as follows: "Only 16 nations have ever achieved a top 3 medal placing in the history of the Summer Olympiad." In consonance with Baimbridge's findings, we find that only 7 nations have won the Olympic Boxing Championships in their history and that USA and Cuba together account for 58.3% of all such championships. However, Baimbridge (ibid, 163) also finds that outcome uncertainty (an indication of the degree of competitive balance) improved in Summer Olympics with boycotts vis-à-vis non-boycotted Summer Olympics (measured by a 20.9% reduction in the ratio of medal-winning to participating nations). The 1980s witnessed boycotts by at least one of the boxing powerhouses (USA, Cuba and Soviet Union) in each of its Summer Olympics (USA in 1980, Soviet Union and Cuba in 1984 and Cuba in 1988). The "standard" HHI was at its lowest in the 1980s (Appendix, Table Two) to reflect, at least in part, the improvement to competitive balance brought about in Olympic Boxing due to boycotts by traditionally strong amateur boxing nations.

Secondly, a "Frequency of Championships HHI" measure is employed (following the generalized model provided by Leeds and von Allmen 2011, 156-157) to calculate the number of championships (i.e., most medal points) won by a nation within a given period, dividing by the number of years in the period, squares this fraction and adds all fractions for all teams. In comparing the past 10 Summer Olympic Games (1976-2012) with the distribution of championships over the period 1998-2008 in Major League Baseball, National Football League, National Hockey League and National Basketball Association and English Premier League Football (Leeds and von Allmen 2011, 156, Table 5.4), boxing is by far the most imbalanced of all the sports. Cuba (1980, 1992, 1996, 2000, 2004 and 2008), USA (1976, 1984 and 1988) and United Kingdom (2012) have won all the Olympic Boxing Championships over the past 10 Olympics, this imbalance should come as no surprise.

Lastly, a difference-of-means analysis is performed (Appendix, Table Four) to gauge competitive balance pre-WWII (the 7 Summer Olympics contested 1904-1936) vis-à-vis post-WWII (the 17 Summer Olympics contested 1948-2012). Here, the summative mean share of medal points earned by the top three nations in each Olympic Games is compared over the two time frames. For example, in 1924, USA (12 points), United Kingdom (10 points) and Denmark (7 points) earned 60.4% of all boxing medal points available). In 1996, Cuba (18 points), USA (8 points) and Bulgaria (7 points) earned 39.3% of all boxing medal points available. Despite the competitive imbalance problems indicated over the past 10 Olympic Games, the situation improved, by this measure, in the post-WWII era.

Discussion and Future Research Implications

By the "standard" HHI measured employed in this study, the 2000's and 2012 Olympics had the greatest competitive balance of any period outside of the boycott-riddled 1980s. The following evidence indicate the decade of the 2010s will improve on competitive balance in Olympic Boxing even further: 1). The anemic showing by the USA in Olympic Boxing in the last decade (only 1 gold medal and 11 total medal points for the male boxers in the Summer Olympics spanning 2000-2012); 2). The introduction of women's boxing in the Summer Olympic Games in 2012 (with China and Russia tying for the Boxing Championship at the 2012 Women's World Boxing Championships held in China) and 3). A tapering-off of Cuba's dominance (with the nation well behind leader Ukraine in the 2011 Men's Amateur World Boxing Championships held in Azerbaijan and "only" a fourth-place finish behind United Kingdom, Ukraine and Russia in the 2012 Olympics) and their position as a non-entity in women's amateur boxing, point to a changing of the guard in Olympic Boxing. Furthermore, the global governing body for amateur boxing, the International Boxing Association (AIBA) has put in place a mechanism to enhance competitive balance in international amateur boxing through its "Road to Dream" project. The program began in 2009 in Assisi, Italy in advance of the 2009 AIBA Men's World Championships to provide financial assistance to amateur boxers and coaches from developing nations to attend intensive international training camps and to compete in international tournaments. In the "Road to London" training camp, held in Cardiff, Wales, February, 2012, 62 boxers participated (who would likely not have had to opportunity to compete at the elite international level in amateur boxing without the financial assistance of AIBA). This program bore fruit in the 2012 Olympics, with participants Mavzuna Chorieva of Tajikistan and Evaldas Petrauskas of Lithuania earning the first Olympic Boxing Medals in their nations' history.

By providing a foundation on the issue of competitive balance in Olympic Boxing, it is hoped that future researchers will follow-up on the topic in several areas. First, the inclusion of women's boxing for the first time in the 2012 Summer Olympics allows for the tracking of competitive balance between men's and women's boxing in this venue. Secondly, as there is significant evidence that greater competitive balance (and therefore outcome uncertainty) enhances attendance (Knowles et al. 1992; McDonald and Rascher 2000; Schmidt and Berri 2001) in sport, a study of attendance and competitive balance in Olympic Boxing would be an attractive addition to the sports economics literature. Lastly, regression analysis in the manner Tcha and Pershin (2003) used to determine competitive advantage in the Summer Olympic Games could be employed to determine the marginal impact a host of variables (average amount spent per athlete, quality of trainers provided, frequency of competition opportunities domestically and regional competitive balance for boxers) have on success in Olympic Boxing would be of interest to researchers in this field.

Appendix

Table 1: Olympic Boxing Tournaments Won (By Medal Points Total)

Nation	Championships
USA	7
Cuba	7
United Kingdom	3
Soviet Union	3
Italy	2
South Africa	1
Germany	1

Table 2: "Standard" Herfindahl-Hirschman Index (HHI)

Olympic Boxing HHI by Decade (Data Only Available for 2012 in the 2010's)										
1900's	1920's	1930's	1940's	1950's	1960's	1970's	1980's	1990's	2000's	2012
4849.82	1015.63	1041.67	1250.00	843.88	1031.03	936.92	779.84	961.59	825.86	786.86

Table 3: "Frequency of Championships" HHI for Past Ten Events (Summer Olympics, 1976-2012) vis-à-vis Select Team Sports, 1998-2008*

Olympic Boxing	NBA	NHL	NFL	MLB	English Premier League Football
0.54	0.28	0.18	0.16	0.14	0.44

*The "Frequency of Championships HHI" in Olympic Boxing for the period 1904-2012 was 0.203.

Table 4: Difference-of-Means Tests by Share of Total Medal Points Earned (Cumulatively) by Top Three Nations: Pre WWII v. Post-WWII

Category	Number of Olympics (n)	Mean Share	Standard Deviation	Two-tailed T-Score	Actual Confidence Level	Statistically Significant Difference?
Pre-WWII	7	67.86	22.50	--	--	--
Post-WWII	17	47.09	8.35	3.37	0.003	Yes

Table 5: 1904-2012 Olympic Boxing Medal Table

Nation	Medal Points	# of Gold	# of Silver	# of Bronze
United States	231	49	23	38
Cuba	154	34	19	14
United Kingdom	99	17	12	24
Soviet Union	98	14	19	18
Italy	93	15	15	17
Germany	83	11	14	22
Poland	68	8	9	26
Russia	49	9	5	12
Argentina	45	7	7	10
Hungary	42	10	2	8
Romania	36	1	9	15
South Africa	35	6	5	7
Kazakhstan	34	6	5	6
France	34	4	7	8
South Korea	33	3	7	10
Bulgaria	31	4	5	9
Canada	30	3	7	7
Ukraine	27	4	4	7
Thailand	26	4	4	6
Ireland	25	2	5	9
Yugoslavia	19	3	2	6
Mexico	19	2	3	7
Finland	19	2	1	11
Denmark	19	1	5	6
China	16	3	2	3
Sweden	16	0	5	6
North Korea	15	2	3	3

Czechoslovakia	13	3	1	2
Mongolia	10	1	2	3
Kenya	10	1	1	5
Japan	9	2	0	3
Venezuela	9	1	2	2
Norway	9	1	2	2
Netherlands	9	1	1	4
Uzbekistan	9	1	0	6
Nigeria	9	0	3	3
Algeria	8	1	0	5
Belgium	7	1	1	2
Uganda	7	0	3	1
Turkey	7	0	2	3
Philippines	7	0	2	3
Australia	7	0	2	3
Puerto Rico	7	0	1	5
New Zealand	6	1	1	1
Spain	6	0	2	2
Azerbaijan	6	0	0	6
Egypt	5	0	1	3
Brazil	5	0	1	3
Dominican Rep	4	1	0	1
Belarus	4	0	2	0
Ghana	4	0	1	2
Chile	4	0	1	2
Cameroon	3	0	1	1
Morocco	3	0	0	3
Colombia	3	0	0	3
Estonia	2	0	1	0
Tonga	2	0	1	0
Czech Republic	2	0	1	0
Georgia	2	0	0	2
Moldova	2	0	0	2
Tunisia	2	0	0	2
India	2	0	0	2
Niger	1	0	0	1

Pakistan	1	0	0	1
Zambia	1	0	0	1
Guyana	1	0	0	1
Bermuda	1	0	0	1
Uruguay	1	0	0	1
Armenia	1	0	0	1
Mauritius	1	0	0	1
Syria	1	0	0	1
Lithuania	1	0	0	1
Tajikistan	1	0	0	1

References

Amegashie, J.A. & Kutsoati, E. (2005). Rematches in boxing and other sporting events. *Journal of Sports Economics* 6(4): 401-411.

Association Internationale de Boxe Amateur (AIBA). Wu hails success of "Road to Dream" project. May 3, 2011 (www.aiba.org).

Association Internationale de Boxe Amateur (AIBA). Road to London begins. February 20, 2012 (www.aiba.org).

Association Internationale de Boxe Amateur (AIBA). Tajikistan and Lithuania achieve first ever Olympic Boxing Medals. August 7, 2012 (www.aiba.org).

Baimbridge, M. (1998). Outcome uncertainty in sporting competition: The Olympic Games, 1896-1996. *Applied Economics Letters*, 5, 161-164.

Balbien, J., Noll, R. & Quirk, J. (1981). The economics of boxing regulation in California. California Institute of Technology, Social Science Working Paper 366.

Ball, D. (1972). "Olympic Games Competition: Structural correlates of national success. *International Journal of Comparative Sociology*, 13, 186-200.

Balmer, N.J., Nevill, A.M. & Williams, A.M. (2003). Modelling home advantage in the Summer Olympic Games. *Journal of Sports Sciences*, 21, 469-478.

Berkowitz, J., Depken II, C. & Wilson, D. (2011). When going in circles is going backward: Outcome uncertainty in NASCAR. *Journal of Sports Economics*, 12(3), 253-283.

Berri, D. et al (2005). The short supply of tall people: Competitive imbalance and the National Basketball Association. *Journal of Economic Issues*, 34(4), 1029-1041.

Chaplin, D. (2011). The economics of boxing: how to differentiate the effort and performance in amateur championships boxing? *Quarterly Review of Sports Science: Economics, Management and Marketing* (Greece), 11(2), 22-30.

Chaplin, D., Halbert, C. & Knapp, A. (2011). Effort and efficiency in elite amateur boxing tournaments. *ACC Journal* (Czech Republic), 17(B), 66-74.

Chaplin, D. (2012). Pay and race in world championship boxing. *Journal of Economics (MVEA)*, 38(1), 43-57.

Del Corral, J. (2009). Competitive balance and match uncertainty in Grand-Slam Tennis: Effects of seeding system, gender and court surface. *Journal of Sports Economics*, 10(6), 563-581.

Dietl, H., Grossman, M. & Lang, M. (2011). Competitive balance and revenue sharing in sports leagues with utility-maximizing teams. *Journal of Sports Economics*, 12(3), 284-308.

El-Hodiri, M. & Quirk, J. (1971). An economic model of a professional sports league. *Journal of Political Economy*, 70, 1302-1319.

Forrest, D. et al. (2005). Home advantage and the debate about competitive advantage in professional sports leagues. *Journal of Sports Sciences*, 23(4), 439-455.

Fort, R. & Quirk, J. (1995, September). Cross-subsidization, incentives, and outcomes in professional team sports leagues. *Journal of Economic Literature*, 33, 1265-1299.

Fort, R. & Maxcy, J. (2003). Competitive balance in sports leagues: An introduction. Comment. *Journal of Sports Economics*, 4(2), 154-160.

Fort, R. (2011). *Sports economics, third edition*. Boston: Prentice Hall.

Humphreys, B. (2002). Alternative measures of competitive balance in sports leagues. *Journal of Sports Economics*, 3(2), 133-148.

Kesenne, S. (2000). Revenue sharing and competitive balance in professional team sports. *Journal of Sports Economics*, 1(1), 56-65.

Knowles, G., Sherony, F. & Haupert, M. (1992). The demand for Major League Baseball: A Test of the uncertainty of outcome hypothesis. *The American Economist*, 36(2), 72-80.

Leeds, M. & von Allmen, P. (2011). *The economics of sports, fourth edition*. Boston: Addison-Wesley.

McDonald, M. & Rascher, D. (2000). Does bat day make cents? The effect of promotions on the demand for Major League Baseball. *Journal of Sport Management*, 14, 8-27.

NationalGrid (2009, September). *Entry Charging Review*, p. 4.

Neale, W. (1964). The peculiar economics of professional sports: A contribution to the theory of the firm in sporting competition. *Quarterly Journal of Economics*, 78(February), 1-14.

Noll, R. (1974). Attendance and price setting. In *Government and the sports business* (Noll, R., editor). Washington: Brookings Institution, 115-157.

Olympic boxing results. Retrieved from www.databaseolympics.com and www.sports-reference.com/olympics/.

Rhoads, S. 1993. The Herfindahl-Hirschman Index. *Federal Reserve Bulletin*, March, 188-189.

Rosca, V. (2012). The political economy of world heavyweight boxing during the great depression. *Theoretical and Applied Economics*, 14(1), 127-142.

Rottenberg, S. (1956). The baseball players' labor market. *Journal of Political Economy*, 64(June), 242-258.

Sanderson, A. & Siegfried, J. (2003). Thinking about competitive balance. *Journal of Sports Economics*, 4(4), 255-279.

Schmidt, M. & Berri, D. (2001). Competitive balance and attendance: The case of Major League Baseball. *Journal of Sports Economics*, 2(2), 145-167.

Scully, G. (1989). *The business of Major League Baseball*, Chicago: University of Chicago Press.

Tcha, M. & Pershin, V. (2003). Reconsidering performance in the Summer Olympics and revealed comparative advantage. *Journal of Sports Economics*, 4(3), 216-239.

Tenorio, R. (2000). The economics of professional boxing contracts. *Journal of Sports Economics*, 1(4), 363-384.

Tenorio, R. (2006). On the competitive structure in professional boxing, or why the best boxers very seldom fight each other. *Handbook on the Economics of Sport* (Andreff and Szymanski, eds.). Cheltenham, UK: Edward Elgar, 364-368.

Zimbalist, A. (2002). Competitive balance in sports leagues: An introduction. *Journal of Sports Economics*, 3(2), 111-121.

Chapter 15

Can Martial Arts Training Protect from Fall Down Accidents?

Hannu Leinonen

Introduction

This is a theoretical framework on the possible benefits of Martial arts in preventing fall down accidents based on review of martial arts research literature for core strength, bone strength and balance (Leinonen 2013, Leinonen, Mälkiä 2013, Leinonen, Mälkiä et al. 2013). Falls and fall down injuries have many definitions, which complicates comparing data from various sources. A generic definition is: "An unplanned descent to the floor with or without injury. All types of falls are included, whether they result from physiological reasons or environmental reasons."(Fall and Injury Prevention - Patient Safety and Quality - NCBI Bookshelf) "No standard for defining, measuring, and documenting injurious falls could be identified among published RCTs."(Schwenk, Lauenroth et al. 2012) Fall down injuries are a serious and well recognized problem for persons over 65 years of age. Every third old person falls every year, half of the fall down accidents result in injuries, and complications increase with age. (Schwenk, Lauenroth et al. 2012, Costello 2008) In a 2-year longitudinal study within the age group of 65-years and over, 35% of the subjects reported fall down accidents, of which over 70% had lead to injuries. Within the age groups 20 – 45 and 46 – 65 years reported equal percentage of fall down accidents leading to injuries, and every fifth reported a fall down accident in a two year period. (Talbot, Musiol et al. 2005) It is obvious that fall down accidents concern all ages. Of course, the consequences of fall downs become more complicated with age. The prevention of fall down accidents should begin as early as possible.

It is difficult to find a suitable theoretical model for fall down accident prevention. Actions and situations related to accidents are versatile and accidents may not have just one cause (Katsakiori, Sakellaropoulos et al. 2009). To structure the multi-causality and versatility of the phenomena we will use a model from a Finnish road safety organisation based on a theory of internal models (Mikkonen 1980, Pidapelivaraa_engl.pdf). (Figure 1.) With small modifications the road safety model is suitable for our framework because most of fall down accidents occur when the subject is walking. "The activity most frequently cited as causing the fall was ambulation in all age-groups and both genders" (Talbot, Musiol et al. 2005). Schema theory is used in various transport domains (Plant, Stanton 2013).

Fall Down Prevention Model

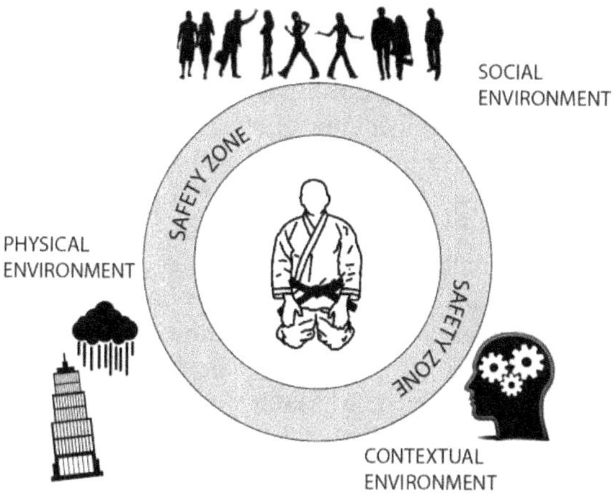

Figure 1: Fall down prevention model (modified from Mikkonen's internal models 1980)

Mikkonen's internal models are based on schema theory with three hierarchical levels of anticipation schemas: "self", "observed situation" and "planned action - goal". Starting from the centre is the first person "self". The first person has his skills, abilities and understanding of his environments - past, present and future and – also motivation and expectations of his own actions. "Safety zone" is the level of risk or barrier of time for reacting to unexpected events. Our willingness to take risks depends on the goals of our actions, but also on contextual situations (environment). Contextual environment is the assignment set to us by an external source. It can be, for instance, a work task. Tasks can affect our behaviour in different situations and also in consequences of accidents. In this model, physical environment also includes weather. One factor is social environment. The factors are separated in this model but in real life the separation is not so clear. Social environment means other people, but would bumping in to someone be a physical environment issue or a social one? At the moment it isn't relevant to categorize. The purpose of the model is to point out that accident prevention is a complicated issue. Further on we will focus on first person's skills and abilities to prevent accidents.

The original model observes accident prevention in three phases; preventing accidents, minimizing injuries and minimizing consequences after the accident has occurred. How can training martial arts help in each phase?

1. Preventing Fall Downs

Fall down accidents can be prevented by affecting external factors, the outer circle of the fall down accident prevention model, or by affecting internal factors, the safety zone and factors inside it. (Figure 1) Martial arts' training affects internal factors, which are our physical and mental abilities, understanding of situations and attitude towards safety. The fall down prevention model includes three hierarchical schemas: self, situation and goal). The "Self schema" is our own mental image of our own abilities and the awareness of our own movements. Our actual abilities affect our performance alongside the mental image we have. The accuracy of schema compared to reality is important concerning safety. Balance and agility are essential when it comes to preventing falling down. Postural control is defined as "the act of maintaining, achieving or restoring a state of balance during any posture or activity" (Pollock, Durward et al. 2000). Postural control has similarities with model of agility (Young 2002).

Experiments with elite karatekas showed that balance may get better by our neural control getting more efficient (Del Percio 2009). It might also be a more optimal control of joint stiffness and antagonist optimal tension. "Long-term Tai Chi exercisers also demonstrated different reflex modulation from a supine to standing position, and long-term Tai Chi practice may lead to a change of Paired Reflex Depression modulation as neuro-adaptation. "(Guan 2011) A review of balance ability and athletic performance is not specific to martial arts, but included judo, stated that "Balance training may lead to task-specific neural adaptations at the spinal and supraspinal levels. It may suppress spinal reflex excitability, such as the muscle stretch reflex during postural tasks, which leads to less destabilizing movements and improved balance ability." (Hrysomallis 2011)

Development of body awareness is most often the reason for better balance. We control our balance by visual information and by proprioseptic feedback. Most important is the vestibular system (Fong 2012). Some martial arts develop balance by improving non-visual sensory information; Tai Chi (Gorgy 2008, Gyllensten 2010), Karate (Violan 1997), Judo (Perrin 2002), Tae Kwon Do (Leong 2011, Hio-Teng Leong 2011). Training of exact positions or slow Tai Chi gait requires sensing your body movements and it develops proprioception. Often in Martial Arts training you cannot visually adjust your posture, but stances are very controlled. In Judo visual information may be important in higher level competitions (Paillard 2002).

Forms (katas) and basic techniques (kihon) in most martial arts are closed skills like ballet dance. Most of martial arts also include an open skill element of sparring where techniques are modified and adjusted to unpredicted situations. "Dancers train for long hours in a very stable environment (in front of a mirror, holding a ramp), then perform freely but in an unmoving space (either in the training room or on stage). They voluntarily generate their own imbalance during their complex chained dynamic choreographic figures. Conversely, both in training and in competition, judoists are constantly subjected to unexpected movements imposed by their opponent in order to make them fall on soft ground (tatami). Therefore, the good performances of judoists in unusual situations, could be due to the fact that training in martial arts develops sensorimotor adaptabilities transferable to posture control in other circumstances."(Perrin 2002)

To conclude Martial Arts can enhance postural balance by developing body awareness and strength and better balance decreases fall down accidents, but cannot prevent all of them (Kalina 2008).

Importance of developing your core muscles is very well accepted. "The importance of function of the central core of the body for stabilization and force generation in all sports activities is being increasingly recognized. 'Core stability' is seen as being pivotal for efficient biomechanical function to maximize force generation and minimize joint loads in all types of activities ranging from running to throwing."(Kibler 2006)

"Effect of swiss ball exercises on some physical and physiological variables and their relationship with kata performance level"(Nagla 2011). Nagla has constructed perfect controlled experiment training with Swiss ball, monitoring strength and improvement of Gankuka Kata performance. Study showed that core strength increased and kata performance got better. Specific core exercise can be used to develop core strength and stability, but more effective might be to disciplines that stress core muscles and do them technically correct. To sum it up "good form will develop core strength" (Leinonen 2013).

"Observed situation schema" is how we interpret current environment and our current action. Review literature of martial arts does not deal with this all that much. Martial arts might enhance timing and anticipation or other people's movements – ability to slip and duck or to react to unexpected pushes or bumps. According to myth martial arts practitioners have a higher level of awareness concerning their surroundings, hence an increased readiness to react. If this is true, it would help prevent accidents.

In reviewed literature we did not find much evidence that martial arts training makes us behave more cautious. "Planned action schema" is the decision to act and the anticipation of a movement's outcome – goal of our action. A long period of Tai chi training (more than 6 years) might change the way a person walks. Tai chi practitioners walk with shorter steps and more cautious than control group (Ramachandran 2007). Martial Arts can affect fear of falling down (Groen 2010) – the anticipation can change in some level.

2. Prevent or Minimize Consequences

To minimize consequences in falling down depends how strong are our passives subsystems like the bones, vertebrae and discs, joints and ligaments, how we can use our active subsystems – muscles and tendons and how well we are monitoring our stability and movements by central nervous system and nerves. According to Panjabi (1992) there is the neutral zone is a region of intervertebral motion around the neutral posture where little resistance is offered by the passive spinal column. Perhaps there is same zone region around passive subsystems in the whole body. The stabilizing system adjusts so that the neutral zone remains within certain physiological thresholds to avoid clinical instability. The martial arts training may help to keep neutral zone.(Panjabi 1992) One serious consequence of fall down accident is breaking bone. Can Martial Arts training strengthen bones? If you build muscle in your training, you will most likely strengthen your bones too (Rittweger 2000). Loads have to be progressive or otherwise changing to stimulate growth or bone density will decrease. "Use it or lose it" and "What you do is what you get". If the workout is challenging, you'll get results. Bone strengthening activities are full body movements, changing directions, fast, high intensity, progressive, continues and 3 times per week about 4 minutes.

It has been observed that most effective to create bone mineral density are weight bearing activities inducing gravitational loading generated as a result of impact with ground. Even such activities which are not causing muscle strength increase can produce positive effects on BMD. Example of weight bearing impact activity is running and weight lifting is weight bearing no-impact activity. Martial arts are most often weight bearing activities including impact with the ground. So many martial arts light training exercises with impact like ukemi or throws can already have positive effect to BMD. (Kohrt, Barry et al. 2009)

A very clear comprehension is that strengthening bones is most effective during growth. Youngster benefit most from bone loading physical activity, but it's also protective during later years. Most Martial Arts include throws and take downs. Breaking a fall is often one of the first techniques taught to beginners. Fall down technique can decrease impact force in hip (van der Zijden 2012, Groen 2010).Teaching breaking a fall "ukemi" has been used for accident prevention – "voluntary motor control is possible within the duration of a fall, even in inexperienced fallers" (van Swigchem 2009). Also safe fall can be learned regardless of sex, age, or body build (Kalina 2008).Save falling down technique can be learned in very short period of training (Weerdesteyn, Groen et al. 2008). Most of these studies are about Judo ukemi. Other Martial Arts have variations of breaking a fall. It would be interesting to compare different techniques and their implication to fall down prevention (Leavitt 2003). In breaking a fall it is important not to direct the force to a weak part of body like wrist. Most of the impact is absorbed by the trunk or directed in a rotational path. Redirecting an impact requires a strong core.

3. Enhance Recovery

Can training of martial arts help you to recover from strains, contusions or broken bones? Traditional martial arts were a combination of healing and damaging. Think of pressure points, they can be used both ways (McCarthy 2008). Healing or even first aid is not taught in most martial art classes, but students get some kind of knowledge how a harmless bruise feels. Major benefit for recovery comes from better fitness due to training. "Cardiorespiratory fitness is an independent predictor of mortality and length of hospital stay and provides significantly more accurate prognostic information than age alone"(Snowden 2013). Muscle strength can be an important factor too in recovery from surgery and decreasing of complications (Valkenet 2011, Logerstedt, Lynch et al. 2013). Pre-surgical exercise interventions may be considered as adjuvant therapy to improve cancer patients' outcomes (Singh 2013). It would be too simple to conclude that good physical condition translates to faster recovery. It helps, but again issue is complicated. Probably one of the most important factors in recovering from a fall down injury is attitude and routine to do required physical therapy exercises. Of course it's very personal how an individual integrates to a social group, but often martial arts clubs form a tribe which in best case scenario will support recovery.

Discussion

Does practising martial arts protect from fall down accidents? Our answer is, it protects, but cannot prevent all injuries. We have used a schema model from Finnish road safety organisation to structure the complexity of prevention of accidents. Practising martial arts addresses only a small portion of the phenomena. Schema model includes three hierarchical mental representations: self, situation and goal. Most of martial arts training benefits are to individuals' skills and abilities and accuracy of schema due to better feedback. Even thou martial arts affect only a small portion of accident prevention, it focuses on the element that is under personal own control. It's the area that we control. We can decide what to do, but we have far less control over environmental factors like weather, physical, social or contextual environment. Martial art is a large spectrum of disciplines and is practised lifelong. To be effective in protecting for injuries practitioner should keep on training to maintain a good physical condition – functional ability. We do not think that martial arts are superior in developing physical abilities to other physical activities, maybe excluding the skill to break a fall. Effectiveness of martial arts comes from personal interest. If training is appealing, it makes it effective. If you are motivated, it's a very good option for developing good balance, agility, core and bone strength and keeping flexible and rolling ukemis. Training martial arts outdoors would be more beneficial compared to a standard dojo or gym class room for fall down accident prevention[1].

References

Fall and Injury Prevention - Patient Safety and Quality - NCBI Bookshelf. Available: http://www.ncbi.nlm.nih.gov/books/NBK2653/ [6/2/2013, 2013].
Pidapelivaraa_engl.pdf. [Available: http://www.liikenneturva.fi/www/en/liitetiedostot/Pidapelivaraa_engl.pdf] [5/29/2013, 2013].
Costello, E., (2008). Update on falls prevention for community-dwelling older adults: Review of single and multifactorial intervention programs. *Journal of Rehabilitation Research & Development*, 45(8), pp. 1135-1152.
Del Percio, C. (2009). "Neural efficiency" of athletes' brain for upright standing: A high-resolution EEG study. *Brain research bulletin*, 79(3-4), pp. 193-200.
Fong, S.M. (2012). Sensory integration and standing balance in adolescent taekwondo practitioners. *Pediatr Exerc Sci*, 24(1), pp. 142.
Gorgy, O. (2008). How does practise of internal Chinese martial arts influence postural reaction control? *J Sports Sci*, 26(6), pp. 629.
Groen. B.E. (2010). Martial arts fall training to prevent hip fractures in the elderly. *Osteoporosis International*, 21(2), pp. 215-21.

---

[1] We thank KIHU - Research Institute for Olympic Sports for its support, which enabled Hannu Leinonen to work full time on this research project.

Guan, H. (2011). Effects of Long-Term Tai Chi Practice on Balance and H-Reflex Characteristics. *American Journal of Chinese Medicine,* 39(2), pp. 251-60.

Gyllensten, A.L. (2010). Stability limits, single-leg jump, and body awareness in older Tai Chi practitioners. *Archives of Physical Medicine & Rehabilitation,* 91(2), pp. 215-20.

Hio-Teng Leong (2011). Low-level Taekwondo practitioners have better somatosensory organisation in standing balance than sedentary people. *European journal of applied physiology,* 111(8), pp. 1787-1793.

Hrysomallis, C. (2011). Balance Ability and Athletic Performance. *Sports Medicine,* 41(3), pp. 221-32.

Kalina. R.M. (2008). Teaching of safe falling as most effective element of personal injury prevention in people regardless of gender, age and type of body build - the use of advanced information technologies to monitor the effects of education. *Archives Of Budo, 2008, Vol.4, pp.82-90,* 4, pp. 82-90.

Katasakiori, P. Sakellaropoulos, G. & E. Manatakis (2009). Towards an evaluation of accident investigation methods in terms of their alignment with accident causation models. *Safety Science,* 47(7), pp. 1007.

Kibler, W.B. (2006). The Role of Core Stability in Athletic Function. *Sports Medicine,* 36(3), pp. 189-198.

Kohrt, W.M. Barryy, D.W. & R.S. Schwartz (2009). Muscle Forces or Gravity: What Predominates Mechanical Loading on Bone?[Report]. *Medicine & Science in Sports & Exercise,* 41(11), pp. 2050-2055.

Leavitt, F.J. (2003). Can martial arts falling techniques prevent injuries? *Inj Prev,* 9(3), pp. 284.

Leinonen, H. (2013). Are Martial Arts good for your Core Strength. *IMAS Quarterly,* 2(1), pp. 35-42.

Leinoned, H. & E. Malkia (2013). Are martial arts good for bone strength? *IMAS Quarterly,* 2(2), pp. 35-48.

Leinonen, H., Malkia, E., & T Vanttinen (2013). Practising martial arts develops balance. *IMAS Quarterly,* 2(3),.

Leonh, H. (2011). Low-level Taekwondo practitioners have better somatosensory organisation in standing balance than sedentary people. *Eur J Appl Physiol,* 111(8), pp. 1787.

Logerstedt, D., Lynch, A., Axe, M.J. & L. Snyder-Mackler (2013). Pre-operative quadriceps strength predicts IKDC2000 scores 6 months after anterior cruciate ligament reconstruction. *The Knee,* 20(3), pp. 208-212.

McCarthy, P. (2008). *Bubishi: the classic manual of combat.* Tokyo ; Rutland, Vt.: Tuttle Pub.

Mikkonen, V. (1980). *Sisäisten mallien teoria liikennekäyttäytymisestä /.* Helsinki] : Helsingin yliopisto.

Nagla, E. (2011). Effect of swiss ball exercises on some physical and physiological variables and their relationship with kata performance level. *Journal of Physical Education & Sport / Citius Altius Fortius,* 11(1), pp. 56-64.

Paillard, T. (2002). Are there differences in postural regulation according to the level of competition in judoists? *Br J Sports Med,* 36(4), pp. 304.

Panjabi, M. (1992). The stabilizing system of the spine. Part II. Neutral zone and instability hypothesis. *Journal of Spinal Disorders.,* 5(4), pp. 390-396.

Perrin, P. (2002). Judo, better than dance, develops sensorimotor adaptabilities involved in balance control. *Gait Posture,* 15(2), pp. 187.

Plant, K.L. & N.A. Stanton (2013). The explanatory power of Schema Theory: theoretical foundations and future applications in Ergonomics. *Ergonomics,* 56(1), pp. 1-15.

Pollack, A.S. Durward, B.R., Rowe, P.J. & J.P. Paul (2000). What is balance? *Clinical rehabilitation,* 14(4), pp. 402-406.

Ramachandran, A.K., (2007). Effect of Tai Chi on gait and obstacle crossing behaviors in middle-aged adults. *Gait Posture,* 26(2), pp. 248.

Rittweger, J. (2000). Bone-muscle strength indices for the human lower leg. *Bone,* 27(2), pp. 319.

Schwenk, M., Luanroth, A., Stock, C., Moreno, R.R., McHugh, G., Todd, C., & K. Hauer (2012). Definitions and methods of measuring and reporting on injurious falls in randomised controlled fall prevention trials: a systematic review. *BMC Medical Research Methodology,* 12(1), pp. 50.

Singh, F. (2013). A systematic review of pre-surgical exercise intervention studies with cancer patients. *Surg Oncol,* 22(2), pp. 92.

Snowden, C.P. (2013). Cardiorespiratory fitness predicts mortality and hospital length of stay after major elective surgery in older people. *Ann Surg,* 257(6), pp. 999.

Talbot, L.A., Musiol, R.J., Witam, E.K., & E.J. Metter (2005). Falls in young, middle-aged and older community dwelling adults: perceived cause, environmental factors and injury. *BMC Public Health,* 5(1), pp. 86.

Valkenet, K. (2011). The effects of preoperative exercise therapy on postoperative outcome: a systematic review. *Clinical rehabilitation,* 25(2), pp. 99-111.

Van der Zijden (2012). Can martial arts techniques reduce fall severity? An in vivo study of femoral loading configurations in sideways falls. *J Biomech,* 45(9), pp. 1650.

Van Swigchem, R. (2009). The effects of time pressure and experience on the performance of fall techniques during a fall. *Journal of Electromyography & Kinesiology,* 19(3), pp. 521-531.

Violen, M.A. (1997). The effect of karate training on flexibility, muscle strength, and balance in 8- to 13-year-old boys. *Pediatric Exercise Science,* 9(1), pp. 55-64.

Weerdestyn, V., Groen, B.E., Van Swigchem, R. & J. Duysens (2008). Martial arts fall techniques reduce hip impact forces in naive subjects after a brief period of training. *Journal of Electromyography and Kinesiology,* 18(2), pp. 235-242.

Young, B. (2002). Is muscle power related to running speed with changes of direction? *Journal of Sports Medicine & Physical Fitness,* 42(3), pp. 282-8.

Chapter 16

Rhythm Skills Development in Chinese Martial Arts

Colin McGuire

'Victory is achieved in the *Heiho* of conflict by ascertaining the rhythm of each opponent, by attacking with a rhythm not anticipated by the opponent, and by the use of knowledge of the rhythm of the abstract'.

Miyamoto Musashi

Introduction

The Book of Five Rings identifies rhythm as a primary concept in not only music and dance, but also combat (1982 edition, p.24-25). A Japanese warrior named Miyamoto Musashi wrote this famous treatise on strategy, swordsmanship, and philosophy in the 17th century, but its principles remain relevant across different martial arts and even in business. Having been both a musician and martial artist for most of my life, I find that the conceptual integration of this approach forms a very compelling tactical methodology. Musical rhythm is an obvious phenomenon, but the rhythm of conflict is a somewhat subtler concept to grasp. When people engage in a physical struggle, whether real or in sport, there is an inherent regularity to the movements of attack and defense. One action leads to the next, and in a stalemate, there is a continuous, reciprocal, sequence of moves. Even when combatants are at a distance from each other, they are generally moving and vying for position, which creates a sort of deadly dance. The ability to control the timing of an altercation provides a definitive advantage, especially if opponents are evenly matched in speed, strength, and skill.

I have trained in a variety of martial arts since 1983 and have found that pedagogical methods surrounding the rhythm of conflict are largely based on practice. At Toronto's Hong Luck Kung Fu Club (康樂武館[1]) for example, once students have acquired a vocabulary of simple movements through repetitive drills, they proceed to apply what they have learned in progressively freer types of training drills and/or sparring. When a student has reached the level of application, they learn by doing and through observing their seniors. While teachers might sometimes speak generally of rhythm, timing, and pace, there is a dearth of detailed verbal instruction on rhythmic tactics. In related scholarly work, Paz-Y-Miño C. & Espinosa (2004) have argued for the use of a regular beat to assist neophyte learners of aikido in practicing their techniques, but John Donohue (2000) has noted that free sparring amongst advanced kendo practitioners occurs with a complex rhythm. In kung fu (功夫), music and dance provide one means of imparting the rhythm skills that play an important roll in bridging the gap between novice and sophisticate martial artist.

This chapter draws on my ongoing fieldwork at the Hong Luck Kung Fu Club to investigate the relationship between music and the martial arts. Although rhythm in a broad sense is ubiquitous amongst the fighting arts, the presence of actual music within such systems is somewhat less pervasive, and certainly infrequently investigated. Some notable exceptions include work being done on the Brazilian martial art of capoeira by Greg Downey (1998, 2002) and Lowell Lewis (1992). Capoeira is a more obvious example of martial arts music because it is always played to the sound of percussion and singing, but the work of these two scholars has helped to establish precedent for related ethnographic studies. The two southern Chinese kung fu styles practiced by my fieldwork consultants are *Choy Lee Fut* (蔡李佛) and *Do Pi* (道派). As an ethnomusicologist, I am applying participant observation methodology to the investigation of music as an aspect of martial culture and have been an active member of Hong Luck since 2008. The present discussion shall be purposefully limited in terms of music theory in order to address a broader audience, but will maintain an ethnographic concern for thick description.

While rhythm is an integral part of training at Hong Luck, the theory surrounding it is largely an implicit element of practice. I am proposing that by identifying methods for rhythm, similar to named methods already used for other aspects of kung fu, students will absorb these principles more easily. I draw here on the tactical games approach advocated by Kozub & Kozub (2004). They postulate that when appropriate strategies are used to structure the application of techniques, combatants understand better what they are doing and are ultimately more likely to be successful. In this case, I am making conceptually explicit what is already an implicit aspect of practice, in order to facilitate acquisition of relevant skills. When I consulted my teachers at Hong Luck regarding this paper, they were initially perplexed by my questions about a link between music and martial arts. After a bit of explanation on my part, they concurred that homologous rhythm skills are found in both, but that they had never thought of it that way. With their blessings, this paper is concerned with the investigation of concepts that pervade Hong Luck's lion dance, percussion music, and kung fu.

---

[1] The Chinese characters used throughout the text are traditional and the Romanizations are colloquial, because this reflects the practice at Hong Luck.

Admittedly, my perspective as both a martial artist and a musician predisposes me to focus on musical rhythm in kung fu. I am not, however, inventing something new, as much as suggesting a new way of understanding something old. Martial artist and movie star Bruce Lee also wrote on the subject of timing in combat and a few of his ideas have gained currency amongst martial artists. Unfortunately, much of Lee's discussion was marred by his confusing choices for terms and an overly pithy exposition (Lee 1975, p.59-68). What I bring to the matter is a musical understanding and specialized vocabulary for discussing rhythm. As a researcher, but also a respectful practitioner, I think it appropriate to formulate my observations based on extant conventions within the Chinese kung fu tradition.

Efficacy in hand-to-hand fighting is an ongoing concern for martial artists, and scholars have also done work in this area since the emergence of hoplology[2] as a nascent academic discipline in the 1970s. In recent publications, Daniele Bolelli (2003) has written on tactical evolution in the relatively new sport of mixed martial arts (MMA) and Joseph Svinth (2003) has done work on the revamped combative programs of the U.S. military. Something both MMA and armed forces martial arts have in common is their reliance on older styles of fighting as sources of techniques and tactics. Unfortunately, in the search for fighting prowess, cultural traditions are often the first thing to be ignored. The hoplological significance of this paper therefore lies not only in its contribution to knowledge of rhythm in kung fu, but also in underlining martial value in a possibly overlooked traditional practice. My teachers, however, cautioned me that introducing such theories too early in a student's training could confuse them, so *caveat lector.*

Grounded in ethnomusicology and hoplology, the present discussion aims to foster understanding of the intersection of rhythm, movement, and strategy. More specifically, and drawing on my ethnographic work in the Hong Luck Kung Fu Club, I will here argue that southern Chinese lion dance (舞獅) and percussion music disciplines the martial body with rhythm in a way that has strategic benefits. First I will provide a description of the lion dance and its music, next I will advance a theoretical frame for this discussion, and lastly I will outline a linked pair of methods for martial rhythm: 'leading' and 'following.'

Lion Dance & Kung Fu

Many diasporic Chinese kung fu clubs feature a ritual performance practice involving a 'gong and drum' percussion ensemble (鑼鼓) and two dancers animating a highly stylized lion costume. Traditional kung fu already incorporates aspects of meditation and cultural rites with self-defense, weapons, fitness, performance art, and personal development into what might be considered a "blurred genre," as proposed by anthropologist Clifford Geertz (1983). At larger kung fu clubs like Hong Luck that also feature lion dance and *sanshou* kickboxing (散手), the boundaries of martial art, sport, and ritual blur even further. Other scholars like Madeleine Slovenz-Low (1994) and Liu Wanyu (1981) have glossed over any significant relationship between lion dance and

---

[2] Hoplology is the study of human combative behavior.

kung fu, reducing it to one of physical fitness, similarity of footwork, and general martial spirit. While lion dance training certainly provides a system of strength, cardiovascular, and agility exercises, it also provides a valuable means of inculcating a sense of rhythm. This embodied knowledge can then be transferred into the practice of kung fu and allows lion dance to make an important contribution to the martial 'habitus.'

Theory

Eminent sociologist Pierre Bourdieu ascribes a functional yet non-conceptual logic to practices such as ritual and sports (1990). He argues that people embody a durable set of dispositions, which are capable of structuring their actions without conscious intention. Bourdieu calls this the habitus and provides us with a useful theoretical perspective for examining functional logic, as given in action. In regards to sport, he says "A particularly clear example of practical sense as proleptic adjustment to the demands of a field is what is called, in the language of sport, a 'feel for the game'" (1990, p.66). According to Bourdieu, the logic of practice allows a similarity of dispositions to be generalized over a range of different situations without recourse to intellectual conceptualization (1990, p.89). It is this economy of practical schema, through the habitus, that explains how rhythm skills acquired by kung fu practitioners involved with percussion music and lion dance are directly applicable to fighting.

Bourdieu cautions us to avoid assigning conceptual motivations where there is only practical logic (1990, p.86-89), but there are two phenomena in Chinese philosophy and kung fu pedagogy which belie this claim. The first is from the neo-Confucian tradition (an important influence on Chinese culture in general), which encourages searching for 'principles' (理) through a process of intuitive induction. This approach has been summarized by Cheng Chun-ying (1974) and applied to kung fu by Carl Becker (1982). A pop culture example of intuitive induction pedagogy lies in the movie *The Karate Kid* (1984). The protagonist Daniel wants to learn karate but must grudgingly polish the car of his inscrutable teacher instead. Only later does he make the conceptual link and discover that "wax on, wax off" is a manifestation of the same principle used in blocking punches.

The second phenomenon is the use of formalized 'boxing methods' (拳法) in Chinese kung fu as a pedagogical and strategic tool. Also translated as 'fist laws', these are concepts used to guide certain types of action; they are ideas that help bring techniques to life, in context. An example of an already existing boxing method is 'linked attack and defense' (連消帶打), which means to use attacks as blocks, to use blocks as attacks, or to block and attack simultaneously. The presence of named boxing methods within kung fu differs from Bourdieu's formulation of the habitus because they structure action with concepts. In regards to the rhythm of conflict, however, an unconscious logic of practice remains the primary guide.

In order to identify rhythmic methods, I will tie together habitus and principles using a method of analysis adapted from dance scholar Susan Leigh Foster. She conceives of physical cultivation systems like sport, acting, etiquette, and particularly dance, as methods of instructing the body with discourses of the self. Foster analyzes what she calls the "body-of-ideas" which is disciplined in the Foucauldian sense to embody the ideals of a system of aesthetics (1997, p.231-232). The premise is that when bodies are taught to relate time, space, and matter through specialized forms of action, there is cultivation of an identifiable model. This model is the conceptual construction of the self as a proponent of a style and informs both mental and physical action within said style. Foster focuses her analysis on the methods of instruction that inscribe the body and the types of movement that characterize the ideals of a dance form. Her approach will provide a framework for analyzing how kung fu students are taught lion dance and what this can reveal about rhythm for the ideal martial body.

Musical Terms

Before discussing the methods I am investigating, it is necessary to clarify some musical terminology used by Hong Luck's lion dance practitioners. My consultants refer to the gestalt of sonic events created by drum, gong, and cymbals colloquially as "the beat". For the purpose of specificity, I am musically separating this structure into pulse, subdivisions of pulse, tempo, rhythm, and phrase. Briefly, the pulse is the metronomic beat you tap your toe to, subdivisions are the beats that come in between the main pulses, tempo is the rate of pulse, rhythms are patterns of subdivisions, and phrases are sequences of rhythm linked together into significant sections. The concept of metre (a recurring cycle of strong and weak beats) used in Western music does not accurately apply to this music – and according to Zhang Boyu, most forms Chinese percussion music either (1997, p.58) – because rhythm patterns and the resulting phrase lengths are variable. Another expression used by lion dancers at Hong Luck is "feeling the beat". Thanks to the pedagogy of professor Steve Otto, I call the main principle that undergirds rhythm perception 'entrainment' and define it as the process that synchronizes two separate rhythmic systems. A simple example of this phenomenon is tapping one's toe to music; the beat entrains one to embody its primary pulse, allowing one to perceive its organization through one's body. The rhythms of lion dancing or of fighting are more complicated than this, but the entrainment principle involved in embodying them is the same.

Leading & Following in Lion Dance

The two tactical methods built on entrainment that I conceptualize here are 'leading' and 'following,' which I shall briefly introduce before expanding on them. The goal remains to make explicit the link between embodied knowledge gained from lion dance and its application in kung fu, in order to increase the understanding of an implicit training regime. Following rhythm allows a lion dance group to synchronize their movements with the beat, but in kung fu, it allows one to track an opponent's movements in order to defend against them and find opportunities to counter. Leading rhythm means the drummer sending aural cues to the lion dancers and the lion dancers sending visual cues to the drummer, but also means controlling an opponent's movements in order to create openings for attack. These two methods are acknowledged at Hong Luck as essential to giving a good lion dance performance because the dancers see very little from under the lion and must follow the lead of the drum. The exception to this is for certain parts of the routine where the lion leads and the drummer must follow their actions with appropriate rhythms.

All students at Hong Luck commence their training with kung fu techniques such as stances, punches, block, and kicks, which they perform following the steady count of the teacher. They must establish a base of fundamentals in the beginners' kung fu classes before advancing to intermediate classes – and intermediate rhythms – including more difficult techniques and combinations thereof, sparring, and lion dance. Not all students choose to participate in all aspects of kung fu, but to become a master there is no other way.

Lion dance training begins with learning different musical rhythms by hearing them and following along with the prescribed movements. Initially, the teacher speaks the rhythm of the drum with a loose set of vocals while guiding the learners through the footwork of the choreography, without using the mask. From there, the teacher plays the drum and the students reiterate the steps they have just been shown. Eventually the students pick up the lion costume and try to perform the sequence with it as well. The dancer who is animating the lion's head learns to track the drum by listening intently to the rhythmic patterns and coordinating movements of his[3] feet and the mask, in time with the music. Meanwhile, the performer who animates the tail learns not only to follow the rhythm aurally, but also to visually follow the movements of the dancer who is moving the head. While some rhythms have very specific steps, in other cases the head dancer is free to select from a range of variations and the tail dancer must follow along.

Soon after beginning to learn the movements of the lion dance, students also start studying the instruments of the percussion ensemble, that is to say, all lion dancers are supposed to learn the instruments and all musicians must learn the lion dance. The percussion ensemble consists of a large drum played with two short, thick, wooden sticks; a flat faced gong played with a small wooden mallet; and one or more pairs of hand-held cymbals. The first instruments to be learned are usually the cymbals, which mostly play the basic pulse. The fundamental challenge is to follow the tempo of the drum, but not (with a few exceptions) the rhythmic elaborations of the other instruments. Those playing the cymbals and the gong learn to watch the drummer for cues made by gestures of the drumsticks and listen for rhythmic or oral prompts regarding the musical structure. The gong player's instructions are to follow the drum, but also to play patterns somewhat more complicated than the cymbals. The person playing the gong is encouraged to follow the main tempo, but places accents on subdivisions that do not always coincide with the drum rhythms, which in musical terms is called syncopation. This, therefore, requires a somewhat higher degree of musicianship to perform.

In some cases, the relationship of leader and follower is reversed, so the ensemble must learn to switch quickly between whom they are following. In sections where the instruments follow the lion, the gong and cymbal players are advised to keep their eyes on the drummer for the purpose of rhythmic synchronization. In order to follow effectively in this case, they must then split

---

[3] The use of masculine pronouns is indicative of the fact that lion dancers are traditionally male. While this policy has recently been softened at Hong Luck, many clients who hire a lion dance continue to demand that it be adhered to.

their attention to also track the lion out of their peripheral vision. In another reversal of entrainment hierarchy, the drummer and gong player follow the pulse of the cymbals in improvisatory sections where they engage in a virtuosic, rhythmic duet.

In the 2000-year-old *Art of War*, Chinese military theorist Sun Tzu wrote that cymbals and drums should be used to "focus and unify people's ears" (2003, p.125). Playing these instruments in kung fu clubs today serves a similar purpose. When it comes to lion dancing, the drum is the recognized leader of the group. The pounding throb of the barrel sized drum sets not only the tempo, but also determines most of the changes between different rhythms and their associated lion movements. The drummer learns to lead the other musicians visually by giving exaggerated clues such as raising the stick extra high before a significant beat. Auditory prompts in the form of specific rhythms or shouts are also used and are part of the structure of the music, which is especially necessary for the lion dancers – who, as previously mentioned, cannot see much from underneath their costume.

In the sections where the dancers lead the musicians, the lion's movements direct the rhythm. The person animating the head accomplishes this by exaggerating certain moves as a prompt. An equally important method of leading is to hesitate or even pause to catch the attention of the drummer, which is perceived as dragging the tempo or suspending an otherwise regular and active dance. On the rare occasions when the person playing the tail leads the ensemble, they learn to do so by placing their hands on the waist of the person playing the head. The tail performer uses tactile signals such as pushing, pulling, and squeezing, to indicate how and when their partner should move for lifts and carries. The musicians are cued visually by the head dancer's responses to these ministrations.

Leading & Following in Kung Fu

Having outlined the functioning of entrainment as leading and following in lion dance, I will now proceed to discuss the same principle in combat. In identifying a latent theory in the practice of lion dance and linking it to the practice of kung fu, I am not suggesting that their rhythms are identical. Rather, there is a methodological homology between them that allows this comparison.

In combat, following is a method that has particular benefit for defence, whether at striking distance or in close range grappling. Self-defence is most effective when one anticipates the attack and is facilitated by the application of the entrainment principle; one feels the opponent's rhythm and synchronizes one's actions to it. Good following also opens opportunities to counter effectively because knowing the timing of an attack gives one the option of placing a pre-emptive or follow-up strike in an offbeat. Bourdieu might say that the habitus developed by syncopating the gong rhythm against the drum rhythm is generalizable to include fitting a counterattack into an opponent's assault. In recognizing an opponent's movement patterns, the height of following is to know what they will do a fraction of a second before they actually do it.

My kung fu teachers' explicit instruction in leading is somewhat stronger than other aspects of rhythm, though they generally still do not conceptualize it in musical terms. Feints and faking are means to lead an opponent to react. By giving a false cue such as a strike launched from slightly too far away to actually land, one is able to draw a response without having to commit oneself. Having established a rhythm through multiple fakes allows one to take advantage of the sequence one has established by attacking outside of it. This is what is called "broken rhythm" – a now-popular term introduced by Bruce Lee (1975, p.62). A similar tactic is to use combinations of real techniques in order to wear down an opponent's defence. Taken rhythmically, this means to execute a pattern of movement and strikes that leads the adversary into a vulnerable position. An alternative to leading an opponent with feints or combinations is to go where they cannot follow by using an unorthodox or complex rhythm, such as a flurry of strikes from different angles aimed at multiple targets. A final application of leading is to control the tempo, which coaches simply call aggression or pushing the pace. Even if one uses uncomplicated rhythms, a fast and sustained onslaught of attacks can overwhelm an opponent who cannot keep up.

Discussion

The fact that many diasporic kung fu clubs have a tradition of music and dance is somewhat remarkable. On the surface, it might seem that martial arts and lion dance simply happen to occur on the same premises for historical or cultural reasons but a deeper reading has turned up another interpretation. Bourdieu's idea of a durable and economical set of dispositions (the habitus) suggests that there are connections between musical rhythm and kung fu. Given that at Hong Luck the same people practice both kung fu and lion dance, the habitus thus formed should be generalizable between the two. Susan Foster's method of analyzing pedagogy in dance was applied to uncover the ideals embodied in the physical practices. I then formulated a linked pair of boxing methods for rhythm (leading and following) based on the homologies I found between martial arts and lion dance. Notwithstanding Bourdieu's insistence that the logic of practice is unconscious, this pair of concepts was styled after already established ones in the kung fu tradition.

In all fairness, alternative perspectives are possible regarding the relationship of rhythm and martial arts. Not everyone who practices lion dance at Hong Luck keeps up with his kung fu and there are kung fu practitioners who never get involved with lion dance. In other styles of martial arts where there is no musical tradition, people still develop rhythm skills and there are sometimes community groups who practice lion dance and have no ties to kung fu. I stand by my statement that martial arts are inherently rhythmic, but I am not saying that they must be musical.

The final connection between lion dance, percussion music, and kung fu is based on my experiences as a participant observer at Hong Luck. People use entrainment to synchronize their rhythms with their partners or opponents through leading and following. I am conducting ethno-musicological research, which biases me towards thinking musically but also provides a focused lens with which to view an under-researched area. My consultants concurred that there are parallels between rhythm concepts in lion dance and kung fu, but that they had never thought of fighting in musical terms. This testimony supports Bourdieu's conception of the habitus as unconscious, but does not preclude people being interested in named methods for the conscious use of rhythm skills in sparring. Victory in conflict is a primary goal of martial arts training and strategy is an important component of winning. By shedding light on competencies that people may already possess, I am assisting in the formation of tactics that build on strengths. Through Foster's method for the analysis of ideals embodied in physical training and the durability of the habitus, understanding of how musical rhythm may be applied in kung fu can be achieved.

Conclusion

As a phenomenon germane to not only music and dance, but also martial arts, Chinese kung fu clubs like Hong Luck inculcate rhythm through lion dance. I have argued in this paper that conceptualizing leading and following as methods embodied in lion dance can facilitate the acquisition of homologous skills by practitioners who also train in kung fu. With all due respect for tradition, I have chosen to identify theory that already exists in practice and phrase it as boxing methods that follow pre-existing modes of communication within kung fu.

In terms of outcomes, these concepts have been beneficial in both my own training and in teaching martial arts to others. Furthermore, I believe my analysis of the functional logic already inherent in the practice of kung fu and lion dance has heuristic value beyond the boundaries of this study, should other people choose to apply it to their own martial arts practices. The rhythm of conflict is important in any style of hand-to-hand combat; leading and following should be considered carefully by martial artists, whether or not they practice lion dancing. Finally, while some advantage may be available merely from an improved understanding of entrainment and rhythm, there is no substitute for practice. Kung fu literally means "skill achieved through effort" and to quote Goethe (often misattributed to Bruce Lee) "Knowing is not enough; we must apply. Willing is not enough; we must do".

References

Cheng, Chung-Ying. (1974). Conscience, mind, and individual in Chinese philosophy. *Journal of Chinese Philosophy,* 2, 3-40.

Becker, Carl B.. (1982). Philosophical perspectives on the martial arts in America. *Journal of the Philosophy of Sport,* IX, 19-29.

Bolelli, Daniele. (2003). Mixed martial arts: A technical analysis of the ultimate fighting championship in its formative years. *Journal of the Asian Martial Arts,* 12 (3), 40-51.

Bourdieu, Pierre. (1990). *The logic of practice.* Translated by Richard Nice. Stanford, CA: Stanford University Press. Original edition, Les Éditions de Minuit, 1980.

Donohue, John. (2000). Sound and fury: Auditory elements in martial ritual. *Journal of the Asian Martial Arts,* 9(4), 12-20.

Downey, Greg. (1998). *Incorporating capoeira: Phenomenology of a movement discipline.* Ph.D. diss, University of Chicago.

---------2002. Listening to capoeira: Phenomenology, embodiment, and the materiality of music. *Ethnomusicology*, 46(3), Autumn, 487-509.

Espinosa, Avelina and Guillermo Paz-y-Miño C. (2004). The rhythm of aikido: Part I. *Journal of the Asian Martial Arts*, 13(2), 44-62.

---------2004. The rhythm of aikido: Part II. *Journal of the Asian Martial Arts*, 13(3), 65-81.

Foster, Susan Leigh. (1997). Dancing bodies. In Jane C. Desmond (Ed.), *Meaning and motion: New cultural studies in dance* (pp. 235-258). Durham, NC: Duke University Press.

Geertz, Clifford. (1983). *Local knowledge: Further essays in interpretive anthropology.* New York: Basic Books.

Jones, David E., ed.. (2002). *Combat, ritual, and performance: Anthropology of the martial arts*. Westport, CT: Praeger.

Karate Kid, The. (1984). Directed by John G. Avildsen. Produced by Jerry Weintraub. Written by Robert Mark Kamen. USA: Columbia Pictures.

Kozub, Francis M. and Mary L. Kozub. (2004). Teaching combative sports through tactics. *Journal of Physical Education Recreation and Dance*, 75(8), 16-21.

Lee, Bruce. (1975). *Tao of Jeet Kune Do*. Santa Clarita, CA: Ohara. Lewis J. Lowell. (1992). *Ring of liberation: Deceptive discourse in Brazilian capoeira.* Chicago, IL: University of Chicago Press.

Liu, Wanyu. (1981). *The Chinese lion dance*. M.F.A. thesis. York University.

Miyamoto, Musashi. (1982). *The book of five rings.* Translated by Nihon Services Corporation. New York, NY: Bantam. Original edition, Japan: letter to Terao Magonojo, 1645.

Slovenz-Low, Madeline. (1994). *Lions in the streets: A performance ethnography of Cantonese lion dancing in New York City's Chinatown*. Ph.D. diss. New York University.

Sun, Tzu. (2003). *The art of war: Complete texts and commentary*. Translated by Thomas Cleary. Boston, MA: Shambala Books. Original edition circa 6th century B.C.E.

Svinth, Joseph R.. (2003). Martial arts meets the new age: Combatives in the early twenty-first century military. In Thomas A. Green and Joseph R. Svinth (Eds.), *Martial arts and the modern world* (pp. 263-270). Westport, CT: Praeger.

Zhang, Boyu. (1997). *Mathematical rhythmic structure of Chinese percussion music: An analytical study of shifan luogu collections*. Ph.D. diss. Turku University.

Part IV: Boxing

Chapter 17
Professional Boxing: Law and Self-regulation

Ian Warren

Introduction

From the mid-19th century, modern western legal processes have had an uneasy relationship with professional boxing or 'prize-fighting'. The historical paradox between criminal prohibitions designed to stamp out competitive boxing and the widespread cultural appeal of fight sports, is perhaps best encapsulated by the words of Sir Arthur Conan Doyle. The juxtaposition of the police inspector's respectable legal aura against the passion of observing a skilful athletic contest illustrates paradox between the protective motives of the criminal law and the emergence of combat as a legitimate sporting custom.

> "The inspector fell in with the procession, and proceeded, as they walked up the hill, to bargain in the official capacity for a front seat, where he could safeguard the interests of the law, and in his private capacity to lay out thirty shillings at seven to one …". (Conan Doyle [1899] 1996: 43).

Prohibitions on assault, battery, public disorder and gambling ensured prize-fighting was a common target of the criminal law until the start of the 20th century. However, criminal prohibition had a limited impact in quelling a popular and highly lucrative professional sport. Most debates focus on whether boxing is a breach of the criminal prohibitions on assault, battery, public disorder and gambling (Gunn and Ormerod 2000; Anderson 2010). However, a more appropriate focus would examine not the overall legality of the sport, but the attitude of police in determining whether a contest warranted formal criminal prosecution. In England and Australia, the lack of reported criminal prosecutions after 1882 suggests competitive boxing for reward, sparring and amateur contests were clearly legal. Only express legislative prohibitions against prize-fighting common to many North American states in the late-19th and early 20th centuries (Million 1938-9), unambiguously prohibited the practice directly. Most prosecutions targeting competitive boxing appear to be a testing ground for the reach of the criminal law. While courts occasionally upheld the legal validity of that test (*R. v. Coney and others* 1882), history shows that private and public boxing clubs promoted a 'scientific' appreciation of the art of physical combat, giving legal legitimacy to a morally contentious sport and ensuring that the risk of physical injury or death would be more common 'from the blow of a cricket ball ... than from a blow of a glove' (*R. v. Young and others* 1866).

The development of a complex self-regulating framework ensures boxing is a popular, lucrative and comparatively safe professional sport. The existence of multiple legal structures cannot possibly eliminate all risks of physical injury, death, or activities that compromise integrity and 'fair play'. However, the history of external legal intervention in professional boxing in the United Kingdom (Anderson 2010) and the United States (Warren 2009) has simultaneously uncovered and perpetuated several profound deficits in the self-governing arrangements in professional boxing. If the objectives of controlled physical combat are to promote positive mental and physical self-development, respect for opponents, healthy athletic competition and transparent management practices, it is arguable that external law has had limited impact in influencing the self-regulatory customs in professional fight sports. In fact, the history of boxing litigation reveals the formal legal system will only proactively overturn decisions relating to the sport's governance when these appear to conflict with other external legal or social requirements.

This chapter provides a truncated description of judicial approaches to scrutinising the regulation of professional boxing throughout the 20th century. The cases are part of a broader sample of two-hundred reported decisions that document the evolution of boxing law between 1805 and 2003 in the United States, Great Britain, Australia, Canada and New Zealand (Warren 2009). These rulings indicate the dominant yet largely misplaced emphasis on boxing as a potential form of criminal violence, underscores a more complex self-regulatory framework that invokes the selective exclusion of certain populations of athletes, while sanctioning various exploitative management and promotional practices. At times, the law strives to correct these errors. However, the overwhelmingly 'hands-off' approach has allowed anomalies in internal governance arrangements to subsist or become entrenched. The argument proceeds in two parts. The first involves a description of licensing bans targeting athletes who are potentially vulnerable to serious injury. The second documents the reluctance of formal law to question licensing rules that facilitate conflicts of interest and other contentious managerial and promotional arrangements. The chapter concludes by suggesting the reluctance of the law to encourage more rigorous scrutiny of fight governance arrangements will invariably sanction the closer surveillance of athletes and their welfare in future.

Safety through Exclusion

As early as 1914, the New York Supreme Court validated a decision by the New York State Athletic Commission (NYSAC) to reject an application for a professional boxing license to protect an applicant from permanent physical injury. Former heavyweight champion 'Ruby' Bob Fitzsimmons, who successfully defended criminal manslaughter charges after his drunken opponent died during an exhibition contest in 1894 (*People v. Fitzsimmons* 1894), sought a license 'to box any person deemed suitable' (Warren 2009, p. 93). Aged fifty-one at the time of the appeal, and with a history of over 390 professional contests, the court affirmed the Commission's legislative authority to prevent any licensed boxing venue from allowing Fitzsimmons to compete. Judicial intervention was only permissible if it was clear the Commission acted 'arbitrarily or capriciously' in denying Fitzsimmons' application. The regulatory structure:

> "... was designed to impose such restrictions upon boxing and sparring contests as would promote its development as a sport, while at the same time this control should be so exercised that certain brutal or dangerous features which have sometimes attended such contests should, as far as possible, be done away with....".

> (Fitzsimmons v. New York State Athletic Commission 1914, p. 835).

This ruling formed the legal basis for endorsing a boxing Commission's decision to reject a manager's license, which in turn could render any contract with a licensed fighter 'null and void' (No author 1942, p. 473). Legally, this preserves a Commission's self-regulatory powers to enforce rules authorised by public legislation, a common framework for regulating professional boxing in the United States and Australia. The United Kingdom adopts an equivalent structure under a private regulatory model (Anderson 2010), which has developed equivalent licensing requirements endorsed by judicial decisions. Courts rarely overturn decisions made under these legally valid self-governing arrangements. For example, English courts validated a decision of the British Boxing Board of Control (BBBC), the private variant of the NYSAC, to withhold agreed match payments under a professional fight contract that could have been technically invalidated because the unpaid fighter was a minor at the time they were signed.

> "Boxers in case of disqualification are only entitled to receive bare travelling expenses, pending the decision of the board or branch on the circumstances of the case, when the board or branch may deal with money as it thinks fit".

> (Doyle v. White City Stadium Limited 1935, pp. 112-113).

The pattern of judicial non-interference is relatively consistent, even if the rules of professional boxing are the product of legislation or private self-governance arrangements. The New Zealand Boxing Association, a private authority, was thus legally justified in requesting a licensed 'athlete who acquired something of a reputation as a trouble maker' to 'show cause' for his threatening behaviour towards a group of visiting Fijian competitors. Interestingly, the professional licensing ban did not prevent this athlete's subsequent registration by the sport's amateur licensing authority (*Stininato v. New Zealand Boxing Association* 1978).

The 'hands-off' approach to reviewing the legality of certain fight rules and their enforcement can produce restrictive prohibitions. Eighty-eight years after the protective ruling in *Fitzsimmons* (1914), an Australian court upheld a decision to deny a professional fighter's license to a person who was 'not registered with the Authority in the calendar year immediately preceding his thirty-sixth birthday'. The athlete's 'ability, both medically and otherwise, to engage in professional boxing was not at issue' (Warren 2009, p. 253). This protective logic translates into rules preventing women from professional competition, even in the face of countervailing human rights provisions designed to prevent sex discrimination. The questionable legal endorsement of moral objections to the 'spectacle of women attacking each other' in competitive boxing and kickboxing, reinforces paternalistic assessments of biological difference to prevent 'injury to the reproductive organs and ... an unborn foetus if a women [sic] were pregnant at the time' of competition (*Ferneley v. Boxing Authority of New South Wales* 2001, p. 741; Warren 2009, p. 249). However, these prohibitionist rationales are not universally accepted. Twenty-six years before the Federal Court of Australia's contentious ruling, New York courts were not prepared to 'hold that women should be precluded from professionally exploiting whatever skills or aptitude they may have in the sport of boxing merely because they are women' (*Garrett v. New York State Athletic Commission* 1975, p. 798).

This contradiction illustrates the highly discretionary nature of formal legal approaches in determining the validity of rules designed to include or exclude participation in professional combat sports. Perhaps the most contentious examples of non-intervention, which persisted at least until 1954, involved the false presumption that inter-racial competition would somehow undermine public order. The formalization of inter-racial bans extended to a United States federal prohibition on the importation or public display of any prize-fight films during the era of Jack Johnson's reign as the first African-American world heavyweight title holder (Warren 2005). Such exclusions sought to prevent 'copy cat' violence by exuberant film viewers rather than to protect actual or aspiring athletes. By the mid-1950s, this protective logic as enshrined in Texas law was deemed unconstitutional by United States federal courts. Interestingly, the court's reliance on 'undisputed' evidence 'that Negro and white professional players have engaged in the same baseball, basketball and football contests in Texas and that no disturbance due to such mixed contests ever occurred' (*I.H. "Sporty" Harvey v. M.B. Morgan* 1954, p. 623) inadvertently reinforces the idea that popular fight-sports have the potential to undermine public order.

Regulating Integrity

In May 2013, the Premier of the Australian state of Victoria expressed his 'fury' over a unanimous decision by the Professional Boxing and Combat Sports Board to grant a promoter's license to a high profile underworld figure. The Board did not consider 'a criminal record that includes illegal gambling, deception, assaulting police, reckless conduct endangering life and burglary' (Campbell and Dowsley 2013) warranted rejecting the application, as internal regulatory oversight would be sufficient to 'police' the applicant. Much public 'outrage' concerned whether the Board should adopt a 'fit and proper person' test that would effectively preclude registration to anyone with a criminal history from involvement in professional fight sports. While 'the fighter is the servant of managers and matchmakers and is the puppet of promoters' (*Oma v. Hillman Periodicals Inc. et al* 1953, p. 723), the emphasis on an individual's prior criminal history overlooks the reality that many contentious management practices have long been accepted by the rules of professional boxing.

All managers and promoters must be licensed under both public or private regulatory models. However, there is limited transparency or 'strict financial disclosure' of contractual and financial arrangements that contribute to the 'oppressive dominance' of athletes (Anderson 2010, p. 185). Regulatory anomalies that encourage exploitative management relationships are open to various sites of external legal review, although contentious rules that allow conflicts of interest and other contentious business arrangements are often legitimised by judicial decisions. While such behaviour is clearly unacceptable in other business fields, 'the increased likelihood of criminal identities and groups interacting with professional athletes and the potential exploitation of these relationships for criminal purposes' (Australian Crime Commission 2013, p. 31) raises numerous questions over integrity in sports management and broader governance processes. Professional boxing offers a pertinent window into governance practices that compromise notions of fair play and athlete welfare that are either immune from systematic external oversight or actively encouraged by the lax enforcement of internal regulatory and licensing requirements.

One key site of vulnerability or potential corruption involves organised match fixing. The 1950s was a particularly torrid era for professional boxing in the United States, with numerous legal cases examining the relationship between match-fixing, deficits in the licensing process and the infiltration of organised crime syndicates in the sport's governance. The link between match-fixing and lucrative betting industries was a particular focus for the greedy or entrepreneurial promoter. Invariably, while athletes could receive considerable short-term financial benefit, there was no guarantee that even the most meticulously rehearsed outcome would go specifically to plan.

> "... [W]hile these parties were in this room the plan of throwing the fight was arranged and it was practiced for Scott and Buchanan to square it off and then the promoter was to step in between them and as he did so Scott was to step back and at this time the other fighter was to throw a punch at Scott and Scott was to go down. All of this was to occur in the third round. This procedure was rehearsed there in the hotel room. Scott further testified that it was arranged between him ... and the promoter for him, Scott, to receive his share of the gate receipts plus one-third of the bets put down. The plaintiff in error was to make the bets. Scott testified that the fight did end in the third round as planned, but that he received a broken vertebra in his neck, which was not planned". (*Casone v. State* 1952, p. 24).

Unlike competitive team sports, it is theoretically easier for two combatants to pre-determine an outcome. However, the prospect of match-fixing is directly linked to the relatively limited number of elite managers or promoters within the fight industry, and the lucrative nature of gaming and other forms of fight revenue. There is considerable demand from actual or aspiring athletes to align themselves with high-profile elite managers and promoters with a track record of success. This market reality provides the setting for various forms of athlete exploitation that are reinforced by several anomalies licensing rules that legitimize conflicts of interest and other forms of malpractice with the potential to compromise integrity in combat sports.

Commonly, a licensing authority must provide reasons for rejecting a management or promotional license. This requirement can be waived where there is clear evidence that the manager 'is dishonest or a drunkard' or:

> "……….suffers from physical or mental ill-health, or is too young, or too inexperienced, or too old, or simply lacks the personality or strength of character required for what no doubt may be an exacting occupation … in most cases the more demanding and responsible the occupation for which the licence is required, the greater will be the part likely to be played by considerations of general suitability of the applicant, as distinct from the mere absence of moral or other blemishes. The more important these general considerations are, the less appropriate does it appear to be to require the licensing body to indicate to the applicant the nature of the 'case against him'.
>
> (McInnes v. Onslow Fane and another 1978, pp. 220-221).

Where no reasons are provided to explain why a license application has been rejected, the case is more likely to be challenged in court. However, it is rare for the court's to overrule a valid licensing decision. When two licensed managers were accused of 'assaulting a referee during a contest at Madison Square Garden on 11 January 1952', and one failed to appear at a NYSAC preliminary hearing, the court, rightly, endorsed the Commission's decision to permanently revoke their professional management licenses (*Eboli v. Christenberry et al.* 1952). However, such decisions only apply in the state where the ban is imposed. Thus, it is technically possible for a manager banned in one jurisdiction to obtain a valid license in another in absence of a truly national (Anderson 2010, pp. 74-75) or transnational regulatory structure.

The external scrutiny of complex fight management contracts raises several additional problems. While all managers, promoters, other fight personnel and contracts relating to major professional contests must conform to licensing requirements, courts are generally reluctant to overturn a Board or Commission ruling to accept or reject a questionable fight arrangement. This principle also applies to remedying any anomalies in licensing rules, or overturning the decisions of statutory or private authorities to reject management contracts, even if, logically, such contracts are designed to directly subvert the regulatory process. One interesting example from the 1940s challenged the decision of the NYSAC to reject a series of contracts for a professional contest that appeared to deliberately flout each of the Commission's rules. The case involved a single contract appointing two managers, instead of the lodgment of separate contracts for each manager. It also provided for higher management fees than those stipulated by the NYSAC's legislative requirements. The court emphatically rejected the claim that the errant contracts were business dealings technically independent of the mandatory licensing regime, because they still involved the organization of a professional boxing contest that must conform to NYSAC's rules. Failure to ensure all managerial contracts are 'filed with the Commission for approval' means they will be declared 'null and void if at any time during its term the manager is not duly licensed by the Commission' (*Casarona v. Pace et al* 1940, p. 727). This essentially invalidates both the contest and the contracts that enable the illicit fight to occur.

> "If a contract which conflicts with the statute and rules in all those respects can be stamped as legal, it seems to me that the entire system of regulation so carefully worked out by the Legislature and the Commission is made a dead letter and practically repealed". (*Baski v. Wallman et al # 2* 1946, p. 31).

Difficulties have arisen in such arrangements under BBBC rules, which enable the dual licensing of fight managers and promoters. Such arrangements have been justified due to the small number of elite professional fight managers in the United Kingdom from the mid-1980s, even though dual licensing was prohibited in the early post-war period. Increased tax liabilities on fight promotions led to demand from within the fight industry for managers to simultaneously have the right to be licensed as promoters (Greenfield and Osborn 1995, pp. 162-163). This arrangement means the interests of the athlete can be subverted by financial gains for the manager as promoter. Two significant legal rulings in the late 1980s challenged the ethics of these arrangements, particularly as young aspiring professional fighters 'unaccustomed to dealing with formal written contracts' are generally ill-equipped to 'bargain on a basis of equality with the managers and promoters with whom they deal' (*Watson v. Prager and another* 1991, p. 493; Warren 2009, pp. 41-43). However, both judicial rulings provided conditional endorsement of BBBC rules that permit dual licensing and the contractual arrangements that enable management and promotional conflicts, because the alternative was to allow for a professional fighter to either remain unmanaged, or to resort to an unlicensed arrangement. These rulings indicate that courts are caught between preserving the integrity of licensing as a process, and upholding the legal validity of rules that undermine athlete welfare by promoting conflicts of interest. It is simply untenable to allow an athlete to seek be managed by someone not endorsed by the licensing authority, hence the conflict is tolerated.

Potential conflicts of interest are by no means unique to the smaller professional fight markets in the United Kingdom or Australia. Perhaps the most contentious promotional dispute involved world-heavyweight challenger James 'Buster' Douglas and Don King, who is considered to have systematically 'exploited the operation of boxing contracts … usually by coercing boxers' into accepting reduced offers for payment (Anderson 2010, p. 160) or signing contracts with restrictive 'first-option' clauses compelling the athlete to compete in subsequent bouts against a fighter in King's stable. On 11 February 1990, Douglas surprisingly defeated title-holder Mike Tyson in Tokyo. King's reaction placed immense pressure on boxing officials to consider the 'monstrous contention that by failing to be precise in his counting the referee had permitted a knockout in the eighth [round] which invalidated a total demolition of Tyson in the tenth' (McIlvanney 1996, p. 203). One of the rulings examining the legal validity of the first-option clause to be invoked after this surprise result highlights King's anger.

> "....King became excited ("jubilant") when Tyson knocked Douglas down, yelling words to the effect that the "fight was over." ... Douglas then got up from the count, causing King to say to the head of the World Boxing Council in loud and profane language, that the referee was "getting his man beat," that the "fight was over" and that it ought to be stopped. King returned to his seat mid-way through the ninth round, World Boxing Council official having taken no action to stop the fight nor having said anything to King. In the tenth round, Tyson was knocked out by Douglas, ending the fight".
>
> (Don King Productions Inc. v. Douglas, Johnson, Golden Nugget Inc. and the Mirage Casino Hotel #3 1990, pp. 766-767).

The complex claims and counter-claims included allegations of defamation, contractual impropriety, conflicting payment agreements and the questionable ability of lucrative multi-million-dollar promotions monopolies to protect the welfare of athletes. All rulings ultimately validated King's arguments and reinforced his influence over fight management and promotions in the United States (Warren 2009, p. 195-198). After losing his title in three rounds to Evander Holyfield later that year, Douglas promptly retired to live from earnings most professional fighters never see. These outcomes indicate that formal law is simply 'part of a conversation' about how complex 'organisational cultures ... are formed, legitimated and sustained' in any self-regulating field (O'Kelly and Wheeler 2012, p. 472).

Conclusions

Just as professional boxing evaded the reach of the criminal law throughout the 19th century, the self-regulating approach to contemporary fight governance is only rarely open to critical judicial review. The formal legal system adopts a 'hands off' approach that is likely to validate tighter surveillance of athletes in future, through the introduction of biological passports and other rule modifications (Anderson 2010, pp. 180-185), rather than greater scrutiny of questionable fight management practices, promotional arrangements and the more rigorous enforcement of public or private licensing requirements. The cases documented in this chapter reveal courts are unwilling to overturn the questionable elements of fight governance under a self-regulatory philosophy. This means any attempts to resolve conflicts of interest and other exploitative management practices are only likely to have merit if they are introduced from within, rather than by way of external requirements determined by the courts, legislation or increased policing activity.

References

Anderson, J. (2010). *The Legality of Boxing: A Punch Drunk Love?* Routledge, London.

Australian Crime Commission (2013). *Organised Crime and Drugs in Sport: New Generation Performance and Image Enhancing Drugs and Organised Criminal Involvement in their Use in Professional Sport*. Commonwealth of Australia. Canberra.

Baski v. Wallman et al # 2 (1946). 63 NYS 2d 26-33.

Campbell, J. and Dowsley, A. 2013. Fury as Mick Gatto wins boxing license. *Herald Sun*, 17 May at http://www.heraldsun.com.au/news/law-order/fury-as-mick-gatto-wins-boxing-licence/story-fni0fee2-1226644816613.

Casone v. State (1952). 246 SW 2d 22-28.

Casarona v. Pace et al. (1940). 22 NYS 2d 726-728.

Conan Doyle, A. (1899: 1996). *The Original Illustrated Arthur Conan Doyle*, Castle Press, New Jersey.

Don King Productions Inc. v. Douglas, Johnson, Golden Nugget Inc. and the Mirage Casino Hotel #3 (1990). 742 F Sup 741-777.

Doyle v. White City Stadium Limited (1935). 1 KB 110-117.

Eboli v. Christenberry et al. (1952). 114 NYS 2d 311-314.

Ferneley v. Boxing Authority of New South Wales (2001). 191 ALR 739-758.

Fitzsimmons v. New York State Athletic Commission (1914). 15 Misc 2d 831-836.

Garrett v. New York State Athletic Commission (1975). 300 NYS 2d 795-798.

Gunn, M. and Ormerod, D. (2000). Despite the law: Prize-fighting and professional boxing. Chapter 2 in S. Greenfield and G. Osborn (Eds.), *Law and Sport in Contemporary Society*, (21-50). Frank Cass, London.

Greenfield, S. and Osborn, G. (1995). A gauntlet for the glove: The challenge to English boxing contracts. *Marquette Sports Law Journal*, 6(1): 153-171.

I.H. "Sporty" Harvey v. M.B. Morgan (1954) 272 SW 2d 621-627.

McIlvanney, H. (1996). *McIlvanney On Boxing*, Mainstream Publishing, Edinburgh.

McInnes v. Onslow Fane and another (1978). 3 All ER 211-224.

Million, E.M. (1938-39). The enforceability of prize-fight statutes. *Kentucky Law Journal*, 27(2): 152-168.

No author (1943). Recent decisions: Administrative law – Power of Commission to declare contracts void under licensing statute. *Columbia Law Review*, 42(3): 473-475.

O'Kelly, C. and Wheeler, S. (2012). Internalities and the foundations of corporate governance. *Social and Legal Studies*, 21(4): 469-489.

Oma v. Hillman Periodicals Inc. et al (1953). 118 NYS 2d 720-726.

People v. Fitzsimmons (1894). 34 NYS 1102-1114.

R. v. Coney and others (1882). 8 QBD 534-570.

R. v. Young and others (1866). 10 Cox CC 371-373.

Stininato v. New Zealand Boxing Association (1978) 1 NZLR 1-30.

Warren, I. (2005). 'Papa' Jack and US Federal interventions. *Entertainment and Sports Law Journal*, 3(1): at http://www2.warwick.ac.uk/fac/soc/law/elj/eslj/issues/volume3/number1/warren/.

Warren. I. (2009). *Outlaw Governance: Boxing and Western Law*, VDM Verlag, Saarbrucken.

Watson v. Prager and another (1991). 3 All ER 487-510.

Chapter 18
Democratizing the Noble Art

Kath Woodward

Introduction

This chapter explores some of the democratic possibilities of boxing which include those for the participation of women and men not traditionally part of hegemonic masculinity in the sport, using the example of western boxing to consider boxing and culture, and especially the links between boxing and cultural forms like film and art (Woodward, 2006). Joyce Carol Oates famously stated that boxing is not drama; it is real and argued that watching boxing on television or at the cinema was a sanitised, poor substitute for actually being there (Oates, 1987). I want to argue that what is so special about boxing is that it is both real and drama and the intensities of boxing are such that the sport can create all sorts of possibilities. Far from being fixed and embedded in traditions, although there are plenty of conventions and traditions in boxing, it also carries the promise of change. Boxing has been called the Noble Art ever since the Marquis of Queensberry's rules were implemented in the second half of the nineteenth century and transformed the sport from prize fighting into something more socially acceptable. This is the conventional wisdom about the civilising process (Elias, 2000), but there is more to the nomenclature. Boxing lends itself to cultural representation which makes and remakes the democratic social inclusion practices of the gym and translates them into cultural forms, like film. Boxing, more than many sports have attracted interpretation into artistic and cinematic forms. The best films about sport have often been what are called boxing films, although such a genre is rarely, if ever, only about boxing. There is something about boxing which inspires and generates films and dramatic representation.

Boxers become part of the popular imagination through their place in movies, whether they are actual fighters or fictional ones like Rocky Balboa, a film character albeit reputedly based on the actual boxer, Chuck Wepner. Some boxers might have passed into cultural oblivion, apart from the memories of the boxing cognoscenti, if it had not been for cinematic representation. Were it not for Robert de Niro's Academy Award winning performance and Martin Scorsese's direction of *Raging Bull*, Jake la Motta might not be still remembered (Tosches, 1997) and if he were his memory would not invoke sophisticated artistic cinematic techniques but probably more technologies of brutish violence. Cinema plays an important role in the re-configuration of heroes and boxing heroes and villains are always implicated in the social and cultural processes through which they are constituted. It is difficult to disentangle the affects of the mechanisms of cinematic reproduction from the materials and objects, here which make up boxing, which are reproduced. What is real is implicated in both.

The emotions which bind boxing fans and the glue of boxing culture are based on memory as well as hopes and dreams. These affects are wound up in the 'real time' of the event, for example of the big fight, which condenses memories of past achievements and failures, the intensities of the moment and the aspirations of futurity (Woodward, 2012b). Memory, re-making and re-stating of the past matters enormously in sport, not least in boxing. Sensation involves emotional encounters which are enfleshed in the relationship between flesh, muscle, sweat, sound, gloves, ropes and the ring itself which can be translated into film. In boxing, flesh has specific capacities and properties which contribute to sensory processes. Flesh and sentience are also implicated in the processes of constructing and regulating authenticity in the reality of being there (Sobchack, 2004). Response to film bridges the gap between film text and spectator through vision, visibility and embodiment, The whole event of the film, as of the fight, is sensory through the organisation of light, movement and matter (Deleuze, 1996, 2002) as in art and expressive systems, which boxing is as drama and as an enfleshed event.

Films and even stage drama seek to recapture the intensities of boxing through different technologies but the interrelationship between actors and performers and spectators and the processes involved are similar. This is evident in the performance of Bryony Lavery's 2010 stage play *Beautiful Burnout* about the three seconds when a boxer drops his guard and the hammer blow which knocks him out is delivered. The play uses movement and movement images and the mobilities of light to create the sensation of the punch and the drama of the play, which is condensed into a limited period of time for the duration of the play and mirrors the duration of the fight.

Boxing films are concerned with the making of heroes, usually through the trope of masculinity. Boxing masculinity is also constituted in relation to femininity through the inclusion of actual women in the narrative or of recognisably feminine traits and attributes and the status of femininity within the fight film genre. This raises questions about the spaces occupied by femininity in these stories of heroic masculinity. Valerie Walkerdine argues that the narrative is central to embodied experience-of the film and of the spectator, however exaggerated the storyline, such as some of the films of the Rocky series (Walkerdine, 1984). Boxing does have the capacity to create alternatives; for example Leila Ali was made through the associations with her heroic father, the legendary Muhammad Ali, as well as through her sporting success; kinship ties are widely enmeshed in the generation of consistencies in boxing. Leila Ali is imbricated in the mix of kinship and family and caught up in the legend that is her father, but she is also part of a sport in which she demonstrated a high degree of competence; it is troubling in some ways but also celebratory of a strong black woman who has been part of the endurance of boxing's power and is part of its transformations. Film is not far removed from the performance of everyday life. In the gym, what matters are the embodied practices of boxing, not who you are outside the gym? Gyms have more recently become formally more gender inclusive and dropped the ban on women boxers. The acceptance of women's boxing as an amateur sport in the Olympics in 2012 means that there are more young hopefuls across the world, even in the powerfully patriarchal Afghanistan, where boxing might be a site of some cultural change.

A Bloody Canvas

I was involved in the process of making a film for the Irish television broadcaster RTÉ, in 2010 which provided some insights into the processes through which boxing is represented and how boxing culture is made. *A Bloody Canvas* (RTÉ, 2010) which was designed to bring together the energies and technologies of art and boxing was directed by Alan Gilsenan and produced by Martin Mahon. This was not an experience of mainstream cinema, but an innovative journey through art and boxing through the life experience of the artist (and former boxer) Sean Scully. The film presents an idiosyncratic journey into the world of the ring by the internationally-renowned abstract painter Sean Scully, who has sustained an interest in boxing and boxers since his childhood in post-war East London and has himself practised both boxing and martial arts. Although the film is primarily concerned with the points of connection between art and boxing, it aims to capture the specificities of boxing, its particular capacities and its enduring appeal. This is effected through conversations, often reinstating the conventional patriarchal networks of older men who reconstruct memories of boxing histories, but these forces are disrupted by different interventions, for example through abstract art, less predictable voices and even eccentric practices. One of the most notable of these eccentricities is probably the Sheffield based Irish trainer Brendan Ingle's Chaplin like dance at the end of the film, which transforms into a parody of the British comic duo, Eric Morecombe and Ernie Wise, who always concluded their television comedy show by they turning their backs to camera and moving away, each kicking their legs sideways in an absurd, affectionately comic performance which captures some of the democratic dimensions of boxing through humour. Boxing is not all 'dark trade' (McRae, 2005). The composition of the film was eclectic and aimed to present an off centre take on boxing, which probably accounts in part for my role in the film too.

As a woman in a largely male assemblage of practitioners and aficionados, my presence was disruptive. It has always been my experience in the research process as a specifically gendered body that I am situated (Woodward, 2008). The sex gender of the researcher is not always marked in sport, even though whether the researcher is identified as male or female is often crucial both to gaining access to the research site and to the relationship between the researcher and the subjects of research (Wacquant, 2004 Woodward, 2008); notably, in sport, through unstated collusions of networks of masculinity (Connell, 1995). Being a woman was more important than whether I had ever boxed or not; if I had boxed I could only have been included as woman boxer and not as part of the networks of hegemonic masculinity than dominates the field. Even the artist Sean Scully had boxed; as is so often the claim of those who occupy the peripheries of boxing and whose central identity is not categorised as being that of a boxer and, of course, by most male researchers (Wacquant, 2004). I was temporarily part of the network as a fan and as a sympathetic commentator. I was interviewed in the gym where I have carried out some of my work and most of this material was included in the film which moved between different locations and images, for example of art work which speaks to boxing in different ways, either abstract as in Scully's own work or through an assemblage of narrative, experience and visual images such as the planes of light and dark in the work of Caravaggio or the dramatic homo eroticized sculptures of Robert Mapplethorpe. There are slippages between what is homo-social and what is homoerotic in boxing.

The focus of the film was on synergies between art and boxing explored by framing elements of the combination of energies and intensities of each field. The film uses the iconography of the ring as a framed space. As David Chandler argues each boxing match is a picture with the ring as frame (1996:13). This frame however carries the movement of the picture image, making it a series of separate still shots (Deleuze, 1983). Scully also visited the world-famous Petronelli Gym in South Boston where Scully talked to Kevin McBride, the Irishman who beat Tyson in the last fight of his career. The ring is acknowledged as the frame of the event as an iconic frame embodying the endurance of boxing legends in an iconography which is shared by the gym in cases such as this. Art plays an important part in the film, at some points with direct links to boxing. The notion of representational art underpins another conversation, located in New York, where Scully interviewed LeRoy Neiman whose reputation as a boxing painter has had considerable influence through the second half of the twentieth century and into the twenty first century. Scully is filmed in his own studio in Ireland and then in Rome, where the artist Caravaggio, himself a pugilist and street fighter. Caravaggio's life story of street fighting lends another strand to the mix of fine art and the art of boxing, the Noble Art, in the film. Scully draws analogies between the artist and the fighter and argues that the fighter like the warrior is always ready to fight (RTÉ, 2010) for example in his paintings of David and Goliath. Caravaggio's own violence on the street is used to situate some of the different materialities that intersect; the regulatory mechanisms of boxing and the brutalities inside and outside that framework. Caravaggio's preoccupation with the depiction of enfleshed sensation and the celebration of erotic masculinity, on occasion through cutting and damaging male flesh invokes the stark contrasts of boxing; the black background, visceral simplicity and flat sculptural moments where miracular moments are made permanent. This resonates with Deleuze's argument about Francis Bacon's paintings, in which he suggests that the essence of painting is experienced as rhythm. 'Rhythms and rhythms alone become characters, become objects. Rhythms are the only characters, the only Figures' (2002: xxxii). Thus Bacon's accomplishment, according to Deleuze, is to show that painting offers a virtual surface for the expression of a logic of sensation that may be the most conducive surface for doing so, at least at the time Bacon was painting.

The Robert Mapplethorpe exhibition in the UK (also in Sheffield at the time) and images of Mapplethorpe's work are presented in contrast to other material but also as unmediated sensation which generates instabilities in much the same ways as boxing can. Boxing is contradictory; it is a skilled and disciplined noble art and also at the same time an affront to civilized society. It is a source of liberation for many practitioners and yet at the same time subject to calls for a ban. These images are underpinned by the connections to homoeroticism. Some sensualities that are more accepted in the art gallery than the gym but the points of connection are visualized as unmediated sensation. There are debates about the homoerotic dimensions of boxing, in film (James, 1996) and in lived experience (Spencer, 2012) but A *Bloody Canvas* put them into discourse through images.

The film moves to and fro between with boxing myths and iconography through a visit to the grave of Gene Tunney, the world heavyweight legend and champion from 1926-1928 who twice defeated Jack Dempsey. The direct engagements with artistic practices are interspersed with frames which include conversations with boxers and trainers, such as with the legendary Irish boxing trainer Brendan Ingle in Sheffield in the UK who provides a discursive mix of the practicalities of the gym and training and claims to the spiritual transcendent qualities of boxing in a surreal display of enthusiasm; another example of the hyperbole which is also an ordinary affect of boxing. Conversations often focus on reflection and the ways in which memory (Woodward, 2011) and is affected by boxing. For example, Scully is filmed in his apartment and studio in Barcelona, where former World Champion Barry McGuigan joins him to 'look back at the mutual fascination between art and boxing, between what they call the men of art and the men of action' (RTE 2010). The moments of reconstituting memory and the conversations between older men are resonant of the strong boxing tradition of making heroes through the framework of the dialogue between the present and the past which so powerfully generates the endurances of hegemonic masculinity.

Even when a boxing film is explicitly about a woman, it is hegemonic masculinity that is largely what dominates the discursive field. More specifically it is patriarchy, the explanatory concept used to explore and understand the dominance of men over women and of older men over younger men. For example, *Million Dollar Baby* (2005), ostensibly the story of a white woman who attempts to follow the more traditionally masculine path of achieving a route out of the trailer park into financial success through the boxing ring in order to support her wayward and dependent family. Clint Eastwood, the film's director also stars in the film as her trainer Frankie along side Hilary Swank as Maggie the boxer, as her trainer Frankie and Morgan Freeman as Eastwood's former sparring partner and friend, Eddie 'Scrap iron' Dupris. Maggie is the vehicle through which the film explores Eastwood's character, Frankie and the problems and the dilemmas of contemporary masculinity (2006, 2009, 2012a 2012c). Frankie's relationship with Scrap, which is deeply imbricated in hegemonic masculinity, takes precedence over Maggie's role as a boxing hero within the familiar storylines of popular culture.

The invisibility of women is also part of their absence from the histories and legends that are the delivery systems of boxing culture as well as the empirical enfleshed absence of women from most gyms, until some increase in their presence, for example in Europe and the USA, relatively recently (Heiskanen, 2012).Change provides evidence of boxing's democratic promise. The real of boxing is not entirely separate from its dramas, but part of the mix. Boxing traditions are made through the capacities of boxing to re-create ordinary affects of masculinity in kinship ties and routine practices as well as through its cultural representations. This is beginning to change, albeit incrementally through increased infiltration of women and of men who seek to engage in the sport and its embodied practices but not its traditions of hegemonic masculinity. Women are starting to occupy some of the space traditionally dominated by a particular version of masculinity and change boxing, not least after the success of the inclusion of the women's sport in the 2012 Olympics.

Women's Boxing

During the games themselves we heard stories of the life choices of boxers like Katie Taylor and especially Nicola Adams which has opened up new ways of thinking which can inform a cultural legacy. These narratives included the traditional biographical journey not dissimilar to that followed by young men on the margins taking the boxing route out of the ghetto. In the case of Nicola Adams this route was produced within a discourse of the intersection of different inequalities (Guardian Women's Boxing, 2012). Adams had experienced marginalisation through her class position and sexuality and as a black woman. Boxing has traditionally been a sport for the investment of physical capital chosen by migrant young men but what is significant about the ways in which women's boxing was put into discourse in 2012 is the inclusion of gendered exclusion and the politics of difference in relation to sex gender and sexuality. Whether large numbers of young women take up the sport or not, it is now at least on the agenda. Sex gender and sexuality are now more explicitly part of the assemblage of what makes up boxing and its culture.

The debate is ambivalent and contradictory in relation to the political possibilities of women's boxing. On the one hand it is expressive of challenge and resistance but on the other the field which women have not entered is one which is also deeply patriarchal and traditional in many of its values. Women who are caught up in a sexual politics of intentionality and resistance now meet the restrictions of the governing bodies of international sport which welcomes the new entrants to boxing with suggestion that women should wear skirts in the ring so that viewers will know that they are watching women and not men (BBC AIBA, 2012) Although the decision was rescinded if it ever got further than a few public statements, it demonstrates the culture of sport and the contradictory nature of what can be read as liberatory and what is repressive. Such statements by regulatory bodies, when others have been issued in relation to women's attire in sports like basketball, also suggest that a simple Orientalist binary (Said 1978) between the progressive west and what is construed as the reactionary east or 'other' is far from convincing. Patriarchy permeates the global culture of sport as it does other fields and social and cultural terrains. The inclusion of the women's event in the games in 2012 is instructive in exploring some of the points of connection and disruption between power axes as well as demonstrating the uneven processes through which change takes place.

Conclusion

Boxing is more multi-faceted than might appear. The sport generates possibilities as well as reflecting social relations and social systems and hierarchies. In this short chapter I have argued for the creative and cultural possibilities of boxing, for example through making a film. My own part in the process of making this film demonstrates the to and fro between inside and outside and the diverse components that make up boxing culture. Drama in the ring and on film is inseparable and is also core to boxing and its democratic promise as well as its socially inclusive actualities.

Boxing stories often narrate the route out of the ghetto within a cultural frame of heroic masculinity but I have argued that these are not the only stories nor are they linear narratives. Boxing is troubling for a whole range of reasons and what seems to be traditional and conventional can always be questioned and disrupted.

References

Chandler, D. Gill, J. Guha, T. and G. Tawadros (1996 [eds.]). *Boxer: An Anthology of London, Institute of Visual* Arts (in VA) Connell, R.W. (1995), Ma*sculinities*, Cambridge: Polity.
Connell, R.W. (1995). *Masculinities*, Cambridge, Polity Press.
Deleuze, G. (2002). *Francis Bacon: The Logic of Sensation*, trans. Daniel Smith. Minneapolis, MN: University of Minnesota Press.
Deleuze, G. (1996). *Cinema I: The Movement Image*, trans. Hugh Tomlinson and Barbara Habberjam
Elias, N. (2000). The Civilizing Process, (2nd edn) Oxford Wiley Blackwell.
Heiskanen, B. (2012) *The Urban Geography of Boxing. Race, Class and Gender in the Ring,* New York, Routledge
Oates, J.C. (1987). *On Boxing*, London: Bloomsbury.
Lavery, B. (2010). *Beautiful Burnout*, Frantic Assembly, Edinburgh, National Theatre of Scotland
McRae, D. (2005). *Dark Trade: Lost in Boxing* Edinburgh, Mainstream Publishing
Sobchack, V. (2004) *Carnal Thoughts: Embodiment and Moving Image Culture*, Berkeley, CA University of California
Spencer, D.C. (2011). *Ultimate Fighting and Embodiment. Violence Gender and Mixed Martial Arts*, New York, Routledge.
Tosches, N. (1997). 'Introduction' in J. La Motta with C. Carter and P. Savage (eds.) *Raging Bull: My Story* 1st edition, new York, de Capo Press pp. vii-xii
Wacquant, L (2004) *Body and Soul. Notebooks of an Apprentice Boxer*, Oxford, Oxford University Press
Walkerdine, V. (1986). 'Video replay: families, films and fantasies' in *Formations of Fantasy*, London: Methuen.
Woodward, K. (2012a). *Sex Power and the Games*, Basingstoke, Palgrave
Woodward, K. (2012b). *Sporting Times*, Basingstoke, Palgrave MacMillan
Woodward, K. (2012c). *Planet Sport*, London: Routledge.

Woodward, K. (2011). The Culture of Boxing: Sensation and Affect, *Sport in History*, Vol.31 (4) (December, 2011):487-503.
Woodward, K. (2009). *Embodied Sporting Practices: regulating and regulatory bodies*, Basingstoke: Palgrave MacMillan.
Woodward, K. (2008). 'Hanging out and hanging about: insider/outsider research in the sport of boxing, *Ethnography*, Vol 9 (4) pp536-560.
Woodward, K. (2006). *Boxing, Masculinity and Identity: The "I" of the Tiger*, London: Routledge.

Films:

A Bloody Canvas, (2010) RTE Dir. Alan Gilseman
Million Dollar Baby, (2005) Dir. Clint Eastwood, Warner Brothers
Raging Bull, (1980) Dir Martin Scorsese USA United Artists
Rocky Series, (1976-2006) Dir. John G.Avildsen, USA Metro-Goldwyn-Meyer, United Artists, Universal Pictures. In order of release:
Rocky, (1976), *Rocky* II (1979), Rocky III (1982), *Rocky IV* (1985), *Rocky V* (1990) and *Rocky Balboa* (2006)

Chapter 19

'Pugilistic Pastoring': Volunteering in Amateur Boxing as Missionary Work

David Chaplin & John Harris

Introduction

Contemplating Mission in the Context of Volunteering in Amateur Boxing

Amateur boxing has long been associated with service to at-risk youth. Father Flanagan's Boys Town in Omaha, Nebraska (USA) utilized the discipline, structure and sportsmanship the sport requires for its mentoring of disenfranchised youth in its racially-integrated boxing club. More recently, Circle of Discipline was formed in 1993 in a poverty-stricken area of Minneapolis, Minnesota (USA) to serve disadvantaged youth through – in part – amateur boxing. Their name and logo represents the 360 degrees of physical, mental and spiritual balance. Restoration Ministries in Harvey, Illinois (USA) coined the slogan, "It's better to sweat in the gym than bleed in the streets" in its inaugural year of 2002 (a slogan that has since been appropriated by many other amateur boxing programs in the United States). Following-up on the theme embodied in Restoration Ministries' slogan, USA Boxing and World Sport Chicago received an Olympic Opportunity Grant from the United States Olympic Committee to form "Gloves, not Guns" in 2007, a program designed as "…a community initiative, which gives kids a free introduction to boxing as an athletic way to improve their lives and fill their time with a positive activity (www.usaboxing.org, 9 January, 2009).

The emphasis on spiritual development witnessed at Circle of Discipline and Restoration Ministries implies a sense of mission in the work these boxing clubs perform. While "mission work" is generally viewed as a distinctly religious exercise -involving either travel to a distant land (i.e., a "mission trip") or a "going-out" into the community and engaging in necessary menial tasks (e.g.,

173

serving meals in a soup kitchen), it will be presented here that those are just a few of the ways in which mission work may be carried out. In the gritty ghetto gyms that dot the urban American landscape, the coaches (trainers) of amateur boxers serve at-risk youth in a meaningful and profound way that contains at least as many of the components of mission work as those mentioned above.

Sport volunteering is a very important category of service to the community. A number of scholars have undertaken research to identify aspects of the role that volunteers play in developing and maintaining sports participation (Nichols and Collins, 2005; Cuskelly, Hoye and Auld, 2006). This has attracted significant attention as sport is often promoted as a means of addressing the widespread obesity epidemic, anti-social behavior and a range of other health and social issues within postmodern society. A study in England found that sports volunteering accounted for 26% of all volunteer activity in the nation in 2002 (cited in Adams and Deane, 2009, p. 120). As such, it deserves a rightful spot as a legitimate form of volunteering - in those cases where there is a significant level of commitment by the volunteer to serving at-risk youth – and fits comfortably into a broad interpretation of the term "mission work". However, the recent move from "sport for good" (stressing external benefits to society) to "sport for sport's sake" (stressing intrinsic benefits of sport) in England noted by Collins (2010, p. 367), provides cause for concern for those sport volunteers who view their role in terms of providing a healthy and (relatively) safe alternative to drugs and street violence through sport, rather than sport itself providing both the means and ends. There has been a marked increase in academic work concerned with volunteering in sport, but it is important to note that volunteering itself is not a new development. Volunteers have always contributed to sport from the very beginning; although it can't be denied that we have witnessed a shift towards more formalized volunteering in the past twenty years. Boxing, like most sports, has always relied on the voluntary contributions of a range of people to provide opportunities for participation.

The recent move away from "sport for good" cited by Collins (ibid) is particularly disturbing in light of boxing's long history (particularly at the amateur level) of providing a host of external benefits to at-risk youth. Dating back to at least the early years of the 1900s, there is substantial evidence, as detailed immediately below, of amateur boxing's external social benefits. In the U.S, the initial movement of what may be dubbed "salvation through boxing" was very much a Midwestern and Catholic exercise. Father Flanagan's Boys' Town in Omaha, Nebraska (USA) was formed in 1917 and utilized the discipline, structure and sportsmanship the sport requires for its mentoring of disenfranchised youth in its racially-integrated boxing club, embracing the slogan, "Sturdy young bodies and stout young hearts" (Boddy, 2008, p. 269). The city of Chicago (USA) has a long history of utilizing amateur boxing in the service of at-risk youth. In June of 1930, the Catholic Youth Organization (CYO) was formed in Chicago by Bishop Bernard J. Sheil (Gems, 1997, p. 300). Sheil is alleged to have provided the following statement on the role of amateur boxing in providing positive role models for at-risk inner-city youth as follows:

> We'll knock the hoodlum of his pedestal and we'll put another neighborhood boy in his place. He'll be dressed in C.Y.O. boxing shorts

and a pair of leather mitts, and he'll make a new hero. Those kids love to fight. We'll let them fight. We'll find champions right in the neighborhood.[1]

More than seventy years later, two Chicago-area organizations continue to carry-on the tradition of CYO. Restoration Ministries in Harvey, Illinois (USA) coined the slogan, "It's better to sweat in the gym than bleed in the streets" in its inaugural year of 2002 (a slogan that has since been appropriated by many other amateur boxing programs in the United States). Following-up on the theme embodied in Restoration Ministries' slogan, USA Boxing and World Sport Chicago received an Olympic Opportunity Grant from the United States Olympic Committee to form "Gloves, not Guns" in 2007, a program designed as "…a community initiative, which gives kids a free introduction to boxing as an athletic way to improve their lives and fill their time with a positive activity.[2]

The discipline and structure provided to amateur boxers in Chicago appears to have put them in good stead for their professional careers, as Wacquant (1992, pp. 232-233) mentions in his study of a ghetto gym in Chicago: "The pros at work in the main gyms in gyms of Chicago in the early 1990s were, as a group, more likely to have completed high school, to be employed and married, and to own a car and checking account than young residents of the city's South Side. It should come as no surprise, therefore, that the legendary author, Nelson Algren, had this to say about Chicago: "…The very toughest kind of town - it used to be a writer's town and it's always been a fighter's town." (1951, p. 69). Such a role for the sport is not unique to this city, of course. There are a number of places throughout the world where boxing is also celebrated for the role it plays in providing focus and direction for youth. Merthyr Tydfil in South Wales has statues celebrating its most famous boxing sons (Johnny Owen, Howard Winston and Eddie Thomas) in the town centre. Here, the sport has been at the heart of the community for generations (see Broadbent, 2006; Smith, 1990). Having identified some of the scholarship relating to volunteering in sport, the next section looks at the works undertaken specific to the sport of boxing.

Motivation for the Study and Other Examples of "Mission Work through Amateur Boxing"

As one of this paper's authors (David Chaplin) has served as a volunteer referee and judge in amateur boxing for seventeen years, we feel that we occupy the "insider" position as boxing researcher presented by Woodward (2008). As such, we have encountered first-hand the positive impact amateur boxing has had on the lives of at-risk youth. The anecdotal evidence, gleaned from many years of ethnographic study in the field, points to amateur boxing literally saving many at-risk youth from the unattractive feasible alternatives to them of prison, an early death as the result of street crime or "running the streets" by developing what Wacquant (1998, p. 345) describes as the boxer's *libido pugilistica* (i.e., their "hunger for the gloves"). Although scholarly research in the field is somewhat

---

[1] Quoted in *The New World*, 6 February, 1931.
[2] www.usaboxing.org, 9 January, 2009

limited, studies by Besant (1912), Fletcher (1992), Nichols (1997), Trimbur (2006, 2007, 2011) and Wright (2008) all provide qualitative evidence of the benefits provided by amateur boxing. Besant (ibid, p. 172) indicates the benefits of "finding amateur boxing" for restless East London youth in the early 1900s: "...They work off their restlessness and get rid of the devil in the gymnasium with the boxing gloves and the single stick; they contract habits of order and discipline; the fruits or their time spent in the club are seen in their after life...". Fletcher (ibid, 1992, p. 60) found that amateur boxing can be a way of maintaining status and respect among peers in amateur boxing without actually having to fight in the streets. In his work titled *Boxing and Society: An International Analysis*, (Sugden, 1996, p. 14), cites "The Father of all Boxing Writers", Pierce Egan (writing in 1812), as providing an example of how boxing could provide a far safer alternative for settling disputes between young gentlemen:

> But what would rather that they should have had recourse to the manly defense of boxing than the deadly weapons of sword and ball (shot); from which a bloody nose, or a black eye, might have been the only consequence to themselves and their families, and neither in their feelings or in their circumstances be injured; reconciliation with their antagonist – faults mutually acknowledged - and perhaps, become inseparable friends ever afterwards.

In an ethnographic study performed at the fabled Gleason's Gym in Brooklyn, New York (USA) Trimbur (2006, pp. 103-104) had the following to say about the role the volunteer coach (trainer) had this to say about the role they play in the lives of the amateur boxers they serve:

> When working with amateurs, trainers perform a unique type of mentoring in which the relationship between mentor and mentee is predicated upon – and successful because of – shared experiences of struggle and accomplishment. This mentoring is explicitly understood by trainers as a form of social work and is an expression of their political consciousness about the failure of society to provide young black and Latino men with guidance and resources necessary to live crime-free lives. The act of training is an active intervention of restorative justice on the part of trainers, as it is employed and explicated narrated as a redemptive tool, and can also be understood as practice of fictive kinship.

In a later study, Trimbur (2011) also demonstrates the positive impact a trainer of amateur boxers can have on instilling a sense of discipline in his or her fighters. In a telling interchange between Trimbur and a Brooklyn-area trainer, the respondent has this to say about his amateur boxer: "I cursed him out three times yesterday and I gave him a long talk about discipline." (2011, p. 345). That is, through the "tough love" of which Trimbur (ibid) writes, these "saints of the ghetto" (trainers of amateur boxers) provide a sense of structure, discipline and responsibility that is missing in all other aspects of their boxers' lives.

Lewandowski (2011, p. 37) confirms the coach's role in maintaining discipline in his ethnographic observations of an amateur boxing gym: "In my experience, individuals who fail to incorporate a coach's constrains into their sparring sessions, either as a result of poor temper or the desire to 'get off' (land heavy blows) are routinely refused the privilege of sparring and tend to give up boxing rather quickly."

A study of Finnish volunteers identified five different role identities, all of which apply to the volunteer amateur boxing coach: "the influencer", "the helper", "the faith-based", "the community-server" and "the success story" (Gronlund, 2011). Lastly, Wright (ibid) provides the most robust framework for serving at-risk youth through amateur boxing though her development of the following "Ten Attributes of Effective Boxing Groups": 1). Provides group members with a new identity; 2). Promotes and offers safety; 3). Provides discipline; 4). Uses defense as a metaphor; 5). Improves impulse control and patience; 6). Develops ability to focus; 7). Teaches commitment and offers meaning; 8). Teaches and provides respect; 9). Relieves stress; 10). Fosters mutual aid. One specific example Wright provides (ibid, p. 150) to develop point #7 is as follows:

> For many group members who experience violence or emotional abuse in their communities, home, schools, or from the police, the safest time in their week is at the boxing gym, Training to be a boxer taps their strengths and helps them learn more about themselves, gain confidence and find a way *out* of violence. This is no paradox: the groups take the familiar experience of fighting they already identify with and sanction it, control it, structure it, refine it, harness it, give the youth ownership of it, and turn it in to an art form to be valued and respected.

Despite the qualitative work on the merits of amateur boxing provided above, a quantitative study of how amateur boxing has served at-risk youth has been missing. We feel this work will provide a solid foundation for quantitative analyses in the benefits of amateur boxing for serving at-risk youth.

The Data Set and Statistical Results

Volunteer coaches of male and female amateur boxers aged 18-25 were surveyed during registration at the 2012 U.S. Amateur Boxing Championships (contested in Fort Carson, Colorado, 26 February to 3 March). While 100 surveys were made available to coaches, only 26 were completed and returned. The objectives of the survey were manifold, as we strove to evaluate 1). How they view their role as a volunteer in amateur boxing, 2). The financial and time commitments they demonstrate as volunteers and 3). The outcomes they have witnessed first-hand in effecting positive changes in the lives of the youth they serve. Detailed responses for the 5 quantifiable questions are provided in the Appendix.

The most extraordinary findings from the survey were related to the time and financial commitments of the volunteer coaches. A remarkable 73% of coaches indicated that they volunteered at least 20 hours per week to serve amateur boxing in this capacity. Considering that the average volunteer in the United

States spends an average of 4.2 hours per week engaged in volunteer work (Chelladurai, 1999, p. 17), this level of time commitment by the majority of amateur coaches in our survey is quite impressive.

Equally impressive were the facts that 81% of coaches spent some money out of their own pocket each month in their support of amateur boxing and 38.5% of all respondents indicated incurring at least $500 out-of-pocket expenses each month as volunteers in the sport. The depth of commitment and the level of seriousness with which volunteer coaches of amateur boxers approach their craft are not surprising, however, for those close to the sport. As Trimbur (2007, p. 2) indicates, "Although they are not paid, many amateurs consider boxing to be their job." It appears this near-religious devotion to amateur boxing applies to the coaches, as well. Even for most professional boxers, something far more profound than financial reward appears to be spurring them on. Wacquant (1995, p. 492) purports, "Given how little money most fighters earn and the multifold privations they must endure…economic payoffs fall woefully short of accounting for the seductions of boxing." A California Institute of Technology Working Paper by Balbien, Noll and Quirk (1981, p. 23) confirm just how impecunious the sport of professional boxing is for most participants, as it was revealed that 77.8% of all boxers competing in California in 1977 earned less than $2,000 that year. That was far below the $6,000 annual "minimum wage income" the authors estimated for 1977. Furthermore, with the exception of those competing in California, professional boxers (excluding world champions) still have no pension plan (Chaplin, 2012). Perhaps it is the unbreakable bond live fan and boxer share that encourages even preliminary boxers to continue to risk their health for such modest financial compensation. Gerald Early, (1988, p. 28) sees the link between these participants in the "fistic drama" as a distinctly religious experience: "In sports, particularly in boxing, the sport is very much like the Christian Communion: We partake of the body and soul of the athlete…touchingly vulnerable." Furthermore, given the near-symbiotic emotional, financial and mentoring relationships that tend to develop between boxer (whether amateur or professional) and coach, the aforementioned privations appear to apply equally-well to the coaches of boxers.

Less startling than the time and financial commitments put forth by coaches, but impressive nonetheless, were responses to the question, "Approximately what percentage of your amateur boxers aged 18-25 have 'turned their life around' as a result of boxing?" The median value reported by coaches to this question was 25%-50%, while nearly 20% of coaches indicated that more than 75% of their athletes had "turned their life around" as a result of amateur boxing.

Discussion and Implications for Future Research

The statistical results provided here confirm what decades of ethnographic study in the field of amateur boxing have purported – the sport provides an attractive alternative to "a life on the streets" (or worse) for at-risk youth. An often overlooked component of the external benefits provided by amateur boxing is the volunteer coach. It may well be that this is because of the social and cultural positioning of the sport, and the very nature of the fight game itself, that the role of coaches has been somewhat overlooked. As summarized in the Appendix, the level of both time and financial commitments invested by these amateur coaches are truly astonishing. From an outcomes perspective, it also impressive to note the percentage of amateur boxers who their coaches believe have "turned their life around" through the sport (Appendix, Question #3).

As the first known study to provide a statistical analysis of the sacrifices coaches of amateur boxers make and the impact they have on the athletes they serve, it is hoped this paper will serve as a foundation for future research in the area. Specifically, data from the athletes themselves on how their coaches and the sport have serve them would complement the data on coaches provided here to provide a more complete picture of the myriad of external benefits provided by amateur boxing. Further work on boxing coaches would also add to the developing work on coaching science and the sociology of coaching that has tended to focus more on team sports. Cuskelly, Hoye and Auld (2006, p. 123) note that "Coaches can facilitate rewarding experiences in sport, especially for younger participants that have direct and significant implications for individual well-being and levels of participation in physical activity." Such a statement seems especially pertinent for a sport such as boxing, given the proven role it as played in offering opportunities for at-risk youth throughout the world.

References

Adams, A. and Deane, J. (2009). Exploring formal and informal dimension of sports volunteering in England. *European Sport Management Quarterly*, 9(2), 119-140.

Algren, N. (1951). *Chicago: City on the Make.* New York: Curtis Publishing Co.

Balbien, J., Noll, R. & Quirk, J. (1981). The economics of boxing regulation in California. California Institute of Technology, Social Science Working Paper 366.

Besant, W. (1912). *East London.* London: Chatto and Windus Publishing.

Boddy, K. (2008). *Boxing: A cultural history.* London: Reaktion Books.

Broadbent, R. (2006). *The big if: The life and death of Johnny Owen.* London, England: Macmillan.

Chaplin, D. (2012). "Blood, sweat and fears: The need for a professional boxers' pension plan". *Journal of Sport and Social Issues*, 36(4), 442-451. DOI: 10.1177/0193723512442202.

Chelladurai, P. (1999). *Human resource management in sport and recreation.* Champaign, IL: Human Kinetics.

Collins, M. (2010). From "sport for good" to "sport for sport's sake" – not a good move for sports development in England? *International Journal of Sport Policy and Politics*, 2(3), 367-379.

Cuskelly, G, Hoye, R. and C. Auld (2006). *Working with volunteers in sport.* London, England: Routledge.

Early, G. (1988). Three notes toward a cultural definition of prizefighting (20-38). In *Reading the fights: The best writing about the most controversial sport* (Oates, J.C. and D. Halpern, editors). New York, Prentice Hall.

Fletcher, M. (1992). *An investigation into participation in amateur boxing.* Unpublished dissertation, MSc in Sport and Recreation Management, University of Sheffield.

Gems, G. (1997). Selling sport and religion in American Society (300-311). In *The new American sport history: Recent approaches and perspectives* (Pope, S.W., editor). Champaign: University of Illinois Press.

Gronlund, H. (2011). Identity and volunteering intertwined: Reflections on the values of young adults. *Voluntas*. Advance online publication. DOI: 10.1007/s11266-011-9184-6.

Lewandowski, J. (2007): Boxing: The sweet science of constraints. *Journal of the Philosophy of Sport*, 34(1), 26-38.

Nichols, G. (1997). A Consideration of why active participation in sport and leisure might reduce criminal behavior. *Sport, Education and Society*, 2(2), 181-190.

Nichols, G and M. Collins (2005). *Volunteers in sports clubs.* Eastbourne, England: Leisure Studies Association.

Smith, D. (1990). Focal heroes: A Welsh fighting class. In *Sport and the working class in modern Britain* (Holt, R., editor). Manchester, England: Manchester University Press.

Sugden, J. (1996). *Boxing and Society: An international analysis*. Manchester: Manchester University Press.

Trimbur, L. (2006). *Living wages: The work of amateur fighters and trainers in postindustrial Brooklyn* (Unpublished doctoral dissertation). Yale University, New Haven, CT.

Trimbur, L. (2007). Between prison and wage labor: Improvising work in an urban boxing gym. Paper Presented at the Annual Meeting of the American Sociological Association, New York, New York, August 11.

Trimbur, L. (2011). "Tough love": Mediation and articulation in the urban boxing gym. *Ethnography*, 12(3), 334-355.

Wacquant, L. (1992). The social logic of Boxing in Black Chicago: Toward a sociology of pugilism. *Sociology of Sport Journal*, 9, 221-254.

Wacquant, L. (1995). The pugilistic point of view: How boxers think and feel about their trade. *Theory and Society*, 24, 489-535.

Wacquant, L. (1998).The prizefighter's three bodies: *Ethnos* 63(3): 325-352.

Woodward, K. (2008). Hanging out and hanging about: Insider/outsider research in the sport of boxing. *Ethnography*, 9(4), 536-561.

Wright, W. (2006). Keep it in the ring: Using boxing in social group work with high-risk and offender youth to reduce violence. *Social Work with Groups*, 29(2-3), 149-174.

Chapter 20

Boxing and Religion: Faith and Heritage in the Sweet Science

Kevin Grace

Introduction

In the 1976 boxing film *Rocky*, the moviegoer hears a trumpet fanfare as the action begins, the now very familiar theme by composer John Williams.[1] It is at once both a sacred and profane call to arms, the common man being summoned to battle and the fans acting as witnesses to a spectacle of man against the gods. And, of course, man against himself in the manner of settling his worldly fate. As the fanfare plays, the camera does a slow pan from the religious image that fills the screen – a crucifix with a bloodied, bowed Jesus Christ hanging on the wall above the action below. Two men, one of whom is the film's protagonist (and supplicant), Rocky Balboa, clutch each other in sweaty fatigue and ultimate resignation. They are in the final minutes of their self-directed Passion Play for the crowd. The pugilists wearily pummel away at each other in the dirty boxing ring and a dozen, perhaps two dozen working-class men either cheer them on or shower them with trash and verbal abuse.

It is a scene so laden with biblical imagery that it seems to approach either cinematic or cultural overkill. But it is also a scene that immediately sets the mood of this urban *noir* experience of fall and redemption that is boxing: the rise of an individual from the masses who seeks salvation for himself as well as redemption for the gritty lives of his cultural peers. He is the man who is jeered, but in the end is acclaimed for preserving and winning eternal life in the manner of myth and pathos. *Rocky* opens with a boxing scene in a Philadelphia church hall, the bout a Catholic parish smoker in an underclass Italian neighborhood. Rocky Balboa is a child born, raised, and glorified through his religious faith and

---

[1] *Rocky,* Directed by John G. Avildson, MGM Studios, 1976.

his ethnic streets. His is the American dream. In reality, however, it is a drama that is played out on different streets, different cities, different nationalities, and different countries. Boxing as both religious drama and as fulfillment of faith breaches cultural borders.

There is an intertwining heritage of boxing and religion, a heritage that has been overtly expressed in numerous ways, from Jewish boxers fighting with the Star of David stitched to their trunks and robes, to Muhammad Ali's conversion to the faith of the Nation of Islam and Mike Tyson's jailhouse conversion to the Islamic faith, to Catholic boxers (*see* Rocky Balboa) blessing themselves as they come out of their corners in answer to the opening bell of the bout. The history of boxing has often reflected an interesting cultural take on violence and faith. Boxing is alternately embraced by and rejected by mainstream religion, while at the same time it is promoting the precepts of Muscular Christianity, being used as an educational tool in Catholic high school and college sports, spanning urban and global religious rivalries (*see,* for example the heritage of boxing in Northern Ireland), and simply rallying fighters in their careers of inflicting damage on one another. There is a distinctive cross-cultural element in boxing that reflects religion in its components of ethics, philosophy, morality, and history. In contemporary religious expression, film and pop culture, urban studies, and literature, the rituals of this sport often follows religious habit and heritage, and through these agents, the sport can lend itself to an understanding of a larger cultural group. As one manifestation, in the professional heyday of boxing in urban America, when cities fostered many boxing clubs and most fan attention was concerned with local matches, promoters often advertised one ethnic fighter against another, such as the Irish against the Italian, or the German against the Pole. Likewise, promotional antics labeled Catholic and Jewish fighters by name or neighborhood. And, in order to stir interest in a cross-cultural bout, it was not unusual for boxers to take on new ethnic names and identities as a ruse for rallying the fans.

As mentioned above, the Catholic imagery in *Rocky* helps form the ethos of that film. The Catholic view of boxing is worth close examination, but initially one must look at an earlier manifestation of religion and boxing, particularly in America, in the philosophy of Muscular Christianity.[2]

Engendered as a 19th century counterpoint to the fear of a feminized male manifestation of Christian belief, and smack within a burgeoning concern with physical fitness, Muscular Christianity had as its basic tenet that a strong body coupled with a strong and intellectually vigorous mind would lead inevitably to strong expression of spirituality and faith in God. After the Young Men's Christian Association (YMCA) was founded in England in 1847 as an opportunity for young adult males employed in trade to uplift their circumstances through formative lectures and readings, the association spread to America a decade later and by the end of the American Civil War in 1865, it was deemed imperative that the YMCA, in addition to those civically invigorating lectures and inspirational literature it provided to the mechanic classes, should also provide the

---

[2] *See* Muscular Christianity: Embodying the Victorian Age, ed. by Donald E. Hall, Cambridge University Press, 1994 and Muscular Christianity: Evangelical Protestants and the Development of American Sport by Tony Ladd, and James A. Mathiesen, Baker Books, 1999.

meads for physical improvement.[3] That is, to establish a program and the wherewithal to re-masculinize the Christian man after past decades of encroaching softness of body and male mental haleness. Gymnasia were incorporated into the building plans of new YMCA facilities, and physical culture and education programs were created. In some YMCAs, boxing became an important part of those programs, establishing pugilism as promise. The realized promise was that a man who could not only defend himself, but prove himself physically dominant as well, while at the same time stoically absorbing punishment, could count himself as a sterling example of manhood. By extension, his community would hold the same view of him. With a belief in God, belief in self-improvement both mentally and physically, the man who embraced boxing would make himself tough in daily affairs and ready for the afterlife.

But certainly the conflict of Muscular Christianity also drew from the efforts of rescuing young men from the cruel effects of cramped urban life and the criminal doings of thugs and wastrels. As immigrants swelled the city populations of mid-19th century America, there was a significant and concomitant rise in the population of the working poor, that is, the working underclass.Segmented by religious predilections, occupations, and ethnicities, the denizens of this new world were created in large measure by the Industrial Revolution, socioeconomic change that fostered a working-wage mentality of how masculinity was defined. The result, with which most urban historians are familiar, was the so-called Bachelor, or, Saloon Subculture.[4] This "homosocial" fraternity of men, expressed and formed in terms proscribed by class and religion, saw in the lower class groupings a celebration of manhood by participation in gambling, drinking, and sport, and, in voluntary associations that included politics, occupational brotherhoods, civic and religious societies, and in gangs. Membership was determined by, and individual worth determined by as well, by validation by the larger group. And it is not a large stress to view these in the same cultural group terms of congregants, ceremony, and communion.

The "sport" engaged in was to an important degree, that of "bloodsport" driven by gambling and defined by the intent to maim or kill the opponent. Bloodsports took the form of dog-fighting, rat-baiting, cock-fighting, and bare-knuckle boxing. These activities, including boxing, were almost exclusively in the Anglo and Irish neighborhoods at first, operating *sub rosa* in times of civic and mainstream Christian opposition. Boxing had as its *raison d'etre* gambling and male camaraderie. It was brutal and sometimes deadly. In this era of boxing's history, bare-knuckle fighting featured rounds which ended only when a pugilist fell to one knee on the ground or could not otherwise continue the bout. Boxing matches could continue for round after round, sometimes into the dozens.

Ostensibly fought by Marquis of Queensbury rules when gentlemen were involved, the back room manifestations of the sport were especially vicious and bloodthirsty, fueled as they were by wagering and drinking on the part of the spectators. Still, in the ring, no matter what the situation, it was always man

---

[3] Getting Physical: The Rise of Fitness Culture in America by Shelly McKenzie, University Press of Kansas, 2013.
[4] The Age of the Bachelor: Creating an American Subculture by Howard P. Chudacoff, Princeton University Press, 1999.

against man, man against his own nature, and man pitted against a formidable destiny imposed by God.

Historically, boxing and the prizefighting ethos that is part of it is Anglo-American and Christian in its origins.[5] That is, it is part of the status quo in the United States, Ireland, and Great Britain, no matter the occasional calls for abolishment. Boxing has always been subject to prevailing standards of morality and ethics, bent as they sometimes are in communities of divided inclination. This was certainly no less true in the matches of the 19th century, and in fact is rather accurate in describing boxing today, particularly the professional incarnation. In the prizefighting world of 18th century Regency England where the sport had its first flowering, there was also sporadic socio-religious disapproval. Communities from time to time have outlawed boxing, making it a nefarious activity as much for the spectacle itself as it was of two men striving to damage one another. This disapproval, whether by local government, church authorities, community organizations imbued with Christian values, was birthed by a determination to eradicate immoral behavior such as drinking, whoring, and gambling. Boxing was not just unsavory; it was viewed as destructive to the social order and the religious pilings that supported it.

The discussion returns to Muscular Christianity and the attempts to codify the qualities of manhood. If boxing could be found to have a socially responsible purpose in making a man fit and self-reliant, forming him into a veritable protector, then by rescuing the inhabitants of the saloon culture and re-channeling the fighting, boxing could then be used to establish a Christian community order, decrease urban crime committed by unacceptable groups of young men, and convince them to reject their evil ways. Thus, if boxing be the tool of God, then so be it. One must ask, then, how the teaching and practice of boxing became a part of an institutional expression of faith like Catholic education in the 20th century, roughly from 1900 to 1960? In his 1952 dissertation that examined the morality of prizefighting, Catholic cleric George C. Bernard attempted to defend the practice of pugilism by viewing it as a means to teach discipline, honesty, physical fitness, and moral awareness.[6] He stated, "Destructive criticism of a national sport is sometimes an imprudent undertaking, especially when such criticism takes the form of condemnation from a moral point of view. Once a sport, or any activity, has been accepted for a long period of time as something good, or at least permissible, any attempt to point out the serious defects of that activity is strenuously opposed...Is there sufficient reason for casting doubt on the morality of an activity which previously had been considered perfectly legitimate when there is good reason to believe that the activity will continue nevertheless?"

In other words, Bernard was quite aware of the brutal nature and the brutal expression of boxing in many circles, and of the version of pugilism that could be supported by the beliefs of muscular Christians. He was opposed to the brutality of boxing but backed the notion that it made one stronger in faith and deed, especially as practiced in the Catholic school gyms and parish community centers

---

[5] The Manly Art: Bare-Knuckle Prize Fighting in America by Elliot Gorn, Cornell University Press, 1986 and Boxing: A Cultural History by Kasia Boddy, Reaktion Books, 2008.

[6] The Morality of Prizefighting by George C. Bernard, Catholic University Press, 1952.

and basements. There was good boxing and bad boxing. He was for one and opposed to the other. His was a specious argument if one considers the primal basic nature of boxing – intentionally inflicting harm on another human being. Whether fighting is professional or amateur does not really matter. Bernard, however, undertook to prove by scripture, theological examination, and philosophical reasoning that some boxing could be considered virtuous. Again, according to Bernard, "...in order to become truly moral and moralizing, [boxing] ought to remain in its place and not go beyond the limits that are assigned to it. In other words, the exercise of the body ought to be subservient to the exercises of the higher factor, the soul. St. Thomas says that three things are necessary to fulfill this condition: that the enjoyment or gratification is not to be sought in words or deeds which are vile, or which or injurious or harmful to our neighbor; that the pleasure derived from the game is not an end in itself, nor that the enjoyment be beyond the limits of reason; and that [boxing] befit the person, the time, and the place, and that all circumstances required for a virtuous act be preserved." Bernard cites the concept of *eutrapelia*, as expressed in Ephesians 5:4 and in his interpretation views boxing as a joy that should be offered up in Christian service.

Bernard attempts a glib approach to religion as an integral part of the sweet science of boxing, and dexterously defends the sport in religious and philosophical contexts. He even cites Clement of Alexandria, who exhorted his followers to hunt and fish, play ball, and try their hand at boxing because "to exert one's strength in the right way and for the benefit of one's health is commendable and manly." This point of view can, therefore, be reduced to one that embraces boxing as social sport that leads to religious cohesion in society.

Again, for all his theological citations perfectly selected to bolster his religious position, Bernard is somewhat categorical in his defense of boxing, stating that "morality of amateur and scholastic boxing must necessarily be more indefinite than those concerning professional prizefighting." In this Catholic view, there is another means to the end for amateurs, that is, victory, rather than the injury of an opponent. Amateur boxing only becomes sinful when the intent is to injure and render the opponent unconscious. One cannot help but wonder if Bernard would support the professional boxing matches sponsored by urban Catholic parishes as a fund-raising tool, a financial endeavor that had a long history in American Catholicism, certainly as long as boxing as a physical education activity in Catholic schools. Were the Catholic professional matches sinful? Was Holy Mother Church using the degenerated form of pugilism for her own ends? It begs the question, in modern parlance, WWRD – "What would Rocky do?" However one interprets the use of boxing for religious ends, and, vice versa, the effect is one way of viewing sport in contemporary society and of acknowledging its role in the maintenance and propagation of a cultural ideal.

In another faith-based cultural heritage, though, the approach has historically been somewhat different than that of the Catholic faith. "Jews entered the ranks of American boxing in large numbers and by 1928 were the dominant nationality in professional prizefighting, followed by the Italians and Irish," according to Allen Bodmer in his elegiac treatment of Jewish prizefighting, *When Boxing Was a Jewish Sport.*[7] As an immigrant class of people in the United States, Jewish fighters saw the sport as a way out of poverty and a chance to achieve a measure of cultural validation in a land where other opportunities beyond sport were often denied them. It was, as Bodmer states, a "mission." After World War II, when educational and employment opportunities opened wider, other "avenues of advancement became available" and boxing was no longer as attractive to young Jewish men. But boxing for Jewish males was a way to exhibit and take pride in their ethnicity and faith. As Bodmer quotes an early Jewish fight promoter, "You take a Jewish boy and sooner or later his race is decried. He tries so much harder to fight back for himself as a representative of all Jews. The knowledge that more than one Jew is on trial when he fights gives him an incentive for training more faithfully and taking greater pride in his work." It is a "sense of sacred mission." In this point of view, the loneliness and singularity of the fighter in the ring is mitigated by a goal of group salvation, of proving religious worthiness and sustaining cultural needs.

More tellingly, Bodmer quotes sociologist Thomas Jenkins, who has traced the history of the dominant nationalities in boxing, concluding that it was second generation urban immigrants who primarily boxed, the succession being English, Irish, Italians, Jews, African Americans, and others. For the "others" category, one could now, in the 21st century, insert Catholic Latinos, and in the case of a recent championship contender, Eastern Europeans. For this latter category, one has only to look at welterweight boxer Dmitry Salita, a native of Ukraine who proudly wore the Star of David on his fighting togs and refused to battle on the Sabbath.[8] And of the Islamic view of boxing, the most prominent athlete has been Muhammad Ali, a fighter who proclaimed his faith with every bout. Though the theology of Ali's Nation of Islam diverges somewhat from mainstream Islam, Ali remains the most visible of Islamic fighters even in his declining years. For Ali, his Muslim faith was regarded more in the public view as one of race rather than religion, and until he became a celebrated statesman of sport following the 1996 Atlanta Olympiad, his faith was often mocked by the public and by the media. In recent times, he has been accorded a fresh and more understanding appreciation of his beliefs.[9]

Former heavyweight champion Mike Tyson is arguably the most brutal boxing personality in the past century.[10] He underwent conversion to Islam while incarcerated in prison after a rape conviction. He has never equivocated about his own violent nature, both in and out of the ring, but has said he approached Islam because of the questions that had always plagued him: Who am I? How do I take my fate in my own hands without being lost and humiliated? How do I reconcile by fear with the view of me as a man consumed with madness? According to Tyson, Islam helped answer those questions, which were stirred in his earliest professional days when his trainer, mentor, and father figure, Cus D'Amato, told

---

[7] When Boxing Was a Jewish Sport by Allen Bodmer, Praeger Publishers, 1997.
[8] http://www.dsalita.com/.
[9] Muhammad Ali: His Life and Times by Thomas Hauser, Simon & Schuster, 1992 and King of the World: Muhammad Ali and the Rise of an American Hero by David Remnick, Random House, 1998.
[10] Iron Mike: A Mike Tyson Reader, ed. by Daniel O'Connor and George Plimpton, Da Capo Press, 2002.

him over and over again that boxing is only partly physical; most of it should be approached in a spiritual way.

Mainstream Islamic beliefs see in boxing a contradiction to the teachings of the Prophet Muhammad. Mas'uud Ahmed Khan, in an erudite consideration of Islam and boxing, sees religious pride in Muhammad Ali, who also transferred this to other Muslims a sense of pride in the sport, "felt by Muslims when a defeated non-Muslim opponent was universal." Stated another way, boxing success by a representative of the underdog outweighs the negative aspects of the sport, something that has always been the case when faith intersects with athletics. But Khan poses the question of whether Muslims should really enjoy and participate in boxing. He looks at the evidence of injury and death and concludes that boxing must be considered *haram,* or forbidden, because of the excessive force directed to the head – the knockout punch being the most desirable outcome of a match for both boxer and fans. Khan quotes the Prophet: "If somebody fights or beats somebody, then he should avoid the face," and refers to a scholar quoting the teachings of the Prophet that it is even wrong to beat an animal on the face. Beyond Islam and relevant to other religions, the face gazes not only upon the earthly works of the Almighty, but eventually upon the face of a god in the afterlife. In a way, Khan's view harkens back to that of Bernard in saying that properly taught, boxing can be a valuable educational tool because of the physical training.[11]

There are other cultural and social aspects to faith and fighting. As an example, exhibit by San Antonio artist Vincent Valdez in 2004 and 2006 cast Jesus Christ as a boxer in a series of charcoal drawings to tell the Passion story, and the artist rendered the crucifixion as a boxing match.[12] The boxer, then, becomes the true Christ, the Everyman who takes our own beatings from the turmoil of daily life and puts them on himself in the ring. At the least, Valdez's view was a provocative take on the topic of faith and boxing.

In the New Life Church in Sioux Falls, South Dakota in 2009, there was the Saturday Night Slam when Pastor Jerry James, a former amateur boxer, used boxing as a religious metaphor for his congregants, much as the Reverend Billy Sunday, a former professional baseball player near the turn of the 2oth century, used that sport in his sermons from 1900 to 1903. These approaches take the spectacle of sport and merge it with religious expression. The Reverend James delivered his message wile in the fight ring, he stated, as a parable for the battles of mankind.[13]

And what of Rocky Balboa? In the film, Rocky wears a crucifix, he crosses himself before battle, and before his big bout with the foe, Apollo Creed, he makes a special detour on his drive to the arena to stop in on his parish priest, asking for blessing before he continues through the dark night streets to meet his fate. In his world, boxing requires the faith to succeed. The boxer, for all the trainers, managers, hangers-on, media, and fans with whom he is constantly surrounded, those minutes in the ring are isolated and alone. There is almost an inevitable destiny of injury and death. To establish a rationale for what he does, to

---

[11] http://www.masud.co.uk/ISLAM/misc/boxing.htm, n.d.
[12] http://www.depauw.edu/news-media/latest-news/details/16858/ and http://glasstire.com/2004/08/02/vincent-valdez-stations/.
[13] http://usatoday30.usatoday.com/news/religion/2009-02-02-church-fights_N.htm.

strive for victory and health, to call upon help, he becomes a willing supplicant to the gods, and in so doing represents cultural norms for both sports and society.

Chapter 21

The Martial Science of Boxing and Its Contribution to Military Close Combat

James R. Lee-Barron

Introduction

This chapter will examine the more obscure aspects of Boxing as a martial science. It will illustrate that the martial history, tradition and virtue of boxing is an undeniable fact albeit one that is rarely, if ever, seriously acknowledged and understood. It will concentrate upon the military applications rather than the normal sporting elements (although it will touch upon certain aspects of sporting competition where deemed appropriate) demonstrating how it has been an integral part of the training of a warrior since ancient times, how it was used to develop "fighting spirit" and how it has continued to provide a major contribution to the origins and development of modern military close-combat techniques in much the same way as certain oriental martial arts. Competition has probably always been an integral part of the human condition. Indeed, isn't evolution itself, with its law of "Natural Selection" a competition to see who is the fittest, fastest, strongest and most suited to survive? Again, competition amongst the human race takes many forms with two of the most important ones being sport, whereby friends can compete with one another and, at the other end of the spectrum, war, whereby enemies can compete against each other. Boxing seems to have played an important role in each of these avenues of competition, and continues to be a popular sport both at the amateur and professional level. Not to mention the thousands of illegal bare-knuckle prize fights that take place every year in different countries around the globe. However, it's worth as a strictly military art of self-defence seems to have become somewhat neglected and ignored. This is a great pity because, as we shall see from the following paper, it was for centuries one of the most important tools in the shaping and training of a warrior and, even in these modern days of "smart weapons technologies" it still has a lot to potentially offer when it comes to instilling skill, determination and the fighting spirit into the hearts and minds of contemporary soldiers.

Martial Arts, Culture, and Society

Martial arts have always had, and must always retain, a certain amount of social and cultural relevance. They play a vital part of such things as sport, religion and warfare, and have been an integral part of the human condition for tens of thousands of years, inspiring invention and ingenuity, aiding people to both conquer and resist, to preserve and destroy in many cultures that can be found around the world, eventually giving birth to a set of rules regarding moral conduct and behaviour known colloquially as the "Warrior code", to which the warrior caste would strictly adhere, and by which they would live and die. Therefore, engineering, science, technology and philosophy have all felt the influence of the "martial arts" and, of course, vice versa. However, when we talk about warriors from the grass roots level, we need to ensure that the people chosen for such an illustrious way of life must be of good temperament and sound judgement and, above all, be made of the "right stuff". After all, having the responsibility of protecting your people is no easy task, and warfare is an extremely violent and bloody affair indeed, so how do you prepare people for such work? The answer lies in their selection and training which together make up a very effective filtering process, enabling the selectors to identify and discard those found not to be worthy or suited to such duties. This is where the basic and brutal hand to hand combat techniques come to the fore because they help prepare a person both mentally and physically for the life of a warrior.

Boxing, with its attention to detail and underpinning aggression is perfect for this task. In addition, a good boxer will learn to use strategy and tactics rather than simply relying solely upon brute force and technique, to eventually defeat an opponent and understand that, in order to realise victory, you must be prepared to suffer and weather a certain amount of pain and hardship. All of which are important lessons for the battlefield, right from the foot-soldier up to the commander-in-chief. Boxing, then, has played an important role in the development of the warrior in many cultures across the world for centuries, and has continued to make such contributions well into the 20th century. Lately, mixed martial arts athletes have come to appreciate the undoubted effectiveness of the "left-jab" or the "right-hook" and, in this manner; it continues to be practiced by not only "boxers" per-say, but other combative athletes as well.

Even so, it's more martial applications, such as being a tool for the training and selection of soldiers, and as part of an integrated system of combat, has become somewhat neglected over the past few years, with people being ignorant (or, perhaps even unwilling?) to acknowledge just how valuable boxing can be in a close combat situation, favouring instead the oriental systems. It is to help draw attention to this military application that this article has been written, and to raise awareness of the fact that boxing is, indeed, a true "martial science" and not simply an exciting and complex combat sport.

The Ancient World

Boxing is one of the most ancient of all the martial arts, and has quite a clear and traceable history when compared to some other forms of combative systems. The term "boxing" itself derives from the "box-like" shape of the closed hand or fist. In Latin, the fist is called "pugnus" so hence the alternative term: "pugilism". Pugnus itself derives from the Greek "pug me", meaning "fist."

Boxing was practiced in one form or another by most of the classical civilisations of antiquity including those of Egypt, Sumer (A form of boxing can be seen in Sumerian Carvings from the 3rd millennium BCE, while an Egyptian relief from about a thousand years later actually shows both participants and spectators. In each case the boxers are bare-fisted) and Crete (where it is even possible to see boxers depicted wearing a primitive type of glove). Even more ancient than this, in 1927 the famous Archaeologist, Dr Ephraim Avigidor Speiser, discovered a Mesopotamian stone tablet while excavating an ancient temple at Khafaje, which is situated very close to Baghdad, Iraq, that depicted two men preparing for a boxing match. This tablet is believed to be some 7000 years old! Fighting with the fists is also described in several ancient Indian texts including the Vedas, the Ramayana and the Mahabharata. In addition, evidence has been found in certain excavations carried out at the site of two ancient cities called Mohenjadaro and Harappa in the Indus valley. However, although fighting using the closed fists would seem to come naturally to most human beings, it was perhaps in Greece that both the sport and science of Boxing began to gather widespread popularity and was organised and developed accordingly.

It was in Greece that Boxing became an Olympic sport (688 BCE), and it was also in Greece that it was refined and recognised as being a valuable tool in the training of the warrior. Boxing is mentioned by Homer in the 13th book of the Iliad (Circa 675 BCE) wherein it is described as being part of the competitive games the Mycenaean's used to honour their dead. At this time, while there were some rules (such as forbidding any clinching or wrestling) there were absolutely no weight divisions, no rings, no rounds and certainly no referee. Boxers would simply pummel each another until one was eventually knocked out or gave up. Consequently, serious injuries and even death were not that uncommon. Pythagoras of Samos, who won the boxing crown at the 48th Olympiad (588 or 584 BCE), is recognised as being the first truly "Technical Boxer", for he was a relatively small man standing about 5ft7in and weighing in at only 160 pounds who, never the less, beat numerous much larger contestants.

As might be expected, it was the warlike Spartans who were to capitalise most with Boxing, recognising it as an effective means of instilling the fighting spirit in the recruit through not only building up levels of courage and tenacity, but also using it as a means of teaching the basics of fighting with the sword, spear and shield. In this manner boxing training became not only an effective unarmed fighting style in its own right, but also served in complimenting the effective use of certain weapons as part of an integrated system of combat training. Spartan society was extremely martial, and they trained hard and long to be efficient soldiers on the battlefield. It is said that they were almost as dangerous unarmed as they were with a weapon. Indeed, this fact is remarked upon by the great historian Heroditus in his account of the battle of Thermopylae, wherein he says: "Those that had them fought with their spears and, when their spears broke, they fought with their swords. When their swords broke, they fought with tooth, nail and fist".

As the popularity of boxing grew it gradually became split and divided, with one branch maintaining the martial aspect in order to compliment the armed prowess of the Hoplite, and the other concentrating upon more sporting applications (albeit quite brutal ones!). Thus, you had the professional soldier on the one hand and the sportsperson on the other. Even Homer tells us of the difference between combat sports and actual combat when he describes the lament of the champion boxer Epeios who pleaded that his incompetence on the battlefield be excused because of his success in sport boxing, saying that it was not possible to be good at all things and that the only place where he wasn't able to fight well was the battlefield itself! (Iliad XXIII) However, he is also credited with designing and building the Trojan horse with the help of Athena, as is told in the (Odyssey IV.265ff and Odyssey VIII.492ff) so, perhaps the poor fellow had a point after all, and we should let him off!

The Etruscans were particularly fond of boxing and were actually the very first to introduce the term "Pugilism" a word that has long since become synonymous with the science and which continues to be used right up to the present day. Later, Boxing became an integral part of the training regime for the Roman Legionaries, with a particularly savage form being adapted for use in the so called "games" of the Arena. It eventually became popular throughout Rome, with all types of people participating including members of the aristocracy (A fight between the agile Dares and the towering Entellus is described at length in the Roman national epic "Aeneid" (1st century BCE)

In 500 A.D., boxing was banned altogether by the Holy Roman Emperor Theodoric the Great for being offensive to the creator as it disfigured the face which was, after all, supposed to be the image of God. However, this edict had little effect outside the major cities of the Eastern Empire and, therefore, boxing continued to evolve as both a sport and a method of self-defence throughout all of Europe but particularly in Italy and especially in the British Isles.

Prize Fighting Era

Boxing resurfaces in strength in England during the early 18th century as "Bare-Knuckle Boxing" sometimes also referred to as" prize-fighting". The first documented account of a bare-knuckle fight in England appeared back in 1681 in a newspaper called "The London Protestant Mercury" with the first English champion being James Figg in 1719. As a well as being the first boxing champion of England, James Figg was also a very adept cudgel-fighter and swordsman and was to play a pivotal role in the boxing renaissance. When he opened his school in London in 1719 Figg made a reasonable living out of teaching young gentleman the art of self-defence by applying the precepts of modern fencing—footwork, speed, and the straight lunge—to fist-fighting. This is interesting in that, as you will recall, Boxing was originally used in order to augment and enhance training with weapons in ancient Greece, whereas now, Boxers learned to throw straight punches, the basis of modern boxing, from fencers. To some extent, it could even be said that boxing replaced duelling with swords and pistols, allowing men of all social classes to defend themselves and their honour without necessarily having to severely maim or kill each other. Despite this connection with fencing, boxing encounters during this early modern era were largely unstructured and highly uncivilized. Boxers fought bare-knuckle (without gloves), and wrestling, choking, throwing, gouging, and purring (kicking and stomping on one's opponent with spiked boots) were commonplace so that, in some respects at least, it bore far more of a resemblance to the ancient Greek Pankration or Japanese Jiu-Jitsu than to the sport we all now know and accept as being boxing today. Also, again like its early predecessor, prize-fighting had no written rules: There were no weight divisions, round limits, or referees. In general, it was extremely savage and very chaotic. The first boxing rules, called the London Prize-Ring Rules, were introduced by the heavyweight champion Jack Broughton in 1743 in an attempt to safe-guard fighters from serious injury and even death. Under these rules, if a boxer was knocked to the ground and was not able to continue after 30 seconds, then they would be considered to have lost the bout. In addition, striking an opponent while they were down and grappling below the waist were strictly prohibited

Although bare-knuckle fighting was in almost every aspect far more brutal than modern boxing, it did allow the fighters a single advantage not enjoyed by today's boxers: The London Prize Rules permitted the fighter to drop to one knee to begin a 30-second count at any time. Thus any fighter realizing he was in trouble had an opportunity to recover to a certain degree in this manner. This is in stark contrast to the modern sport of boxing, wherein intentionally going down will cause the recovering fighter to lose points in the scoring system. Furthermore, as the contestants did not have heavy leather gloves and wrist-wraps to protect their hands, a certain amount of restraint was required when striking to the head. It is perhaps due to this that, although severe injuries were sometimes incurred by the fighters, there were no actual deaths ever recorded from "bare knuckle" fighting. This would later change drastically with the introduction of the boxing glove, which protected the fighter's hands so well they were able to execute full-force punches to the head, with the result sometimes proving fatal.

In 1838 the London Prize Ring rules were expanded and were subjected to further revision in 1853. These were eventually replaced by the famous Marquis of Queensberry rules in 1867. It was the introduction of this modern set of rules, together with a High-Court ruling in 1882 which declared that bare-knuckle matches were "an assault occasioning actual bodily harm", (despite the very clear consent of the fighters), that saw the gradual demise of prize fighting eventually giving birth to what we know as "modern boxing"

That said, the effectiveness of even this modern, refined boxing as a martial science cannot be denied. For example: On December 31, 1908, in Paris, France, heavyweight boxer Sam McVey knocked out Jiu-Jitsuka Tano Matsuda (Jiu-Jitsu) in ten seconds. And, in another bout held on January 12, 1928, in Yokohama, Japan, Packey O'Gatty, a bantamweight boxer, knocked out another Jiu-Jitsuka called Shimakado with a single punch in less than four seconds!

Bartitsu or Baritsu

Mention must also be made here of a certain gentlemen by the name of Edward William Barton-Wright who, after returning to the UK from three years in Japan, incorporated certain boxing techniques into his new, exciting and eclectic martial art which he called "Bartitsu". This was, perhaps, the original "mixed martial arts" (although its main goal was that of self-defence rather than any kind of sporting application) and was truly an ingenious innovation that incorporated ideas and techniques from fencing, wrestling, Jiu jitsu, savate, cane, boxing and even how to use your Bowler hat as a self-defence tool!

"Bartitsu", (later to become known as "Baritsu") provided people with a truly integrated form of self-defence and became quite popular for a short period of time at the turning of the 19th to the 20th century, and it was this martial art that Sir Arthur Conan Doyle chose to arm his great literary creation Sherlock Holmes with. In "The adventure of the empty house" Holmes tells his friend, Dr. Watson about his victory over his nemesis and arch-enemy Professor Moriarty during their fateful encounter at the Reichenbach Falls, explaining it was thanks to "Baritsu, or the Japanese system of wrestling, which has more than once been of use to me" It is thanks to this mis-spelling that "Bartitsu" came to be remembered as "Baritsu", and that the western influences such as that of boxing, were almost completely disregarded in favour of the Oriental. Even so, this brief historical episode is still yet another endorsement to the continuing use of boxing as a martial art rather than simply a combat sport, and that is why I have alluded to it (albeit in passing) here.

The Military

It was this obvious effectiveness, together with its strict set of "Gentlemanly rules" that caused the military, and especially the officer class, to recognise boxing as being of some very real worth in the basic training and battlefield prowess of their soldiers. However, there was one particular officer who saw even further: Captain William J. Jacomb. The First World War has gone down in the record's as being the worst managed conflict in history. This was largely due to the fact that most of the senior officers involved had undergone their basic training and fought their first military campaigns in the 19th century. That meant they had cut their soldierly teeth upon massed cavalry charges and infantry organised into lines and squares, and so had thought that they could continue to engage the enemy in this manner in the 20th century, even with its machine guns, air support, communications, mustard-gas and modern artillery pieces. These outdated and obsolete strategies and tactics were to soon turn the battlefields of World War One into muddy, bloody acres of "no-man's-land", honeycombed with thousands of trenches that actually ended up interlocking in some cases. In such an inhospitable and dangerous type of terrain it was not uncommon for patrols from opposing sides to "bump" into each other with little or even no warning. Consequently, the fighting was often of a very desperate nature, taking place at extremely close-quarters. It is as a direct result of this that both sides began experimenting with various hand to hand combat systems including Japanese Jiu Jitsu, in order to help provide their troops with that much needed "edge" on the battlefield.

William J. Jacomb was an officer in the Canadian army who had a lot of experience as a boxing coach at various universities as well as in the military. It had come to his attention that it was the soldiers who had a basic knowledge of boxing who also seemed to make the best bayonet fighters. He immediately started to design a programme of instruction for the army that combined standard boxing drills with the efficient use of the bayonet and put forward a proposal to his superiors that this training should be made available to as many troops as possible. In 1916, Jacomb was appointed as an instructor to the Bayonet fighting and Physical Training Staff of the Canadian Army in order to teach his methods of boxing/bayonet to a specially selected group of soldiers most of whom already possessed a certain amount of boxing training and experience, with the idea being that they would then return to their individual units as instructors in close-quarter combat. The students were divided into classes of 20 with each course being of 21 days duration during which time a lot a material had to be covered and learnt. Jacomb himself says:

> "Physical courage is perhaps the most common of virtues, but the courage of a soldier, and especially in the bayonet fighter, is a courage borne of confidence and ability to fight and to defend himself. I do not believe there is any other form of exercise which develops this as quickly as the practice of boxing. Secondly, and fortunately, bayonet fighting is so near akin to boxing that the practice of boxing develops skill in bayonet in less time, with less expense, and with fewer casualties".

As already stated, the urgent need and importance for effective hand to hand fighting (particularly Bayonet) had already been identified and acknowledged due to the nature of the conflict and the appalling conditions in which it was fought, so Jacombs's endeavours in this area were both supported and encouraged. The official 1916 manual on Bayonet Training says that:

> "The spirit of the bayonet must be inculcated into all ranks so that they will go forward with the aggressive determination and confidence in superiority borne of continual practice, without which a bayonet assault will not be effective".

From the outset, Jacombs course was well received and deemed to be an outstanding success turning out as it did confident and competent instructors for the army. Later, in 1918, Jacomb published a book entitled "Boxing for Beginners" outlining his methods. It consisted of three parts with the first describing how to box, the second describing the relationship of boxing to bayonet fighting and the third on how to organise a boxing tournament. In his conclusion to the chapter regarding the relationship between boxing and bayonet fighting, Jacomb states the following:

> "Every man who is going to carry a rifle and bayonet should learn to box to help him use the bayonet. He should be taught by men who have had experience in boxing. His bayonet fighting should be taught by a teacher of that subject. If the instructor is good at both, so much the better. The pupil must always be taught that the point of his bayonet is the best end of his weapon."

This is very similar to telling a boxer to keep his opponent on "the end of the Left-jab" or to concentrate on long-range "Outfighting". However, Jacomb did also demonstrate and teach how "In-fighting" boxing tactics and techniques could be adapted for use with a rifle and bayonet, especially by utilising the butt- end of the rifle to deliver "Hooks" and "Upper-Cuts" to dispatch a foe quickly and efficiently. Captain Jacombs' training courses were very well received, being a resounding success with the troops who found what they learned helped to keep them alive in the trenches.

Conclusion

Boxing or, as it is sometimes (very rightfully) known: "The noble art of self-defence" is, without a doubt, a true martial science. It has contributed to the training of soldiers almost since the beginning of recorded history. Whether it be aiding a 'Hoplite' in effective sword and shield drills, affording the officer class a non-lethal alternative to duelling, or enhancing the use of the bayonet in 20th Century warfare. It has demonstrated its effectiveness on the battlefield, in the sporting arena (against other martial arts) and as an effective means of self-defence, as taught by James Figg and others. Indeed, to this day, an extremely savage form of boxing known as ?Milling" is used to help select soldiers for the elite airborne units of the Parachute Regiment in the United Kingdom, with similar applications being employed in the units of other armies around the word. I, myself, have experimented with boxing drills as a means teaching basic short-blade techniques, and have found this to be extremely worth-while. As a martial science that has proven itself consistently over literally thousands of years, it is my opinion that boxing still has a great deal to offer. At the very least, it is a fantastic method for keeping fit, healthy and focused and also improves balance, coordination and confidence in the individual. Thus, by learning boxing a person will be far more able to defend themselves both on the street and in battle (we should remember here that successful bayonet charges have been recorded in both the Falklands (Guards Brigade/Parachute Regiment July 1982) and Iraq (Argyle and Sutherland Highlanders, May 2004).

Boxing should be regarded as being much more than the sport we see. It is a bono fide martial science, and should, therefore be accepted, respected and appreciated as being such.

References

Barton-Wright, & E. W. March (1899) "The new art of self-defence: How a man may defend himself against every form of attack." *Pearsons Magazine* 7

Beaumont, N. (1997). Championship Streetfighting: Boxing as a Martial Art. Boulder: Paladin Press.

Collins, N. (1990). Boxing Babylon. New York: Citadel Press.

Crowther, N. B. (2007). Sport in Ancient Times. Westport, Connecticut and London Press

Dempsey, J. (1983). Championship Fighting: Explosive Punching and Aggressive Defense. Downey, CA: Centerline Press.

Donnelly, N. (1881). Self Defence or the Art of Boxing, Weldon and Co

Early, G. (1994). The Culture of Bruising: Essays on Prizefighting, Literature, and Modern American Culture. Hopewell, NJ: Ecco Press.

Eustathius, 1324.18 (translation to English from Sweet, W. E. (1987). Sport and Recreation in Ancient Greece: A Sourcebook with Translations. New York and Oxford: Oxford University Press.)

Frost, K. T. (1906). Greek Boxing. *The Journal of Hellenic Studies*

Gilbey, J. F. (1986.) Western Boxing and World Wrestling: Story and Practice. Berkeley: North Atlantic Books.

Haffner, C. and D.E. Lusitant (1996). Blood and Honor at the First Olympics. [Motion Picture]. United States: Greystone Communications, Inc.

Homer, the Iliad, Book 13 (Circa 750-650BC)

Homer, the Odyssey IV .265ff and Odyssey VIII.492ff (Circa 750-650BC)

Jacomb, W. J. (1918). Boxing for Beginners. Lea & Febiger. Philadelphia and New York.

Michel, E. B. (1897). Fencing, Boxing and Wrestling (Fourth edition), Part 2 "Boxing and Sparring".Longmans, Green and Co

O'Dell, D. & O. F. Snelling. (1995). The Boxing Album: An Illustrated History. New York: Smithmark Publishers.

Odd, G. (1989). The Encyclopedia of Boxing. Secaucus, NJ: Chartwell Books.

Speiser, E. A. (1937). "New discoveries at Tepe Gawra amd Khafaje" *American Journal of Archaeology*, Vol. 41, No. 2 (Apr. - Jun.)

Sweet, W. E. (1987). Sport and Recreation in Ancient Greece. New York: Oxford University Press.

Virgil, Aeneid (1st century BC)

Chapter 22

The Sweet Science: Boxing as Sport and Spectacle

Guy Spriggs

What is thus displayed for the public is the great spectacle of Suffering, Defeat, and Justice. Wrestling present's man's suffering with all the amplification of tragic masks.[1]

Roland Barthes (1957)

Each boxing match is a story – a unique and highly condensed drama without words. Even when nothing sensational happens: then the drama is "merely" psychological.[2]

Joyce Carol Oates (1986)

Introduction

As they wait for the bullfights to begin in Ernest Hemingway's book *The Sun Also Rises,* Jake Barnes and Brett Ashley look over a wall, watching as bulls are corralled into the arena. Jake leans over the wall, noting the aggressive maneuvers of the bull, "striking into the wood from side to side with his horns, [making] a great noise" (Hemingway, 2003/1926, p. 143). After Brett comments on the strength and beauty of the bull, Jake instructs her on exactly what she's seeing: "'Look how he knows how to use his horns,' I said. 'He's got a left and a right

---

[1] Barthes, R. (1972). *Mythologies.* (A Lavers, Trans.). New York, NY: Hill and Wang. (Original work published 1957).
[2] Oates, J.C. (2006). *On Boxing.* New York, NY: Harper Perennial. (Original work published 2002).

just like a boxer'" (Hemingway, 2003/1926, p. 144). Although she cannot accurately read the bull's actions at first, Brett is fascinated by the display and eventually understands the image as communicated by Jake, saying, "I saw it [...] I saw him shift from his left to his right horn" (Hemingway 2003/1926, p. 144).

In "The World of Wrestling," Roland Barthes writes that professional wrestling is not a sport but instead a "...spectacle of excess," partaking "...of the nature of the great solar spectacles, Greek drama and bullfights" (1972/1957, p.15). Wrestling is framed by Barthes as something akin to a dramatic play, a staged performance with characters and conventions and archetypal roles. But Barthes also suggests that wrestling is a spectacle because its meaning is communicated by individual intelligible images, relying on outward, exaggerated expressions throughout the match. In this way, wrestling is juxtaposed with boxing, a "Jansenist sport, based on a demonstration of excellence," defined by the finality of its result rather than being a sum of singular meanings (Barthes 1972/1957, p. 15-16). In '*The Sun Also Rises*', Hemingway demonstrates that bullfighting too is similarly viewed and read by its spectators, but has his characters communicate the meaning of the moment by relating it to boxing, comparing the movements of the bull to having a left and a right just like a boxer. This moment suggests that, for both characters Jake Barnes and author Ernest Hemingway, boxing can be *read:* like wrestling, boxing produces individual moments that offer meaning aside from – and often times, in the absence of – a final, conclusive image of superiority. But boxing cannot be similarly translated: boxing can only be understood through boxing – or, as Joyce Carol Oates suggests, "boxing isn't really a metaphor, it is the thing in itself" (2006/2002, 102). In this way, then, it is possible to conceive of boxing as a spectacle: an arena where meaning is communicated through signs and narrative, where stories follow the idealized "pattern of Justice" that Barthes observes in the world of wrestling (1972/1957, p. 22).

As a result of its ever-expanding history and in-ring limitations (time limits, judges), boxing has become more than just a sport – something other than a struggle for individual superiority. As Norman Mailer suggests (1990/1988), boxing is a language of the body: a boxer uses the entire body to communicate meaning to the opponent, to the referee, to the judges, and to the crowd. Boxing is a sport – based on the demonstration of excellence – but it is also spectacle in the tradition of Barthes – a language system based on signs and excess. As a result, this dual reality leaves boxing to communicate meaning through an inherently flawed system of language, creating a massive middle ground of slippage in defining identity between what is real or authentic and what is not.

Joyce Carol

In her writings on boxing, Joyce Carol Oates contends that "Professional boxing is the only major American sport whose primary, and often murderous, energies are not coyly defected by such artifacts as balls and pucks" (2006/2002, p. 185). While Oates's writings are integral to a critical understanding of contemporary prizefighting, her assertion about the unmediated singularity of boxing is misleading: there are undoubtedly artifacts that exist in the ring and inform boxing, they merely don't take the shape of externalized score-keepers like pucks and balls. The accessories of boxing are the stuff of Barthes's seminal text *Mythologies:* everyday objects taken as natural – their cultural significance overlooked, their ability to create and impart meaning obscured. Apart from the atmosphere and environment of a prizefight – themselves indicators of spectacle of a different sort – the most obvious device that separates *boxing* as a sport from *fighting* as a barbaric and illegal activity is the boxing glove. Gloves have the practical function of safety, cocooning the hand with padding that protects both boxers. In order to understand boxing as a spectacle, however, one must see the value created by the boxing gloves as a sign and the way(s) they can be utilized to communicate meaning. Gloves are typically colorful and shiny, which allows the spectator to more clearly follow the punch and observe the damage it causes. Similarly, gloves are covered in leather, creating loud, palpable *snaps* for shots to the head and cringe-worthy *thuds* for shots to the body. Boxing gloves are typically the subject of much debate before a big title bout: heavier punchers want smaller gloves, allowing for more of their punching power to be delivered without cushioning; defensive experts lobby for bigger gloves, giving them larger targets to avoid and more opportunity to block; boxers facing opponents who cut easily arrange for white gloves, so that any bleeding that occurs will be more easily seen. Without such props, the moments created during a boxing match are less intelligible, leaving the meaning of the boxing match in the final image, creating definition in the hope of a clear outcome where one competitor is standing while the other is not.

Another reality of the ring – as previously mentioned – is that even in the middle of the most furious exchange the boxers are not truly alone. In the introduction to her book *Boxing: A Cultural History,* Kasia Boddy features a 1912 watercolor by William Roberts entitled *The Boxing Match, Novices,* which she reads as the conveyance of the "relentless succession of contenders, champions and palookas that makes up the history of boxing" (2008, p. 7). What Roberts's art more accurately displays, however, is the multitude of figures that factor in to what is inevitably a contest between two men: there is the manager ushering his boxer up the ring steps, the ring attendant holding open the ropes, the announcer introducing the bout, the trainer fanning down his boxer with a towel, and more individuals whose function(s) are not as clear. Boxing, then, does not suffer from a lack of individualized images, but instead risks being unintelligible because its moments can be filled with so many indicating figures that the images can potentially become overly saturated with meaning.

Most importantly, however, Boxers are overseen by what Oates calls the "shadowy third" (2006/2002, p. 8) – the referee, who, as in the world of wrestling, mediates the bout and acts as the representative of the rules. The main function of the referee is to make sure that the rules are followed and enforced, but he also plays an integral role in communicating the meaning of the action to the audience. It is easy to ignore the referee when watching a bout, but when potentially meaningful or ambitious moments occur, he becomes the most visible figure in the ring. Although the knockdown creates an intelligible image of superiority, its meaning is not complete without the referee's count, as otherwise there is nothing to distinguish a knock*down* (a temporary moment of excellence) from a knock*out* (the definitive, finalized moment of excellence). The referee reminds us of another important truth: boxing is not fighting – all meaning in boxing is predicated upon the existence of an agreed-upon and understood set of rules, without which meaning ceases to be. David Chandler calls similar attention to the referee, writing that the "rules not only gave boxing the basis for its current structure but perhaps more significantly transformed its visual imagery, its character as a spectacle" (1996, p. 13). The ability of the spectator to view the boxing match as a succession of meaningful images, then, is predicated upon the role played by the referee, representing the rules that govern the ring and signifying value for those watching the bout. As Oates reminds us, the referee is "central to the drama of boxing" – the referee "makes boxing possible" (2006/2002, p. 47).

An infamous example of boxing's reliance on language took place on April 6, 1987 – the night "Marvelous" Marvin Hagler defended his middleweight championship against "Sugar" Ray Leonard in Las Vegas, Nevada. Hagler had been champion for nearly seven years and conventional wisdom suggested the fan-favorite Leonard had little chance to win. The fact that Leonard was eventually awarded a hotly-contested split decision is less important, however, than the manner in which he won. Like the iconic Muhammad Ali, Leonard was a showman, boxing in an unnatural style and appearing "to be perpetually on the brink of disaster" (Oates, 2006/2002, p. 193). More than that, Leonard was also a master of boxing language, and thus knew that he did not have to be superior to Hagler – to *beat* Hagler – in order to be victorious. This bout reveals Leonard's ability to exploit the accessories of boxing, particularly his boxing shoes. Rather than wearing the traditional boots, Leonard donned shoes with red tassels affixed to each ankle. Unlike the boxing glove, which has practical as well as theoretical function, Leonard's boots served only one purpose: drawing the eye of the spectator to the movement of his feet, exaggerating his movement and making him appear as the faster, more mobile boxer. By attacking Hagler and then sliding away using long strides, Leonard was able to make Hagler seem slow and ineffective, communicating the message that Hagler was unable to close the distance and attack.

This bout also reveals Marvin Hagler's unwillingness to utilize the language of boxing. Hagler's boots were also fitted with tassels, but he made no attempt to use them to the desired effect. In other words, Hagler recognized the capacity for language – the potential for communication – in the ring, but was unwilling or unable to *speak*. Moreover, Hagler, who was skeptical of judges' ability to accurately score a bout, often claimed that his fists were his judges, meaning that he would always knock out his opponent instead of letting someone else decide the winner ("The tale of Hagler: Leonard," 2003). He had finished all but one opponent in his twelve title defenses, creating unmistakable final images: one fighter standing and victorious while the other is fallen, vanquished. Leonard, on the other hand, admitted that his strategy was to attack furiously at end of each round, creating the image of activity rather than actually sustaining offense – in his words, to "steal the round" ("The tale of Hagler: Leonard," 2003). According to boxing analyst Larry Merchant, Hagler felt the decision was stolen from him because he was not as glamorous as Leonard ("The tale of Hagler: Leonard," 2003), but the reality is that he lost because he was not as fluent in the language of boxing. It is little surprise that Hagler says, "I don't see what everybody sees. This man never beat me" ("The tale of Hagler: Leonard," 2003): Hagler's performance demonstrates that even boxers themselves often fail to grasp the intricacies of boxing's system of signs. The ambiguity and subjectivity in viewing classic bouts such as this one reiterate that even the most carefully constructed language system has limits – what is signified or intended can have any number of received meanings.

Every action in boxing is an opportunity to create meaning – not necessarily to define boxing as a metaphor for life (as Oates suggests), but to communicate through intelligible images. The epigraph to Rotella's *Cut Time: An Education at the Fights* features a quote from boxer Terronn Millett, who declares, "We both come to punish the person. The difference is I think about some of the things I want to throw. I don't throw them wild and out of context. My punches have meaning" (2003). The function of the accessories of boxing – as implied by Millett's comment – is rooted in a desire to find meaning in the individual moments of the contest. Whereas wrestling is built around the clear presentation of suffering, creating the need for unmistakable gestures and signs, the reality of the suffering in boxing means that it often lacks the indicators that make wrestling seem so approachable and lucid to Barthes. In other words, a boxer taking damage in a contest is compelled to look strong and appear unfazed specifically because he is being hurt. This is precisely the reason why boxing can appear unintelligible: boxers do not "sell" punches by expressing suffering equivalent to the blows they have absorbed. Instead, boxers achieve legendary status by their ability to receive punishment, spurned on by commentators who note how particularly tough boxers are able to *eat up punches* and *walk through power*. Therefore, reading the value of particular moments in boxing is predicated upon the execution of a specific action – whether it be a devastating blow or an artful dodge – rather than the reaction of the one receiving the punch or the one whose punches misses the mark.

As a result, Oates's reference to "The old boxing adage [...] that you cannot be knocked out if you see the blow coming" (2006/2002, p. 13) has implications for spectators as well as boxers themselves. Simply put, punches that are not clearly seen cannot be scored, and therefore images cannot be clearly constructed to show which boxer is superior. Because boxing involves less overtly developed signs and less indicators of suffering, viewers have to learn what to look at – as Brett Ashley does in *The Sun Also Rises* – in order to understand the value of what they see. Boxers are nevertheless engaged in a real struggle, the subject of real violence and aggression, and thus not inclined display their suffering. Watching boxing and trying to find meaning in the reactions of the boxer being punished can be entirely counterproductive, as signs of outward suffering can also be used by boxers to indicate a false or reversed meaning. Often times a boxer who receives a punishing blow will rub his face and make it appear as if he barely felt the punch when in reality he was badly hurt, offering this outward display of imperviousness in hopes of affecting his opponent's confidence. Indeed, the opposite is also true: it is not rare to see boxers appear to be hurt, faking wobbly legs or instability, in an attempt to trick the opponent and draw him in. Simply, in boxing there is not the same one-to-one, mathematical relationship between sign and meaning as there is in professional wrestling. Carlo Rotella observes this phenomenon in the career of Muhammad Ali, writing, "Ali, more than anyone, play-acted in and out of the ring so habitually that his opponents had trouble figuring out what effect their punches actually had on him" (2003, pg. 102). Boxers *pretend,* and this is precisely why the accessories of boxing are so necessary and valuable: to amplify the meaning of each action in the absence of the clearer, more deliberate images of suffering present in wrestling.

The natural question that follows recognition of the language of boxing is *what:* what is the meaning or image being contested in the language system created and utilized by boxing? Oates describes boxing as "a purely masculine activity [that] inhabits a purely masculine world" (2006/2002, p. 70), presenting the embodiment of right manhood through a story, "a unique and highly condensed drama" (2006/2002, p. 8) – echoing Barthes's connection between spectacle and dramatic theater. Boxing should also be read along the lines of justice – a battle between good and evil – instead of just a display of masculinity or a demonstration of excellence, framing it in a manner that can create questions surrounding its legitimacy. In the HBO television show *Legendary Nights,* boxing writer Ralph Wiley notes that certain boxers are stuck in a specific role as hero or villain, saying that "Usually in boxing one of the fighters is portrayed as this gallant figure and the other is sort of portrayed as Grendel" ("The tale of Pryor: Arguello," 2003). Because of the massive hype that precedes and surrounds most big name title bouts in modern boxing, the roles being played by the boxers in the contest can often be determined outside of the ring, established in the threats and looming violence of a press conference. But boxing is also full of examples where the villain is created in the ring through the foul play and rule-breaking Barthes uses to identify the bastard in professional wrestling (1972/1957). The clearest, most intelligible moments in boxing occur in the form of fouls: low blows, elbows, headbutts, and rabbit punches (those thrown to the neck or back of the head) always illicit immediate, unmistakable responses from the victim and cause the boxers who committed the foul to be showered with boos. Boxing is therefore not relegated to a pure demonstration of excellence, but can also take part in the "great spectacle of Suffering, Defeat, and Justice" (Barthes, 1972/1957, p. 19). Moreover, while also providing a stage for boxers to perform acts of masculinity, the ring also is also the site of opposition: "struggles between opposing qualities, ideals and values" (Boddy, 2008, p. 7). Boxing has long been a site for individuals – mostly men – to prove themselves, but while the ring may offer fertile ground for the establishment and defense of identity, that same ground is also, at best, unstable.

The Story of Boxing

Roland Barthes argues that wrestling is not sadistic because the viewer sees the image of suffering rather than the reality (1972/1957), but with boxing there is both: the reality of suffering and the language system communicating a larger meaning. Furthermore, in the ring there are also a sequence of individual moments and a story, both pointing toward a central idea we understand as boxing. We are left, then, with Barthes's view of wrestling as "a sum of spectacles, of which no single one is a function" (1972/1957, p. 16) and Oates's claim that "Each boxing match is a story – a unique and highly condensed drama without words" (2006/2002, p. 8). Boxing is indeed the sweet science, as it always implied what Barthes refers to as "a science of the future" (1972/1957, p. 16), but boxing necessitates being read as a spectacle because the final image of a match in itself is not always absolute. "Because a boxing match is a story without words, this doesn't mean that it has no text or no language," Oates argues, "only that the text is improvised action; the language a dialogue between the boxers of the most refined sort" (2006/2002, p. 11). Boxing does have a language, communicated through right hooks and slips and showmanship, operating in a manner distinctly different than the sign-system of the world of wrestling, but nevertheless generating the value necessary to give meaning to each bout. Boxing is not, then, a sum of spectacles of which no single one is a function, but a sum of spectacles of which *all* are a function. The realities of the ring are no less genuine as a result of this complexity: boxing does not cease to be violent or "real" because it employs signs and language in producing meaning. Nevertheless, because boxing is still a sport in spite of these spectacular qualities, it is increasingly difficult to observe and read and understand – or to recognize its claims on identity as legitimate or authentic.

References

Barthes, R. (1972). *Mythologies.* (A. Lavers, Trans.). New York, NY: Hill and Wang. (Original work published 1957).
Boddy, K. (2008). *Boxing: A Cultural History.* London: Reaktion Books.
Chandler, D. (1996). Introduction: the pictures of boxing. In D. Chandler (Ed.), *Boxer: An Anthology of Writings on Boxing and Visual Culture* (13-25). Cambridge, MA: The MIT Press.

Hemingway, E. (2003). *The Sun Also Rises.* New York, NY: Scribner. (Original work published 1926).

Mailer, N. (1990). King of the Hill. In J.C. Oates & D. Halpern (Ed.), *Reading the Fights* (121-149). New York, NY: Prentice Hall Press. (Original work published 1988).

Merchant, L. (Writer), & Sheehan, M. (Director). (2003). The tale of Hagler: Leonard [Television series episode]. In R. Bernstein & R. Greenburg (Producers), *Legendary nights.* New York, NY: Home Box Office.

Merchant, L. (Writer), & Sheehan, M. (Director). (2003). The tale of Pryor: Arguello [Television series episode]. In R. Bernstein & R. Greenburg (Producers), *Legendary nights.* New York, NY: Home Box Office.

Oates, J.C. (2006). *On Boxing.* New York, NY: Harper Perennial. (Original work published 2002).

Roberts, W. (1912). *The Boxing Matches, Novices.*

Rotella, C. (2003). *Cut Time: An Education at the Fights.* New York, NY: Houghton Mifflin Company.

Part V: Capoeira

Chapter 23

A Multi-dimensional Model of the Martial Arts: How Biological, Psychological, Social, and Spiritual Factors Interact in Brazilian Jiu-Jitsu & Capoeira[1]

John T. Sorrell & Itaborá Ferreira

'Preoccupied with a single leaf, you won't see the tree'

Takuan Soho

Introduction

To consider the Martial arts from any other perspective than a multi-dimensional and multi-layered model would not only serve as an injustice to the depth and dimension of Martial arts but also would severely neglect much of the richness and essence of what is comprised within, and derived from, these dynamic art forms. To exclude or remove any of the elements that make-up the martial arts would indeed result in losing sight of the tree. It would be akin to attempting to remove the flour, water, and other ingredients from a cake after it has been baked. Unless one is a skilled chemist or alchemist, it is not possible. These individual elements are part of the whole, fused together to make it what it is. Furthermore, if it were possible to take away these elements, the end result would no longer be

---

[1] Preparation of this manuscript was supported in part by Behavioral Health Psychology Services and the Institute of Brazilian Fitness. A previous version of this material was presented at the 2010 Sport and Society International Conference, Vancouver, Canada. The authors would like to express their sincere appreciation to Nancy G. Sorrell, RN, ND, and PhN. for reviewing and providing valuable comments on a previous version of this chapter.

a cake, just individual or a combination of ingredients that when eaten would neither resemble nor taste anything like the rich, delicious cake out of the oven and frosted with icing. Similarly, leaving out the biological, psychological, socio-cultural, and spiritual components of a discussion on the experiences of a martial artist would be bland, underwhelming, and deficient in the richness that is offered by the arts.

While it may be difficult for some to reflect on the Martial arts without also considering the biological, psychological, socio-cultural, and spiritual elements imbedded therein, it is not an ubiquitously shared or accepted perspective in medicine, psychiatry, or psychology (see Ghaemi, 2010, for a review). Generally speaking, even within the focused area of sports psychology, many theories of human behavior have been applied towards the study of sports and sport-related activities (e.g., Anshel, 2012; Armitage & Connor, 2001; Nesti, 2004). Through critical analysis and thinking, teaching, and research, however, perhaps one day there will be a unified model to specifically guide our understanding of what influences the martial arts and the martial art practitioner. It is with this focus in mind that the following chapter is written. Moreover, we strive to encourage a comprehensive analysis and investigation into the multidimensionality of Martial arts in general and the Brazilian martial arts, Brazilian Jiu-Jitsu and Capoeira, in particular.

The Biopsychosocialspiritual Model (Fitch et al. 2003)

'Flow with whatever may happen, and let your mind be free: Stay centered by accepting whatever you are doing. This is the ultimate'.

Chuang Tzu

To achieve our primary goal, we will help the reader gain a greater appreciation for the Brazilian martial arts by supporting their understanding of a multi-factorial model of human behavior that has been used for many years in health care research and practice, the 'Biopsychosocialspiritual Model' (Fisch, Titzer, Kristeller, et al., 2003; Whitford, Olver, & Peterson, 2008). First, we will provide an introduction and overview of the biopsychosocialspiritual model and each of its components. Second, a brief review of literature will be provided that supports this conceptualization as it applies to human behavior and the martial arts. Next, we will highlight and discuss the biopsychosociospiritual elements within Brazilian Jiu-Jitsu and Capoeira. Last, we will discuss important psychological principles to be considered in future research to facilitate the expansion of our understanding and knowledge base of these Brazilian art forms.

We bring to this textbook a chapter that is based on a perspective that, we hope, can bring a deeper understanding of how the martial artist can benefit from their practice, as well as a solid, empirically based conceptualization for the academic researcher to embrace in their quest to better understand the concepts discussed. Although we will focus on two Brazilian martial arts that collectively have been part of our lives for over 45 years (Capoeira and Brazilian Jiu-Jitsu) the information within this chapter can be applied, conceptually and practically, towards any martial art form.

The biopsychosocial model was comprehensively described by George Engel in an effort to expand the one-dimensional medical model used in psychiatry in the mid-1970's (Engel, 1977). The spiritual element of the multi-layered human experience first appeared in the 1920's, however, when Viktor Frankl introduced spirituality into psychology (e.g., Marseille, 1997). Since the development and early years of the biopsychosocialspiritual model, research has supported it as a particularly useful way to understand the dynamic, and often complex, nature of the human experience (Brady, Peterman, Fitchett, et al., 1999; McGee & Torosian, 2006; Puchalski, 2008; Whitford, Olver, & Peterson, 2008). While the medical model has focused predominantly on a biological approach to understanding disease, the biopsychosocial model examines both disease and illness; with differences in the way illness is expressed being a function of complex interactions among biological, psychological, and socio-cultural variables, all of which impact the individual's perception and response to illness (Turk & Monarch, 2002).

As is depicted in Figure 1, the biopsychosocialspiritual model is a multidimensional conceptualization of human behavior. It is a layered model that entails biological processes, psychological factors, socio-cultural influences, and spiritual elements that together interact to motivate and influence behavior in many ways (Sulmasy, 2002). Within the practice of clinical psychology, patients receive information about how their psychological experiences can influence their life in general and their health, behavior, and life functioning in particular. This educational process may include a biopsychosocialspiritual formulation that is geared towards discussing neurobiology (e.g., neurochemical transmission), cognitive processes (e.g., the way that you think about or have expectations about an experience), emotional factors such as fear, anxiety, and anger, social influence such as role models, education level, and cultural practices, and spiritual elements such as the belief in a higher power, faith, and/or sense of connection to nature or God. Taken together, as it typically is explained to the patient, these four processes interact, contribute to who we are as individuals, and influence what we do and don't do in our lives. With this basic appreciation of the biopsychosocialspiritual model in psychotherapy, patients are more likely to understand the purpose and rationale for different treatment recommendations that coincide with each element of the model. Within the context of chronic pain management, for example, it may be clear for a patient as to why they would see a physician to address pain (e.g., for medication, injections, or diagnostic procedures such as x-ray, MRI, or CT scan). On the contrary, the patient may not have a clear appreciation as to why they would work with a psychologist and attend to their psychological experience in the treatment of chronic pain. After hearing about the biopsychosocialspiritual model, and how physiology is influenced by psychological, socio-cultural, and spiritual variables, the patient may be more open to a multidisciplinary treatment approach and therefore have a greater likelihood of contacting effective treatment outcomes, which include increased physical and emotional functioning and reconnecting with important areas of life (see Turk & Gatchel, 2002, for a review).

Elements of the Biopsychosocial Model and the Environment

'Sword and mind must be united. Technique by itself is insufficient, and spirit alone is not enough'.

Yamada Jirokichi

Biology

There are several aspects of an individual's physiology that make up the biological component of the biopsychosocialspiritual model. Examples include the circulatory and respiratory systems, muscle fiber types (slow twitch and fast twitch), and the skeletal system, which taken together are heavily influenced by genetics.

At a neurobiological level, another aspect of the biological component of the biopsychosocialspiritual model, our brains are made of billions of neurons and neural connections among them. Together, neurons and their connections create pathways by which a combination of electrical and chemical messages is transported from one neuron to another to initiate and maintain functioning. Indeed, neurons are considered "the most specialized cells and most sensitive type of tissue of all biological systems" (Dispenza, 2007, p. 73) and are vital to our existence.

Each biological system, including the neurobiologic system, and their functions are influenced by genetics as well as the environment within which the individual lives. For years, and even to this day, there has been debate about which was more important in influencing human behavior; nature (that is the biology of the person such as genetics) or nurture (or the environmental elements and life experiences that one has throughout the lifespan). Through the course of this controversy, research and clinical work suggested that neither one nor the other was more or less important above and beyond the other. Rather, it has been suggested that both play critical roles in how we live, adapt, and move forward in life and in sports (see Davids & Baker, 2007, for a review).

Within the brain, neural connections are clearly a product of heredity (or genetics); however, these connections also are influenced by the environment and how the individual interacts with various experiences in the environment. Stimulating environments, rich with excitement, are more likely to facilitate neural changes realtive to dull, boring, or underwhelming environments. In mice, for example, a 15 percent increase in total numer of brain cells was observed when they lived in enriched environments compared to when they lived in conventional, less stimulating environments (van Praag, Kempermann, & Gage, 1999). This process is called neurogenesis and also occurs in humans (see Gage, 2002, for a review). Neurogensis is a process by which damaged brain cells are repaired or new brain cells are produced all together. Similar to the aforementioned example, the human brain changes with new experiences and to a greater extent with more simulating environments. Draganski and collegues (2004) found that when people learn a new skill and practice daily for three months, there are significant changes in the specific parts of the brain that are used in the performance of that new skill. Moreover, after practice of the new skill is stopped, the brain returns to its previous state before the new skill was learned (Draganski, Gaser, Busch, et al., 2004).

Nature & Nurture

An illustration of the interaction between nature and nurture can be seen in the large discrepancies between chronological and physiological age. Tina Turner, for example, will be 74 this year and arguably is one of the most spirited and enthusiastic musical artists to have hit the stage. She does not fit the stereotype of what some might consider a "70-something year old woman in their twilight years." With hits like "What's love got to do with it", she continues to rock the stage wherever she performs. Her spunk, energy, and zest for life keeps her going and shows how there can be a mismatch between chronological age and her physiological age.

A second example illustrating the wide gap between chronological and physiological age is seen in the accomplishments of Bert Morrow. At the age of 90, Bert won three gold medals in the 2003 San Diego Senior Olympics for three different events, the 80 meter hurdles, 100 meter sprint, and 200 meter sprint. There are not many 90-year-olds who can jump a single hurtle let alone be competitive in hurdling and win multiple gold medals in the Senior Olympics. With the right combination of genetics and proper diet, social support, and life experiences, many individuals can be very active into late adulthood. It is an interaction between biology and social factors that can make this more likely; the essence of the model we are presenting.

Regardless of how much life experience we have, however, there is a limit to the degree of change that will occur in our brain or to our bodies. For example, it is unlikely that any human will sprout wings and be able to leap off of a cliff and fly away to safety. There also are normal age-related changes that everyone goes through over time. Newborn babies sleep nearly 20 hours a day or more and spend a large period of time in REM sleep, a stage of sleep where dreaming occurs. It also happens to be an important stage of sleep for growth and rest. It is normal to spend less time in this period of sleep as we enter adulthood and then begin to spend more time in REM sleep in older adulthood. These are normal changes that occur and are probably less influenced by nurture than other naturally occurring biological changes in the body.

Neurons

Other normal changes that occur in the body over time can be seen in neuron development and migration. The human brain is not fully developed at birth. Neurons multiply as the child gets older and, by age 6, there are many more neurons than when the child was born. The individual is more capable and skilled at performing any number of tasks as the individual interacts with his or her environment and the brain changes over time with these life experiences. This is a natural developmental progression and is seen neurologically with the observation of a greater proportion of gray matter in the brain as we age. Although not more important than genetic influences, nurture is critical for one to meet their genetic potential.

Several factors influence the degree to which we meet our genetic potential. For example, physical, intellectual, social, vocation, spiritual, and emotional experiences impact the way that our brain develops (exactly the concept behind the biopsychosocialspiritual model). Stressors in our environment have significant influence on our lives and the way that our bodies and brains develop and function. There are many sources of environmental stress; such as financial hardship, weather, natural disaster, and limited resources. It can feel like we are coming unraveled when we are overwhelmed with stress. Think back to a resent stress in your life. How did it make you feel physically and psychologically? What was your experience?

As it turns out, the impact on brain development is quite profound when young children are exposed to environmental stress by way of impoverished or understimulating environmental conditions (see Child Welfare Information Gateway, 2009 for a review). The impact of neglect and understimulation in a growing child can have unbelieveablely negative effects on the brain size and functioning. Researchers have found that the brain of children who experienced severe neglect were significantly smaller compared to that of a healthy child living in a socially diverse, rich environment with a broad range of life experiences (Perry, 1997; Perry & Pollard, 1997).

Taken as a whole, by changing what one does in their life, he or she can change the wiring of their brain. In the words of Robin Williams from the movie, Mrs. Doubtfire, "Go pump some neurons! Expand your craniums!" This is not just a silly line in a movie. It is reality and warrants thoughtful consideration.

Lifestyle

We know that lifestyle has an important impact on brain development, processing, and functioning. Therefore, if you are willing to work, your brain can literally grow; developing new neurons, new pathways becoming more efficient, and expanding the efficiency of those that already exist. To help promote these neurobiological changes, one can decrease exposure to environmental toxins, improved diet, exercise regularly, and manage stress (McEwen, 2012; Somayajulu-Nitu, Domazet-Damjanov, Matei, et al., 2008). To emphasize this point, enriched environments, broadly defined, can lead to improved sensory stimulation, motor activity, information processing, as well as opportunities for brain development, learning, and memory. Enriched environments also increase neurogenesis and neuroplasticity and localization of neurons in the brain (Kempermann, Fabel, Ehninger, et al., 2010).

The Importance of Psychology

When discussing an individual's psychological experiences, a clinician often specifies the cognitive (e.g., thoughts, attention, and memory) and the emotional elements of an experience. Cognitive Behavioral Therapy, a type of treatment in psychology, emphasizes the influence of thoughts and emotions on behavior (see Butler, Chapman, Forman, & Beck, 2006, for a review). Negative thoughts or expectations about an upcoming experience, for example, will likely influence one's emotions from calm and pleasant towards more anxious or stressed. The function of these emotions is to prepare the individual for action. In the case of having an expectation of danger in a situation, the "fight or flight" response activates in the service of self-preservation and longevity of life. To illustrate this process, imagine that a student is preparing for her final exams at the end of the semester in college. She thinks to herself, "There is no possible way that I'm going to pass this final! I don't understand any of this material. I'm just wasting my time trying to memorize all this information." In response to this thought, she begins to feel anxious and worries that she will fail the class and the semester. The anxiety and stress triggers more negative expectations of failure in life and rejection by her friends and family. With such overwhelming anxiety and negative thoughts, the student decides to drop the class and receive an incomplete rather than face the final exam and the scenario that she created in her mind about the outcome of taking the test (before she actually took the exam!).

As thinking and emoting creatures, our psychological experiences are all around us and happening all the time. The psychological experience can range from negative, maladaptive beliefs and emotions such as depression, shame, guilt, anxiety, and anger to positive, confident beliefs and emotion such as joy, happiness, gratitude, hope, and love. An essential detail to consider in the experience of psychological functioning is that these cognitive and emotional responses do not occur in a vacuum. That is to say that while biological variables influence psychological responses, thoughts, beliefs, and emotions are not just happening randomly; there are interactions with the environment in important ways.

A wonderful and classic example of environmental influence on psychological development is found in the work of Harry Harlow in the late 1950's and early 1960's. Harlow's research showed that when given the choice between surrogate parents (a parent made of either wire mesh or soft cloth), rhesus monkeys chose "mommies" with soft, cuddly fabric over those made of wire, even when wire frame moms had milk dispensers. The conclusion of Harlow's work was that contact comfort during development was even more important than food in the development of affection and love, as evidenced by the baby's choice of being close to the surrogate made of soft cloth (Harlow, 1958).

It is well established within behavioral and cogntive behavioral theories in psychology that cognitive and emotional responses occur in context and are relative to the environmental conditions in which they are observed. Due in part to a combination of what is referred to as respondent and operant conditioning processes (Poling & Braatz, 2001), for example, a thought or emotion may be more likely to occur in one context relative to another. To illustrate this concept, think about an individual who enters a medical setting. While this person typically may be very calm and relaxed in most situations of his life, when he enters the dentist's office there is a profound anxiety response and thought that he will not make it out of this experience alive, or at least without significant pain and emotional distress. A number of emotional and environmental determinants of why this person might react in this manner have been discussed (see McNeil, Sorrell, & Vowles, 2006, for a review) and suggest a complex interaction between biological preparedness, previous experiences in the dental office, and immediate environmental stimuli that set the occasion for this patient's anxiety response. Moreover, there are a number of interventions that can be implemented to reduce the likelihood of this patient's anxiety interfering with treatment, including providing education and information about treatment (Sorrell, McNeil, Gochenour, & Jackson, 2009) or increasing the patient's ability to start or stop an uncomfortable aspect of treatment (Ludwick-Rosenthal & Neufeld, 1988).

Similar to biological elements within individuals, psychological experiences interact in important ways with the environment to influence human behavior. The introduction of psychotherapy into the environment for an individual struggling with an emotional problem, for example, can not only change the way they experience their emotional struggle but can change their neurobiology as well (Chiesa, Serretti, & Jakobsen, 2013; Lutz, Herwig, Opialla, et al., 2013).

The Importance of Sociology

Socio-cultural factors also have an enormous impact on the individual and their experiences within the larger group context. Examples of sociological variables include age, gender, ethnicity, economic status, occupation, and region of residence, to name a few. These variables will undoubtedly impact what the individual contacts in his or her life, their experiences with what they contact, as well as the biological factors within the individual. Poor socioeconomic status, for example, has been shown to be significantly linked with lower levels of cerebellar gray matter volume in a neurologically healthy group of males (Cavanagh, Krishnadas, Batty, Burns, et al., 2013). This information underscores the interaction among socio-cultural factors and neurobiology.

Socio-cultural factors also influence psychological elements of the individual. For example, a sense of belonging and identification with a group can help shape what is appropriate behavioral and emotional reactions in various situations. According to the World Health Organization (2009), "Cultural and social norms do not necessarily correspond with an individual's attitudes (positive or negative feelings towards an object or idea) and beliefs (perceptions that certain premises are true), although they may influence these attitudes and beliefs if norms become internalized" (p. 4). While the culture may not necessarily dictate each individual's attitudes and beliefs within that culture, there is no question that there will be influence by virtue of proximity and interaction with that environment (e.g., Langston, Gould, & Greenberg, 2007). Despite the strong influences of socio-cultural factors on the formation of attitudes and beliefs about stigmatized social issues, there is evidence that said beliefs, and the behaviors that surround them, can be altered in a positive manner for both the individual as well as the culture within which that person resides (e.g., Lunasco, Goodwin, Ozanian, & Loflin, 2010).

A concept in social learning theory (Bandura, 1977) that influences human behavior is referred to as behavior modeling (see Taylor, Russ-Eft, & Chan, 2005, for a review). Behavior modeling states that learning is a process that occurs in the environment through observation; the observed is the "model" and the actions the model is engaged in become the learned behavior for the individual observing as long as it is reinforced. Role models are used, such as our parents, for example, to determine what is good for us and what we should do in life.

Looking at an advertisement for bubble gum, you cannot help but wonder who decided to market this product depicting an adult male smoking a cigarette with a young boy looking up to him with a smile from ear to ear. The caption at the top of the box (which is shaped exactly like a box of cigarettes) reads, "Just like dad!" Perhaps it was the tobacco industry or the candy industry that was well educated about social learning theory and the influence modeling can have on behavior. Regardless, by taking advantage of this process, the bubble gum advertisement targeted children using social norms of the time to market and sell their product. There is no way to tell what the impact was on future smoking behavior of children who used the bubble gum product versus those who did not; however, social learning theory would suggest an influence towards smoking behavior later in life.

One of the most recognized experiments in modern psychology that demonstrates the impact of behavior modeling on learning is referred to as the "Bobo Doll Experiment" (Bandura, Ross, & Ross, 1961). In this study, children observed adults interacting with a Bobo Doll in an aggressive manner (e.g., hitting and throwing the doll). Compared to children who did not observe this behavior in the study, those who viewed the aggressive adults behaved significantly more aggressive and literally mimicked the actions they observed. Thus, starting at a very young age, our environment and those within our environment influences learning and behavior, for better or for worse that shape the way we conduct ourselves and lead our lives in the future.

An interesting statistic that we believe reflects, at least to some degree, behavior that is influenced by socio-cultural factors is the difference in suicide rates between the United States and Brazil. There was an average of 11.1 suicides per 100,000 people in the US and 4.3 in Brazil, in 2005 and 2008, respectively (World Health Organization, 2011). In 2002, the United States ranked 43rd in the world whereas Brazil was ranked 73rd; the country with the highest suicide rate was Lithuania in the same year.

The leading cause of suicide is untreated depression (Conwell, van Orden, & Caine, 2012; Conwell, Duberstein, Cox, et al., 1996; Szanto, Mulsant, Houck, et al., 2003), and while one might argue that the United States has more access to modern resources and treatment options for depression compared to Brazil, there are data that suggest lifetime prevalence estimates of depression to be greater in higher income countries (e.g., United States) compared to low- to middle-income countries (e.g., Brazil) (see Bromet, Andrade, Hwang, et al., 2011, for a review). It has been suggested that depression is an illness of the wealthy (Koplewicz, Gurian, & Williams, 2009) and occurs more in countries where there is a greater disproportion of income inequality (Wilkinson & Pickett, 2009).

While perhaps speculative, there also seems to be differential emphasis on values between these industrialized countries that may contribute to the aforementioned statistics. Of course not ubiquitously, but generally, for example, there is a large emphasis on career, work, and advancement in the United States; and while these values may be important in Brazil as well, we believe there is greater emphasis placed on family connection, social bonding, and living with less attachment to material items in Brazil compared to the United States. It is this differential emphasis on what is most important that may serve as a protective factor for Brazilians relative to Americans when it comes to unhappiness and depression leading to suicide. Research into this hypothesis clearly is warranted and could have profound implications for socio-cultural practices around the world (i.e., life values and priorities).

Indeed, the social environment and social support are important variables to consider in the context of understanding human behavior. Social support can have vital implications for an individual's ability to cope through adversity, especially during times of need, to facilitate healthy behavior and to adequately prepare our youth for the future (Byrnes & Miller, 2012).

Spirituality

While socio-cultural factors such as family history, ethnic and cultural practices, and exposure to religious and spiritual practices will undoubtedly influence one's sense of spirituality, there is utility and importance in examining spirituality as a separate element from other social variables and expanding the biopsychosocial model to reflect a slightly more comprehensive and detailed biopsychosocialspiritual model.

Spirituality means different things, for different people, at different times, in different places and cultures, and there has been debate throughout the history of psychology about what it is exactly and whether or not there is a distinction between spirituality and religion (Zinnbauer, Pargament, Cole, et al., 1997), relevance in psychotherapy for spirituality (Plante, 2007), and an impact of spirituality on health outcomes (George, Larson, Koenig, & McCullough, 2000). Both religiosity and spirituality are multidimensional concepts that warrant operationalization to best understand the impact on the life of the religious or spiritual individual (George, et al., 2000).

In a comprehensive review of the impact of spirituality on health, George and colleagues (2000) define spirituality as "the feelings, thoughts, experiences, and behaviors" that result from the pursuit of the sacred; '...a divine being, higher power, or ultimate reality, as perceived by the individual' (p. 104). The second part of this definition distinguishes spirituality from other social and personal phenomena (Berger, 1967). The authors cite several studies that are part of a large area of research that support a significant relation between spirituality and the onset of many medical problems, including cardiac disease, emphysema, liver disease, hypertension, and disability. Attendance at religious services was found to be the strongest predictor of illness prevention; in other words, the more that an individual attended services, the less likely they were to develop significant medical problems from illness.

From the point of view in behaviorism, a behavior analysis of spirituality is not only possible but also provides good reason to do so in the analysis of self-awareness and therapeutic processes that occur in the treatment setting (Hayes, 1984). In a conceptual analysis of spirituality, Beringer (2000) undescores the pursuit of that which is 'sacred' as fundamental to spirituality. Thus, in behavioral terms, spirituality can be examined, at least in part, by focusing on the thoughts, emotions, physiological experiences, and behaviors (George, et al., 2000) of the individual who searches for a higher power; a perspective that is very much in accordance with that which is proposed in this chapter.

Spirituality can provide structure or a sense of purpose in life, connectedness to self, others, nature, God, a higher power, or serve as a compass by which one uses to guide their actions in life. It also provides a level of transcendence, or the sense that there is more to life than the material or practical and activities that give meaning and value to the individual. Looking through a spiritual lens gives us a structure to facilitate making sense of life events that at times may be incomprehensible.

Moreover, a wonderful, deep, and meaningful way of coping with hardships and suffering that every human is prone to experience at some point in life can be found within the framework of spirituality. Having the structure to make sense of an adverse life experience that, on the surface, makes no sense at all may be what helps to carry that individual through the adversity and reduce the onset of illness (George et al., 2000).

The Biopsychosocialspiritual Model in Martial Arts

> 'Physical strength (hard work), mental strength (perseverance) and spiritual strength (love & acceptance) are the keys to continuous growth'.
>
> Rickson Gracie

Applying the biopsychosociospiritual model to martial arts provides a comprehensive structure to facilitate understanding of the research that has come from the martial arts. Research exploring the benefits of martial arts on physical and mental health find improvements in muscle strength, power, balance, coordination, agility, flexibility, blood pressure, and energy. There also is evidence that practicing martial arts increases self-confidence, self-esteem, and concentration along with improvements in emotional well-being such as decreased depression, anxiety, anger, impulsivity, and stress (see Martin, 2006; and Vertonghen & Theeboom, 2010, for reviews). Moreover, when the experienced martial artist goes without training, there is evidence of severe mood disturbance even after only one week of abstinence (Szabo & Parkin, 2001).

While the vast majority of studies examine the impact of martial arts on physical and emotional health, there also are more subtle positive outcomes from training martial arts (Martin, 2006). In combination with the Buddhist/Taoist philosophy and specific training methods and goals, Martin suggests that traditional martial arts are "an effective way of transmitting desirable values and, over time, indoctrinates students with the idea of respect, a sense of consequence, a sense of personal responsibility, and a sense of connection to the self through a strong mentor / student relationship" (pp. 1-2). Martin's position underscores the socio-cultural and psychological influences imbedded in the practice of martial arts.

The psychosocial benefits of Tai Chi have been found to be extensive (see Zhang, Layne, Lowder, and Liu, 2012, for a review). In a randomized control trial, for example, the effects of Tai Chi for 60-minutes twice a week were examined on physical functioning in older adults (Li, Harmer, McAuley, Duncan, et al., 2001). Participants who practiced Tai Chi significantly improved physical functioning; with 65% increasing to moderate-vigorous activity such as running from daily activity such as walking compared to those in a control group that did not participate in the Tai Chi regimen.

In a case report by Massey and Kisling (1999), a 76 year-old woman was treated with chronic and severe spinal cord compression secondary to multiple cervical disk problems. She did not respond to various interventions such as medication, rest, and traditional physical therapy. Following 8 weeks of physical therapy adapted from Tai Chi and Kung Fu, 20 minutes per day, she was symptom free. This is not to suggest that martial arts are "better" than traditional medical interventions, but rather that it can be a beneficial addition to medical treatments and should be considered to broaden the scope of treatment for patients who seek medical intervention.

A study by Focht, Bouchard, & Murphey (2000) looked at the impact of martial arts training on pain perception. Students from an introductory karate class trained 1-2 times per week for 60 minutes. After 14 weeks, students had significantly higher pain threshold levels and decreased pain intensity during an experimentally induced pressure pain task.

Kimura and colleagues (2005) examined the effects of Nishino breathing technique on immunological activity (as measured by the natural killer cell [NK]) and stress levels. The Nishino breathing was developed by Kozo Nishino, a master of martial arts, in an effort to develop Ki (...an internal life energy or a spiritual energy). Similar to Chinese qigong practice, Nishino breathing involves visualization of internal energy flow, slow body movements, and the emission of life energy from one's hand.

After a single 90-minute class, there was a significant increase in NK cells and a significant decrease in stress for those individuals who practiced this breathing method. These data suggest the importance of the breathing practice during martial arts and the potential benefit it can have on immunological regulation (Kimura, et al., 2005).

The use of visualization and mental imagery has been proposed to be an excellent strategy for developing skills for martial artists (Lajcik, 2008). Lajcik, a renowned wrestler and Mixed Martial Artist, describes a type of visualization called mental rehearsal. He explains how visualization can be used to reinforce the neuromuscular pattern of proper fighting technique. Indeed, many sports psychologists recommend visualization prior to performance (see Suinn, 1997, for a review), and can trigger physiological reactions in the body similar to those that are experienced when actually doing the activity (Hecker & Kaczor, 1998).

The impact of mental imagery on the performance speed of Judo practitioners was examined by Louis, Guillot, Maton, et al., 2008. Three groups in the study were instructed to either imagine performing techniques slowly, at fast pace, or as normally practiced. After 4 weeks of training, 3 sessions per week, there was a clear and significant difference between the 3 groups on actual performance speed. Results indicated that the actual speed of performing the techniques matched the visualization practiced over the 4 weeks relative to their speed at baseline; fast imagery group was faster, slow imagery group was slower, and normal speed imagery group did not change significantly from baseline.

In a research series that examined the health benefits of Capoeira, Mestranda Edna Lima of Long Island University, NY, found that 8-weeks of Capoeira practice had measurable benefits. Students experienced 3-5% reductions in body circumference and 10% reduction in body fat. Mestranda Lima continues to do excellent work measuring the benefits of this Brazilian martial art (Lima, 2007).

Indeed, spirituality has been examined broadly in sport (Watson & Nesting, 2005); however, despite frequent colloquial reference to spirituality in martial arts, there is a dearth of academic literature that systematically examines this element (Boylan, 1999). Nevertheless, spirituality is an integral part of the martial arts and has been extensively discussed (e.g., Boylan, 1999, 2001; Gilham, 2004; Klens-Bigman, 2000). Mihaly Csikszentmihalyi comments on the biopsychosocialspiritual aspects of the martial arts in his book, *'Flow: The psychology of optimal experience'* (1990). He states that:

> '….martial arts were influenced by Taoism and by Zen Buddhism, and thus they also emphasize consciousness-controlling skills. Instead of focusing exclusively on physical performance, as Western martial arts do, the Eastern variety is directed toward improving the mental and spiritual state of the practitioner. The warrior strives to reach the point where he can act with lighting speed against opponents, without having to think or reason about the best defensive or offensive moves to make. Those who can perform it will claim that fighting becomes a joyous artistic performance, during which the everyday experience of duality between mind and body is transformed into a harmonious one-pointedness of mind. Here again, it seems appropriate to think of the martial arts as a specific form of flow"

Csikszentmihalyi, p. 106

Indeed, Jackson and Csikszentmihalyi (1999) describe the 9 components that best describe the mindset of flow; originally there were 4 (Csikszentmihalyi, 1975) and then 8 components (Csikszentmihalyi, 1993). The flow components of optimal experience include 1) Challenge-skills balance, 2) Action-awareness merging, 3) Clear goals, 4) Unambiguous feedback, 5) Concentration on the task at hand, 6) Sense of control, 7) Loss of self-consciousness, 8) Transformation of time, and 9) Autotelic experience. Although an in-depth discussion of each component characterizing flow of optimal experience would go beyond the primary scope of this chapter, research examining optimal experience consistently finds that when individuals are doing something enjoyable (regardless of whether it is sport, work, video gaming, or other activity), they describe their state of mind in similar terms (Csikszentmihalyi, 1975; Jackson, 1995; 1996). Examples of how consciousness was described include 'being in the zone, focused, on auto, nothing else matters, flowing, and in the groove' (Jackson & Csikszentmihalyi, 1996).

There is a quality within the flow experience that has a spiritual element and may help an athlete feel the connection between their sport and a sense of transcendence. The flow experience has been examined and conceptual aspects of it applied to the religious experience (Neitz & Spickard, 1990). Thus, given the aforementioned in regard to flow and optimal experience, it seems to serve as a potentially helpful framework to not only further apply towards the physical activity elements of martial arts but the spiritual aspects as well.

In a randomized clinical trial with HIV/AIDS patients, McCain and colleagues (2005) evaluated the effects of Tai Chi on a number of variables, including spiritual/existential well-being. Results suggested that those patient who were randomized into the Tai Chi intervention group had higher spiritual/existential well-being, perception of social support, and more frequently used appraisal-focused coping strategies following treatment compared to before they started the intervention. Martial arts teach a broad range of values and skills that include communication skills, assertiveness, empathy, courage, humility, perseverance, gentleness, perseverance, respect for others, responsibility, and dedication, among others. The benefits are appreciated by those who practice these arts while research validates the positive effects of martial arts on the body, mind, and spirit.

Biopsychosocialspritual Model and Brazilian Martial Arts

'I'm always in control of my possibilities and knowledge of my possibilities; emotionally, technically, and spiritually. That's what jiu-jitsu gave me'.

Rickson Gracie

When we closely examine the Brazilian martial arts, there are rich, multifaceted layers to these practices with each element of the biopsychosociospiritual model represented. The most obvious element of the model is the biological system and how it is stimulated by the physical activity of Brazilian Jiu-Jitsu and Capoeira. Given that these martial arts involve movement and exercise, neurobiological changes will occur as the practitioner progresses in their training (Kempermann, Fabel, Ehninger, Babu, et al., 2010). The tradition and cultural influences on these practices also are profound (e.g., Assunção, 2005) and have survived the test of time. For some individuals who practice Brazilian Jiu-Jitsu and Capoeira, there is a deep spiritual connection, sense of being in the moment (or "flow"), and personal, metaphysical growth that occurs within the art forms.

The psychological elements involved in these Brazilian art forms also are profound. For example, anxiety, fear, or worry can be experienced by anyone stepping onto the jiu-jitsu mat for the first time or even for the seasoned veteran black belt preparing to compete in a tournament. These emotions are so common before tournaments that chances are, if you are not nervous before a match, you are not getting ready for jiu-jitsu. Moreover, when the Brazilian Jiu-Jitsu practitioner does not train for several days, they become irritable, stressed, and easily frustrated. While this statement may be somewhat anecdotal, as we are not aware of any empirical research that supports this claim specifically in Brazilian Jiu-Jitsu, there is research that supports the occurrence of severe mood disturbance for the Shotokan karate practitioner after one week of training deprivation (Szabo & Parkin, 2001). Further, if the practitioner is truly passionate and deeply fond of Brazilian Jiu-Jitsu, there could be a true sense of loss, grieving, and ultimately depression if they were unable to practice this art form again secondary to injury or some other uncontrollable, traumatic event (see Heil, 1994; and Kubler-Ross, 1969, for reviews).

A significant degree of interaction among each system within the biopsychosocialspiritual model occurs at all times while the Brazilian martial artist practitioner trains. As an example to illustrate these interactions, consider the Capoeirista who travels to attend a Roda where she does not know anyone. She is alone and has no specific person to support her and to share in the experiences of the event.

The music begins, the Roda forms, and everyone begins to clap and sing. She feels a combination of excitement and anxiety as she sings a familiar song and looks around realizing that there is not one single familiar face. The players begin to play and the games are fierce. She witnesses two players who are kicked hard enough that they can no longer participate in the Roda. Her heart is pounding, adrenaline pumping through her body, and her legs feel weak as if she were standing on Jell-O. She thinks to herself, "This is going to be a rough and painful day."

After a while, the Capoeirista starts to find her "flow", she begins to connect with a sense of calm and peace drawn from the spiritual connection she has with this beautiful art form. Feeling ready to enter the game, she buys with someone she has been watching and seems to be fairly non-aggressive. The moment she enters, the opposing player changes her tone to anything but non-aggressive. The beat of the music speeds up and the kicks begin to fly faster than she was prepared for seeing from this player. Out of nowhere a 'meia-lua de 'frente' skims past the right side of her head but she 'esquivas' just at the right moment. Her body "knew" what to do at that very moment the kick was coming and she did not have to even think about the escape and ensuing counter attack. After what seems like several minutes, but actually was only about 90 seconds, the game is over and the Capoeiristas embrace in a hug that speaks volumes of the respect they have for one another, their shared passion, and the art form itself. The visiting Capoeirista has made a friend for life and is welcome back to this annual event anytime she wishes to attend.

Many who read the aforementioned example and have trained Capoeira can relate in one way or another; each element of the biopsychosocialspiritual model are happening with the Roda for each participant. The Capoeirista in the example is hardwired to react in situations where threat is perceived. The sympathetic response, also referred to as the 'Fight or Flight or Freeze' response, is an automatic reaction. This response has evolved to protect the individual from danger; by fighting to protect oneself, fleeing from danger by running away, or freezing, staying very still to blend into the surroundings and avoiding threat.

Generally, this sympathetic response is adaptive particularly when it comes to protecting the individual from immediate threat (escaping a predator); however, the utility of this response in Brazilian Jiu-Jitsu and Capoeira is not particularly beneficial. For example, freezing and fleeing are not going to help expand or improve one's skill set, training, and development as a practitioner of the arts. Similarly, becoming blinded by rage or aggression will not help the Brazilian martial artist either. Indeed, overriding the biological system and finding "flow" (Csikszentmihalyi, 1990) as an alternative will not only assist the practitioner with optimal experience in the martial art but also will help to generalize this response more broadly in other areas of life. As previously discussed, the only way to truly alter the fight, flight, or freeze response is through direct life experience. Practice, training, and otherwise "being in the action" are necessary for the brain to make the neurobiological connection and changes to "override" this otherwise adaptive response.

By way of direct life experience and interactions on the jiu-jitsu mat or in the Roda, one learns that these martial arts have elements of danger but also are fun, exciting, and full of rich experiences. Through the practice of these Brazilian martial arts, and other forms of martial arts and physical activity, the brain makes new neural connections, helping the body to be more efficient with movement and function; fear is reduced and self-confidence built; community and relationships are assembled through cooperation, culture, and trust; and spiritual paths are paved to guide the practitioner towards a higher purpose. The practitioner learns about him- or herself. In jiu-jitsu, the roll never lies. The experiences within the roll are real and the consequences are deniable. Self-preservation, emotional, physical, and spiritual growth will result if one is open to the learning opportunities in the roll; if not, the practitioner's career in Brazilian Jiu-Jitsu will be short lived.

Conclusions and Future Directions

'Forget about past mistakes and focus your energy on the victories of tomorrow'.

Grand Master Carlos Gracie Sr.

We hope that this chapter has been successful in providing understanding of a multidimensional structure to the many dimensions involved in Brazilian Jiu-Jitsu and Capoeira, two dynamic martial arts rich with stimulating socio-cultural influences, functional movements, and potential to help the practitioner find calmness that not only fills there martial arts training but also spans across all areas of their life. A majority of the sports psychology research examining the biological, psychological, socio-cultural, and spiritual effects of human behavior focus on sports in general and only a small amount of research specifically examines the impact of martial arts on these factors. An extremely small percentage has considered Brazilian Jiu-Jitsu and Capoeira in any type of research let alone research from a biopsychosocialspiritual perspective.

Good evidence supports a range of benefits that can be drawn from the martial arts for the practitioner. There is no reason to believe that these data would not generalize to the Brazilian martial arts. Nonetheless, in practicing sound scientific doctrine, it is an important venture to design, conduct, and evaluate the impact of Brazilian Jiu-Jitsu and Capoeira on physical and mental health, socio-cultural variables, and spirituality of the martial artist.

Areas of theory and research within clinical psychology that may provide useful in future projects examining Brazilian martial arts include mindfulness and acceptance (Hayes, Follette, & Linehan, 2004) as well as the impact these processes have on the brain functioning of the practitioner (Siegel, 2007). The benefits that have come from therapies using mindfulness and acceptance principles have been quite remarkable with a broad range of patient populations (e.g., Cramer, Haller, Lauche, Dobos, 2012; Marchand, 2012; Vøllestad, Nielsen, Nielsen, 2012; Witklewitz, Lustyk, Bowen, 2013).

As with the constantly evolving games of jiu-jitsu and Capoeira, research and theory also will evolve over time. In this regard, clinicians, researchers, and martial arts practitioners all may someday truly understand and appreciate the depth of what these art forms are, what they have to offer the world, and release their potential to anyone and everyone willing to experience them.

References

Anshel, M.H. (2012). *Sport psychology: From theory to practice* (5th ed.). San Francisco: Benjamin-Cummings.

Armitage, C. J., & Connor, M. (2001). Efficacy of the theory of planned behavior: A meta-analytic review. *British Journal of Social Psychology, 40,* 471-499.

Assunção, M. R. (2005). *Capoeira: The history of Afro-Brazilian martial arts.* Oxon: Routledge.

Bandura, A. (1977). Self-efficacy: Towards a unifying theory of behavioral change. *Psychological Review, 84,* 191-215.

Bandura, A., Ross, D., & Ross, S. (1961). Transmission of aggression through imitation of aggressive models. *Journal of Abnormal and Social* Psychology, 63, 575-582.

Berger, P. (1967). *The sacred canopy: Elements of a sociological theory of* religion. New York: Doubleday.

Beringer, A. (2000). In search of the sacred: A conceptual analysis of spirituality. Journal of Experiential Education, 23, 157–165.

Boylan, P. W. (1999). Aikido as spiritual practice in the United States. (Master's Thesis). Western Michigan University, Kalamazoo, Michigan.

Boylan, P. W. (2001). Spiritual practice in Budo. *The Iaido Journal, January,* Retrieved from http://ejmas.com/tin/tinart_boylan_0201.htm.

Brady, M. J., Peterman, A. H., Fitchett, G., Mo, M., & Cella, D. (1999). A case for including spirituality in quality of life measurement in oncology. *Psychooncology, 8,* 417-428.

Bromet, E., Andrade, L., Hwang, I., Sampson, N., Alonso, J., Girolamo, G., Graaf, R., Demyttenaere, K., Hu, C., Iwata, N., Karam, A., Kaur, J., Kostyuchenko, S., Lepine, J-P., Levinson, D., Matschinger, H., Mora, M., Browne, M., Posada-Villa, J., Viana, M., Williams, D., & Kessler, R. (2011). Cross-national epidemiology of DSM-IV major depressive episode. *BMC Medicine, 9,* 90-106.

Butler, A. C., Chapman, J. E., Forman, E. M., & Beck, A. T. (2006). The empirical status of cognitive-behavioral therapy: A review of meta-analyses. *Clinical Psychological Review, 26,* 17-31.

Byrnes, H. F., & Miller, B. A. (2012). The relationship between neighborhood characteristics and effective parenting behaviors: The role of social support. *Journal of Family Issues, 33,* 1658-1687.

Cavanagh, J., Krishnadas, R., Batty, G. D., Burns, H., Deans, K. A., Ford, I., McConnachie, A., McGinty, A., McLean, J. S., Millar, K., Sattar, N., Shiels, P. G., Tannahill, C., Velupillai, Y. N., Packard, C. J., & McLean,

J. (2013). Socioeconomic status and the cerebellar grey matter volume. Data from a well-characterised population sample. *The Cerebellum, June 2013*, 1-10. DOI:10.1007/s12311-013-0497-4.

Chiesa, A., Serretti, A., & Jakobsen, J. C. (2013). Mindfulness: Top-down or bottom-up emotion regulation strategy? *Clinical Psychology Review, 33*, 82-96.

Child Welfare Information Gateway (2009). Understanding the effects of maltreatment on brain development. [Available at: www.childwelfare.gov/pubs/issue_briefs/brain_development/], [Accessed on 26 June 2013].

Conwell, Y., Duberstein, P. R., Cox, C., Herrmann, J. H., Forbes, N. T., & Caine, E. D. (1996). Relationships of age and axis I diagnosis in victims of completed suicide: A psychological autopsy study. *The American Journal of Psychiatry, 153*, 1001-1008.

Conwell, Y., Van Orden, K., & Caine, E. D. (2012). Suicide in older adults. *Psychiatric Clinics of North America, 34*, 451-468.

Cramer, H., Haller, H., Lauche, R., Dobos, G. (2012). Mindfulness-based stress reduction for low back pain. A systematic review. *BMC Complementary and Alternative Medicine, 12*, 1-8.

Csikszentmihalyi, M. (1975), Beyond Boredom and Anxiety, Jossey-Bass, San Francisco, CA.

Csikszentmihalyi, M. (1990). *Flow: The Psychology of Optimal Experience*, Harper and Row, New York.

Csikszentmihalyi, M. (1993). *The Evolving Self: A Psychology for the Third Millennium*, New York: Harper Collins.

Davids, K., & Baker, J. (2007). Genes, environment and sport performance: Why the nature-nurture dualism is no longer relevant. *Sports Medicine, 37*, 1-20.

Dispenza, J. (2007). *Evolve your brain: The science of changing your mind.* Deerfield Beach: Health Communications, Inc.

Draganski, B., Gaser, C., Busch, V., Schuierer, G., Bogdahn, U., & May, A. (2004). Neuroplasticity: Changes in grey matter induced by training. *Nature, 427*, 311-312.

Engel, G. L. (1977). A need for a new medical model: A challenge for biomedicine. *Science, 196*, 129-136.

Ferrin, K. (2009). *What's age got to do with it?* Volume II, Red Zone Publishing. Norman, OK.

Fisch, M., Titzer, M., Kristeller, J., Shen, J., Loehrer, P., Jung, S., Passik, S., & Einhorn, L. (2003). Assessment of quality of life in outpatients with advanced cancer: The accuracy of clinician estimations and the relevance of spiritual well-being – A Hoosier Oncology Group Study. *Journal of Clinical Oncology, 21*, 2754-2759.

Focht, B. C., Bouchard, L. J., & Murphey, M. (2000). Influence of martial arts training on the perception of experimentally induced pressure pain and selected psychological responses. *Journal of Sports Behavior, 23*, 232-244.

Gage, F. H. (2002). Neurogenesis in the adult brain. *The Journal of Neuroscience, 22*, 612-613.

George, L. K., Larson, D. B., Koenig, H. G., & McCullough, M. E. (2000). Spirituality and health: What we know, what we need to know. *Journal of Social and Clinical Psychology, 19,* 102-116.

Ghaemi, S. N. (2010). *The rise and fall of the biopsychosocial model: Reconciling art and science in psychiatry.* Baltimore: The Johns Hopkins University Press.

Gilham, G. (2004). Culture in the martial arts: On the Japanese culture in today's Budo. *Guelph School of Japanese Sword Arts, July,* Retreived from http://ejmas.com/proceedings/GSJSA04gilham.html.

Harlow, H. (1958). The nature of love. *American Psychologist, 13,* 673-685.

Hayes, S. (1984). Making sense of spirituality. *Behaviorism, 12,* 99-110.

Hayes, S., Follette, V., & Linehan, M. (2004). *Mindfulness and acceptance: Expanding the cognitive-behavioral tradition.* New York: Guilford Press.

Hecker, J. E., & Kaczor, L. M. (1998). Application of imagery theory to sport psychology: Some preliminary findings. *Journal of Sport and Exercise Psychology, 10,* 363-373.

Heil, J. (1994). Understanding the psychology of sport injury: A grief process model. *Temple Psychiatric Review, May, 3 & 10.*

Jackson, S. A. (1995). Factors influencing the occurrence of flow in elite athletes. *Journal of Applied Sport Psychology, 7,* 135-163.

Jackson, S. A. (1996). Toward a conceptual understanding of the flow experience in elite athletes. *Research Quarterly for Exercise and Sport, 67,* 76-90.

Jackson, S. A., & Csikszentmihalyi, M. (1999). *Flow in sports: The keys to optimal experiences and performances.* IL: Human Kinetics.

Kempermann, G., Fabel, K., Ehninger, D., Babu, H., Leal-Galicia, P., Garthe, A., & Wolf, S. (2010). Why and how physical activity promotes experience-induced brain plasticity. *Frontiers in Neuroscience, 4,* 189-198.

Kimura, H., Nagao, F., Tanaka, Y., Sakai, S., Ohnishi, S. T., & Okumura, K. (2005). Beneficial effects of the Nishino breathing method on immune activity and stress level. *The Journal of Alternative and Complementary Medicine, 11,* 285-291.

Klens-Bigman, D. (2000). Spirituality in the martial arts – An overview of the issues. *Guelph School of Japanese Sword Arts, July 21,* Retrieved from http://ejmas.com/proceedings/GSJSA00klens.htm.

Koplewicz, H. S., Gurian, A., & Williams, K. (2009). The era of affluence and its discontents. *Journal of the American Academy of Child & Adolescent Psychiatry, 48,* 1053-1055.

Kubler-Ross, E. (1969). On death and dying. New York: Macmillan.

Lajcik, T. (2008). Developing fighting techniques through visualization. *Journal of Asian Martial Arts, 17,* 78-86.

Langston, V., Gould, M., & Greenberg, N. (2007). Culture: What is its effect on stress in the military? *Military Medicine, 172,* 931-935.

Li, F., Harmer, P., McAuley, E., Duncan, T. E., Duncan, S. C., Chaumeton, N., & Fisher, K. J. (2001). An evaluation of the effects of Tai Chi exercise on physical function among older persons: A randomized controlled trial. *Annals of Behavioral Medicine, 23,* 139-146.

Lima, E. (2007). Capoeira workout fitness standards Long Island University world dance program. [Available at: www.ednalima.com/html/university2007.html#study], [Accessed on 23 June 2013].

Louis, M., Guillot, A., Maton, S., Doyon, J., & Collet, C. (2008). Effect of imagined movement speed on subsequent motor performance. *Journal of Motor Behavior, 40,* 117-132.

Ludwick-Rosenthal, R., & Neufeld, R. W. (1988). Stress management during noxious medical procedures: An evaluative review of outcome studies. *Psychological Bulletin, 104,* 326-342.

Lunasco, T. K., Goodwin, E. A., Ozanian, A. J., & Loflin, E. M. (2010). One shot-one kill: A culturally sensitive program for the warrior culture. *Military Medicine, 175,* 509-513.

Lutz, J., Herwig, U., Opialla, S., Hittmeyer, A., Jancke, L., Rufer, M., Grosse Holtforth, M., & Bruhl, A. B. (2013). Mindfulness and emotion regulation – An fMRI study. *Social Cognitive and Affective Neuroscience,* first published online: April 5, *2013,* DOI: 10.1093/scan/nst043.

Marchand, W. R. (2012). Mindfulness-based stress reduction, mindfulness-based cognitive therapy, and Zen meditation for depression, anxiety, pain, and psychological distress. *Journal of Psychiatric Practice, 18,* 233-252.

Marseille, J. (1997). The spiritual dimension in logotherapy: Viktor Frankl's contribution to transpersonal psychology. *The Journal of Transpersonal Psychology, 29,* 1-12.

Martin, D. (2006). *The psychological benefits of martial art training: What most instructors know but can't articulate.* Greeting Line – Document pp. 1-7. [Available at: www.southern-crossmartialarts.com/documents/10BENEFITS_OF_MA_ARTICLEv3.pdf], [Accessed on 26 June 2013].

Massey, P. B., & Kisling, G. M. (1999). A single case report of healing through specific martial art therapy: Comparison of MRI to clinical resolution in severe cervical stenosis: A case report. *The Journal of Alternative and Complementary Medicine, 5,* 75-79.

McCain, N., Elswick, R. K., Gray, D. P., Robins, J., Tuck, I., & Walter, J. M. (2005). Tai Chi training enhances well-being and alters cytokine levels in persons with HIV disease. *Brain, Behavior, and Immunity, 19,* E50.

McEwen, B. S. (2012). Brain on stress: How the social environment gets under the skin. *Proceedings of the National Academy of Sciences, 109,* 17180-17185.

McGee, M. D., & Torosian, J. (2006). Integrating spiritual assessment into a psychiatric inpatient unit. *Psychiatry (Edgmont), 3,* 60-64.

McNeil, D. W., Sorrell, J. T., & Vowles, K. E. (2006). Emotional and environmental determinants of dental pain (pp. 79 - 97). In D. I. Mostofsky, A. G. Forgione, & D. B. Giddon (Eds.), Behavioral Dentistry. Ames, IA: Blackwell.

Neitz, M. J., & Spickard, J. V. (1990). Steps toward a sociology of religious experience: The theories of Mihaly Cxikszentmihalyi and Alfred Schutz. *Sociology of Religion, 51,* 15-33.

Nesti, M. (2004). *Existential psychology and sport: Theory and application.* New York: Taylor & Francis.
Perry, B. D. (1997). Incubated in terror: Neurodevelopmental factors in the 'cycle of violence' In J. Osofsky (Ed.), *Children, Youth and Violence: The Search for Solutions*, (pp. 124-148). New York: Guilford Press.
Perry, B. D., & Pollard, R. A. (1997). *Altered brain development following global neglect in early childhood.* [Available at: www.ou.edu/cwtraining/assets/pdf/handouts/2010/Altered%20brain%20 development%20following%20global%20neglect.pdf], [Accessed 26 June 2013].
Plante, T. G. (2007). Integrating spirituality and psychotherapy: Ethical issues and principles to consider. *Journal of Clinical Psychology, 63,* 891-902.
Poling, A., & Braatz, D. (2001). Principles of learning: Respondent and operant conditioning and human behavior. In C. M. Johnson, W. K. Redmon, & T. C. Mawhinney (Eds.), *Handbook of organizational performance: Behavior analysis and management* (pp. 139-166). New York: The Haworth Press.
Puchalski, C. M. (2008). Spirituality and the care of patients at the end-of-life: An essential component of care. *Omega (Westport), 56,* 33-46.
Siegel, D. (2007). *The mindful brain: Reflection and attunment in the cultivation of well-being.* New York: Norton & Company.
Somayajulu-Nitu, M., Domazet-Damjanov, D., Matei, A., Schwartzenberger, E., Cohen, J., & Pandey, S. (2008). Role of environmental and inflammatory toxicity in neuronal cell death. *The Open Toxicology Journal, 2,* 26-41.
Sorrell, J. T., McNeil, D. W., Gochenour, L. L., & Jackson, R. (2009). Evidence-based patient education: knowledge transfer to endodontic patients. *Journal of Dental Education, 73, 1293-1305.*
Stanley, A. Q. (2011). Benefits of Teacher 'Connections' in Stressful Educational Settings. *International Journal of Children's Spirituality, 16,* 47-58.
Suinn, R. M. (1997). Mental practice in sport psychology: Where have we been, where do we go? *Clinical Psychology: Science and Practice, 4,* 189-207.
Sulmasy, D. P. (2002). A biopsychosocial-spiritual model for the care of patients at the end of life. *The Gerontologist, 42,* 24-33.
Szabo, A., & Parkin, A. (2001). The psychological impact of training deprivation in martial arts. *Psychology of Sport & Exercise, 2,* 187-199.
Szanto, K., Mulsant, B. H., Houck, P., Dew, M. A., & Reynolds, C. F. (2003). Occurrence and course of suicidality during short-term treatment of late-life depression. *Archives of General Psychiatry, 60,* 610-617.
Taylor, P. J., Russ-Eft, D. F., & Chan, D. W. (2005). A meta-analytic review of behavior modeling training. *Journal of Applied Psychology, 90,* 692-709.
Turk, D., & Gatchel, R. (2002). *Psychological approaches to pain management: A practitioner's handbook* (2nd edition). New York: Guilford Press.
Turk, D., & Monarch, E. (2002). Biopsychosocial perspective on chronic pain. In D. Turk & R. Gatchel (Eds.), *Psychological approaches to pain management: A practitioner's handbook* (2nd edition, pp. 3-29). New York: Guilford Press.

van Praag, H., Kempermann, G., & Gage, F. H. (1999). Running increases cell proliferation and neurogenesis in the adult mouse dentate gyrus. *Nature Neuroscience, 2,* 266-270.

Vertonghen, J., & Theeboom, M. (2010). The social-psychological outcomes of martial arts practise among youth: A review. *Journal of Sports Science and Medicine, 9,* 528-537.

Vøllestad, J., Nielsen, M. B., Nielsen, G. H. (2012). Mindfulness- and acceptance-based interventions for anxiety disorders: A systematic review and meta-analysis. *British Journal of Clinical Psychology, 51,* 239-260.

Watson, N.J., Nesti, M. (2005). The Role of Spirituality in Sport Psychology Consulting: An Analysis and Integrative Review of Literature, *Journal of Applied Sport Psychology, 17,* 228-239.

Whitford, H. S., Olver, I. N., & Peterson, M. J. (2008). Spirituality as a core domain in the assessment of quality of life in oncology. *Psychooncology, 17,* 1121-1128.

Wilkinson, R., & Pickett, K., (2009). *The spirit level: Why more equal societies amost always do better.* London: Allen Lane.

Witkiewitz, K., Lustyk, M. K., & Bowen, S. (2013). Retraining the addicted brain: A review of hypothesized neurobiological mechanisms of mindfulness-based relapse prevention. *Psychology of Addictive Behaviors, 27,* 351-365.

World Health Organization (2009). Violence prevention the evidence: Changing cultural and social norms that support violence. Switzerland: WHO Press.

World Health Organization (2011). Suicide rates per 100,000 by county, year, and sex. [Available at: http://www.who.int/mental_health/prevention/suicide_rates/en/index.html], [Accessed on 29 June 2013].

Zhang, L., Layne, C., Lowder, T., & Liu, J. (2012). A review focused on the psychological effectiveness of Tai Chi on different populations. *Evidence-Based Complementary and Alernative Medicine, 2012,* 1-9.

Zinnbauer, B. J., Pargament, K. I., Cole, B., Rye, M. S., Butter, E. M., Belavich, T. G., Hipp, K. M., Scott, A. B., & Kadar, J. L. (1997). Religion and spirituality: Unfuzzying the fuzzy. *Journal for the Scientific Study of Religion, 36,* 549–564.

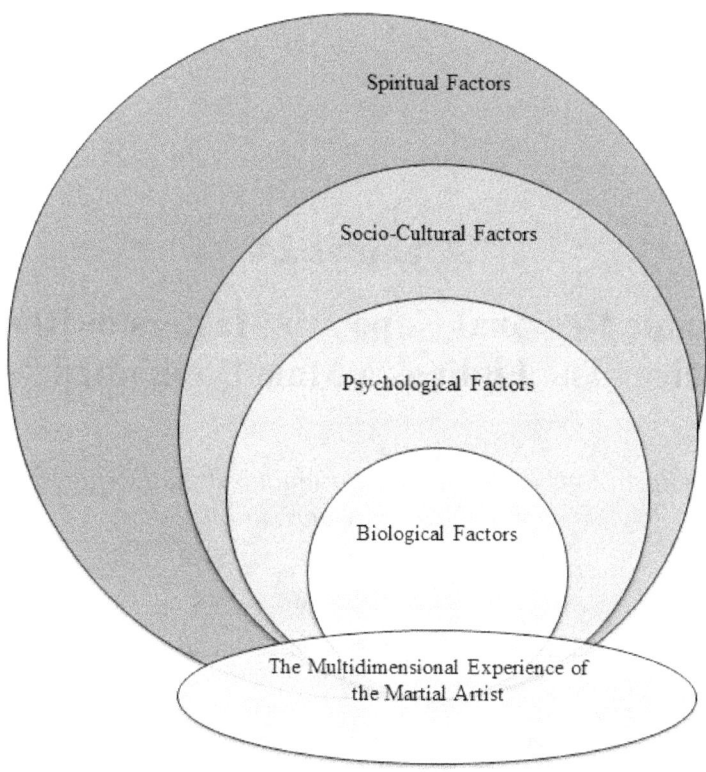

Figure 1: A visual representation of the biopsychosocialspiritual model applied towards the multidimensional experience of the martial artist. The dynamic experience occurs at the intersection of each factor in the layered model.

Chapter 24

Female Regional Capoeira Masters in Rio de Janeiro: The Fight as a Male Dominated Area[1]

Eliane Glória Reis da Silva Souza, Fabiano Pries Devide, Sebastião Josué Votre, & Mauricio Murad

Introduction

It is known that some elements of the physical culture of movement, represented by fights and some sports, can, to an extent, be interpreted as a male-dominated area. Thus, the characteristics that encompass some activities historically built by people can sustain the argument that practices such as *capoeira*, judo and football were and, in some instances, still exhibit male characteristics (DEVIDE, 2005; 2011).

When the issue of women in male-dominated areas is analyzed, the term gender arises, being widely adopted in studies of various fields of knowledge. The term was coined by feminist scholars in the United States, and was translated and adopted in Brazil in the 1970s, within the scope of the second feminist wave (SCOTT, 1995; DEVIDE et al., 2011).

The term gender can be interpreted as a cultural construction that distinguishes the sexes and proposes that it be understood as a constituent of the individual's identity. This can have several definitions, but the consensus is that the anatomical sex, in the biological perspective, does not correspond to the differences and inequalities produced and reproduced among men and women in society, and that these were fruits of social and cultural construction (SCOTT, 1995; LOURO, 2010).

It is uncontested that women's rights and gender equality in Brazil have made significant advances, and they are certainly the result of actions that have

---

[1] Extracts from a Master's Thesis defended in 2011 entitled: Regional *capoeira*: social representations of female masters and graduates on their integration and role in teaching the fight in Rio de Janeiro – Salgado de Oliveira University.

taken place in recent decades in many sectors of our society. Therefore, the results of these advances can be seen by all. Especially regarding the field of physical practices, such as sports and fights, these are no longer just for men; the arguments of virility, strength and the biological representations of the frail, maternal and docile body of women no longer sustain these discourses (Romariz, Votre, Mourao 2012).

In the current scenario, sports and fight – since they are activities of physical contact and symbolically represent a space built to develop and enhance features such as virility, aggressiveness and fighting – were culturally considered a "male thing", inherent to building a male identity. However, after nearly a century of struggles and achievements, women participate in virtually all levels of Olympic sports and fights, allowing for the saying that "today, all sport modalities are for men and women" (Romariz, Votre & Mourao, 2012 p. 220).

The fact that women participate as athletes or in positions of command or power does not mean females are broadly and unrestrictedly accepted in sports. Therefore, it can be said that female fighters are sometimes excluded and treated with overt and covert attitudes of prejudice that question their femininity or sexual identity, causing the sexuality of these women to be questioned, creating stereotypes and stigmatizing labels or questions as to their power of leadership (Devide, 2005).

In light of the discussions regarding Gender Studies and female *capoeira* masters, some questions arose, such as: what are the social representations of female regional *capoeira* masters on their integration and role in teaching the fight in Rio de Janeiro? How did they advance in this practice? What strategies or tactics did they employ or currently employ to achieve the status of master?

The goal was to identify elements of social representations of female regional *capoeira* masters on their integration and role in guiding the teaching of *capoeira* in Rio de Janeiro.

The study is justified by the fact that it discusses some issues related to Gender Studies that focus on the integration of women in male-dominated areas, since this topic has been increasingly scrutinized and debated.

Capoeira: Origins and Women's Participation in the 20th Century

Capoeira can be understood as a form of struggle since slaves yearning for freedom used it as a tool. Tubino (2007) states that the fight is practiced by playing *capoeira*, which requires two *capoeira* practitioners for its development, creating an ambiguity between fight and game.

It is an expression of popular culture, recently declared a cultural heritage of Brazil. According to the Institute of Historical and Artistic Heritage – (Iphan: 2008 & 2009), it is practiced in approximately 150 countries, with about six million followers in Brazil alone (Vieria, 2004); *capoeira*, the circle and the role of instructor or master were included in the "Book of Forms of Expression" and in the "Book of Knowledge" in 2009.

Araújo (2009) recognizes that the inclusion of women in *capoeira* is a recent phenomenon. The classic styles of *capoeira* (Angola and Regional) have traditions nurtured and passed on for generations through men. Consequently, *capoeira* is seen in a male perspective.

At this point, I will expose some clippings or discursive fragments that derived from recorded interviews, reports and records made by some masters, being the result of a historiography assembled by *capoeira* practitioners themselves, and by some historians of popular culture, in order to record the memory of (fe)male *capoeira* practitioners in Bahia and Rio de Janeiro.

Among the scant historical records of the presence of women in *capoeira*, in the nineteenth century, we can quote a black female *capoeira* practitioner Maria Felipa de Oliveira. Her name is associated with the black uprising of July 10, 1822, against the Portuguese fleets, which resulted in the independence of Bahia, and is celebrated on July 2, 1823 (Abreu, 2005).

In the early twentieth century, between the 1920s and 1930s, according to an interview of Master Relâmpago (*"Lightning"*), Atenilo dos Santos, by Master Itapoan in Salvador, he reports that there were two female *capoeira* practitioners who liked the beat, an African fight currently extinct, and samba: Salomé, sung in *capoeira* circles and *Maria dos Anjos*. Both were students of the *capoeira* practitioner nicknamed "Doze Homens" (*"Twelve Men"*) (Almeida, 1988, p. 51). Another woman known in Salvador and sung on circles is *Dona Maria do Camboatá*. Also mentioned is "Maria Homem", a woman who played *capoeira* and fought in the streets (Oliveira & Leal, 2009). These women practiced *capoeira* during a period of history in which *capoeira* was illegal for men and women, and fights were forbidden to women.

Almeida (1986) reports that in Bahia, according to information from Master Acordeom, women were not part of the *capoeira* scene during the period mentioned above, but, around 1940, Master Bimba trained a woman named "Maria Doze Homens" ("Maria Twelve Men") and a group of women to participate in an International Festival. The referred to presentation existed but the initiative was discontinued. Most of the women who participated in *capoeira* over the decades were confined to the circles, as spectators. In the same period, in Angola *capoeira*, Master João Grande, in an exclusive interview, said he had met a female *capoeira* practitioner nicknamed "Chicão" who was wild and never lost to anyone (Abreu & Castro 2009).

At the State University of Rio de Janeiro, in the 1950s, Professor João Lyra Filho was responsible for the inauguration of the first "Capoeira" course at the university level. He is one of the pioneers in promoting a course of this nature in Brazil, which had about one hundred women who actively participated in the course (Murad, 2009). In that same decade, also in Rio de Janeiro, Master Artur Emídio trained several women, among them Brazilian tennis champion, Lucy Maia (Lace, 2006).

Master Itapoan explained that in 1961, in Bahia, Master Bimba surprised everyone when he recorded his first vinyl record containing only voices of women[2] in the chorus of songs. A true pioneer since it was the first time that women sang in a *capoeira* music album; a record that gave visibility to these women on *capoeira* circles. The earliest records of the active participation of

---

[2] The women who sang the chorus in Master Bimba's Album were: Alice dos Santos, Helenita Maria dos Reis, Creusa Maria dos Reis, Edna dos Santos, Dulce do Sacramento, Zélia and Tutuca (wife and daughters of the master) (verbal information provided by Master Itapoan for our survey).

women in Brazilian Student Games, specifically the XIV Brazilian Scholastic Games - Technical Regulation of Capoeira (Souza, 2011) took place in the 1980s.

Methods

The survey has a qualitative, exploratory and documentary design (Thomas; Nelson & Silverman, 2007). As an instrument of data collection, we used a non-directive, semi-structured interview. The script was validated by five expert judges as well as by four teachers and two regional *capoeira* masters of Rio de Janeiro.

The survey's group of interviewees consisted of ten women entitled regional *capoeira* "masters". Despite having identified 12 female masters, since in order to participate in this survey, they should have the recognition of the *capoeira* community, be teaching classes for children and/or adults, and have at least 20 years of practice in the fight, two were excluded because they did not meet the criteria.

Data analysis was carried out based on the use of the theoretical references of the Content Analysis (Bardin, 2008), which provided the category entitled "*capoeira*: a male-dominated area". To interpret the statements of the interviewees we used key elements of the Theory of Social Representations (Moscovic, 1978) - information, attitude and field of representation-, of Discourse Analysis (Orlandi, 2008) - polysemy, discursive interdictions and dispersion; of Ethnomethodology (Coulon, 1995) - indexicality, reflexivity, reportability and notion of member, and Gender Studies (Scott, 1995). These key elements are approaches that have convergences and complement each other, because they are focused on language as a means of production, interaction and interpretations of everyday social practices of people (Orlandi, 2008).

Interviewees

From a data survey record, below we present some characteristics of the group of interviewees in order to identify and discuss issues such as: maternity, family, marriage, double work shifts and how they interact with *capoeira*, because we still live in a society with residual patriarchal characteristics that still offers barriers to women who practice *capoeira* and other physical activities considered male-dominated areas.

The group of interviewees consisted of female *capoeira* masters who practice and teach this fight, contributing in a unique way for its inclusion in a scenario considered male. All have diplomas or statements issued by Federations or documents issued by founding masters of original groups, confirming their titles. Moreover, they have documentary iconographic media, analog or digital photographs, posted on social networking sites[3], or on their blogs.

---

[4] Such as: YouTube, Facebook, Twitter and Orkut.

Of the ten interviewees, eight have college degrees[4] and two completed secondary education. Of the university graduates, five have an undergraduate degree in Physical Education, one has a graduate degree and two have a non-degree graduate course; and the others have training in Psychology, Administration and Educational Psychology, with a non-degree graduate course.

The age of the interviewees ranges from 34 to 50 years old, with 20 to 33 years as *capoeira* practitioners; with regard to their role in teaching *capoeira*, the youngest began in 1996 and the oldest in 1981. Nine interviewees are natives of Rio de Janeiro and one is from Minas Gerais, five are married (two are mothers); one is divorced, without kids; and four are single, without kids.

A relevant datum on single participants is the option not to have child(ren). According to Lessa (2005), in the 1930s, the bodies and behaviors of women were watched. The traditional family was valued, and women were expected to fulfill their purposes: marry and procreate, considered at the time, their social functions. Unmarried women were considered a threat, because they broke away from the dominant representation, standards and social order, competing with men in the labor market. Consequently, single women suffered from stereotypes of being "lesbians", "hysterical feminists" or "ugly".

It is important to highlight the relevance of feminist theories, which sought to break away from the socio-historical, culturally constructed order. However, there are changes in the construction of femininity focusing on the social behavior of women who are taking greater control of their lives, their desires and their gender and sexual identities, which includes the option to stay single and without kids (Devide, 2005; Meyer, 2008).

Capoeira as a Male Dominated Area

In general, interviewees faced resistance from their family when joining *capoeira*, on account of racial prejudice, but also for being an activity that has a male identity. Most reported that the father, mother or both presented resistance against them joining the fight, claiming that *capoeira* was a "male thing" that made women masculine or that could influence the choice of sexual identity.

Cordeiro (2010), in a study of *capoeira* practitioners in Pernambuco, clarifies that the agonistic body practices, as is the case of *capoeira*, while considered a "male thing", of male hegemony, shape bodies and minds, emerging doctrines that establish roles for men and women, shaping attitudes and behaviors, making emerge prejudices related to women who join the fight.

Louro (2010) believes that the discourse on gender somehow encompasses sexual issues, being important to deconstruct the understanding guided by the male and female binary, for men and women develop and live masculinities and femininities that differ from hegemonic ones. Some activities considered masculine can create confusion about gender and sexual relations. In this regard, interviewees broke the barrier of disapproval of their parents, prejudice and homosexual stigmas, because they are often labeled and may suffer by having

---

[5] In a study by Souza, Ramos and Devide (2010), with *capoeira* instructors, it was found that, in general, women who are *capoeira* instructors need more training to perform the same functions as men, reflecting a gender inequality.

made choices that differ from the hegemonic heterosexual norm, and, currently, it is evident that after nearly four decades of women's presence in *capoeira* many changes have taken place in the scenario. According to an excerpt of a statement by master (M), M1 said that values have changed as to the inclusion of women in *capoeira*.

> When I started training, there were very few women in capoeira. My parents did not want me to practice capoeira, they used to say it was a *man's sport*. There was social prejudice, family prejudice... of men and women ... Mother and/or father, the men themselves. Unfortunately. Then the story began to change, and these *resistances became less intense (M1)* (emphasis added).

According to Orlandi (2008), AD should investigate the discursive, ideological formations that underlie the discourse. Regarding the path in *capoeira*, in the discourse of the interviewees, i.e., their insertion and permanence in *capoeira*, each one reflected and produced a discourse based on their social reality as a member of their group or *capoeira* community. It is possible to infer that their statements are directly related to their history, their social class, where they live, among other things. Based on feminist studies that draw attention to differences among women (Louro, 2010), we can state that since they are different their discourses contain the various realities they experienced. There are many variants, such as: white, black, heterosexual, homosexual, urban, different social classes. However, regardless of existential differences, the impediment was due to women being the result of a patriarchal cultural model that prevented them from practicing *capoeira*, somehow they underwent a similar process and subverted the order by entering and remaining in *capoeira*.

This reality is present in other studies that investigate women in *capoeira*. In the discourse produced by the interviewees of Bruhns (2000) and Cordeiro (2010), the practitioners of *capoeira*, who train in Rio de Janeiro and in other states (Pernambuco and Bahia), which have been part of this scenario of masculine identity for nearly 40 years, indicate that in these states *capoeira* was considered inappropriate by the family because they deemed it a "male thing".

> I started through a *friend* who insisted I go watch (...) *my mother did not like it (...) (M4)* (emphasis added).

However, a female master presented a singularity in her discourse, saying that a dance teacher, who was also a *capoeira* instructor, took her to get to know the fight. This female master is different from most others that have men as idols and models. Her role model is a female master recognized in Rio de Janeiro, Sueli Cota, who is part of the imaginary of almost all interviewees. It is important to mention that she is the youngest of the masters, with 20 years of practice. Therefore, she lived at a time when barriers had already been overcome by the pioneers.

> *My first instructor was a woman.* But my father was against it, he thought it was a black thing, he had a lot of prejudice (...). I met Master

> Sueli Cota. Something that stuck in my mind was an event organized by the students of Master Paulinho that I attended ... In 1993, in Niterói, and Master Sueli was there. With her daughter in her arms, she was presented as a master. *It was the first female master I saw. It influenced me, it inspired me (M6).*

Based on the discourse of the interviewees, when they talk about their paths, they speak openly about the opposition of the family, friends, they criticize the medium in a stinging manner, as if they were complaining. However, we noticed that they do not speak of the possible prejudice of their masters, since they are ordinary people who may be subject to influences of the social environment in which they live and, therefore, are likely to influence the people who are part of their social circle; after all, they are still the ones who determine who ascends or not in the group in which they are inserted.

Moscovici (1978) in his study of social representations called this situation "pressure of inference", which brings forth as a result a discursive production with a frequency of ready answers that are common among the group, not resulting in exposure. A fact that we observed in this study, when interviewees make use of terms such as: "many understood", who? Being implicit and unspoken; "criticism" by whom? "Under pressure", by whom? These are evidence of prejudice suffered when they were not masters, but they do not specify the social actor, who holds the power to decide such situations, they preserve their masters.

> By being married to a master, I was under a lot of pressure. A lot, a lot, a lot. *Not by the master,* but by the community, right? (M2) (emphasis added).

Through excerpts from interviewees, as for the influence of the family in relation to their insertion and *capoeira* practice. Most state that:

> *My mother did not like it (...) (M3) (emphasis added);* my mother did not accept it. But she did not say it (...). My *parents* were against it (...) *(M5)* (emphasis added).

As explained by Louro (2010), the family plays a very important role in the development of identities, self-esteem and motivation of the person who practices some form of physical movement. Having the encouragement of the family is crucial for the proper development of this body practice. Aldemam (2004, p. 209) reports that "certainly not all women interested in sports could count on the support of their families". However, he warns that support is important for women to progress in the body practice of their choosing; it is important to mention that the resistance are for both genders and that these barriers become more pronounce and encounter family resistance especially when it crosses the gender frontier (DEVIDE, 2005). Many stated that currently their families are enthusiasts and proud of them being *capoeira* instructors.

A point in the discourse of the interviewees that arouses interest is the way they express themselves. According to Louro (2010), language is endowed with meanings that can represent, reflect or reproduce behaviors, gestures or words that carry prejudices, stigmas and stereotypes, and some expressions may be used to identify powerless and oppressed groups, which could characterize gender inequality.

> Since there are many more men, women are unable to "play" and sometimes the men do not let them [women] play, *it seems natural* for men, sometimes without malicious intent, whatever, but it happens, someone of a higher rank needs to step in, with the right skills to get more respect, *right*? You see very few women participating, *you notice that, right? (M2)* (emphasis added).

We identified the use of euphemisms in the statements of interviewees when discussing certain topics with the use of polite expressions, or even, the need for acceptance at the end of the statements made in a safe and consistent manner and non-recognition of the culturally constructed. This fact is explained by Lakoff (1975) and Louro (2010) who affirm the importance of women to talk about their experiences and their situations in society so that they can assume their voices. We live in a world that is somehow still structured by men, which forces women to develop skills in order to enhance their own thoughts and experiences. At times, the statements of the interviewees contained doubts and hesitations, especially when their personal experiences are not in accordance with the myths and values that relate to women in *capoeira*.

Today, there are many female *capoeira* masters in almost all Brazilian states and abroad, their participation is increasing in the medium, among the best known females masters in Rio de Janeiro we identified: Sueli Cota, Rufatto, Borboleta, Siomara, Baixinha, Magali, Thiara, Francesinha, Tida and Márcia and abroad we have: Cigarra and Suelly[5]. There are also many new female masters inserting themselves is the universe of African-Brazilian culture, however this number reflects a numerical inferiority in relation to men (Souza & Devide, 2011).

Conclusions

The number of women giving *capoeira* classes is rising in Brazil as well as in other countries. Many female Brazilians, from almost all regions of the country, particularly from the southeast and northeast, are working abroad. Today, there are several foreign instructors who teach *capoeira* and other elements of Brazilian popular culture abroad. We need to rewrite the History of Women in *capoeira* and place them as the focal point of studies.

In their circulating discourses, the interviewees anchored their thoughts and desires, which, notably, were founded on their daily social practice. These revealed and depicted the reality of Rio de Janeiro, of yesterday and today, regarding the presence of women in *capoeira* in the state of Rio de Janeiro. Their statements contained certain situations, behaviors and attitudes that demonstrate

---

[5] The first foreign female master is American. She lives in San Francisco, California and is a student of Master Acordeom, disciple of Master Bimba.

the need to "fight" and "waddle" in order for *capoeira* to become a place of equality for all.

It is suggested that further studies investigate the achievements of female *capoeira* practitioners who acted in the past and were responsible for the beginnings of the History of Women in *capoeira* in Brazil, contributing for the empowerment of women in sports and Brazilian society, in order to allow future generations to live together in a harmonious society in terms of gender relations.

References

Abreu, F. J. (2005). Capoeiras, Bahia, século XIX: imaginário e documentação. Salvador: Vogal
Abreu, F. J. & M.B. CASTRO (2009). Capoeira – Encontros/Capoeira. Rio de Janeiro: Beco do Azougue.
Almeida, B. (1986). Capoeira – a Brazilian art form. USA/California: North Atlantic Books.
Almeida, R. C. (1998). Mestre Atenilo – o "Relâmpago" da Capoeira Regional – Depoimento. Salvador: UFBA.
Adelman, M. (2003). Mulheres atletas: re-significações da corporalidade feminina. *Revista Estudos Feministas, Florianópolis*, v. 11, n. 2, p. 445-465, jul./dez.
Alves-Mazzotti A. J. (2002). "O Planejamento de Pesquisa Qualitativa". In: Alves-Mazzotti A. J. & F. Gewandsznajder (Org.). O Método nas ciências naturais e sociais. São Paulo: Thompson, p. 147-178.
Araujo, R. C. (2009). "A Mulher traz para a roda o seu próprio universo". In: ABREU, F. ; CASTRO, M. B. Capoeira – Encontros e capoeira. Rio de Janeiro: Beco do Azougue, p.198-205.
Bardin, L. (2008). Análise de conteúdo. Lisboa: Edições 70.
Brasil. M. E. D. (2009). Parâmetros curriculares nacionais. Educação Física, Terceiro e Quarto Ciclos. Brasília, MEC/SEF, 1998. Disponível em: </http://portal.mec.gov.br/seb/arquivos/pdf/ttransversais.pdf/>. Acesso em: 22 set. 2009.
Bruhns, H. T. (2000). Futebol, carnaval e capoeira – entre as gingas do corpo brasileiro. Campinas: Papirus.
Cordeiro, I. C. A. (2010). A Mulher entrou na roda: olhares femininos sobre a capoeira de Pernambuco. Recife: Prefeitura de Recife.
Devide, F. P. (2005). Gênero e mulheres no esporte – história das mulheres nos jogos olímpicos modernos. Ijuí, RGS: Editora UNIJUI, 2005.
Devide,, F. P. et al. (2013). Estudos de gênero na Educação Física Brasileira.In: Revista Motriz, Rio Claro, v.17, n.1, p.93-103, jan./mar. 2011. Disponível em: < http://dx.doi.org/>. Acesso em: 13 mar.
Instituto Do Patrimonio Historico E Artistico Nacional-Iphan. Disponível em: </ http://portal.iphan.gov.br/portal/pesquisa.do>. Acesso em: 25 ago. 2008.
Lakoff, R. (1975). Language and woman's place. Nova York: Harper and Row.
Lessa, P. (2005). Mulheres, corpo, e esporte em uma perspectiva feminista. Motrivivência, Santa Catarina, ano XVII, n. 24, p. 157-172, jun.
Lace, A. (2010). A mulher na capoeira. Jornal da Capoeira – Crônica (2006). Disponível em:

<http://www.capoeira.jex.com.br/cronicas/a+mulher+na+capoeira/>. Acesso em: 24 set.

Louro, G. L. (2010). Gênero, sexualidade e educação: uma perspectiva pós-estruturalista. Petrópolis, RJ: Vozes.

Meyer, D. E. (2008). "Gênero e educação: teoria e política". In: Louro, G. L.; Felipe, & J.; Goeller, S. V. (Orgs.). Corpo, gênero e sexualidade – Um debate contemporâneo na educação. 4. ed. Petrópolis/Rio de Janeiro: Vozes. p.9-27.

Moscovici, S.(1978). A representação social da Psicanálise. Rio de Janeiro: Zahar.

Murad, M. (2009). Sociologia e Educação Física – diálogos, linguagens do corpo, esportes. Rio de Janeiro: Editora FGV.

Olivera, J. P. & L.A.P. Leal (2009). Capoeira, identidade e gênero – ensaios sobre a história social da capoeira no Brasil. Salvador: EDUFBA.

Orlandi, E. P. (2008). Discurso e leitura. Campinas: Unicamp.

Scott, J. (1995). Gênero: uma categoria útil de análise histórica. *Educação e Realidade, Porto Alegre*, v. 20, n. 2, p. 71-99, jul/dez.

Simoes, A. C. (2004). O Universo das mulheres nas práticas sociais e esportivas. In: Simoes, A. C. & J.D. Knijnik (Orgs.). O Mundo psicossocial da mulher no esporte – comportamento, gênero, desempenho. São Paulo: Aleph. p. 23-45.

Souza, E. G. R. S. (2011). Capoeira Regional: representações sociais das mestras e formandas sobre sua inserção e atuação no ensino da luta no Rio de Janeiro. 2011. 167 f. Dissertação (Mestrado) – Programa de Pós-Graduação Stricto Senso em Ciências da Atividade Física, Universidade Salgado de Oliveira, Niterói.

_____. (2010). Capoeira: sua História e as Relações de Gênero. IN: Congresso Regional de Historia – Anpuh – Associaco nacional de Historia, 14, 2010, Rio de janeiro. Anais ... Rio de Janeiro: Numen.

Souza E. G. R. S. & F.P. Devide (2009). "Capoeira uma luta brasileira – Interfaces com a história da cultura brasileira, a Educação Física Escolar e as relações de gênero". In: Ferreira, W. S.; Menezes, P. F. (Orgs.). Lutas – Potencial educativo e formativo das lutas. Rio de Janeiro: Viagraf p. 61-68.

Souza, E. G. R. S.; Ramos, M. R. F. & F.P. Devid (2010). Capoeira e Promoção de Saúde na Educação Física Escolar. In: Congresso Nacional de Educacao Fisica Escholar - Encontro Nacional de Educação Física Escolar – ENFEFE/UFF, 13, 2010, Niterói – Rio de Janeiro. Anais ... Rio de Janeiro.

Souza, G. C. & L. Mourao (2011). Mulheres no tatame: o judô feminino no Brasil. Rio de Janeiro: Mauad X: Faperj.

Thomas, J. R.; Nelson, J. & S.J. Silverman(2007). Métodos de pesquisa em atividade física. São Paulo: Artmed, 2007.

Tubino, M. J. G. (2007). Dicionário Enciclopédico Tubino do Esporte. Rio de Janeiro: Senac Rio.

Vieria, S. L. S. (2004). "Capoeira". In: DaCosta, L. P. (Org.). Atlas do Esporte no Brasil. Rio de Janeiro: Shape. p. 39-40.

Chapter 25
Capoeira: An Example of Sustainable Sport

Andrea Cristiane Alves da Cunha & Renata Osborne

Introduction

Capoeira is a multidimensional sport; for some people it is an art, for others a dance, a game, a ritual or a fight. It has a long history, was originated in times of slavery in Brazil, has survived, and nowadays is very valued as a manifestation of the Brazilian culture. We can say that Capoeira blossomed over time, and it is now appreciated not only in our country but also in many other countries.

Vieira (2004) explains that Capoeira is a game, a ludic physical activity that uses legs, arms and head, practiced by doubles based on attacks, elusive and insinuation movements having music played by artisanal instruments and singing by the group involved. It can be employed as gymnastics, dance, sport, art, martial art, folklore, recreation and theater.

It was created by the slaves in Brazil, black men and women who were brought from Africa, especially, Angola (Iório and Darido, 2005). It was a strategy to resist, to survive in face of oppression. Vieira (2004) explains that Capoeira was originated in the 18th century, as a dance-fight, was forbidden by law until 1940; became institutionalized as a sport in 1941 and expanded nationally and internationally since then. In 2004, there were approximately six million of capoeiristas in Brazil and Capoeira International Federation include federations in Canada, Argentina, Portugal, Holland, France, Germany and Australia and acknowledges Capoeira practice in 156 other countries. According to Lussac (2010), Capoeira was recognized as a Brazilian cultural immaterial patrimony in 2008 by the National Institute of Historic and Artistic Patrimony, and its next step is to be a candidate as a humanity patrimony by UNESCO.

Figueiredo (2002) in his research about physical education and environmental education points out that Capoeira only recently has been introduced in Brazilian schools. For the author, the importance to teach Capoeira in schools is not only about learning our past history or folkloric patrimony, but to understand a world view that questioned the efficiency concept and various patterns of modern western society. In this sense, Teixeira, Osborne and Souza (2012) explicate that Capoeira started as a manifestation against the slave regime, and now is a popular practice that still combats ethnocentrism, which fosters prejudices and discriminations against black people, their rituals, drums and identities.

The literature about Capoeira has treated its history of oppression and overcome, but little was written on unique present practices and future perspectives. This situation generated our research problem. We, the authors, are: an instructor of Abadá Capoeira and a professor of Salgado de Oliveira University. The first one has the experience in Capoeira and the second one has been researching physical education, sport and sustainable development; we have been discussing the connections between these points of view, betting in a fruitful combination. The text we are presenting is one of the products of a work in progress.

Sustainable Sport

Before sustainability concepts there was the ecological movement that questioned economic development of capitalist and socialist societies, which both generated environment destruction, threatening the ability of humans to survive in the long term. It revealed an ethical crisis in which human beings should change their view of the world, from a dominant and egoistic point of view to a respectful and cooperative posture towards each other human being and nature.

Nowadays sustainable development is a well known term to a kind of development able to meet present and future society needs, which depends on respecting ecosystem limits. It is also an intelligent and holistic development that balances economic, social, cultural and environmental dimensions in order to improve life conditions.

For UNESCO (2005), the concept of sustainable development continues to evolve, but can be defined as encompassing three key components: society, environment and economy, having culture as an underlying dimension. The first component is about understanding the role of different institutions in change and development as well as the role of democratic and participatory systems; the second component is about the conscience that environment is fragile in face of certain human activities; and the third component is about knowing the limits and potential of economic growth with its consequences on society and environment. The three components must be integrated in order to promote a sustainable development, and the values, languages and world views associated with culture influence how those components are worked together in different contexts. The Decade of Education for Sustainable Development (2005-2014), leaded by UNESCO, aims to promote positive values and changes towards sustainable development.

Sustainable development is complex and multifaceted endeavor that depends on ethical principles and political will. There are many important key words of sustainable development, but we would like to emphasize the word change, not any change, but one that improves life conditions for all, humans and non-humans. On that matter, UNESCO (2005) affirms: "Sustainable development is not about maintenance of the status quo, but rather about the direction and implications of change" (p.14)

The world of sport has been participating in the discussion of sustainable development. As explained by Jägeman (1997), everywhere sport has been developed in wrong directions and pollution in nature threatens sport practice; therefore, sportsmen cannot ignore environmental problems and their responsibilities. But, as Costa (1997) states, sport is ambivalent because it can increase environment destruction or contribute to raise awareness towards environment conservation.

One basic thing to judge if sport is being not friendly to the environment is to assess its impact. The International Olympic Committee (1997) classifies sport activities as able to cause low or high impact. The first one refers to sports that do not significantly change the ecosystem, while the second one requires substantial destruction of the ecosystem.

There is always some impact in any activity but is different, for example, the impact of practicing jet sky compared to surfing in the beach. The kind of environmental impact is very important in assessing the need to limit or promote some sport practice if we intend to improve quality of life. Another important issue to consider is everyone's right to play sports, so in planning sports development we need to ask which ones are able to be widely practiced.

Joining the idea of meeting the present and future needs, respecting the right to play sports and improving life conditions of the whole community (humans and no-humans), there is the following definition of sustainable sport: "Sport is sustainable when it meets the needs of today's sporting community while contributing to the improvement of future sport opportunities for all and the improvement of the integrity of the natural and social environment on which it depends" . (Chernushenko, 2011, p. 21)

In Chernushenko's definition, we would like to emphasize the idea of sport opportunities for all, because when sport is used with exclusion logic, it becomes unsustainable as it strikes the right of everyone to have access to sport opportunities.

This is something that United Nations advocates; in 2003, for example, their agencies united in a task force to utilize sports in activities related to development and peace. In their view, the concept of "sport for all" is central to understanding their goals. Their aim "is not the creation of new sporting champions and the development of sport but rather the use of sport in broader development and peace-building activities" (United Nations, 2003, p. 2). And in 2005, United Nations launched the International Year of Sport and Physical Education to promote education, health, development and peace, with clear messages on drug abuse prevention and cultivation of values such as respect, teamwork and tolerance.

Abadá Capoeira

One of the steps of our research was to analyze documents from the Group called Abadá Capoeira. They were images of the many practices of the group, headed by Master Camisa, who provided explanations for the documents meanings. The selected documents from Abadá Capoeira included their own newspaper, posters of events, pictures, music CD, images from facebook and their blog. The main categories created were based on theory related to the role of sports in sustainable development, while the subcategories emerged from the data.

The first block of documents was categorized as telling the history of Capoeira. One of the images from facebook is a picture of a painting that shows a farm, a group of black women and men slaves around two of them who were dancing and fighting, while a man was playing a drum. The people around were doing different things, some were dancing and clapping hands, while some looked like they were just in their way to work and stopped to watch. It looked like a daily moment of leisure.

Another image is a drawing of two black men fighting in a farm environment and a guard jumping a fence going towards the men. There is a date on the drawing, 1813. It transmits the idea of a combat that went beyond the two fighters; it was a social fight, slaves were not obeying the rules and were fighting for their space in society. They were showing their strength, resistance and ability to fight, while the guard representing the system was trying to stop them.

The second block of images was about past Masters of Capoeira and the present leader, how they lived and their unique contributions for Capoeira. This is very important for the group, the memory of what was done before and who did it and the feeling of recognition and gratitude. It is a way to make the spirit of those who passed away alive among the group, and to acknowledge their present leader.

The third block of documents was on the Master Bimba Educational Center. This place was built in a rural environment, designed to look like a *quilombo*, which was a hiding place in Brazil for fugitive slaves in the past. Camisa says it is a modern *quilombo* that continues to resist. It has abundant flora and fauna. There Camisa goes to have moments of reflection and also it is a place to hold events, seminars and courses. Camisa loves animals and there are pictures of him with horses and with a macaw on his arm or on his Capoeira instrument called *berimbau*. At the Education Center, animals that were born and raised in captivity are brought to be free, they get help and live without cages at the Center. "The animals conquered their freedom like Capoeira did" are words of Camisa.

The fourth group of documents refers to social projects organized by Abadá Capoeira. There are many creative projects involving communities, art, education and music. Camisa explains that Capoeira is an art that includes many arts. Through many creative events Capoeira send messages of solidarity, union and peace.

One of the posters is about Community Games that were held in Rocinha *favela* that welcomed others *favelas*. In this event there was a lecture about the dangers of drugs consumption. Camisa explains that this was an event for peace and that Capoeira has the power of harmonizing relationships between communities.

Another poster with the title "Take me out of the streets" is about a project in Portugal that used Capoeira to assist homeless children. Camisa has always worked to improve life conditions and reverse poverty and abandonment of communities; he has always fought for social justice.

One of the documents is the music lyrics of Abadá Capoeira CD, which contains music composed for social and ecological campaigns held in their various events. It has the following messages: peace, disarmament, harmony, no to deforestation, no to fauna and flora destruction, no to ocean pollution, wise consumption of water, recycling, blood donation, combat to a disease caused by a mosquito, drivers' education, and no to drugs consumption. Master Camisa explains that Capoeira serves community.

Camisa has always encouraged the practice of Capoeira for everyone; Abadá Capoeira organizes special classes and events for children, women, people with disabilities and elderly. There are pictures and posters of all of these groups; one of the pictures that caught our attention is one of a guy without his two legs playing Capoeira with another man without disability. The guy without legs was in an upside position, sustaining his upper body by his two hands on the floor.

The fifth group of documents is posters of Abadá Capoeira games, when there is always a campaign. It is a way that Abadá finds to be useful and contribute to a more conscious, just and less consuming society. Some of the images express symbioses between Capoeira, man and nature. An example is an image of a tree combined with a man in a handstand position (Capoeira movement). His arms form the roots of the tree, his upper body is the trunk, and his legs are the branches. Examples of campaigns announced were: for harmony between capoeira, nature and ecology; reforestation; care for fauna and flora; better use of water, oil recycling and solid waste recycling.

Master Camisa told that Abadá Capoeira's events and ecological campaign were very successful and their intention is to sensitize people for an ecological behavior, a constant concern with the place we live. In his opinion, everyone can help, stopping throwing away garbage on the streets is a beginning, and then there is the need to care for air, trees, animals and specially human beings.

The last group of documents is posters and pictures of Abadá international events held in Brazil and in other countries. The games characterize the movement of Capoeira sportivization. The search for performance is also a characteristic of Abadá school, which work with profession training.

There is a big class in Copacabana beach that is the closing of the international events of Abadá Capoeira. On this day the winners of the world games are presented, the various groups such as the ones with special needs and elderly do their presentations, and there are messages and actions of ecological and social campaigns.

The table below presents a synthesis of the results presented.

Abadá Sustainable Capoeira	
Dimensions of sustainable development	**Philosophy and actions of Abadá**
cultural	History of Capoeira and its role in the political context of Brazil
	Valorization of predecessor and present Masters of Capoeira
	Values: solidarity, respect, peace, progress, social justice, harmony, community service

social	Games in favelas
	Participation of various groups: children, youth, women, people with disabilities and elderly
	Health and citizen education
environmental	Low impact
	Love and care for animals
	Campaigns of reforestation, oil recycling, solid waste recycling, wise consumption of water
economic	Realization of big international events
	High performance training
	Professional training

Final Remarks

We worked with the hypotheses that Capoeira is a sustainable sport, and we concluded that it is now and can be in the future if it continues in a positive way. People suffer from a world where the economic interests still subjugates life flourishing. There is too much violence, environmental destruction, poverty and hunger, which are unsustainable realities. It is still time to resist and change. Capoeira is an example of resistance and search for a better place to live. It is a strong group that was able to survive past oppression and has been fighting for peace, education, health and social justice. The slaves who created Capoeira had to conquer freedom in the past, but our present society still deals with freedom issues. Nowadays it is more about how we are going to use our freedom with responsibility. The ecological movement shows the interrelatedness between people and the environment, and demands limits to human activities. We can say that Capoeira is using its freedom with social responsibility. As presented in this text, Capoeira promotes respect for past, present and future generations and the environment; respect is a central value to sustainable development. To learn Capoeira is to do much more than incredible movements, is to learn a way of being and relating full of wisdom. Capoeira is about knowing history and making part of it by being proactive.

Capoeira is versatile, can happen in any place, outdoor or indoor, has low impact on the environment. It is simple, can be practiced by everyone, and very rich in meanings and possibilities. It is a path of enchantment, so necessary to foster balance between the rational and artistic mind. Abadá Capoeira contributes to sustainable development in diverse ways: being in tune with a holistic view, promoting inclusion, educating children and youth, valuing female participation in Capoeira, propagating messages of no consumption of illegal drugs, promoting campaigns of blood donation, leading campaigns on fauna and flora preservation, reforestation and recycling. Nowadays Abadá Capoeira sends us a message of strength, beauty and hope that we are glad to register. We recommend future studies on sustainable sports versus unsustainable ones because the concept of sustainable sport can help in planning worthwhile sport practices.

References

Chernushenko, D. (2011). Promoting Sustainability in Sport and Through Sport: An Industry Veteran Looks Back, and Forward, and Issues a Challenge. In K. Gilbert (Ed.), *Sustainability and Sport* (pp. 15-21). Champaign: Common Ground.

Costa, L. (1997). Introdução. In: Costa, Lamartine P. da (Ed.), *Meio ambiente e desporto:* uma perspectiva internacional, (pp. 23-29). Faculdade de Ciências do Desporto e Educação Física, Universidade do Porto, Porto.

Figueiredo, R. P. (2002). *Educação Física para Educação Ambiental: uma relação a ser construída na transitoriedade.* (Unpublished Master's Dissertation). Universidade de Brasília, Brasília.

Jägeman, H. (1997). Perpetrator and victim sport's relationship with the environment. In: COSTA, Lamartine P. da (Ed.), *Meio ambiente e desporto:* uma perspectiva internacional, (pp. 183-194). Faculdade de Ciências do Desporto e Educação Física, Universidade do Porto, Porto.

International Olympic Committee (1997). *Manual on Sport and the Environment*, Lausanne, International Olympic Committee.

Lussac, R. M. P. (2010). A Polivalência da multifacetada Capoeira. *RevistaDigital*, 14 (142), [Available at: www.efdeportes.com], [Acessed 28th August 2012].

UNESCO (2005). *United Nations decade of education for sustainable development 2005-2014: Draft International Implementation Scheme.* [Available at: http://portal.unesco.org/education/admin], [Accessed 11th May 2005].

United Nations (2003). *Sport for development and peace: Towards Achieving the Millennium Development Goals. Report from the United Nations Inter-Agency Task Force on Sport for Development and Peace.* [Available at: http://www.un.org/wcm/webdav/site/sport/shared/sport/pdfs/Reports/2003_interagency_report_ENGLISH.pdf], [Accessed 15th August 2013].

United Nations (2005). International Year of Sport and Physical Education [Available at: http://www.un.org/wcm/content/site/sport/home/resourcecenter/publications], [Accessed 15th August 2013].

Teixeira, F. F., Osborne, R., & Souza, E. G. R. S. (2012). A prática do ensino da Capoeira nas escolas: perfil e visão do capoeirista. *Corpus et Scientia*, 8(2), 1-15.

Vieira, S. L. S. (2004). Capoeira. In L. P. DaCosta (Ed.), *Atlas do Esporte no Brasil:* atlas do esporte, educação física e atividades físicas de saúde e lazer no Brasil, (pp. 39-40). Shape, Rio de Janeiro.

Chapter 26

Capoeira as an Art of Living: The Aesthetics of a Cunning Existence

Greg Downey

Introduction

As we rode the bus together, I asked Natinho, a veteran practitioner of *capoeira*, the Afro-Brazilian martial art and dance I had travelled to Salvador to study, how he fared in a weekend capoeira *roda* or 'ring.' Although we trained together at the *Grupo de Capoeira Angola Pelourinho*, named for the Salvador's historic Pelourinho neighbourhood, I heard that he had ventured to the nearby school of *Mestre* or 'Teacher' João Pequeno (Little John) for a roda. Capoeira rodas are the primary performance events for the genre, where practitioners come together to 'play' (*jogar*) the acrobatic fight-dance. Weekend rodas at João Pequeno's academy were long, meandering events, with pairs of players randomly matched against each other for five or ten minutes at a time (longer if they were particularly adept). The rodas started slowly and went on for hours. Mestre João Pequeno was in his eighties and, still playing if a bit less flexibly than he once did, he often gave players more leeway than our own teacher, *Mestre* Moraes, allowed. The result was sometimes disarray, even an occasional brawl.

Natinho was not happy about his weekend performance. Although capoeira 'games' (*jogos*) are inconclusive, practitioners constantly evaluate their own and each other's performances. Natinho told me that he could not get in the right frame of mind. His initial attempts to start were too agitated, too tense; he said he was *parado*, 'stopped.' His game was ugly, and he could not respond fluidly to his adversary's attacks. The veteran player had returned to the 'foot' of the orchestra to restart the game two, three times, listened carefully to the music, tried to calm himself, before he finally felt like things went well and his performance 'rolled.' Natinho described taking control of his inner state, willing his body to become relaxed, and accepting the orchestra's rhythm as a guide to his actions.

Finally, the game went well, and he was pleased with how he played; he felt he had confirmed his status as a player deserving some renown.

As he told me the story, I felt Natinho seized upon it to teach me. As a novice practitioner, helping him to instruct small classes in Salvador's urban periphery, I struggled even more severely with myself in the roda. Natinho reminded me that this was one of the central challenges of practice and offered some consolation. I was not alone: even a veteran could find himself nervous, overly aggressive, and incapable of relaxing into the flow of the roda and music. His story drew my attention to the techniques he used to manipulate his own internal state, allowing himself to become more susceptible to external factors that were crucial to a virtuoso performance.

Capoeira is an acrobatic Afro-Brazilian danced martial art, training for a game descended from African challenge dances, the pastimes of urban toughs in Brazil, and the feast day performance games from the plantation regions around the Bay of All Saints, in the north-eastern state of Bahia. Heir to a tradition of both thuggery and resistance to racist oppression, combining violence and artistry, and a once-persecuted black art that has become a source of national pride, capoeira performances embody a number of tensions. A good game, one that players and audiences alike savour, requires a shifting, unstable balance between cooperation and competition, aggression and playfulness. With this sort of ambivalence at its heart, and no definitive way of resolving a game—practitioners have long struggled against the expectation that a 'sport' should produce a clear winner[1]—aesthetic judgment is both essential and extremely difficult.

At the heart of capoeira aesthetics is the dynamic that Natinho described: the art requires one to control one's own internal state (emotions, tension, mood, receptivity to perceptions, attention, mental state) so that one's performance is an appropriate response to an adversary, the music, the environment, and the unfolding of a game. To understand capoeira aesthetics requires not merely learning to judge a performance visually based on local values and standards, but also coming to perceive the internal state of players through the way that they move and respond to each other. The inseparability of internal state and external performance make capoeira training a form of psycho-physical discipline, a shaping of oneself and one's reactions over time, and makes capoeira aesthetics a judgment of a person's developing character.

Capoeira performance and the aesthetic judgment of how a person plays, from this perspective, are not judgments of representations or creativity, nor are they Romantic assessments of how authentic a performance is to a person's 'true self.' Rather, aesthetic evaluations are assessments of a person's work on themselves, how a performer is progressing in his or her pursuit of becoming a fully-fledged *capoeirista*, a practitioner of the art who embodies its principles. Aesthetic appraisal in this setting bears more than a passing resemblance to a psychological diagnostic process, where a performance is judged as symptomatic of a practitioner's internal state, including both long-term pursuit of proficiency and that person's current condition, such as the ability to achieve the relaxation

---

[1] Downey, G. (2002). 'Domesticating an Urban Menace: Efforts to Reform Capoeira as a Brazilian National Sport,' *International Journal of the History of Sport* vol. 19, no. 2, pp. 1-32.

necessary for responsive play. In Natinho's case, he found his agitated, dissipated mental-emotional state made it impossible for him to perform up to his own standards.

Treating capoeira as a form of artistic self-cultivation highlights the relationship between disciplined training in the art and programs for the 'care of self,' such as those that Michel Foucault explored in some of his final works.[2] Although Foucault's exploration of what he called the 'aesthetics of existence' arose, in part, from his studies of Greek philosophy, he alluded to contemporary examples in the artistic lifestyles of subcultural groups, such as the dandy described by Baudelaire and sadomasochists Foucault himself encountered in California. Viewing capoeira through the lens of Foucault's concern with self-cultivation helps us to understand indigenous capoeira aesthetic evaluation among practitioners better than considering a game or roda as an isolated performance.

My hope in this chapter is that my own apprenticeship in capoeira will help me to shift the scale of the account, telling a different story about the politics of capoeira aesthetics than the typical sociological narrative of social domination and resistance. This smaller-scale person-centred account better recognizes the hard work of taking the self as a project and the challenges of turning one's body and life into a work of art. This perspective does not dispel politics from the account but rather changes the scale of the political frame, a move in keeping with discussion in the introduction to this volume of how a revived consideration of aesthetics seeks to escape from uniform political narratives about art. That is, rather than reducing artistic labour to the representation of a story we already know about domination and resistance, racist hegemony and aesthetic revolt, for example, I hope instead to help readers understand why the stakes are so high for individuals, why they would devote themselves so completely to a game in which they cannot even achieve decisive victory: one's own life and (nick) name are at stake.

Background

As an art form, Lowell Lewis has characterized capoeira as a 'blurred genre,' borrowing the term from Clifford Geertz, because the art combines elements of game, athletic contest, improvised dance, techniques for self-defence, musical genre, and vehicle for oral history transmission.[3] Practitioners train extensively, many for years or even decades, to engage in improvised games. They seek to trip, head butt, kick, or otherwise out-manoeuvre an adversary, demonstrating greater agility, foresight, and wile in a kind of one-up-man-ship with no clear resolution of the contest in the roda or 'ring'. At the same time, players must also harmonize

---

[2] A number of works demonstrate this trend, but see especially Michel Foucault. *The Use of Pleasure: Volume 2 of The History of Sexuality.* Translated by Robert Hurley. New York: Vintage, 1985; *The Care of the Self: Volume 3 of The History of Sexuality.* Translated by Robert Hurley. New York: Vintage, 1986; *Technologies of the Self: A Seminar with Michel Foucault*, edited by Luther H. Martin, Huck Gutman, and Patrick H. Hutton. Amherst: University of Massachusetts Press, 1988.

[3] J. Lowell Lewis. *Ring of Liberation: Deceptive Discourse in Brazilian Capoeira.* Chicago: University of Chicago Press, 1992, p. 1; Clifford Geertz. *Local Knowledge: Further Essays in Interpretive Anthropology.* New York: Basic Books, 1983.

their movements with the instrumental music provided by a group of musicians that makes up one side of the capoeira roda. Players are admired for physical ability and technical proficiency but also for a sly sense of humour, dramatic timing, and an acute eye for an opportunity to act decisively, even cruelly. A practitioner may also be recognized for his or her spontaneous improvisations or humorous sung comments upon the games of other players, as the whole gathering performs together, usually for their own enjoyment. Full proficiency, at least in the schools I studied most closely, requires mastering all roles in the performance: player, song leader, musician, teacher, oral historian, even manufacturer of musical instruments.

When capoeira practitioners play in the roda, the dominant performance form of the art, even an untrained observer will inevitably recognize that aesthetic concerns influence the action. Although the game may be at heart a struggle or 'fight' (*luta*), as practitioners will point out, the movement techniques are so flamboyantly excessive, so unnecessarily acrobatic and indirect, that the combative nature of the art may be submerged. For this reason, some describe the art as a *dança-luta*, a 'dance-fight.' During play, practitioners remain in constant motion through a swaying step, the *ginga*, which varies among individuals, styles, and in relation to the music. Practitioners ornament their movement in ways that have nothing to do with any obvious objective, such as evading an adversary's techniques or tripping an opponent, using a range of cartwheels, wrist spins, fluid headstands, and acrobatic moves referred to collectively as *floreios*, 'flourishes.' Many practitioners argue that floreios are an essential part of a game, not only because they beautify the event, but also because they distract an adversary and conceal more direct attacks.

Expert capoeiristas, however, do not contrast starkly artistry with violence, but see some of the most aggressive techniques, if well-timed and appropriate, as crowning aesthetic achievements. One informant, for example, described a veteran player admiringly as 'perverse' (*perverso*) and 'evil' (*malvado*), shaking his head at the veteran's extraordinary resourcefulness in finding ways to befuddle and take down his opponents. For this reason, aesthetic evaluation of a technique, an attack, or an escape is very much about its fitness or suitability to the situation in which it took place; even an effective technique can be judged ugly if it is poorly timed, inappropriate, or suggests that the attacker's internal state is not well-suited to play. As one capoeira instructor told me, each technique did not have a proper form because it had to conform to circumstances.

Style and the Sociology of Aesthetics

During my field research in Salvador, all aesthetic judgments of capoeira performance were shaped, in part, by a contrast between different styles of the art, often described as a polarity between a traditionalist *Capoeira Angola* style and *Capoeira Regional*, a form of the art created in the twentieth century by Mestre Bimba. I worked most closely with practitioners of Capoeira Angola, the style of the art considered more ludic, dance-like, and African. Although I had extensive contact with practitioners of the more vigorous, athletic, martial, and high speed forms that my closest colleagues labelled, 'Capoeira Regional,' apprenticeship-based fieldwork demanded that I ally myself with a single school and practice a specific style. Some teachers claimed to provide students with a foundation in the art as a whole, synthesizing the various styles; the *angoleiros* or practitioners of Capoeira Angola with whom I worked scoffed at the idea that such a synthesis was even possible.

In fact, the stylistic field was far more complicated than the contrast between Regional and Angola, 'modern' and 'traditional,' might suggest. For example, practitioners that my fellow angoleiros labelled uniformly 'Capoeira Regional' disagreed amongst themselves about stylistic issues, some cleaving as conservatively to the teachings of the style's founder as any traditionalist angoleiro. These former students of Mestre Bimba, the creator of Regional, pointedly criticized styles of the art that, in their eyes, exaggerated martial or acrobatic tendencies, featured additional innovations, or even tried to reincorporate practices from Capoeira Angola that Mestre Bimba had excluded. Likewise, angoleiros disagreed pointedly on a host of issues, especially aesthetic concerns about ideal movement styles, the proper pace of play, or how much individual creativity ought to be allowed. The school with which I was mostly closely associated, the Grupo de Capoeira Angola Pelourinho (GCAP), for example, attracted outside criticism from fellow angoleiros who felt that Afrocentric members exaggerated kinesthetic traits considered 'African,' such as a highly-ornamented staccato ginga, because of cultural politics.

Members of GCAP demonstrated an aesthetic preference for certain kinaesthetic traits in movement, as I have discussed at length elsewhere.[4] Specifically, they favour a varied pace in games rather than the uniform high velocity found in some rodas; 'closed' over 'open' positions, appreciating postures that contain the body more tightly and remain in close proximity to an adversary; 'soft' movements which conform to relations between the bodies rather than 'hard,' abrupt motions with greater kinaesthetic integrity; and greater variation in the interactive flow of games than found in some rodas. My colleagues in GCAP tended to criticize other styles, not only for aesthetic reasons, but for the social implications that they imputed to them; other rodas were not simply 'ugly,' they were 'whitened,' 'bourgeois-fied,' 'aggressive,' 'distorted,' or disrespectful of tradition. In contrast, the group was criticized by some for resisting creative change, ignoring the art's pugilistic tradition, and being overly pious or precious about stylistic embellishment. As several outside critics cautioned me, if they played with someone who danced around like a member of my home group, they would not hesitate to kick a dancing angoleiro in the chest or knock him out of the roda.

Within this environment of vigorous disagreement about proper practice and style, I assumed when I started my field research that aesthetic judgments of performance would be social critique by artistic means. Influenced by the work of Pierre Bourdieu, everyday aesthetics appeared to me to be socially motivated forms of distinction and tactics to increase group status.[5] In his program for a sociology of sport, Bourdieu explains how individuals choose to take up different sports in sociological terms: 'In short, the determining element of the system of

---

[4] Downey, G. (2005). *Learning Capoeira: Lessons in Cunning from an Afro-Brazilian Art.* New York: Oxford University Press.
[5] See especially Pierre Bourdieu, *Distinction: A Social Critique of the Judgement of Taste.* Translated by Richard Nice. Cambridge: Harvard University Press, 1984 (1979).

preferences is here the relation to the body, to the way the body is put into action, which is associated with a social position and an innate experience of the physical and social world.'[6] To the degree that these preferences are sociologically determined and hierarchically related—as Bourdieu has argued is the case for most cultural fields—the range of stylistic difference within sport or movement discipline reflects and reproduces social distinctions.[7]

In fact, from a sociological perspective, aesthetic judgments among my informants *did* look like thinly veiled tactical moves of hierarchy, marking both the aesthetic judge and the target of appraisal simultaneously, demonstrating the taste of the viewer at the same time that they placed a performer into a social-stylistic landscape. My initial research impulse was to figure out how the various styles of moving were organized by traits such as class or race. How were certain ways of moving judged to be particularly 'African' or 'authentic' or 'working class' or 'bourgeois' or 'modern'? This sociological lens lent suspicion to my hermeneutics, an assumption that aesthetic judgment was not merely socially embedded but socially motivated.

But the closer I came to the art, the longer my own apprenticeship continued and the deeper my own commitment to performance, the less compelling I found sceptical sociological explanations for aesthetic judgments. I found myself making the same aesthetic judgments as my informants, being as thrilled by a virtuoso performance as they were, and as disdainful of soulless games as the most acerbic among them. Although they disagreed whether a person's ginga should be smoothly flowing or baroquely intricate, for example, I found practitioners across stylistic divides shared admiration for certain virtuoso performers, thrilled to the same games, and seemed to admire certain traits even if they disagreed about the proper procedure for starting a game, which instruments should be in the orchestra, or which songs were appropriate for a game. In their big public events, practitioners of Capoeira Regional placed virtuoso angoleiros in positions of honour and stopped everything to watch when they entered the roda. Even in the most Afrocentric groups, I saw grudging respect for cagey players of Regional, adept enough to enter tradition-bound rodas of Capoeira Angola and play with savvy and grace.

Running against the folk sociology of capoeira style that practitioners argued about overtly, and that my readings in the sociology of bodily kinesthetics anticipated—who was really 'authentic,' whether a style was 'whitened,' whether certain innovations 'appropriated' or 'distorted' the art beyond recognition—was

---

[6] Pierre Bourdieu, *In Other Words: Essays Towards a Reflexive Sociology.* Translated by M. Adamson. Stanford: Stanford University Press, 1990, p. 157.

[7] A number of sociologists of sports have followed Bourdieu's programmatic call to explore the relationship between social groups' kinaesthetic preferences in sport and their habitual relationships to their own bodies. Perceptive examples include Suzanne Laberge and David Sankoff, 'Physical Activities, Body *Habitus*, and Lifestyles,' in J. Harvey and H. Cantelon, eds., *Not Just a Game: Essays in Canadian Sport Sociology.* Ottawa: University of Ottawa Press, 1988; and Christian Pociello, *Le Rugby, ou la Guerre de Styles.* Paris: Editions A. M. Métalilié, 1983. For a more well-developed discussion of the influence of Bourdieu in this field, see Jean-Paul Clément, 'Contributions of the Sociology of Pierre Bourdieu to the Sociology of Sport,' *Sociology of Sport Journal*, vol. 12: pp. 147-157, 1995.

a shared appreciation of virtuoso achievement. Although sociological critiques may assert that an individual's style is the product of his or her social position, closer phenomenological examination reveals that emulating models of good performance is, in fact, quite difficult, and players fail to achieve proficiency more often than they succeed. Instead of movement technique being a simple manifestation of one's social character, kinesthetic style is the result of social relations of training and an arduously produced, intentionally cultivated relation to one's own body, developed in practice, that partially constitutes an emergent social identity. Devotees of capoeira face shared phenomenological challenges—movement-restricting shame, brittleness from fear of confrontation, tentativeness in unfamiliar ways of moving, and the demand for unprecedented mobility and corporeal articulation. The different styles in which they play are, in effect, different ways of confronting similar sets of challenges posed by experience. The social taxonomy of style reveals itself to be a product, at least in part, of the phenomenology of practice.

Because of capoeira's history as an oppressed art, with stylist variants embraced by both implicitly racist groups and, more recently, militant Afrocentrists, aesthetic critique in the art frequently appears political. Practitioners and analysts alike have become adept at using aesthetic assessments—and critique of aesthetic judgment—as sociological statements, seeming either to assert distinction or to resist cultural hegemony. Focusing on the phenomenological implications of aesthetic judgment in capoeira, rather than its sociological entailments, does not remove aesthetics from the political realm, but rather shifts the scale on which we consider politics as advocated in the introduction. From a politics of group hierarchy and distinction, we shift the ground to an aesthetics of artistic self-formation.

One obstacle to writing a non-sceptical account of aesthetic judgment in this environment, especially when indigenous debates about the meaning of style offer ample food for a delightful meal of suspicious political interpretation, is the fear of appearing to be an aesthetic partisan. If I plunge too enthusiastically into a discussion of capoeira aesthetics, my own position, including my partisan devotion as an angoleiro, might become too obvious. In fact, many anthropological analyses of performance intentionally try to remain blind to the aesthetic judgments made by practitioners or deafen themselves to the sound of local musics, thereby refusing to be socialized into indigenous sensibilities. Anthropologists refuse to write which performances are good, bad, beautiful, ugly, virtuoso or inept—even if they are not moved uniformly by all—because of a reluctance to judge art by ethnocentric standards and because we recognize that indigenous critics themselves disagree so vehemently. In place of aesthetic judgments, anthropological analyses of performances such as dance often seek refuge in representational theories of art, conspiring along with Western theories of dance from the proscenium stage that treat bodily activity before the audience as standing for (or 'dancing for') something else, typically a narrative, set of archetypes, or abstract concepts. In this neutral interpretive frame, the anthropologist asks what is communicated, rather than how effective, successful or good a particular performance might be.

In the case of capoeira, I am advocating that we may understand the artists' aspirations much better by embracing their aesthetic standards because these judgments, however conflicting, lead us beyond a superficial politics of aesthetics—a suspicious hermeneutics that many of my Afrocentric subjects wielded as adeptly as any post-structuralist anthropologist—to an existential aesthetics of existence. On this deeper phenomenological level, beneath an ideologically motivated dispute about the sociology of aesthetics among practitioners, we find a shared concern for how capoeira might help a person to live in an unequal, dangerous, dishonest social world. For practitioners of Angola and Regional, as well as proponents of hybrid and discredited styles, this long-term project of self fashioning entails taking control of one's own body, perceptions, and habits, sharpening one's awareness of and responsiveness to the world, and becoming a cunning actor. But it also means judging many fellow practitioners to be inadequate. Ultimately, capoeira offers a path to heroic self formation, the chance, however elusive, of becoming renowned for one's own achievements and admired for one's cunning.

Cunning as an Aesthetic Principle

Ultimately, practitioners admire *malícia*, even referring to it as the 'fundamental' or underlying secret of capoeira play.[8] In contrast to its English cousin, 'malice,' the Brazilian term, malícia, especially among capoeira adepts, denotes positively valued aspects of character and aesthetics. For this reason, malícia is better translated as 'cunning' or 'craftiness,' although the term denotes a broad constellation of qualities: wariness, quick wit, savvy, unpredictability, opportunism, playfulness, viciousness, dramatic flair, and a talent for deception. Although *malicioso* traits may be morally ambivalent, they are universally admired and intentionally cultivated among capoeiristas.[9] A technique is more likely to be respected for being malicioso than for being technically precise, strong, or quick; that is, timing an attack so that it takes advantage of an adversary's momentary lapse is more important than the form of the technique. Even the most basic unwritten rules of the game can be broken if the breach demonstrates malícia. When an opponent clamped a leg 'scissors' on me before a game started, the attack was ugly, not because it violated a sense of fair play, but because it was not decisive *enough* and simply left us tangled together.

The antonym of malícia, as it is used by capoeiristas, is 'naïveté,' but it is also being openly aggressive or too obvious about one's intentions. The cardinal aesthetic flaw, according to this framework, is not ugliness, but being predictable, insufficiently quick to respond, tentative, or too easily duped. Through apprenticeship in capoeira, the student should learn more than just physical techniques; he or she should discover how to avoid being a sucker or a rube

---

[8] Mestre Nestor Capoeira, for example, titled one of his books *Capoeira: Os Fundamentos da Malícia* (Rio de Janeiro: Editora Record, 1992). In his discussion of Candomblé, Afro-Brazilian religious practice, religious scholar Paul Johnson defines fundamentos as 'secret, foundational matters' (*Secrets, Gossip, and Gods: The Transformation of Brazilian Candomblé.* Oxford: Oxford University Press, 2002, p. 4). On malícia, see also Barbara Browning, *Samba: Resistance in Motion.* Bloomington, Indiana: Indiana University Press, 1995; Downey, *Learning Capoeira*; Lewis, *Ring of Liberation*, pp. 32-33 ff.).
[9] See also Lewis, *Ring of Liberation*, p. 49.

(*otário*), both in the roda and in everyday life, and how to slyly pursue an advantage, even if it means deception or rule-breaking.

Capoeiristas and scholars who study the game often argue that the art's appreciation of cunning indicates its origin as a 'weapon of the weak,' to borrow a phrase from James Scott, developed by slaves and the *lumpen-proletariat*.[10] Experience in the roda is supposed to teach a player that the game—'like life,' I was told *repeatedly*—is an unequal struggle. Individuals start from different positions and encounter unequal opportunities. Capoeira is a body of techniques best suited to serve the weaker party in a conflict, allegedly like guerrilla warfare, with which it is often compared.[11] Through the use of malícia, a frail, disadvantaged individual might overcome a more powerful, better-armed adversary. Along these lines, the development of capoeira is often recounted as a series of asymmetrical conflicts in which malícia served to help defeat physically or numerically superior adversaries. Cunning was the great equalizer in the hands of the oppressed underdog.

An aesthetic appreciation for malícia shapes even very basic kinaesthetic preferences. My angoleiro colleagues said that they favoured a more baroque, ornamented ginga, or basic step, because it was less obviously aggressive and created more opportunities to beguile or deceive an opponent than the more regular and rhythmically uniform ginga of Capoeira Regional practitioners. They criticized more openly aggressive styles for being 'obvious,' arguing that the initial stages of attacks could be cloaked in extraneous motions from more dance-like gingas.

The aesthetic appreciation of malícia, unlike an ethos of 'sportsmanship,' means that capoeira audiences respond positively to deft breaches of the rules, clowning during a game, sneaky tricks, and even feigning injury to gain an advantage—the kind of 'subterfuge' for which Brazilian soccer players are internationally notorious. The contrast with Euro-American athletic self-imagining and aesthetic appreciations of athletic contests could not be more marked. Sports in the Olympic and British traditions exhaustively set about eliminating unfair advantages and creating an idealized 'level playing field'; capoeiristas favour trickery and assume contests will be unequal.

This aesthetic preference extends to historical myths; whereas past conflicts in the United States, for example, are often recast as tales of pure, fair competition in which superior ability or character could prevail—Western gunfights cinematically refigured as high-noon, face-to-face showdowns when they were often treacherous, bullet-in-the-back affairs—capoeira conflicts are recounted as archetypal cases of trickery, even when they were not. For example, a victory by legendary capoeira practitioner, Ciríaco, over a Japanese jujitsu

---

[10] James C. Scott, *Weapons of the Week: Everyday Forms of Peasant Resistance.* New Haven and London: Yale University Press, 1985; Scott specifically examines the dynamic of arts of the 'week' in *Domination and the Arts of Resistance: Hidden Transcripts*. New Haven, CT: Yale University Press, 1992. Capoeira, because it combines martial art and artistic expression, would seem an ideal exemplar of the way art acts as resistance as Scott outlines, a persuasive macro-political narrative that might obscure the existential dynamic this chapter explores.

[11] For example, in Muniz Sodré, *A Verdade Seduzida: Por um Conceito de Cultura no Brasil.* Rio de Janeiro: Editora CODECRI, 1983, p. 213.

champion in a prize fight in 1909 is often told with glee as an example of malícia. Capoeiristas claim Ciríaco prevailed with a treacherous surprise attack before the match officially started. In fact, contemporary newspaper accounts of the fight reported that Ciríaco abided by the match's guidelines, securing victory after several rounds of intense action.[12]

One essential dimension of malícia that the English word "cunning" does not capture well, however, is playfulness. Capoeiristas sometimes appear to use humour in spite of, or as a defence against, the inherent injustice and peril of the world. Perhaps in this regard, malícia differs most from 'malice.' Unlike a malicious individual, a person who is malicioso is a sly trickster, ever vigilant, not only for an adversary's vulnerabilities, but also for a chance to enjoy a good laugh. Nevertheless, alongside this humour and joyfulness stolen in the face of hard realities, malícia encompasses acts that border on cruelty.

Knowing which pole of these various dichotomies is appropriate requires an ability to read instantaneously each moment, to know what is appropriate or anticipated, and sometimes to defy these expectations. Capoeira is not merely a 'blurred genre'; players intentionally 'blur' the activity, fluctuating between theatre, farce, play, and open hostility for tactical advantage. In order to perceive and respond so quickly, a capoeira practitioner has to remain calm and relaxed, almost indifferent to the game itself or else that player's own intentions or emotions might cloud the ability to react fluidly. In GCAP, our teacher, Mestre Moraes, would refer to this quality as 'softness' (*moleza*), pointing out that the body had to remain free of tension if it was to squeeze through 'openings,' or vulnerabilities, and if it was to avoid being struck or pinned down by another player's attacks. When Natinho struggled with himself and became 'stopped,' he needed to relax, to become 'softer,' and thus more responsive to the music and flow of the game. To achieve this in a stressful situation, facing an aggressive adversary and with one's own reputation at stake, required multiple attempts in his case, but the result was a state of mind and fluidity of body that allowed Natinho to play artfully, replying with cunning to the 'rolling' of the game.

Foucault on the Aesthetics of Self

According to Marli Huijer, Michel Foucault ended his published work with the admonition, 'Make life a work of art.'[13] Seemingly a strange finale to an eclectic intellectual career, some theorists have gone on to argue that, in fact, during the last years of his life, Foucault's thought was dominated by an interest in philosophy as an art of living. The shift to a concern with regimes of self-care was widespread; it appears in Foucault's historical reflections on Classical ethics in the second and third volumes of *The History of Sexuality*, in his interviews, and even in his personal life, especially his embrace of sadomasochism.[14] An interest that arose from reading Greek philosophical writings on the good life, the art of

---

[12] See Downey, 'Domesticating an Urban Menace,' for a longer discussion.
[13] Marli Huijer. 'The aesthetics of existence in the work of Michel Foucault,' *Philosophy and Social Criticism*, vol. 25, no. 2, pp. 61–85. 1999.
[14] See also James Miller. *The Passion of Michel Foucault*. New York: Simon and Schuster, 1993.

caring for the self, led Foucault to allude to how, in our own context, we might 'make life a work of art.'

Although philosophy is typically treated as the pre-eminently theoretical and analytical field, Alexander Nehamas points out that, since Classical Greek thought, philosophers have also insisted that philosophy should be a prescriptive 'art of living.'[15] In this stream of thought—practiced by many of the same ancient figures considered crucial in the development of abstract philosophy—doing philosophy was advocated, not only as a rigorous intellectual practice, but also as a guide for living. Prior to the denigration of the body in Christian philosophy, Western thinkers considered deeply how the correct treatment of the body might produce both virtue and public renown, guiding behaviour in an environment in which no single sacred text oriented a universal morality. Foucault was fascinated, he explained, by techniques 'which permit individuals to effect by their own means or with the help of others a certain number of operations on their own bodies and souls, thoughts, conduct and way of being, so as to transform themselves in order to attain a certain state of happiness, purity, wisdom, perfection, or immortality.'[16]

In contemporary academic philosophy, the Delphic principle, 'Know yourself,' has come to overshadow the pragmatic admonition, 'Take care of yourself.'[17] One could argue that contemporary Western discussion of the art of living is now dominated by self-help books, pop psychology, physical fitness, religion, self-help gurus, 'life coaches,' and fashion commentary. Nehamas suggests that the rare modern thinkers who do maintain a concern with self cultivation are literary theorists, historians or anthropologists (he singles out Montaigne and Nietzsche, along with Foucault).

According to Foucault, in Antiquity, prior to the rise Christianity, 'the will to be a moral subject, the search for an ethics of existence, was principally an effort to affirm one's liberty and to give to one's own life a certain form in which one could recognize oneself, be recognized by others, and in which even posterity could find an example.'[18] That is, Classical care of the self entailed the pursuit of both autonomy and aesthetics, freedom and the recognition of others. As Foucault explained in an interview with Herbert Dreyfus and Paul Rabinow, this aesthetic relationship to the self was not a universal morality:

> ... it was reserved for a few people in the population; it was not a question of giving a pattern of behavior for everybody. It was a personal choice for a small elite. The reason for making this choice was the will

---

[15] Nehamas, Alexander. *The Art of Living: Socratic Reflections from Plato to Foucault*. Berkeley: University of California Press, 1998.
[16] Foucault, *Technologies*, p. 18.
[17] Foucault, *Technologies*, pp. 19 & 22.
[18] Michel Foucault, 'An Aesthetics of Existence,' translated by John Johnston. In *Foucault Live (Interviews, 1966-84)*, edited by Sylvère Lotringer. New York: Semiotext(e), 1989, p. 311.

to live a beautiful life, and to leave to others memories of a beautiful existence.[19]

The second and third volumes of *The History of Sexuality*, then, are not so much dedicated to sexuality in isolation as to the development of Classical technologies with which to care for the self, the techniques through which one could cultivate a 'beautiful existence.' Huijer points out that, according to Foucault, two of the principle ways in which Classical subjects endeavoured to create an aesthetic relationship to their 'selves' were through sexuality and friendship.[20]

According to Nehamas, philosophers who advocate the construction of self generally employ writing as the vehicle, both to realize the aesthetic life and to allow others to examine it. He explains:

> ….it is difficult to imagine that one can formulate one's own art of living without writing about it because it is difficult to imagine that the complex views that such an art requires can be expressed in any other way. Further, unless one writes about it, one's art will not be able to constitute a model for others in the longer run.[21]

In fact, Nehamas likely overestimates the necessity of writing; other arts might serve as the vehicle both for meditating upon and sharing an art of living. Certainly, when Foucault focused on dandyism and sadomasochism as contemporary exemplars of self-care as aesthetic work, he signalled that literary inscription was not the only technology of self-cultivation that he recognized. One could argue that some contemporary artists, especially those who blur the boundaries between life and performance, or engage in creative self 'branding,' are finding ways to make an aesthetic life as a model for others.

For Foucault, however, the 'aesthetics of self' was not merely a concern with one's body or reputation. As he writes in the conclusion to, 'What Is Enlightenment?':

> The critical ontology of ourselves has to be considered not, certainly, as a theory, a doctrine, nor even as a permanent body of knowledge that is accumulating; it has to be conceived as an attitude, an ethos, a philosophical life in which the critique of what we are is at one and the same time the historical analysis of the limits that are imposed on us and an experiment with the possibility of going beyond them.[22]

Ultimately, for Foucault, the project of 'critique' is an experiment in self-transformation: 'I shall thus characterize the philosophical ethos appropriate to the critical ontology of ourselves as a historico-practical test of the limits that we

---

[19] Michel Foucault, 'On the Genealogy of Ethics: An Overview of Work in Progress.' In *The Foucault Reader*, edited by Paul Rabinow. Translated by Catherine Porter. New York: Pantheon, 1984, p. 341.
[20] Huijer, 'Aesthetics of existence,' p. 62.
[21] Nehamas, *Art of Living*, p. 8.
[22] Foucault, 'What Is Enlightenment?', p. 50.

may go beyond, and thus as work carried out by ourselves upon ourselves as free beings.'[23]

Not every physical discipline is a technology of self-production according to this definition because many do not involve questioning social domination or carving out a space for autonomy and individual creativity. As Markula and Pringle discuss, for example, many athletes enrol in forms of physical discipline that entail greater and greater subordination of their individuality as they achieve more elite levels.[24] Ballet dancers, likewise, might be seen as a limit case of how the body can be subordinated to external ideals, as Anna Aalten details in her phenomenological study of the 'ruthless' way in which dancers treat their own bodies, even when injured.[25] That is, if we are to consider capoeira a Foucauldian project to 'make life a work of art,' demonstrating that the body is taken as the object of disciplined labour is not sufficient; an aesthetic existence in this sense demands creativity and autonomy, or it is simply another disciplinary technology to produce beautiful but docile bodies.

Because Foucault focused so heavily on the long-standing relationship in Western thought between sexual restraint and morality, and because of his own personal life (which he insisted affected his academic work), his thinking about projects to realize freedom and test limits tended to turn to sexual practices. But he also makes it clear that the mode of aesthetic transcendence inevitably depends upon the historical specificity of the moment in which we find ourselves carrying out work upon ourselves. In Baudelaire's account, for example, Foucault finds a heroic attitude toward modernity in the dandy's 'ascetic elaboration of the self,' an expression of freedom and creativity in which the dandy, recognizing his situation, sought to invent himself in a way that transgressed his own limits by making his body, actions, dress, and daily life a work of art.[26]

Capoeira as an Art of Self

Capoeira is *mandinga* [sorcery], it's cunning, malícia. It's everything that the mouth eats. Attributed to Mestre Pastinha

Most capoeira practitioners consider the late, legendary Mestre Pastinha, founder of the first academy of Capoeira Angola, one of the most eloquent, poetic practitioners of capoeira's 'old guard.' Among his many enigmatic sayings, the aphorism that capoeira is 'everything that the mouth eats' (*tudo que a boca come*) is probably the most frequently cited; practitioners like both the definition of capoeira he offers and his poetic insistence that capoeira, ideally, influences every

---

[23] Foucault, 'What Is Enlightenment?', p. 47.
[24] Pirkko Markula and Richard Pringle. *Foucault, Sport and Exercise: Power, Knowledge and Transforming the Self*. London and New York: Routledge, 2006.
[25] Anna Aalten, 'Listening to the Dancer's Body,' in Chris Shilling, ed., *Embodying Sociology: Retrospect, Progress and Prospects.* Malden, MA: Blackwell/Sociological Review, 2007, p. 110.
[26] Michel Foucault, 'What Is Enlightenment?' In *The Foucault Reader*, p. 42; see also Anita Seppä's account of Foucault's radically pluralist version of aesthetics and its implications for feminism, in Seppä, 'Foucault, Enlightenment and the Aesthetics of Self,' *Contemporary Aesthetics*, Vol. 2, 2004 (online journal: http://www.contempaesthetics.org).

action of a capoeirista. That is, capoeira shapes one's comportment inside and outside of the roda; other practitioners told me that capoeira was a 'way to live.' Similarly, Nestor Capoeira suggests that malícia is capoeira's 'philosophy,' but in qualifying that term, alludes to this sense in which capoeira differs from a form of 'knowing' the self: 'It is not something that can be understood with the use of the mind — in spite of the fact that it is, itself, a form of understanding.' Malícia is, rather, 'the perspective of the capoeirista, his way of facing life, the world, and other people... this specific type of vision of things, this type of perception of the universe... this type of wisdom.'[27] Nestor's ambivalent grappling with the term, 'philosophy,' may even arise from the severing of analytic and practical philosophies in Western traditions; the sense he seeks is the 'care of self' stream within philosophy.

The permanent state of alertness and opportunistic cunning instilled in the game ideally extends beyond it, becoming a principle that orients a practitioner in daily life. The transformation wrought by capoeira apprenticeship should be thorough-going, affecting every gesture and action. As folklorist, Ordep Serra, described in a newspaper column in honour of Mestre Pastinha, when Serra first went to the mestre's school, the wizened old teacher said that he was going to teach Serra how 'to walk' after seeing the way that the young man moved.[28] During my fieldwork, practitioners offered countless examples of the ways that capoeira training indirectly transformed their lives: where and how they stood and walked in city streets, how they dealt with conflict, their physical health and abilities, and their own sense of themselves. A practitioner's entire life will be made over through the training in the art of capoeira.

In a society like Brazil where race, class, public comportment, and violence figure so centrally in social hygiene and are a locus for control, it can hardly be surprising that aesthetic projects of self construction that Foucault conceived of as primarily sexual, might instead take up these themes and build upon Afro-Brazilian forms of expression.[29] When a capoeirista learns to overcome bodily shame and pushes beyond learned inhibitions on movement—especially within a performance framework that emphasizes the potential for 'African' expression within all people, no matter what their descent—that practitioner is engaged in an experiment in freedom specific to his or her social world and encultured body.

But the case of capoeira is also intriguing for the ways that it defies Foucauldian expectations, premised on the examples of Classical philosophy and contemporary subcultures, of how 'care for the self' might enjoin personal transformation. Ironically, two aspects of the ethical self-cultivation that Foucault

---

[27] Nestor, *Fundamentos*, pp. 121-122.
[28] See Downey, *Learning Capoeira*, pp. 30-31, for Serra's account and a longer discussion.
[29] For examples of work discussing these themes, one can turn to such classical anthropological and literary works on Brazil as Roberto DaMatta, *Carnivals, Rogues, and Heroes: An Interpretation of the Brazilian Dilemma*. Translated by J. Drury. Notre Dame, Indiana: University of Notre Dame Press, 1991 (1979); Gilberto Freyre, *The Masters and the Slaves: A Study in the Development of Brazilian Civilization*. Second English edition. Translated by S. Putnam. Berkeley: University of California Press, 1986 (1933); Peter Fry, *Para Inglês Ver: Identidade e Política na Cultura Brasileira*. Rio de Janeiro: Zahar Editores, 1985; or Antônio Cândido, *On Literature and Society*. Translated and edited by H. S. Becker. Princeton, New Jersey: Princeton University Press, 1995.

found central to Classical self-care are reversed in capoeira. Foucault recognized 'truth' and 'friendship' at the centre of Greek aesthetics. By contrast, capoeira practitioners see deception and a deep suspicion of social relations as crucial to responsible self-cultivation, as a reflection of the true nature of a hostile world. If aesthetics in capoeira is often a way to judge the internal state of the practitioner, this inner state is emphatically alert, wary of everyone including close colleagues, and selectively deploying truth and deception for tactical advantage. That is, if the Greeks advocated transcending their condition, even their mortality, through truth and friendship, capoeira practitioners assert that the only route to transcending, sometimes even surviving within, an inherently treacherous world, is to face it with awareness and cunning.

Marli Huijer suggests that Foucault's problematization of friendship as part of an aesthetics of existence runs counter to common depictions of urban social life as fleeting, transitory, and superficial, thus providing a critique of our lax attitudes toward relationships in our daily lives:

> You are packed like sardines in the Tube; you touch everyone lengthily and intensively, and you get out at the next stop without knowing anything about anyone; you pick up a man or woman on the street or at a club, gratify your desires and forget all about him or her. In the depiction of this kind of contact, there is nothing that makes life worthwhile. Foucault refuted this depiction by problematizing the touches and collisions with others: isn't it precisely these confrontations and touches that present us with an opportunity to go beyond what we are in the present, to transform ourselves?[30]

While Foucault might have exhorted us to transform ourselves in these fleeting relations, capoeira practitioners advocate a heightened sensitivity to the danger of even passing moments of contact. For capoeiristas, the primary deception of modern urban life, with its touches and collisions, is that all these chance encounters are merely happenstance; no, many of them are traps. As Ângelo Decânio, student of Mestre Bimba, wrote of his teacher's lessons: there were 'dangers at corners, doorways, and over-hangs... behind a door left open or at the thick trunk of a tree.' The world is not indifferent to our presence but rather lying in wait. Whereas Foucault calls for a 'permanent critique' and a 'permanent creation of ourselves in our autonomy,' malícia demands a permanent heightened suspicion and a wilful production of layers of deception in which to cloak one's own goals.[31]

Just as Foucault resists the idea that one can withdraw from relations of domination through critique, capoeiristas do not call for ascetic renunciation or even excessive bitterness about the treacherous state of the world. As Mestre Nestor Capoeira writes, 'Life is a struggle? Life is a fight? The player perceives that capoeira is teaching him to *dance* within the fight!'[32] Nestor asserts that it is through malícia, including a sense of humor and a playful spirit, that the adept is

---

[30] Huijer, 'Aesthetics of existence,' p. 72.
[31] Foucault, 'What Is Enlightenment?', pp. 42 & 44.
[32] Nestor Capoeira, *Capoeira: Os Fundamentos*, p. 125.

able to derive amusement from hardship, in part to counteract the long-term psychological effects of constant wariness. The mestre says that this ludic dimension of malícia helps a capoeirista avoid such pitfalls as cynicism, an 'arid' disposition, and 'egotism'.[33] In the face of a treacherous world, capoeira teaches a practitioner to take advantage of opportunities to play, even in dire circumstances; at the very least, appearing innocent of the dangers is one of the first weapons in a capoeiristas arsenal.

Reflecting on Kant's discussion of enlightenment, Michel Foucault suggests that 'modernity' is a distinctive 'attitude': 'a mode of relating to contemporary reality; a voluntary choice made by certain people; in the end, a way of thinking and feeling; a way, too, of acting and behaving that at one and the same time marks a relation of belonging and presents itself with a task.'[34] If modernity is, in part, 'an attitude,' then capoeira might be seen as an especially sceptical, alert, even paranoid 'countermodernity' (Foucault's term), a wariness and distrust of others and the security of civil interactions. In addition, with a strong phenomenological grounding in a sense of the past, particularly through the use of music, a capoeira ethos strongly counter-acts the notion of a break with the past, especially traditionalist forms of the art.[35] Rather than grasping the heroic in the present, or projecting into a progressive future, capoeira performance surrounds the practitioners, even haunts them, with a sense of past treachery and heroism.

Conclusion: Epic Self Imagining

To enter the roda is to present oneself as an aesthetic project, to expose to the community's scrutiny one's inner state through one's movements, so that the self as a work of art can be judged. If a practitioner's skill and self-control are strong enough to demonstrate malícia, no matter what an adversary does, the player's renown will grow. Seizing upon opportunities in the roda, impressing other practitioners with one's deft sense of humour or 'perverse' ability to exploit an adversary's vulnerabilities, generate a reputation for being malicioso. If a player's legend grows enough, that capoeirista might be invited to 'baptise' a new student at another capoeira school, be given one of the lead instruments in a public event, or even hear his or her name sung in the salutations that precede a roda. Ultimately, one might be judged a 'mestre' by the whole community.

Individual performances, however, are not really what are being judged in the sense that one's status as a mestre is a cumulative accomplishment: over and over again, the community must perceive that a person's character has been transformed by the art until malícia seasons every action. As one capoeirista explained when he showed me how a wary handshake was actually a sign of respect, to inspire just a little bit of fear, a measure of extra caution in other practitioners, was a sign of respect. When a person received wary handshakes, he or she was being recognized as malicioso.

---

[33] Ibid., p. 128.
[34] Foucault, 'What Is Enlightenment?', p. 39.
[35] On the production of an immediate felt sense that the 'sinister' past endures, see Greg Downey, 'Listening to Capoeira: Phenomenology, Embodiment, and the Materiality of Music,' *Ethnomusicology* vol. 46, no. 3: pp. 487-509.

As discussed in the introduction to this volume, demonstrating and assessing capoeira performance depends fundamentally on visual knowledge. Players and knowledgeable observers recognize that how one moves both demonstrates one's internal state and ongoing development as well as, importantly, it can be used to manipulate one's own experience and character. When Natinho returned to the foot of the orchestra repeatedly to calm himself, he used performance techniques to achieve the emotional conditions necessary to perform well. Likewise, an astute, artistically sensitive audience will not be impressed by flashy, superficial techniques; audience members can perceive in their actions if players are nervous or afraid, lack self control, or cannot respond to the flow of the game. And over the longer term, as a teacher studies a novice, aesthetic judgments serve to guide instruction, as a perceptive mestre perceives through students' movements the current state of proficiency, diagnosing what lessons need to be passed along next.

Foucault's account suggests that most 'art of living' philosophers encourage individuals to fashion the self into *someone*. Nehamas suggests that 'creating' or 'fashioning' a 'self,' in this way of thinking, is to become 'a *character*, that is, someone unusual and distinctive': 'To become an individual is to acquire an uncommon and idiosyncratic character, a set of features and a mode of life that set one apart from the rest of the world and make one memorable not only for what one did or said but also for who one was.'[36] Labouring on the self in obscurity is insufficient as an 'aesthetics of self,' for the same reason that most artists do not create material artworks or performances to be concealed: part of the goal is to place one's creativity before the community.

The end goal of capoeira practice, then, is not just a moment of performance, but a carving out of a public identity, renown, even a legend, both inside and outside the roda. The aesthetic object that is constructed is one's life as a *bamba* ('tough guy'), a *mestre* (teacher), or a *capoeira* (the older use of the term as designating a person rather than the art). The ideal is to become 'someone,' a named persona, known widely from one's *nome de guerra* or 'war-name.'

When I first encountered the custom of giving *appelidos* or 'nicknames' in capoeira, practitioners told me that they were a historical legacy of oppression. According to legend, thugs who once battled police with *capoeiragem* (capoeira techniques) took nicknames to conceal their identities, like criminal aliases. In contrast, the contemporary practice much more closely resembles corporate naming or commodity branding; practitioners seek memorable nicknames in order to become more quickly remembered and recognized; famous practitioners bear colourful nicknames like Samuel 'Beloved of God,' Antônio 'Pig Mouth,' Green Snake, Black Cat, Traitor, Hillbilly, even Prick.

The goal is at once pragmatic and idealistic; the pragmatic effect of one's renown travelling far and wide is that one will be invited to travel, paid to teach seminars, and called upon to share one's wisdom. Becoming 'someone' in capoeira generates economic opportunity. The idealistic dimension is that one will fight the crushing anonymity that faces many popular artists in Brazil. If a capoeirista can become so well known that he or she is celebrated in the

---

[36] Nehamas, *Art of Living*, pp. 4-5.

louvação, the musical salutes that precede capoeira games, he or she will have turned the tide against forgetting and created a life as an artistic achievement.

References

Aalten, A., (2007). Listening to the Dancer's Body. In C. Shilling (Ed.), *Embodying Sociology: Retrospect, Progress and Prospects* (pp. 109-125). Malden, MA: Blackwell/Sociological Review.

Bourdieu, P. (1984 [1979]). *Distinction: A Social Critique of the Judgement of Taste* (R. Nice, trans.). Cambridge, MA: Harvard University Press.

Bourdieu, P. (1990). *In Other Words: Essays Towards a Reflexive Sociology* (M. Adamson, trans.). Stanford, CA: Stanford University Press.

Browning, B. (1995). *Samba: Resistance in Motion*. Bloomington, IN: Indiana University Press.

Cândido, A. (1995). *On Literature and Society*. H. S. Becker (Trans. & Ed.). Princeton, NJ: Princeton University Press.

Capoeira, N. (1992). *Capoeira: Os Fundamentos da Malícia* [Capoeira: The foundations of cunning]. Rio de Janeiro, Brazil: Editora Record.

Clément, J.-P. (1995). Contributions of the Sociology of Pierre Bourdieu to the Sociology of Sport. *Sociology of Sport Journal, 12*, 147-157.

DaMatta, R. (1991 [1979]). *Carnivals, Rogues, and Heroes: An Interpretation of the Brazilian Dilemma* (J. Drury, trans.). Notre Dame, IN: University of Notre Dame Press.

Downey, G. (2002a). Domesticating an Urban Menace: Efforts to Reform Capoeira as a Brazilian National Sport. *International Journal of the History of Sport, 19*(2), 1-32.

Downey, G. (2002b). Listening to Capoeira: Phenomenology, Embodiment, and the Materiality of Music. *Ethnomusicology, 46*(3), 487-509.

Downey, G. (2005). *Learning Capoeira: Lessons in Cunning from an Afro-Brazilian Art*. New York, NY: Oxford University Press.

Foucault, M. (1984). *The Foucault Reader* (C. Porter, trans.). P. Rabinow (Ed.). New York, NY: Pantheon.

Foucault, M. (1985). *The Use of Pleasure: Volume 2 of The History of Sexuality* (R. Hurley, trans.). New York, NY: Vintage

Foucault, M. (1986). *The Care of the Self: Volume 3 of The History of Sexuality* (R. Hurley, trans.). New York, NY: Vintage

Foucault, M. (1988). *Technologies of the Self: A Seminar with Michel Foucault*. L. H. Martin, H. Gutman, and P. H. Hutton (Eds). Amherst, MA: University of Massachusetts Press.

Foucault, M. (1989). *Foucault Live (Interviews, 1966-84)*. S. Lotringer (Ed.). New York, NY: Semiotext(e).

Freyre, G. (1986 [1933]). *The Masters and the Slaves: A Study in the Development of Brazilian Civilization* (S. Putnam, trans.). Second English edition. Berkeley, CA: University of California Press.

Fry, P. 1985. *Para Inglês Ver: Identidade e Política na Cultura Brasileira* [For the English to See: Identity and Politics in Brazilian Culture]. Rio de Janeiro: Zahar Editores.

Geertz, C. (1983). *Local Knowledge: Further Essays in Interpretive Anthropology.* New York: Basic Books.
Huijer, M. (1999). The aesthetics of existence in the work of Michel Foucault. *Philosophy and Social Criticism, 25*(2), 61–85.
Johnson, P. (2002). *Secrets, Gossip, and Gods: The Transformation of Brazilian Candomblé.* New York, NY: Oxford University Press.
Laberge, S., & Sankoff, D. (1988). Physical Activities, Body *Habitus*, and Lifestyles. In J. Harvey & H. Cantelon (Eds.), *Not Just a Game: Essays in Canadian Sport Sociology* (pp. 267-286). Ottawa: University of Ottawa Press,
Lewis, J. L. (1992). *Ring of Liberation: Deceptive Discourse in Brazilian Capoeira.* Chicago: University of Chicago Press.
Markula, P., & Pringle, R. (2006). *Foucault, Sport and Exercise: Power, Knowledge and Transforming the Self.* London: Routledge.
Miller, J. (1993). *The Passion of Michel Foucault.* New York, NY: Simon and Schuster.
Nehamas, A. (1998). *The Art of Living: Socratic Reflections from Plato to Foucault.* Berkeley, CA: University of California Press.
Pociello, C. (1983). *Le Rugby, ou la Guerre de Styles* [Rugby, or the War of the Styles]. Paris: Editions A. M. Métalilié.
Scott, J. C. (1985). *Weapons of the Week: Everyday Forms of Peasant Resistance.* New Haven, CT: Yale University Press.
Scott, J. C. (1992). *Domination and the Arts of Resistance: Hidden Transcripts.* New Haven, CT: Yale University Press.
Seppä, A. (2004). Foucault, Enlightenment and the Aesthetics of Self. *Contemporary Aesthetics, 2*, Retrieved from http://hdl.handle.net/2027/spo.7523862.0002.004
Sodré, M. (1983). *A Verdade Seduzida: Por um Conceito de Cultura no Brasil* [The Truth Seduced: For a Concept of Culture in Brazil]. Rio de Janeiro, Brazil: Editora CODECRI.

Part VI: Social Issues

Chapter 27

The Highway to Hooliganism? An Evaluation of the Impact of Combat Sport Participation on Individual Criminality[1]

Craig Jenkins & Tom Ellis

Introduction

This U.K. study is concerned with whether and how combat sports, such as martial arts and full contact fighting sports such as boxing, affect the potential criminality of participants. This was accomplished using principles derived from cognitive behavioural treatment and risk factor-based intervention, which has seen a rapid growth of interest, following the passing of the Crime and Disorder Act 1998 (here-after CDA 1998).

The CDA 1998 contained a series of crime tackling policies aimed directly at young offenders and the general youth population (Muncie, 1999, p. 147). Identification of risk factors featured as a crucial element of the CDA 1998, with the primary focus on: poor parental supervision; poor discipline; truancy; and unstable homes (Home Office, 1997 p. 5). The Youth Justice Board (here-after YJB), constituted under the CDA 1998, additionally included low income and aggressive behaviour (Anderson et al., 2005 p. 4). These risk factors relate primarily to: family; school; community; and personal experiences (Anderson et al., p. 3). The YJB's crime reduction strategy therefore relied heavily on both community-based crime prevention schemes and offender treatment programmes.

---

[1] Please note: This chapter was originally published in the International Journal of Police Science and Management, Vol. 13 No. 2, (2011), pp. 117–131. We are grateful for the journal's permission to reproduce the article herein.

Between 1999 and 2002, the YJB implemented 42 intervention schemes costing over £4.5 million. Eight of these interventions (involving 3,350 youths) were sport/physical activity/leisure-based (Hurry & Moriarty, 2004 pp. 4–20). Additionally, sport-based interventions are being implemented across the UK, including: Positive Futures; Police Community Boxing Clubs; Sport in the Community; Sport England; Splash/Splash Extra; and Midnight Basketball. However, with the exception of Police Community Boxing Clubs, there appears to be no inclusion of combat sports within the schemes despite their increasing popularity. Mixed Martial Arts (MMA), otherwise known as cage fighting, is widely considered to be the fastest growing sport in the world, grossing over US$200 million in 2007, with an impressive list of celebrity fans, and gaining increased popularity in many countries, including the UK (Davies, 2008). Given the popularity and spread of modern and traditional combat sports, the need for our study is perhaps overdue. First, however, it is important to summarise the relevant existing evidence.

Sports Participation

Recent research has suggested that those involved in structured and supported leisure activities are less likely to take part in antisocial behaviour and offending (Mahoney & Stattin, 2000, p. 123). Conversely, those involved in activities lacking structure and support are at the highest risk of engagement in young offending, and have the most deviant peers (Abbot & Barber, 2007, p. 59; Mahoney & Stattin, 2000, p. 123; Mahoney, Stattin, & Magnusson, 2001, p. 509). Furthermore, this is particularly important for reducing youth crime in rural areas (Meak, 2006 pp. 100–101). As noted, sports and physical activity-based interventions have featured heavily in tackling youth crime and antisocial behaviour. Offering outdoor sports such as canoeing as an incentive to enrol in life skills workshops, Fairbridge projects represented five of the YJB's eight sports and physical activity programmes between 1999 and 2002 (Astbury, Knight and Nichols 2005, pp. 84–85). The others included the Duke of Edinburgh's Award and two Midnight Basketball programmes (Hurry & Moriarty, 2004, pp. 4–20). In an impact evaluation of all 42 YJB intervention programmes, Hurry and Moriarty (p. 58) found a 25 per cent reduction (i.e. a 60 per cent reoffending rate) in reoffending compared with the year before enrolment. However, there was no comparison group available to establish evidence of a significant benefit (Hurry & Moriarty, p. 58). Indeed, the small number of evaluations relevant to UK sports programmes can be regarded as indicative rather than definitive, as shown in Table 1.

Table 1: UK sport-based crime reduction scheme summary

Programme	Programme Structure	Evaluation Outcome
Fairbridge Programme	Outdoor sports participation limited to 1st week • E.g. climbing and canoeing for the initial week. Then opportunity to enrol in: • outdoor pursuit courses • life-skills workshops	• No evidence of a long term crime reduction • Reduced the circumstances which put youths at risk of offending Sport played a vital role in fostering pro-social relationship with program supervisors and catalyst for personal development. (Astbury, Knight, & Nichols, 2005)
Midnight Basket ball (The original United States Programme)	• Basketball leagues set up between 10am and 2pm in inner city areas in the United States	• Cities with midnight basketball schemes showed significant decreases in crime rates (inc. property and violent crime). (Hartmann and Depro 2006)

Examples of other sports-based interventions include: 'Summer Splash' schemes, using sports such as kayaking and football (Loxley, Curtin, & Brown, 2002, p. 8); Sport England and Best Value through sport initiatives (Sport England, 1999); summer camp programmes including baseball, basketball and field hockey (Haynes, Rife, & Laguna, 2005, p. 41); Police Community Boxing Clubs (Metropolitan Police Service, n.d.); Positive Futures (Ramella, as cited in Smith & Waddington, 2004, pp. 281–282); the West Yorkshire Sports Counselling Association; and the Hafotty Wen 14 peaks programme (Nichols & Crow, 2004, p. 273). Additionally, Sport England and local authorities have provided sport-based community regeneration schemes in deprived areas (Neighbourhood Renewal Unit, 2003), resulting in the development of the Tuckingmill Skate Park in 2004 (Sport England, 2005, p.15) and the X-site Skate Park, Skegness, boasting a 17 per cent reduction in reported crime since opening in 2006 (Sport England, n.d.a, pp. 11–12).

Theoretical Underpinnings of Sports Interventions and their Critics

The theoretical understanding of how such sports programmes might reduce crime can be summarised as follows:

- Cathartic: all sport entails elements of violence that releases and channels aggression that would otherwise lead to violent crime and therefore educates 'men' into conscious and responsible self-control (Lorenz as cited in Dunning, 2005, p. 905).
- Diversionary: diverting youths away from time spent committing crime (Nichols, 1997, p. 183; Nichols & Crow, 2004, pp. 269–270).
- Providing natural excitement: sating individuals' quest for excitement otherwise quenched through crime or drugs (Nichols, p.183; Coalter, and Elias & Dunning, both studies as cited in Smith &Waddington, 2004, p. 284).
- Developing cognitive competencies: contributing to increased self-esteem, self-control and a sense of achievement also linked to increased employability (Loxley et al., 2002 p.10; Nichols, pp. 185–187; Nichols & Crow, p. 270).

There are inevitably critics. Smith (as cited in Dunning, 2005, p. 910) argues that sport can facilitate violent behaviour since participants are trained to see opponents as nonhuman. Feminist treatments of aggressive sports as a method of crime reduction have also been critical. Table 2 outlines the key findings from studies; all from the USA, arguing that participation in aggressive sports increases 'violent masculinities'. It would seem then, that from the research summarised in Table 2, increased contact and aggression in sports can only lead to more violence and crimes against women. Inevitably, there are also criticisms that could be levelled at these findings. First, feminist studies have failed to account for the effects of aggressive sports on female participants. They focus only on sports that have a predominantly male following and male sports teams, ignoring aggressive contact sports with female participants or competitive female sports teams.

Table 2: US research on the negative impact of aggressive sports participation

Study	Sample/Method	Findings
Hoffman (1986). Cited in Dunning (2005), p.911. (USA)	• 200 college campuses in 1986. • Analysed college police case records.	• Football & basketball 38% more frequently involved in sexual assault.
Koss and Gaines (1993), pp.94-108. (USA)	• 530 undergraduate males. • 140 were athletes. • Analysed self reported sexually aggressive acts (inappropriate touching to rape).	• Basketball & football players were significantly more likely to be sexually aggressive (inc males involved in other sports). • Alcohol use & athletic participation were 2 of 4-variables accounting for 11% variance in levels of sexual aggression.
Nelson (1994). Cited in Dunning (2005), p.911. (USA)	• 10,000 students at Towson State University. • Analysed recorded incidents from the Campus Violence Centre.	• Athletes were 16% of campus population. • Commit 55% of acquaintance rapes in 1991. • Commit 33% of 862 sexual assaults on campuses over 3 years in 1980s.
Crosset, Benedict and McDonald (1995). Cited in Dunning (2005), p.911; Woods (2007), p.295. (USA)	• 107 cases of sexual assault. • In 10 division 1 schools 1991 – 1993. • Analysed police records, judicial affairs and reports.	• Male athletes were 3% of campus population. • Commit 19% of sexual assaults & 35% of domestic assaults. • Basketball players show disproportionately high number of sexual assaults.

Forbes, Adams-Curtis, Pakalka and White (2006), pp.447-455.	<ul><li>147 males at private, Midwestern university inc.101 aggressive sport athletes (football, basketball, wrestling and soccer).</li><li>Analysed self reported: relationship aggression and coercion, sexism, rape myth and violence acceptance, and attitude toward homosexuals.</li></ul>	<ul><li>Aggressive sports participants committed more psychological and physical aggression (inc injury to partners) & sexual coercion of partners.</li><li>Also more sexist and hostile towards women, accepting of violence, less tolerant of homosexuality.</li></ul>

Second, the sports selected in the studies in Table 2 are subject to interpretation regarding aggression and contact. For example, American football is rightly regarded as aggressive. Much like rugby, its fast paced and unavoidable physical contact makes an 'aggressive' classification appropriate. However, basketball is a *non-contact* sport. Players are only allowed to make contact with the ball, not another player's body. Physical violence occurs as a result of the unsporting character of the rule breaker. Similarly, excessive physical contact in soccer results in a foul; it is not a licit feature of the game. These criticisms therefore lead us on to a consideration of the main focus of our study: combat sports.

Combat Sports

This study focuses on sports which encompass a regular and unavoidable engagement in interpersonal violence, aggression and contact, i.e. combat sports. This pushes our focus to an extreme end of the sports spectrum, but one that therefore reduces ambiguity when interpreting what constitutes a violent or aggressive sport.

Only a handful of US and European studies have given consideration to combat sport and crime reduction, which remains an under-researched area. Table 3 provides a summary of the key studies and their findings.

Table 3: Summary of research on the effects of combat sport participation

Study	Sample/Method	Findings
Trulson (1986), p.1131 (USA)	<ul><li>34 male school students identified as delinquent by the Minnesota Multiphasic Personality Inventory (MMPI) & Jackson Personality Inventory (JPI).</li><li>Group 1: traditional taekwondo lesson 3x1 hour\per week, for 6 months.</li><li>Group 2: same as group 1 but modern adaptation, lacking philosophical elements</li><li>Group 3: no intervention.</li><li>MMPI and JPI repeated after training.</li></ul>	<ul><li>Group 1: decreased aggression and anxiety, increased self-esteem & value orthodoxy</li><li>Group 2: large increase in aggressive behaviour observed</li><li>Group 3: No change in any personality measures.</li></ul>
Fletcher (1992). Cited in Nichols (1997), p.184 (UK)	<ul><li>Unknown number of amateur boxers (gender unknown) in unpublished study of amateur boxing club.</li><li>Observations and interviews.</li></ul>	<ul><li>Participants less likely to engage in street violence due to increased self-esteem and self-control</li></ul>
Endresen and Olweus (2005), pp.468-476 (Norway)	<ul><li>477 male school students with varied participation in combat sports: boxing; kickboxing; wrestling; karate; judo & taekwondo.</li><li>3 groups of participants</li><li>1 group of non-participants</li><li>Before, during & after measures: self reported antisocial behaviour, violence and total anti social involvement test</li></ul>	<ul><li>Untroubled boys participating in fighting sports become more prone to antisocial behaviour.</li><li>Manifested as violent and non-violent behaviour changes: starting fights, using weapons, truancy and vandalism</li><li>Negative effects persisted long after participation ceased.</li></ul>

Palermo, Di Luigi, Dal Forno, Dominici, Vicomandi, Sambucioni, Proietti and Pasqualetti (2006), pp.656-659 (Italy)	• 13 male and 3 female children aged 8 to 10, diagnosed with behavioural problems associated with delinquency. • Group 1 enrolled on a 10 month karate programme: 3 lessons per week. • Group 2: no intervention. • Before & after measures of intensity, adaptability and mood regulation	• Participating youths showed greatly improved behaviour • Observed a diversion from potentially criminal behaviour, e.g. disobedience and aggressive temperaments.
Wright (2006), pp.149-171 (USA)	• Unknown number of male youths from boxing clubs in impoverished areas of New York & San Francisco. • Interviews & observations to measure boxing's potential to reduce violence in the community.	• Identified 10 effects of boxing associated with reduction in violence and crime (see Table 4).

Table 4: Wright's (2006) 10 benefits of boxing training

❑ Identity based on valuing respect and pride above toughness	❑ Ability to focus and for longer periods of time
❑ Provides/promotes safety during dangerous high crime periods (including emotional safety from the boxing group	❑ Gaining a sense of meaning, hope and self-esteem beyond losing friends/relatives to violent crime, incarceration or encountering violence in daily life
❑ Emotional skills aiding development into law abiding adults	
	❑ Learning respect for others
❑ Using defence as a metaphor for conflict resolution	❑ Relieving stress which could otherwise be released as violence
❑ Learning patience/becoming less impulsive	❑ Promotes and provides mutual aid/support from the group training atmosphere

From these studies, it is clear that the field is under-researched and there is no reliable of comprehensive picture. Wright's (2006, pp.158–171) in-depth approach has provided the most comprehensive list of benefits, in this case, for boxing training participants.

The positive benefits of combat sports are also found in Fletcher's (as cited in Nichols, 1992, p. 184) and Palermo et al.'s (2006) studies. In Fletcher's case (where less is known about the detail of the study), emotional control was gained through boxing, while for Palermo et al. (p. 654), when taught appropriately, martial arts could be effective in reducing problem behaviour.

Trulson's (1986) study is the most nuanced and perhaps the most important in thinking about the type of approach to combat sports that would be most appropriate for interventions with offenders. It was clear that the traditional philosophical and psychological elements were vital to being effective in reducing risk factors associated with offending. If these elements were removed, Trulson (p. 1131) found that combat sport was associated with increased criminal behaviour. Consider the role of the referee in traditional compared with non-traditional combat sports. Those participating in MMA will continue to strike an unconscious opponent until the referee intervenes, whereas a traditional martial artist shows control, using only the necessary amount of force to win a bout.

Another significant challenge comes from a different perspective. Endresen and Olweus's (2005) study represents the strongest challenge to the use of combat sports to reduce criminal behaviour since they found that fighting sports could increase criminality among untroubled youths. From an interventions perspective, this can be seen as analogous to 'overdosing' minor offenders with interventions, which is known to be likely to increase their criminal behaviour. Endresen and Olweus therefore pose the intriguing question of whether those without criminal involvement should be participating in combat sports.

It seems that sport and recreation-based crime reduction strategies have some theoretical and empirical, if contested, justification. However, not much attention has been given to justifying the use of combat sport-based interventions. First, little is known about the effects of varying styles of combat sports which vary in levels of aggression, interpersonal contact and machismo. Second, there is little research aimed at the effects of combat sport participation on grown adults of both genders, as the focus is nearly always on male youths. Paradoxically, because of the ethical issues (not to mention bureaucracy) involved in researching those under 16 years, our focus is exclusively on adults. Finally, there has been little focus on how continued combat sport participation can address the needs of those at risk of criminality through 'values of sport' (Sport England, n.d.b) such as educational/economic benefits and community inclusion. Given the paucity of research and the level of potential dissonance in the results, we felt it was timely to carry out our own investigation. Importantly, our research is the first we are aware of to include male *and female* participants. In order to address what we see as the weaknesses of much of the feminist perspective research on the negative impact of 'contact' sports, we also evaluate the relationship between socio-cultural areas of risk and voluntary participation in sports, where the distinction between 'contact' and 'noncontact' is extremely clear.

Methodology

We carried out our research during the spring of 2009 in a coastal city in the UK on two combat sport clubs. The first author was able to negotiate access through his active participation in combat sport, providing a hitherto unique perspective. Participants completed questionnaires anonymously at the two clubs' training facilities during training sessions. The semi-structured questionnaire included 7-point Likert scale statements and some qualifying open questions. The former were designed to measure the impact of combat sports on the potential risk factors experienced in areas of everyday life. The latter were designed to allow the respondent to expand on the reasons for a particular response to the Likert statements. The Likert component of the questionnaire produced a very respectable Cronbach's Alpha reliability score of 0.718.

We gathered a sample of 50 regular participants from the two clubs. While club records were not sufficient to carry out a systematic sampling exercise, the numbers involved compare favourably with many of the previous studies most commonly referred to in this area, some of which do not even include the number of subjects. The clubs practised different approaches, with one using traditional Korean Taekwondo (similar to Karate) while the other used the hybrid sport of K1, ensuring a variation in combat sports. K1 combines training in multiple traditional fighting styles, and therefore was selected to represent the majority of the sample. However, in K1 the spiritual aspects of the training styles are removed, leading one to question its potential to decrease criminal tendencies in participants (Trulson, 1986, p.1131). We ensured that 20 per cent of the sample was female, both to match the overall gender balance in the two clubs, and to address the absence of females in the existing studies. Table 5 summarises the sample characteristics.

Table 5: Sample characteristics by gender and club

	Male	Female	All
K1 Club	24	9	33
Taekwondo Club	16	1	17
Total	40	10	50

Participants' ages ranged from 16 to over 40 with 44 per cent of the sample between 21 and 30 years of age. 60 per cent participated for between two and six hours a week in combat sports. Overall participation ranged from one to ten hours per week. 58 per cent had been training at their respective club for between one and ten years, and the remainder for under a year. 64 per cent of respondents had had alternative combat sport experience, 14 per cent of whom had experience in five or more alternative combat sports. Taking these points into consideration, the sample represents a relatively wide range of combat sport participants.

Results

The results are presented under headings representing the major four categories of risk identified in the literature review: social and community impact; impact on sense of self; behavioural impact; and economic and educational impact. An additional section addresses combat sport experience and gender issues.

For the purposes of analysis and table content, the Likert questions were regularised so that in all cases below, a score of 1 is the strongest possible agreement with a statement and a score of 7 is the strongest possible disagreement. The overall mean for all Likert statements was 2.3, indicating that respondents felt combat sport participation had had a generally positive impact on their lives regarding a reduced risk of offending.

Social and Community Impact

Participants responded to four key statements (see Table 6), with two additional questions measuring the extent to which combat sport has changed their social life and how. The mean response to the four key statements was 1.7, indicating that participants perceive themselves to have fostered stable relationships with family and non-deviant friends and are more included in the community, since participating in combat sport.

Table 6: Community and Social Impact

	N	Mean	Std. Deviation
Effect on family relationships	50	1.5	1.111
Peer influence of other participants	50	1.58	1.43
Effect on relationships with friends	50	1.68	1.316
Feel part of the community	50	2.22	1.502

Participants' responses overall, to statements about the impact of combat sport on relationships with family and friends, achieved a mean score of 1.5 and 1.68 respectively (see Table 6). Additionally, the statements encountered 80 per cent and 72 per cent maximum agreement respectively. The implication is that large proportions of participants could have experienced a strengthening of family and friend relationships as a result of involvement in combat sports. The peer effect of other participants was seen as a positive influence on their behaviour, with a mean response of 1.58 (see Table 6) with 80 per cent of the sample responding with maximum agreement, indicating that the social life at the training facility positively influences many participants.

Regarding the extent to which participants' social lives had changed, the mean response of 2.22 shows that 72 per cent of participants believe that combat sports have changed their social life. When asked to expand, 60 per cent of participants highlighted gaining a combat sport-specific social life, with other members in and out of training. Considering that the majority of participants believed club members to be a positive influence, their increased involvement in one another's social lives should be considered constructive.

Impact on Sense of Self

This small but important section was based on responses to two statements and one question qualifying the impact of combat sport participation on self-esteem. Participants considered combat sports to be a highly important part of their identity and a positive impact on self-esteem acquiring mean responses of 1.78 and 2.1 respectively (see Table 7). The qualitative responses showed that 42 per cent of respondents cited increased confidence since participating in combat sports, as the reason for increased self-esteem.

Table 7: Impact on sense of self

	N	Mean	Std. Deviation
Forms part of a proud identity	50	1.78	1.055
Changed self-esteem	50	2.1	1.266

Behavioural Impact

Participants were asked to comment on four statements evaluating the impact of combat sport participation on their behaviour (see Table 8). There were also two qualitative questions for explanation and one question measuring the extent of changes in conflict resolution (see Table 8 'makes me deal with conflict differently'). The overall mean for responses to the four behavioural statements was a positive 2.2, indicating that respondents believed that combat sport participation has helped them control aggressive/violent behaviours, deal better with stress, and be less likely to commit violent assault or use controlled substances.

Table 8: Behavioural Impact

	N	Mean	Std. Deviation
Makes me less violent/aggressive toward others	50	1.66	1.189
Helps me cope with stress	50	2.08	1.322
Less likely to engage in violent assault	50	2.54	2.002
Less likely to engage in drug abuse	50	2.66	2.086
Makes me deal with conflict differently	50	2.9	1.876

The violence and aggression statement's mean response of 1.66 (see Table 8) indicates that the sample of respondents feel that they have not been made more violent or aggressive by participating in combat sport. Furthermore, 62 per cent of the sample experienced a possible reduction in perceived violent and aggressive behaviour since participating.

When asked if they were less likely to engage in violent assault ($M=2.54$) and drug abuse ($M=2.66$) the positive responses indicate that the respondents perceived their risk of engagement in these activities had decreased. However, when asked to offer a reason, 24 per cent of the sample failed to comment. The 38 participants who responded showed that the primary reason was increased self-control since participating in combat sport (26.3 valid per cent). However, the second highest response indicated that combat sport participation had no impact on the perceived likelihood of engagement in the offences for many participants. When coupled with the lack of response, it was not possible to be certain whether combat sport participation materialises into reductions in violent and drug-related offences.

Participants felt that they dealt with conflict differently since participating in combat sports, with a mean of 2.9 (see Table 8). When asked to expand, 44 participants highlighted two common themes: increased self-control (30 per cent); and increased confidence in their ability to deal with conflict (22 per cent).

Economic and Educational Impact

Participants responded to five statements (and expanded on two) on economic and educational impact (see Table 9). With a mean of 3.0, the sample perceived combat sports to have: improved work and educational/leisure balance; mildly improved performance; and not distracted them from completing important economic and educational functions (see Table 9).

Table 9: Economic and educational impact

	N	Mean	Std. Deviation
Improved work/leisure relationship	50	2.64	1.467
Distracts me from important tasks	50	2.92	1.816
Improved education/leisure relationship	46	3.17	1.387
Helps do better in education	49	3.24	1.575
Helps do better at work	50	3.28	1.703

The work/leisure relationship statement received a positive mean response of 2.64 (see Table 9). Further analysis revealed that despite an 18 per cent neutral response, 74 per cent of the sample perceived themselves to have experienced improvements in their work/leisure relationship. The two key reasons offered were that combat sports allowed participants to relax (26 per cent) and allowed a healthier lifestyle through increased energy (14 per cent).

Large proportions of the sample took a neutral stance (48 per cent) or failed to respond (8 per cent) to the statement regarding education/leisure relationship which makes a conclusive finding difficult. However, when asked to expand, 18 per cent of the sample cited an increased level of focus since participating in combat sport, helping them balance leisure and education better.

The results for educational and economic effects did yield some pronounced positive influences. For example, 68 per cent believed that combat sports did not distract them from important tasks. This indicates that combat sport participation possibly helped them to focus on important economic and educational tasks. Furthermore, even with a 34 per cent neutral response, 52 per cent of the sample ($N = 50$) felt that combat sports 'helps them do better at work'. The same question was applied to education ($N = 49$) with similar results (28 per cent neutral response and 54 per cent positive response).

Extent of Experience of Combat Sport

'Experience' was characterised by: hours per week; number of years participating in the current combat sport; and number of alternative combat sports experienced. A moderately negative correlation ($r = -0.241$) was discovered between hours training per week and the mean extent of impact. This indicates that participants with a greater level of involvement perceive combat sport to have had a greater impact on their life (see Table 10).

Table 10: Weekly participation and extent of impact

Weekly Participation (Hrs)	Mean Extent of Impact
<2	3.2
>2 - <6	2.6
>6 - <10	2.1
>10	1.5

A moderately negative correlation ($r = -0.258$) was discovered between experience in the current combat sport and the mean perceived nature of impact. This indicates that the longer participants stayed connected to the combat sport club, the more positive they perceived its impact to be.

No correlation was found between weekly participation (hours), experience in the current combat sport (years), or the number of combat sports participated in, and the perceived extent of impact. Furthermore, the research indicates that the number of combat sports participated in does not alter the respondents' perceived nature of impact.

Gender

Importantly, there were no significant differences between males' and females' responses in any aspect of the study, with equally positive general means for all Likert responses of 2.3 (males) and 2.1 (females). Similarly, the responses to statements measuring the extent of combat sport impact attained mean scores of 2.5 for both males and females.

Discussion

The existing literature and evidence revealed an explicit, mostly positive relationship between socio-cultural risk factors and leisure/sports-based offender programmes. This research has sought to extend the examination of this relationship to participation in combat sports.

The importance of non-deviant social networks appears in much of the existing literature (Loxley et al., 2002; Mahoney, 2000; Nichols, 1997; Nichols & Crow 2004). As such, many of the community crime reduction strategies and sport-based interventions include the use of group based activities to develop pro-social relationships. Our findings suggest that combat sport participation can strengthen relationships with family and friends and provide participants with non-deviant peer networks. This represents a reduction in the exposure to risk factors associated with the community. The combat sports we studied are not team sports, but they appear to provide a similar encouraging and supportive atmosphere to that encountered in boxing clubs studied by Wright (2006). Based on these results, the use of combat sports could be recommended for interventions aimed at group offenders, such as gang members, or as a pre-emptive attempt to reduce the community and social risk factors experienced by individuals lacking the support of the family unit. Given the lack of combat sports-based interventions, these benefits appear to have been neglected by the Ministry of Justice and the National Offender Management Service in England and Wales.

Connected with the fostering of non-deviant peer networks is the issue of self-esteem. Both have been categorised by Nichols and Crow (2004, p. 270) under the umbrella of pro-social developments. This leads to a consideration of the impact of combat sport participation on an individual's sense of self. A striking finding from our research is that combat sport forms an important part of the participants' identities with which they are proud to be affiliated. In turn, combat sports increased the self-esteem of participants through increased self-confidence. Fletcher (as cited in Nichols, 1997, p.184) and Wright (2006, pp.154–164) also discovered increased self-esteem among boxing participants. The main question is how this change reduces crime. Nichols and Crow (p.169) argue that self-esteem increases as individuals spend more time with appropriate role models and non-deviant peers. In turn, they no longer feel the need to engage in image boosting antisocial behaviours. Considering the perceived social and community benefits that combat sport has provided our respondents (the current sample), it appears to support Nichols and Crow's argument. The implication is that the combat sports could be used within crime reduction strategies aimed at moderating antisocial behaviour by countering the risk factors affecting an individual's sense of self.

Previous studies suggest that participation in combat sports can act as a moderator for behavioural problems associated with offending by: reducing aggressive temperament (Palermo et al., 2006; Trulson, 1986; Wright, 2006); aiding individuals to cope better with stress (Wright); reducing instances of assault and drug abuse (Fletcher, as cited in Nichols, 1997, p. 184; Nichols, 1997; Coalter; and Elias & Dunning, both studies as cited in Smith & Waddington, 2004, p. 284); and enabling individuals to control emotions in conflict situations (Fletcher; Palermo et al.; Wright).

The implication is that these changes in behaviour could represent distancing from the behavioural risk factors highlighted by Anderson et al. (2005, p. 4), such as aggressiveness and disobedience (Palermo et al., p. 654).

Expanding sports-based programmes can also reduce crime by meeting the excitement needs, usually gained by committing crime or using controlled substances (Nichols, 1997, p.183; Coalter; and Elias & Dunning, both studies as cited in Smith & Waddington, 2004, p. 284). This effect would be increased if the excitement gained from the participation matched elements of risk involved in offending. Thus, introducing elements of danger, such as the risk involved in combat sports, could be beneficial to sports-based programmes. The same is to be said of the long-term personal development and pro-social development, since crucial elements are increased self control, self-esteem and self-discipline. In summary, one could argue that combat sports-based interventions would potentially be ideal for addressing behavioural risk factors, and targeting violent and emotionally impulsive offenders.

Evidence provided by the current research shows that combat sport participation can improve educational and economic performance (Loxley et al., 2002; Mahoney, 2000; Nichols, 1997; Nichols & Crow, 2004); and improve work/leisure relationships. Furthermore, evidence suggests that improvements in the participants' behavioural risk factors contribute to protection from economic risk factors. Our research suggests that the primary reason for educational and economic improvement was increased relaxation. When coupled with the perceived stress relief benefits of combat sport participation, it is possible to argue that behavioural improvements had a positive impact on economic risk factors. Nichols and Crow; Nichols; and Loxley et al. all argued that improved cognitive development can lead to employment through sport-based programmes. Therefore, the use of combat sport participation within training, education and employment intervention schemes could result in long-term crime-reduction benefits. However, in this study, we could not address the extent to which improved work/leisure relationships or work performance materialise into real economic advantage such as increased opportunities, income and qualifications.

Similar difficulty is encountered when discussing educational improvements which are confined primarily to combat sports as a use of leisure time. For Mahoney and Stattin (2000, p. 123) and Mahoney et al. (2001, p. 509) constructive leisure time is participation in structured events such as team sports. Unconstructive leisure includes low structure groups, such as those encountered at youth recreation centres. The participating combat sports clubs used high levels of structure and hierarchy, making them consistent with a constructive use of leisure time. This would make participants less likely to drop out of education and offend (Mahoney, 2000, pp. 512–513). Our study could not include youths under 16 years of age and more research is needed before being able to make an empirically grounded recommendation regarding the crime reduction benefits of combat sports, through improved educational performance. We can suggest that our adult respondents felt that combat sport participation had reduced their exposure to economic and educational risk factors. However, economic improvements relate more to reduced behavioural risk factors and the structure of the activity.

Conclusions

Despite the limitations of the current research, this small but innovative study has successfully evaluated the impact of combat sport participation on individual criminality.

It has shown that combat sport participation can act as a protective factor which distances participants from socio-cultural and individual risk factors in the behavioural, economic and social spheres. It has also indicated that combat sport represents an appropriate activity to be utilised within crime reduction strategies that aim to address these risks. Furthermore, it has indicated that combat sport has the potential to help treat violent offenders, gang/group offenders and emotionally charged impulsive offenders.

It does not, however, prove decisively that combat sport will rid participants of any risk that they might offend. There are more complex structural risk factors that combat sports cannot address for which more extensive, representative and controlled longitudinal research is required, if one is to fully understand the impact of combat sport participation.

We feel this study provides a clear indication that the 'what works' agenda cannot be considered complete whilst combat sport continues to show significant potential to be examined in more detail. A larger study is required that can address the following issues. First, the reliability of respondents' perceived impact of combat sports needs to be measured against actual behaviour. Thus, future research would benefit from using more objective measurements such as reoffending/reconviction rates and additional psychological behavioural instruments. Second, the sample consisted of individuals who voluntarily participate in regular combat sports and there is therefore a need for an evaluation within the context of offender treatment programmes. It is likely that combat sport would still be subject to offender self-selection, as coerced participation would not only be ethically and politically unpalatable, but would work against 'what works' selection criteria. Third, our research is effectively a small, innovative pilot study and needs to be expanded to incorporate a much larger sample, including proportionate sampling of women and children. Finally, and most importantly, future research should include a control or comparison group of noncombat sports participants.

References

Abbot, B., & B. Barber, (2007). Not just idle time: adolescents' developmental experiences provided by structured and unstructured leisure activities. *Australian Educational and Developmental Psychologist, 24*(1), 59–81.

Anderson, B., Beinart, S., Farrington, D., Langman, J., Sturgis, P., & D. Utting,(2005). *Risk and protective factors*. Youth Justice Board.

Astbury, R., Knight, B., & G. Nichols (2005). The contribution of sport-related interventions to the long-term development of disaffected young people: an evaluation of the Fairbridge program. *Journal of Park and Recreation Administration, 23*(3), 82–98.

Davies, G. (2008, 18 January) *UFCs Are Here To Stay*. Retrieved 27 March 2011 from
http://blogs.telegraph.co.uk/sport/garethadavies/3665421/UFCs__are_here_to_stay/

Dunning, E. (2005). Violence and sport. In W. Heitmeyer & J. Hagan (Eds.), *The international handbook of violence research* (pp. 903–920). Dordrecht, Holland: Kluwer Academic Publishers.

Endresen, I., & D. Olweus (2005). Participation in power sports and antisocial involvement in preadolescent and adolescent boys. *Journal of Child Psychology and Psychiatry, 46*(5), 468–478.

Forbes, G., Adams-Curtis, L., Pakalka, A., & K. White (2006). Dating aggression, sexual coercion, and aggression-supporting attitudes among college men as a function of participation in aggressive high school sports. *Violence Against Women, 12*(5), 441–455.

Hartmann, D., & B. Depro (2006). Rethinking sports-based community crime prevention: a preliminary analysis of the relationship between Midnight Basketball and urban crime rates. *Journal of Sport and Social Issues, 30*, 180–196.

Haynes, C., Rife, E., & L. Laguna (2005). The impact of a summer camp program as a secondary prevention measure for at-risk youth. *Crime Prevention and Community Safety: An International Journal, 7*(3), 37–49.

Home Office. (1997). *No more excuses: a new approach to tackling youth crime in England and Wales* (Cm. 3809). London: HMSO.

Hurry, J., & V. Moriarty (2004). *Education, training and employment projects: the national evaluation of the Youth Justice Board's education, training and employment projects.* London: Youth Justice Board.

Koss, M., & J. Gaines (1993). The prediction of sexual aggression by alcohol use, athletic participation, and fraternity affiliation. *Journal of Interpersonal Violence, 8*(1), 94–108.

Loxley, C., Curtin, L., & R. Brown (2002). *Summer Splash schemes 2000: findings from six case studies* (Crime Reduction Research, series paper 12). London: Home Office.

Mahoney, J. (2000). School extracurricular activity participation as a moderator in the development of antisocial patterns. *Child Development, 71*(2), 502–516.

Mahoney, J., & H. Stattin (2000). Leisure activities and adolescent antisocial behaviour: the role of structure and social context. *Journal of Adolescence, 23*, 113–127.

Mahoney, J., Stattin, H., & D. Magnusson (2001). Youth recreation centre participation and criminal offending: a 20-year longitudinal study of Swedish boys. *International Journal of Behavioural Development, 25*(6), 509–520.

Meak, R. (2006). Social deprivation and rural youth crime: young men in prison and their experiences of the 'rural idyll'. *Crime Prevention and Community Safety, 8*, 90–103.

Metropolitan Police Service. (n.d.). *Youth boxing club is knockout.* Retrieved 16 February 2009, from http://cms.met.police.uk/met/boroughs/barking_and_dagenham/04how_a re_we_doing/news/youth_boxing_club_is_a_knockout

Muncie, J. (1999). Institutionalized intolerance: youth justice and the 1998 Crime and Disorder Act. *Critical Social Policy, 19*, 147–175.

Neighbourhood Renewal Unit. (2003). *Joint working in sport and neighbourhood renewal* (Report 9). London: Office of the Deputy Prime Minister.

Nichols, G.. (1997). A consideration of why active participation in sport and leisure might reduce criminal behaviour. *Sport, Education and Society, 2*(2), 181–190.

Nichols, G., & Crow, I. (2004). Measuring the impact of crime reduction interventions involving sports activities for young people. *Howard Journal, 43*(3), 267–283.

Palermo, M., Di Luigi, M., Dal Forno, G., Dominici, C., Vicomandi, D., & A. Sambucioni,et al. (2006). Externalizing and oppositional behaviours and

Karate-do: the way of crime prevention: a pilot study. *International Journal of Offender Therapy and Comparative Criminology, 50*, 654–660.

Smith, A., & I. Waddington (2004). Using 'sport in the community schemes' to tackle crime and drug use among young people: some policy issues and problems. *European Physical Education Review, 10*, 279–298.

Sport England. (n.d.a). *Active England case studies*. Retrieved 8 January 2010, from http://www.sportengland.org/search.aspx?query=neighbourhood+renewal+unit

Sport England. (n.d.b). The value of sport monitor. Retrieved 17 April 2011, from http://www.sportengland.org/research/value_of_sport_monitor.aspx

Sport England. (1999). *Best Value through sport:the value of sport to local authorities*. Retrieved 27 March 2011 from http://www.toolkitsportdevelopment.org/html/resources/5C/5C6D9742-7A45-4906-A1E3-0B7132A89051/best%20value%20through%20sport%20authorities.pdf

Sport England. (2005). *Spatial planning for sport and active recreation, guidance on SportEngland's aspirations and experience v1.0.* Retrieved 8 January 2010, from http://www.sportengland.org/search.aspx?query=neighbourhood+renewal+unit

Trulson, M. (1986). Martial arts training: a novel 'cure' for juvenile delinquency. *Human Relations, 39*, 1131–1140. Woods, R. (2007). *Social Issues in Sport*. Champaign, IL: Human Kinetics.

Wright, W. (2006). Keep it in the ring: using boxing in social group work with high-risk and offender youth to reduce violence. *Social Work with Groups, 29*(2), 149–174.

Table 1: UK sport-based crime reduction scheme summary

Programme	Programme structure	Evaluation outcome
Fairbridge Programme	Outdoor sports participation limited to 1st week • Eg, climbing and canoeing for the initial week. Then opportunity to enrol in: • outdoor pursuit courses • life-skills workshops	• No evidence of a long-term crime reduction • Reduced the circumstances which put youths at risk of offending • Sport played a vital role in fostering pro-social relationship with programme supervisors and catalyst for personal development (Astbury, Knight, & Nichols, 2005)
Midnight Basketball (The original United States programme)	• Basketball leagues set up between 10pm and 2am in inner city areas in the United States	• Cities with midnight basketball schemes showed significant decreases in crime rates (inc. property and violent crime) (Hartmann & Depro, 2006)

Table 2: US research on the negative impact of aggressive sports participation

Study	Sample/Method	Findings
Hoffman (as cited in Dunning, 2005, p. 911)	• 200 college campuses in 1986. • Analysed college police case records.	• Football & basketball 38% more frequently involved in sexual assault.
Koss and Gaines (1993, pp. 94–108)	• 530 undergraduate males. • 140 were athletes. • Analysed self-reported sexually aggressive acts (inappropriate touching to rape).	• Basketball & football players were significantly more likely to be sexually aggressive (inc. males involved in other sports). • Alcohol use & athletic participation were two of four variables accounting for 11% variance in levels of sexual aggression.
Nelson (as cited in Dunning, 2005, p. 911)	• 10,000 students at Towson State University. • Analysed recorded incidents from the Campus Violence Centre.	• Athletes were 16% of campus population. • Commit 55% of acquaintance rapes in 1991. • Commit 33% of 862 sexual assaults on campuses over three years in 1980s.
Crosset, Benedict, and McDonald (as cited in Dunning, 2005, p. 911); Woods (2007, p. 295)	• 107 cases of sexual assault. • In 10 division 1 schools 1991–1993. • Analysed police records, judicial affairs and reports.	• Male athletes were 3% of campus population. • Commit 19% of sexual assaults & 35% of domestic assaults. • Basketball players show disproportionately high number of sexual assaults.
Forbes, Adams-Curtis, Pakalka, & White (2006, pp. 447–455)	• 147 males at private, Midwestern university inc. 101 aggressive sport athletes (football, basketball, wrestling and soccer). • Analysed self-reported: relationship aggression and coercion, sexism, rape myth and violence acceptance, and attitude toward homosexuals.	• Aggressive sports participants committed more psychological and physical aggression (inc. injury to partners) & sexual coercion of partners. • Also more sexist and hostile towards women, accepting of violence, less tolerant of homosexuality.

Table 3: Summary of research on the effects of combat sport participation

Study	Sample/Method	Findings
Trulson (1986, p. 1131) (USA)	• 34 male school students identified as delinquent by the Minnesota Multiphasic Personality Inventory (MMPI) & Jackson Personality Inventory (JPI) — repeated measures. • Group 1: traditional taekwondo lesson 3×1 hour/per week, for 6 months. • Group 2: same as group 1 but modern adaptation, lacking philosophical elements • Group 3: no intervention.	• Group 1: decreased aggression and anxiety, increased self-esteem & value orthodoxy • Group 2: large increase in aggressive behaviour observed • Group 3: No change in any personality measures.
Fletcher (as cited in Nichols, 1997, p. 184) (UK)	• Unknown number of amateur boxers (gender unknown) in unpublished study of amateur boxing club. • Observations and interviews.	• Participants less likely to engage in street violence due to increased self-esteem and self-control
Endresen and Olweus (2005, pp. 468–476) (Norway)	• 477 male school students with varied participation in combat sports: boxing, kickboxing, wrestling, karate, judo & taekwondo. • 3 groups of participants • 1 group of non-participants • Before, during & after measures: self-reported antisocial behaviour, violence and total antisocial involvement test	• Untroubled boys become more prone to violent and non-violent antisocial behaviour changes: fights (inc. weapons) truancy and vandalism • Negative effects persisted long after participation ceased.
Palermo et al. (2006, pp. 656–659) (Italy)	• 13 male and 3 female children aged 8 to 10, diagnosed with behavioural problems associated with delinquency. • Group 1 enrolled on a 10-month karate programme: 3 lessons per week. • Group 2: no intervention. • Before & after measures of intensity, adaptability and mood regulation	• Participating youths showed greatly improved behaviour. • Observed a diversion from potentially criminal behaviour, eg, disobedience and aggressive temperaments.
Wright (2006, pp. 149–171) (USA)	• Unknown number of male youths from boxing clubs in impoverished areas of New York & San Francisco. • Interviews & observations to measure boxing's potential to reduce violence in the community.	• Identified 10 effects of boxing associated with reduction in violence and crime (details in text).

Table 4: Wright's (2006) 10 benefits of boxing training

- Identity based on valuing respect and pride above toughness
- Provides/promotes safety during dangerous high crime periods (including emotional safety from the boxing group)
- Emotional skills aiding development into law abiding adults
- Using defence as a metaphor for conflict resolution
- Learning patience/becoming less impulsive
- Ability to focus and for longer periods of time
- Gaining a sense of meaning, hope and self-esteem beyond losing friends/relatives to violent crime, incarceration or encountering violence in daily life
- Learning respect for others
- Relieving stress which could otherwise be released as violence
- Promotes and provides mutual aid/support from the group training atmosphere

Table 5: Sample characteristics by gender and club

	Male	Female	All
K1 Club	24	9	33
Taekwondo Club	16	1	17
Total	40	10	50

Table 6: Community and social impact

	N	Mean	Std. deviation
Effect on family relationships	50	1.5	1.111
Peer influence of other participants	50	1.58	1.43
Effect on relationships with friends	50	1.68	1.316
Feel part of the community	50	2.22	1.502

Table 7: Impact on sense of self

	N	Mean	Std. deviation
Forms part of a proud identity	50	1.78	1.055
Changed self-esteem	50	2.1	1.266

Table 8: Behavioural impact

	N	Mean	Std. deviation
Makes me less violent/ aggressive toward others	50	1.66	1.189
Helps me cope with stress	50	2.08	1.322
Less likely to engage in violent assault	50	2.54	2.002
Less likely to engage in drug abuse	50	2.66	2.086
Makes me deal with conflict differently	50	2.9	1.876

Table 9: Economic and educational impact

	N	Mean	Std. deviation
Improved work/leisure relationship	50	2.64	1.467
Distraction effect on important tasks	50	2.92	1.816
Improved education/ leisure relationship	46	3.17	1.387
Helps do better in education	49	3.24	1.575
Helps do better at work	50	3.28	1.703

Table 10: Weekly participation and extent of impact

Weekly participation (hrs)	Mean extent of impact
<2	3.2
>2–<6	2.6
>6–<10	2.1
>10	1.5

Chapter 28

Synchronizing Modernity: Panama Al Brown and the Fight Game in France, 1926–1938

Bennetta Jules-Rosette

'Al Brown is a mystery. In the domain of boxing and in that of literature, we speak the same language.... Beware, sports fans. You will constantly find yourselves in the presence of a prince of the ring, a phenomenon, a sorcerer, an acrobat, a psychologist, a specter... a poet, in short: a boxer'.

[Jean Cocteau, 1938]

Preamble

Alfonso Teofilo Brown (1902-1951) was an extraordinary, pivotal figure in early twentieth-century boxing. The evolution of Brown's career and his rise to fame as the world bantam-weight champion in 1929 paralleled much of the history of boxing and its increasing regularization during this era.[1] The Marquis of Queensberry's rules and the London Boxing Ring Rules brought some order to the field during the late nineteenth century.[2] Standardized gloves, attire, ring size, weight classes, and weigh-in rules were established. Similar rules were also put

---

[1] I gratefully acknowledge the assistance of sociology student Stephen Reynders of the University of California, San Diego for his research on the history of boxing, rules of the fight game, and press coverage of Al Brown. I would also like to thank J. R. Osborn of Georgetown University and Lea Marie Ruiz-Ade of the UCSD Art, Culture, and Knowledge (ACK) Group for their helpful comments on this manuscript.

[2] Boxing historian Alexander Johnston (1947: 12-17) provides a cogent summary of prize fighting and ring rules as they emerged during the nineteenth century. In spite of the Queensberry Rules and the London Prize Fighting Rules for gloved contests, the regularization of boxing and the codes of enforcement evolved gradually. See also Loïc Wacquant (2004: 125) on the sociological sanctity of boxing rules.

into place in other sports, such as soccer, at that time. However, as late as the 1930s, many rules and standards of sportsmanship that were technically in place were not actually enforced in professional boxing.

The lines between street fighting and professional boxing were often blurred, as fighters shuttled between weight categories and engaged in a wide range of illicit behavior in the ring. Although they came under increasingly close scrutiny by local and international boxing commissions and federations, managers and promoters were also at fault. Pushing boxers to meet unreasonably demanding schedules and subjecting fighters to questionable medical risks were among the drawbacks of the profession and a source of recurrent conflict between boxers and their promoters. The issue was one of synchronizing modernity inside and outside of the ring by bringing a set of rational legal rules into play within a gladiatorial sport. Synchronizing modernity is the balance among performance in the ring, the rules and regulations of boxing, and the life of the athlete. In boxing, synchronization consists of timing and performance in the ring, some of which is rule governed as well as stylistic (i.e., rounds, combinations, pacing, and footwork). Hartmut Rosa (2013: 6-7) relates this type of synchronization to the emergence of modern bureaucratic institutions in which the regulation of time is an essential aspect of social control.

The first decades of the twentieth century were accompanied by new vistas for the mass consumption of leisure pursuits as an escape from the increasingly bureaucratized and time-bound structures of labor (Gorn, 1986: 250). Athletes, performers, and celebrities became the icons of modernist popular spectacles as exemplars of the world of play who, at the same time, worked hard to maintain their image. Brown was caught up in the conundrums and paradoxes of modernity's challenge. This discussion examines Brown's biography with regard to the tensions and changes emerging in boxing as a performance and a profession during the heyday of his career. This approach is known as semiography, a research method that uses the tools of socio-semiotics to excavate the narratives, images, and representations that constitute the public and private lives of biographical subjects (Jules-Rosette, 2007: 5-7). Within semiography, each of Brown's matches may be also viewed as a cultural signifier in which the wins, knockouts, and losses create a sequence of infinite semiosis leading to Brown's championship belts.

Training: From the Streets of Panama to the Boulevards of Paris

Al Brown began his career on the streets and in the small gyms of Colón, a suburb of Panama City. As an adolescent, he watched informal boxing matches organized by US sailors on the back lots of the town. Eventually, he became part of the Strand gym where he received formal training in the techniques and rules of boxing. On March 19, 1922, fighting under the name of Kid Teofilo, Brown became Champion of the Isthmus in a six-round bout against José Moreno. Accruing several knockout victories, Brown continued to fight in Panama until early 1923. In an interview with newspaper columnist Vaughn Bryant (1943: D5), Brown erroneously claimed that he was only 13 years old at the time. Signing up as a mess hand on a rickety cargo ship bound for New York, Brown secretly disembarked in Hoboken, New Jersey and made his way to New York City.

Brown's professional fighting career slowly began to unfold at this point, and the blueprint for his training practices emerged. In New York, Brown trained at Billy Grupp's gym, once a local landmark institution that now no longer exists. There he encountered Leo Flinn, an entrepreneur and boxing aficionado. After a brief series of negotiations, Flinn and his partner, trainer Dai Dallings, agreed to sponsor Brown, changing his professional name from Kid Teofilo to the more trendy Panama Al Brown, in the tradition of another currently popular fighter Panama Joe Gans. The contract with Flinn was the first of many exploitative relationships into which Brown would enter during the course of his boxing career. According to Brown, Dallings informed him that his first bout would be in front of 20,000 spectators. In his journal, Brown explained (Arroyo, 1982: 22):

> 'After the weigh-in, Dallings told me to go get some lunch. I wasn't hungry, and I went to sit on a bench in Central Park and wait until I had to go to the ring. I had a satchel containing my new boxing shoes and my new trunks, violet with black stripes. I didn't yet have a boxing robe, but instead used a towel that I put over my shoulders to enter the ring'.

At this point, Brown was scheduled to earn $40.00 per round, with Flinn and Dallings taking 75% of the earnings. This arrangement left Brown with barely enough money to eat. According to his journal, Brown cleared a total of $20.00 after his initial fight for Flinn and Dallings. Brown wrote:

> "I understood for the first time what an American manager could be for a black boxer; rarely an honest man, never a friend" (Arroyo, 1982: 23).[3]

While in New York between 1923 and mid-1926, Brown engaged in over 30 bouts, often fighting as frequently as three to four times a month with little extra time for training and recovery. Brown lost only four of these fights. In 1925, Brown developed a friendship with manager Eddie MacMahon and a French ex-amateur boxer, motorcyclist, and restaurateur, Villepontoux. Together MacMahon and Villepontoux challenged Flinn's management plan and ultimately took over Brown's contract.

Meanwhile, Villepontoux, who had decided to close his New York bistro and return to France for financial reasons, convinced MacMahon that he should take two fighters with him—Al Brown and Jimmy Brown (no relationship to Panama). Villepontoux had been close to Sénégalese light-heavyweight champion Louis Fall Siki ("Battling Siki"), and based on this experience, he thought that France would offer a fertile and lucrative terrain for young black fighters, who would be embraced with enthusiasm as exotic curiosities rather than marginal box office attractions (Benson, 2006: 232-233).

Arriving in Paris in the fall of 1926, Brown went to work immediately. Villepontoux arranged for Al to be sponsored by fight promoter Jeff Dickson

---

[3] Throughout his career, Al Brown kept a detailed journal in which he recorded his daily experiences and analyzed his own fighting style. In his biography of Brown, Eduardo Arroyo (1982: 38-39) quotes copiously from Brown's journals, in particular with regard to his first impressions of Paris and his descriptions of conflicts with managers and promoters.

from Mississippi and manager David Lumiansky from Massachusetts, both Americans with a detailed knowledge of the European fight scene and its circuits. Dickson remained a promoter of Al's fights almost until the end of Brown's European sojourn. Lumiansky, however, had a more spotty and uneven career riddled with scandals and accusations from local governments, boxing commissions, and the fighters themselves.

From the moment that Brown reached Paris, Dickson scheduled him for a year of fights from November 10, 1926 through December 10, 1927. Of the ten fights scheduled by Dickson for 1926 and 1927, Brown won five by early round knockouts. Two of Brown's three losses during this period were against a fighter who was to become his archrival, Henri Young Scillie, the Belgian welterweight champion who studied Brown's fighting style closely. Scillie carefully avoided Brown's signature right to the jaw and pummeled Brown with incessant jabs and body shots. Nonetheless, one of Scillies' victories was by decision in the tenth round, and none was by knockout. During this period, Brown honed his elegantly choreographed fighting style and adhered closely to his strategy of early knockouts, described at length in his journals.

By 1929, Luminansky and Dickson thought that Brown was ready for a championship bout in the bantamweight category. Brown's record was strong, and his maturity and reputation as a fighter had evolved. However, Lumiansky and Dickson also believed that for the title to be credible, the championship match would have to be fought in the United States. Brown defeated Gregorio Vidal in Long Island on June 18, 1929, thereby winning the world bantamweight championship. Between 1929 and 1934, Brown maintained a full fight schedule that included at least two successful championship bouts a year and an average of ten to twelve fights annually. Nevertheless, in 1932, the National Boxing Association and the New York State Boxing Commission ruled that Brown did not defend his belt frequently enough, and they declared the bantamweight title vacant (Johnston, 1947: 371-372; Fleischer and André, 1959: 304-305).[4] This type of conflict was not new to Brown, who initially had difficulty obtaining licensing to fight in New York during the early 1920s. The situation was compounded by the questionable conduct of Brown's early managers. Brown himself considered some of his problems to be racially motivated. But during an era when race did affect all sports in the United States and without strong managerial support, Brown had difficulty making his case and claims known publicly until his temporary suspension and the disqualification of his manager in 1933. His performance in the ring was also influenced by his extravagant lifestyle. In order to explore this dimension of Brown's career, it is helpful to examine the social context in which he operated in Black Paris and how he was perceived outside of the ring.

---

[4] Alexander Johnston (1947: 371-376) and Nat Fleischer and Sam André (1959: 287 and 304-305) argue that Brown fought abroad primarily because his bantamweight title was in dispute in the United States. However, Brown left for France three years before his US title fight. Arroyo (1982: 233) criticizes the work of these authors as erroneous ("*truffée d'erreurs et de faux resultants*") and argues for a more balanced understanding of Brown's motives and career trajectory.

Panama Al Brown and Black Paris

When Brown arrived in Paris in 1926, the Jazz Age was in full swing. Al went directly to rue Fontaine in Montmartre, the center for African-American expatriates and artists. His social life, at least in his early days in Paris, revolved around this community and not the world of gyms and other athletes. It could even be argued that Brown, who is purported not to have been able to stand the sight of blood in the ring, attempted to finish his fights as rapidly as possible (including one knockout in 18 seconds) so that he could visit his favorite haunts. Brown is famously quoted as stating: "To live, I need, first of all, 20,000 bottles of champagne. The rest comes later" (Arroyo, 1982: 85; Stovall, 1996: 68).[5] Describing his outfit upon arriving in Paris, Brown stated that he wore a checkered cap, a light beige suit, and matching suede shoes, which created a "sensation." The shoes became Brown's signature trademark. During his affluent period, Brown often traveled to Italy to purchase custom-made shoes and to London to have his suits tailored. It is said that he changed suits up to six times a day. Brown viewed fashion as an integral aspect of his assimilation into French society and into the fast-paced life of Black Paris. Part of the psychology of this sort of dandyism (later to become known as *sape*, or dressing for ambiance, in the circles of African Paris) is the idea of standing out from the crowd in order to achieve social acceptance.

The cabarets, music halls, clubs, and hotels lining the avenues of Montmartre were the center of a vibrant nightlife in which black and white, proletarians and élites, and artists and their patrons came together to share the excitement of moments suspended in time and space from the quotidian drudgery and repetition of the world of work. Montmartre became an official commune of Paris in 1860. Right after the Franco-Prussian war in 1870, the Sacré-Coeur basilica, a Byzantine-style structure, was built to fulfill a vow of penitence made by French Catholics. Located on top of a hill known as the Butte, the basilica is the pinnacle of Montmartre. At the foot of the hill is the Place Pigalle, the hub of Montmartre's nightlife. It is in this world of entertainment, sexual freedom, and flowing alcohol that Brown felt at home and was revered as a charismatic personality. When Brown's boxing fame and affluence increased, he involved himself more and more in the heady life of the Parisian Jazz Age and its aftermath.

During the early 1920s, African-American artists, musicians, and writers, some of whom were World War I veterans, settled in Montmartre. According to social historian Tyler Stovall (1996: 47): "Throughout this period, Montmartre remained the undisputed center of black expatriate life in Paris." Key figures in this community included the owner of Le Grand Duc cabaret Eugene Jacques Bullard, who was a former boxer; restaurateur Florence Jones and her family at Chez Florence; and performers Bricktop (Ada Louise Smith), Josephine Baker, and Sidney Bechet. Brown imbibed the rhythms and choreography of their exciting performances and introduced some of these rhythms into his skillful footwork in the ring (Jackson, 2003: 56-57). American expatriates, French artists and intellectuals, and an assortment of European luminaries and tourists

---

[5] Brown's extravagance, described by biographers and historians (Stovall, 1996: 67-68), could be interpreted both as a publicity ploy and a strategy of cultural assimilation.

frequented the clubs of Montmartre and were part of Brown's social world.[6] Some of these connections crystallized, becoming increasingly important to Brown as his boxing career in Europe progressed and faltered. Other venues connected with the nightlife of Black Paris were also incorporated into Brown's offstage repertoire, including the Maisons-Lafitte where he stabled race horses as well as his Bugatti sports car and the race tracks and casinos of Deauville and the Riviera, where Brown thought nothing of spending thousands of francs a day in the pursuit of pleasure.

In addition to these activities, Brown became a dedicated humanitarian in France. He helped Marcel Griaule, Georges-Henri Rivière, and Josephine Baker to raise funds for the 1931 Mission Dakar-Djibouti in which Griaule conducted research and collected artifacts across the African continent for the Musée de l'Homme (Jules-Rosette, 1998: 26-30). At this time, the worlds of art, in particular surrealism, museum science, and performance intersected in Paris as a key moment of negotiating modernity (Clifford 1988: 136-138). Brown's scheduled ten-round bout at the Cirque d'Hiver with French postal worker turned boxer, Roger Simendé, was the main event. All funds were donated to Griaule's anthropological expedition, of which Brown was a proud sponsor. Brown proclaimed that he was boxing "to increase the knowledge about and understanding of Africa" (Jules-Rosette, 1998: 28). He freely contributed to surrealist artistic projects and other musical spectacles held in Black Paris. Brown also lent his financial support to French political candidates. He benefited from these humanitarian efforts by being considered as a successful and leading figure in African-American Paris of the 1920s and 1930s.

In discussing Brown's visibility in Black Paris, Stovall compares his trajectory with that of historian, scholar, and author Anna Julia Cooper. He argues that both figures had been victims of racism and exclusion in the United States but found acceptance and success in Paris. According to Stovall (1996: 68): "Paris both facilitated and witnessed their triumphs, confirming in the minds of many African Americans its reputation for sophistication, tolerance, and generosity…"

A more apt comparison with Brown, however, is performer Josephine Baker, whose panache, sense of style, sexual aura, and humanitarianism paralleled Brown's. While the black body iconically represented savagery, primitivity, and sexual freedom in 1920s France, both Brown and Baker constantly juxtaposed primal imagery and urbane elegance in their performances on and off stage (Jules-Rosette, 2007: 152-154). Brown wore a championship boxing belt, and Baker donned a banana belt, designed by Jean Cocteau and graphic artist Paul Colin, for her public. These two symbols semiotically mirrored each other. This homology is further reinforced when we consider Frantz Fanon's notion of the riveting audience gaze through which the "crushing objecthood" of the self and seminude black bodies is torn apart by combined corporeal and historico-racial schemata (Fanon, 1967: 109-111). In the cases of Baker and Brown, the belt as a cultural signifier highlights the distinctiveness of their performative personae while also drawing attention to the primal imagery of the seminude black body.

---

[6] When Brown's boxing career began to decline, his artistic and social contacts in Paris, in particular Jean Cocteau, Coco Chanel, and the Vicomte de Noailles, became important sources of personal and financial support (Steegmuller, 1970: 432-434).

Thus, the black performer remained imprisoned within stereotypes of exoticism and difference (Sharpley-Whiting, 1999: 10).

Figure 1: Publicity photograph of Alfonso Teaofilo Brown and his Bantamweight belt use in the fight against French Boxer Roger Simendé, April 15, 1931. Reproduced from the files of Phototèque, #D.80.652, Musée de l'Homme, Paris

A closer look at Brown's lifestyle reveals a darker side of the expatriate immigrant experience. In his journals, Brown mentions his desire to return to Panama, where he claimed a woman was waiting for him. In Paris, he lived in hotels and transitory apartments, and he was often on the road boxing for weeks and months at a time. Combined with heavy scheduling by his managers and Brown's own need for a constant flow of financial resources to sustain his elegant lifestyle, Brown was an itinerant fighter with an unstable home life. Although he had many contacts in Paris, he had few lasting relationships apart from those with his managers and later with Jean Cocteau.

In this sense, Brown was a loner—a fish out of water—for whom boxing and the ring provided the main anchor of his life. The managerial and professional obstacles that he encountered as a fighter could not be eluded.

Management and Obstacles

Following his 1929 bantamweight win, Brown's managers and promoters scheduled fights for him in England, France, Wales, Belgium, Denmark, Switzerland, Italy, Tunisia, and Algeria. These fights included four championship matches in which Brown retained his belt in spite of claims to the contrary by the

New York Boxing Commission and the California Athletic Commission. According to fight historians Nat Fleischer and Sam André (1959: 304): "Brown's record was so good that he was universally recognized as champion." His boxing performance is amazing to witness in the surviving film clips, but serious problems and disagreements arose concerning his title and his management.

Lumiansky organized a championship match for Brown with Kid Francis in Marseilles on July 10, 1932. Brown claimed to be pleased about this arrangement because, for a change, he was fighting within his own bantamweight class rather than with random contenders selected by Lumiansky and Dickson for promotional purposes, including fighters ranging from the flyweight to the heavyweight categories. There were two official judges for the fight, one of whom was an American, Mr. Sparks, selected by Lumiansky. Kid Francis was a native of Marseilles, and many locals had wagered on his victory. When Sparks proclaimed Brown the winner of the 15-round bout by points, the crowd went into an uproar. Sparks' score card and wallet were stolen, and he was viciously attacked by the mob. Some members of the crowd also attempted to set the ring on fire. The fight was declared a draw, and Lumiansky and Brown were eventually found hiding in the gym shower as the mêlée continued. The next day, the French Boxing Federation launched an investigation of the fight as well as the ensuing brawl, and declared Brown the official winner by points. They also announced that no further championship boxing matches were to be held in Marseilles in the near future. If the French Boxing Federation had not intervened, the championship fight might have been considered a "foul out" in order to protect the bets on Kid Francis.[7] This incident was only one among many in which Lumiansky placed his client in jeopardy. On the other hand, Dickson attempted to lighten Brown's schedule and protect the fighter's interests.

In 1933, Lumiansky organized a series of fights for Al in England, including a championship bout with Johnny King that Brown won in 15 rounds. At the end of that year, Brown left for North Africa under suspension because of a missed fight in England, but Lumiansky continued to book him for more matches there, promising to pay him based on a new contract. The contract stipulated a down payment of $5,000 per year for Lumiansky in addition to 35% of all of Brown's earnings for life. Brown claimed that Lumiansky had already taken 75% of his earnings, and he launched a publicity campaign against him in the boxing press. Ultimately, Lumiansky was disqualified as a boxing manager by the New York State Athletic Commission, the British Boxing Board of Control, the French Boxing Federation, and the International Boxing Union, and Brown was temporarily suspended from fighting in Europe. Lumiansky parted ways with Brown at the end of 1933, while Dickson stayed on as the fight promoter. Lew Burston, a temporary manager, flew in from New York to take charge.

---

[7] The "foul out" rule making it impossible to win or lose a fight based on a foul was heavily used in the criminalized demimonde of boxing betting (Williams, 1954: 66-70). In matches ending with a foul, bets cannot be paid. The foul also opens the door for the fighters to request a rematch. The 1932 Kid Francis fight in Marseilles comes close to being a foul out, and indeed Brown did have a victorious rematch with Kid Francis in Paris in 1934.

Brown fought eight matches in 1934, winning five, including a title rematch with Kid Francis in Paris. Under the new management and the training of Lew Burston and Bobby Diamant, with Dickson still on board as a promoter, Brown's situation had not improved. His contract was unregulated and exploitative. He also continued to view himself as under pressure to defend his disputed championship belt. In Algeria, Brown had suffered from a fractured jaw and a broken right hand, which interfered with his famous right cross. He had also started to lose even more interest in training and spoke repeatedly of returning to Panama. Dickson and Diamant scheduled a championship fight between Brown and Baltazar Sangchili for June 1, 1935 in Valencia, Spain. The betting was heavily in Sangchili's favor, and Brown was reluctant to fight him having lost a nonchampionship bout to him earlier that year.

During his stay in North Africa, Brown was rumored to have secretly married an Algerian woman in Oran (Arroyo, 1982: 158-159). In the absence of concrete recordings of Brown's actual interactions with his colleagues, managers, and promoters in 1934, following is an ethnographic reconstruction based on historical facts about what transpired as Brown prepared for his 1935 title bout with Sangchili in Spain (Jules-Rosette, 2010: 84-86).

Jeff Dickson and Al Brown are Talking in Jeff's Montmartre Office, February 10, 1934

JEFF: Panama, we have just a little more than a week until your first fight in Paris since the end of the suspension. How're you feeling?

AL: My teeth still hurt. And I miss my wife.

JEFF: What the heck are you talking about? You can't possibly be serious about that woman from Oran.

AL: Well, I married her.

JEFF: That marriage isn't legal, and you know it. If I find out that it is, we'll have it annulled. You don't have any time for marriage in this business. Not now, anyway, while you're trying to make a big comeback, and we're getting you squared with the Boxing Commission.

AL (smoldering): Maybe I just won't box anymore. I'll go back to North Africa and live a peaceful life with my wife on my earnings from Paris. I'm tired of being treated like this.

JEFF: Let me remind you that you are under contract, and you owe a lot of money. If the Boxing Commission clears you, you're still the World Champion. But you'll have to defend your title against Victor Young Perez on February 19 and against Kid Francis in April. Both of these fights are scheduled for Paris. If you win these fights and most of the others, we'll schedule a new season for you next year. But you'll have to defend the championship again, and that's going to be a tough fight... Baltazar Sangchili in Spain.

AL: Once I have my teeth fixed and my jaw heals, tough fights won't be a problem. But what about my wife?

JEFF: That's history. Don't look back. I'm going to take care of everything.

AL: I'll bet you will.

Al turns abruptly and leaves Jeff's office, slamming the door behind him. He runs into Lew Burston, his new manager, in the hallway.

LEW: Going somewhere, Brown? I want to talk to you.

AL (in anger): Not now, Burston. Jeff's waiting for you inside.

LEW (enters Jeff's office): We've got to do something about Brown. He's completely out of control.

JEFF: Oh, he's just a little upset about the woman he left in Oran. I'll take care of it.

LEW: And will you take care of his training too? We've got to call the gym.

JEFF: I already have. They're sending Bobby Diamant over. He's on his way now.

A knock on the door and Bobby Diamant enters. He greets Lew and Jeff. The three of them begin to plan the championship bout with Baltazar Sangchili in Spain.

Brown was in poor form for the Sangchili fight and lost after 15 rounds. Implicating his own trainer Bobby Diamant and Sangchili's henchmen. Brown claimed that his water bottle had been poisoned and that he had been illicitly drugged before the fight. Sangchili's supporters countered that Brown, who was not prepared for the fight, had been out all night carousing in Valencia and that Sangchili was the legitimate winner by points. However, the New York State Athletic Commission and the National Boxing Association in the United States ignored Sangchili's claim for the world bantamweight belt, arguing that the title had long since been vacated. Although it did not mark the end of his boxing career, the June 1935 loss to Sangchili was the beginning of Brown's demise. He had been defeated by the rules of the ring as well as the obstacles that he faced outside of it.

Bending the Rules of the Ring and Beyond

Reflecting on boxing as it existed during Al Brown's prime returns us to several interrelated issues concerning the synchronization of modernity and the institutionalization of sports. The field of management was loosely controlled during Brown's era. Al left the United States to box in Europe where he thought that brighter opportunities awaited him. Yet, he was still saddled with a series of managers from the United States who viewed Europe as an arena of opportunity and golden gains for themselves and their expatriate clients. These managers blatantly ignored the pronouncements and decisions of the US and world boxing commissions. They also shamelessly exploited fighters with overboxing and underrepresentation. Ringside betting and backdoor deals were rampant and threatened the respectability of boxing as a sport and a profession.

Some of these activities were facilitated by the nature and quality of ringside judging. Contemporary championship bouts have three to five judges, instead of two, whose score cards are made public and appear on the screen and the Internet during televised fights. Instant replays make it possible to review close and problematic judgment calls interactively both during and immediately after fights. Ring quality can also be assessed visually and on video during fights, making it possible to correct minor problems that might affect the fighters on the scene and the quality of the match right away.

Spectatorship has also changed with millions of viewers watching fights in real time on television or the Internet. Viewers and commentators respond by sending in their own score cards through Twitter to rival those of the official judges. The fight becomes a reality not only immediately but beforehand via countless videos and Internet interviews with the fighters as they train for a bout. In fact, this pre-fight publicity substitutes for actual fights, thereby reducing the amount of time that well-known professional fighters actually spend in the ring defending their titles. The ambiguity of these titles is also reduced by increased regularization and coordination of boxing commissions and federations around the world.

Media in Brown's time consisted of radio, newspapers, boxing magazines, and brief newsreel clips. Only radio was instantaneous but, lacking a visual component, it also left a great deal of room for subjective judgment calls. The semiotics of spectatorship in contemporary boxing is complex, and spectators include a large, active, and multilayered network of onsite and online audiences. That said, the immediacy and excitement of ringside spectatorship still remains salient in contributing to the outcomes of matches. By commenting on the fighters, referees, and judges, and egging on the fighters to be more vigorous, the ringside audience becomes an integral part of the spectacle. According to sports columnist Joe Williams (1954: 76): "The promoter wants it that way too. Red meat sells better than chocolate fudge at the box office." This type of active spectatorship raises questions about the role the audience plays in maintaining what sociologically constitutes the sanctity of the rules of the game.

Although aggressive audience responses were common in Al Brown's era as well, as evidenced by the audience uproar over Battling Siki's initially disputed 1922 victory against French light-heavyweight champion Georges Carpentier and Brown's 1932 Marseilles fight with Kid Francis, the immediate impact of the audience has now expanded, making each fight its own performative, multimedia microcosm.[8] Commentators, journalists, and online kibitzers also engage in their own battles outside of the ring about ambiguous and disputed fight results. Thus, while the categorization of weight classes, the physical condition of the fighter, and the rules of the ring are under systematic technical scrutiny in contemporary boxing, with digital scales, drug tests, glove inspections, and real-time video playback, audiences still crave the ringside stimulation and excitement of a successfully, dramatically, and artfully fought match.

Brown's Later Career

Shortly after the loss to Sangchili in 1935, Brown retired from fighting and went underground. He earned a living by shadowboxing and dancing in the clubs and dives of Montmartre. Sometime in early 1936, Marcel Khill, a North African colleague and protégé of Jean Cocteau, discovered Brown shadowboxing in a Parisian cabaret and took Cocteau there to reacquaint the two (Steegmuller, 1970: 427-428).[9] Brown and Cocteau probably first met in about 1930, but they had not remained in close contact, although Cocteau knew about the Sangchili loss.

As a surrealist poet and playwright, Cocteau was fascinated by Brown's exoticism, elegance, and power in the ring. He also viewed his reconnection with Brown as the perfect opportunity to embark on a new avocation, boxing management, starting with the rehabilitation of the ex-champion. After persistent persuasion, Cocteau convinced Brown to join him in this scheme. Even though they both knew that Sangchili was not considered to be a legitimate world champion, they concocted the goal of winning a rematch with him as a way of restoring Brown's self-esteem and reputation as an undisputed champion in the world of boxing. A 1936 interview with a reporter in Paris depicts Brown as preparing to make a comeback (*Meriden Record*, January 24, 1936: 4):

> "Breaking into a tap dance—a habit he acquired making spare change as an attraction at Paris cabarets—Brown asserted "I'm just as fit as a fiddle now. There have been a lot of reports going about that I'm getting old and decrepit. Why, I'm only thirty years old, which is very young for a bantamweight."

With the backing of Coco Chanel, Cocteau established a training camp for Brown at Aubigny in the French countryside of Champagne. Under the watchful eyes of an American trainer, Bob Robert, Brown was placed on a strict exercise, diet, and sparring régime. After four months, Cocteau affirmed that Brown had regained

---

[8] The fight game is a form of spectacle on many levels extending from the technical performances of the fighters and the referees to the active participation of the audience. Jonathan Markovitz (2011: 54-55) discusses the "media lynching" of some black athletes whose spectacular performances have been impugned for allegedly racial reasons.

[9] There are various accounts of Al Brown's relationship with Jean Cocteau. Francis Steegmuller, Cocteau's biographer, indicates that Cocteau was obsessed with his rehabilitation project and with Brown himself, although his knowledge of boxing was slim (Steegmuller, 1970: 428-434). Claude Arnaud (2003: 508-514) is more cynical, referring to Brown as a "dandy," a "ghetto kid," and a "drain on Cocteau's energy." Nevertheless, Arnaud admits that Cocteau's rehabilitation project was at least partially successful.

his punching power, timing, speed, and agile footwork. With the assistance of Jeff Dickson, Cocteau began to book Brown for fights in France and Switzerland in 1937 and 1938.

Al did not disappoint his new manager, winning all of the fights booked for him, most of them by knockout. Brown's first fight in 1937 was on September 9 in Paris against André (Tiger) Régis, a former featherweight champion of France. Brown knocked out Régis after a startling one minute and four seconds of the first round (*Milwaukee Journal*, September 10, 1937: 9). These fights also included the long awaited victorious rematch with Baltazar Sangchili held in Paris on March 4, 1938 and another victory against the International Boxing Union's world flyweight champion Valentin (*Tintin*) Angelmann in 10 rounds (*Milwaukee Journal*, April 14, 1938). Throughout this period, Cocteau launched a relentless publicity campaign for the boxer. He published articles in French sports magazines, wrote poems about Brown, referring to him as an ebony Adonis, and had a collection of photographs taken in which he often appeared at Brown's side. During the 1920s and 1930s, several major French journals and magazines covered sports. *L'Auto*, founded in 1900 and operating until the German Occupation, covered the fights of Battling Siki and Al Brown's bouts. It was followed later in the 1930s by a weekly magazine, *L'Écho des sports* (Benson, 2006: 240). The daily newspaper, *Paris-Soir*, also expanded both its sports and its entertainment coverage during the 1930s, including Brown's fights and Josephine Baker's performances.

Cocteau contacted all of these sources in addition to publishing his own independent poems and press releases about Brown. In spite of these successes, Cocteau's management was not taken seriously in boxing circles. Cocteau's principal English-speaking biographer Francis Steegmuller (1970: 434) argues that his obsession with Brown was a Jazz Age fantasy that had outlived its time. Claude Arnaud (2003: 509), another Cocteau biographer, describes Brown as a broken-down "has been" for whom Cocteau served as a guardian angel.

Still under Cocteau's management, by the end of 1938, Al once again retired from the boxing ring and started a shadowboxing act at the Cirque Médrano in Montmartre (which earlier had also been the subject of some of Toulouse-Lautrec's sketches) and afterwards on the road with the Cirque Amar. Brown's performance at the Cirque Médrano was preceded by transvestite trapeze artist Barbette who parodied accepted gender stereotypes in her act (Bloom, 2008: 192-193). Cocteau designed the stage sets and costumes for Brown's performance in which he wore white tails and a top hat and shadowboxed with himself. Later, a Basque beret was added as an accessory to his costume. When these theatrical productions folded, Brown briefly opened his own cabaret, the Kit-Kat Club, in Toulouse. Commenting on this episode in Brown's life, cultural critic Peter Bloom (2008: 193) states: "Through the illusionism of theatrical display, sexual and racial terms were exposed as constructed categories, fictionalized within the ropes of the boxing ring..." Another aspect of this illusionism was Brown's strategy of converting his flamboyant life outside of the ring into the main event, an event about which he had considerable misgivings. The very racism that Brown had sought to escape by leaving the United States resurfaced in the form of exoticized public performances for a French audience that parodied both his identity and his chosen profession. Under Cocteau's tutelage, Brown ended by theatrically simulating his own performance as a boxer.

The Final Score Card

Calculating Al Brown's final score card relies on creating a conceptual balance between his professional record and his private life. As a boxer, despite his efforts to avoid the obstacles of racism, exploitation, and poverty while he rose to fame in the United States, Brown felt compelled to pursue his boxing prime in France. There he found an atmosphere of tolerance for his personal lifestyle, but he remained an alienated and marginal loner, admired by many fans but close to few people. Throughout his career, Brown was exploited by unscrupulous managers and retained little agency over his professional trajectory. Even after dismissing Lumiansky, his first manager in Paris, Brown was plagued by a series of corrupt managers who attempted to use his talents for their own benefit. To a certain extent, Brown was complicit with these managers as long as their strategies led him to more visibility and fame.

Brown's personal situation was complicated by the uneven regulation of the fight game in the 1920s and 1930s, including murky title claims, shady ring behavior, weight class blurring and fraud, illicit betting practices, and excessive risk-taking activities on the part of athletes that marred the sport and led to the demise of many fighters (Keith Gilbert, 2005: 8-9). Yet, this sense of *anomie* was also part of boxing's dynamism and chaotic appeal. Confronted by a host of problems inside and outside of the ring, Brown persevered, not leaving France until the eve of the German Occupation in 1939 when many American expatriates departed. Contemporary twentieth-century boxers such as Muhammad Ali and Sugar Ray Leonard used Brown as a role model in the ring, studying his rapid footwork and punching style. Brown's story is one of heroic courage, success, and suffering in a sport that both made him a celebrity and robbed him of his fame and fortune.

Figure 2: Publicity program cover photograph for the Brown-Simendé fight held on April 15, 1931. Reproduced from the files of the Photothèque, #C.80.604.493, Musée de Homme, Paris.

Conclusions

By weaving together biography and social history as part of Brown's narrative and semiography, this discussion highlights the interrelation between rules of the game and the larger social context of boxing. The social environments in which fighters perform place constraints on their agency behind the scenes and in the ring. Boxing's social context also extends beyond the total configuration of the rules in the fight game to the unwritten politics of sports and the ongoing negotiation of management.

This semiography of Al Brown and the world of boxing emphasizes how the backstage contracts and the negotiations of management operate as cultural signifiers that shape the frontstage main event as a dramatic performance in powerful and subtle ways.[10] In turn, these interactions are filtered through the biographies of fighters as they use the world of combat sports to carve out a source of recognition for themselves. Al Brown, regarded by many sports fans as an undisputed iconic and popular champion whose official title was constantly challenged, is certainly no exception to the process of social and cultural shaping

---

[10] In his discussion of dramatic realization, Erving Goffman argues that the performance of prizefighters represents a case in which the public performance of a frontstage activity matches the completion of a backchannel task. He states: "These activities allow for so much dramatic self-expression that exemplary practitioners—whether real or fictional—become famous..." (Goffman, 1959: 31). However, this statement does not take into account the discrepancy between the frontstage and backstage performances that are involved in the scheduling, staging, and wagering on a fight.

in the fight game. Although Brown continued to box after his return to New York and Panama in 1939, he never again achieved the prowess of his golden years in France. In 1941, he made yet another comeback, winning the featherweight title of Panama from Leo Torres (Bryant, 1943: D5). During this period, Brown ran a nightclub and continued to be adored by local fans. Through his diverse activities in France in the 1920s and 1930s at a magical time, Al Brown reached the pinnacle of his professional performance and stood at the crossroads of art, science, entertainment, and boxing.

Appendix: Panama Al Brown's Fight Record*

1922			
19 Mar	José Moreno	Colón, Panama	W6
22 Apr	Montalbo Kid	Panama	KO2
21 May	Battling Miller	Panama	KO5
29 July	Ernie Rijkogel	Panama	KO4
8 Sep	Kid Pelkey	Panama	KO4
7 Oct	Jeff Clarke	Panama	KO6
9 Dec	Sailor Patchett	Panama	W15
1923			
11 Feb	Pedro Troncoso	Panama	W6
22 Aug	Johnny Breslin	New York, NY	D4
13 Oct	Bernie Hyams	NY	KO3
16 Nov	Jackie Harris	NY	W4
12 Dec	Willie Darcey	NY	W12
1924			
12 Apr	Willie Farley	NY	KO1
21 Apr	Tommy Murphy	NJ	ND10
3 May	Bobby Burns	NY	KO7
24 May	Joe Colletti	NY	W12
7 Jun	Willie LaMorte	NY	W12
28 June	Al Kaufman	NY	KO1
9 Aug	George McNally	NY	KO4
30 Aug	Joey Russell	NY	W10
8 Sep	Johnny Harko	NH	W10
13 Sep	Willie Salter	NY	KO1
27 Sep	Billy Marlowe	NY	W10
25 Oct	Frankie Ash	NY	KO1
11 Nov	Tommy Milton	NY	W15
6 Dec	Jimmy Russo	NY	L10
1925			
3 Jan	Jimmy Russo	NY	W10
19 Feb	Davey Abad	NY	W6
3 Mar	Willie LaMorte	NJ	ND10
11 June	Frankie Murray	PA	LDQ1
27 June	Dominick Petrone	NY	W6
22 Aug	Eddie Flank	NY	W10

21 Sep	Joey Ross	NJ	ND10
3 Oct	Bobby Green	NY	W10
16 Oct	Johnny Breslin	NY	W10
14 Nov	Marty Gold	NY	W10
12 Dec	Tommy Hughes	NY	W10
1926			
6 Feb	Dominick Petrone	NY	L10
20 Mar	Eddie O'Dowd	NY	W12
10 Apr	Willie O'Connell	NY	D6
23 Apr	Abe Goldstein	NY	L10
21 May	Teddy Silva	NY	KO3
5 June	Jacques Pettibone	NY	KO4
26 June	Billy Marlowe	NY	KO4
8 Jul	Pete Zivic	NY	W10
6 Aug	Harry Forbes	NY	W12
2 Sep	Joe Ryder	NY	WDQ4
9 Sep	Davey Adelman	NJ	ND10
10 Nov	Antoine Merlo	Paris	KO2
1 Dec	Roger Fabregues	France	KO1
14 Dec	Henri Scillie	France	D10
1927			
25 Jan	Edouard Mascart	France	KO5
8 Mar	George "Kid" Socks	France	KO5
2 Apr	Eugene Criqui	Paris	W10
10 May	Young Cyclone	France	W10
18 Oct	Albert Ryall	France	KO2
22 Nov	Henri Scillie	France	L12
10 Dec	André Routis	France	L10
1928			
23 Mar	Benny Schwartz	NY	W10
10 Apr	Eddie Nugent	OH	WDQ2
21 Jun	Billy Shaw	NY	KO1
13 Sep	Kid Francis	NY	W12
23 Oct	Alf "Kid" Patterden	Paris	D15
14 Nov	Johnny Cuthbert	France	D12
18 Dec	Harry Corbett	France	W15
1929			
9 Jan	Gustave Humery	France	KO1
24 Mar	Domenico Bernascon	Spain	W10
9 Apr	Joe Cadman	Paris	KO3
18 Jun	Gregorio Vidal	Long Island City, NY	W15
	Won World Championship		
3 Jul	Vic Burrone	NJ	W10
16 Jul	Vernon Cormier	ME	KO4

26 Jul	Battling Battalino	Hartford, CT	L10
28 Aug	Knud Larsen	Denmark	W12
1930			
25 Jan	Pinky Silverber	Cuba	W10
8 Feb	Johnny Erickson	New York, NY	WDQ4
	Retained Championship		
18 Feb	Johnny Canzoneri	PA	W10
14 Mar	Tommy Paul	NY	D6
15 Apr	KO Morgan	OH	WDQ7
21 Apr	Al Gillette	MA	KO9
5 Jun	Milton Cohen	CT	KO1
16 Jun	Johnny McCoy	MA	KO7
18 Jun	Benny Brostoff	NJ	KO2
24 Jun	Mickey Doyly	PA	W10
4 Jul	Calvin Reed	MD	KO4
23 Jul	Domenico Bernasconi	Brooklyn, NY	W10
29 Aug	Johnny Vacca	CT	KO3
4 Oct	Eugene Huat	Paris	W15
	Retained Championship		
22 Oct	José Girones	Spain	D10
8 Nov	Nic Bensa	France	W10
1931			
11 Feb	Nic Bensa	France	W10
9 Mar	Willie Farrell	England	KO3
31 Mar	Douglas Parker	England	KO11
13 Apr	Jack Garland	England	W15
15 Apr	Roger Simendé	France	KO3
23 Apr	Julian Veerbist	France	KO8
21 May	Teddy Baldock	England	KO12
15 Jun	Johnny Cuthbert	England	LDQ8
25 Aug	Pete Stastol	Montréal	W15
	Retained Championship		
21 Sep	Ginger Jones	Wales	KO9
27 Oct	Eugene Huat	Montréal	W15
	Retained Championship		
18 Nov	Art Chapdelai	Canada	KO7
15 Dec	Newsboy Brown	Los Angeles, CA	L10
1932			
4 Jan	Speedy Dado	Los Angeles, CA	L10
15 Mar	Golfball Bernard	MA	W10
18 May	Dominique DiCea	France	W10
28 May	Luigi Quadrini	Wales	KO5
31 May	François Machtens	France	W10
13 Jun	Nel Tarleton	England	D15
18 Jun	Eugene Huat	France	W10

25 Jun	Vittorio Tamagnini	Milan	L10
10 Jul	Kid Francis	Marseilles, France	W15
	Retained Championship		
17 Aug	Roland LeCuyer	Canada	KO6
19 Sep	Émile Pladner	Toronto	KO1
	Retained Championship		
26 Sep	Mose Butch	PA	W10
20 Oct	François Machtens	Belgium	W10
23 Oct	Nicolas Biquet	Belgium	W10
14 Nov	Émile Pladner	France	KO2
1 Dec	Dick Burke	England	W10
3 Dec	Henri Scillie	Belgium	D10
8 Dec	François Machtens	France	W10
1933			
9 Jan	Henri Poutrain	France	W10
5 Mar	Johnny Peters	England	W15
18 Mar	Dominico Bernasconi	Milan	W12
	Retained Championship		
30 Apr	Tommy Hyams	England	KO9
7 May	Arthur Boddington	England	KO4
13 May	Dick Burke	England	KO12
12 June	Dave Crowley	England	W10
3 Jul	Johnny King	London	W15
	Retained Championship		
1 Oct	Georges LePerson	Algiers	W10
12 Nov	Alfredo Magnolfi	Casablanca, Morocco	W10
9 Dec	Luigi Quadrini	Oran, Algieria	W10
1934			
19 Feb	Victor Perez	Paris	W15
	Retained Championship		
7 Apr	Maurice DuBois	Switzerland	KO2
16 Apr	Kid Francis	Paris	W15
	Retained Championship		
17 May	Gustave Humery	France	LDQ6
30 Jun	Johnny Edwards	Switzerland	L10
1 Nov	Victor Perez	Tunis	KO10
9 Dec	François Machtens	France	W10
24 Dec	Freddie Miller	France	L10
1935			
2 Mar	Henri Barras	France	W10
9 Mar	Gustave Ansini	France	D10
18 Mar	Baltazar Sangchili	Valencia, Spain	L10

12 Apr	Luigi Quadrini	Spain	W10
24 Apr	Javier Torres	Spain	KO2
1 Jun	Baltazar Sangchili Lost World Championship	Valencia, Spain	L15
11 Sep	Pete Sanstol	Oslo, Norway	L10
1937			
9 Sep	André Régis	France	KO1
23 Sep	Maurice Huguenin	France	KO3
8 Oct	Francis Augier	Switzerland	KO2
25 Nov	Joseph Decico	France	W10
22 Dec	Victor Perez	France	KO5
1938			
4 Mar	Baltazar Sangchili Purportedly Regained Championship	France	W15
13 Apr	Valentin (*Tintin*) Angelmann	France	KO8
1939			
22 Apr	Cristobal Jaramillo	NY	KO4
6 May	Mariano Arilla	NY	KO3
1941			
14 Jul	Leocadio Torres	Panama	KO6
26 Jul	Battling Nelson	Panama	KO4
7 Sep	Kid Fortune	Panama	KO2
26 Oct	Eduardo Carrasco	Panama	L10
1942			
8 Mar	Eduardo Carrasco	Panama	L10
30 Aug	Leocadio Torres	Panama	D15
4 Dec	Kid Fortune	Panama	W10

* *This fight record is quoted from*

http://members.tripod.com/newsbrown/panamastats.html, July 12, 2013.

References

Arnaud, C. (2003). *Jean Cocteau*. Paris: Éditions Gallimard.
Arroyo, E. (1982) *"Panama" Al Brown: 1902-1951*. Paris: Éditions Jean-Claude Lattès.
Benson, P (2006). Battling Siki: A Tale of Ring Fixes, Race, and Murder in the 1920s. Fayetteville: University of Arkansas Press.
Bloom, P. (2008). French Colonial Documentary: Mythologies of Humanitarianism. Minneapolis: University of Minnesota Press.
Brown, Panama Al, Website 2013

http://members.tripod.com/newsbrown/panama.html, July 12.
Brown, Panama Al, Official Fight Record 2013
    http://members.tripod.com/newsbrown/panamastats.html, July 12.
Bryant, V.M. (1943). "'Panama Al' Brown Quits Ring." Ohio: *Youngstown Vindicator* (April 11): D5.
Clifford, J. (1988). The Predicament of Culture: Twentieth-Century Ethnography, Literature, and Art. Cambridge, MA: Harvard University Press.
Cocteau, J. (1938) "Open Letter on Panama Al Brown." Quoted in Cocteau, Jean. *Poésie et journalisme.* Paris: Belfond, 1973.
Fanon, F. (1967). *Black Skin, White Masks.* Trans. Charles Lam Markmann. New York: Grove Weidenfeld. (Originally published as *Peau noire, masques blancs.* Paris: Éditions du Seuil, 1952.)
Fleischer, N. & S. E. Andre (1959). *A Pictorial History of Boxing.* London: Spring Books.
Gilbert, K. (2005). "Introduction." In Keith Gilbert ed., *Sexuality, Sport and the Culture of Risk*, pp. 7-16. Oxford: Meyer and Meyer Sport.
Goffman, E. (1959). The Presentation of Self in Everyday Life. New York: The Overlook Press.
Gorn, E.J. (2003). The Manly Art: Bare-Knuckle Prize Fighting in America. Ithaca, N.Y.: Cornell University Press.
Jackson, J.H. (2003) Making Jazz French: Music and Modern Life in Interwar Paris. Durham, NC: Duke University Press.
Johnston, A. (1947). Ten–And Out!: The Complete Story of the Prize Ring in America. New York: Ives Washburn.
Jules-Rosette, B. (1998) *Black Paris: African Writers Landscape.* Urbana: University of Illinois Press.
Baker J. (2007). in *Art and Life: The Icon and the Image.* Urbana: University of Illinois Press.
2010 *Never KO'd: The Al Brown Story.* La Jolla, CA: Unpublished manuscript.
Markovitz, Jonathan 2011 Racial Spectacles: Explorations in Media, Race, and Justice. London: Routledge, Taylor and Francis Group.
Meriden Record 1936 "Panama Al Brown on Comeback Trail." Paris: Associated Press (Jan. 24): 4.
Milwaukee Journal 1937 "Panama Al Wins." Paris: Associated Press (Sept. 10): 9.
1938 "Panama Al Brown Stops Frenchman." Paris: Associated Press (April 14): 6.
Photothèque of the Musée de l'Homme, Paris: Mission Dakar-Djibouti Collection, 1931.
Rosa, H. (2013). *Social Acceleration: A New Theory of Modernity.* Trans. Jonathan Trejo-Mathys. New York: Columbia University Press.
Sharpley-Whiting, & T. Denean (1999). Black Venus: Sexualized Savages, Primal Fears, and Primitive Narratives in French. Durham, NC: Duke University Press.
Steegmuller, F. (1970). *Cocteau: A Biography.* Boston: Little, Brown and Company.
Stovall, T. (1996). Paris Noir: African Americans in the City of Light. New York: Houghton Mifflin.

Wacquant, L. (2004). Body and Soul: Notebooks of an Apprentice Boxer. New York: Oxford University Press.
Williams, J. (1954). *TV Boxing Book*. New York: D. Van Nostrand Company.

Chapter 29

Mixed Martial Arts [MMA]: Social Interactions and Inclusion in the Brazilian Favelas

Orestes Manoel da Silva[1] & Carla Rocha Araujo[2]

Introduction

In mid-nineteenth century, Brazil sports were presented "as an incipient social practice, with low levels of conflict and demands, as well as a lack of secondary interests and minimal intervention by the state[3]" (Linhales, 1996, p. 204). However, over time this reality began to change and sports have become an activity with systems of expanded interests, incorporating a variety of actors and conflicts (Giovanni, 1995; Rojek, 1995; Veblen, 1983), subject to increasingly wider commitments, shifting from an activity with an end in itself to an effective instrument with external purposes.

Currently, sports are firmly inserted in society; it is considered a socio-cultural phenomenon and it is regarded as a social right. According to Article 217 of the Brazilian Constitution, "the State shall foster the practice of formal and informal sports, as a right to all[4]"(Brasil, 1988). Despite being a duty of the State we note that the promotion of sports does not occur solely through government agencies. Sports policies for children and adolescents have been the goal of the

---

[1] Researcher at Federal University of Rio de Janeiro at Sports Law (FND-UFRJ), Researcher at Laboratory studies of Urban Social Culture and Member of the Olympic Committee Games at OAB (Order the Attorneys of Brazil).
[2] Researcher at University Gama Filho (Brazil) and PhD Student at Univerity of Porto - Faculty of Sport (Portugal)
[3] Translate to English by the authors: "como prática social incipiente, com baixos níveis de conflito e de demandas, ausência de interesses secundários e pouca intervenção por parte do Estado"
[4] Translate to English by the authors: "é dever do Estado fomentar práticas esportivas formais e não formais, como direito de todos"

public, private and third sector – ONG's (Bretãs, 2007; Guedes & al., 2006; Melo, 2004). Therefore, numerous projects arise throughout the country in order to promote sports activities for children and youth outside of school hours through different initiatives. These initiatives, called "socio-sports projects", are gaining prominence in the media and society (Melo, 2004, 2005). For a better understanding of these initiatives, it is necessary to investigate what has been proposed - through documents and the perspective of managers, teachers and volunteers – as well as what has been searched for children, teenagers and their keepers.

There are many reasons for children and teenagers to practice a particular physical activity and sports, and sociability is one of the motives. Young people urge to belong to a certain group and this may be a main factor to get involved with sports. For Weinberg & Gould (2001) children embrace sports because of it's an opportunity for personal relationships and fostering new friendships. Sociability, friendship and capability are rules that manage social acceptance and the development of essential skills in order to prepare children and teenagers to grow adequately by preparing them for adulthood. According to Farinatti (1995), children are exposed to many opportunities for social contact through interaction, which contributes to their development. Therefore, being with friends, belong to a group or making new friendships, has an important role in their psychological, moral and ethical development.

Within the scope of social sporting projects, the actions that have been disseminated in society have been consolidated in a bottom up movement, that is, these projects are often established based on the actions of individuals, groups and organizations that mobilize around a common goal. The reverse movement, from top to bottom, the targeted involvement of the government is also present, considering projects such as: *Boxe Vidigal* of the *Todos na Luta* Institute, in the Vidigal community and the *Luta pela Paz* Sports Center, in the Maré community. However, the number of actions that have been taking place from the bottom up in Brazil appears to be a typical phenomenon of the late twentieth and early twenty-first century that deserves the attention of academia.

MMA: Mixed Martial Arts

MMA is a fighting activity where athletes don't need to follow a specific martial art, and therefore the 'technical' name is Mixed Martial Arts. This sport allows the use of any techniques or blow from several martial arts such as *boxing*, *jiu-jitsu*, *karate*, *judo*, *muay thai*, among others. A good fighter has control of most of the key martial arts blows and knows how to use them at the right time (Brandão, 2011)

The first record of a sport such as MMA dates back to Greece in 648 BC. Pankration, a combination of two Greek words, *pan* (meaning all or several) and *kratos* (meaning strength), was a fusion of boxing and wrestling. The decline of Pankration overlapped with the rise of the Roman Empire. Mixed fighting lost popularity to sports like boxing and wrestling, which were more widespread in the West.

At the end of 1800 already MMA events occurred. Fighters representing a huge variety of styles, including several wrestlers, Greco-Roman wrestlers and many other forms of martial arts would square off in competitions and games throughout Europe. The first fight between a great boxer and a wrestler in modern times took place in 1887 when John L. Sullivan, the world heavyweight boxing champion at the time, entered the ring to face his Greco-Roman wrestling coach William Muldoon and was knocked out in two minutes. The next fight occurred in the 1890s when the future heavyweight boxer champion Bob Fitzsimmons faced champion Greco-Roman wrestler Ernest Roeber.

Another early example of MMA is the martial arts called *Bartitsu*, founded in London in 1899. This was the first known martial art to combine Asian and European styles and the one that organized events similar to modern MMA throughout England, by putting European and Japanese champions against players of various European wrestling styles.

In 1925, the fights that mixed different martial arts returned to the world stage thanks to a Brazilian family. The history of modern MMA is closely linked to the history of the Gracie family. Carlos Gracie learned to fight judo with Mitsuyo Maeda, a Japanese instructor who lived in the same region. Later, Carlos taught the sport to his brothers and gradually adapted judo rules and moves, leading to the development of Brazilian jiu-jitsu.

The name MMA became popular due to Rick Blume, president of Battlecade[5] in 1995. Since then this sport became hugely popular because of Pay Per View and the rivalry between Boxing and Professional Wrestling.

MMA competitions have undergone significant changes since the first Ultimate Fighting Championship (UFC) in 1993, notably with the adoption of the Unified Rules of Mixed Martial Arts. The overall risk of injuries in MMA is now comparable to other sports combat, including boxing.

UFC is a Brazilian-origin mixed martial arts organization currently managed by Zuffa Entertainment and headed by the American Dana White. Fighters of this sport practice different martial arts such as jiu-jitsu, boxing, Olympic wrestling, Thai boxing and karate, among others.

MMA is dangerous and its competitors are exposed to serious risks of injury every time they step into the Octagon[6]. As a result, MMA fighters receive more care and precautions than other athletes in most sports. With supervised fights, magnetic resonance before and after fights, four doctors close to the Octagon, two ambulances for emergencies and mandatory testing for steroids. These organizations have led to a higher level of safety and quality in sports.

UFC was an idea of Rorion Gracie as a way to promote and spread jiu-jitsu in United States. His intention was to show jiu-jitsu as a dominant martial art and attract the attention of new pupils. The purpose was achieved successfully and Royce Gracie won three of UFC four first editions.

UFC had some successful at the beginning but many problems emerged in subsequent editions that conducted to the crash of the organization. The final UFC 4 match, exceeded the time allotted for pay-per-view, which prevented those who bought to watch the end of the fight between Royce Gracie and Dan Severn. Royce won after more than 15 minutes of uninterrupted combat. Furthermore, the

---

[5] Part of General Media International and *Penthouse* editor.
[6] Designed by Rorion Gracie based on gladiator combats. It is 9 meters across and 1.80 meters in height. The angles prevent fighters from being stuck in a corner without the possibility of escaping.

brutality of the initial UFC fights generated a negative reaction from some sectors of US society, which led to the outright banning of the event is some states. UFC became a sport of the ghetto, supported primarily by fans that exchanged information and fight videos in certain online forums.

After a long battle for approval and at the brink of bankruptcy, in 2011 the Semaphore Group met with Station Casino executives, Frank and Lorenzo Fertitta and boxing promoter Dana White. A month later, January 2001, the Fertittas and Dana White bought UFC for US$ 2 million and created Zuffa, the championship's patent controlling company. With tie connections with Nevada Athletic Commission (in which Lorenzo Fertitta had been a member), Zuffa secured approval to hold fights in Nevada in 2001. Shortly thereafter, in Ultimate 33, the competition returned to American pay-per-view cable television.

Ultimate continued to grow in popularity after Zuffa purchased it, due to heavy advertising, major sponsorships, pay-per-view and DVD sales. With major events in famous places like the Trump Taj Mahal Casino and MGM Grand Arena and increased pay-per-view sales, Ultimate landed its first television deal with Fox Sports and with The Best Damn Sport Show, which held the first mixed martial arts fight on American cable television, in June 2002, in Ultimate 37 (Vitor Belfort versus Chuck Liddell). Soon after, Feature Story News began broadcasting the best moments of the fights. In Ultimate 40, pay-per-view purchases yielded US$ 978,150 in a lineup that had the fight between Tito Ortiz and Ken Shamrock as its main event. Despite the success, Ultimate was still in debt and, in 2004, Zuffa had lost US$ 78.5 million with the purchase. Currently, UFC is the biggest MMA Company in the world and its market value is around US$ 1 million dollars.

MMA bouts are held in the Octagon. The Octagon was designed by Rorion Gracie and is based on gladiator combats. It is 9 meters across and 1.8 meters in height to ensure the safety of the fighters. Its angles prevent fighters from being stuck in a corner without the possibility of escape. In the Octagon, none of the martial arts has an advantage.

Title fights are divided in five rounds and non-title fights in three. Each round lasts five minutes and the fighter rests for a minute after each one. The round-by-round score takes place as follows: 10 - 10: even; 10 - 09: slight advantage; 10 - 08: domination and 10 - 07: total domination. The evaluation criteria are relative to the performance of the fighters on each round. MMA wins are by KO, Submission and Judges' Decision.

UFC is currently divided into eight categories, according to the weights of the fighters: Flyweight over 52.1 kg and under 56.6 kg; Bantamweight between 56.6 kg and 61.2 kg; Featherweight between 61.2 kg and 65.7 kg; Lightweight above 65.7 kg to 70.3 kg; Welterweight between 70.3 kg and 77.1 kg; Middleweight between 77.1 kg and 83.9 kg; Light Heavyweight fighters between 83.9 and 92.9 kg and Heavyweight from 92.9 kg to 120.2 kg (Mancilha, 2012).

In MMA events, fighters must use equipment such as mouth guards, gloves, jockstrap, shorts and remain barefoot. Prohibited areas are the hair, eyes, back of the neck, cervical spine and genitals. Kicks, stomps and knees to the head of a grounded opponent are considered illegal blows. Throwing an opponent out of the Octagon, 12-to-6 elbow strikes, pile driving, bites and pinches are also prohibited.

The most popular Brazilian MMA fighters are Anderson Silva (Middleweight), Maurício Shogun (Light Heavyweight), Lyoto Machida (Light Heavyweight), José Aldo (Featherweight), Rodrigo Minotauro (Heavyweight) Vitor Belfort (Welterweight), Júnior Cigano (Heavyweight) and Rogério Minotouro (Light Heavyweight).

The striking techniques used in MMA are punches, kicks, knee blows, elbows blows and grappling techniques are clinches, submissions, and takedowns, etc. Since MMA has no international regulatory body, rules may differ between organizations. While the legality of elbow blows, stomps and others may vary, there is a universal ban on the use of "techniques" such as biting, groin strikes, eye gouging, hair pulling, blows to the back of the neck and spine, holding the ropes/fence and pulling small joints.

Today fighters must train a variety of styles to counterattack the moves of the opponent and to continue to be effective throughout the fight. For example, a stand-up fighter, or a fighter who prefers to fight standing up, will have few opportunities to use his/her skills against a fighter who is specialized in submissions and who has good takedowns[7]. Many traditional disciplines remain popular as a way for a fighter to improve aspects of his/her game.

Despite media resistance in disseminating this sport, MMA is undergoing a real transformation and is entering a new phase in Brazil, mainly driven by three factors, which are the professionalization of the sport, the exponential growth of the fan base and the success of Brazilians fighters abroad. We observed that the media turns UFC fighters into a new type of worker, because they meet advertising mechanisms. Therefore, it is clear that the popularity of UFC fighters is directly linked to their relationship with the media and public passion. This passion generates returns for media outlets and advertisers that go beyond the financial scope. Proof of this is bank BMG, which sponsors the fighter Vitor Belfort, the vice-president of the bank says that the return on investment in football is on average five times the investment in marketing, while Vitor Belfort has a rate of return of nine times. UFC is tantamount to profitability in the form of concepts such as innovation, rejuvenation, dynamism and vigor to the sponsoring companies (Cabral, 2012).

Moreover, the participation of national idols who fight in the UFC on TV shows is fiercely disputed by broadcasters, because the mere presence of a fighter, especially Anderson Silva, increases ratings.

MMA is currently being disputed on every continent. The countries providing the most fighters are the US, Brazil, Canada, UK, Japan and Sweden.

UFC officially announced its first ranking of the best fighters in the competition. The ranking is divided into weight categories. Brazil has a representative in all of them, with 11 fighters among the top 10 in their category. In the last update on 07/09/2013, Jon Jones overtook the first spot left by Anderson and now leads in the category of best athlete of all weight classes, the so-called pound-for-pound: 1st Jon Jones (USA), 2nd Georges St-Pierre (Canada); 3rd Anderson Silva (Brazil); 4th José Aldo (Brazil); 5th Benson Henderson (USA);

---

[7] Takedowns – the deliberate act of taking the opponent down in martial arts and combat sports.

6th Cain Velasquez (USA); 7th Demetrious Johnson (USA); 8th Renan Barão (Brazil); 9th Dominick Cruz (USA); 10th Chris Weidman (USA).

Among the Brazilian fighters, Anderson is a phenomenon, both inside and outside the UFC octagon. He managed to take MMA to a level never before seen in Brazil. Inside the Octagon, he has an aggressive fighting style and a lot of movement, which makes him one of the most admired UFC fighters. Creative inside the Octagon, 'Spider' is able to perform at a high standard when striking and on the ground and provokes his opponent with feints. Currently, the bouts of the Middleweight champion are hardly predictable: it is unclear whether it will end in a knockout, submission or by points. When up against opponents in the Ultimate Fighting Championship, the Brazilian fighter often dances around to confuse rivals and dodge blows. Anderson Silva's ability to dodge is compared to that of Muhammad Ali (regarded by many as the biggest name in boxing history) and the Brazilian fighter is currently considered the most important name in MMA. Anderson Silva admires and imitates his American role model. This type of movement allows him to put down his guard, as was seen in the bouts against Forrest Griffin, Demian Maia and Yushin Okami. Outside the Octagon he depicts an image that contradicts other MMA fighters, he is more of a "family man", charismatic, cheerful, a father of five and has an unusual voice that he himself jokes about. Discreet in his personal life, 'Spider' enjoys appearing in public alongside his children who actively participate in his UFC career by entering the Octagon with the champion and even acting as sparring partners.

The Middleweight champion of the world's biggest MMA event, Anderson Silva recently entered into three major sponsorship contracts with Sport Club Corinthians Paulista, Multinacional Nike and fast food chain Burger King, in addition to commercials for automaker Ford and Budweiser (Rudnick, 2011).

In Brazil, UFC events are broadcast live via pay-per-view on the Combat channel and were rebroadcast on the open access TV channel RedeTV from 2009 to 2011. On August 28th, 2011, UFC Rio was broadcast live on Brazilian open access TV RedeTV. The first broadcast by Rede Globo took place on November 12th, 2011. It will be the holder of the broadcasting rights until 2012, which includes all competitions in Brazil and three combats abroad.

It is important to remember that much has changed in MMA since 1998, when UFC first came to São Paulo. Over the past 15 years, it has become a billion dollar company that draws fans to its events around the world. The most important change, despite the prejudice, has been the participation of women. On December 6th, 2012, the American fighter Ronda Rousey made MMA history by becoming the first female UFC champion and the first female fight in the history of the franchise was announced between Rousey and Liz Carmouche, on February 23th, the main event of UFC 157 (Stagliorio, 2013).

The first female fight in the UFC had to overcome the resistance of the organization's president, Dana White. However, he took advantage of the hype around Rousey and initiated events with women. Besides the two athletes who fought that tonight, UFC has four other female fighters: Alexis Davis, Cat Zingano, Miesha Tate and Sara McMann. Brazil has two representatives in the UFC, the first Brazilian female fighter hired was Amanda Nunes, followed by Jéssica Andrade who replaced Miesha Tate in the UFC held on July 27th, in Seattle – USA (Passos, 2013).

With so many changes in MMA and the rise of its popularity, we cannot ignore the official launch of the Brazilian MMA Confederation - CBMMA, in March of 2011 in São Paulo, which was attended by the Minister of Sports Aldo Rebelo, the State Secretary of Sports José Benedito Pereira Fernandes and the Municipal Secretary of Sports Bebetto Haddad. Its objective is to act in a very well planned manner in order to minimize mistakes and work toward the development of the sport. To do so, it has established partnerships with the Ministry of Sports, the Department of Sports of the Municipality of São Paulo, the Chamber of Deputies, the Legislative Assembly, FILA, CBLA, FEPALO, SEADESP, IDT-CEMA, ABIH-SP and many others, which will contribute to the achievement of all its objectives. Among them, the establishment of the Brazilian MMA Ranking so that athletes can evolve into professional fighters and become eligible to participate in major tournaments, leagues and national and international competitions, promoting the growth of the sport in Brazil. In addition to holding professional and amateur MMA championships in Brazil with selection taking place at the state championships organized by the federations, which currently number 25 in the country among the 26 Brazilian states and the Federal District.

Image Rights of the MMA Professional

Due to the possibility of making images available, it is understood that they are legally marketed, both by the will of the holder, as well as through the intrinsic necessity of his/her condition and/or commercial interests.

The appreciation of the commercial image of the athlete is not something new. This phenomenon precedes the most sophisticated television broadcasts, when the narrative transmitted on the radio led to the exposure of certain athletes who stood out before an audience. With advances in technology and facilities to reproduce images of athletes, there was a significant appreciation of the image, which created a lucrative market.

Take for example the fighter Anderson Silva who, after his MMA popularity, become the first athlete to sign with 9INE (footballer Ronaldo's, the phenomenon, Sports Marketing Agency), of the WPP communications group and of entrepreneur Marcus Buaiz. In addition, Anderson Silva signed a six-month contract with Burger King and with the Ford campaign. The license agreement for use of the image is ideal for disseminating the athlete because the image is not the object of the contract, but its license for the use.

With regard to the contractual issue, Ambiel & Santos Junior (2002) article, in a translation of Paul Roubier book, state that the license simply grants the right of exploring the image, while the right itself remains in the hands of its holder.

Bittar (1995) notes that contracts should specify the purpose, conditions of use, time, term and other circumstances that make up the content of the business interpreting it restrictively, i.e., remaining the other uses not expressly stated as an asset of the licensor. These contracts may not cause the curtailment of individual freedom or extended sacrifice of their celebrity status and the agreement that provides such provision will be nullified as a clause of protest.

With regard to consent and its extent, Ezabella (2006) explains that the holder of the image has the power to choose when and how the image will appear in public whether on billboards or newspapers, if there is a provision in the agreement for its use. It is understood that not only unauthorized uses are unlawful, but so are those that exceed the limits specified in the contract.

The appreciation of the professional athletes' image and often their personification by the public as a "hero" makes them recipients of very attractive economic investments, as well as their sponsors and employer. Therefore, their image can be used to garner sponsors, sell shirts of the sport they are engaged in, toys, promote sporting events through television commercials, magazines ads and sports websites.

The license agreement for use of the image, entered into between the sporting organization and the athlete will be executed in writing, containing expiration date, compensation, purpose, practical use, etc. In addition, since it is an exclusive right, the athlete may terminate it at any time, and civil courts will be in charge of examining the damages caused by a breach of contract.

In sports, the license agreement for use of the image may suffer two violations: lack of consent and unauthorized use, and in this regard, there are two appellate decisions of the Supreme Court of Justice (STJ), presented by Minister Sálvio Figueiredo Teixeira:

> "**I** – Image rights contain a double content: moral, because of right of personality; proprietary, because based on the principle that lawfully no unjust enrichment shall take place at the expense of others" (v. appellate decision of 02.23.99, v.u. Fourth Panel of the RSP 74473/RJ); and
>
> "**I** – Image rights constitute an exclusive right of personality, protecting the right of the individual to oppose the dissemination of this image, in order to protect his/her private life".
>
> **II** - (Not available at this time)
>
> **III** – The use of a citizen's image for economic purposes, without his/her proper authorization, constitutes unjust enrichment and is subject to damages.
>
> **IV** – When dealing with image rights, the obligation to demonstrate the improper use of the exclusive right does not need to contemplate proof of damages. In other words, the damage is the improper use of the image for lucrative purposes, without the need to demonstrate material or moral damage". (appellate decision of 10.25.99, v.u. Fourth Panel of the RESP45305/SP).

Please Note that the above decisions confirm the violations to which the image is subject, and such violations may be found in sports contracts.

Socially Oriented Sports Projects in Poor Communities

Considering that sports in contemporary society are a significant strategy of social transformation, besides fulfilling human yearnings, a broader and grounded perspective analysis is needed, where favoring and ratification of access through existing legal diplomas help the process of dissemination and democratization, protecting the rights guaranteed to Brazilians citizens. However, other benefits can be attributed to sports such as access to other human rights, mainly through the interaction with the educational process and health promotion, as well as emerging as a basic component of citizenship, which is also a right guaranteed by Article 1 of the CRF of 1988 and Article 5 of the ECA – Children's and Adolescent's Statute (Machado & Silva, 2013)

The relation between sports and low-income communities is evident. According to Murad (2007), the sports-related activities performed in these communities, which he calls "sports schools", have achieved significant results in the management of social violence rates. Murad (2007) also states that such sports initiatives are accepted, valued and encouraged by all recognized international bodies.

According to Figueiredo (2002), the physical education professional connected to social sciences, attempts to achieve changes in society through its practice, seeking to correlate the practice of sports with social transformation. It is important for the pursuit of this improvement to occur inside the community. Tubino & al (2007) says that the "International Charter of Physical Education and Sport of UNESCO (2006), written in 1978 and circulated in 1979, established the right to sports and physical activities" (p. 36). The demand for these rights formed new sports concepts, such as educative sports (educational sports) and leisure sports (participation sports).

With the right to access sports activities, the Sport for All movement arises, which, according to this authors (Tubino et al., 2007) is considered an example of participation sports, allowing universal access regardless of people's financial condition or biotype. According to Gomes & Constantino (2005), the initiative of the movement is a set of sports activities whose objective, in different angles, is the socialization and physical fitness of practitioners.

DaCosta (2007) sees Sport for All as a movement that provides socialization and physical fitness, aimed at transforming highly competitive and school sports into mass community sports, including leisure, health, community development, social inclusion, civility, humanization of cities, appreciation of nature, the practice of sports, the practice of organized sports and enhancement of community service. Furthermore, the term "contemporary sports" comes up, which, according to Tubino (2003), is a socio-cultural phenomenon whose practice is considered a universal right and that highlights the development of values such as solidarity, brotherhood and cooperation that are necessary values for human society. Gomes & Constantino (2005) define Sports Projects for Social Inclusion as systematic and ongoing professional intervention projects, excluding those that only perform sporadic activities, such as games or tournaments, summer camps, living streets, among others.

In several Brazilian cities, some communities are building projects with MMA geared towards social inclusion. Among them, we can highlight the Usina Citizenship Project in effect for 16 years in the city of Rio de Janeiro, and on August 18th, 2011, the Manguinhos Refinery Training Center was inaugurated, coordinated by former fighter Pedro Rizzo. The Manguinhos MMA Training Center has an official-sized octagon and accommodation for athletes to rest between workouts and to house them during their stay in Rio de Janeiro (Hackradt, 2011).

Rizzo supervises 225 young people who practice various fighting styles: judo, jiu jitsu, boxing, capoeira, muay thai and wrestling. Sports are essential to mold adults who are responsible, determined and committed to the welfare of society.

In Rio Grande do Sul, in the city of Novo Hamburgo, the Sports and Culture Association created the MMA Golden Fighters event. The event was set up to encourage amateur and professional sports, and especially to support social projects at the municipal level.

Implemented by various institutions of the Government of Bahia, the Pact for Life Program has former world heavyweight champion Junior Cigano as one of the main star. The objective of the program is to help reduce the levels of violence in the region, focusing on the reduction of crimes against life and property. One of the strongest work fronts of the program is confronting crack and other drugs, with the expansion of the Psychosocial Care Centers network, prevention and detoxification of patients, as well as integrated actions in the areas of sports, employment and education.

Former TUF Brazil fighter Wagner Galeto, whose last fight took place at UFC 147 in Belo Horizonte, concerned with social causes gives an example of conscience and fair play by heading a project against drugs in partnership with the sports brand Rudel Sports that promotes the Fight Against Drugs project. The project is carried out at the *Amigos da Vida* (Friends of Life Association), where the fighter is a member and promotes Muay Thai and MMA classes, as well as other activities with regulars and visitors in order to use the sport in the fight against drugs and promote the exchange of experiences and success stories.

Evangelista Cyborg began his martial arts career in 1996 when he made his first MMA fight debut. A black belt in muay thai, kickboxing, jiu-jitsu and wrestling, Cyborg has fought in international MMA tournaments, such as Pride (Japan) and Strikeforce (United States). The fighter opened an MMA training center in the city of Uberlândia (Minas Gerais), where he intends to develop social projects. In addition to developing athletes, the fighter says he wants to help the personal development of young people and sees the sport as the best path to do so.

The objectives of these projects are the physical, moral and social development of children and adolescents in poor communities, transmitting notions of citizenship and expectations of future professions so that project participants become participative, responsible and productive adults. Training MMA leads to the physical, moral, emotional, social and cognitive development of the individual by requiring the practitioner to exercise self-control, respect for rules and the opponent, discipline, responsibility in training sessions and live a well-regulated life, without vices and bad habits. Undeniably, as exposed by Melo (2005), sports training has the power to integrate, harmonize, provide a sense of belonging and unite people. Melo (2005) goes on to say that, sports alone cannot solve all social problems, but they can surely contribute to citizenship and social inclusion in the improvement of social indicators. The author states that "few social phenomena are able to exercise so much social inclusion as sports" (p.67).

The Importance of MMA in Brazil and its Involvement in Social Causes

UFC is one of the major MMA events in the world. To be in the ring and make the night even more interesting, many fighters earn hundreds of thousands of dollars either by winning or losing in the Octagon. The money given to each one depends on several factors, but the most relevant is the importance of the fight for the event. Monetary values would surely lead anyone to want to enter the ring and start swinging – or even get beat up!

The Ultimate Fighting Championship holds an average of 30 events a year. To pair off so many fights, the UFC has a large number of fighters, which includes boxing, wrestling, Muay Thai, Jiu-Jitsu and Judo fighters, as well as other styles. UFC currently has over 340 fighters divided across 8 divisions. Until the end of 2012, Brazil had dominated half of the UFC weight classes with Anderson Silva (84kg category), José Aldo (66kg), Junior Cigano (above 93kg) and Renan Barão (61kg). However, Cigano lost the title to Cain Velasquez at UFC 155 in December 2012 and Anderson lost the Middleweight belt at UFC 162 in July 2013.

According to the website MMA Brasil, there are 60 Brazilian fighters in the UFC roster. Among them, 8 held a UFC belt: Murilo Bustamante (Middleweight, UFC 36 only one successful title defense); Vitor Belfort (Light Heavyweight, UFC 46); Anderson Silva (Middleweight, UFC 64 with 9 successful title defenses as of August 2011); Rodrigo Minotauro (Heavyweight (interim), UFC 81); Lyoto Machida (Light Heavyweight, UFC 98 with one successful title defense); Maurício Shogun (Light Heavyweight, UFC 113); José Aldo (Featherweight, three successful title defenses as of January 2012) and Junior Cigano (Heavyweight, UFC On FOX 1 with one successful title defense as of May 2012). Other Brazilians won UFC tournaments such as Royce Gracie (UFC 1, UFC 2 and UFC 4), Marco Ruas (UFC 7) and Vitor Belfort (UFC 12).

The image of a successful athlete exerts great influence on the population. With this in mind, state governments and municipalities see the opportunity of launching projects and campaigns in poor communities aimed at combating violence through MMA fighters. Proof of this is the project launched by the Governor of Rio de Janeiro, Sérgio Cabral, in 2009. An agreement between the government and Bitetti Combat, which supports the project for poor communities called "Fight for Pacification" (Cruz, 2009) until 2016. In addition, in May 2013, the state government of São Paulo joined the "Count to 10 Campaign", launched by the National Council of the Prosecution Office, which aims to encourage a culture of tolerance on a day-to-day basis to prevent homicides caused by traffic altercations and misunderstandings between neighbors and family members. The São Paulo state government prepared 10,000 campaign ads containing messages of peace of professional athletes, which includes UFC fighter Anderson Silva and judo Olympic champions Sarah Menezes and Leandro Guilheiro. Moreover, ads will be aired on TV and a jingle on the radio (S. Fernandes, 2013).

Individually, MMA fighters are opening spaces to serve the residents of poor communities in several states in Brazil. When he was officially presented as an athlete of Corinthians, in September of 2011, Anderson Silva said his goal was to change the heroes of Brazil by making fighters role models for society. "UFC has a really cool project, which is to hold events at military bases, a social work to bring the sport to another atmosphere. Remove it from violence. War. We have the power to change the world and we are doing it" (B. Fernandes, 2011).

In October 2011, the former champion inaugurated the Anderson Silva Training Center at Corinthians, which among its activities serves children and young people who are interested in becoming part of the social project of the center. The idea of the club is that between 100 and 120 children and adolescents aged from 7 to 15 begin to fight and learn everything that martial arts have to offer, such as concentration and respect (Padeiro, 2011).

MMA fighters Rodrigo Minotauro and Rogério Minotouro, of the *Irmãos Nogueira* Institute, are going to set up a social project for poor children in the town of Uberlândia, in Curitiba. The "Team Nogueira" project, which has been present in Rio de Janeiro and Salvador for 5 years, gets its first edition in Paraná. It is a grassroots social project aimed at developing champions. In weekly classes children will learn various martial arts and, through them, discipline, conduct and determination. In Rio de Janeiro, the project reaches seven poor communities, including the Alemão complex and Manguinhos. Altogether, the project reaches 1,050 children aged from 4 to 17. Besides the social project, the Nogueira brothers have three gyms in the United States, two in Europe, in Switzerland and Japan. In early August, the duo opened the first Team Nogueira gym in Curitiba, in the Água Verde community (Kern, 2012).

The first Fighting Center in Amazonas state, the Diego Trindade Fighting Center, opened in March 2013. The event was attended by the reigning MMA world featherweight champion, José Aldo and his trainer André Pederneiras. According to the Municipal Department for Sports, Recreation and Youth, the project will include boxing, capoeira, judo, jiu-jitsu and wrestling. Children in the project are accompanied by a social worker, for monitoring and completion of a registration with the Secretaria de Assistência Social e Direitos Humanos (Department of Social Welfare and Human Rights) to assess the needs of the families and to provide assistance such as milk donations, enrollment in *Bolsa Família* (a social welfare government program), among others (Victor, 2013).

Fighter Wanderlei Silva, one of the world's biggest MMA legends and owner of the Wand Fight Team gym, owner of a large training warehouse near the famous casino strip in Las Vegas, says he wants to set up a gym in Brazil of the same size as the American one and offer free classes. He wants to provide a space where poor students can train, shower, eat and return home. Wanderlei believes that "Education is Sport", but practicing Sports is expensive because you have to pay for transportation, equipment, food, etc., and as a result, many athletes end up quitting. Wanderlei said he received this support and now wishes to return the favor by helping other young people. He hopes to use the knowledge he has acquired and the friends he has made around the world to raise funds to create his social project. Wanderlei states that it is difficult to create a social project in Brazil because the public views such projects and NGOs negatively: the majority believes that such initiatives are designed to misallocate funds and not to help communities in need. However, he makes it clear that although he has enough money to live, he cannot use this money to do social work. He wants to use the incentives prescribed by law to enable the creation of this project with a good structure and get many people out of poverty.

Conclusions

The socially oriented sports projects are regarded as a space that protects children and adolescents from drug abuse, drug dealing and violence. In addition to protecting children and adolescents from certain ailments, it is believed that sports projects also protect such youth from the harsh reality that many experience in their homes, since such youth live in less than ideal conditions and are constantly exposed to violence, child labor, crime, drug dealing and drug abuse. These programs provide different types of sports education, reinforce classroom content, and foster the engagement of participants. One of the main objectives of the project is to promote behavioral improvements in children and adolescents. Among all the activities developed in social projects, sports stand out as a tool that can promote positive socialization through the incorporation of values in the construction of citizenship, besides attracting participants.

Since its inception, MMA has been strongly related to the concept of putting on a show. MMA presentations have a set of technological apparatus designed to provide the spectator with a lively experience of the show (Zorzanelli, 2008). Throughout all stages of the MMA life, we noted a strong tendency to make adaptations of all kinds in order to satisfy the needs of a larger number of people. It ceased to be a dispute between martial arts and turned into its own sport, where the main objective is combining sports technique for the show. Rules were designed to ensure physical integrity and prevent the risk of death so as not to harm the most important values of society: the right to life.

MMA is the fastest growing sport in the world and has captured fans of all ages, irrespective of social class, race, religion or nationality. Currently, it is no longer ostracized by mainstream media, which used to associate it with violence. It is still a new sport that is being consolidated in Brazil. The hiring of world-class athletes by UFC, such as Anderson Silva, José Aldo, Junior Cigano, Wanderlei Silva, Vitor Belfort and others, led to the opportunity of negotiating the publicity of their image in order to raise funds, sell products and promote the UFC brand in the domestic and international markets.

The major MMA stars that earn high salaries in a single combat and even sign multi-million dollar advertising contracts have become major references for poor people who dream of escaping poverty. Due to their inability of afford a gym where they could train, residents of poor communities look for social projects in order to train MMA. The projects do not function as a promise to turn participants into superstars hired by the UFC, but they promote the inclusion of these citizens who have been forgotten by the government. Becoming a major star of the octagon is possible, ultimately depending on the student's talent and perseverance.

It is believed that the Training Centers maintained by big clubs such as Corinthians develop fighters. Brazil has the potential of doing so, because Brazilians are natural fighters. As stated by Anderson Silva, his goal is to change the heroes of Brazil by making fighters role models of society. To do so, we need to train more MMA champions who are willing to fight to change the history of poverty and minimize the social differences between the world of comfort and the world of slums.

References

Ambiel, C. E., & W.G.S. Junior (2002). Relação entre contrato de trabalho e contrato de licença de uso de imagem. . *Revista Instituto Brasileiro de Direito Desportivo, 1*.

Bittar, C. A. (1995). *Os direitos da personalidade*. Rio de Janeiro: Forense Universitária.

Brandão, L. (2011). Tudo Sobre MMA, 21 September 2011, from http://revistaup.com/2011/07/tudo-sobre-mma/

Brasil. (1988). *Constituição da República Federativa do Brasil: promulgada em 5 de outubro de 1988*. Brasília: Senado Retrieved from http://www.senado.gov.br.

Bretãs, A. (2007). Onde mora o perigo? Discutindo uma suposta relação entre ociosidade, pobreza e criminalidade. *Educação, esporte e lazer, 9*.

Cabral, M. (2012). BMG joga na retranca: Principal patrocinador do futebol brasileiro, o banco mineiro vai reduzir quase pela metade o investimento nos clubes. Retrieved 28th July 2013, from http://www.istoedinheiro.com.br/noticias/78258_BMG+JOGA+NA+RE TRANCA

Cruz, E. (2009). Governador do Rio vira padrinho do MMA., 30th June 2013, from http://gustavonoblat.blog.terra.com.br/2009/08/04/governador-do-rio-vira-padrinho-do-vale-tudo/

DaCosta, L. (2007). Princípios do Esporte para Todos. In A. C. Almeida & L. DaCosta (Eds.), *Meio Ambiente, esporte, lazer e turismo: Estudo e pesquisa no Brasil de 1967-2007* (Vol. 1, pp. 97-99). Rio de Janeiro: Gama Filho.

Ezabella, F. L. (2006). *O direito desportivo e a imagem do atleta*. São Paulo: IOB Thomson.

Farinatti, P. T. (1995). *Criança e Atividade Física*. Rio de Janeiro: SPRINT.

Fernandes, B. (2011). O UFC tem ajudado a quebrar o paradigma de esporte violento - enterview to Anderson Silva. *Terra Magazine*, 26th June 2013, from http://terramagazine.terra.com.br/mmamanoamano/blog/2011/10/17/o-ufc-tem-ajudado-a-quebrar-o-paradigma-de-esporte-violento-diz-anderson-silva/

Fernandes, S. (2013). São Paulo aposta em Tolerância para reduzir homicídios por motivos fúteis Retrieved 26th June 2013, from http://www.redebrasilatual.com.br/cidadania/2013/05/sp-inicia-campanha-para-evitar-morte-por-brigas-especialistas-pedem-desarmamento-8028.html

Figueiredo, R. P. (2002). *Educação Física para Educação Ambiental: Uma relação a ser construída na transitoriedade*. (Master), Universidade de Brasilia, Brasília.

Giovanni, G. d. (1995). *Mercantilização das práticas corporais: O esporte na sociedade de consumo de massa*. Paper presented at the Encontro Nacional da Historia do Esporte, Lazer e Educacao Fisica, Curitiba.

Gomes, M. C., & M.T. Constantino (2005). Projetos esportivos de inclusão social - PIS - crianças e jovens. In L. DaCosta (Ed.), *Atlas do esporte no Brasil*. Brazil: CONFEF.

Guedes, S. L., et al. (2006). *Projetos sociais esportivos: notas de pesquisa*. Paper presented at the XII Encontro Regional de Historia.

Hackradt, B. (2011). Rio de Janeiro recebe espaço inédito para prática de MMA Retrieved 28th June 2013, from http://terramagazine.terra.com.br/mmamanoamano/blog/2011/08/16/feras-do-mma-apoiam-projeto-social/>

Kern, M. F. (2012). Projeto dos Irmãos Nogueira será implantado no Uberlância Retrieved 1st July, 2013, from http://www.gazetadopovo.com.br/blogs/suburbana-em-campo/projeto-dos-irmaos-nogueira-sera-implantado-no-uberlandia/

Linhales, M. A. (1996). *A trajetória política do esporte no Brasil: interesses envolvidos, setores excluídos.* (Master), Universidade Federal de Minas Gerais - Faculdade de Filosofia e Ciências Humanas, Belo Horizonte.

Machado, T., & O.M. Silva (2013). Esporte uma estratégia na efetivação dos direitos constitucionais das crianças e do adolescentes. In A. Vargas (Ed.), *Direito no desporto: cultura e contradições*. Rio de Janeiro: Letras Capital.

Mancilha, H. L. F. (2012). *Mixed Martil Arts: evolução e crescimento. Direito desportivo & esporte: Temas selecionados* (Vol. 4). Salvador: Instituto de Direito Desportivo da Bahia (IDDBA); Instituto Mineiro de Direito Desportivo (IMDD).

Melo, M. P. (2004). Lazer, esporte e cidadania: Debatendo a nova moda do momento. *Movimento, 10*(2nd), 105-122.

Melo, M. P. (2005). *Esporte e juventude pobre: Políticas públicas de lazer na Vila Olímpica da Maré*. Campinas - SP: Autores Associados.

Murad, M. (2007). *A violência e o futebol: Dos estudos clássicos aos dias de hoje*. Rio de Janeiro: Editora FGV.

Padeiro, C. (2011). Anderson Silva inaugura octógono no Corinthians para ter projeto social na aposentadoria Retrieved June, 2013, from http://esporte.uol.com.br/lutas/vale-tudo/ultimas-noticias/2011/10/24/anderson-silva-inaugura-octogono-no-corinthians-para-ter-projeto-social-na-aposentadoria.htm

Passos, A. (2013). Jéssica Andrade é a primeira Brasileira a lutar no UFC. Retrieved 04/07/2013, 2013, from http://www.superlutas.com.br

Rojek, C. (1995). Veblen, leisure and human need. *Leisure Studies, 14th*(2nd), 73-86.

Rudnick, F. (2011). Anderson Silva fenómeno na luta e no marketing fecha com novos e grandes patrocinadores Retrieved 8th July 2013, from http://www.gazetadopovo.com.br/blog/lutalivre/?id=1154043&tit=anderson-silva-fenomeno-na-luta-e-no-marketing-fecha-com-novos-e-grandes-patrocinadores

Stagliorio, C. (2013). UFC 98 - UFC 2013: O que mudou no UFC de lá para cá? Retrieved 4th July, from http://www.boxingtown.com.br

Tubino, M. J. G. (2003). Movimento esporte para todos: da contestação do esporte de alto nível à atual promoção da saúde. *Boletim FIEP*.

Tubino, M. J. G., Garrido, F. A. C., & F.M. Tubino (2007). *Dicionário Enciclopédico Tubino do Esporte*. Rio de Janeiro: SENAC Editions.

UNESCO. (2006). *Marco estratégico para a UNESCO no BRASIL*. Brasilia: UNESCO.
Veblen, T. B. (1983). *A teoria da classe ociosa: um estudo económico das instituições*. São Paulo: Abril Cultura.
Victor, S. (2013). Manaus ganha primeiro centro de lutas com a participação de José Aldo, 20th July 2013, from http://www.d24am.com/esportes/lutas/manaus-ganha-primeiro-centro-de-lutas-com-a-participacao-de-jose-aldo/81786
Weinberg, R. S., & D. Gould (2001). *Fundamentos da Psicologia do Esporte e do Exercício*. Porto Alegre: ARTMED.
Zorzanelli, M. (2008, July). A vitória do Vale Tudo. *Época*.

Chapter 30

Developing Emotional Intelligence through the Martial Arts

Chris Moser and Cheri Hampton-Farmer

Introduction

In ancient times the martial arts were developed as a form of military defense. When heavy artillery became the weapon of choice, marital arts remained as a method for self-defense but also became a source for personal development and physical activity that emphasizes either psychological maturation or skill acquisition (Columbus & Rice, 1998; Lantz, 2002). Consequently, the martial arts have existed for more than 3000 years and have experienced recent growth with an increase of 3.8 million participants in 1993 to 4.6 million in 2004 (Sports Business Research Network, 2008) and the number of martial arts schools in the U.S. increased by almost 1,000 from 1999 to 2003 (Ko & Kim, 2010) with hundreds of different styles (Lakes & Hoyt, 2004). Today, most participants believe the martial arts are capable of producing both physical and psychological benefits like agility as well as focus and enhanced self-esteem (Ko & Kim; Weiser & Kutz, 1995).

Like many sports, training in the traditional martial arts includes both skill and character development. Although all martial arts disciplines embody unique cultural beliefs, values, and practices, each discipline differs based on the specific martial art and its adaptation to the cultural and social situation where it is practiced. The values learned throughout the training in traditional martial arts temper aggressiveness by teaching students to respect their trainer, those of a higher rank, and each other. This pervasive thinking influences behavior both in and outside the gym. Therefore, values imbedded in the martial arts training encourage positive behavior. Because these values produce positive outcomes, the martial arts have become a sport of choice for self-improvement seeking children, adults, and elderly.

Psychological Benefits of Martial Arts Training

Parents see the benefits of martial arts and often enroll children in the martial arts to reinforce or develop values such as respect and enhance ability to focus. Lantz (2002) analyzed interviews with parents and children enrolled in martial arts and identified behavioral changes that emerged as a result of martial arts training. Parents reported higher levels of respect in themselves and their children. This value is reflected in honorifics used during training and through nonverbal means of bowing to show respect to the instructor. Similarly, Noel (2009) found greater confidence among women in a martial arts self-defense class claiming that training changed perception about female vulnerability to one of equality in physical and mental ability.

Self-reflection

The non-physical practice of meditation, an integral part of this sport, yields many physiological gains along with psychological benefits (Binder, 1999; 2007). Meditation, which includes rhythmic breathing that steadies the pulse, de-clutters thinking, and sharpens the senses, begins most martial arts training sessions to help students focus and prepare for training. It has the added benefit of being a stress reliever, enhancing both physiological and psychological well-being. Like martial arts students, college students found meditation to help them become more observant and identify appropriate responses in communication (Huston, 2010). However, technique without values may increase rather than reduce aggression. Musashi (1982) and Nonsanchuk and MacNeil (1989) found techniques learned in martial arts could be used aggressively to overpower an individual or to mitigate a conflict. Likewise, Trulson (1986) found an increase in aggressive behavior among delinquent adolescents when meditation and philosophy teaching were absent in martial arts training.

Social Integration

Although competition, especially in a combat sport, may encourage aggressiveness, when values like respect for others permeate training sessions, students benefit from the natural outcomes of cooperation, collaboration, and belonging. Law (2004) explains how learning traditional martial arts can be beneficial for individuals of all ages, but specifically for adolescents. He argued that because traditional martial arts do not emphasize competition like modern martial arts, there is greater collaboration. Law suggested that the traditional martial arts practices meet the basic human needs of safety, belonging, power, and self-actualization. Students develop self-esteem through group work that builds community and a sense of belonging. He argued that power needs are met through empowerment as students receive affirmation and achieve attainable goals. These positive effects ward off the potential for negative ones like bullying that result with competitions in which individuals jockey for a single position. Law further confirmed that adolescents in the traditional martial arts show signs of higher self-esteem, lower anxiety, and higher levels of independence.

Self-confidence

The ability to assess a situation, choose the appropriate response, and succeed develops self-confidence, a building block of self-esteem. Families reported confidence-building as a reason for training in the martial arts and perceived an increase in self-respect as a result in Lantz (2003). Similarly, Angleman et al (2008) found higher levels of self-efficacy, while Ball and Martin (2012) found reduced fear among victims of sexual assault due to martial arts training (Angleman et al, 2008).

Conflict Management and Diminished Physical Aggression

Due to philosophical training in martial arts that encourages restraint rather than aggression, trainees find alternate ways to manage conflict. Twemlow, Biggs, Nelson, Vernberg, Fonagy, and Twemlow (2008) found decreased aggression in males participating in the Gentle Warrior Program designed to teach helpful by-standing advocating anti-bullying. Lakes and Hoyt (2004) found an increase of self-regulation among students enrolled in their elementary school's LEAD program, a martial arts training that replaced physical education. They referenced a distinction of martial arts that other sports do not possess: success is based on improvement which enables more individuals to participate and succeed. The authors claimed:

> "Martial arts philosophy emphasizes effort and determination more than 'natural' ability, making it an attractive and feasible activity for children not naturally drawn to sports or for children who do not view themselves as 'athletic.' Because progress in the martial arts is based on improvement, not just the achievement of a particular standard, martial arts training may be more amenable to children who struggle to achieve the required standard in other sports". (p. 299).

Unlike competitive sports, where only winners are rewarded, success in Martial Arts training is measured by one's personal goal achievement. Aggression is more likely to occur in competitive sports when the goal is to prevail over one or more individuals. Because participants in Martial Arts training compete with themselves, the potential for conflict is diminished. Additionally, during training participants exercise peaceful ways to manage conflict.

Conflict Management

Although martial arts techniques can be used to be combative, training encourages conflict management in a peaceful way. Parish's (2007) interview with Zeb Glover, former bodyguard for the Dalai Lama and martial arts instructor, indicated that martial arts training encourages restraint. Glover argued that having the confidence to use martial arts in a combative way but exercising self-control is an effective way to manage conflict. Glover encourages showing empathy and approaching a conflict by building a relationship with a potential assailant. Parish suggests these methods could be used in health care settings when restraining a violent patient may be necessary. Morrison (2009) concluded that state of mind controls the way an individual responds during a confrontation. He argued:

> "State management refers to your ability to control your emotions during a violent incident to such a degree that you can access your skills and deal with the danger. State access means cultivating your ability to shift into the most resourceful state(s) of mind and body before, during and after the altercation. Both elements are closely related to mind-set". (p. 87).

He further suggested that individuals must conduct a self-assessment. Self-reflection, a part of intrapersonal communication, enables the individual to quell emotions and control thoughts which lead to positive results. Golden (2005) enumerated the benefits of managing conflict through martial arts like Aikido which emphasizes preparedness through mental strength. He argued that knowing how to overpower an opponent by assessing their behavior and physical attributes and applying a strategy that minimizes physical harm will serve the individual well. Like Golden, Morrison (2009) argued that martial arts training helps individuals develop a state of mind that enables the individual to manage fear and ultimately gain the confidence to face opposition.

While many studies point to the benefits of martial arts training, some have shown no significant behavioral differences. When Strayhorn, a child and adolescent psychiatrist, noticed an influx in number of clients who enrolled in the martial arts as early as Kindergarten to gain confidence and increase focus, the observation prompted a behavioral study about children who continued participation in martial arts from kindergarten through fifth grade. Although their findings indicated a higher dropout rate from third to fifth grade, they found little evidence that martial arts training altered behavior in the classroom (Strayhorn & Strayhorn, 2009).

Populations Who Benefit from Martial Arts Training

Martial arts training is not just for children. Adults often join when they see what their children are able to achieve. Both authors of this chapter were introduced to the martial arts through their children and joined a program after observing their success. Some families join martial arts programs to increase family time and support one another through the levels. Additionally, the elderly are beginning to realize the benefits of martial arts. Brudnak, Dundero and Van Hecke (2002) found increased stamina and improved balance among those engaged in Taekwondo training. Additionally, they found participants in the study were motivated and wanted to continue with the training.

A large body of research has reported affective, cognitive, social, and behavioral benefits from martial arts training. Affective factors associated with martial arts training include higher self-esteem, a more positive response to physical challenges, greater autonomy, emotional stability, assertiveness, and self-assurance or self-confidence. Cognitive factors influenced positively by martial arts training include concentration and a greater awareness of mental capacities as well as a cultivation of that potential. Social benefits of martial arts training include learning to be more respectful of others (Lakes & Hoyt, 2004). These reported benefits of martial arts training are similar to what has come to be known as emotional intelligence.

Emotional Intelligence

Although skill and intellectual ability contribute to one's proclivity for success, Goleman (1995) claimed success is based on 20% IQ and 80% other factors, like emotional intelligence. Emotional intelligence (EI) includes emotional responses that inform decisions and prompt action. Mayer and Salovey (1997) explain that emotional intelligence are those personal attributes that influence thought. They defined EI as:

> "….the ability to perceive emotions, to access and generate emotions so as to assist thought, to understand emotions and emotional knowledge, and to reflectively regulate emotions so as to promote emotional and intellectual growth" (p. 5).

Goleman (1995) argued that individuals with high levels of emotional intelligence have the ability to identify emotions in oneself, an intrapersonal attribute, and others and provide the appropriate response, an interpersonal attribute (Gardner, 1993; Mayer & Salovey, 1990). In a later study, Goleman (1998) found EI, rather than technical skill, to be a greater contribributor to leader success. A number of scientific investigations empirically measured the effects of EI on life quality, academic/occupational success, resistance to stress, health and the quality of social/marital relationships, to name a few most significant outcomes. Taken together, these studies indicate that EI is an active and essential ingredient of life success and happiness (Nelis, Quoidbach, Mikolajczak & Hansenne, 2009).

Developing Emotional Intelligence

In addition, there is an emerging consensus that EI competencies can be developed and that improving EI competencies is essential for leadership development. Awareness is crucial for any long-term change to occur and must be intentional. This awareness requires one to make a choice to continue managing emotions the way they always have or experiment with using emotions in a different way. Learning programs, when complemented by coaching sessions, have resulted in significant improvement in assertiveness, emotional self-control or impulse control, problem solving, emotional self-awareness, accurate self-assessment, initiative, self-confidence, achievement, adaptability or flexibility and optimism (Carrick, 2010). Emotional intelligence is born largely in the brain's limbic system, which governs feelings, impulses, and drives. Research indicates that the limbic system learns best through motivation, extended practice, and feedback. Therefore, strategies for developing EI competencies require intentionality, persistence and practice in order to produce lasting results. (Rangarajan, 2009).

Martial Arts Values and Practices Reflected in EI

The mastery of most sports requires self-discipline and develops personal characteristics like independence, cooperation, leadership, self-respect, and focus. Likewise those who excel in the martial arts by reaching the level of black belt, possess or have developed these personal characteristics which are reflected in higher levels of emotional intelligence (EI), a predictor of success. Corporate language borrows credibility from Black belt rankings with designations like Six Sigma Black Belt Certification, black belt leader, and black belt commission. Moreover, leaders are encouraged to espouse martial arts values as noted in books like *Think Like a Black Belt* (2010) and *Leading People The Black Belt Way* (2006).

Excelling in the martial arts can be attributed to a number of factors. Although natural ability and physical skill may contribute to one's success in the martial arts, individuals who possess qualities such as self-discipline, perseverance, and other personal qualities are more likely to achieve the rank of black belt. Just as certain EI competencies and attributes contribute to one's effectiveness in life and as a leader, those who reach the level of black belt must also possess certain qualities and attributes that enable them to achieve a high level of success and distiction in their martial art.

Emotional Intelligence Levels among Black Belts

Utilizing the BarOn Emotional Quotient Inventory (EQ-i), Moser (2013) examined the emotional intelligence of 77 adult martial artists representing a variety of martial arts disciplines who held a rank of 1st degree black belt or higher. The EQ-i is a scientifically validated instrument created to assess emotionally intelligent behavior and probe one's use of these emotional and social skills in terms of frequency and intensity and reports a total EQ score, five composite scale scores, and 15 EQ subscale scores. Moser and Hampton-Farmer (2013) investigated whether black belt martial artists possess higher levels of emotional intelligence than the general population and to identified those specific emotional quotient subscales that appear to contribute to their success in the martial arts.

Emotional Intelligence Reflected in Martial Arts Values

The EQ-i data revealed that the sample black belt group's total EQ mean was greater than the mean of 100 found among the general population. In addition, the sample black belt group scored higher than what would be found in the general polulation on each of the five EQ-i composite scales (intrapersonal, interpersonal, stress management, adaptability, and general mood), as well as in each of the 15 subscales measured by the EQ-i. A noteworthy finding of this study is that the highest EQ- i subscale scores for the black belt group were found in stress tolerance, assertiveness, self awareness, and self actualization, which are attributes imbedded in martial arts training.

The results of this study suggest that not only do adult black belt holders in this study possess a higher overall level of EI than that found in the general population, but the black belt group scored higher than the general polulation in all five composite scales and 15 subscales of IE measured by the EQ-i. These findings are consistent with prior research investigating the psychosocial benefits of participating in the martial arts. The parallels between the dimensions and competencies that comprise EI and the reported outcomes and benefits of participating in the martial arts would suggest that the higher than average EI levels of the black belt participants in this study may be a contributing factor regarding their ability to achieve a high level of success and distinction in their martial arts discipline. However, the high EI levels reported in this study cannot be attributed solely to one's attainment of a black belt or participation in the martial arts since participation in this study was voluntary and no attempt was made to control for the effects of self-selection.

It appears that many of the beliefs, values, and practices embodied in the traditional martial arts could contribute to EI development among its participants. In addition, research suggests that EI development occurs through motivation, extended practice, individualized attention and feedback (Goleman, 1998), all of which are integral to martial arts training. Moreover, black belt leaders are held in high regard among martial arts students and exert a great deal of influence on the behavior of others through modeling those values, qualities, and attributes deemed important to their martial arts discipline.

References

Angleman, A. J., Russo, S. A., Shinzato, Y., & V. B. Van Hasselt (2009). Traditional Martial arts versus modern self-defense for women: Some comments. *Aggression and Violent Behavior,* 14, 89-93.

Ball, K. & Martin, J. (2012). Self-Defense training and traditional martial Arts. *Sport, Exercise, and Performance Psychology,* 1(2), 2157-3905.

Bar-On, R. (2007) BarOn Emotional Quotient Inventory Technical Manual. Canada: -Health Systems Inc.

Binder, B. (1999; 2007). Psychosocial Benefits of the Martial Arts: Myth or Reality? A Review. http://userpages.chorus.net/wrassoc/articles/psychsoc.htm

Bouchard, J. (2010). *Think Like A Black Belt.* United States: San Chi Publishing.

Brudnak, M. A., Dundero, D., & F.M. VanHecke (2002). Are the 'hard' martial arts, such as the Korean martial art, TaeKwon-Do, of benefit to senior citizens?

Carrick, L. A. (November, 2010). Demystifying the EI quick fix. *T&D,* 61-63.

Columbus, P.J., & D. Rice (1998). Phenomenological meanings of martial arts participation. *Journal of Sport Behavior,* 21(1), 16-29.

Gardner, L. & C. Stough (2002). Examining the relationship between leadership and emotional intelligence in senior level managers. *Leadership and Organization Development Journal,* 23, 68-78.

Golden, B. (2005). Using aikido principles for conflict resolution in and out of the practice hall. *Journal of Asian Martial Arts,* 14(1), 74-81.

Goleman, D. (1998b). What makes a leader? *Harvard Business Review,* 76, 93-104.

Huston, D. (2010). Waking up to ourselves: The use of mindfulness meditation and Emotional Intelligence in the teaching of Communications. *New Directions for Community Colleges, 151,* 39-50.

Ko, Y. J., & Y.K. Kim (2010). Martial arts participation: consumer motivation. *International Journal of Sports Marketing & Sponsorship, 11*(2), 105-123.

Lakes, K. D., & W.Y. Hoyt (2004). Promoting self-regulation through school - based martial arts program. *Applied Departmental Psychology, (25),* 283-302.

Lantz, J. (2002). Family development and the martial arts: A phenomenological study. *Contemporary Family Therapy 24(4),* 565-580.

Law, D. R. (2004). A choice theory perspective on children's Taekwondo. *International Journal of Reality Therapy, 24*(1), 13-18.

Mayer, J. D. & P. Salovey (1997). What is emotional intelligence? In P. Salovey & D. J. Sluyter (Eds). *Emotional development and Emotional Intelligence,* NY: Basic Book.

Mayer, J. D. & P. Salovey (1990). Emotional Intelligence. *Imagination, Cognition, and Personality, 9,* 185-211.

Morrison, L. (2009). Lessons learned during a 30 year quest to master reality-based fighting games. *Black Belt,* 84-89.

Moser, C. (2013). [Emotional Intelligence levels among black blacks]. Unpublished raw data.

Moser, C., & C. Hampton-Farmer (2013, April). Emotional Intelligence among black belts: Predictor of success. Paper presented at the annual Center for Scholastic Achievement Conference, Scotsdale, AR.

Musashi, M. (1982). The book of five rings. Toronto: Bantam Books.

Nosanchuk, T.A. & M.L. MacNeil (1989). Examination of the effects of traditional and modern martial arts training on aggressiveness. *Aggressive Behavior 15,* 153-159.

Nelis, D., Quoidbach, J., Mikolajczak, M., & M. Hansenne, (2009). Increasing emotional intelligence: (How) is it possible? *Personality and Individual Differences,* 47, 36–41.

Noel, H. (2009). Un-doing gendered power relations through martial arts? *International Journal of Social Inquiry, 2(*2), 17-37.

Parish, C. (2007). When might is right. *Nursing Standard, 21*(24), 18-19.

Rangarajan, P. (2009). Emotional Intelligence and the quality manager: Beauty and the best? *The Journal for Quality & Participation, 31*(4), 31-34.

Strayhorn, J. & J. Strayhorn (2009). Martial arts as a a mental health intervention for Children? Evidence from the ECLS-K. *Child and Adolescent Psychiartry and Mental Health, 3,*(1), 3-32. doi:10.1186/1753-2000-3-32.

Trulson, M. E. (1986). Martial arts training: A novel "cure" for juvenile delinquency. *Human Relations, 39,* 1131-1140.

Twemlow, S. W.; Biggs, B. K.; Nelson, T. D.; Vernberg, E. M.; Fonagy, P. & S.W. Twemlow (2009). Effects of participation in a martial arts–based anti-bullying program in elementary schools. *Psychology in the Schools,* 45(10), 947- 959.

Warneka, T., H. (2006). *Leading people the black belt way*. Cleveland, Ohio: Asogomi Publishing International.

Weisner, M., Kutz, I., Kutz, S., & D. Weisner, D.(1995). Psychotherapeutic aspects of the martial arts. *American Journal of Psychotherapy, 49*(1), 118-127.

Part VII: Research on the Individual Martial Arts

Chapter 31

Approximately 'As Real as It Gets': Naturalistic Mythologies, Biological Determinism, and MMA's Symbolic Environment of Originary Violence

Matthew P. Ferrari

'Fighting - I don't care what color you are, or what language you speak, or what country you live it, we're all human beings and fighting's in our DNA. We get it and we like it. Before a guy ever hit a ball with a bat, or a ball went through a hoop, there were two guys on this planet and somebody threw a punch, and anybody who was standing around was watching it'.

Dana White, UFC President (cited in Martin, 2010, para. 7-8)

Introduction

The Ultimate Fighting Championship (hereafter UFC) has established itself as the pre-eminent cage fighting organization on the planet, and its high-profile President Dana White regularly contends that 'fighting is in our DNA'. A sentiment echoed in the company's tagline, "As Real As It Gets." Now better known as "mixed martial arts" (MMA), the owner of Bear Essential Combat MMA gym, Bear St. Clair, shares this popular belief, claiming: "...it's a primordial thing, and if you get down to the basic instinctual thing of what we are, we are animals. Combat and territory and superiority and genetic selection and survival is ingrained in every single last one of us" (as cited in Mayeda, 2008, p. 122). As if to highlight this point a commercial for Tapout MMA apparel digitally transforms a fighter's eyes into that of a wild animal. The ubiquitous Venum

MMA logo on fighters' shorts or t-shirt creates direct visual analogies between human and non-human predation. However, as Julia Corbett (2007) explains, "...an individual needs no direct experience with untamed environs to know what an eagle or cougar represents and is valued for" (p. 165). MMA's promotional imaginary, I argue here, exploits naturalistic/naturalizing mythologies, suggesting the sport's ambiguous social status, and also its historical lineage to myths of spiritual (masculine) regeneration via "nature." By one important definition, social myth "comes into play when (...) social or moral rule demands justification, warrant of antiquity, reality, and sanctity" (Malinowski, p.107). Or, as Roland Barthes (1957) explains it: "We reach here the very principle of myth: it transforms history into nature. (...) Myth is depoliticized speech" (p.129). In other words, we can do this because it has always been done – it is "natural." The category of (wild) "nature" and notions of what is "natural" are often complicit in – even directly equated to – the operation of myth in the popular imaginary (Evernden, 1992). Allow me to briefly trace further some of the contours of what Varda Burstyn (1999) labels the "symbolic-ideological experience" (p.24) of modern sport, for the specific context of MMA.

In MMA, symbolic transformation is suggested through fighters' nicknames; the fighter (and by extension of fighting) is often simultaneously substituted by (metaphor) –and associated with (metonym) – wild nature: Randy "The Natural" Couture (also known as "Captain America"); Anderson "The Spider" Silva; Andrei "The Pitbull" Arlovski; Dan "The Beast" Severn. Or, there is the journalist who characterizes the fighter as a "wild man" (Walshaw, p.50). "Animals MMA" identifies one martial arts academy in Yonkers, NY, with a banner inviting you to "join the pack!" There is the iconography of the cage, literal and symbolic container for wildness, and technological mediator of wild nature. Accompanying the cage, there are many reflexive body performances and rituals invoking wild "nature." For example: Quinton Jackson's trademark wolf howl while wearing an oversized chain-link around his neck; Forest Griffin's chest-beating gorilla mimetics; B.J. Penn licking the blood off his gloves as a predator might clean its paws; or Rashad Evans and Jon Jones' ritual of crawling into the cage on all fours – all signifying an affinity with wild nature. Symbolic transformations in MMA are enacted through a promotional imaginary that manipulates binaries symbolically in the manner typical of myth. Such mythmaking encourages perceptions and categorizations of difference, from good to bad, human to superhuman, natural to supernatural, human to animal, secular to sacred (Burstyn, 1999). While all modern sports arguably supply society with a powerful "...strategy for regeneration and renewal" (Mrozek, 1985, p. 26) through their marketing and myth-making, MMA more overtly condenses and expresses many of these principle binaries in its promotional imaginary. These symbolic transformations are part of a wider semiotic profusion constellating around MMA culture, or, what I like to think of as "MMA's burgeoning wild kingdom" (Ferrari, 2009).

Masucci and Butryn (2013) contend that a key dimension still largely missing from the scholarly work on MMA are analyses of its media representations, including assessments of the social implications associated with the UFC's successful branding and commodification of violence. This chapter seeks to remedy this absence. While most modern sports exist as a social context for transcending or escaping the mundane through forms of "symbolic-ideological experience," I make the case here that MMA's particular sport form, its cultural origins, and the contested conditions of its social emergence combine to produce a distinctive symbolic economy of masculine regeneration. Myths in all cultures "...are crucial in defining what is natural, normal, and legitimate" (Burstyn, 1999, p. 22). And yet, somewhat paradoxically, the transgression of such socially constructed parameters of the "natural" and "normal" also become integral to strategies of self re-creation, regeneration, transcendence, even salvation (Soper, 1995). MMA's current institutional status and social forces cannot be adequately understood without a thorough accounting of the agency in its operative myths and symbols – especially those present in MMA media, advertising, and related public discourse.

MMA's Social Trajectory and Sport-form as Approximated "Reality"

MMA's overall social trajectory, from its tabooed status as "human cockfighting" towards broader social acceptance, directly informs its promotional imaginary. This evolution parallels an institutional trajectory from an initial "de-sportizing" of traditional martial arts (no-holds-barred fighting), through to a "re-sportized" status involving official sanctioning bodies, strict rules and regulations, more mainstream commercial sponsorships, and the most elite levels of athlete/fighter training and development (Van Bottenburg and Heilbron, 2007). MMA's social history and technical development carries disruptive implications for the fences we ensconce demarcating categories of "primitive" and "civilized". Furthermore, the sports' strategic "technological minimalism" (Downey, 2007), and an ontological status as "mixed" (martial art), comprise its organizing principle – a desire (albeit for commercial ends) to (re)produce some archaic notion of "real" or "natural" fighting. However, exploiting nature/culture binaries while explicating the origins of sport is not a new phenomenon.

Interrogating the naturalness of sport, social historian Allen Guttmann (1979) explains that "...sports as we know them today are not the natural, universal, trans-historical physical activity forms they are commonly thought to be, played in roughly the same way by all peoples in all periods of human history" (p.33). And yet while attempting to explain the socio-psychological basis of sport, Guttman's (1979) only apparent recourse is to invoke these categories, proposing that "the emotional function of the game may be primitive, even atavistic" (p. 125). Football and rugby as social phenomena, for example, and are explained as providing "an outlet to the primitive desire to bang into people" (Guttmann, p. 130). The social historian's evident recourse to such structural binaries is related to how a creative marketing imaginary taps into narratives of sports' emotional function as linked to something "natural, universal, trans-historical."

The emergence of MMA as a martial art in its own right is rooted in the desire to answer longstanding questions about which "traditional" martial art is most effective in "real" combat. The popular success of martial arts films narrativizing this question beforehand (e.g. *Bloodsport*, 1988) may have played some part in the original conception of the UFC by a PPV executive and a movie producer. MMA was –at least as incarnated by the UFC– born in the commercial imperatives of televised spectacle. Institutionally, however, Van Bottenburg and

Heilbron (2006) explain MMA's emergence as a "de-sportizing" of traditional martial arts' modern formats and institutional structures; or, in other words, through the "reduction of rules and regulations in pursuit of greater authenticity, blurring the boundary between martial arts and real fighting" (p. 269). Then, realizing the limited market for such an extreme spectacle of violence, MMA underwent a gradual re-sportization, adopting stricter rules and regulations, and gaining wider acceptance.

Borrowing the concept of "sportization" from Norbert Elias (1971), Van Bottenburg and Heilbron adopt the argument that the history of sportization is linked to the "civilizing process," requiring the "pacification of everyday life" where physical violence is permitted only in socially sanctioned forms (2006, p. 263). The success of the civilizing process demands physical violence is rendered socially, even morally, reprehensible, with modern sport the main exception. If the link between the sportization of physical combat and the civilizing process is accepted, it follows that MMA's initial de-sportizing involved, in some sense, a regression from the social values of civil society, encouraging a socio-psychological marketing imaginary rooted in signs of wildness, where the symbolic boundaries between human/animal, primitive/civilized, nature/culture, and wild/tame are strategically breached. Masucci and Butryn's (2013) recent finding – that newspaper coverage of the UFC (formed in 1993) from the mid 1990s was characterized by "moral panic" –supports this view.

The visual spectacle of an MMA fight is also integral to encouraging a myth of the "real" or "natural". The image of minimally clothed men (and now, with increasing visibility, also women) punching, kicking, and grappling on the ground to the point of either submission or unconsciousness surely suggests a pre-modern, animalistic struggle for survival. After all, one principle way humans are distinguished from animals, Turner points out, is our need to "cover nature (genitals) with culture (the loin cloth)" (2008, pp. 5-6). Yet as Greg Downey (2007) argues, drawing from Marcel Mauss (1973), one should not "...assume that the (nearly) naked human body is not already a technological artifact, shaped by cultural training techniques and subject to social dynamics" (p. 203). That is to say, despite outward appearances –those leading to its now famous labeling by John McCain as "human cockfighting" – MMA is "more technically sophisticated than instinctually savage" (Downey, 2007, p. 202). Downey's argument is that MMA has worked to create "...the closest approximation of 'real' fighting permitted under the law" (2007, p. 206), but is not "real" or "natural" in any absolute sense.

Thus, compared to other modern sports, MMA's promotional imaginary benefits and draws from the sports' impression of eliminating cultural artifice (e.g. large boxing gloves) that may inhibit "real" or "natural" fighting. A form of what Downey calls "technological minimalism" (2007, p. 211), MMA combat is less mediated by gear or other artificially introduced technical apparatuses that would mitigate the diversity of available fighting styles. The cage, for example, is not in itself more "natural" than the boxing "ring," but is primarily in place to allow for a wider range of martial arts, in particular grappling forms (e.g. jujitsu, judo and wrestling). Ultimately, fighting (and the UFC) in MMA's current sport form is an approximated reality, though not exactly "As Real as it Gets."

Nature, Myth, and the "Primitive" in the Social Authorization of Cage Fighting

> "We never speak about nature, without at the same time speaking about ourselves."
>
> (Kate Soper, 1995, p. 73)

Elsewhere I have argued that MMA culture is a privileged site for what Neil Everden understands more generally as the "social creation of nature" (1992). A dimension of MMA's promotional imaginary appropriates signs and symbols of wildness, with "nature" configured as primitivity, exploiting a popular metaphysical/spiritual (i.e. fixed, transhistorical) conceptualization (as opposed to a scientific or realist one) of human-on-human violence, effectively naturalizing it (Ferrari, 2013). For example, another outgrowth of MMA's growing popularity is the proliferation of apparel and gear companies like "Spider Instinct," "Venum," "Untamed MMA," "Pitbull MMA," or "Badboy" (to name but a few) that produce t-shirts, gear, logos, and multi-media with fragmentary plant and animal features such as wings, thorns, fangs, eyes, claws, and horns. Animals, beasts, and other natural phenomena are common motifs in mythological traditions. In this respect, Dorothy Norman (1969) argues that heroes are frequently revealed/made through their triumphant confrontation with animals (natural and supernatural), but also transformed, where the figure bonds, merges, or acquires some of the animal's powers (pp 56-58). That is, defeating "nature" then allows the hero to wear the beast in some expressive manner. Fighters and fans alike "sport" these symbolic "natures" (Ferrari, 2013). Animal and plant imagery stand in here not as individuals, but as "species representatives," as "shorthand" symbols for human values (Corbett, p. 207; Hansen, p.138). The iconic elements of animals and plants signify defensive and aggressive mechanisms in the natural world, combined in expressive ways with other graphic elements (and of course, brand names). MMA t-shirts (as part of sponsorships worn during ritual walk-outs and elsewhere) might be viewed as analogous to the myriad tattoos "worn" by fighters. The t-shirts are often graphically similar to fighters' tattoos, affording the fan greater symbolic vicinity to, and participation in, their mythic transformation through violent confrontation (Ferrari, 2013). Burstyn (1999), in making the argument that sport be seen as "secular sacrament," posits the athlete as "the living mythic symbol bearer" (p. 18). The MMA fan can thus ascribe or overlay themselves with the same distinct set of naturalizing symbols so often inscribed on fighters' flesh. This stylistic mode of appropriating "nature" is complicit with the process of symbolic transformation, standing as one discrete dimension (among others) of MMA's commodification of "nature" and myth.

In explaining why images of nature – and cultural notions of what is "natural" – are so frequently exploited in advertising and popular culture, Anders Hansen explains that associating things with the natural world "..serves to hide what are essentially partisan arguments and interests and to invest them with moral or universal authority and legitimacy" (2010, p.136). Neil Evernden (1992), drawing on Roland Barthes, explains nature as sign:

> 'Nature has become a powerful part of our vocabulary of persuasion. But even that puts it too mildly, for it is often treated as the very realm of the absolute. To be associated with nature is to be placed beyond human caprice or preference, beyond choice or debate. When something is "natural" it is "the norm," "the way," "the given." This use of "nature" affords us a means of inferring how people ought to behave –including what objects they ought to associate with, that is, buy'. (pp. 22-23)

So, for example, determining the answer to that enduring question of whether or not violence and aggression are in fact "natural" to men, a biological instinct, or evolutionary adaptation, is beside the point. These qualities or behaviors are reified through their representation and repetition as "nature" in public discourse, popularly treated as true, beyond question, and inevitable. Thus, as Corbett (2006) explains, nature's success as a marketing device is "not so much what nature is, as what nature means to us" (p. 165). MMA's appropriation of nature happens in terms of the "primitive." Soper (1995) argues that, historically, "nature" as a concept is frequently configured "as primitivity." These and key associated categories effectively construct and "police" definitions of the "human." As Soper (1995) argues:

> 'Western configurations of nature –notably its association with the "primitive," the "bestial," the "corporeal" and the "feminine" –reflect a history of ideas about membership of the human community and ideals of human nature, and thus function as a register or narrative of human self-projections'. (p. 10)

Thus "nature" serves as a conceptual device for both promoting and challenging social conventions and human norms. Performing the role of binary "other" for codifying the terms of humanity and civilization, "nature" and the "primitive" (and associated categories) have been of crucial significance to any number of discourses and disciplinary regimes. Soper (1995) articulates the socio-historical processes for defining the "human" as a series of "exclusions." She explains, "what is proper to humanity (…) has been thought in relation to a number of excluded dimensions, of which the 'primitive', the animal, the corporeal, are the most notable" (1995, p. 74). And yet, as mentioned earlier, these excluded dimensions become the fertile ground upon which people seek spiritual regeneration, indeed:

> 'Civilized thinking no sooner constructed its own 'humanity' by way of a contrast with wild bestiality and primitive savagery than it discovers within the excluded domain of the 'natural' its own intrinsic nobility. (…) [nature] has served both as a conceptual tool through which humanity thinks its difference from the rest of animality and as an assertion of its communiality with it'. (Soper, 1995, pp. 78-81)

When myths are deployed in MMA through ritual, ideologies about the naturalness and nobility of human-on-human aggression are implicated. According to Mircea Eliade (1963), through their ritual enactments, myths function to authorize (natural and social) phenomena (like human violence) by transporting participants to a "primordial" or "sacred" time (pp 18-20). Eliade explains: "myth tells how, through the deeds of Supernatural Beings, a reality came into existence, be it the whole of reality, the Cosmos, or only a fragment of reality –an island, a species of plant, a particular kind of human behavior, an institution" (1963, pp. 5-6). But perhaps most significantly for MMA is myth's dual purpose of justifying and rejecting society, for myth articulates the basis of civilization, but also the supposed dangers in too much of it.

The "primitive" serves as a tool in MMA discourse for rejecting social norms and building myths of origins for human violence. According to Kurasawa, primitiveness "represents a related set of beliefs and values generated to explain rhetorically what Euro-American societies have become in relation to their pasts and futures" (2002, p. 2). However, it is important to make the distinction between the "primitive" as a powerful racist discourse of "evolutionary distancing" –one which Western civilization has historically used to define itself and justify countless atrocities– and a "socio-psychological primitivism" more closely associated with the alienated modern subject's romantic or nostalgic impulse to re-access their "natural" or untamed selves (Fabian, 1983; Torgovnik, 1990; White, 1985). Thus the "primitive" now more often refers to an "internal" other, rather than the "external" other which was the problematic subject of early work in physical anthropology and 19th century social-evolutionary discourses (Kurasawa, 2002; White, 1985).

Torgovnik argues that in the 20th century primitivism went from being a discourse used to justify the imperialistic subjugation of other populations, to a "medium of soul searching and self-transformation" for the Western subject (1997 p. 13). Or, put another way, the "primitive" is a myth employed "to radically put into question existing institutions, values, and habits" of society (Kurasawa, 2002, p 2-3). Primitivism, according to Hayden White, represents a form of wildness responding to desires to "escape the obligations laid upon us by involvement in current social enterprises" (1985 p.170). To that end, White contends, it "simply invites men to be themselves, to give vent to their original, natural, but subsequently repressed desires, to throw off the restraints of civilization and thereby enter a kingdom that is naturally theirs" (1985, p. 171). For Lovejoy and Boas (1965) primitivism is more generally understood as a "backwards looking habit of mind," accompanied by the impulse to recover "what has been lost" in industrial modernity (p. 7). Yet primitivism's "invitation" to men is, in many cases, inextricably tied to gendered master narratives responsible for naturalizing and rationalizing the masculine aggression and domination of a patriarchal economic and gender order.

Heroism and Symbolic Transformation in MMA

Barthes (1957) points out that the "knowledge contained in a mythical concept" – as in hero forms, for example – "is often confused, made of yielding, shapeless associations" (p.119). But it is still possible and instructive here to delineate some of MMA's different "styles of heroic masculinity" (Burstyn, 1999, p. 36), for example, along the lines of race and class. Consider the example of former UFC middleweight champion Rich Franklin, who fits the style of middle-class hero.

Before Franklin became champion he was, as one journalist put it, "a mild mannered high school math teacher" whose "life would have amounted to nothing more than PTA meetings and grading papers" (Anderson, 2010, para. 2). Another explains how Franklin "pulls off the Clark Kent outside the cage, Superman inside" (Dure, 2010, para. 7). Or, simply, "Rich Franklin, former math teacher –current badass" (Childs, 2009). The general fascination with Franklin's story, the "nice guy teacher turned MMA fighter" (McClintock, 2011), is nearly always expressed through good/bad, nice/mean, domestic/wild, gentleman/beast binaries. In Franklin's symbolic transformation, as with many fighters whose personal backgrounds seem generally incommensurate with their status as cage fighters, there are clear echoes of myths where heroic masculinity is revealed through a confrontation with the wild/nature –through the challenge of being forced from a domesticated (tame) occupation to a wild one (e.g. hunting, survival, combat) (Womack, 2003, pp 190-191). Franklin exemplifies a type of MMA heroism where being "intelligent", and having "civilized" skills is a remarkable and hero-structuring dynamic when opposed to the wild/natural imaginary of cage fighting. This heroic style, involving adaptability and interchangeability between realms tame and wild, is evident with many other fighters. Shane Carwin is almost always depicted through his dual identity as civil engineer and fighter, and a related pattern is evident when commentators and journalists commonly highlight fighters with higher education degrees. These transformations echo one of the most common myth-themes, "the quest," in which the hero leaves his everyday (civilized) life under the threat of some natural or man-made calamity (Slotkin, 1973). According to Slotkin, this is perhaps the most important of American myths, in which the hero mediates "between civilization and savagery," and is fundamentally a "lover of the spirit of the wilderness, and his acts of love and sacred affirmation are acts of violence against that spirit and her avatars (…)," but also bring about his "initiation into a new life or higher state of being or manhood" (pp. 21-22).

Another heroic style is linked to working class and military ideals. This style is less associated with intelligence or technologies of civilization, but instead expressed along "the carnal plane" of muscularity, physical bravery and sacrifice (Burstyn, 1999, p.37). Notable examples here might include: Clay "The Carpenter" Guida, former union framer; Forrest Griffin, former Police Officer; and Brian Stann, former U.S. Marine and Silver Star recipient. Fighters transformed in this style are more likely to be characterized through more ambiguous metaphysical, romantic categorizations, in terms of their "heart," "spirit," and "will" rather than in terms of intelligence, technique, or strategy. In discussions of fighters in general, though, there is often talk of one's "heart" or "spirit." A metaphysical construction of "nature" substitutes here for the unquantifiable, ineffable, or imaginary dimensions of human physical potential. When so much of modern sport has become quantification through statistics, historicizing (i.e. temporalizing) canons, and high-tech enhancement (i.e. P.E.D.'s, equipment, spectator viewing ecologies), "nature" stands in for human potentialities and what cannot be measured or quantified, becoming a crucial part of the symbolic-ideological experience for athletes and fans (Ferrari, 2009).

However, with styles of heroic transformation based in naturalistic myth, there is an associated possibility for symbolic incarnation as the "beast," bad boy, wild man, monster (i.e. psycho-path), and related terms complicit in social myth-making associated with "male animal ideology" (Bordo, 1999). Often these myth-images and artifacts are used for positive idealization, but also occasionally for negative attribution and symbolic "othering." For example, Clay Guida's fighter prowess is partly substantiated, in his own words, as a "blue-collar work ethic" (i.e. hard work, sacrifice) (as cited in Lee, 2010), but is transformed by UFC commentator Joe Rogan in terms of socio-psychological forms of wildness. Rogan says of Guida (and Diego Sanchez), "you couldn't ask for two more psychotic dudes to fight each other –this is a dog fight man" (Rogan, 2009). Rogan often labels the fighter (especially those who tend towards brawling rather than technique and strategy) a "wild man," though as White (1978) asserts, "in modern times the notion of the Wildman has become a psychological category rather than an anthropological one (…), Wildness now tends to be conflated with notions of psychosis (…) (pp. 178-179).

Other fighters inspire distinct combinations of heroic forms and symbolic transformation. Anderson "The Spider" Silva is known to wear masks, literally and symbolically (Wayne, 2011). Silva manages to encompass the myth of (super-human) "artist," predatory (non-human) animal, and debased fantastical creature (sub-human). Silva, regarded as MMA's best pound-for-pound fighter, is often elevated to "artist-as-hero" status because, as with the heroic principle ascribed "great" artists, he has so successfully mastered and then strategically flouted forms and conventions, effectively transcending his medium, and thus aided in our own spiritual "revivification" (Norman, 1969). One journalist, invoking several contrasting forms of MMA symbolic transformation, claims Silva "is not some sociopath committing acts of violence in a locked cage for money. He is an artist who creates his work live and under the most hostile circumstances possible" (Rios, 2013, para 6). Another writer describes Silva's performances as "a living art installment" (Hunt, 2013, para 13), while also constructing the fighter through analogy to a wild predator relying on "his superior reactionary skills and general prowess before finishing off his prey" (para 10). So when Silva was improbably defeated for the first time in over six years, his style of flouting rudimentary principles of striking defense, occasionally viewed as a sign of "disrespect" for his opponents, but also comprising his main "artistic" tactic –the "clowning" and "showboating" by which he lured opponents into his counter-striking style– he went from hero to hero-buffoon, from god to "troll." Icarus burnt by the sun. One journalist exclaims of the loss: "Silva is also a straight-out troll. He has more ways to show he's bored by or disdainful of an opponent than most of his rivals have techniques" (Marchman, 2013, para. 2). But, "Silva had finally trolled too hard" (Marchman, 2013, para. 16). However, using trolls –as one creature of myth understood as "nature-beings," associated with darkness, as "human-like" but not fully human (Lindow, 1978)– has problematic racial implications, but is only one example from a wider naturalistic symbolic imaginary associated with MMA.

Thus, symbolic transformation in MMA often negotiates the more socially ubiquitous heroic styles in configuration with naturalistic myths that rely on constructed "nature" in terms of 'primitivity' and wildness. We see in these myth-narratives variations on the hero quest involving the hunt (a direct confrontation with the wild), where variations involve, on the one hand, the possibility for spiritual regeneration, and on the other hand moral danger through the attenuation of humanness. As Slotkin (1973) explains it: "Through the ordeal and discipline of the hunt and its culmination in violence, the hero has achieved a regeneration of the spirit" (p.551). However, by becoming "assimilated" to the wild, the hero "runs grave moral risks:" "He may partake so much of the flesh of wild, hunted things that he becomes like them" (p. 552). Delving further into MMA's range of naturalistic myth-artifacts and images further reveals this ambivalence between the hero's potential for spiritual regeneration or salvation by merging with "nature," and their potential for becoming too much the "beast," involving socio-biologically inflected notions of latent animality.

Myths of Natural Process and the Re-inscription of Originary Violence

The casual, biological determinist worldview expressed by St. Clair at the outset underwrites MMA's socio-psychological imaginary, as it does more generally for popular social Darwinist modes of interpreting human behavior. Certainly the most high profile purveyor of this naturalistic mythology is UFC president Dana White, who proclaims: "Fighting – I don't care what color you are, or what language you speak, or what country you live it, we're all human beings and fighting's in our DNA. We get it and we like it" (as cited in Martin, 2010, para 7). MMA's commercial viability may not depend on this popular belief, but its marketing and promotional imaginary certainly benefits from creatively communicating it. For example, primitivism's "…backwards looking habit of mind" is evident in one of the UFC's recent commercials for *The Ultimate Fighter 15* reality TV show (TUF). Playing on the "March of Progress" scientific illustrations, a linear visual depiction compressing millions of years of human development, *Evolution* (Zuffa, 2012) depicts the progress from ape, to cave man with a club, to the final image of a modern day MMA fighter in the cage. Or, take for instance the trailer for *The DNA of GSP* (2013), a documentary on UFC fighter Georges St. Pierre. The film's topic is introduced by cross-cutting between slow-motion footage of GSP fighting in the cage, with that of two wolves fighting, accompanied by a voice-over stating: "…for the wolf, it's live or die, and for us in the ring, it's live or die" (Svatek & Manchester, 2013).

MMA's imaginary of wildness is also evident in the names of its television programs, like *UFC Unleashed*, or Bellator MMA's *Fight Master*. And in the names and marketing imagery of myriad MMA schools, such as the "New Breed" academy, with a cobra in its logo; "Predator MMA"; "Evolve MMA"; "Tiger MMA"; "Wolfslair MMA." The fighters themselves often qualify the ineffable aspects of their own martial prowess by deploying naturalistic myth-artifacts. Johnny Hendrix explains how he goes into "beast mode" (as cited in Daniels, 2013) during fights. Forest Griffin says of the basis of his will to fight: "That's just the way I am. I'm just a dog" (as cited in Borchardt, 2013). Vitor Belfort announces that his next opponent, Luke Rockhold, will be "fighting a lion" in the cage (as cited in Hall, 2013).

Our relationship to animals is established and perpetuated through master narratives dating back to classical Western thought and literature. One important sense of the "primitive," Torgovnik explains, "…begins with the discontinuities separating human bodies, animals, and inanimate things – and seeks to bridge the gap" (1997, p. 7). Animals are capable of embodying desirable qualities, such as power, strength, speed, bravery, and spirit (Magdoff & Barnett, 1989). Hence their common use in advertisements, from cars to sports teams. Animals are claimed to have been the first subjects in painting, and possibly even the first metaphor (Berger, 2009). John Berger locates the human desire to look at animals in their position at the "intercession between man and his origins" (Berger, 2009, p. 253). Animals serve as a central value concept, often configured symbolically in opposition to "the social institutions which strip man of his natural essence and imprison him" (Berger, 2009, p.257). We use animals and nature symbolically to communicate human values, and while people tend not to take them (too) literally, they still have the discursive function of naturalizing certain kinds of behavior, and elevating those capable of successfully performing it into the realm of the mythic and timeless. Or, as Fabian defines the naturalizing function of such forms of symbolic transformation, its subjects become problematically "separated from (historic) events meaningful to mankind" (1983, p.13).

Masculinist cultural appropriations of "nature" and the "primitive" are often a defensive reaction against the perceived threats of feminization, alienated labor, over-civilization, and related challenges to hegemonic masculinity (Bederman, 1995; Bordo, 1999; Rotundo, 1993). The "masculine primitive" (Rotundo, 1993) –or what Susan Bordo (1999) labels "male animal ideology" and "primal masculinity"– creates a problematic "double bind" between social expectations of wildness and civility, a particular challenge for young men to safely achieve and regulate. The "double bind" of masculinity –the contradictory messages we impose on boys telling them to be "animals" or "beasts" in sport and competition, yet civilized gentleman outside those arenas– is associated with "the male animal as ideology" (Bordo, 1999, p. 245). Bordo links this ideology directly to modern organized sports, seen as a direct response to anxiety over "the repressive effects of civilization and its softening of men," which responds with "fantasies of recovering an unspoiled, primitive masculinity," and carries with it "a flood of animal metaphors" (Bordo, 1999, p.249).

Male animal ideology is underwritten by the facile belief in a causal link between genes and human behavior, men as natural warriors and hunters, a world where "boys will be boys." This sort of popular social Darwinism is based in overly reductive naturalistic explanations, which in turn manifest in naturalistic mythologies of violence. Conversely, scientific consensus holds that human behavior is too complex to be explained by a single gene (Turner, 2008). Biological evidence alone for male aggression is not conclusive, and studies suggest that prevailing narratives of ideal masculinity, and a wider habitus of violence, are more directly responsible for male aggression (Kimmel, 2000).

One of the more contested issues surrounding the study of social mythologies is whether their narratives, artifacts, and images more often serve as a cultural means to explain and celebrate natural phenomena (i.e. scientific or empirical realities), or instead to rationalize, justify, and naturalize particular social (e.g. economic) interests and ideals. Social myths, of course, rely on language, with which we can effectively "create nature." Regarding this conundrum, Everden (1992) asks a crucial question: "If our use of language has allowed us to conflate social norms and nature, then what might we be obscuring? Are we destined to always mistake our cultural norms for 'nature'" (p.27)? There is still a great deal of ambiguity and disagreement on the question of the innateness of human aggression and violence. Famed sociobiologist E.O. Wilson (1996) submits that while many species, including humans, "are capable of a rich, graduated repertoire of aggressive actions. The key is the environment: frequent intense display and escalated fighting are adaptive responses to certain kinds of social stress" (p.88). It should be no surprise then that MMA promotional narratives often embellish certain kinds of social stressors, like manufactured personal attacks (e.g. "trash talk"), or providing for family members, where often no other motivation is offered except that the opponent is taking money from their pocket, food from their table. (In fact, questions surrounding fighter pay, potential fighter unions, and the troubling –though by no means unprecedented– financial logic of the UFC's contract and pay structure are coming under increasing critical scrutiny lately). Still, according to Wilson (1996), the biological evidence alone "cannot be used to justify extreme forms of aggression, bloody drama, or violent competitive sports practiced by man" (p. 88). That is, what genes "prescribe" for certain is only "the capacity to develop certain behaviors and the tendency to develop them in various specified environments," but not specific human behaviors like aggression (Wilson, 1996, p.89). And while the human "urge to affiliate with other forms of life," positively or negatively, "is to some degree innate" –and even that a genetic bias towards aggression is evident, especially in males– there is no conclusive evidence that "it constitutes a drive searching for an outlet" (Wilson, pp. 7, 87). Rather, our social environment, its institutions and sanctioning mythologies, (re)produces a "naturalistic fallacy," one "which uncritically concludes that what is, should be" (Wilson, p. 93).

Institutions of masculinist cultural (re)production, especially those focused on physical violence, are responsible for perpetuating such popular notions. McBride (1995) finds that "male territorial games" –a designation perfectly suited to MMA, though not a sport he addresses specifically– in fact produce and legitimize the mythical origins of their own violence:

> 'As the ground on which a masculinist culture is renewed, male territorial games are the reenactment of an originary violence which establishes the parameters of the patriarchal order. The practice of male territorial games produces its antecedant, creates the memory that founds the present on a legitimized past. It is a reinscription of a founding violence, of a violence that founds itself, which is legitimated precisely because of its iterability. The violence of male territorial games is justified, not because it has always been that way, but rather it has always been that way because it is so now'. (pp. 110-111)

However, it is too limiting to suggest that the "primitive" and the "natural" have only been symbolically appropriated in the name of patriarchy and human oppression. In postmodern cultural production the "primitive" becomes, as Torgovnik puts it, a "general marketable thing –a grab bag primitive" (1990, p.37). The "primitive" and the "natural" are now free-floating signifiers, and may also be appropriated for pro-social and pro-environment causes, among others.

Looking Ahead: Spiritual Regeneration or Market Logic

Sport, Burstyn (1999) explains, is "remarkable for its ability to express two apparently contradictory sets of qualities: on the one hand, modernity, abstraction, efficiency, science, concept, and mind; on the other, the past, archaism, worship, emotionality, sex, and the body" (p. 21). This essay has focused more on the latter, but future research would benefit from developing a synthesis of the two interrelated poles of MMA – the interdependent forward and backward-looking public discourses. For example, elsewhere I have argued that contemporary sport as a whole exhibits a "dark techné" –a simultaneous idealization and anxiety over the high techno-cultural (sporting) body (Ferrari, 2010). However, where a sport like football, as evidenced in, for example, Nike's "Alter-Ego" commercial for its Pro Combat Apparel, is more likely to express ambivalence towards the (forward-looking) high-tech, in this instance by tethering it to a form primitivism, MMA's dark techné involves the recuperation and idealization of a (backwards-looking) low techno-cultural (sporting) body, as expressed in the Tapout's "Hammerhands" commercial (Ferrari, 2010).

In this vein, future scholarly work on MMA might also consider how the UFC's forward-looking global expansion (a "territorial business game") has given MMA a bright future as a socially legitimate (though not uncontested) global sport, but with the aid of a backwards-looking rationalization and naturalization of its originary violence based in a naturalistic fallacy. Arguably MMA promoters like Dana White have benefited from the symbols and rituals that help enact a mythic sanctioning of their violent commodity, giving MMA (and associated forms of violence) its own version of primeval origins rooted in human biology. It makes sense then that the U.S. Marines formed a promotional partnership with the UFC, with military combat increasingly harder to romanticize (i.e. "sell") in its frightening state of high-tech distancing and associated cowardice and alienation, MMA's naturalistic mythologies are ennobling by symbolic association.

Yet, as Eliade (1963) argues, myths not only explain and describe origins, they also function to provide spiritual renewal and rebirth. I would ask in these instances where myth and metaphor purportedly describe natural phenomena or processes (violence, aggression, combat), where does this leave traditional martial arts' holistic, spiritual, and eco-centric ideals? That is, how well does the current MMA marketplace discourse fit with martial arts' traditional ideals, which are often thought to help people "become more moral, more non-violent, more peaceful, and less aggressive" (Becker, p.20). It is well established that many traditional Asian martial arts took direct inspiration from nature, most notably in the imitation of animal movements, a legacy still preserved in the names of moves (and entire styles) in Kung Fu, Tai Chi, and Karate. Traditional martial arts are intertwined with holistic, eco-centric philosophies thought to foster self-awareness of one's place and interconnectedness within the natural world. According to Becker (1982), martial arts "…are held to confer on the practitioner a sort of wisdom or knowledge of the processes, nature, and flow of the universe, with which the martial arts are said to harmonize the practitioner's own actions" (1982, p.24). MMA's promotional imaginary, as I've sketched here, points to how the nature-spirituality dimensions of such ancient practices have been translated and transformed within the contemporary Euro-Western marketplace.

But does MMA's growth justify the hope that more people will be influenced by traditional martial arts' eco-centric ideals or spiritualism?

Some fighters are known to meditate in nature, like UFC star Jon Jones who has a preflight ritual of "finding some running water" outside and drawing power from its "limitlessness" (Wildmind Meditation, 2011; Levaux, 2012). Some fighters have recently participated in public campaigns for PETA, like Jake Shields' leading role in the organization's video game, "Cage Fight: Knock Out Animal Abuse" (Simon, 2013). Peta's campaign posters are revealing in how fighters' social status can be used to promote eco-centric ideals because of a symbolic vicinity to wild nature (and at least in part due to their celebrity), as social-symbolic mediators between the tame and the wild, civilized and primitive. One poster states: "I'm living proof that you can run further, train harder, and pack a meaner punch without eating animals. I'm Jake Shields, and I'm a vegetarian" (PETA2, 2010). In a separate campaign, fighters Norman Wessels and Tito Ortiz speak up against the circus and dogfighting (respectively): "I choose to be in the ring, animals don't. Boycott the circus. Leave wild animals where they belong –in the wild" (PETA2, n.d.). A poster with fighter Richard Quan proposes tattooing as an alternative to wearing animals skins: "Ink not Mink: Be comfortable in your own skin, and let animals keep theirs" (PETA Asia-Pacific, 2012). While other athletes and celebrities have participated in similar PETA campaigns (especially in the wake of the Michael Vick dogfighting scandal), the recruitment of MMA fighters benefits both MMA and PETA in distinct ways. Participation humanizes the fighter (cage fighters can be vegetarians?!) by contrasting them with wild nature, highlighting fighters' individualism (choice, free-will, subordination of instinct), and might even aid in improving the sports' overall social status. While for PETA, the fighters' symbolic affinity to forms of (socio-psychological) wildness undermines the "human" in those people who would act contrary to the campaign's values. On yet another register, fighters as symbolic intermediaries between the wild and tame might be thought to have special knowledge of, and access to, wildness, having triumphed in their confrontation with the wild through the (symbolic) quest or hunt, and thus (as is the general operation of social mythologies) lending credibility to the campaign's moral policing and social construction of the "human". So, finally, shall we take the view that MMA cultivated its own mythic promotional imaginary out of social need, to benefit fighters and fans, to provide a form of human revivification or spiritual regeneration? Or, does the specificity of these naturalistic mythologies, their relationship to a specific sport form, favor the view that MMA's still tenuous social status requires the undergirding of myth to continue its rapid economic growth? Either way, MMA stands as a distinct cultural site for the (re)production of myths and narratives which articulate human-on-human violence as inevitable – as merely "human nature."

References

Amos, C. (2013). The DNA of GSP: Official Trailer for Georges St-Pierre Documentary. *Bleacher Report*. Retrieved from http://bleacherreport.com

Anderson, W. (2010). From Teacher to MMA Legend: The Journey of Rich "Ace" Franklin. *BleacherReport.com*. Retrieved from http://bleacherreport.com

Bederman, G. (1995). *Manliness & civilization: A cultural history of gender and race in the United States, 1880-1917*. Chicago: University of Chicago Press.

Berger, J. (2009). *Why look at animals?* London: Penguin.

Bordo, S. (1999). *The male body: A new look at men in public and in private.* New York: Farrar, Straus and Giroux.

Borchardt, S. (2013). A dog's life: A look back at the UFC career of Forest Griffin. *Bloody Elbow*. Retrieved from http://www.bloodyelbow.com

Burstyn, V. (1999). *The rites of men: Manhood, politics, and the culture of sport*. University of Toronto Press.

Childs, B. (2009). Rich Franklin –Former Math Teacher, Current Badass. *Asylum*. Retrieved from http://www.asylum.com

Corbett, J. B. (2006). *Communicating nature: How we create and understand environmental messages.* Washington, DC: Island Press.

Downey, G. (2007). Producing pain: Techniques and technologies of no-holds-barred fighting. *Social Studies of Science*, 37, 2, 201-226.

Daniels, S. (2013). Johnny hendricks: GSP doesn't know if he's 100% ready, mentally. *Bloody Elbow*. Retrieved from http://www.bloodyelbow.com

Dure, B. (2010). Rick Franklin keeps trash talk light ahead of Liddell fight. *USA Today*. Retrieved from http://usatoday30.usatoday.com/sports/mma

Eliade, M. (1963). *Myth and reality* (Vol. 31). New York: Harper & Row.

Elias, N. (1971). The Genesis of Sport as a Sociological Problem, in E. Dunning (Ed.), *The Sociology of Sport: A Selection of Readings* (pp. 88–115). London: Frank Cass.

Evernden, L. L. N. (1992). *The social creation of nature*. JHU Press.

Fabian, J. (1983). *Time and the other: How anthropology makes its object*. New York: Columbia University Press.

Ferrari, M. P. (2013). Sporting nature(s): Wildness, the primitive, and naturalizing imagery in mma and sports advertisements. *Environmental Communication: A Journal of Nature and Culture*, 7(2), 277-296.

Ferrari, M. P. (2010) Dark techné in sports advertisements. *Flow Journal*. 11(8). Retrieved from http://flowtv.org

Ferrari, M. P. (2009) MMA's burgeoning wild kingdom. *Flow Journal*. 10(3). Retrieved from http://flowtv.org

Guttman, A. (1978). *From ritual to record: The nature of modern sports*. New York: Columbia University Press.

Hall, C. (2013). UFC on FX 8's Luke Rockhold says Vitor Belfort "will get his." *Bloody Elbow*. Retrieved from http://www.bloodyelbow.com

Hansen, A. (2010). *Environment, media and communication*. London: Routledge.

Hunt, L. (2013). Did Anderson Silva take a dive? No, here's why. *Sports Illustrated*. Retrieved from http://sportsillustrated.cnn.com/mma/news

Kimmel, M. S. (2000). *The gendered society [electronic resource]*. Oxford University Press.

Kurasawa, F. (2002). A requiem for the "primitive." *History of the Human Sciences*, 15, 3, 1-24.

Lee, R. (2010). Exhausting Clay Guida. *Fight! Magazine*. Retrieved from http://www.fightmagazine.com

Levaux, A. (2012). UFC 145: Jon Jones on water, spies, his book of moves, Rashad's top game, JDS. *Bleacher Report*. Retrieved from: http://bleacherreport.com

Lindow, J. (Ed.). (1978). *Swedish legends and folktales*. Univ of California Press.

Lovejoy, A. O., & Boas, G. (1965). *Primitivism and related ideas in antiquity: Contributions to the history of primitivism*. New York: Octagon Books.

Magdoff, J., & Barnett, S. (1989). Self-imaging and Animals in TV Ads. *Perceptions of animals in American culture*, 93-100.

Marchman, T. (2013). Anderson Silva, the UFC's troll king, wins again. *Deadspin*. Retrieved from http://deadspin.com

Martin, D. (2010). Dana White: Fighting's in our DNA. *MMA Weekly*. Retrieved March 4, 2010, from http://www.mmaweekly.com

Masucci, M., & Butryn, T. M. (2013). Writing about fighting: A critical content analysis of newspaper coverage of the Ultimate Fighting Championship from 1993-2006. *Journal of Sports Media*, 8(1), 19-44.

Mauss, M. (1973). Techniques of the body. *Economy and Society*, 2, 1, 70-88.

Mayeda, D. (2008). *Fighting for acceptance: Mixed martial artists and violence in American society*. iUniverse.

McBride, J. (1995). *War, battering, and other sports: The gulf between American men and women*. New Jersey: Humanities Press.

McClintock, P., & Kit, B. (2011). UFC champ Rich Franklin's story headed to the big screen. *The Hollywood Reporter*. Retrieved from http://www.hollywoodreporter.com

Norman, D. (1990). The hero: myth, image, symbol. New York, Cleveland: World Publishing.

PETA Asia-Pacific (2012). MMA fighter Richard Quan talks ink, not mink! Retrieved from: http://blog.petaasiapacific.com

PETA2 (2010). Vegetarian and Strikeforce champion Jake Shields. Retrieved from http://www.peta2.com

PETA2 (n.d.). Tito Ortiz says, "I choose to be in the ring. Animals don't". Retrieved from http://www.peta2.com

Rios, T. (2013). Stopping the troll. *Sports on Earth*. Retrieved from http://www.sportsonearth.com/article/53082604/

Rotundo, A. (1993). *American manhood: Transformations in masculinity from the revolution to the modern era*. New York: Basic.

Simon, Z. (2013). PETA launches "Cage Fight: Knock Out Animal Abuse" with Jake Shields. *Bloody Elbow*. Retrieved from http://www.bloodyelbow.com

Slotkin, R. (1973). *Regeneration through violence: The mythology of the American frontier, 1600-1860*. University of Oklahoma Press.

Soper, K. (1995). *What is nature? Culture, politics, and the non-human*. Oxford: Blackwell.

Torgovnick, M. (1990). *Gone primitive: Savage intellects, modern lives*. Chicago: University of Chicago Press.

Torgovnick, M. (1997). *Primitive passions: Men, women, and the quest for ecstasy*. New York: Alfred A. Knopf.
Turner, B. S. (2008). *The body and society: Explorations in social theory*. Sage.
Van, Bottenburg, M., & Heilbron, J. (2006). De-sportization of fighting contests. *International Review for the Sociology of Sport*, 41, 3-4.
Wayne, M. (2011). Vitor Belfort knows Anderson Silva is a good man, despite the mask he wears. *MMA Junkie*. Retrieved from http://www.fightline.com
White, H. V. (1985). *Tropics of discourse: Essays in cultural criticism*. Baltimore: Johns Hopkins University Press.
Wildmind Buddhist Meditation. (2011). Ultimate Fighting Championship light heavyweight champ Jon Jones meditates before big fight. Retrieved from http://www.wildmind.org
Wilson, E. O. (1996). *In search of nature*. Island Press.
Womack, M. (2003). *Sport as symbol: images of the athlete in art, literature and song*. McFarland.
Zuffa & UFC. (2012). Promo – Evolution. *The Ultimate Fighter – Season 15*. Retrieved from: http://www.tvweb.com/shows/the-ultimate-fighter/season-15—promo evolution

Chapter 32

Approaches to the Historical Acculturation of Judo

Haimo Groenen

Introduction

Cultural History of Judo, Acculturation and Assimilation of Japanese models

Judo differs in the world of sport through its Japanese origins and international development. Its history is rich in relations and influences between East and West (Brousse, 2000a, 16). As perfectly illustrated by Michel Brousse concerning the French case (2000a, 17), "....the history of judo is like that of a cultural object, which is assimilated then transformed by the society that integrates it". Cultural history thus constitutes a useful tool to understand the establishment and diffusion of judo, and the acculturation processes involved, particularly in Europe (Brousse, 2000b, Groenen, 2005a). The original orientations of the Japanese discipline should therefore be understood.

When Kano Jigoro founded judo in the late 19th century, he created an educational method on a physical, moral and mental level.[1] The two founding principles of judo, i.e. mutual aid and prosperity, and optimal use of physical and mental energy, accentuated its axiological specificity. Kano created the conditions for educational combat. The martial art thus broke with the traditional techniques of jiu-jitsu,[2] albeit partially taking inspiration from them. The various judo techniques (throwing, holding, strangling, joint-lock) were categorised together as Kodokan, from the name of the school founded by Kano to study the "gentle way". The Kodokan Method was based on three forms of practice rooted in the

---

[1] On the origins of judo and the work of Kano, see, for example, Brousse (1996, 14-31; 2000a, 34-55).

[2] Jiu-jitsu is a set of forms of confrontation, using bare hands or minimal weapons.

tradition of Japanese martial arts: *randori*[3] (free practice without individual victory), *kata* (technical demonstrations between partners, embodying judo's values, and technical and tactical foundations), and *shiai* (competition). Judo was also influenced by two references from the East, *Bushido Code* (samurai moral code) and *Zen* (independent school of Buddhism). And in line with Japanese society, it formed an extremely hierarchised environment based on grades (*dan*) representing the judoka's technical, combative and moral values. Yet because of his life course, Kano was also influenced by scientific, pedagogical and sporting references from the West.

From the early 20th century, Kano strove to diffuse his method internationally, in particular through a number of foreign trips. Further Japanese experts also played their part by settling permanently in Europe or the United States, for example. Following the Second World War, the American authorities required that Japanese judo be purely sport oriented (Brousse, 1996, 127). The first world judo championships in Tokyo in 1956 furthered its international development. Yet, it was judo's Olympic inclusion in the 1964 Tokyo Games that marked a decisive turning point in its sportification and *occidentalisation* (Guttmann, 1988, 54; Guttmann, 1994, 138; Guttmann & Thompson 2001, 178). The 1960s revealed, more broadly, the sportification, democratisation and massification of Kano's Method (Brousse, 2011). Despite such developments, the Japanese maintained a long-standing influence over the world of judo, in particular through techniques, and pedagogical and training models. The origins of judo, the sporting superiority of the Japanese and their rankings highlighted this Japanese domination.

Cultural history has undergone varying developments throughout the world, in relation to the subjects of study engaged in, the theoretical references used and the definition of the concept of culture (Chartier, 2008; Rioux & Sirinelli, 1997; Poirrier, 2008). Michel Brousse refers explicitly to a judo culture, in the sense that its practitioners share a set of values, representations and practices that are transmitted and continued socially (Brousse, 2000a, 16-18; Brousse, 2011, 60). This anthropological meaning has been adopted here to define culture as a coherent and structured whole, structuring the ways of living and thinking of a given social group, and shared and transmitted within it. In judo, this culture articulates not only values, symbols, representations and beliefs, but also rituals, norms and practices, as well as techniques, equipment and institutions (Groenen, 2007, 199). The cultural history of judo reveals the acculturation processes that have marked its development through time, particularly in France (Brousse, 2000a, 2000b; Groenen, 2005a, 2005b, 2007), Belgium (Groenen, 2005a, 2007, 2008) and the United States (Brousse, 2011). Further historical, sociological and anthropological works have examined cultural transformations occurring in judo, e.g. in British and French judo (Goodger & Goodger 1980; Goodger 1981a; Goodger, 1981b; Kim, 1999).

This chapter aims to highlight the acculturation processes that have crossed and orientated the history of judo in Europe, through a number of significant examples supported by the available literature. Acculturation is defined with reference to the anthropological works of Melville Jean Herskovits and Roger

---

[3] Japanese terms are written here in italics and the singular.

Bastide, and in relation to the concept of assimilation. Assimilation implies complete internalisation by a dominated group of the culture of a dominant one. Yet, such reproduction is nearly always accompanied by acculturation phenomena, corresponding to the set of processes that result from contact between social groups belonging to different cultures, and leading to changes in the initial cultural models of one or both groups (Cuche, 2001, 54-58). The transformations resulting from actors' active strategies may be distinguished from those, much slower ones, linked to contact of the Japanese art with the society in which it is established (Brousse, 2000a, 20).

Judo's development in France and Belgium will be studied first, in order to examine the establishment of specific cultural foundations, then the 1960s, as a testament to judo's sportification. Indeed, France is a perfect illustration of the acculturation of the Japanese model of the development of Judo.

Acculturation of Judo in France: Affirmation of a French specificity

Having discovered jiu-jitsu in Palestine, Feldenkrais travelled to Paris to continue his studies in physics. While there, he discovered judo, in 1933, during a demonstration given by Kano.[4] Feldenkrais then set up the *Jiu-Jitsu Club de France* (JJCF) in 1936, *"....the club behind the origins of French judo"* (Brousse, 2000a, 26), which was attended by a male, scientific and intellectual elite. The pioneer of French judo played a key role in giving judo its own identity in relation to jiu-jitsu. Feldenkrais' assimilation of Kano's method may be seen in the definition of judo and its founding principles, techniques, exercises and gradings (Groenen, 2005a). Yet, Feldenkrais also innovated. He initially valorised jiu-jitsu to meet practitioners' expectations, then devised a rational pedagogical method based on a deductive approach integrating various branches of scientific knowledge (anatomy, biomechanics, physiology, psychology, psychoanalysis). The latter orientated teaching and enhanced technique analysis. While traditional Japanese teaching used a global and intuitive approach, Feldenkrais valorised students' intellectual understanding and verbal technical instructions. He gave meaning to learning by identifying principles of action. In this way, Feldenkrais wished to adapt to the rationality associated with the French mind. Last but not least, his method expressed his scientific and professional culture, and was in tune with the social characteristics of the first enthusiasts. Scientific acculturation led to "cultural reinterpretation" (Cuche, 2001, 55-56). The social positions of the first practitioners explained their enthusiasm for judo ethics (Clément, 1987). In line with the *Bushido Code*, respect became one of the cardinal values of French judo. Judo's appeal came about within the context of an emerging new middle class, embodied by the engineer. It was Kawaishi, however, who ensured the development and success of French judo.

Kawaishi left Japan for the American continent in 1925, and spent time in London. With the Kodokan grade of 4th Dan, he taught different martial arts during his trips. Kawaishi arrived in Paris in 1935. On the strength of his expertise and charisma, he quickly held a dominant position in the JJCF, then at

---

[4] Concerning Feldenkrais' biography and method, see particularly Brousse (1996, 2000a) and Groenen (2005a, 2005b).

the French Federation of Judo and Jiu-Jitsu founded in 1946. Kawaishi remained true to the fundamental spirit and values of Japanese judo, yet considered that judo's development in France required him to adapt his teaching to Western mentalities.[5] Kawaishi reserved a place for jiu-jitsu, in accordance with practitioners' interest in self-defence, and valorised the competitive sport dimension. The first French Championship, set up in 1943, facilitated the recognition of judo on the French sports scene, and the orientations promoted by Kawaishi ensured the development of French judo. From the 1950s, it opened up to the middle classes who demonstrated a growing interest in judo's sport dimension. The Kawaishi Method highlighted acculturation of the Kano Method. Kodokan gave techniques names referring to concrete meanings or images (e.g. *o-soto-gari:* major outer reaping), and categorised them, in particular according to the body parts used (leg, arm, etc.). Kawaishi gave each technique a French name and a number indicating learning progression. *O-soto-gari* thus became "1st leg throw", i.e. the first leg technique to be learnt. In this way, he rationalised the pedagogical content. Acculturation also affected gradings. Kodokan distinguished *kyu*, intermediate grades to black belt, and *dan* (starting at black belt level). Kawaishi created intermediary coloured belts between the white and brown ones.[6] With them, he associated technical knowledge, learning progression, a practical exam and mental fitness test. Not only motivational levers, grades were also conveyors of a common culture. Indeed, the Kawaishi Method became the cornerstone of French judo culture. Finally, Kawaishi modified certain exercises, as in "Kawaishi randori" and "competition randori". His rational approach was also intuitive, based on students' own research and a low number of explanations provided by the master. Kawaishi's biography itself clearly highlighted acculturation of the Kano Method. His training at Butokukwai (rival school of Kodokan) and familiarisation with Western culture through his university studies and trips, as well as his discovery of judo competitions in England and his collaboration with Feldenkrais, were all decisive elements. Yet, Kawaishi was also a visionary. He quickly expressed great ambitions for French judo, which he wished to free from Japanese influence (Brousse, 2000a, 370). Kawaishi created a hybrid model that lay at the crossroads of Eastern and Western cultures, associating the French model and a Japanese man. Through judo, Paris confirmed its status as cultural "production circle" (Sirinelli & Sot, 1995).

The principle of cultural adaptation, introduced first by Feldenkrais, then Kawaishi, left a permanent mark on French judo. The creation of a French teaching method in 1964 (Groenen, 2002, 2011), followed by a French judo school, confirmed a national specificity. The history of Belgian judo, on the other hand, illustrates a contrary trend, since it shows, above all, receptivity to foreign, and mainly Japanese, models.

---

[5] Concerning the biography and method of Kawaishi, see particularly Brousse (1996, 2000a) and Groenen (2005a, 2005b).

[6] Belt progression is as follows: white, yellow, orange, green, blue, brown. Judo has 10 *dan* grades.

Judo Establishes Itself in Belgium

Although jiu-jitsu was present in Brussels as early as 1905, judo only established itself in Belgium at the time of the Liberation,[7] as the result of different foreign influences according to the linguistic community. Historically, Belgium was divided between the Flemish, Walloons and a German minority. The first, from Flanders in the north, officially spoke Dutch. The second, from Wallonia in the south, were French-speaking. Finally, the third was confined to the south-east of the country. The capital, on the other hand, was bilingual.

Fleming François Van Haesedonck discovered the Japanese discipline in Holland, although his training mainly concerned self-defence. He nevertheless founded the first Belgian judo club in Antwerp in 1945. On the French-speaking side, Jean-Marie Falise was introduced to judo during the war through contact with a Frenchman, and opened a judo club near Charleroi in 1947. Georges Ravinet took a similar initiative in the Brussels-Capital Region. Unable to form an association in Belgium for lack of competent instructors, these pioneers perfected their skills in one of the main centres of European judo, JJCF. Kawaishi put them in touch with one of his best students and French champion, Jean de Herdt. For the Belgian pioneers, therefore, JJCF constituted a cultural relay for the discovery of judo. They immediately adhered to the Kawaishi Method. From 1948 on, De Herdt ensured the establishment of judo in Belgium, in line with the mission entrusted by Kawaishi to diffuse judo internationally according to his method. De Herdt became the Federal Technical Director of the Belgian Federal Association of Judo and JiuJutsu (AFBJJJ), founded in 1949.

Quite unlike the French case, Belgian judo did not constitute an area where new teaching methods were created. On the contrary, its history shows assimilation of foreign models, primarily French and/or Japanese. In 1953, the Kawaishi Method was abandoned in favour of the Kodokan Method, represented by Ichiro Abe. Residing in France since 1951, this Japanese expert was called upon by the AFBJJJ to replace de Herdt. France thus constituted an "intermediary" for importing the traditional Japanese model. Receptivity of Belgian judo to foreign models showed a trend that had more broadly marked the history of Belgian sport since the 19th century, while France, along with England, constituted a central reference. More generally, Belgium had always been open to foreign influences, through its position at the crossroads of Western European cultures. France historically represented a predominant cultural model, including in Flanders. Geographical and linguistic proximity alike also facilitated cultural transfers. The importance of French judo was also the result of its European influence, of the fact that Kawaishi was an eminent Japanese expert and that his method was exported to Belgium by a great, high-ranking champion. The subsequent choice of the Kodokan Model showed the dominance of Japanese judokas and models in Europe, with Abe's technical expertise, considered superior, also playing a part in the change in models.

Yet, the conditions in which Belgian judo established itself and diffused led to the unwished acculturation of foreign models. Judo developed gradually and its presence remained relative following the setting-up of the AFBJJJ. The lack of

---

[7] Concerning the history of jiu-jitsu in Belgium, see Neyens (1988). On the development of judo in Belgium, see Groenen and Terret (2008).

high-ranking masters until 1948 explained the approximate and imperfect representation of judo. Even in the early 1950s, judo was still being confused with jiu-jitsu, and its values, founding principles and philosophical foundations were generally fairly unknown by instructors and judokas. The techniques and specific practices of judo were likewise affected by being only partially known. The diffusion strategy for judo in Belgium highlighted this situation, in comparison with the French one. French pioneers trained instructors before authorising new clubs to open, with every instructor being, in principle, black belt level. This guaranteed the unity of French judo and the diffusion, in its true form, of the Kawaishi Method, which served as a basis for instructors' training. In Belgium, on the other hand, the development of clubs preceded the training of high-ranking instructors. In 1951, ten Belgian judokas were awarded black belt level, although there were already 68 judo clubs (Groenen, 2005a). At the time, it often happened that a green belt judoka was responsible for teaching judo, and that deviations from the reference model occurred, particularly in the values, technique and practices. In addition, judo's establishment occurred within a context of slow democratisation in sport. The first Belgian judokas did not belong to any social or intellectual elite, as in France, and showed less interest in judo's philosophical dimension.

The tendency to assimilate foreign models left a permanent mark on the history of judo in Belgium. The Kodokan Method has, to this day, constituted a central reference, even if the sportification of judo resulted in receptivity to other models, for example Russian. Interestingly the 1960s saw a break in Europe between a martial art and traditional Japanese judo, and judo as a sport. France underwent a process of sport acculturation.

Sport Acculturation of Judo in France during the 1960s

During the 1950s, the French Judo Federation (FFJ) worked for the development of judo as a sport and prepared an elite for international gatherings,[8] while remaining true to the original definition of judo. At the same time, several actors, such as Alain Valin and Robert Boulat, physical education teachers keen on other combat sports, campaigned for a strictly sporting version of judo, although this remained a minority idea (Brousse, 1996, 2000a; Groenen, 2005a). The following decade, however, witnessed a decisive change of direction in the sportification of judo. In 1960, the Olympic inclusion of judo for the upcoming Games in 1964 showed the westernization and sportification of the discipline. From 1960 on, the FFJ organised competitions based on weight classes, hitherto opposed since considered contrary to judo's spirit and principles.[9] French judo incorporated a norm from other combat sports and a principle already adopted by various European countries and for the Olympiads.

Elected as Federal President in 1961, Claude Collard implemented a policy aimed at making judo a major national mass sport, capable of shining at the international level. Preparation for the Games constituted the priority objective

---

[8] The first European Judo Championship took place in Paris in 1951.
[9] Concerning this episode on weight classes, see especially Brousse (1996, 2005a) and Clément (1984).

orienting Federal sports policy as a whole.[10] The Federation made the sport dimension its aim and *raison d'être*. The Olympic preparation programme combined action aimed at both the elite and masses. The idea was to spark motivation for sport in the young, and develop judo as a sport at school and university. Competitions were set up for different age and practitioner categories. These measures reflected the principle of Coubertin's pyramid, widespread in France and according to which "from the masses would come the elite". The measures were implemented as part of the State's proactive sports policy concerning mass and elite sport, and in the context of sport development in France. Against the background of the Cold War, sport (and in particular the Olympic disciplines) was a tool to be used for the greatness of France, as promoted by Gaullism. A former international competitor with a 4th *dan* in judo, Collard was a versatile sportsman who had been working, since 1956, for the development of judo as a sport, without nevertheless forgetting its other dimensions and cultural foundations. He was able to count on the support of Robert Boulat, an ally devoted to the cause and responsible for Olympic preparation at the FFJ in 1962. This former wrestler constituted a "cultural conveyer" (Rioux, 1997) for importing cultural norms and references from the sports and physical education milieus with which he sustained close relationships. This could be seen in training for the elite, which increased in frequency, intensity and duration. In addition, a comprehensive physical training programme was henceforth added to judo training. Developing strength and physical fitness became a priority theme, resulting in the use of new practices, such as bodybuilding and jogging. The sportification of training was linked to models that were internal and external to judo, and mainly foreign. In a context of wider international judo gatherings, reference norms were set by the world elite. The Japanese held a dominant position, followed closely, in particular, by the Russians. International competitions were a "medium" (Rioux, 1997, 17) for the diffusion of new norms and models. Although the FFJ sought to reproduce the Japanese or Russian form of training, this assimilation project met with sociocultural obstacles linked, more especially, to the slow development of French university judo, athletes' social conditions and fears related to overtraining. At the same time, the training of high-level athletes (in particular American and Russian) became a reference for judo, which was likewise influenced by athletics, considered in France as a fundamental sport. It was thus external sports references that led to sport acculturation.

The development of judo among the young[11] also contributed. Judo became a means of sport and physical education for the young, quite beyond any philosophical references. Physical education in schools demonstrated this (Groenen, 2011). Within the context of school physical education, judo was incorporated into official school content in 1967. In accordance with the concepts developed by the pioneers of school judo (particularly Valin and Boulat), judo was understood solely as a combat sport. All references to the specific principles and values of judo disappeared, in favour of sports ethics (Groenen, 2013). Boulat

---

[10] On Federal sports policy during the 1960s and the preparation of the 1964 Olympics, see particularly Brousse (1996), Groenen (2002, 2012b).
[11] In 1962, 50% of Federal members were under 16 years old; in 1965, the figure rose to 60%.

also developed a transversal teaching method, based on technical similarities between wrestling, judo and sambo. Sport acculturation of school judo thus redefined values, techniques and pedagogy.

Sportification, however, was not widespread. Although women had been practising judo since the 1930s, social and cultural resistance, linked to the dominant gender norms within the FFJ and French society, hindered the sportification of women's judo (Brousse, 1996, Groenen, 2005c). The first official women's competitions were, in fact, only set up by the FFJ in 1972.

Conclusion

While the examples presented here are not sufficient for an exhaustive analysis of judo's acculturation in Europe, they lay down heuristic markers. Acculturation of the Japanese model occurred through a wide variety of references and factors. To varying degrees, and depending on the periods and social spaces under consideration, it modified several essential cultural foundations of judo, including purposes, values, ranks, techniques and practices. Singularities and similarities appeared between France and Belgium, with both countries lending themselves particularly well to the cultural history of judo (Groenen, 2007). There, a dual process of acculturation and assimilation of lastingly influential Japanese models may be observed. Yet, assertion of a national specificity through a method and a French School of Judo constituted a unique case at the international level. Conversely, Belgian judo showed strong receptivity towards foreign models. Sportification of French training during the 1960s resulted from a plurality of foreign influences, particularly Japanese, with Japanese judo itself having evolved and incorporated sports references. As a result, instead of being analysed purely in terms of westernization, sportification of judo should rather be considered according to the dialectical relationships between East and West.

Acculturation of judo would gain from being analysed historically in connection with the dominant cultural models and social milieus concerned, with the actors and cultural relays likely to introduce and legitimate new references or initiate cultural reinterpretation, as well as with the diffusion and circulation mechanisms, and common mediums involved. Acculturation is the result of several factors, in particular actors' concepts (linked themselves to their biographical path) and the conditions under which judo established itself and diffused (in relation to the social characteristics of practitioners and milieus concerned). Teaching and training methods likewise played a decisive role. They were a product of both judo culture and the process through which the culture was built and transmitted, and therefore diffused and evolved (Groenen, 2005a, 52).

This overview opens up perspectives for comparative approaches in Europe. Sportification of judo was likewise observed in Great Britian in the 1960s (Goodger, 1981a, 1981b), but appeared slower than in France. Sportification of women's judo also expressed national specificities. By way of example, the first women's competitions were set up in England, France and Belgium respectively in 1966, 1972 and 1974 (Groenen, 2005c, 2012a). These time intervals should be interpreted with regard to the concepts of influential actors, to gender norms and the resistance to women's emancipation, which has marked the history of the countries under consideration.

References

Brousse, M. (1996). *Le judo: son histoire, ses succès*, Genève, Liber.
Brousse, M. (2000a). *Les origines du judo en France de la fin du XIXe siècle aux années 1950: Histoire d'une culture sportive*, PhD. diss., University of Bordeaux 2.
Brousse, M. (2000b). L'historiographie des arts martiaux. In A. Terrisse (Dir), *Recherches en Sports de combat et en Arts martiaux. État des lieux* (pp. 21-34). Paris, Editions Revue EP.S.
Brousse, M. (2011). Ondes de choc: conflits politico-culturels et évolution du judo mondial, in Terret T. (Dir.), *Histoire du sport et géopolitique* (59-75). Paris, L'Harmattan.
Chartier, R. (2008). Postface, in P. Poirrier (dir.) *L'histoire culturelle: un « tournant mondial » dans l'historiographie ?* (pp. 189-196). Éditions Universitaires de Dijon, Dijon.
Clément, J. P. (1984). Catégories de poids en sport de combat, éthique sportive et ethos de groupe, in N. Midol (Coord.), *Anthropologie des techniques du corps* (pp. 283-290). Editions STAPS, La Gaillarde St Aigulf.
Clément, J. P. (1987). L'itinéraire du judo dans la société française (1936-1970): pour une problématique de l'intégration. *STAPS,* Dossier STAPS – Ecrit 1 – CAPEPS, novembre 1987, 129-144.
Cuche, D. (2001). *La notion de culture dans les sciences sociales*, Paris, La Découverte.
Goodger, B. C. (1981a). *The Development of Judo in Britain: A Sociological Study*, Ph.D. diss, University of London.
Goodger, J. M. (1981b). *Judo: A Changing Culture*, Ph.D. diss., University of London.
Goodger. B. C. & J.M. Goodger (1980). Organisational and Cultural Change in Post-War British Judo, *International Review of Sport Sociology*, 1 (15), 21-48.
Groenen, H. (2002). Le renouvellement de la politique de la fédération française de judo au milieu des années 1960. In K. Szikora, P. Nagy, S.-J. Bandy, G. Pfister, & T. Terret (Eds.), *Sport and Politics* (pp. 255-262). Budapest: HUPE.
Groenen, H. (2005a). *L'ukemi, le randori et le kata. Une histoire culturelle des méthodes d'entraînement en judo: étude comparée France Belgique de l'entre-deux-guerres à la fin des années 1950*, Ph.D. diss, University of Lyon 1.
Groenen, H. (2005b). Les méthodes d'entraînement dans le judo français de 1936 à 1957: entre assimilation de modèles d'entraînement japonais et spécificités nationales, in G. Gori Gigliola, T. Terret (Coord.), *Sport and Education in History* (362-367). Sankt Augustin, Akademia Verlag.
Groenen, H. (2005c). La pratique du judo féminin en France et en Angleterre de l'entre-deux-guerres au début des années 1970: entre traditions et sportivisation, entre tutelle masculine et émancipation, in T. Terret T. (Dir.), *Sport et genre. XIXème-XXème siècles*, Vol. 1 : *La conquête d'une citadelle masculine* (pp. 223-242). Paris, L'Harmattan.
Groenen, H. (2007). Une histoire culturelle et comparée des méthodes d'entraînement de judo en France et en Belgique: intérêts et limites, in

M. Lämmer, E. Mertin, T. Terret (Eds.), *New Aspects of Sport History* (pp. 197-206). St Augustin, Academia Verlag.

Groenen, H. & T. Terret (2008). L'influence de la France dans l'implantation du judo en Belgique entre 1945 et 1953. *Stadion*, 34, 123-236.

Groenen, H. (2011). La promotion d'un judo éducatif pour la jeunesse par la FFJDA entre 1968 et 1990: le poids des méthodes fédérales, in J.-F Loudcher & J.-N. Renaud (Coord.), *Education, sports et combat et arts martiaux* (pp. 151-166). Grenoble, Presses Universitaires de Grenoble.

Groenen, H. (2012a). The Early Development of Women's Judo in Belgium from the Liberation to the late 1950s: Emancipation, Sport and Self-defence, *The International Journal of the History of Sport*, Vol. 29, Nr 13, 1819-1841.

Groenen, H. (2012b), La préparation des premières olympiades de judo en France (1960-1964): acculturation, assimilation et sportivisation. Communication at the *15e Carrefours d'Histoire du sport, Accueillir, organiser et célébrer les Jeux olympiques*, Colloque international, 29-31 October 2012, University of Rouen.

Groenen, H. (2013, under press). L'enseignement du judo en Education physique en France sous l'angle de l'éthique : une acculturation scolaire, in *Ethique, sports de combat et arts martiaux*. Presses de l'Université Toulouse 1 Capitole, Collection défense et sécurité.

Guttmann, A. (1988). ""Our Former Colonial Masters": The Diffusion of Sports and the Question of Cultural Imperialism", *Stadion*, Vol. 14, Nr 1, 49-63.

Guttmann, A. (1994). *Games and Empires: Modern Sports and Cultural Imperialism*, New York, Columbia University Press.

Guttmann, A. & L. Thompson (2001). *Japanese Sports: A History*, Honolulu, University of Hawaii Press.

Kim, M. O. (1999). *L'origine et le développement des arts martiaux. Pour une étude anthropologique des techniques du corps*, Paris, L'Harmattan.

Neyens, K. (1988). Onstaan en evolutie van judo in België, *Bijdrage tot het Archief voor de Moderne Sport,* Diss., Katholieke Universiteit Leuven.

Poirrier, P. (2008). Introduction: pour une histoire comparée de l'histoire culturelle, in P. Poirrier (dir.) *L'histoire culturelle: un « tournant mondial » dans l'historiographie ?* (pp. 9-13). Éditions Universitaires de Dijon, Dijon.

Rioux, J. P. (1997). Introduction. Un domaine et un regard. In J.-P. Rioux & J.-F. Sirinelli (Dir.) *Pour une histoire culturelle* (pp. 7-18). Paris, Seuil.

Rioux, J. P. & Sirinelli J. F. (Dir.) (1997). *Pour une histoire culturelle*, Paris, Seuil.

Sirinelli, J. F. & M. Sot (1995). L'histoire culturelle, in F. Bédarida (Dir.), *L'histoire et le métier d'historien en France 1945-1995* (pp. 339-349). Paris, Editions de la Maison des sciences de l'homme.

Chapter 33

Understanding Martial Arts in the Light of Japanese Mesology and Systemic: The Case of Shintaido's W*akametaiso Kata*

Pierre Quettier[1]

'One cannot not communicate'.

(Waztlawick et al., 2000 p.52),

Introduction: The Three Ethical "Excluded Middles"

Wishing to clarify the conditions for intelligent communication, around the year 350 BCE Aristotle formulated the "principle of excluded middle" as the third "law of thought." Following the "principle of non-contradiction," stating that of two contradictory propositions, either one or the other could be true, he developed further the "principle of excluded middle," forbidding the existence of a third possibility in between[2].

For humanity itself, these resulted in three "excluded middles," corresponding to three levels of human *ethos*. These are:

---

[1] Pierre Quettier is an Associate Professor at Paris 8 University. He has been practicing Japanese martial arts since 1976 and is a holder of several of the highest ranks of various disciplines within the Shintaido School. His ongoing research has been conducted with the guiding principle of "knowledge transmission" (today a part of the field of Knowledge Management or KM) in mind.

[2] I owe use of the "excluded middle" concept to A. Berque's *mésologie*, based on the Japanese philosophy of "betweeness." For a more exhaustive, yet accessible, presentation of the three principles, see "Laws of thought" and "Law of excluded middle" on Wikipedia. See also http://ecoumene.blogspot.fr.

- Relating to its personal existence, a human being is considered as either "mind" or "body" with nothing in between;
- Relating to social existence, a human being is considered as either "self" or "other" with nothing in between;
- Relating to ecumene (Berque, 2000, see below), a human being should be thought of as either "culture" or "nature" with nothing in between.

We know that mind (self and culture) "won" as a matter of fact, are at the very source of these principles, and this eventually culminated "in thought" in Descartes *cogito (ergo sum)*. Meantime, the "excluded middle" principle and its incarnations percolated down to national and continental cultures *via* various situational vectors (religion, education, politics, health care, sciences, etc.) working jointly in one, the other or a combination of the three ethical "excluded middles". These premises yielded the fantastic outcomes we know in sciences, allowing humanity to control its own destiny. On the other hand it also yielded a lot of suffering to antagonist minds/bodies, selves/communities and cultures/naturesand their conjunctions. When reaching global scale development of today, the 'price to pay' seems to become dangerously threatening for the very existence of humanity and many signs today indicate that in various fields of existence we are, at individual, community and cultural levels, reactively or proactively, looking for "remedies" to these sufferings and their radical outcomes.

My hypothesis is that martial arts could play a humble yet important role in this regard. In the perspective of this chapter, my second hypothesis will be that remedies would better be designed by taking all three aspects of the problem, and their combinations, into consideration. To present and discuss these, I shall at first introduce as briefly as possible a number of interacting scientific theories, both eastern and western, that offer interesting categories for analysis of martial arts practices. Then, after introducing and detailing a *kata* (仕方, gestural sequence) of the shintaido school of martial arts, *wakametaiso kata*, in action-research posture, I shall step back and proceed to analysis.

Method: Japanese Mesology[3]

It is obvious for anyone who understands the Japanese culture — by practicing one of its numerous folk arts, such as martial arts, for example — that it actually does not consider a separation of mind/body, self/other or culture/nature in its development. It distinguishes them but at the same time it conjoins them, in themselves and among themselves. This Japanese *ethos* is well accounted for by the researchers of the Kyoto school of philosophy, among whom T. Watsuji and K. Nishida are the most known in western languages.

---

[3] I use the term as developed by A. Berque to translate the concepts of human existence formulated by Japanese philosophers. I qualified it as "Japanese" in order not to confuse it with the more restrictive sense of the term in English.

Between Culture and Nature

One of the main concepts of Watsuji's works is *fudô* (風土, ecumene or milieu)[4]. To demonstrate it, Watsuji proposes to examine the phenomenon of "cold." He explains that, being exposed to a cold atmosphere, we may experience the feeling of "becoming cold" as the entrance of this surrounding coldness into our body. But, we might also consider that the phenomenon of coldness has continuously been part of our experience under the form of "temperature" In fact, from as far back as we can remember, haven't we always *felt* more or less hot, warm, chilly, cold or comfortable, according to situations? Therefore, between "us" and "our environment" we may consider a third entity (a "middle") made of our *feelings*[5] and our *interpretations* of surrounding phenomena, but also of our actions on them, their reactions and so on. Eventually, these interactions — physical, chemical, sensitive, interpretative, etc. — between the world elements (including humanity) aggregates to form the "milieu" or ecumene (Berque, *Ibid.*) by which we belong to each other. We know nothing of "humanity" or of "nature" in themselves but we know of them or we stand in a sensitive, cognitive and practical milieu from which we continuously *experience* them *at once*[6].

Between Self and Other

Watsuji pointed out that the expression "human being" in Japanese is rendered by the word *ningen* (人間), which means "being between" and the capacity underlying it is rendered by the word *aidagara* (間柄), which means "betweeness" or "mediance", as A. Berque puts it. Our relation to others is thus placed under the same sensitive and cognitive totems as our relation to environment. As for coldness or warmness, we may agree that, from mother/father, to close and distant family members, to friends, to enemies, to colleagues, and so on, we have always felt various emotions, impressions, intuitions and the like in relation to interactions with them (*i.e.* "among us"). The "Other" can thus be considered as having, and actually has, been "in" us as well as "with" us on a continuous ground of shared feelings and meanings, thus creating the *lebenswelt*[7] that is as necessary to us humans as are water, bread and air.

K. Nishida called *basho* (場所, place) this "common ground" we share and contribute building whenever we are in relation with each other. This use of a spatial word by Nishida is most appropriate as this social matrix is for members "already there". Today, the concept is intensely used in Knowledge Management to define various "places"— including electronic media— of active knowledge sharing (Nonaka, 2007, 23-25).

---

[4] Fudô, meaning literally "climate", is the title of one of main works of T. Watsuji. In French, we owe its translation to A. Berque (2011).
[5] Standing for "emotions", "impressions", "intuitions" and the like.
[6] Berque names this experience "trajection" (*ibid.* : 308).
[7] This *lebenswelt* (or "life-world") being is, according to Husserl (1970), the ground from which social sciences should never stray.

Between Mind and Body

Last and closest, a third mediance similarly trajects the mind/body relation. Occurring at the innermost levels however, it could not be accounted for "in fact" until after the First World War, when brain-damaged soldiers were treated by physiologists and observed by phenomenologist Maurice Merleau-Ponty (2002). Differences in patients' behaviors led researchers to understand the roles of certain specific areas of the brain and thus to shed light on consciousness itself. Y. Yuasa (1987, p. 167-201) and A. Berque (2011 p. 305-318) both relate M. Merleau-Ponty's findings and the way they clarify Watsuji's basic layout of the mind/body mediance. However, nowadays, numerous researchers in neurobiology or neuropsychology are plowing the field with increasingly interesting results. Not surprisingly, all of them refer in their works to those of philosophers. The following relate to some of the researchers and their work:

- Damasio (1995), revealed the prominent role emotions play in the decision process and came out with the "somatic marker" concept uniting both mental and physical inner entities (namely representations and emotions) in the common function of "deciding" (considered the corner stone of "reason") ;
- Alain Prochiantz (1997), presenting brain development— from a first cell's DNA to a fully functional organ— demonstrated the emergence of the neuronal *homunculus* by which we introject, through actual worldly interactions, our body scheme and various entities from our environment, into our brain's neuronal connexions.
- F. Varela and H. R. Maturana (1922), doing researches on immunity, demonstrated that the immune systems of vertebrates were capable of operating a coupling of action and perception that enabled them to create a closure and meet constraints from environment; hence to behave as cognitive entities, without neurons in some cases (Varela, 1994). From these they derived the systemic concepts of "enaction" and "autopoiese," theorizing the emergence of the individual mind.

Thus T. Watsuji, by proposing his set of concepts outlining the culture/nature and self/other mediances, offered a matrix within which it was possible to think about mind/body mediance as well (Yuasa, 1987). In that regard, martial practices may be thought of as directly addressing this medial entity, not only body nor mind but between and both; our medial "self."

Highlighting Martial Arts

Martial arts refer to open conflict; which is, according to common sense, the exact opposite of communication. When one wins, the other loses or they come to a tie… and go on; it is quite simple. Now, let us take a phenomenological look at the conflict process itself and, in order to do so, let's "decide" to see it as did the Palo Alto psychologists who decided to act "as if" every sign of mental disorders they saw in their patients (like shouting, muteness, aggressiveness, self-mutilation, etc.) were not "miscommunications" or "refusals of communication" but "different ways of communication"[8]. Being incapable of verbal communication, patients had turned to non-verbal communication. From that point they could start interpreting patients' signs as meaningful messages. More so, when possible, they entered into communication with them using the same "codes" (non-aggressively however). This often yielded surprising results and, in time, completely new theories and psychotherapies could emerge.

In my understanding, that is exactly what martial arts are doing: martial artists may choose to consider that a person coming to the point of aggressiveness (less-verbal or non-verbal) is a person faced with a difficulty to communicate but trying to communicate "anyhow" in order to be understood or, at least, heard. What such a person needs once this point has been reached is not some admonition to turn back to verbal communication, but to enter a space of action and interaction in (safe) continuity with his/her present feelings; a space of non-verbal communication. Martial arts aim at training people so that they become able to do exactly that. Furthermore, in so doing, martial arts create spaces (*ba* 場, equally pronounced *jo*, as in *dojo* 道場— "the place of the way") of experience that especially attract people having precisely these kinds of problems of miscommunication— the "not being heard", "not being understood" or "being misunderstood" complex, in many disguises.

That is how martial arts look right into the eyes of the dragon of self-other "mis-mediance" and propose "re-medies" for this specific mismediance, and therefore as we shall see for the mind/body mismediance and for the culture/nature mismediance as well. Or, to be more precise, that is "what" they do. "How" they do it may be further clarified. This we can do using G. Bateson's systemic theory of learning and communication.

Method: A Systemic Theory of Learning and Communication

The above mentioned Palo Alto psychotherapists based their new psychotherapeutic practices on G. Bateson's (1999) works. In turn G. Bateson had drawn his models from an active participation in the collective works that elaborated, after the Second World War, a new, teleological, paradigm for sciences and technologies: the systemic paradigm. One of the key models G. Bateson elaborated was "the categories of learning and communication" model (1999, p. 279-308). I find this model most useful for elucidating how, starting from physical, agonistic, practices, one may gradually raise oneself to higher, and possibly the highest, levels of social, intellectual and spiritual accomplishments.

Bateson develops four levels of learning. At each level, the subject solves specific problems and, in so doing, acquires the ability to solve the class of problems to which they belong. In turn, each class of problem poses problems of a totally different nature. Starting from zero, each new level is generated when the subject, having understood the previous class of problems, enters a 'class of classes' (i.e. a meta-class) and so on. These levels are:

---

[8] By presupposing that "one cannot not communicate" (*ibid.*) as they did, one establishes *de facto* the primacy of intentionality, therefore of consciousness, in the subject, in one form or another.

- *Zero*: The automatic action arising from integrated learning. Bateson named it so because there is no actual learning. It is often qualified as "Pavlovian" in reference to the final stage of Pavlovian learning.
- *One*: The adaptive action. It achieves a sequence of problem solving.
- *Two*: The mastery of the framework of action. Bateson called it *deutero-learning*, standing for "learning how to learn." Solving problems dialogically increases the subject's ability to solve future problems. Innovation capacity thus grows exponentially and becomes maximized within a given framework of action.
- *Three*: Overcoming and controlling frameworks. For example, when moving suddenly from a "reward reinforcement system" to a "punishment reinforcement system," some subjects do not overcome the deception and then regress while some, eventually after a short downtime, integrate the new meta-rule and go on. By so doing they not only keep learning but acquire a third level meta-ability to "change frameworks" (first one, then again and again, until mastering "change of framework" itself) The more one goes through the de-phasing confusion/re-phasing clarification caused by this learning experience, the more one develops a "stable stand point"— *i.e.* a consciousness, an awareness or self[9]— allowing one to go through it safely and so gain the meta-ability to survive the fundamentally unpredictable nature of an "ecumenal" (in Berque's sense) life-world.[10]

More about Martial Arts

Having "communication" as the primary intention, as demonstrated above, martial arts problem-solving situations are fundamentally medial. Bateson's categories of "learning and communication" show us how a martial *dojo* could be a place, a kind of laboratory, to live through experiences enabling the self to develop abilities of increasing medial complexity (the self "within itself," the self in social interaction, and the self in "ecumenal" interaction).

Results: Field Data

In a recent communication,[11] I introduced the typical karate practice of *tsuki* attack vs. *gedan-barai* receiving, named *chi-no-kata* in shintaido. Although this practice is clearly martial (win, lose or draw), I insisted that it should be considered as a purely symbolic practice, a semiosis. For this paper I shall present a peaceful-looking practice, of the types that are sometimes called "inner practices." Its "deep martiality" will appear at later stages of the process.
Wakametaiso (seaweed exercise)

---

[9] In this, I am following G. H. Mead, who defines the "self" as the interactional product of "I" (what I am originaly, my ipseity) and "generalized other" (what I am as a member of society, my identity).
[10] That is, a life-world within which "nature" is allowed a role.
[11] "Body & awareness" colloquium in Zadar (2011).

The Wakametaiso partner practice is a relatively recently developed technique of a school of martial arts which emerged during the counter-culture movement of the sixties, the Shintaido school. An outgrowth of several martial filiations, this school had especially developed the metaphorical and symbolic effectiveness of martial practices as a proactive adaptation to the coming "information society", which we are fully in now. Wakametaiso kata may be practiced with one partner, with multiple partners, or by oneself (relating to "ecumene"). Sub-phases exist that are used to teach beginners, which I shall not detail here.

With One Partner

Description : After a mutual bow, Partner «A» stands still and closes his/her eyes, imagining being a seaweed under water or a tall prairie grass in the wind. When «A» seems ready, partner «B», like a sea current or a wind coming from afar, pushes «A»'s upper body at shoulder level, again and again coming from different angles. In the first stage, «A» shouldn't lose balance. After a while «B» might push at hip or knee levels as well. Pushes gradually increase in frequency and intensity, always without causing loss of balance. After a while however, «A» may start moving, *i.e.* losing and recovering balance again and again, eventually rolling and so on.

The exercise could finish there. In this case, after a climax of movement, «B» would decrease frequency and intensity, bringing «A» back to stillness, then stopping and preparing to switch roles.

«A»'s experience: «A» is right away put in a paradoxical situation by the *kata's* framework (much as when faced with a Zen *koan*): resistance is not possible and displacement is not possible either. The solution appears quickly: affirming the lower part of body while softening the upper part. The process is greatly eased by calling on metaphors: "as if" rooted yet as flexible as seaweed (a *wakame*) or a blade of prairie grass; "being" a seaweed or a blade prairie grass. This is what the name of the *kata* is intended for. When pushes increases with frequency and intensity, eventual loss of balance gives instant feedback of a break into the mind-body continuum (a glimpse of inattention, a thought followed unduly, a mental, yet untimely, anticipation of one's partner's intention, etc.). When movement is allowed into the process, «A» receives the suggestion to do it "as if" weighted by a "heavy ballast down there" (much as a seaweed carrying a piece of rock). Movement from a fixed location and eventual rolling bring about a "cleaning of [the doors of] perception" (Blake, 1994, p. 25-26),[12] which in turn increases the capacity to receive «B»'s "attacks" to the point of "anticipation"[13].

---

[12] "*... But first the notion that man has a body distinct from his soul, is to be expunged; this I shall do [...by] melting apparent surfaces away, and displaying the infinite which was hidden.*
If the doors of perception were cleansed everything would appear to man as it is, infinite ..."

[13] As these anticipations can sometimes be so well-timed and repetitive, practitioners conceive the existence of some telepathic phenomena (intention being perceived as soon as it is intended) to explain it. These conceptions eventually end up in what is known as "the *ki* theory." Scientific measurement of these phenomena (Yamamoto *et al.*, 2001) is not

When «B»'s influence finally decreases and stops, «A» enters a space of quiet martial meditation: body thoroughly vertical, relaxed and with deep sensitivity to the surrounding "milieu."

«B»'s experience: For lack of space, I shall not detail «B»'s experience. We note however that it takes quite a long time for beginners to stop "acting small" (pushing locally and mecanically) even when told to "look far," "use whole body movement," or "move like a current coming from a distance." From this we see that this ability to "attack" properly is also linked to a sensitivity to milieu (from a distance, into the distance).

With Several Partners

After the first switching of roles, the one-to-one exercise speeds up, gradually allowing mutual influence: pushing (attacking) and receiving on one side or the other, at one level or another or with any combination of these, while maintaining the dynamics of the movements, *i.e.* receiving/attracting a push on one side of the body while letting the other side push a "dead"— unmoving— part of the partner's body ("as if" attracted to it) to make it come alive. Many such interactive games become possible while playing with perceptions and representations of the situation. Advanced practitioners often feel that the various *kata* they have learned in their careers suddenly come alive in their medial-bodies (Berque, 2009, p. 295) and start acting efficiently according to the situation.

Then, as interactions heat up, a given pair of practitioners might cross paths with another pair in the *dojo* and start interacting with them. This usually happens with explicit permission from the leading instructor (as this could be dangerous for unprepared persons). As this spreads out, the whole situation quickly turns into a kind of "battlefield" with people initiating or receiving attacks at any time to anyone in the way. This creates a highly stochastic situation within which one may find one's way toward efficient mental/pragmatic (level two) strategies yielding better results (*i.e.* "keep moving," "follow the path of attack," "abandon expectations" and so on).

Uniting with "nature"

At a certain point of development of the group practice, each person and the group seemingly experience an expansion of feeling to a point of "fusion" into surrounding "nature" (some kind of deep relation with "what is" *hic* and *nunc*) or with "the idea of nature" or "ecumene", as A. Berque calls it more rightly. It is a group experience but altogether it is a "return" to oneself for each practitioner. This phase— sometime excited but most of the time meditative— brings an end to the practice.

---

quite convincing. Experimental conditions themselves (*i.e.* the fact of experience itself) creating the problem, they should be measured in actual *dojo* situations, and this has not been possible so far to my knowledge.

Discussion: Mediating Vertical and Horizontal Accomplishments

Part One: Vertical Accomplishments

Vertical accomplishments are analyzed according to Bateson (1999) categories. Level one: Research on sports being already very rich with such demonstrations, I shall not develop how physical abilities (mechanical, organic and emotion-related, such as stability, flexibility, adaptability, sensitivity to "weak signals," reactivity, dynamism, calm, etc.) may be gained by practicing a physical discipline like *wakametaiso*.

Level two: Instead, considering Bateson's categories of learnings, I would like to insist on *deutero-learning, the* "learning of learning" that may be realized. A. Damasio (1995, p. 215-258) showed us that it is the conjunction of emotions (feelings, sensations, intuitions, etc.) with representations (signs, symbols, memory , etc.) that makes the "somatic marker" which is kept in stock to be reactivated next time a similar situation demanding a reaction is met. This partly explains the cognitive efficiency of metaphors. This is how something that was learned in depth in a *dojo* can be memorized and semiotized to be reactivated in time of need.

In *wakametaiso*, when in the first phase one learns how to "root" one's lower-self while at the same time softening one's upper-self, one gains, with experience, the mastery of specific inner states and their combinations that may be used when confronted with a situation where normal routines in job, family life, etc. are disturbed. Similarly, when one learns, in the second phase, how to sort out confused feelings in order to regain stability after having been disturbed from physical balance, one gains, with experience, "somatic markers" that may serve as emotional and/or mental hints when facing heavier life-disrupting challenges.

Level three: The experimental quality of practices (a *dojo* is a place of interactions designed so that one may learn by essays and errors) allows one to live many similar, yet slightly different, situations and to extract the essence of them. This allows a practitioner quick acquisition of meta-expertise and distance. "Blooming" at intellectual (verbal) and existential levels, these learning pieces interact with personal and cultural values.

In *wakametaiso*, when having learned, in the third phase, how to follow one's intuition in a chaotic situation to find one's way easily from one partner to the other in a dynamic crowd, one gradually learns how to depart from specific situations and reach a distanced and self-centered consciousness— yet one still adequately sensitive to weak signals— allowing one to process the details of situations while keeping global attention. These abilities are readily transferable into daily life.

For people living in fast-changing societies where the capacity to adapt to, to surf, and to control flows of information is so important, the *wakametaiso* practice may indeed appear as symbolic and serve as a potential educational vector for useful survival abilities.

Part Two: Horizontal Accomplishments

Abilities learned in the *dojo* may thus find their ways into the daily social lives of practitioners *via* human complex meta-learning capacities. Speaking of and for itself, that could be considered sufficient. On the other hand, social (second level) learning may be greatly improved (*i.e.* transferred to daily life) using the circumstances of the group's social life.

A school of martial arts practice is a "place," in Nishida's sense, where people of different horizons gather, without choosing each other, for the purpose of improving themselves by interacting among themselves with the guidance of physical *kata* and under the direction of a teacher. The organization of the practice (*dojo* care, assisting the teacher, logistics for regular classes and occasional seminars, finances, etc.) thus creates occasions for social interactions which, if taken seriously by teachers themselves (that is if it is considered by them as a personal and social discipline), put the learner in real, yet supportive, situations of life interactions. This extended conception of the *dojo* thus works as a kind of transitional space between *dojo* life and real-life worlds. In Japan, this is taken most seriously and all forms of social interactions, in and out of *dojo*, are ruled by *shikata* (仕方 - meaning "etiquette", "manners" or "best practices").[14]

Kata and *shikata* are thoroughly codified by martial arts and Japanese culture. As this culture has a rich martial background (a martial way of life) and strong "ecumenal" drive (a relation to "nature"), the *kata* and the *shikata* reflect these. As is clearly demonstrated by the three phases of *wakametaiso kata*, which may be found in other Japanese and Asian martial arts in one form or another, and by the gradual "spaces of accomplishment" of the educational organization of the school, the three dimensions of human ethics mentioned at the beginning ought to be considered— to be studied, to be accomplished— as a continuum of hyper-relating[15] phenomena. This continuity is in itself a medial accomplishment consubstantial, thus corollary as well as complimentary, with the specific personal, social and ecumenal dimensions of self-development.

This has many implications for the teaching— *i.e.* the training of teachers— of Japanese, and possibly Asian, martial arts outside their original culture (Quettier, 2011); implications that dearly demand research and intellectualization by academic and practitioners' communities if we want their cultural assets to be understood and transferable into non-Asian physical education curricula.

Conclusions

Martial arts have always adapted to technological and social changes in order to keep serving the needs for protection of people living in a given era. In Japan, there was a dramatic change (a change of system) in the Meiji era, when the samurai caste was dissolved as modern warfare made its entrance. Their "art of living," facing death with honor, or "warrior's way" (*budo*, 武道), was thus split into the techniques (*jutsu*, 術) the warriors (*bu*, 武) had been practicing and

---

[14] This is so true that mention of a high martial arts ranking lin a CV is highly valued by Japanese companies' recruiters.
[15] I use the prefix as in internet's hyper-link.

became as many ways (*do*, 道) by themselves. That is how *ju-jutsu* became *judo*, *ken-jutsu* became *kendo* and so on. And these new "arts of living" survived and evolved constantly from then on, more practiced in civil society as "way of life" than simply as fighting techniques.

In this chapter, I have briefly shown how a new technique from a contemporary school would embody the vertical development of an individual person from practical learning to life learning. Then, I have shown how such technical and personal development is further reinforced in the horizontal accomplishments of the art in the social and cultural aspects of a school's life.

References

Bateson, G. (1999). Steps to an ecology of mind: collected essays in anthropology, psychiatry, evolution, and epistemology. Chicago, Ill.; Chichester: University of Chicago Press ; Wiley.

Berque, A. (2009). Ecoumène : Introduction à l'étude des milieux humains. Belin.

Blake, W. (1906). *The marriage of heaven and hell*. Boston, J. W. Luce and company. Retrieved from http://archive.org/details/marriageofheaven00blak

Husserl, E. (1970). The crisis of European sciences and transcendental phenomenology; an introduction to phenomenological philosophy. Evanston: Northwestern University Press.

Damasio, A. (1995). Descartes' Error: Emotion, Reason, and the Human Brain. Penguin Books.

Ichijo, K., & I. Nonaka (2007). *Knowledge creation and management: new challenges for managers*. Oxford; New York: Oxford University Press.

Maturana, H. R., & F. Varela (1992). *Tree of Knowledge* (Rev Sub.). Shambhala.

Merleau-Ponty, M. (2002). *Phenomenology of perception*. London; New York: Routledge.

Prochiantz A. (1997). *Les anatomies de la pensée - A quoi pensent les calamars?* Odile Jacob.

Quettier, P. (2011), *Les deux temps de la conception japonaise d'inculturation – Sogo to shoetsu – Intégrer et transcender,* La métamorphose des cultures : sociétés et organisations à l'ère de la globalisation, dir. Lardellier, Editions Universitaires de Dijon (p.113-125).

Thomas, W. I., & D.S. Thomas (1938). *The Child in America;: Behavior Problems and Programs*. A.A. Knopf ;

Varela, F. J. (1994). A Cognitive view of the immune system. *World Futures, 42*(1-2), 31–40. doi:10.1080/02604027.1994.9972495

Watsuji, T. (2011). *Fûdo : Le milieu humain*. Trad. A. Berque, CNRS.

Yamamoto, et al., (2001). "Mini- symposium – a remote action experiment." *Journal of International Society of Life Information Science* 19.

Yuasa, Y (1987), *The Body: Toward an Eastern Mind-Body Theory*. Trans. Thomas P. Kasulis. New York : SUNY Press.

Chapter 34

Mixed Martial Art Viewership Motivation: An Analysis of Motives in Mixed Martial Arts Viewership

Yongjae Kim

Introduction

Mixed martial arts (MMA) is a combat sport which gives professional fighters the opportunity to test their abilities against other martial artists from around the world. The sport of MMA is performed by athletes who train a mix of various fighting styles in quest of developing superior stand-up and ground fighting techniques. MMA became an instant hit in the United States (US) when the Ultimate Fighting Championship (UFC) created sport consumer demand for MMA during the early 1990s. However, political controversy toward the legalization of mixed arts events did exist as the sport was not yet regulated in many US states (Cheever, 2009).

In 2001, the UFC was reorganized under the guidelines of state athletic commissions in efforts of establishing the UFC's brand of MMA as a legitimate and sanctioned entity that could make its way into the mainstream sport scene. Under new guidance, the UFC began to experience rapid growth by continually meeting consumer demand for entertainment. Most importantly, the UFC began promoting a refined image which highlighted the importance of fighter safety in MMA. The UFC brand is turning into a sanctioned and regulated entity that protects the safety of its fighters while preserving the integrity of the athleticism the sport requires.

Today, given a dramatic increase in interests for the sport of MMA, the UFC has become one of the most popular sport brands among young men. The popularity of MMA is evidenced by the fact that TV viewership peaked at 5.2 million during a single main event in 2013 (Andrews, 2013). According to the

Simmons Research Database (2010), by comparison to major professional sports in the US, the UFC's fanbase increased their total number of fans by about 14% (and 30% among avid fans in 2010). Clearly, MMA has become a new and popular violent combat sport proliferated by television around the world.

Despite its ever-increasing popularity and the tremendous growth of the mixed martial arts (MMA), there is a significant lack of empirical research studying the motivational factors that drive sport consumption towards UFC branded MMA events. Previous studies (e.g., Cheever, 2009; Kim, Greenwell, Andrew, Lee, & Mahony, 2008) were methodologically limited particularly with respect to construct validity and reliability and a theory-based approach of understanding spectator motivations for attending MMA events. Therefore, it is necessary to develop a comprehensive conceptual framework of MMA viewing motivation to fill the conceptual void existing in the current literature. The Use and Gratifications paradigm (U&G) was adapted as a theoretical framework to guide this study. It suggests that media user selection and continued use of televised MMA is based on their needs and satisfaction (Ruggiero, 2000). This U&G approach to the media users' activity has provided valuable insight into the understanding of MMA viewership. The current study is the first attempt to understand the psychological profile of MMA fans with a rigorous statistical procedure, and will serve as a benchmarking study for future investigation of this growing sport consumer segment. Therefore, guided by Uses & Gratifications theory, the purpose of this study was two-fold: (1) examine what motivational dimensions lead to televised MMA viewing, and (2) develop and test a comprehensive MMA motivation scale.

Theoretical Background: A Uses and Gratifications Perspective

The Uses and Gratifications theory (U&G) assumes that people are actively involved in media choice and usage to fulfill their needs and wants, in that audiences play an active role in media selection and usage (Blumler & Katz, 1974). The psychological communication perspective was established in an attempt to understand what people do with the media, rather than how the media impacts people (Katz, Blumler, & Gurevitch, 1974; Rubin, 1994). The primary purposes of the U&G approach are to explain the psychological needs that motivate audiences to use media, and to examine needs, motives, and media behavior (Katz et al., 1974; Rubin, 1994). With the emphasis on the role of audience initiative and activity, the U&G paradigm provides a theoretical approach to examine audiences' psychological process during while using media in particular contexts (Eighmey & McCord, 1998; Papacharissi & Rubin, 2000; Ruggiero, 2000).

Given the recent developments of the electronic information age, the notion of audience activity has become an important construct for conducting audience analysis (Ruggiero, 2000). If audiences are aware of not only their needs but also how to gratify their psychological needs by selecting appropriate media (Katz et al., 1974; Rubin, 1994), then perhaps they will take the initiative in selecting and using media content from a number of alternatives (e.g. television) to best satisfy their needs and desires (Ferguson & Perse, 2000; Katz et al., 1974; Rubin, 1994). This activity is directed by prior motivation, interests and preference, and involvement of users with media (Blumler, 1979; Levy & Windahl, 1984). In addition, this audience activity is especially crucial when examining what leads to an individual's choice for the type of media and the continuing use of a medium and its content to satisfy specific needs (Swanson, 1987).

Uses and Gratifications of Viewing MMA

In the uses and gratifications literature, previous studies have investigated audiences' motivation and decision to use a certain type of media as a new technology moves into the stage of mass communication (Elliott & Rossenberg, 1987). While previous research has not yet examined reasons for watching MMA, there have been several empirical endeavors to identify motives for sport media consumption. In the rapid growth of the sport industry, many researchers have examined psychological and behavioral aspects of sport consumers to understanding sport consumption motivations (e.g., Funk, Mahony, Nakazawa, & Hirakawa, 2001; Milne & McDonald, 1999; Trail & James, 2001; Wann, 1995). However, Sloan (1985) argued that motivations vary across different sport consumption contexts. As such, these earlier scale measures would not be applicable to MMA consumption contexts.

In an attempt to identify a set of common underlying dimensions for MMA motivations, Kim et al. (2008) adopted existing sport spectator motivation measures. Based on a review of the current literature, the ten motivational factors were identified: drama/eustress, escape, aesthetics, vicarious achievement, socializing, sport interest, national pride, economic factor, adoration, and violence. The study found that one of the most prominent factors was sport interest and drama and also there were gender differences in motives. More recently, Cheever (2009) employed the U&G framework to examine users' motivations for televised MMA viewing. The study found six dimensions of gratifications: violence (sensational and violent qualities of MMA), competition (sport aspect of MMA), better than other sports, underdog qualities, external sources (social interaction), and internal forces (personal interest in martial arts). However, the findings were methodologically limited particularly with respect to construct validity and reliability. While the study has contributed to the MMA spectator motivation literature, there is a need to employ a rigorous statistical procedure and a theory-based approach of understanding spectator motivations for attending MMA events. More importantly, motivational factors such as knowledge application and gambling on event do not emerge in the study even though sport fans with a preference for aggressive sports tend to engage in sport betting in violent sports with their own sport knowledge (Wann & Ensor, 1999).

With the growing popularity of MMA and the advancement of media technology, a more complete understanding of the MMA spectator motivations is needed among researchers and marketers. Although previous research has some limitations, the findings of previous studies provide insights into the understanding of motivations for MMA consumers and point to a "gratifications" approach that can serve as a starting point in understanding audience experiences with MMA viewing. Accordingly, it is imperative to identify unique motivations of the MMA viewing based on the U&G theory as a theoretical framework.

Method

Following the scale development procedure advocated by Churchill (1995), this study implemented a two-stage scale development procedure to validate an instrument for measuring motives for MMA consumption. First, focus groups were conducted to identify the primary reasons why people watch MMA on TV in order to develop instrument items. Second, a confirmatory factor analysis was utilized to validate the scale constructed to assess MMA motivations. The following section provides a detailed discussion of the instrument development procedure.

Focus Groups and Instrument Construction

The first step in the scale development process was the generation of statements for survey items assessing MMA viewing motivations. Focus group sessions were employed with a total of 21 undergraduates enrolled in sport management classes at a medium-size East Coast university in the United States. Based on the focus group findings, relevant items were modified and developed using a 7-point Likert-type scale ranging from *1 = Strongly Disagree* to *7= Strongly Agree* and randomly placed within the survey.

In order to determine the appropriate number of factors to retain, an exploratory factor analysis (EFA) was conducted using a convenience sample of 201 undergraduate students at the same university. For the purification of the instrument resulting from the EFA, the researchers began with an assessment of content and face validity through an expert review panel. The experts provided valuable feedback regarding the removal of scale items, alternate groupings of items, and the specific content of items assessing each factor. Based on the feedback from the expert panel, a final scale structure was developed for the second stage of the research study.

Instrument Validation

In order to validate the MMA viewing motivation scale, the refined scale was administered at MMA.tv Forums, one of the popular online MMA forum communities. The site was chosen as the sample frame because of the large membership and very active interaction among the members. Once the self-selected respondents visited the hyperlink address to the online survey questionnaire, respondents selected the desired answer and clicked the submit button at the end of the page. A total of four hundred fifty nine (459) respondents were obtained through a web-based survey, of which 412 (male = 386 and female = 26) were deemed usable. A confirmatory factor analysis (CFA) was then conducted using AMOS 18 to verify the internal consistency and the construct validity of the MMA viewing motivation scale. Convergent and discriminant validity were also evaluated in order to develop a more comprehensive understanding of the scales construct validity.

Results

Focus Groups

The data from the focus groups resulted in 71 initial statements for the scale. After reviewing each statement, three independent content evaluators retained 22 statements viewed as potential discriminators. The evaluators reached 95% agreement when interpreting and placing the items into specific factors. Differences among evaluators were discussed and agreement was reached on the placement of the remaining responses. The 22 items were then developed into an initial pool of the scale.

Exploratory Factor Analysis

Using the correlation matrix, the Bartlett test of Sphericity and the Kaiser-Meyer-Olkin (KMO) measure of sampling adequacy index (0.853) were used to assess the appropriateness of the data for factor analysis (Hair, Anderson, Tatham, & Black, 1998). Given the values met all recommended levels of adequateness; factor analysis was deemed the next appropriate step in the scale development process. Consequently, a principal axis exploratory factor analysis with varimax rotation was then conducted on the 22-item measure.

In order to determine the appropriate number of factors to retain, a variety of criteria were used (Comrey, 1978; Fabrigar, Wegener, MacCallum, & Strahan, 1999). The Kaiser criterion, suggested 6 factors (Nunnally & Bernstein, 1994), while the scree-test revealed a substantial drop in the plot after reaching both 2 and 6 factors, suggesting either solution is appropriate. Finally, the overall interpretability of the loading scores (Fabrigar et al., 1999) suggested retention of 5 factors. In contexts such as these where procedures suggest different numbers of factors, Comrey (1978) suggests choosing a model that produces the most readily interpretable and theoretically sensible pattern results while still retaining the statistical validity and reliability. As such, the 5-factor model was selected as the most appropriate. The results indicated that the selected 5 factors, 20-item measure accounted for 87.7% of the total variance explained.

Expert Panel Review

Based on feedback from expert reviewers, the scale was further refined with the elimination of several additional items and the renaming of one factor. For example, the item stating, "I can get information about fighters' techniques and their profiles through TV watching" was originally believed to represent a Knowledge Application factor. The majority of experts suggested, however, that this item does not contribute to the factor and was thus dropped from further analysis. In addition, three items with highest loadings for each latent variable were selected for scale validation process in an attempt to minimize the number of items in this present study. Accordingly, four items with relatively low loading were additionally dropped out from the final questionnaire. Also, as suggested by the expert panel, the Social Interaction factor was renamed to Socialization in order to better reflect the conceptual makeup of the items representing that factor.

As a result, the final five-factor solution contained 15 items and was accepted as the most appropriate. The first factor, labeled Arousal/Sensation seeking, captures an individual's need for varied, novel and complex sensations and experiences. The second dimension, Competition/Vicarious Achievement, depicts an individual's needs to experience a vicarious pleasure or feeling through fighters' success and performance. Knowledge Application, the third dimension, represents an individual's need to test their own competence and prediction by using knowledge about fighting styles and fighters while watching MMA. The fourth factor, Sport Betting, captures the economic value of MMA events (gambling on event). The fifth dimension, labeled Socialization, reflects the desire for individuals to develop and maintain human relationship through MMA viewing.

Characteristics of MMA viewers

The demographic profile of the 412 respondents for the validation of the scale using confirmatory factor analysis is presented in Table 1. The findings indicated that the majority of MMA TV viewers were male (96.1%), single (76.5%), and well educated (at least 78.9% had some post-secondary education). Additionally, 70.1% were Caucasian, and 97.3% were between 18-39 years of age.

Scale Validation

The measurement model with all five constructs was submitted to a confirmatory factor analysis (Anderson & Gerbing, 1988) using AMOS 18. Based on the recommendations of Hu and Bentler (1998; 1999), several fit indices and their cutoff criteria were selected to assess the overall fit of the model. Hu and Bentler (1999) suggest that for the ML method, a cutoff value close to .95 for CFI and TLI, a cutoff value close to .08 for SRMR, and a cutoff value close to .06 for RMSEA are interpreted as a relatively good fit between the hypothesized model and the observed data. Table 2 shows that the overall fit of the measurement model revealed a good fit of the model to the data given that each index met their respective recommended cutoff levels.

As reported in Table 2, the chi-squared value (158.69) was statistically significant at $p < .05$ ($df = 80$). This indicates that the given model's covariance structure is significantly different from the observed covariance matrix. However, sample size and non-normality can have a great effect upon the chi-squared statistic (Finch, West, & MacKinnon, 1997; Hair et al., 1998). Therefore, a variety of other indices were used and indicated good model fit. The CFI is derived from a comparison of a restricted model with a hypothesized model (Bentler, 1990), and the value of .986 suggests evidence of adequate fit. The values of the TLI reflect a good fit to the data (Bentler, 1990), with a value of .982 indicating that the model accounts for 98.2 % of the variance and covariance of the variables, but relative only to the hypothesized model (Browne, MacCallum, Kim, Andersen, & Glaser, 2002). The SRMR is intended to measure the absolute misfit of the data, based on standardized residuals (Browne, et al., 2002), and the value of .045 is interpreted as a good fit (Kelloway, 1998). The RMSEA is a measure of the average difference between the estimated population and model variances and covariance's (Kelloway, 1998). The RMSEA value of .049 indicated a close fit to the model. In summary, the overall fit indices for the model reveal a good fit of the model to the data.

Reliability and Validity of Scale

The reliability of the scale was assessed using both composite reliability and a confirmatory factor model with five constructs. The reliabilities for all five factors met the minimum level of .70 recommended by Nunnally and Bernstein (1994), and ranged from .860 to .962. The AVEs calculated using the CFA results are significantly greater than the recommended .50 criterion level (Fornell & Larcker, 1981), ranged from .542 to .881 (see Table 2). Analysis of these data suggested that the overall reliability of the MMA viewership motivation scale was acceptable.

The psychometric properties of the five constructs and indicators were then assessed with respect to convergent validity and discriminant validity. Each indicator's loading on its underlying construct, the reliability of the constructs, and the AVE were all used as measures to assess convergent validity (Bagozzi & Yi, 1988; Fornell & Larcker, 1981). Table 2 presents the loadings and the t-values of the indicators included in the model. All factor loadings exceeded .50 and each indicator was significant at the .01 level. In addition, each indicator's loading is greater than twice its standard error (Anderson & Gerbing, 1988), and the corresponding t-values were significant for its specific factor. The adequate values of AVEs for each factor indicate that the amount of variance explained by the constructs was greater than the variance explained by measurement error. These results suggest that the measurement model possesses sound convergent validity.

Discriminant validity is demonstrated when the squared correlation between one construct and any other is lower than the AVE for each construct (Fornell & Larcker, 1981). The results of the AVE test of discriminant validity are shown in Table 3, and clearly indicate that the five independent variables are distinctive from each other. As such, the results suggest the measurement model exhibited a good level of model fit, as well as evidence of sound convergent validity and adequate discriminant validity.

Discussion and Implications

To date, little empirical research has been conducted to examine psychological aspects of MMA viewers. This study represents one of the first attempts to provide empirical evidence to this area of research through a rigorous statistical procedure and a theory-based approach of understanding spectator motivations for viewing televised MMA events, and provides new insights into the psychology and characteristics of MMA fans.

These findings provide important implications for both sport marketers and advertisers. This demographic information of MMA spectators is helpful for sport marketers in developing effective communication strategies to reach their target market. Demographic characteristics of MMA viewers suggest that a wide range of age groups now enjoy MMA events and the majority of the MMA fans are male. The age range of the MMA spectators in the current study is between 18 and 56 years old with a mean age of about 24.6 years old. This provides evidence that MMA viewing is spread across a wide age spectrum, and a variety of generations. With regards to gender differences, MMA fans are predominantly male between the ages of 18-39. This research supports that the majority of MMA viewers do indeed fall within the highly desirable male 18-34 demographic (Levine, 2005). As this target market becomes more and more difficult to reach as they spread their leisure time over a variety of activities, the practice of advertising in MMA represent a valuable tool to reach this demographic.

Through a uses and gratifications paradigm, this research examined what psychological needs are satisfied through MMA consumption and produced a five motivational dimension scale that reflects the unique aspects of MMA viewership. As expected, the findings of this study support that human interaction exists in the MMA consumption setting. That is, the motivation factor labeled Socialization, and the items that comprise it lead to speculation about social context of MMA viewing in which sport fans interact with and form friendship with other fans. More importantly, it also seems likely that MMA fans are seeking personal gratification in that they enjoy the opportunity to develop and maintain the new social relationship by sharing experience and knowledge (e.g., how fighters' strategies and techniques vary) with like-minded fans in their peer group. Moreover, the motivation factor, Knowledge Application reflects a desire to test his/her own competency and outcome prediction by applying sport knowledge to a fighting event. In other words, sport fans are seeking opportunities to gratify a psychological need to test their knowledge related to fighters' ability and strategies while watching MMA, comparing their decisions against the decisions of fighters or managers in the event.

In addition to Knowledge Application, the motivation factor, Sport Betting reflects a desire for potential monetary gains through wagering on MMA events. In other words, sport fans are seeking its economic value. In competitive sport context, it is necessary that the MMA viewers first understand the rules of the sport, various fighting styles, and strategies to bet on its outcome. This leads to a speculation that most MMA viewers are knowledgeable about the sport of MMA and fighters.

Furthermore, the results of the current study are encouraging for the continued understanding of motivation for sport consumption. An identification of two dimensions, Sensation Seeking and Competition/Vicarious Achievement, is consistent with the findings of previous research explored motives for sport consumption behaviors (e.g., Gantz, 1981; McDonald, Milne, & Hong, 2002; Recours, Souville, & Griffet, 2004; Trail & James, 2001). The prominent gratifications sought by MMA viewers were Arousal/Sensation Seek. The motivation factor shows that watching MMA satisfies the need for varied, novel, and complex sensations and experiences. In particular, Competition/Vicarious Achievement motive identified in MMA viewership is very similar to self-esteem found in the general sport motivation literature. It can be implied that MMA provide spectators with opportunity to experience vicariously achievement from fighters' success through identifying with fighters in real life sport settings.

The findings of current study point towards specific implications for both scholars in the field of sport management and marketing and managers in the sport industry. With the demographic information of MMA viewers, this study may be useful to researchers who want to better understand the psychology of combat sport consumers, given motivation is central to attitudinal and behavioral outcomes of media use (Palmgree, Wenner, & Rosengren, 1985; Papacharissi & Rubin, 2000; Rubin & Rubin, 1982). A better understanding of motives for MMA viewing will enhance the explanation of attitudes and behaviors associated with the MMA viewership in general. Furthermore, understanding of MMA viewers and their motives also help develop effective promotional strategies for sport marketers.

Limitations and Future Research

Similar to all research endeavors, there are limitations to the generalization of the present study that are necessary to address in future research. First, this research was based on only one MMA fans community in the US. This will limit generalizing the results to other fans in different areas of the world. Specifically, spectators under different cultures may seek different gratifications from MMA viewing. As such, cultural variables should be considered in future research to develop a more comprehensive motivation scale.

The second limitation of the study is that this study did not examine specific motives for media disuse, but rather only the needs of the audience that influence MMA viewership. From U & G perspective, many researchers suggest that individuals are actively engaging in avoiding certain media behavior to gratify specific needs and desires (Stafford & Stafford, 1996). As such, the importance of examining motives for avoidance of media use has been highlighted when investigating motives for a certain media use. This issue was not taken into consideration in the current study. Thus, the examination of the motives for avoidance of media use should be included in future research. Additionally, future research might be wise to use structural equation models to investigate the effects of the motives for media disuse and media use on actual usage such as frequency and time spent watching MMA.

References

Andrews, K. (January 29, 2013). *MMA Crossfire – Audience peaks at 5.2 million during main event of UFC on Fox 6*. Retrieved June 10, 2013 from http://o.canada.com/2013/01/29/mma-crossfire-audience-peaks-at-5-2-million-during-main-event-of-ufc-on-fox-6/

Anderson, J., & D. Gerbing (1988). Structural Equation Modeling in practice: A review and recommended two-step approach. *Psychological Bulletin*, 103(3), 411-423.

Bagozzi, R., & Y. Yi(1988). On the evaluation of structural equation models. *Journal of the Academy of Marketing Science*, 16(1), 74-94.

Bentler, P. (1990). Comparative fit indexes in structural models. *Psychological Bulletin*, 107(2), 238-246.

Blumler, J. (1979). The Role of Theory in Uses and Gratifications Studies. *Communication Research*, 6(1), 9-36.

Blumler, J., & E. Katz (1974). *The Uses of Mass Communications: Current perspectives on gratifications research.* In. Beverly Hills, CA: Sage Publications.

Browne, M., MacCallum, R., Kim, C., Andersen, B., & R. Glaser (2002). When fit indices and residuals are incompatible *Psychological Methods*, 7(4), 403-421.

Cheever, N. (2009). The Uses and Gratifications of Viewing Mixed Martial Arts. *Journal of Sports Media,* 4(1), 25.53.

Churchill, G. (1995). *Marketing Research: Methodological Foundations* (5th international ed.). London: The Dryden press.

Comrey, A. (1978). Common methodological problems in factor analytic studies. *Journal of Consulting and Clinical Psychology*, 46(4), 648-659.

Eighmey, J., & L. McCord (1998). Adding value in the information age: Uses and gratifications of sites on the World Wide Web. *Journal of Business Research* 41(3), 187-194.

Elliott, W. R., & W. L. Rosenberg (1987). The1985 Philadelphia Newspaper Strike: A Uses and Gratifications Study. *Journalism Quarterly*, 64 (4), 679-687.

Fabrigar, L., Wegener, D., MacCallum, R., & E. Strahan (1999). Evaluating the use of exploratory factor analysis in psychological research. *Psychological Methods*, 4(3), 272-299.

Ferguson, D., & E. Perse 2000). The World Wide Web as a Functional Alternative to Television. *Journal of Broadcasting and Electronic Media*, 44(2), 155-174.

Finch, J., West, S., & D. MacKinnon (1997). Effects of sample size and nonnormality on the estimation of mediated effects in latent variable models. *Structural Equation Modeling*, 4(2), 87-107.

Fornell, C., & D. Larcker (1981). Evaluating structural equation models with unobservable variables and measurement error. *Journal of Marketing Research*, 18(1), 39-50.

Funk, D.C., Mahony, D.F., Nakazawa, M. & S. Hirakawa (2001). Development of sport interest inventory (SII): Implications for measuring unique consumer motives at sporting events. *International Journal of Sports Marketing and Sponsorship*, 3, 291-316.

Gantz, W. (1981). An Exploration of Viewing Motives and Behaviors Associated with Television Sports. *Journal of Broadcasting*, 25, 263-275.

Hair, J., Anderson, R., Tatham, R., & W. Black (1998). *Multivariate Data Analysis* (5th ed.). Upper Saddle River, NJ: Prentice Hall International Inc.

Hu, L. & P. Bentler (1998). Cutoff Criteria for Fit Indexies in Covariance Structure Analysis: Conventional Criteria Versus New Alternatives. *Structural Equation Modeling,* 6(1), 1-55.

Hu, L. & P. Bentler (1999). Fit Indices in Covariance Structure Modeling: Sensitivity to underparameterized model misspecification. *Psychological Methods,* 3(4), 424-453.

Katz, E., Blumler, J., & M. Gurevitch (1974). Uses and Gratifications Research. *The Public Opinion Quarterly*, 37(4), 509-523.

Kelloway, K. (1998). *Using LISREL for structural equation modeling: A researcher's guide*. Thousand Oaks: Sage Publications.

Kim, S., Greenwell, T.C., Andrew, D.P.S., Lee, J. & D.F. Mahony (2008). An analysis of spectator motives in an individual combat sport: A study of mixed martial arts. *Sport Marketing Quarterly*, 17(2), 109-19.

Levy, M., & S. Windahl (1984). Audience activity and gratifications: A conceptual clarification and exploration. *Communication Research*, 11(1), 51-78.

Levine, R. (2005, October). Reaching the Unreachables. *Business* 2.0, 6 (9), 108-116.

McDonald, M., Milne, G., & J. Hong (2002). Motivational Factors for Evaluating Sport Spectator and Participant Markets. *Sport Marketing Quarterly*, 11(2), 100-113.

Milne, G.R., & M.A. McDonald (1999). *Sport Marketing: Managing the Exchange Process*. Sudbury, MA: Jones and Bartlett Publishers.

Nunnally, J., & I. Bernstein (1994). *Psychometric theory* (3rd ed.). New Yotk: McGraw-Hill.

Palmgreen, P., Wenner, L., & K. Rosengren (1985). "*Uses and Gratifications Research: The Past Ten Years,*". In K. E. Rosengren, L. A. Wenner & P. C. Palmgreen (Eds.), Uses adn Gratifications Research: Current Perspectives (pp. 11-37). Beverly Hills, CA: Sage.

Papacharissi, Z., & A. Rubin (2000). Predictors of Internet usage. *Journal of Broadcasting & Electronic Media,* 44(2), 175-196.

Recours, R. , Souville, M., & J. Griffet (2004). Expressed Motives for Informal and Club/ Association-based Sports Participation. *Journal of Leisure Research*, 36(1), 1-22.

Rubin, A. (1994). *Media Uses and Effects: A Uses and Gratifications Perspective*. In J. Bryant & D. Zillmann (Eds.), Media effects: Advances in Theory and Research. Hillsdale, NJ: Lawrence Erlbaum Associates.

Rubin, A., & R. Rubin (1982). Older persons' TV viewing Patterns and Motivation. *Communication Research*, 9(2), 287-313.

Ruggiero, T. (2000). Uses and gratification theory in the 21st century. *Mass Communication & Society*, 3, 3-37.

Simmons Research Database (2010). The UFC Fan Base. Retrieved June 11, 2013 from
http://mmapayout.com/2010/11/the-ufc-fan-base/?utm_source=feedburner&utm_medium=feed&utm_campaign=Feed%3A+Payout+%28Payout%29&utm_content=Google+Reader.

Sloan, L.R. (1989). The Motives of Sports Fans. In J.H. Goldstein (Ed.) *Sports, Games, and Play: Social & Psychological Viewpoints* (2nd Ed.), 175-240. Hillsdale, N.J.: Lawrence Erlbaum Associates.

Stafford, T., & M.R. Stafford (2001). Identifying motivations for the use of commercial Websites. *Information Resources Management Journal*, 14(1), 22-30.

Swanson, D. (1987). Gratification seeking, media exposure, and audience interpretations: Some directions for research. *Journal of broadcasting & electronic media,* 31(3), 237-254.

Trail, G., & J.D. James (2001). The Motivation Scale for Sport Consumption: Assessment of the Scale's Psychometric Properties. *Journal of Sport Behavior*, 24(1), 108-127.

Wann, D. L. (1995). Preliminary validation of the sport fan motivation scale. *Journal of Sport & Social Issues*, 20, 377-96.

Wann, D. L., & C.L. Ensor (1999). Further validation of the economic subscale of the Sport Fan Motivation Scale. *Perceptual and Motor Skills*, 88(2), 659-660.

Table 1 Demographic Profile of MMA Spectator

Demographic Information	Total(%)
N	412 (100)
Sex	
Female	16 (3.9)
Male	6 (96.1)
Age	
< 20	111 (26.9)
20-29	207 (50.2)
30-39	72 (17.5)
40 ≤	22 (5.3)
Marital Status	
Single	315 (76.5)
Married	81 (19.7)
Divorced	16 (3.9)
Education	
High School Graduate	87 (21.1)
Attending College	200 (48.5)
College Graduate	138 (27.7)
Professional/Graduate School	11 (2.7)
Ethnicity	
Black/African American	23 (5.6)
Native American	8 (1.9)
Hispanic	26 (6.3)
White/Caucasian	289 (70.1)
Asian or Pacific Islander	59 (14.3)
Other	7 (1.7)

Note: ( ): Percentages may not add to 100 % due to rounding.

Table 2 Composite Reliabilities (ρ), Average Variance Extracted (AVE), Factor Loadings, Standard Errors and t-values for the MMA viewing motivation scale Confirmatory Factor Analysis.

Factors and Items	ρ	AVE	Factor Loading	CR
Knowledge Application (3)	.904	.726		
I like challenging myself to see how many I get right in future outcomes.			.901	
I apply my knowledge about fighters and techniques/strategies while watching MMA.			.899	25.37
I apply my fighting knowledge to predict future outcomes of match-ups.			.809	21.33
Sport Betting (3)	.933	.813		
One of the main reasons for watching MMA events is because I can bet on it.			.943	
MMA events are enjoyable if I can bet on the outcome.			.916	31.76
Making wagers is the most enjoyable aspect of being a MMA fan.			.859	27.14
Competition/Vicarious Achievement (3)	.946	.843		
I feel like I have won when my fighter wins			.928	
I feel proud when my fighter beats other.			.962	36.92
I feel a sense of accomplishment when my fighter plays well.			.879	28.96
Arousal/Sensation Seeking (3)	.860	.542		
I get excited when my fighter comes on to the cage.			.715	
A fight is more excited when the outcome is not decided until the very end.			.924	16.34
I find myself on the edge of my seat during a competitive MMA match-up.			.811	15.52
Socialization (3)	.962	.881		
An important aspect of watching MMA events includes discussing how fighters' strategies and techniques vary.			.949	
Watching MMA events provides opportunities to interact with other like-minded individuals.			.972	45.29
Watching MMA provides me with opportunities to be with others.			.914	35.59

Note. Likelihood-ratio chi-square (χ^2) = 158.69, df = 80, p = .000; Tucker-Lewis Index (TLI) = .982; Standardized Root Mean Square Residual (SRMR) = .045; Comparative Fit Index (CFI) = .986; Root Mean Square Error of Approximation (RMSEA) = .049.

Table 3 Correlations among Factors

	Mean (SD)	KNOW	SBET	VA	ARO	SOC
Knowledge Application (KNOW)	4.63 (.948)	.726				
Sport Betting (SBET)	3.97 (1.091)	.590**	.813			
Competition/ Vicarious Achievement (VA)	4.53 (.871)	.564**	.462**	.843		
Arousal/ Sensation Seeking (ARO)	4.77 (.846)	.484**	.396**	.507**	.542	
Socialization (SOC)	3.95 (1.040)	.162**	.133**	.142*	.200**	.881

Note: * $p < .05$, ** $p < .01$

The figures underlined represent AVE; Figures below the AVE line are the correlations between constructs; No correlations failed the AVE (Average Variance Extracted) discriminant validity test.

Chapter 35

The Importance of Education and Morality in the Martial Arts

Keith Gilbert

'There is no guarantee cast in stone....only the process of constant evaluation of what the subject is about, in the minds of interested, informed and concerned individuals, will at least give it a fighting chance'.

Peter Lofthouse[1] (1992)

Introduction

From the outset it can be clearly stated that being involved in the production of this book has enabled me to better understand the nuances of the martial arts and their impacts and benefits on global society. Certainly, because of my previous involvement in judo I thought I had a broad knowledge of most of the martial arts and their individual quirks, idiosyncrasies' and mechanics. I was wrong. Furthermore, after working closely with the authors and on the individual chapters in this book I have come to realise the intricate and sometimes unconventional world of martial arts often operates below the radar normally embodied by other major sporting organisations. In this regard and undeniably, there is a definite lack of community and indeed societal knowledge regarding the positive aspects of the martial arts as they have become far to glamorised and in

---

[1] Lofthouse, P. (1992). Forward; In K. Gilbert (1992). *Towards an Understanding of Physical Education*, Queensland University of Technology Press. Brisbane, Australia. Peter was Head of the School of Human Movement Studies at Queensland University of Technology, Brisbane, Australia. He was an amazing lecturer who taught me all I know about the teaching of dance and primary physical education teaching. I am indebted to him for his belief, patience, trust and friendship.

many ways they display the reverse intentions and negative connotations portrayed through aggressive and brutal behaviour in film and other media outlets. Rather than support the positive and good aspects of fighting, film and media have actually turned off whole generations of people who think that competing in the martial arts involves large amounts of shouting, spinning, flying and bloodletting. This fantasy martial arts movie world rather than support the martial arts has tended to turn people off to the sports themselves. In this regard there is a real need for further positive marketing and educational development of the individual sports on a global basis through the International Federations and the IOC. The aim in this brief chapter is to take a closer look at the education and moral processes which are highly important to the continued development of the martial arts. In doing so I argue that the issues raised by the authors in this book are not just about participation but also about the theoretical perspectives of the martial arts. Consequently, what follows are some thoughts and perspectives on the role of the key elements of education, morality and ethics in the future development of the martial arts.

Education

Through the development of this book it is clear that there has been one recurring theme and that theme is *education*. The following points to be made here revolve around the education process required to market the martial arts, develop the martial arts and maintain the skills over time so that each generation does not lose the particular physical skills in order to save the sports in their original historically grounded formats. An important part of the continued education process revolves around the written rules and regulations which determine each martial art and sets them apart from each other and also regulates change. If we further investigate the education potential of the martial arts we come to understand that virtually all of the martial arts are taught indoors and in educational institutions of some kind. For example: schools, universities, dojos, halls, gymnasiums, community centres and monasteries and involve some form of formal physical and mental training. As such it can be clearly stated that there is definitely education occurring through martial arts and an educational balance being achieved between practical and academic which does not necessarily occur with other sports. That being said as practitioners we must continue to be diligent and maintain the need for improved coach education programmes which offer further standard certification and university education which provides degrees and higher degrees and deliver respectability, morality, ethics, values and links to the individual federations and intellectual aspects of martial arts. It is believed that this academic respectability argument is modest and devalued in some of the martial arts. Indeed, it requires more credence in the clubs and individual martial arts themselves in order to maintain and argue for funding and increased resources in the future. Along with this form of education comes the increasing importance of managing individuals, teams and clubs within an increasingly competitive sports world. Management education and financial club management is becoming more and more important and is virtually non-existent in the martial arts at the grass-roots levels. In relation to this point we desperately need to up-skill our leaders.

There have been throughout this book many comments as to the effects of the martial arts on troublesome or difficult children, youth and adults. In actuality there is no doubt that the benefits to troubled individuals of competition and the values which martial arts exude are immense but perhaps this also requires further certification so that individuals can improve their personal lives and also be supported by the martial arts to receive better employment prospects. Trainers need to be educated in order to support these important developments in the benefits to the community of martial arts. Basic courses for the participants in the development of a curriculum vitae, literature and math would also be of considerable benefit to individuals who function at the lower end of our communities. There could be courses developed to teach 'integrity' and 'anti-bullying' and these would fit nicely into the curriculum development of many schools and colleges across the world. The argument could be that these additions to the martial arts also build the notions of capacity and capital amongst our disadvantaged youth. Capacity building is an important aspect of our work in the martial arts and should be high on our outcomes list. Indeed, the United Nations Development Program (UNDP) has placed a high emphasis on the building of capacity which it defines as '...the ability of individuals, institutions and societies to perform functions, solve problems, and set and achieve objectives in a sustainable manner'[2]. All these attributes are already happening in the martial arts but have not been fleshed out in order to develop people fully. If we further break the term down then we realise that 'capacity building' relates significantly to the development of individuals and institutional capacity. Indeed, community martial arts training should involve increasing and supporting health of our participants, making them aware of the environment and also be linked strategically to local government initiatives. Too often we go off on our own separate tracks and the champions for the martial arts are not necessarily skilled in the development of our problem children and youth. Much of the life skill development occurs through osmosis and the practical aspects of the martial arts themselves. When I was the team manager of the Exmouth School Judo team many years ago it became increasingly clear to me that the notion of capacity building can and must be enhanced by the sustainability of a martial arts programme over time. The development of management structures which train and educate individuals to organise their competitors training and practice can only be beneficial to the community whether in the sport or political community contexts.

Because most martial arts programmes are about education and physical and mental skill development it would be relatively easy to provide capacity building exercises for the coaching curriculum. In short then we need to debate and come up with solutions which are specific to individuals - gender and age - or community based – relationships and shared norms – when capacity building through use of the martial arts. Perhaps the main way in which martial arts education programs can assist is in the development of strategies which emphasis management and quality of life issues. This is especially important if we argue that the definition of capacity building is: 'The societal activities and resources that strengthen the skills, abilities of people and community groups to take

---

[2] Please see the UNDP website for more information regarding the building of 'capacity' in developing nations. (http://www.undp.org/content/undp/en/home.html)

effective action and leading roles in development of their communities' then the martial arts have all the attributes to support this definition[3].

Hand in hand with the notion of capacity building through martial arts goes the building of potential in people known as 'social capital' (Bourdieu, 1983; Putman, 1993) which has been defined by Bourdieu (1983, p.249) as:

> 'Social capital is the aggregate of the actual or potential resources which are linked to possession of a durable network of more or less institutionalized relationships of mutual acquaintance and recognition'.

And by Putman (2000, p. 19) as:

> 'Whereas physical capital refers to physical objects and human capital refers to the properties of individuals, social capital refers to connections among individuals – social networks and the norms of reciprocity and trustworthiness that arise from them. In that sense social capital is closely related to what some have called "civic virtue." The difference is that "social capital" calls attention to the fact that civic virtue is most powerful when embedded in a sense network of reciprocal social relations. A society of many virtuous but isolated individuals is not necessarily rich in social capital'.

It is clear that the martial arts lends themselves to the social aspects of youth development and in particular the development of social capital and in Putman's mind 'social capital allows citizens to resolve collective problems more easily' thus the development of social capital through the martial arts seems a forgone conclusion. Nothing could be easier perhaps? However, as mentioned previously, what I found in this book is that the social capital often occurs simply through osmosis and not as a planned and developed outcome of the martial art itself. We need to be more thoughtful and proactive in our interactions with community leaders and youth. We need to teach patience, character building and the use of positive aggression in our interactions with our pupils. I feel that the aspects of capacity building and social capital is under developed and can be further explored through the martial arts and requires further research, perhaps through masters or PhD study, in order to provide supplementary support to the individuals in disadvantaged situations and more importantly to better support the martial arts in our communities. Indeed, learning is implicit in the development of capital and by association learning is implicit in the development of martial arts.

Education manifests itself in other ways through its connection with the martial arts. In coaching for example where grand masters, leaders and coaches should be cognizant of some of the commonplace physical education teaching strategies such as experiential learning, situated learning and other particular styles of teaching and learning. In general all martial arts educators should be constantly upgrading their qualifications and attempting to get better at how they get their important messages across to participants in their individual martial art. Most all of the individuals who I spoke with in the preparation of this book have

---

[3] Definition taken from (http://en.wikipedia.org/wiki/Capacity_building).

been involved in some form of martial art as a competitor. All were very adamant that you can't learn about the martial arts unless you compete and they believed solely in learning by doing. I am sorry to say that their perspective is old fashioned and a misnomer propagated by individuals who think that education is not as important as practice. The sooner they upgrade with qualifications outside of their martial arts sport the better the sports will become and in turn they could produce more champions and experts to keep their sport in the forefront of the public's minds. Granted the martial arts are the only sports that have internal qualifications built in through the awarding of belts but there should be more work produced which highlights the benefits of martial arts to the development of the 'whole human being' and this can only be achieved through extended education practices run through our school and higher education institutions.

Morality and Ethics

I recognise that in any project which works directly with human beings there needs to be moral and ethical practices put into place in order to maintain some form of life values to which we all adhere. Without a measured response to the deep philosophical underpinnings of martial arts themselves we cannot expect to make significant changes for the better and *changing individual's morality*, ethical understanding and life values are important to the betterment of humankind. Again through the writing of this book I have come to understand that the incorporation of the perspectives of all people involved in the martial arts is a priority and if we leave out the recipients of the individual sports in our thinking then we open ourselves to the phenomenon of 'drop out' which happens regularly within individual martial arts programmes. Indeed, this is a phenomenon which requires further research. It is important to attempt to instil morality and ethics and values through our program planning in 'martial arts development' across the world. Indeed, how do we change others morals and values in order to respect life and family through the medium of the martial arts in an ethical manner? We achieve this by involving them in sports which have integrity, morality and wisdom inbuilt. The martial arts fit all of the previous criteria and should be better marketed by CEO's and Directors of the individual sports in order for the sports to progress into the future.

Conclusive Statement

This chapter relates to some of the important directions which the martial arts need to follow in the future. The key elements being education, morality and ethical behaviour. Without further consideration of all three areas and the strong messages which they can provide to the public then some forms of martial arts will become less important and be in danger of extinction.

References

Besterfield, D. H., Besterfield-Michna, C., & M. Besterfield-Sacre (1999). Total Quality Management, Prentice Hall, USA

Bourdieu, P. (1983) The Forms of Capital. In J. Richardson (Ed.) Handbook of Theory and Research for the Sociology of Education (New York, Greenwood), pp. 241-258

Deneulin, S., & L. Shahani (2009). An Introduction to the Human Development and Capability Approach: Freedom and Agency. Sterling, VA: Earthscan.

Fingeld, D.L. (2003). Metasynthesis: The state of the art – so far, *Qualitative Health Research*, vol.13, no. 7 pp. 893-904

Hauge A.O. & K. Mackay (2004). Monitoring and Evaluation for Results: Lessons from Uganda. Capacity Development Brief 3, World Bank (pdf).

Holden, M; Mackenzie, J. & R. VanWynberghe (2008). Vancouver's promise of the world's first sustainable Olympic Games. *Environment & Planning C: Government and Policy,* Vol.26, pp 882-905.

Legg, D. & K. Gilbert (2011). Paralympic Legacies, Commonground publishing, Illinois, USA

Leifried, K.H.J. & C.J.McNair (1994). A Tool for Continuous Imporovement, Harper Collins, USA.

Lister, R. (2005). Being Feminist (Politics of Identity – VIII). Government Opposition , Vol. 40, Issue 3, pp. 442-463 Summer 2005.

Putnam, R. D. (1993) 'The prosperous community: social capital and public life' in the *American Prospect*, 4:13

Sachs, G. (2005). The End of Poverty: Economic Possibilities for our time. Penguin Press

Thompson, I. and Cox, A. (1997), Don't imitate, innovate, *Supply Management*, pp. 40-3

Tomasello, M. (1999). "The Human Adaptation for Culture" in *Annual Review of Anthropology* vol. 28: p.514

Tylor, E. B. (1871) *Primitive Culture*, Harper & Row. New York 1958 p.16

Notes on Contributors

Richard Bailey is a professor of sport, physical activity, and public policy in the Faculty of Education, Health, and Leisure at Liverpool John Moores University, Liverpool, U.K.

Stanley Blue is a PhD student in the Sociology Department at the University Lancaster, U.K.

David Brown is a reader in the sociology of sport and physical culture at Cardiff School of Sport, Cardiff Metropolitan University, Cardiff, U.K.

David Chaplin is an associate professor of economics in the School of Business at Northwest Nazarene University, U.S.A.

Andrea Cristiane Alves da Cunha is completing her master's in physical activity & sciences at Salgado de Oliveira University in Niterói, Brazil.

Orestes Manoel da Silva is a researcher at the Federal University of Rio de Janeiro in sports law (FND-UFRJ), Brazil.

Eliane Glória Reis da Silva Souza is a doctoral student in exercise science and sports at Gama Filho University, Brazil, and holds a Master of Science in physical activity from Salgado de Oliveira University and is an expert in history and popular culture.

Marianne Dortants is an assistant professor in the University of Utrecht, Netherlands.

Greg Downey is an associate professor in the Department of Anthropology, Faculty of Arts, Macquarie University, Australia.

Tom Ellis is a research associate in the Institute of Criminal Justice Studies at the University of Portsmouth, U.K.

Matthew Ferrari is a doctoral candidate in the Department of Communication at the University of Massachesetts, Amherst, U.S.A.

Itaborá Ferreira is very experienced and has been practising capoeira since 1974. He is also a two-time Brazilian jiu-jitsu World Champion and Brazilian jiu-jitsu Pan American Champion.

John Fulton is a principal lecturer in the Faculty of Applied Sciences at the University of Sunderland, U.K.

Keith Gilbert is a professor of sport sociology and sport management in the School of Health, Sport, and Bioscience at the University of East London, U.K.

Kevin Grace is the head and university archivist of the Archives & Rare Books Library of the University of Cincinnati, U.S.A.

Haimo Groenen is a senior lecturer attached to the SHERPAS laboratory at the University of Artois, France.

Cheri Hampton-Farmer is chair of the Communication Department at the University of Findlay, U.S.A.

Jennifer Hardes is a PhD student and lecturer in the Department of Physical Education at the University of Alberta, Canada.

John Harris is a reader in international sport and event management in the Department of Business Management at Glasgow Caledonian University. U.K.

Bryan Hogeveen is currently an associate professor in the Department of Sociology at the University of Alberta, Canada.

Craig Jenkins is a research associate in the Institute of Criminal Justice Studies at the University of Portsmouth, U.K.

Brian Jones is an assistant professor in kinesiology and health science at Georgetown College, U.S.A.

Bennetta Jules-Rosette is a distinguished professor of sociology and director of the African & African-American Studies Research Centre in theDepartment of Sociology at the University of California, San Diego, U.S.A.

Anna Kavoura is a PhD student in sport psychology in the Department of Sports the University of Jyväskylä, Finland.

Yongjae Kim is an assistant professor in the Faculty of Sports Management at Kutztown University. U.S.A.

Marja Kokkonen is a researcher at the University of Jyväskylä, Department of Psychology, University of Jyväskylä, Finland.

Jamie Lee-Barron is a professor and director of the Institute for Martial Arts and Sciences, U.K.

Hannu Leinonen is a practitioner and PhD student at the University of Jyväskylä, Finland.

Sergio Mendoza is the chief operating officer at Plaza Mexico, a Mexican grocery store and restaurant in Southern Idaho, U.S.A.

Colin McGuire is a PhD candidate in ethnomusicology at York University, Toronto, Canada.

Chris Moser is an assistant professor in the College of Education at the University of Findlay, U.S.A.

Mauricio Murad has a PhD in sociology of sport from the Faculty of Sport at the University of Porto, Portugal, and is a graduate in social science. He is currently an associate professor (retired) at the University of the State of Rio de Janeiro, and a professor of sociology teaching masters at Salgado de Oliveira University.

Renata Osborne is a professor of qualitative research at the Physical Activities and Sciences Master's Program of Salgado de Oliveira University in Niterói, Brazil.

Fabiano Pries Devide has a degree in physical education from the Federal Rural University of Rio de Janeiro, and MS and PhD degrees in physical education and culture from the University Gama Filho. He is currently a professor of physical education at the University Federal Fluminense.

Pierre Quettier is an associate professor at Paris 8 University, France.

Carla Rocha Araujo is a researcher at University Gama Filho, Brazil, and a PhD student at University of Porto—Faculty of Sport, Portugal.

Tatiana V. Ryba is a professor at Aarhus University, Denmark

Baris Sentuna is a professor in sociology at Balikesir University, Turkey.

John T. Sorrell is a licensed psychologist in behavioral health & psychology Services, San Francisco, U.S.A.

Guy Spriggs is a professor in the College of Arts and Sciences at The University of Kentucky, U.S.A.

Charles Spring is an academic and subject coordinator for sport at the University of Derby, Buxton, U.K.

Marc Theeboom is the head of the department and works as a full professor in the Faculty of Physical Education and Physiotherapy and the Faculty of Psychology and Educational Sciences of the Vrije Universiteit Brussels.

Maarten van Bottenburg is the head of the department and a professor of sport development at Utrecht University School of Governance.

Jikkemien Vertonghen works as an assistant professor in the Department of Sports Policy and Management (Faculty of Physical Education and Physiotherapy) of the Vrije Universiteit Brussel (VUB).

Sebastião Josué Votre has a post-doctoral degree in the sociology of sport from the University of Strathclyde, Scotland. He holds a doctorate from PUC-RJ in sociolinguistics and he is a professor at UFRJ (retired) from the University Gama Filho. Currently he is a member of the University Federal Fluminense and works in the CEDES network of the Ministry of Sports in Brazil.

Ian Warren is a senior lecturer in criminology in the School of Humanities and Social Sciences, Faculty of Arts and Education at Deakin University, Australia.

Kath Woodward is a professor in sociology at the Open University in the U.K.

Index

A

Accidents, 136, 137, 138, 139, 141
Adolescents, 283, 312, 321, 323, 324, 329
Aesthetic, 3, 5, 6, 106, 107, 115, 248, 249, 250, 251, 252, 253, 254, 255, 257, 258, 259, 260, 262, 263
Aesthetics of self, 258, 263
Aggression, 9, 24, 25, 30, 38, 39, 41, 44, 46, 79, 151, 190, 203, 221, 223, 248, 270, 271, 272, 273, 275, 278, 283, 284, 329, 330, 343, 344, 348, 349, 350
AIBA, 129, 133, 170
Aikijitsu, 109
Analysis, 15, 46, 69, 76, 77, 79, 90, 111, 114, 117, 120, 123, 126, 127, 129, 130, 147, 152, 179, 180, 208, 216, 223, 227, 228, 233, 258, 277, 279, 284, 320
Anthropologist, 146, 253, 254
Anxiety, 96, 209, 213, 217, 220, 221, 226, 228, 273, 329, 348, 350
Aristotelian goals, 107
Arrhythmia, 118, 120, 121, 122, 123
Arrhythmia, 121
Art, 3, 4, 5, 6, 7, 8, 9, 10, 15, 27, 40, 41, 43, 45, 56, 57, 60, 64, 67, 68, 69, 70, 71, 72, 73, 74, 75, 78, 80, 81, 93, 105, 106, 107, 108, 109, 110, 111, 140, 141, 145, 146, 153, 156, 165, 166, 167, 168, 169, 177, 189, 192, 194, 196, 201, 207, 208, 219, 220, 221, 223, 225, 226, 238, 240, 243, 247, 248, 249, 250, 251, 252, 253, 255, 256, 257, 258, 259, 260, 262, 263, 295, 305, 313, 314, 328, 333, 334, 340, 341, 346
Art form, 69, 72, 106, 177, 207, 208, 220, 221, 223, 238, 249
Art of self, 189, 192, 196
Art of War, 5, 105, 150, 153
Asian martial arts, 40, 50, 55, 56, 70, 74, 75, 76, 350
Attitudes, 21, 24, 41, 96, 122, 123, 214, 231, 234, 237, 261, 283
Avatars, 345

B

Bailey, vii, 49, 52, 55, 56
Balance, 8, 15, 90, 91, 93, 99, 101, 125, 126, 127, 128, 129, 130, 134, 135, 136, 138, 139, 141, 142, 143, 173, 196, 217, 219, 245, 248, 276, 279, 291, 303, 331
Beautiful movements, 6
Behaviour, 3, 14, 22, 24, 25, 34, 38, 39, 40, 41, 42, 68, 118, 137, 157, 159, 190, 257, 267, 268, 270, 273, 274, 275, 277, 278, 281, 283, 284
Behaviour change, 118, 273
Being, 3, 4, 6, 7, 8, 9, 12, 16, 18, 22, 23, 26, 30, 34, 35, 39, 42, 51, 59, 60, 68, 69, 72, 73, 75, 78, 79, 80, 83, 84, 88, 89, 90, 91, 92, 93, 94, 98, 105, 109, 113, 114, 118, 120, 122, 139, 145, 152, 165, 166, 168, 179, 181, 182, 185, 186, 187, 189, 190, 191, 192, 194, 195, 196, 199, 201, 202, 203, 204, 209, 213, 216, 217, 219, 220, 222, 224, 226, 227, 230, 232, 234, 235, 236, 241, 242, 245, 251, 252, 253, 254, 255, 256, 257, 262, 268, 275, 282,

295, 297, 298, 312, 313, 314, 315, 316, 324, 329, 344, 345, 367, 371
Belonging to war, 4, 8
Biological, 68, 87, 92, 94, 158, 162, 208, 209, 210, 211, 213, 214, 220, 221, 222, 230, 231, 343, 347, 349
Biological determinism, 87
Biological differences, 94
Biological factors, 214
Biology, 87, 93, 210, 211, 350
Biopsychosocialspiritual, 208, 209, 210, 212, 216, 221, 222, 229
Black belt, 6, 13, 18, 25, 45, 61, 78, 82, 111, 220, 321, 333, 334, 335, 336
Black Paris, 293, 294, 295, 310
Body, 3, 4, 5, 7, 9, 16, 18, 29, 32, 33, 34, 36, 45, 56, 57, 67, 68, 69, 70, 71, 72, 73, 74, 75, 76, 78, 79, 80, 81, 83, 84, 85, 88, 90, 91, 94, 96, 98, 99, 100, 101, 102, 108, 118, 121, 129, 138, 139, 140, 142, 146, 147, 148, 160, 167, 178, 182, 185, 199, 200, 211, 218, 219, 220, 221, 222, 231, 234, 236, 244, 247, 249, 251, 252, 253, 254, 255, 256, 257, 258, 259, 260, 272, 293, 295, 316, 331, 339, 341, 350, 371
Body capital, 32, 33, 36
Bodyguard, 330
Bourdieu, 29, 32, 33, 34, 35, 36, 68, 69, 70, 72, 75, 85, 147, 150, 151, 152, 251, 252, 264
Boxing adage, 203
Boxing club, 29, 30, 31, 33, 34, 35, 156, 173, 174, 182, 273, 274, 281, 284
Brazilian jiu-jitsu, 78, 79, 80, 81, 82, 83, 85, 314
Broken bones, 140
Brutal, 7, 118, 157, 183, 184, 186, 190, 192, 193

C

California Athletic Commission, 297
Capital, 29, 33, 34, 35, 36, 68, 69, 71
Capoeira, 145, 152, 153, 230, 231, 232, 233, 234, 235, 236, 237, 238, 239, 244, 247, 248, 249, 250, 252, 253, 254, 255, 256, 259, 260, 261, 262, 263, 321, 323
Care of self, 249, 260
CDA, 267
Ceteris paribus, 125
Champions, 30, 31, 79, 89, 175, 178, 201, 242, 314, 322, 323, 324
Character building, 30, 32
Children, 2, 19, 21, 22, 25, 26, 39, 44, 46, 212, 215, 233, 243, 244, 245, 274, 283, 312, 313, 317, 321, 323, 324, 328, 329, 330, 331, 335
Chinese lion dance, 146, 153
Chivalry, 9, 14
Choy Lee Fut, 145
Chronological, 211
Close combat, 59, 60, 61, 64, 190
Close quarter, 61, 65
Coach, 17, 72, 83, 84, 176, 177, 178, 194, 314
Cognitive psychology, 118
Cold War, 58
Combat, 2, 4, 5, 6, 8, 33, 39, 44, 49, 51, 58, 59, 60, 61, 62, 64, 69, 70, 71, 88, 97, 105, 108, 111, 113, 114, 119, 142, 144, 146, 150, 152, 155, 156, 158, 160, 189, 190, 191, 192, 194, 195, 243, 244, 267, 268, 272, 273, 275, 276, 277, 278, 279, 280, 281, 282, 283, 304, 314, 316, 324, 329, 340, 341, 345, 350
Combative, 30, 79, 146, 153, 190, 191, 250, 330
Community development, 9, 320
Competitive balance, 125, 126, 127, 128, 129, 130, 134

Confidence, 3, 7, 16, 21, 24, 25, 33, 36, 41, 177, 195, 196, 203, 217, 222, 278, 279, 281, 329, 330, 331, 332
Conflict management, 330
Constructed, 88, 89, 111, 112, 113, 139, 202, 203, 234, 237, 263, 302, 340, 343, 346
Contextual environment, 141
Contusions, 140
Coordinated, 9, 320
Crane, 74
Creativity, 6, 248, 251, 259, 263
Criminal law, 155, 162
Criminality, 267, 275, 282
Cuba, 128, 129, 130, 131, 307
Cultural history, 179
Culture, 3, 14, 23, 45, 72, 75, 77, 87, 88, 89, 90, 93, 109, 145, 147, 165, 166, 167, 169, 170, 171, 182, 183, 184, 214, 222, 225, 226, 230, 231, 232, 237, 240, 241, 322, 339, 340, 341, 342
Cunning, 108, 254, 255, 256, 259, 260, 261, 264

D

Dance, 3, 4, 5, 6, 8, 10, 84, 138, 143, 144, 145, 146, 147, 148, 149, 150, 151, 152, 153, 167, 226, 235, 240, 247, 249, 250, 253, 255, 261, 301, 390
Definition, 2, 3, 4, 5, 8, 9, 10, 13, 69, 98, 110, 136, 179, 200, 216, 242, 259, 339
Degree, 12, 13, 17, 18, 29, 30, 31, 33, 34, 35, 50, 125, 126, 128, 149, 166, 183, 193, 211, 212, 215, 221, 234, 252, 331, 333, 349
Dehydration, 97, 99, 100, 101
Democracy, 14
Depression, 21, 134, 213, 215, 217, 220, 226, 227
Derrida, 83, 85, 115
Development, x, xi, 2, 4, 5, 7, 13, 14, 15, 16, 19, 27, 29, 32, 33, 34, 35, 36, 40, 41, 43, 44, 45, 51, 54, 68, 77, 94, 102, 119, 146, 156, 157, 173, 174, 177, 179, 189, 190, 209, 211, 212, 213, 221, 224, 227, 231, 236, 241, 242, 244, 246, 255, 257, 258, 263, 269, 274, 281, 282, 283, 284, 313, 314, 318, 320, 321, 328, 332, 334, 335, 340, 347, 359
Developmental, 41, 42, 43, 45, 211, 283
Diuretics, 99, 100
Do Pi, 145
Dragon, 74
Durkheim, 73, 76

E

Economic capital, 29, 36, 68
Ecosystem, 241, 242
Education, 2, 12, 13, 16, 18, 19, 20, 22, 26, 34, 51, 55, 106, 123, 142, 183, 184, 209, 214, 227, 234, 240, 242, 243, 244, 245, 246, 279, 282, 284, 321, 324, 345
Educational impact, 277, 279
Elements, 5, 9, 38, 39, 51, 54, 72, 73, 79, 81, 152, 162, 168, 189, 207, 208, 209, 210, 212, 214, 219, 220, 222, 230, 231, 233, 237, 249, 270, 273, 275, 281, 331, 342
Elite female, 98
Embodied experiences, 79
Emotion, 55, 84, 213, 224, 226
Emotional intelligence, 332, 333, 334, 335
Enlightenment, 258, 259, 261, 262, 265
Entertainment industry, 38
Environment, 13, 25, 51, 60, 101, 137, 138, 139, 200, 210, 211, 212, 213, 214, 215, 224, 241, 242, 243, 245, 246, 248, 251, 253, 257, 349
Esquivas, 221
Ethics, 3, 14, 76, 109, 161, 182, 184, 256, 257

INDEX 403

Ethnographic, 29, 88, 89, 90, 93, 119, 145, 146, 175, 176, 177, 178, 298
Eutrapelia, 185
Evolution, 51, 119, 146, 156, 189, 290, 340

F

Faith, 59, 60, 83, 177, 181, 182, 184, 185, 186, 187, 209
Fat, 98, 219
Feel, 1, 3, 4, 7, 22, 42, 69, 72, 73, 79, 92, 113, 118, 147, 175, 177, 180, 212, 213, 219, 221, 278, 281, 283
Feminine, 90, 91, 166, 343
Feminists, 234
Fight or flight, 213
Fighting, 1, 2, 6, 8, 9, 13, 14, 32, 33, 39, 42, 44, 51, 53, 54, 55, 58, 61, 64, 65, 74, 75, 78, 81, 87, 99, 117, 118, 121, 122, 145, 146, 147, 148, 151, 152, 155, 163, 168, 177, 180, 182, 183, 184, 185, 186, 187, 189, 191, 192, 193, 194, 195, 196, 200, 201, 218, 219, 221, 225, 231, 243, 245, 267, 268, 273, 275, 276, 291, 292, 293, 297, 301, 313, 317, 321, 335, 338, 339, 340, 341, 345, 347, 349
Film, 158, 165, 166, 167, 168, 169, 171, 181, 182, 187, 297, 347
First general definition, 4
Fitness, 2, 10, 21, 30, 32, 33, 46, 100, 118, 119, 140, 143, 146, 182, 184, 226, 250, 257, 320
Flemish, 43
Focus, 14, 15, 16, 18, 29, 31, 52, 68, 72, 73, 109, 137, 146, 150, 155, 159, 168, 169, 175, 177, 179, 208, 222, 231, 267, 270, 272, 274, 275, 279, 328, 329, 331, 333
Foucault, 94, 118, 121, 123, 249, 256, 257, 258, 259, 260, 261, 262, 263, 264, 265

Friendship, 258, 261, 292, 313, 390

G

Gauntlet, 126, 163
Gender, 32, 33, 87, 88, 89, 90, 91, 92, 93, 94, 96, 134, 142, 167, 170, 214, 230, 234, 236, 237, 238, 273, 276, 277, 302, 344
Gender dynamics, 88
God, 182, 184, 192, 209, 216, 263
Gong and drum, 146
Grapplers, 98, 99, 100, 101, 102, 103
Greco-Roman, 313
Guttman, 340

H

Hamaguchi, 15, 19
Hand to hand combat, 59, 65, 190, 194
Hand to hand fighting, 64, 195
Heat illness, 100, 101, 103
Heredity, 68, 71, 210
Heritage, 68, 70, 75, 182, 185, 231
Hero, 35, 169, 175, 203, 319, 342, 344, 346
HHI, 128, 129, 130
History, 5, 8, 9, 12, 14, 15, 39, 48, 50, 72, 74, 76, 78, 81, 85, 96, 107, 128, 130, 156, 157, 159, 174, 180, 182, 183, 185, 186, 189, 191, 194, 196, 199, 201, 216, 223, 232, 235, 240, 241, 243, 245, 249, 253, 290, 299, 304, 314, 317, 324, 339, 340, 341, 343, 359
HIV/AIDS, 220
Hooliganism, 114
Hugging, 111, 112, 114
Human, 2, 4, 7, 8, 22, 56, 59, 75, 79, 81, 107, 108, 112, 118, 121, 122, 143, 146, 158, 185, 189, 190, 191, 208, 209, 210, 211, 214, 216, 217, 222, 227, 241, 244, 245, 319, 320, 326, 329, 338,

339, 340, 341, 342, 343, 344,
345, 346, 347, 348, 349, 350,
351, 366
Human aggression, 343, 349
Human movement, 4
Humanity patrimony, 240
Humble, 27, 65, 82, 119
Hwarang, 74

I

Illegal drugs, 245
Image rights, 319
Imbalance, 128, 129, 133, 138
Improve life conditions, 241, 243
Injuries, 2, 32, 39, 44, 45, 46, 89, 93,
    120, 121, 136, 137, 141, 142,
    191, 193, 314
Injury, 8, 30, 35, 39, 44, 45, 97, 110,
    120, 121, 136, 140, 142, 143,
    156, 158, 185, 187, 193, 220,
    225, 255, 272, 314
International federations, 2
Internet, 70, 300
Intimate, 15, 82, 83, 84, 111, 112

J

Jansenist, 199
Jeet Kune Do, 50, 153
Jiu-jitsu, 43, 220, 222, 223, 313,
    314, 321, 323, 359
Judo, vii, ix, 9, 15, 17, 27, 38, 42,
    43, 46, 53, 55, 56, 71, 73, 77, 78,
    81, 87, 88, 89, 90, 91, 92, 93, 94,
    95, 96, 103, 109, 110, 118, 138,
    140, 143, 218, 230, 273, 313,
    314, 321, 322, 323, 341, 355,
    358, 359, 360
Judokas, 87, 88, 89, 90, 91, 92, 93,
    94

K

Karate, 6, 14, 15, 16, 18, 19, 20, 27,
    38, 39, 42, 43, 44, 45, 50, 51, 55,
    56, 70, 73, 74, 78, 81, 118, 138,
    143, 147, 153, 218, 273, 274,
    276, 285, 313, 314, 350
Kata, ix, 51, 139
Katas, 110
Kawaishi, 358
Kickboxing, 17, 38, 39, 42, 43, 45,
    47, 50, 81, 146, 158, 273, 321
Kicking, 24, 53, 117, 167, 193, 341
Knights, 14
Knowing, 50, 56, 150, 241, 245,
    260, 261, 331

L

Law, 14, 155, 156, 158, 162, 163,
    164, 189, 240, 274, 323, 341
Learning, 12, 13, 15, 18, 19, 22, 25,
    29, 34, 35, 36, 50, 51, 52, 53, 54,
    55, 56, 60, 61, 62, 63, 73, 75, 80,
    81, 83, 108, 110, 149, 196, 212,
    214, 215, 222, 227, 240, 248,
    329, 332
legality, 155, 158, 316
Legitimacy, 38, 70, 74, 156, 203,
    342
Leisure time, 282
Lexicon, 79
Lifestyle, 80, 212, 279, 293, 296,
    303
Lineage maps, 68, 73
Lineage maps, 68
Literature, x, 5, 41, 43, 65, 79, 125,
    126, 128, 130, 136, 139, 182,
    208, 219, 241, 276, 280, 290,
    347
Live or die, 347
Logic of practice, 67, 75, 147, 151,
    152
Ludic, 240, 250, 262

M

Male, 33, 36, 76, 87, 89, 90, 91, 92,
    93, 94, 96, 98, 129, 149, 167,
    168, 177, 182, 183, 214, 230,

231, 232, 233, 234, 235, 270, 273, 274, 275, 346, 348, 349
Male animal ideology, 346, 348
Male dominated, 92, 93
Male thing, 231, 234, 235
Malvado, 250
Martial arts, x, 2, 3, 4, 5, 6, 7, 8, 9, 10, 12, 13, 14, 15, 16, 17, 18, 19, 21, 22, 25, 26, 27, 38, 39, 40, 41, 42, 43, 44, 45, 46, 47, 48, 49, 50, 51, 52, 53, 54, 55, 56, 60, 61, 67, 68, 69, 70, 71, 72, 73, 74, 75, 76, 78, 79, 81, 82, 83, 85, 88, 91, 93, 105, 108, 109, 110, 111, 112, 114, 118, 136, 137, 138, 139, 140, 141, 142, 143, 144, 145, 146, 151, 152, 153, 167, 189, 190, 191, 196, 207, 208, 217, 218, 219, 220, 222, 223, 224, 225, 227, 228, 267, 275, 313, 314, 315, 316, 321, 323, 324, 328, 329, 330, 331, 333, 334, 335, 336, 339, 340, 341, 350, 365, 374
Martial science, 189, 190, 193, 196
Martially functional, 6
Masculinist culture, 349
Media, 38, 40, 51, 52, 71, 80, 81, 95, 96, 110, 113, 117, 186, 187, 233, 301, 313, 316, 324, 339, 342
Medications, 100
Mestre, 238, 247, 250, 251, 254, 256, 259, 260, 261
Metanarratives, 74
Military, 13, 14, 15, 59, 60, 61, 64, 65, 109, 146, 150, 153, 189, 190, 194, 225, 323, 328, 345, 350
Military close combat, 61
Mind/body dichotomy, 7
Mindset, 65, 79, 91, 219
Mission work, 173, 174
Mixed martial arts, viii, ix, 7, 39, 44, 45, 46, 49, 72, 86, 97, 117, 118, 119, 123, 124, 146, 152, 171, 190, 194, 268, 312, 313, 314, 315, 338
MMA, ix, 39, 82, 117, 118, 119, 120, 121, 122, 123, 146, 268,
275, 312, 313, 314, 315, 316, 317, 318, 320, 321, 322, 323, 324, 325, 326, 338, 339, 340, 341, 342, 343, 344, 346, 347, 349, 350, 351
Modernity, 76, 111, 259, 262, 291, 295, 300, 344, 350
Moleza, 256
Monkey, 74
Morality, 182, 184, 185, 257, 259
Multi-dimensional, 19, 207
Muscle cramping, 99, 101
Musical rhythm, 146, 149, 151, 152
Myths, 169, 237, 255, 339, 340, 343, 344, 345, 346, 348, 350, 351

N

Narratives, 74, 170, 171, 249, 291, 340, 344, 346, 347, 348, 351
NATO, 65
Naturalistic mythologies, 348, 350, 351
Nature, 2, 4, 5, 6, 17, 18, 25, 26, 56, 58, 62, 64, 75, 76, 87, 112, 126, 158, 160, 170, 178, 184, 186, 194, 195, 199, 209, 210, 211, 216, 224, 225, 232, 241, 242, 244, 250, 261, 280, 300, 320, 339, 340, 341, 342, 343, 345, 346, 348, 350, 351, 370
Negative thoughts, 213
Nehamas, 257, 258, 263, 265
Neurons, 210, 211, 212
New York Boxing Commission, 297
Noble art, 169, 196
Non-formal learning, 34, 36
Non-formal learning, 34, 36
Nutrition, 98, 99, 118, 119

O

Olympic Judoka, 119
Olympics, 77, 108, 128, 129, 130, 131, 135, 167, 170, 197, 211, 361

Oppression, 240, 241, 245, 248, 263, 349
Originary violence, 349, 350
Others, x, 2, 3, 18, 25, 27, 34, 35, 41, 49, 73, 78, 79, 82, 83, 84, 85, 94, 97, 102, 103, 126, 152, 156, 163, 170, 186, 196, 216, 220, 234, 235, 240, 243, 257, 258, 261, 262, 268, 274, 278, 298, 313, 314, 316, 318, 319, 320, 323, 324, 329, 332, 334, 342, 349
Outcomes, 26, 38, 39, 40, 42, 43, 46, 47, 134, 140, 152, 162, 177, 179, 209, 216, 217, 228, 300, 328, 329, 332, 334

P

Pain, 7, 8, 9, 33, 73, 117, 118, 190, 209, 213, 218, 224, 226, 227
Panama Al Brown, ix, 290, 292, 294, 305, 310
Parado, 247
Pedagogical, 41, 144, 147
Pedagogical, 50
Performance, 6, 21, 53, 54, 55, 63, 89, 98, 99, 100, 101, 103, 113, 133, 135, 138, 139, 142, 143, 146, 148, 153, 166, 167, 199, 202, 210, 218, 219, 224, 226, 227, 244, 245, 247, 248, 249, 250, 251, 252, 253, 258, 260, 262, 263, 279, 282, 291, 293, 295, 297, 302, 304, 315
Perverso, 250
Philosophy, 72, 83, 107, 144, 147, 152, 162, 182, 190, 217, 249, 256, 257, 260, 329, 330, 365
Physical capital, 32, 33, 36, 68, 170
Physical capital, 34, 36, 68
Physical education, 15, 44, 56, 106, 185, 240, 241, 320, 330, 390
Physical environment, 137
Physiological, 99, 102, 136, 139, 142, 211, 216, 218, 329
Planning, 242, 246, 285
Positive role models, 174
Positive youth development, 42
Positive youth development, 45
Poverty, 80, 173, 186, 243, 245, 303, 323, 324
Power sports, 40, 44, 47, 283
Powerful, 9, 26, 41, 72, 255, 304, 339, 343, 344
Prevention, 41, 44, 48, 55, 121, 136, 137, 138, 140, 141, 142, 143, 216, 228, 242, 267, 284, 285, 321
Primitivism, 344, 347, 350
Prize fighting, 165, 193, 290
Pro-environment, 349
Psychological, xi, 27, 39, 40, 41, 45, 47, 89, 96, 99, 198, 208, 209, 212, 213, 214, 217, 220, 222, 224, 226, 227, 228, 248, 262, 272, 275, 283, 313, 328, 329, 340, 341, 344, 346, 347, 351
Punching, 53, 117, 200, 302, 303, 341
Punish, 94, 202

Q

Queensbury rules, 183

R

Racism, 295, 302, 303
Real, 7, 16, 23, 25, 33, 52, 55, 63, 64, 65, 70, 80, 92, 94, 110, 111, 112, 113, 114, 126, 137, 144, 151, 165, 166, 169, 194, 199, 203, 204, 222, 282, 300, 301, 304, 316, 340, 341
Reality, 51, 111, 114, 138, 159, 160, 166, 182, 199, 200, 202, 203, 204, 212, 216, 235, 237, 262, 300, 312, 324, 335, 339, 341, 344, 347
Recognition, 17, 25, 36, 43, 203, 233, 237, 243, 252, 257, 304
Referee, 160, 162, 175, 191, 199, 201, 275

Religion, 75, 76, 89, 180, 182, 183, 185, 186, 187, 190, 216, 223, 257, 324
Research, 2, x, 9, 10, 13, 17, 24, 26, 39, 40, 41, 43, 46, 51, 52, 53, 56, 71, 74, 88, 89, 90, 93, 94, 95, 98, 100, 123, 126, 136, 141, 151, 167, 172, 174, 175, 179, 180, 208, 209, 210, 213, 216, 217, 218, 219, 220, 222, 223, 240, 241, 242, 250, 251, 252, 268, 270, 271, 273, 275, 276, 280, 281, 282, 283, 285, 290, 291, 295, 331, 334, 350, 365
Respect, x, 3, 14, 21, 23, 25, 35, 51, 72, 152, 156, 161, 176, 177, 193, 217, 220, 221, 237, 242, 244, 245, 252, 262, 274, 321, 323, 328, 329, 330, 333, 342
Rhythm, 4, 5, 54, 120, 122, 144, 145, 146, 147, 148, 149, 150, 151, 152, 153, 168, 247
Rhythmanalysis, 118, 120, 123
Right stuff, 190
Roda, 238, 247, 248, 249, 250, 251, 252, 255, 260, 262, 263
Racred, 181, 186, 216, 223, 257, 339, 344, 345

S

Salvador, 232, 238, 239, 247, 248, 250, 323, 326
Salvation through boxing, 174
San Diego academy, 80
Scholarly, 2, 74, 145, 175, 339, 350
Sculpture, 108
Second general definition, 5
Self, 3, 7, 14, 16, 21, 24, 25, 26, 27, 30, 32, 35, 36, 40, 41, 45, 49, 50, 56, 59, 60, 72, 76, 83, 88, 94, 109, 118, 137, 138, 141, 146, 148, 156, 157, 162, 181, 183, 184, 192, 194, 196, 213, 216, 217, 219, 222, 236, 248, 249, 253, 254, 255, 256, 257, 258, 259, 260, 262, 263, 270, 271, 272, 273, 274, 277, 278, 279, 281, 283, 295, 301, 304, 321, 328, 329, 330, 331, 332, 333, 334, 335, 340, 343, 344, 350, 370
Self-cultivation, 56, 249, 258, 260
Semiography, 291, 304
Sharing, 112, 134, 258
Shintaido, ix, 365
Shot of pain, 7
Shotokan karate, 220
Shotokan Karate, 50, 56, 71
Silent codes, 68
Skill, 3, 4, 40, 52, 53, 54, 59, 60, 62, 82, 83, 109, 138, 141, 144, 152, 190, 195, 210, 221, 262, 328, 332, 333
Skill development, 3, 4, 40
Slaves, 231, 240, 243, 245, 255
Sleep deprivation, 100
Snake, 7, 74, 263
Social environment, 25, 137, 216, 226, 236, 242, 304, 349
Social Interactions, ix, 312
Socialisation, 34
Society, 2, 29, 33, 35, 36, 42, 46, 76, 89, 90, 91, 93, 107, 109, 111, 113, 169, 174, 176, 185, 188, 191, 230, 231, 233, 237, 238, 241, 243, 244, 245, 260, 294, 312, 313, 315, 319, 320, 321, 322, 324, 339, 341, 344, 370
Socio-cultural, 68, 208, 209, 214, 215, 216, 217, 222, 275, 280, 282, 312, 320
Socioeconomic status, 214
Socio-historical processes, 343
Sociological lens, 252
Sociology, 34, 36, 39, 44, 47, 79, 179, 180, 226, 251, 252, 254, 290
Space, 4, 5, 61, 72, 79, 80, 82, 85, 91, 93, 94, 138, 148, 168, 170, 231, 243, 259, 294, 323, 324
Spectacle, 117, 158, 181, 184, 187, 198, 199, 200, 201, 203, 204, 300, 301, 340, 341
Spectatorship, 110, 111, 113, 114, 300

Spiritual, 3, 4, 8, 10, 39, 51, 72, 108, 110, 169, 173, 187, 208, 209, 212, 216, 217, 218, 219, 220, 221, 222, 223, 224, 226, 227, 276, 339, 342, 343, 346, 347, 350, 351
Spiritual regeneration, 343, 347, 351
Spirituality, 75, 182, 209, 216, 217, 219, 222, 223, 225, 227, 228, 350
Sport, 2, 3, 12, 14, 16, 19, 29, 30, 31, 32, 40, 41, 42, 43, 44, 45, 46, 47, 48, 53, 55, 69, 71, 87, 88, 89, 91, 92, 93, 94, 95, 96, 98, 105, 106, 107, 108, 109, 110, 115, 117, 118, 119, 120, 121, 123, 125, 127, 128, 130, 144, 146, 147, 155, 156, 157, 158, 159, 165, 166, 167, 170, 171, 172, 173, 174, 175, 178, 179, 180, 182, 183, 184, 185, 186, 187, 189, 190, 191, 192, 193, 194, 196, 199, 204, 208, 219, 224, 225, 227, 231, 235, 240, 241, 242, 246, 248, 251, 252, 268, 269, 270, 272, 273, 275, 276, 277, 278, 279, 280, 281, 282, 283, 284, 285, 291, 300, 303, 313, 314, 315, 316, 318, 319, 321, 323, 324, 328, 329, 339, 340, 341, 342, 345, 348, 349, 350, 351
Sport for all, 242
Sport initiatives, 269
Sportization, 341
Sports, 2, 4, 8, 9, 12, 13, 14, 15, 16, 26, 33, 38, 39, 40, 41, 42, 43, 44, 45, 46, 47, 49, 53, 88, 91, 96, 97, 98, 99, 102, 105, 106, 107, 108, 109, 110, 111, 112, 113, 114, 125, 126, 127, 129, 130, 134, 135, 139, 147, 153, 155, 156, 158, 159, 165, 170, 174, 178, 179, 180, 182, 188, 192, 208, 210, 218, 222, 225, 230, 231, 236, 238, 242, 243, 251, 252, 267, 268, 269, 270, 271, 272, 273, 275, 276, 277, 278, 279, 280, 281, 282, 283, 284, 290, 291, 293, 295, 300, 302, 304, 312, 313, 314, 316, 319, 320, 321, 324, 328, 330, 333, 339, 340, 341, 348, 349, 351, 361
Sports coaching, 15, 16, 17
Sportsmanship, 173, 174, 255, 291
Spring, 276
Square off, 314
Standard, 18, 50, 127, 128, 129, 136, 141, 195, 317, 330
Stereotypes, 231, 234, 237, 296, 302
Strains, 140
Street-cred, 26
Street-cred, 23
Strength training, 90
Students, x, 2, 10, 13, 15, 18, 21, 22, 23, 24, 25, 26, 35, 46, 50, 52, 61, 62, 63, 64, 67, 69, 72, 78, 80, 81, 83, 87, 110, 140, 145, 148, 149, 195, 217, 218, 232, 236, 251, 263, 271, 273, 323, 328, 329, 330, 334
Super-conscious, 85
Superhuman, 339
Supernatural, 339, 342
Supine, 138
Survive, 55, 59, 61, 65, 68, 69, 73, 126, 189, 240, 241, 245
Sustainable development, 241, 242, 243, 245, 246
Sustainable sport, 242, 245, 246
Sweet science, 180, 185, 204
Symbolic-ideological experience, 339, 340, 345
Symbolism, 68, 74
Synchronizing modernity, 291
Syncopation, 118, 121, 122, 123, 149

T

Taekkyeon, 75
Taekwondo, 38, 39, 42, 43, 45, 46, 71, 74, 78, 108, 109, 110, 118, 141, 142, 273, 276, 331, 335

Tai Chi, 7, 13, 27, 47, 55, 70, 73, 74, 138, 139, 142, 143, 217, 218, 220, 225, 226, 228, 350
Taoism, 219
Target groups, 42
Targets, 25, 58, 151, 200
Teaching, 12, 13, 14, 15, 18, 22, 24, 26, 43, 50, 51, 52, 55, 61, 62, 63, 64, 68, 71, 152, 184, 191, 192, 196, 208, 230, 231, 233, 234, 261, 328, 329, 335, 390
Techniques, 5, 8, 23, 50, 51, 52, 53, 54, 55, 61, 62, 65, 69, 71, 74, 78, 79, 80, 81, 87, 99, 108, 118, 120, 138, 140, 142, 143, 145, 146, 147, 149, 151, 166, 189, 190, 194, 196, 218, 225, 248, 249, 250, 254, 255, 257, 258, 263, 291, 313, 316, 329, 330, 341, 346
Technological, 324, 339, 340, 341
Technological minimalism, 340, 341
Thai boxing, 314
The art of living, 257
Theeboom, vii, 38, 39, 40, 42, 47, 51, 56, 71, 77, 217, 228
Third general definition, 9
Tiger, 74, 172, 302, 347
Time, x, 2, 4, 5, 8, 14, 15, 18, 22, 23, 25, 32, 34, 39, 41, 43, 49, 50, 51, 58, 61, 62, 63, 67, 68, 72, 78, 79, 80, 81, 82, 84, 85, 90, 92, 95, 103, 110, 112, 113, 119, 120, 121, 122, 127, 128, 129, 130, 137, 141, 143, 148, 149, 157, 158, 159, 161, 166, 168, 173, 175, 176, 177, 178, 179, 182, 183, 184, 185, 191, 193, 194, 195, 199, 211, 213, 215, 217, 219, 220, 223, 232, 234, 235, 240, 245, 247, 248, 249, 252, 258, 262, 270, 274, 281, 282, 283, 291, 292, 294, 295, 296, 298, 300, 301, 302, 305, 312, 313, 314, 318, 319, 331, 342, 344, 346
Touch, 69, 81, 82, 83, 84, 189, 261

Tough, 32, 176, 183, 202, 263, 299
Traditional, 3, 8, 12, 31, 33, 39, 40, 41, 42, 45, 46, 48, 49, 50, 51, 52, 53, 54, 55, 58, 71, 73, 75, 91, 92, 108, 109, 118, 128, 145, 146, 170, 171, 201, 217, 218, 234, 251, 268, 273, 275, 276, 316, 328, 329, 334, 335, 340, 350
Training, 2, 12, 13, 14, 15, 18, 21, 22, 25, 26, 27, 30, 31, 32, 33, 44, 45, 46, 49, 51, 53, 54, 55, 59, 61, 63, 64, 65, 68, 72, 73, 79, 81, 82, 87, 89, 90, 91, 92, 97, 98, 99, 101, 102, 103, 108, 109, 110, 111, 112, 117, 118, 119, 120, 121, 122, 123, 129, 137, 138, 139, 140, 141, 143, 145, 146, 147, 148, 149, 152, 169, 176, 186, 187, 189, 190, 191, 192, 194, 195, 196, 217, 218, 220, 221, 222, 224, 226, 227, 234, 235, 244, 245, 248, 249, 253, 260, 273, 274, 275, 276, 277, 280, 282, 284, 285, 291, 292, 298, 299, 301, 321, 323, 328, 329, 330, 331, 333, 334, 335, 340, 341
Transnational, 160
Transport domains, 137
Trouble maker, 157

U

Uchikomi, 53, 54
UFC, 78, 80, 81, 111, 112, 114, 118, 124, 314, 315, 316, 317, 321, 322, 324, 325, 326, 338, 339, 340, 341, 344, 346, 347, 349, 350, 351
Ugly, 6, 234, 247, 250, 251, 253, 254
Ultimate Fighting Championship, 78, 112, 118, 314, 317, 322, 338
United Nations, 41, 48, 242, 246
Universities, x, 17, 194
University graduates, 19, 234
USA, 2, 19, 20, 128, 129, 130, 153, 169, 172, 173, 174, 175, 176,

238, 270, 271, 273, 274, 316, 317

V

Value, 14, 33, 38, 54, 55, 69, 107, 128, 146, 152, 178, 200, 201, 202, 203, 204, 217, 245, 273, 285, 315, 329, 348
Values, 2, 3, 9, 14, 15, 29, 38, 88, 89, 90, 109, 170, 180, 184, 204, 215, 217, 220, 235, 237, 241, 242, 248, 275, 320, 322, 324, 328, 329, 333, 334, 341, 342, 344, 348, 351
Violence, 1, 2, 6, 21, 25, 40, 41, 48, 108, 110, 114, 117, 118, 156, 158, 166, 168, 174, 177, 180, 182, 203, 227, 228, 245, 248, 250, 260, 270, 272, 273, 274, 278, 283, 285, 320, 321, 322, 323, 324, 339, 341, 342, 343, 344, 345, 346, 347, 348, 349, 350, 351
Visual information, 138

W

Wacquant, 31, 32, 33, 36, 37, 42, 47, 79, 86, 117, 119, 124, 167, 171, 175, 178, 180, 290, 311
Walking, 137, 218

Weapon, 110, 191, 195, 255, 328
Weight, 12, 32, 80, 89, 90, 96, 97, 98, 99, 100, 101, 102, 103, 119, 120, 140, 191, 193, 290, 291, 301, 303, 316, 322, 360
Weight cutting, 100
Weight reduction, 96, 97
Wildness, 339, 341, 342, 344, 346, 347, 348, 351
Wing Tsun, 18
Winning, 6, 105, 106, 109, 110, 111, 112, 113, 114, 127, 128, 152, 166, 181, 293, 298, 301, 302, 305, 322
Wrestling, 32, 40, 43, 98, 122, 191, 193, 194, 199, 201, 202, 203, 204, 272, 273, 313, 314, 321, 322, 323, 341
Wushu, 15, 43, 71, 77

Y

Youth, 2, 3, 31, 38, 39, 40, 41, 42, 43, 44, 46, 47, 101, 173, 174, 175, 177, 178, 179, 180, 216, 228, 245, 267, 268, 282, 284, 285, 313, 324

Z

Zen Buddhism, 51, 219

www.ingramcontent.com/pod-product-compliance
Lightning Source LLC
Chambersburg PA
CBHW070805300426
44111CB00014B/2428